THEORY AND METHODS OF SOCIAL RESEARCH

JOHAN GALTUNG

THEORY AND METHODS OF SOCIAL RESEARCH

OSLO: UNIVERSITETSFORLAGET
NEW YORK: COLUMBIA UNIVERSITY PRESS

BASIC SOCIAL SCIENCE MONOGRAPHS FROM THE
INTERNATIONAL PEACE RESEARCH INSTITUTE, OSLO

No. 1. Johan Galtung: Theory and Methods of Social Research. 1967

© UNIVERSITETSFORLAGET 1967
REVISED EDITION 1969

ORIGINALLY PUBLISHED IN NORWAY BY
UNIVERSITETSFORLAGET, OSLO

PUBLISHED IN
THE UNITED KINGDOM BY
GEORGE ALLEN & UNWIN, LTD., LONDON
AND IN THE UNITED STATES OF AMERICA BY
COLUMBIA UNIVERSITY PRESS, NEW YORK
(Library of Congress Catalogue Card Number 67–26343)

PRINTED IN DENMARK BY P. J. SCHMIDTS BOGTRYKKERI, VOJENS

To the memory of
my beloved father

Preface

For one who has entered the social sciences via mathematics and natural science, a feeling of oversophistication in much of what today is presented in social science methodology can be very strong. There are two kinds of this oversophistication. There is the conscientious philosophical scrutiny of the foundations of social research, and there is the equally conscientious elaboration of complex details in the techniques. But however laudable these efforts, the former easily leads to sterile debates where the plain fact that quite a lot of contemporary sociology simply *works* is lost in efforts to apply philosophical categories developed by people who often are unacquainted with contemporary sociology and have little or nothing constructive to offer. And the latter may lead to technicalities based on assumptions rarely or never met with in actual social research; nevertheless, these refinements are adhered to simply because they exist in the vernacular of social research.

The present work is an effort to stay in the middle of the road, discussing the properties of social data with a view to weaknesses and strengths of various approaches. No attempts will be made to go deeply into foundations or technicalities — the attempt is rather to present the reader who is already acquainted with the elements of general methodology, and social science methodology in particular, with an analytical outline. Thus, the present work will neither serve as an introduction nor as a handbook. The hope is that it may be useful as an integration of widely scattered approaches in data collection, data-processing, data analysis, and theory formation.

Just a few words about the plan of this book. It is divided into two parts, Data Collection and Data Analysis, where the second part is actually divided into three subparts: Data processing (chapters 1–3), Data analysis (chapters 4–5), and Theory formation (chapter 6). In the first chapter of Part I the key concept of the whole text is presented: the data matrix which has *m* rows for the units to be explored and *n* columns for the variables used to explore them. *Data collection,* then, is about how to fill the matrix with data; *data processing* deals with the steps from that point to the point where any distribution of any number of variables can be obtained; *data analysis* is concerned with how to use the distributions to test any proposition about the units that may be phrased in terms of the variables; and *theory formation* is concerned with systems of propositions linked by a relation of implication. Thus, the text touches unevenly upon most of contemporary social science methodology (with experimental techniques and historical analysis as two of the most important exceptions). Obviously, not everything is treated equally thoroughly — but the intention never was to give a complete text on social science methodology. Rather, the intention has been to try to integrate things usually kept apart: techniques of data collection, techniques of analysis, statistical methods, and some philosophy of science. The effort has been made to show how the theory and method of social research is enriched if concepts and insights from all of these disciplines can be brought into the limelight at the same time. To what extent the effort is successful is another matter.

Readers may well complain that the level of abstraction varies considerably from chapter to chapter, from section to section and even with any section. Mathematical and philosophical analyses are found side by side with some petty details about the administration of surveys and sorting of punched cards. To this one might reply: true, it makes uneven reading. *But these are the tools of our trade, in the social sciences.* All of this is needed, and much, much more; the range of knowledge and experience required is unlimited. Knowing more one can always do a little better; do research that is more faithful to social reality and yields more penetrating insights. Not all is equally attractive to everybody, to say the least. But if some social scientists feel beyond the more manual and administrative details and others define themselves as below the most involved details of analysis the result is very often bad social science. For these levels of abstraction have to coexist in our minds.

Originally the material for this book consisted of papers intended for publication as articles. However, the occasion to give systematic courses in methodology stimulated the effort to link these articles together in a more coherent framework. Particularly important in this connection has been teaching experience in "developing countries" where there is a particular need for a coherent presentation of the whole field — and also less of the unfortunate tradition of fragmented teaching of methodology so often found elsewhere.

The first draft of the present work was written in Pátzcuaro, México, during the summer of 1958, and the work was completed when the author was a UNESCO professor at the *Facultad Latinoamericana de Ciencias Sociales* (FLASCO), Santiago, Chile, 1962/1963 and 1965. The work is based on lectures on methodology given at Columbia University 1957/1959; at the University of Oslo, 1959 and 1960/1962; at FLACSO, Santiago 1962/1963 and 1965; and at the *Centro di Ricerche Industriali e Sociali* (CRIS), Torino, spring 1964. I am deeply indebted to eager and perceptive students at all these places, to Professors W.J.Goode, Paul F.Lazarsfeld, Sverre Holm, Peter Heintz and Dr. Anna Anfossi for their invitations to lecture on methodology and their encouragement and stimulation or methodological work; and to Professors Arne Næss and Gustav Marthinsen, who were my first teachers in methodology at the University of Oslo. I am particularly grateful to FLACSO, to Professor Peter Heintz, the creative director of the Latin-American School of Sociology, to my "counterpart" Professor Edmundo Fuenzalida for his excellent translation into Spanish and very useful discussions, and to UNESCO for the practical arrangements that made the completion of the work possible. Special thanks are due to Ståle Seierstad, Gudmund Iversen, Nils Petter Gleditsch, Nils Halle and Else Sandved, Oslo; and to Simón Schwartzman, Belo Horizonte, for their helpful criticism and constructive assistance; and to Thordis Saxlund, Consuelo Barros and Lily Bianchi for patient and efficient secretarial work. My final expression of gratitude goes to Universitetsforlaget, Oslo, and to Susan and Tord Høivik — for untiring cooperation in the processing of the manuscript as well as imaginative suggestions.

Needless to say, the responsibility for the conclusions rests entirely with the author.

Oslo/Santiago, June 1965. *Johan Galtung*

Contents

Part I. Data Collection

Part II. Data Analysis

PART I

Data Collection

1. The Data Matrix

1.1. *The tripartite form of data*

Social science *data* are obtained when a social scientist records facts about some section of social reality, or has facts recorded for him. It is customary to say that the data must have some kind of empirical reference located outside the social scientist himself, and we shall follow this tradition.

Although data in social science, with its enormous span in subject matter, take on very many different forms, there is a common structure that in most cases presents itself readily and in other cases is easily imposed on the data. This structure has three parts, but they appear under different names in different contexts.

First of all, and most importantly, there are the *elements of analysis,* or *units of analysis,* such as human beings (respondents) in a survey or laboratory experiment, or nations in a comparative study of properties of nations, or more complex units. These units have one thing in common insofar as they form the subject matter of social science inquiry: they either consist of human beings or of products of human beings, as when a content analysis is made of newspaper clippings.

Secondly, there are the *dimensions* or *variables* one wants to explore in connection with the units, such as 'energy output per capita' in studies of underdeveloped nations, or responses to certain strategic questions in an election study. Sometimes this can be more properly phrased as a set of *conditions* under which one wants to study the units, or a set of *stimuli.* We shall use the language of variables when dealing with units that are imponderables in the sense that they cannot (in an artificial or natural way) be presented a set of conditions so that the social scientist can study the outcomes – and we shall use the language of conditions or stimuli in cases where this is possible. But as general term, 'variable' will be used.

Thirdly, there are the *values* of the units on the variables studied, or, in the other language, the *responses or outcomes* when the units are exposed to the stimuli or to the conditions under which the social scientist wants to study them.

Thus, we have these three parts that can be said to form the structure of social science data, expressed in the variable-language; in the language of conditions, stimuli and responses (SR-language); and in what may be called the survey-language:

Table 1.1.1. *The three parts of data, expressed in different terms*

general terms	dimensions	units	values
variable-language	variables studied	units of analysis	values on variables
SR-language	conditions, stimuli	units of analysis	outcomes, responses
survey-language	psychological objects	subjects, respondents	responses

It is difficult to choose between these terminologies, because they are not at all synonymous. We shall therefore have to use some combinations of the terms, or to select the language that seems most appropriate for the occasion. To avoid many of the difficulties stemming from this and to avoid distinctions that are very often unnecessary, the following simple symbols will be introduced:

Table 1.1.2. *Symbols for the three parts of social science data*

part of data	dimensions, variables	units of analysis	values, responses
symbol for one element	S,V,X	O	R
symbol for a class of elements	S,V,X	O	R
symbol for the number	n	m,N	r

To take an example: the typical survey study starts out with the confrontation of m respondents (O) with n questions (S) or 'psychological objects' in Thurstone's terminology, so that for each question S_j and each respondent O_i there are r_j different possible responses, R_j. Or to take another example: one can make a comparative study of m nations by listing their values R on a set of n variables of social disorganization, S – such as alcoholism, mental insanity, general criminality, homicide, and suicide, for a given year. If, in addition to this, the change in rates over a period of years is studied, the original tripartite structure is preserved by multiplying the five rates of dis-

organization by, say, the fifteen years, so that altogether 75 variables appear
The structure of the data remains the same; units of analysis are seen against
a number of specified dimensions.

If we accept that most data can be presented by these three parts, the
concept of the *data matrix* then follows. The data matrix is a way of arranging data so that the tripartite form is particularly visible:

Table 1.1.3. *The data matrix*

$$
M =
\begin{array}{c}
 \\
O_1 \\
O_2 \\
O_3 \\
\cdot \\
\cdot \\
O_i \\
\cdot \\
O_m
\end{array}
\left\{
\begin{array}{cccccc}
S_1 & S_2 & S_3 & \ldots\ S_j & \ldots\ S_n \\
R_{11} & R_{12} & R_{13} & \ldots\ R_{1j} & \ldots\ R_{1n} \\
R_{21} & R_{22} & R_{23} & \ldots\ R_{2j} & \ldots\ R_{2n} \\
R_{31} & R_{32} & R_{33} & \ldots\ R_{3j} & \ldots\ R_{3n} \\
\cdot & \cdot & \cdot & \cdot & \cdot \\
\cdot & \cdot & \cdot & \cdot & \cdot \\
R_{i1} & R_{i2} & R_{i3} & \ldots\ R_{ij} & \ldots\ R_{in} \\
\cdot & \cdot & \cdot & \cdot & \cdot \\
R_{m1} & R_{m2} & R_{m3} & \ldots\ R_{mj} & \ldots\ R_{mn}
\end{array}
\right\}
$$

In this scheme, R_{ij} is the response unit no. i gives to stimulus no. j; or, in
other words, the value for unit no. i on variable no. j. This is exactly the
form in which data appear if there is one punched card for each unit, one
column for each variable, and one punch for each value – and the cards
are run through a machine that lists for each card what is punched in the
card. Further, this is the form of the data a headmaster has in his protocol
with the names of the students vertically, the subjects taught at school horizontally, and the grade achieved by student no. i in subject no. j in the
appropriate square.

In technical language, the data matrix is the mapping of the cartesian
product $O \times S$ on $\underline{R}$, or, in other words: the idea is simply that *there shall be
one value R for each combination* (O, S). The form of the data matrix itself,
and this definition, yield the first three principles of data-collection:

(1) *Principle of comparability*:
    The statement '(O_i, S_j) is mapped on R' must be either true or false for
    all i, j and R included in $\underline{R_j}$.
(2) *Principle of classification*:
    For each stimulus S_j the set of response categories $\underline{R_j}$ shall yield a
    classification of all pairs (O_i, S_j) $(i = 1, \ldots, m)$.
(3) *Principle of completeness*:
    For each pair (O_i, S_j) a value R_{ij} must be found empirically.

These three principles require comments.

11

Looking at one vertical row in matrix M in Table 1.1.3, we see the idea is simply that the same stimulus shall be presented to all units of analysis, e.g., the *same* question shall be asked of all respondents. The emphasis is on 'same': the stimulus shall not be changed from one object to the other. This, however, is only what is already included in the definition of the matrix. The *principle of comparability* now says in addition that each such combination of a given stimulus with a unit of analysis shall be *meaningful,* in the sense that it shall be either true or false that a combination (O_i, S_j) gives any value in the set $\underline{R_j}$. By means of this principle, stimuli, units, and responses are made commensurate. If O_i is a nation, S_j a direct question on marital status, and $\underline{R_j}$ the set consisting of the elements 'married', 'unmarried', 'widow(er)', and 'divorced', then any combination is neither true, nor false, but simply meaningless.

Comparability, thus, is achieved when the three sets are tuned to each other so that the condition mentioned in principle (1) is fulfilled. This means, for instance, that questions must appear in appropriate translations in a comparative survey, but it does not mean that a question in a survey 'must have the same meaning' for all respondents, so long as it only has some meaning. Comparability in our sense is a weaker requirement, but it nevertheless means that one horizontal row can be compared with another, because the R's in the entries are not meaningless.

If now two units are found to be different on one dimension S, we may split the difference into two components – one 'real' component and one 'semantic' component – and attribute the difference observed to some function of these two components. We may even claim that all difference is due to a semantic component, as is the case when verbal disagreement co-exists with factual agreement. And it may be that the semantic and real components cancel each other out so that the net result is an observed similarity that may be said to be spurious. But all this is a question of interpretation, irrelevant to the field of data-collection, unless the aim is to reduce the semantic component as much as possible. We should notice, however, that it is not self-evident that the semantic factor constitutes an 'error' in a survey study, or that nations' crime-rates cannot be compared because they are based on different penal codes. An ambiguous question is nevertheless a question, and a study of how persons react to a question of that kind may yield important information as to how they would react to that sentence in everyday life. And even though crime-rates would change if they were based on a universal criterion, much research can be based on a comparison of rates based on discrepant definitions – for the simple reason that the rates may tell something about *how that which is called crime* differs from one country to another.

12

The *principle of classification* now adds three more constraints on the choice of the sets S, O and R. What it says is that for every stimulus S_j, the set of possible responses R_j shall form a classification – i.e., for each pair (O_i, S_j) there shall be *one* (exhaustiveness) *and only one* (mutual exclusiveness or single-valuedness) R_{ij} on which the pair can be mapped. (Ideally, there shall also be a *fundamentum divisionis*.) When this condition is fulfilled, we are guaranteed a response for each possible combination of unit and stimulus, and a *single* response. In the construction of questionnaires this is known as the principle that the respondent shall check one and only one answer or category. When he is given a so-called 'multiple choice', he is in fact given a set of stimuli, one for each category, so that there are *two* responses for each stimulus, *select or reject*. And this is a classification as good as any, it is a dichotomy.

The first two of the three principles concern the logic of the matrix and the three sets on which it is based. The third *principle of completeness* deals with the empirical job of completing the matrix and says simply this: *leave no cell open*. This *desideratum* is easily pronounced but not easily fulfilled, so all we have is a norm that the amount of cells with 'no information', 'no answer', etc. shall be kept 'as low as possible'. Whereas the first two principles can be adhered to before the data are obtained by seeing to it that the stimuli or variables apply to all units and that all sets of response categories form classifications, the third principle can only be adhered to in the process of collecting the data and afterwards. Here such things as techniques of keeping refusal rates low through appropriate legitimation of the research, or ways of tracing almost unavailable data, enter. But there is also the possibility *post hoc* of inspecting the distribution of empty cells in M and deleting appropriate O's and S's *to get rid of a maximum of empty cells with a minimum of deletions*. As a rule of thumb 10% may be taken as the absolute limit of empty cells allowable in any column or any row in M, while 5% is more advisable. But in some cases it may still be valuable to keep an O or an S even though both principles concerning empty cells have been infracted. For one reason, 'no answer' may also be an answer, and can be treated as a response. And to change O and S is to change the design.

The general technique, then, is to count the number of DK's and NA's for each O and each S and get the distribution. More often than not, a small percentage of the O's and S's will account for a great percentage of the DK's and NA's – and these are the obvious candidates for refusal. Only rarely will the DK's and NA's be randomly scattered in the data matrix.

If m as usual is the number of units, n the number of dimensions and r the average number of response categories, the figure $W = m \cdot n \cdot r$, or rather written as (m, n, r) is the *characteristic* of the matrix. W is a figure that indicates how much work is involved in a data collection process, although more importance should be attached to m and n than to r. r tells how finely the measurement discriminates between responses and must evidently be at least 2.

The basic choice in any research plan concerns the numbers m and n. A project with the dimensions (300, 20) is obviously very different from a project of the type (20, 300). The researcher will have to make his choice, and we shall call the ordered pair (m, n) the *research strategy* of the project. The next section is devoted to some reflections on different types of strategies.

Finally, some words about how r depends on m and n. There is no reason why it should depend on n: to add a variable does not change the number of values for the preceding variables. But r may be said to depend on m. Strictly speaking, we can always have elements, units to measure. With one unit we need to specify only one value – the correct one. The variable will consist of that value and its negation, the last comprising all other possible values. As m increases, we will need more values; but r will tend to increase more slowly, the greater m becomes. Having more units makes for difficulties of discrimination between units, and this leads to the grouping of similar units together. Often the variable used will not be strictly uni-dimensional, so that the exact location of two units relative to each other will be disputable – a conflict which can only be solved by establishing cruder categories, i.e. lower values of r. The researcher must try to obtain the general divisions, leaving out some details and problems a comparison of many units entails.

1.2. *The number of units and variables*

The numbers m and n are of crucial importance for the evaluation of any process of data-collection, both from a theoretical and a very practical point of view. The lowest value of m is 1 (as when only one person or nation is investigated), and the lowest value of n is also 1 (as in elections when only one question – which is your party or candidate? – is asked). In general, we get the combinations of possible values of m and n shown in Table 1.2.1. This Table should be taken *cum grano salis*. Nothing is indicated in the main diagonal, although such combinations may well occur. The typical intensive and extensive types of research appear as extremes, with boxes characterizing much of what is usually found in the twin sciences of psychology and sociology as neighboring cells. There is this difference, however: to the psychologist, the unit of analysis is almost always the living organism, to the sociologist it may in addition be some kind of collective. If the collective is

14

Table 1.2.1. *The combinations of values of m and n*

n = number of dimensions	one	few	many
many	*intensive* research (depth psychology, case studies)	psychology	
few	journalism		sociology
one		enquête	*extensive* research (elections, gallup)
	one	few	many → m = number of units

the nation, the historian might perhaps be placed where the psychologist is now placed, with his emphasis on the more casuistic aspects of the units of analysis. This does not mean that upper left-hand corner approaches can not be generalizing, however – but to the extent that the researcher wants to generalize on the level of the unit of analysis, *replication of the whole data matrix is necessary*. With very extensive research, generalizations can be obtained by the use of sampling techniques and statistical inference, or simply by dividing a large sample in smaller subsamples and testing hypotheses on one subsample after the other. On the other hand, not much can be said as a result of extensive analysis, since the researcher knows so little about each unit.

Clearly, the ideal is the (many, many) combination: as many units and as many dimensions as possible. We assume, however, that the word 'many' is used in such a way that this is impossible, for lack of resources like time, energy, personnel and money. The availability of these important factors and skills in the handling of different types of data will always lead the researcher in specific directions, and he may be so conditioned to one of the types in Table 1.2.1, that the others are virtually nonexistent to him. But any combination of *m* and *n* may be of some value, and a research tradition that dogmatically outrules one or more of the combinations only demonstrates its own limitations. On the other hand, each cell has its style and calls for specific skills that only rarely are found within one person, but easily could be found within one research team. For it seems obvious that a given problem in most cases can be approached better by a suitable *combination* of methods than by one single method or (*m*, *n*) combination. The field calls for knowledge of different approaches and a tolerant view of the virtues and drawbacks of the various combinations, but no real metamethodology exists, to guide us systematically in the choice of composite strategies.

Instead of simply listing arguments pro and con the nine cells, we shall do essentially the same thing, but in a way that also gives the methodological background for the importance of the data *matrix* in social science research. If we have $m = 1$ or $n = 1$, the matrix is said to *degenerate* (into a row or column vector, respectively, or into one response if we have both $m = 1$ and $n = 1$). There are good reasons why these degenerate data matrices are problematic.

Let us imagine that $m = 1$, i.e. that we have chosen only one unit for study. If we merely want to know a certain unit as well as possible, this may be justified if we have selected exactly the unit we want to study. If, however, our purpose is to study a social system, and we have selected one informant for that purpose, the unit studied is not the same as the unit selected. The situation becomes at once problematic: why exactly *this* informant, when we know that all informants will differ somewhat? This also applies if, instead of studying a social system, we are studying a social category. *One* unit picked at random or systematically will always be one unit only; and even though the unit may coincide with the arithmetic mean, or be the leader or whatever else, there will be other units different from the chosen one.

In chemistry or in physics there is often no problem of finding *le cas pur*. When the chemist wants to establish a proposition about sulphur he can use any lump of chemically pure sulphur (provided its crystalline form is irrelevant to the experiment) and treat it as a true and pure representative of sulphur, S.[1] If a social scientist wants to study The Norwegian Voter, it would simplify research enormously if he could find the pure voter, the one person who would be the representative of all Norwegian voters, so that all that was necessary would be to ask him or watch his behavior. At present, the belief in the possibility of finding *le cas pur,* on the individual or collective level of analysis, seems to have disappeared completely from social research.

There can be the same argument about the case of $n = 1$, i.e. the case where only one question is asked, in survey research. Imagine a dimension has been singled out for study, such as 'cosmopolitan vs. local orientation in general'. The standard procedure today would be to select a set of questions designed to 'tap' this dimension, ask all questions, and base the analysis on some kind of aggregate index formed with the questions asked as items. One would rather not limit the survey to one question alone. Why exactly that question – why could not another question do, or why not at least supplement the information given by the first question? There are exceptions to this principle of many questions for the same dimension, however. When simple background information is asked for, or when an attitudinal dimension that has occurred very often in everyday debate is investigated, the survey researcher seems justified in limiting himself to one question alone. Gallup polls fall in either or both of these categories, which makes them methodologically justifiable from this point of view. But on the other hand, it is difficult for this very reason to use gallup data in an analysis where more abstract concepts of a more theoretical and less commonsensical kind occur.

There are other, more positive, reasons why the degenerate cases should be avoided, however. They can be listed as follows:

Table 1.2.2. *Reasons for avoiding the cases m = 1 or n = 1*

Reasons for	More than one unit	More than one dimension
negative reason	lack of belief in *le cas pur*, why this unit rather than the other?	lack of belief in *la question pure*, why this stimulus rather than the other?
the use of dispersion	more than one unit makes it possible to see differences, variations, and to avoid stereotyping[2]	more than one question or dimension makes it possible to see patterns of response, to see one response or value in a context
the use of correlation	the correlation of responses to different questions is one of the main tools of analysis, and can be applied only with a certain number of units and at least two dimensions	

For the analyst used to working with statistical data (i.e., data that can be put in the form of a complete data matrix), the third reason is of overwhelming importance; the whole set of arguments is in a sense the basis on which he works. There is no substitute for the kind of analysis he can make, while it may, of course, be argued that there are other valuable approaches based on data where $m = 1$ or $n = 1$. At some level of the analysis, one is always studying one unit only, as when a survey is made of *US* males and their sexual behavior. The community study addresses itself to one community, but within that community it is usually advisable to get a complete data matrix based on well-chosen individual units and dimensions. But interest in one unit does not imply any belief in the *Einmaligkeit* position.[3]

2 *

One of the most famous examples of the idea of studying a phenomenon by studying *le cas pur* is found in Durkheim's *Les formes élémentaires de la vie religieuse*. His *Introduction* presents a brilliant case for his method, even if it may appear less acceptable today than when it was first published (Paris, 1912). He says at the very beginning:

Nous nous proposons d'étudier dans ce livre la religion la plus primitive et la plus simple qui soit actuellement connue, d'en faire l'analyse et d'en tenter l'explication. Nous disons d'un système religieux qu'il est le plus primitif qu'il nous soit donné quand il remplit les deux conditions suivantes: en premier lieu, il faut qu'il se rencontre dans des sociétés dont l'organisation n'est dépassée par aucune autre en simplicité: il faut de plus qu'il soit possible de l'expliquer sans faire intervenir aucun élément emprunté à une religion antérieure. (Page 1).

And he says further:

A la base de tous les systèmes de croyances et de touts les cultes, il doit nécessairement y avoir un certain nombre de représentations fondamentales et d'attitudes rituelles qui, malgré la diversité des formes que les unes et les autres ont pu revêtir, ont partout la même signification objective et remplissent partout les mêmes fonctions. Ce sont ces éléments permanents qui constuient ce qu'il y a d'éternel et d'humaine dans la religion; ils sont tout le contenu objectif de l'idée que l'on exprime quand on parle de la religion en général. (Page 6).

Here, we have two important ideas. First of all a division of a social institution into two parts which may be called the *essential* and the *accidental,* and the simple equation:

Social institution = *essential* part + *accidental* elements
(*chose sociale*)

The essential evidently represents the condition *sine qua non,* 'l'idée que l'on exprime quand on parle de la religion en generale'. Durkheim expresses this equation almost in our words when he says:

L'imagination populaire ou sacerdotale n'a encore eu ni le temps ni le moyen de raffiner et de transformer la matière première des idées et des pratiques religieuses; celle-ci se montre donc à nu et s'offre d'elle même à l'observation qui n'a que moindre effort à faire pour la découvrir. L'accessoire, le secondaire, les developpements de luxe ne sont pas encore venus cacher le principal. Tout est réduit à l'indispensable, à ce sans quoi il ne saurait y avoir de religion. Mais l'indispensable, c'est aussi l'essentiel, c'est à dire ce qu'il nous importe avant tout de connâitre. (Page 8).

Secondly, there is the idea that the essential part is found in its most pure form in primitive societies, and in general, the more primitive the better. In other words, the idea is that the society somehow starts out with 'la matière première', and to this is added, by processes of evolution and diffusion 'l'accessoire, le secondaire, les developpements de luxe'.

Since nobody seems to have disputed one of the basic propositions of the evolutionists, that social change tends to be in the direction of more rather than less complex forms (with *division de travail* and its concomitant growing complexity of the status-network as one of the dimensions) one will not dispute that some social institutions may be more *simple* at lower levels of social organization in general. But this, even if tenable more generally than we are willing to assume, is not the same as saying that these institutions are more *pure*. Simplicity is not the same as purity.

Two very basic ideas may facilitate the acceptance of Durkheim's conception of working with *le cas pur,* which led him to the intensive second-hand study of the Arunta tribe. First of all, there is the classic distinction between *universalia* and *particularia,* corresponding to our distinction between the essential and the accidental, a distinction between the general idea and the inessential extra characteristics (such as the famous *color* of the horse, exactly *which* objects are defined as sacred, etc.). If we introduce here the equally classic dispute between the realists and the nominalists, we can conceive of a continuum of attitudes in this conflict, instead of the traditional two positions: the realist *ante rem* (the universalia have an independent existence 'prior' to the things that are the manifestations) and the nominalist *in rebus* (the universalia have no such existence, they are only names of abstractions from the things). Some intermediate positions would be as follows:

We may take the position that 'things' (i.e. the denotata of the idea, of the universalia) can be arranged according to how many particularia they possess, thus starting with the purest approximations to the idea itself, adding to it the more complex forms exhibiting more accidental elements, more particularia, more of 'le secondaire' to use the terminologies employed. But even if it is possible to arrive at a linear or partial ordering of the 'things', it is only interesting if this variable (degree of 'purity') is highly correlated with some other variable. At this point, the second basic cultural idea enters: the idea that the variable is correlated with evolutionist stages, whatever that is. Even if Durkheim did not have this idea, he had the idea of 'des sociétés dont l'organisation n'est dépassée par aucune autre en simplicité', and the idea that this is where one would have to look to find 'les formes élémentaires de la vie religieuse'. The difficulty is that 'simplicité', even though it may work as a global characteristic of a society, does not seem to work for all parts of the society, as the kinship systems of 'primitive' societies show clearly. Nevertheless, the position is interesting, as a kind of modified *ante rem* position; not *ante* all social institutions, but *ante* the existence of the religious institutions in our societies.

Another intermediate position could take as its point of departure the equation presented above and conceive of it not, as above, as a *temporal* relation with the accidental characteristics added with time, but as a *spatial* relation with the accidental characteristics superimposed on the essential ones; not only analytically distinguishable, but also empirically distinguishable. Any owner of a motorcycle will know what is essential and what is not as his cycle deteriorates, but he will also know that it is always possible to predicate more of the parts of the motorcycle than the property that is its functional *sine qua non*. For instance, he may conclude that he can do without the gas tank as long as he has a bottle and a tube to the carburator, but the predicate 'bottle' is still an inessential characteristic. Still, there may be degrees to which the accidental may be empirically removed so as to reveal the essential in its naked form: 'Celle-ci se montre donc a nu'.

The scientific utility of these positions is generally held in low esteem today. The dominant current position is nominalist, and the derisive term used for any tendency to attribute independent existence to the universalia is 'reification', whether this independence is *ante rem,* early evolutionist, or as empirical categories.[4] All these positions will include analysis, logical and/or empirical, as a tool in the hunt for the essential. Posed against this is the current practice of distinguishing between the *extension* (denotation) and *intension* (connotation) of a concept, and to include in the intension only the properties that are *necessary* for the inclusion of an element in the extension. Together the properties forming the intension will constitute a necessary and sufficient condition for inclusion in the extension.

It is not necessary to attribute to Durkheim such labels as 'quasi-realist' and 'evolutionist'. A person may be anti-realist and anti-evolutionist, whatever this may mean, and still proceed almost exactly as Durkheim did, although possibly with a different introduction, stressing simplicity more than purity ('matière première'). But, with the commonly held views on the relation between ideas and things indicated above, another procedure emerges more easily: that of studying a sample of units that all fall under the idea of 'religious institutions', and using their variations as an analytical tool. This may be coupled with case analyses which would not only include the Arunta, but also highly modern religious systems.

Thus the criticism of Durkheim's type of methodology includes at least these elements: (1) ('anti-realist') that the religious institution or any other institution should be seen in its social context, which invariably involves 'accidentals', and studied in its context, not isolated; and (2) ('anti-evolutionist') that global characteristics such as 'primitive' may characterize societies as wholes by emphasizing the simplicity of certain institutions, but this characteristic does not necessarily apply to other parts of the society. By analyzing many units, no judgment as to purity is needed, nor any more or less arbitrary isolation of the essential from the accidental.

In retrospect, it may be said that the modern methodology of extensive research or research with a high number of units in general presupposes readily available resources, in terms of money, energy, time, and manpower. The intensive methodology compatible with Durkheim's line of reasoning is also compatible with the library model of the academic man of the past century. Thus, there are interrelations here between methodology, very basic ideology, and the social structure of social research, that may themselves lead to severe conflicts.

In the history of sociological methodology or social science methodology in general, a considerable amount of ideology has been invested in different cells in Table 1.2.1, or subsets of cells – claiming that these cells represent the optimal combinations in the search for scientific knowledge about social reality. Emotional investment seems to be higher, the more off-diagonal is the position to be defended. We prefer a more even distribution of ideological investment, since that seems to be more in line with what actually happens in contemporary social research. It looks as if the scientific process itself invariably will bring one to most of the cells if the usual canons of scientific research are to be followed. Thus, it may well be that the first germinal suspicion leading to a research project in the mind of a sociologist was located in the left hand bottom corner as a remark made by one person responding to one question. Research may then extend legitimately horizontally by asking a number of people the same question, or vertically by asking the same person a number of different questions. Sooner or later, the two dimensions of units and variables will probably have to be brought together, at least implicitly, thus bringing the process towards the diagonal, at a low or high level probably more dependent on resources than on methodological ideology.

It may be that the final *confirmation* will have to be obtained by means of projects located on or close to the diagonal, but it may also be that the first (and perhaps lasting) *insights* are obtained closer to the axes. Thus, we do not compare the extensive with the intensive as much as we compare the asymmetric with the symmetric research strategies. Very intensive research will probably have a low yield in confirmation value relative to general propositions, and we assume a certain generality to be the aim, because of the low number of units. Similarly, very extensive research will not contain a sufficient number of variables to control for relevant conditions and test at least some of the many alternative hypotheses that are bound to appear in the researcher's mind. Thus, the most fruitful philosophy with regard to the Table seems to be a combination of two 'both-ands': both research of the extensive kind and research of the intensive kind, *and*, leading to both high m and high n.

If our contention that the different ideologies regarding choice of research strategy represent different phases in the scientific process is correct, then we should expect the holders of the different ideologies to have some kind of connection with these different phases. We have no empirical data here, only the more intuitive impression that the researcher who is insight-oriented, in search of perspectives more than confirmation, tends to argue in favor of off-diagonal strategies, and more often than not in favor of intensive research case-studies, etc. Similarly, the confirmation-oriented researcher, less concerned with 'perspectives', more concerned with 'hard facts', is often found to argue in favor of his specialty in the upper right hand corner, and often also in favor of extensive strategies. In the latter case, he can often be beaten with his own arguments, since a scarcity of variables will hardly offer the rock basis necessary to explore alternatives and, eventually, discard $n-1$ hypotheses in favor of the n'th one. However this may be, it is of less interest, since we are concerned with normative methodology, not with descriptive methodology – with what researchers should do more than with what they actually do. We only note in passing that symmetric ideologies in this field seem to be hard to harbor for reasons well known to students of tolerance of ambivalence, and particularly because the folklore of contemporary science seems to have imposed some kind of opposition between the two. It is often as if one has to be either in favor of intensive or in favor of extensive research, either 'case' or 'survey' oriented.

And the same applies to the difference between the so-called *nomothetic* ('generalizing') and *ideographic* ('singularizing') sciences: it is often exaggerated. Both kinds of sciences develop propositions and both kinds of sciences link propositions together in theories by means of implication relations. In other words, both kinds have description as well as explanation as their goal. But whereas the propositions in ideographic sciences are about limited and contiguous time-space regions ('France under Louis XIV', 'the Italian city-state during the Renaissance', etc.), the propositions in the nomothetic sciences deal with phenomena that (at least in principle) can be found over a wide field of noncontiguous space-time regions ('the relation between rapid industrialization and political stability'). Thus, we can picture the relationship as follows:

Diagram 1.2.3. *The relation between nomothetic and ideographic sciences*

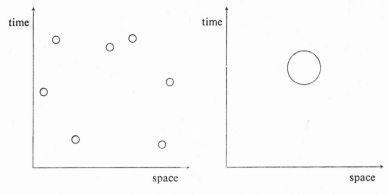

nomothetic: non-contiguous
space-time regions

ideographic: contiguous
space-time regions

Slogans like the difference between 'saying very little about very much' and 'saying very much about very little' do not capture the essential point: the propositions in the ideographic sciences are programmatically limited to a contiguous region (usually one interval in the history of one nation, or of some selected aspect of one nation), whereas the propositions in the nomothetic sciences know of no such boundaries. The regions relevant for their testing are usually scattered over a wide field, and there is no need to fill in the gaps between them with knowledge.

Obviously, the total field of an ideographic monograph *may* be wider than the total field of a nomothetic monograph, as when one person is writing the history of the industrial revolution in Britain and another person is testing hypotheses about worker-entrepreneur relations in a number of establishments in that period, in that nation. Also, obviously, the borderlines between the two are by no means sharp. Rather, they represent two different foci: the detailed, realistic, concrete description and explanation of something meaningfully interrelated; and the testing of general, less realistic, more abstract propositions about something scattered and not in the same sense interrelated by the unity of time, space and action, like classical drama.

As is usual with dichotomies, they have a tendency to polarize not only thinking but also people. That the two supplement each other is so obvious as not to need any justification: generalizing science can give singularizing science hints about what to look for of theoretical interest, singularizing science can give generalizing science data to test its hypotheses. But the difference is not simply along an explanation/description axis. Ideographic science has the advantage of giving explanations that are realistic in the singular case in the sense of taking into account a more nearly sufficient number of factors; generalizing science has the descriptive advantage of surveying a larger field, for which reason it can develop categories meaningful in a wider context.

This is particularly important in connection with the often disputed relationship between *synchronic* social science (dealing with phenomena that take place anywhere in space, but within a relatively narrow time-interval) and *diachronic* social science (dealing with phenomena that take place anywhere in time but within a limited space region). The relations between them can, perhaps, be depicted in the following way:

Table 1.2.4. *The relation between synchronic and diachronic social science*

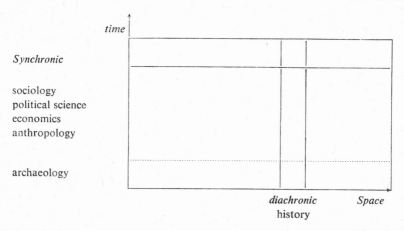

But the difference between, for instance, sociology and history, is not merely in terms of synchronic vs. diachronic. Sociology tends to be more nomothetic, history to be more ideographic. The total set of sociological work may cover space relatively well in a set of interlocking monographs, one dealing with family relations anywhere, one with power structure anywhere, etc. What is missing would be ideographic, synchronic science: the really good set of treatises about the sociology of a given region in space, say a nation. This is found in anthropology and in community studies, but perhaps at the expense of general insights. Correspondingly, the total set of historical and much anthropological work may fill both time and space by joining works about adjacent and contiguous space-time regions. What is missing here would be nomothetic, diachronic science connecting all this knowledge in theoretical frameworks that know no limitations in space and time, operating at the level of individuals and of social structure.

24

It is a deplorable state of affairs that keeps sociology and history apart institutionally at the universities, thus separating not only the synchronic and diachronic approaches, but, to a considerable extent, also the nomothetic and ideographic approaches.

Tearing down these artificial barriers would obviously call for team-work and institutional cooperation. This could probably most easily be done at new universities, perhaps also in developing countries, where unfortunate academic practices of the past have not formed a tradition too sacred to be tampered with. Theoretically, we should be able to bring forth a more general science of man, exploring relations both in space and time, in contiguous and noncontiguous regions at the explanatory and descriptive levels, all within the same project. This would, of course, require a much better basis in terms of synchronic, descriptive social science (*sociography*, descriptive sociology) and diachronic, descriptive social science (*historiography*, descriptive history) than we have today. But, with modern methods of data storage, this should not be too difficult.

Since the approach of the present text is mainly nomothetic, it may be worth while to give these thoughts more substance by spelling out what this would mean, say, in terms of IBM cards. The classical unit of synchronic social science has been the individual. A great step forward is made by adding higher level units, provinces, nations etc. A further advance is made by the analysis of pairs, triples etc. of units at any level (individual or collective), since this permits the inclusion of relational variables (see 2.1). So the step we suggest here is simply to add the dimension of *time*. A nation could thus be regarded not only as a spatial unit, but as a 'space-time chunk'. We could take the last 150 years' history of the nation (provided it has been in existence that long) and divide this in intervals of, say, five years each, a total of thirty space-time units. If the same could be done for, say, all Latin-American *nations* we would get close to 600 units of analysis. If the same could be done for all *pairs* of Latin-American nations, even only within a period of fifty years, we would get $10 \cdot \binom{20}{2} = 1900$ units of analysis, and we could explore the interaction of time and space on international relations. Keeping *nation* constant would yield diachronic analysis, keeping *time* constant would yield synchronic analysis, giving both dimensions free play would give the kind of analysis (nomothetic variety) towards which social science is no doubt heading.

Thus, the arguments for more than one unit of analysis are by no means arguments for survey and public opinion studies only – although it may be said that these studies have shown the way since they were easiest to carry out. Rather, they are arguments for imagination in choice of units within the space-time region where data can be obtained, and arguments for breaking down institutional barriers in the choice of such units.

This work is concerned with a methodology based on the idea of sampling, both on the unit and on the variable side, and on the idea of skepticism where the choice of only one unit or only one variable is concerned. This should not be confused with a nomothetic orientation, although it will generally be associated with it. A researcher studying a contiguous space-time region will also generally use sampling, for instance of a king's letters or actions. How, then, should one characterize this type of methodology, in very broad terms? One effort may be as follows.

A problem defines a set of space-time regions, continuous or not, as relevant for the study. For the geologist it may be a mountain, for the oceanographer a part of an ocean, for the sciences of man the regions discussed above, and so on. The scientist has two goals: the search for invariances (propositions), and the search for explanations of invariances (theories). To do this, he sooner or later has to encounter data, and if he does not have a theory and a set of hypotheses that indicate where to look, he has to sample units. The geologist could collect test samples of stone, the oceanographer of the ocean, and analyse them with regard to such variables as location and composition, temperature, etc. The social scientist will make his kind of sampling from the space-time continuum. The units will be exposed to a systematic analysis in terms of the variables introduced, by means of methods to be described and similar methods.

One problem of this methodology is its way of atomizing entities – the 'ocean-ness of an ocean' and the 'mountain-ness of a mountain' may disappear in the process. The method is antiholistic, unless it is combined with a method based on several levels of analysis to be described in I, 2.1.

Another problem can be phrased as follows. Imagine you want to study the game of chess. Will you do this by using the rules, or by sampling moves and analyzing them in terms of 'variables'? The answer is, of course, that what the researcher does will depend on whether he knows the rules or not, and that the type of scientific activity described, prescribed and analyzed in the present work is most applicable to problems where the rules are not known. The person observing a game of chess for the first time in his life will get many insights by simply watching it and inferring regularities, and more so by doing it in a systematic way. By the audacity and imagination associated with theory-formation he may eventually hypothesize and verify the rules of chess as regularities of behavior in chess-players. But this would require good sampling, and also replications with several dyads of players; and he may in the process discover regularities (hilariousness in the person

26

who says 'check-mate') that he may have difficulties in distinguishing from the rules as ordinarily conceived of. That it would be foolhardy to do all this if the rules were already known (except to check the extent to which the rules are adhered to) does not invalidate the approach in the cases where 'rules' are not known – as in most of the problems studied by the social sciences. Neither should this be confused with the truism that one will not discover legal rules by studying overt behavior – unless one studies overt behavior of judges or others associated with due process of law. Only empirical regularities can be inferred.

Essentially, thus, the present methodology is inductive, and although it will be greatly facilitated by hypotheses *a priori,* it is above all the methodology of *discovery* not only of confirmation. It is as such we feel it is of particular relevance to the social sciences – nomothetic or ideographic, diachronic or synchronic.

1.3. *Observation and inference*

Data in social sciences, as in other sciences, are based on sense-observations; and one criterion of quality-rating has to do with the *immediacy* of the datum. A check in an answer-box is a datum, not the inference that the respondent is for or against something. A smile is a datum, the inference is that the smiling person is in a happy mood is not, etc. A datum is what is *observed,* is *manifest* or *phenotypical;* not what is *inferred,* as *latent* or *genotypical.* Our concern in this presentation of data-collection is always with manifest data, never with the latent, with what can be inferred.

The word observation is used here and elsewhere to include all forms of sense-perceptions used in the recording of responses, as they impinge on our senses. We make, however, a distinction between a response and a datum – a *response is some manifest kind of action, a datum is the product of the recording of the response.* The road from the response to the datum is winding, involving among other things such difficulties as intra- and inter-personal perceptual variations, variations in the usage of symbols to record the impressions of the responses (the semantic aspect), etc. Thus, it is a distinct desideratum to make the last part of this sequence as short as possible:

Table 1.3.1. *The stimulus to datum sequence*

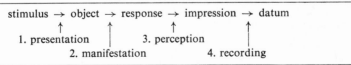

A response is observable, a datum is observed.

There are two important conditions imposed on scientific observations as opposed to other observations, and these conditions delimit to some extent what can properly be regarded as manifest data. Imagine that the phenomenon observed is *repetitive,* and that it is *constant* (e.g., a man who gives the same answer to the same question, a person who reacts the same way in the same experimental situation, etc.). It seems quite reasonable to require of repeated observations of this object that they shall yield constant data, regardless of whether the observations are made by one observer or by different observers. *If repeated observations of a constant phenomenon by the same observer yield constant data, the observation is said to be intrasubjective or reliable. If repeated observations of a constant phenomenon by different observers yield constant data, the observation is said to be intersubjective.* (It should be noticed that in both cases we are dealing with definitions with reduction-sentences.)

These two requirements, reliability and intersubjectivity, can be used together as definiens of the loosely used term 'objectivity'. The requirements serve to rule out from the sphere of scientific observation, observations that are unstable, hasty and hazy, insufficiently standardized – and observations that belong to one particular person's subjective perception only and cannot be shared by others. Obviously, it is necessary to talk of *degrees* of reliability and intersubjectivity, and exactly where the borderline is to be drawn is a problem that perhaps can best be decided *ad hoc.*

Reliability and intersubjectivity have to do with the two components of the observation process here called perception and recording, and have nothing to do with either the presentation of the stimulus or the manifestation of the responses in the respondent. Whether a constant stimulus produces a constant response is an entirely different question; it has (by definition) to do with the *constancy of the object* (the unit of analysis) and nothing to do with the observation process. It is often regarded as desirable to find stimuli that easily yield constant responses, but this desideratum is somewhat unrealistic. Firstly, stimuli may appear constant without being so, because the context in which they appear relevant for the objects is not constant. An example is when the 'same' question is asked for the second time in a panel study. Secondly, if stimuli render constant responses, this may be an indication that the stimuli are too crude, since the responses do not reflect the minute oscillations we may safely assume to take place in the human mind. This, then, is an argument for using more than one stimulus to tap the same 'dimension' – as we certainly have no desideratum requiring constancy also of the objects.

To summarize: in addition to the principles for the construction of a data matrix, we have introduced two new principles:[5]

(4) *Principle of intrasubjectivity or reliability*:
Repeated observation of the same responses by the *same* observer shall yield the same data.
(5) *Principle of intersubjectivity*:
Repeated observation of the same responses by *different* observers shall yield the same data.

In this connection, a principle of validity is often mentioned, with the understanding that an observation is valid if one has observed what he wants to observe. Validity thus obviously has to do with the relation between the manifest and the latent. Since observations by definitions always are at the manifest level, we can formulate the principle as follows:

(6) *Principle of validity*:
Data shall be obtained of such a kind and in such a way that legitimate inferences can be made from the manifest level to the latent level.

Since the concepts of manifest and latent have not really been defined, we shall postpone further argument, and not make use of the principle of validity. Actually, data are always valid in *some* context, with regard to *some* latent dimension – and this weakens the concept of validity somewhat. Validity becomes a question of whether or not data can be used for exactly the purpose they were designed to meet. This again is a question of some kind of awareness prior to the data-collection that may be of great importance, but also may play a minor role, as in a more descriptive and exploratory study.

1.4. *Classes of variables and models for research*

In social science analysis, *individuals* are most frequently used as *units of analysis*. The individual can be characterized, and has been characterized, by means of an enormously high number of variables. The number is high for two reasons: the individual is the usual level of human interaction, and hence the level where the need for discrimination in perception and communication is most acutely felt and developed; and secondly, the possibility of verbal interaction with individuals makes verbal responses with their immense variety possible.

We need some kind of order in this variety, some kind of typology and suggest two bases for classifying variables characterizing individuals.

First of all, the value an individual has on a variable may be *public* or *private*. By a 'public variable' we mean a variable where the individual values are known and *known to be known* by others. Examples are age, sex, race, creed (more often than not), occupation, income (at least in broad terms, compare public access to tax protocols), address, family of origin, data about the family of procreation, etc. By a 'private variable' we mean a variable where the individual values certainly *may* be known, but others have no legitimate claim on knowing the values. Examples are IQ, plans for the future, whether one is authoritarian or not, attitudes and behavioral patterns of different kinds. A person may make his opinion with regard to the EEC or the NATO publicly known, but this does not imply that his attitude is a public variable, because he may also withhold it from human interaction.

Secondly, a person's value on a variable may be *permanent* or *temporal*. By the latter we mean that knowledge of a person's value at one point in time yields a relatively poor basis for a prediction of his value at some later time; but if the value is permanent, the basis for prediction is very good. Obviously, the borderline between what is most properly called a 'temporal' value and what should be called a 'permanent' value is far from clear – and the same applies to the borderline between 'public' and 'private': how many people have a legitimate claim before a value is public? Is IQ, known to the school psychologist, a public variable? 'Public', relative to what systems, etc. But the distinctions, nevertheless, have great heuristic value. If we combine them, we get the following fourfold-table:

Table 1.4.1. *A typology for variables characterizing individuals*

	Permanent values	Temporal values
Public values	(background variables)	impossible
Private values	(personality variables)	(attitudinal and behavioral variables)

This typology has four cells, but one of them is void because of a sociological proposition that can be phrased as follows: Institutionalized interaction is based on relevant *public* variables (i.e., variables where the values of a specific individual are known publicly and, hence, can be legitimately used in interaction); but if variables shall yield a basis for lasting interaction, they must be predictable, which means that the individual values must show a certain degree of *permanence*. The values must be cognized and recognized, *which means that the public variables cannot be temporal*. It should be added that *most* human interaction is not institutionalized and takes place on the basis of cues of a more evasive and ephemeral nature. Characteristic of inter-action is that it may start with a basis in more private and even temporal values, but as the interaction catches on and becomes institutionalized there will be a change in the character of the values used as a basis, towards the public and permanent. A public value can never be temporal, because a temporal value does not yield sufficient basis for public interaction.

In the remaining three cells some terms have been put. They should not be regarded as completely coextensive with the meaning these cells have been given by definition. Rather, the meaning of a 'background variable' is a variable which is public and permanent *within a given system of interaction,* e.g., the Norwegian society. 'Chairman' of a local organization is not a public value when Norway as a whole is taken as a system of reference, but 'occupation' is, because of its relevance in the national context. In the con-text of the local organization, however, it may be irrelevant whereas 'chair-man' will be highly relevant. Typical background variables are age, sex, geographical location, occupation, etc. When we say that they are permanent, we do not deny the possibility of mobility – we mean only 'permanent within a period'.

The variables that are 'public *and* permanent' place the individual in the social matrix, or in the social structure, if one wants to use that term. The set of values on the background variables gives, for the individual, his social personality. For that reason these variables are often called 'structural vari-ables', a term we prefer not to use because it may lead to a confusion of levels of analysis. The background variables characterize *individuals,* but when they are called 'structural', one is thinking of the structure of *societies.*

By 'personality variables' we mean variables that may be hidden even to the individual himself and require the skill of a psychologist to be assessed. The essential characteristic is their permanence. Since we usually have the idea that permanent variables are of a more latent character, whereas the manifest variables yield less permanent values for the individuals, personality variables will usually be what we have called latent variables. Again, 'per-manence' does not mean that change is impossible, but it means that there are time intervals that are long enough to be of importance, within which the fluctuations are insignificant.

The third category contains the rest: all kinds of behavioral and attitudinal variables or other variables that can be used to characterize an individual and that are neither public, nor permanent. Most data we get by means of a questionnaire or an interview-investigation fall in this category. Since the only factor these variables have in common, according to this scheme, is their property as temporal variables, we have no better term than 'behavioral elements'. Responses to interviews and questionnaires are then classified as behavior (speech reactions, verbal behavior).

Hence, what this typology amounts to is a division of variables characterizing individuals into background variables, personality variables and behavior elements. Actually, a quite similar scheme can be used, for instance, with regard to nations; and the fruitful application of this scheme lies in the field of the analysis of units that are human beings, or nations, or any actor.

Usually, these analyses take place with a certain model in mind, which may or may not have been made explicit by the researcher. Typically, the thinking is in terms of regarding the 'temporal' behavior elements as somehow produced or caused by the background variables, or personality variables, or both. Essentially, these are the four models that seem to be most current in the literature:

Table 1.4.2. *Models for the relations between the types of variables*

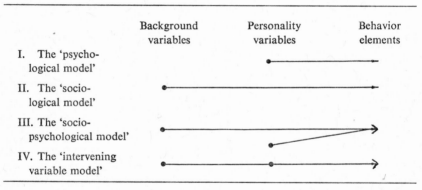

The researcher should have a relatively clear picture as to what he has in mind. The terms chosen for the models are, again, not coextensive with the content given to the models by the diagram, but also more often true than false.[6]

The difference between the third and fourth models is as follows: in the fourth model, the idea is that a certain social condition defined by a set of background variables produces (more often than not) a certain personality structure; and this personality structure, in turn, produces (more often than not) certain behavior elements. But, in the third model, the personality characteristics are not seen as steps on the road, so to speak, but as independent sources producing the behavior elements jointly with the social background characteristic.

Imagine that we have developed powerful indices of social background and of personality, so that either can be successfully analyzed by means of one variable (for instance, by choosing some measure of the 'center-periphery' dimension for social background and of the 'open mind – closed mind' dimension for the personality characteristic, thus incorporating much of contemporary thinking). A powerful design for the study of behavioral elements, whether they are overt (actions) or covert (attitudes) would be as follows:

Table 1.4.3. *Design for the study of behavioral elements*

Social background variables

		1 2 3 .... a	Total
Personality variables	1 2 3 · · · b		
	Total		

The design would study how behavioral elements vary with both social background and personality. To do this, an $a \times b$ design is necessary, if the social variable has a levels and the personality variable b levels. The design lends itself to interpretations both of types III and IV, to be treated in II, 5.3.

To appreciate the idea of the design, let us consider some typical truncated designs that are often used. Models I and II would use only the vertical and horizontal marginals, respectively, of the design. This may not be objectionable, although the correlations will probably be lower than they could be, because at each social level there will be much personality variation unaccounted for, and at each personality level there will be much social variation unaccounted for. Still, general tendencies in terms of social structure or personality structure may be obtained. What is really objectionable is to base the analysis on models I or II and use samples from only some of the rows or columns in the design. In sociological research, this would mean sampling only people with certain personality traits; in psychological research, it would mean sampling only people with certain social background characteristics. The sociologist is saved from this fallacy more often because of the difficulty in using psychological data as sampling criteria; but the psychologis will often be tempted to sample the most easily accessible or the most extraordinary, thus overselecting central and peripheral social categories, respectively, like political science based on Western societies.

3 *

This is one of the main points in the important methodological critique of *The Authoritarian Personality* by Hyman and Sheatsley.[7] As they say about 'sampling the heterogeneous national population':

Such a population has one often overlooked virtue, which would have improved the quality of the analysis and cast doubt on certain conclusions in '*The Authoritarian Personality*'. For such a sample reveals the extent and social location of attitudes. Without this knowledge, interpretation is difficult and often dangerous. Thus, one might well find in a national sample that a particular attitude is most universal. Yet this same attitude, studied in a small homogeneous group, may appear to be deviant. Lacking national norms, one would attempt to explain the latter finding in terms of some *idiosyncratic* personality process, when in reality it is highly correlated with a major social fact. – But if the researcher, because of his sampling design, cannot tell whether the given attitude is normative for the general population, he may seek the explanation in the wrong place. (Pp. 67-68).

One may object to the reasoning presented here that if 'group' in 'small homogeneous group' above stands for social group and not for social category, then the rare is also the deviant, even if it is common in larger contexts. But the general argument is important, and extends not only to rates and percentages but also to correlations, i.e. to attitudinal organization:

– inquiries into the *organization* of sentiments /cannot/ afford to ignore sampling considerations in the study in the course of the study design and analysis of the results. We feel that the slighting of this matter by the authors is unsound methodology, and from a practical standpoint it tends to perpetuate the implication that the level of organization of sentiments is a kind of universal, an intrapsychic process which bears little relation to environmental conditions. (P. 60).

We shall show later that, by suitably biasing his sample, the analyst can in many cases obtain almost any correlation he wants between two attitudes. In the idea of sampling one particular social category, e.g. the famous students taking courses in Introductory Psychology, there is an easily recognizable case of *le cas pur* thinking, or 'a kind of universal' as Hyman and Sheatsley express it. They then go on to quote a large number of research reports to the effect that attitudinal correlations vary with such factors as *age* ('children became more consistent in their moral traits as they grew older') and *education* (research showing increasing correlation between prejudice and authoritarianism with education). Obviously, generalizations from one social category to the entire society are not permissible, hence the importance of the complete design.

In this design there is no implicit assumption that social background and personality are independent. Indeed, a considerable research tradition in

34

social psychology shows that these are dependent. What is important is to try to get data covering all cells, even if the design is to be handled in one of the two collapsed forms (models I and II). If the two basic variables are both recorded for all units, there is always the possibility of controlling for the effect of the second variable, so that extensions in the direction of models III and IV may be made.

The relation between the two variables can best be explored by means of a research model of a fifth type:

Table 1.4.4. *A model for relations between the types of variables*

	Background variables	Personality variables	Behavior elements
V. The 'social-psychological model'	●————————————▶		

We have not included this among the others, since it does not touch directly on behavior elements, and obviously will have to be based on research according to models III or IV – since we shall assume that the personality variables are latent, and the behavior elements manifest, and we can only obtain manifest data. This model will yield distribution of personality traits over social categories, and hence a kind of knowledge indispensable in research according to model IV.

It should be emphasized that the uni-directedness of the arrows in the five models should not be taken as more than rules of thumb. Thus, personality may be seen as an independent variable and such background variables as occupation or education as the dependent ones – although the models may easily and even fruitfully be saved by defining *seeking* occupation and education as a behavioral element. In general, the models reflect the present stage of social science thinking, but they will have to be refined in subsequent chapters in order to serve as guides for research.

Models III and IV are interdisciplinary and call for the pooled skills of the psychologist and the sociologist, if the units are individuals. Hence, they are models for research teams, unless we can assume that adequate knowledge is possessed by one and the same researcher, or that the sociologist can hand over to the psychologist, and *vice versa,* sufficiently good instruments to be used by the un-initiated.

It should be emphasized that although we have used as examples units that are *individuals*, the whole scheme in this section is equally applicable to units that are groups, or nations. Thus, *background variables* would place nations in the international system (as big, powerful, poor, etc.); then there would be variables describing the domestic system of the nation (economically, politically, culturally, etc.); and finally, the variables describing how nations act in the international system (voting in the UN, acts of conflict and cooperation, etc.). Correspondingly, one would get five major models of research, all of them very meaningful.[8]

A distinction very often made in this connection is that between *independent* and *dependent* variables. In mathematics these terms are frequently used to point out a certain asymmetry in the way a functional relation is *presented,* but mean very little more. In empirical sciences the terms can only be used if there exists some model, even of the vaguest kind, of the relationship between the variables studied. Models may take on many forms, note for instance the five basic models in social science research mentioned above; but they usually have in common the idea of 'something somehow producing something else'. In this idea the two elements leading to the conceptions of independent and dependent variables are clearly seen. We can give three applications:

(1) If the model is any of the five discussed above (or any other involving the same types of variables), *then the independent variable is the variable most to the left*, with the dependent variable to the right.
(2) If the model is causal, *then the causal variable is the independent variable*, with the effect as the dependent variable.
(3) If there is a time-order among the variables, *then the preceding variable is the independent variable.*

Finally, a point relating the choice of variables to applied social science should be made. Applied social science shall *yield a basis* for directives concerning social science and differs from general social science discourse only in one thing: 'right', but the directives themselves can be formulated by others. Applied social science differs from general social science discourse only in one thing: it should make its conclusions in terms of variables that are *manipulable*. A causal relation where there is no possibility of manipulating the independent variable for technical, economic, ethical, or other reasons is of little value to the practitioner. This is actually a case against applied social research according to model I above, since personality factors are so difficult to change.[9] It is not so much a case against models II and IV, however, particularly not in a culture where 'social engineering' is somehow regarded as more feasible than 'human engineering'.[10] Whatever one's philosophy here may be, the choice of basic model should be well considered before a project is started, and the general purpose of the study should be examined before irreversible decisions concerning the choice of independent variables are made.

2. Units

2.1. *Levels of analysis*

The choice of unit is probably the first decisive choice made in most investigations. Once made, it is hard to reverse: the procedure will be built up around this choice. For that reason it is essential to have a clear picture of the spectrum of possible units, so that the choice based on the research problem may be a fruitful one, and not only a traditional one.

Sociology is often defined as the science of social interaction, from which it should follow that the unit of sociological analysis should be a social actor. In most sociological analyses this will be the case, and in the majority of them the choice will fall on the prototype of the social actor, the human individual. A considerable percentage of sociological work is done on the assumption, it seems, that most insights can be gained by studying the individual, carefully sampled, and pooling the results from analyses of this type to get information about social structure.

Two basic objections may be relevant to this kind of study. First, one may argue that it implies an atomistic conception of society, viewed as a heap of individuals, with structural factors discounted or presumed mirrored in the single individual. Secondly: the concentration on the individual as social actor, because it is easy and looks convincing, may lead away from considering other units of analysis. These objections will be formulated more precisely as a typology of units of analysis is developed. A physical analogy: it is like a conception of matter where the atoms form no superunits (molecules) and are not related to each other, like the inert gases.

Hence, there are two basic facts about units of analysis in sociology, and other sciences, that should be taken into account. First of all, the human mind usually sees some basis for generating sets of elements or units so that a unit only rarely is seen as completely unique. Rather, it is seen as one element in a set of units that somehow are of the same kind. This has two important concequences: a unit may be seen, judged, measured not only in absolute terms but also relative to other units of the same kind belonging to the same set. And it may often be fruitful to look for the *structure* of this set, i.e. for the set of relations defined for the elements in the set.

Secondly, it often happens that the set of units itself is a unit of analytical interest, and this unit may again generate a set of interest in some context. If the set is an age *category*, i.e. persons 13-19 years old, the unit as such may be of less interest, but if it is a teen-age gang it may be of considerable interest. Generally, the units that can also be conceived of as social actors, such as political subdivisions of a country, firms, groups and subgroups are most easily singled out for attention.

However, at this point a completely open mind with regard to the nature of the units should be maintained. Thus, the unit may not be an empirically definable actor, but could be a category of some actors or subcategories. The units need not be human or biological at all at any level, but most cases would have to be related to human interaction as *products* of such action, or *conditions* for them, etc. Space and time categories could also be used; much interesting analysis can be made by using a time interval, e.g. a year or a month as a unit of analysis, filling it with meaningful variables.

In general, then, instead of conceiving of the universe of social science discourse as consisting of unrelated elements:

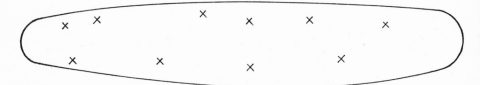

it shall be conceived of as consisting of units grouped together to form new units at different levels, and related to each other at the same level. Any theory of data-collection should take into account these two factors: that units at the same level may form a structure, and that different levels are related to each other by relations of inclusion.

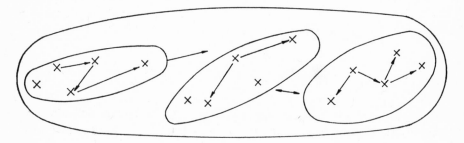

Taking all this into account, it should be possible to build relatively complex structures into the data-collection and consequently into the analysis itself.

Starting with the individual, superunits can be constructed, and since this is indeed the nature of the social process, methodology will have to reflect it. A useful distinction often made between three kinds of superunits is as follows:

(1) *The category*, which is a set of units with no structure.
(2) *The system*, which is also a set of units, but with a binary interaction relation that is 'weakly connected'; all units are connected, but not necessarily directly.
(3) *The group*, which is a system, but with a binary interaction relation that is 'strongly connected'; all units are directly connected with each other.

The following diagram illustrates the difference, and gives some terms:

Diagram 2.1.1. *A typology of collectivities of first order*

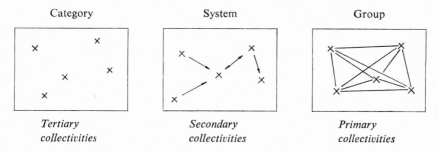

Category	System	Group
Tertiary collectivities	*Secondary collectivities*	*Primary collectivities*

We may now go on to form collectivities of a higher order:

Table 2.1.2. *Collectivities of second order*

Second level→ First level ↓	Tertiary collectivities	Secondary collectivities	Primary collectivities
Tertiary collectivities	sets of age categories	impossible	impossible
Secondary collectivities	lists of firms, nations	a nation as community of communities	a military alliance
Primary collectivities	list of families	a village as community of families	a party organized in 'cells'

Once a tertiary collectivity is reached, there is no longer an actor, hence nothing that can interact, hence no possibility of grouping categories together to form secondary or primary collectivities of higher order. Of course, it serves no purpose to continue this kind of construction process. In practice, the researcher will hardly ever work at more than three levels: the individual, the collectivities of first order, and the collectivities of second order. In addition to this, however, there will be a need for a subunit to the individual, a 'level 0', which will be commented on later. Thus, in the choice of units the researcher should always have a clear idea of (1) which level or levels of action are to be investigated, and (2) which degree of structure exists at the various levels. Our scheme represents three major possibilities.

The same reasoning applies to *products* of human interaction, e. g. printed matter. A newspaper as a unit has subunits (articles) and sub-subunits (themes in the articles); and it has superunits (volumes) and super-superunits (volumes of the newspapers in that city). In these sets there are various degrees of structure, depending on which relations we focus on.

The question is now how to exploit this richness when selecting the variables to use. We shall treat this topic in the present chapter, to throw more light on the choice of units.

Lazarsfeld and Menzel, in their important article on the subject, distinguish between the following types of variables[1]:

Table 2.1.3. *The Lazarsfeld-Menzel system of variables*

| | absolute properties | properties that are based on | | |
		distribution	structure	inclusion
unit, level n	'absolute'	'comparative'	'relational'	'contextual'
unit, level $n+1$	'global'	'analytical'	'structural'	(only one subunit)

The terms they introduce are as useful as any. It should be emphasized that with this scheme each unit can be characterized in the following five different ways:

(1) *By reference to itself only* (absolute, global).
   'Rating' is an example, where measurement is carried out on the unit alone, no knowledge of subunits, superunits or other units at the same level being necessary. Actually, there is no reason to use both terms 'absolute' and 'global'; the first term may do, since the nature of the variables are exactly the same at the two levels, and the same unit may well be a superunit in one but a subunit in another context.

(2) *By reference to other units in the same set* (comparative).
   'Ranking' is the typical example, where the measurement is carried out on the unit, but relative to other units of the same kind. The trans-

formation of absolute scores to percentage scores or to sigma scores is another example. The measurement still refers to the single unit, but is carried out by means of the properties of the other units in the reference-set. Instead of 'comparative', these variables may be called 'relative'.

(3) *By reference to the structure of the set* (relational).
The term 'relational' covers the meaning very well. The variables still characterize the units themselves, but the property is no longer a property the unit has alone or relative to some other unit, but a relation the unit has to another unit. If the units are individuals, the sociologist would, as a rule, like to characterize the individual in terms of his interaction network with other individuals. Thus, relational properties belong to a unit by virtue of its being in a set, and by virtue of the set having a structure.

(4) *By reference to the subunits.*
Here, we get two subcases:
   (a) *Reference to the distribution of the subunits* (analytical).
   The typical example is the rate, the average, the dispersion, of all three kinds of subunit variables (absolute, comparative, and relational).
   (b) *Reference to the structure of the set of subunits* (structural).
   An example may be 'cyclical' vs. 'open' structure of communication networks.
The terms suggested are useful, although 'synthetic' might be just as good as 'analytical'.

(5) *By reference to the superunits* (contextual).
Here the unit is simply given the property of being a *member* of the superunit, and the superunit is characterized in an analytically relevant way. The superunit may then be characterized by means of global, analytical or structural variables.

Obviously, this list starts again for each new level. A group may be characterized by structural variables, but also by relational variables that relate the group to other groups of the same kind. The difference between levels is thus well taken care of, as well as the structure. In other words, the Lazarsfeld-Menzel scheme seems to satisfy these two desiderata quite well. As these authors argue themselves: 'Obviously no one wants to make methodological classifications for their own sake. They are, however, useful in reminding us of the variety of research operations that are possible, and in clearing up misunderstandings'.[2]

Looking at the first three types of variables in the list, we should notice that they refer to increasing degree of complexity on the level of the unit. Take away the structure of the set of units, and *relational* properties lose their meaning. This is the case when the set of units is a category which by definition has no structure (e.g., one of the traditional social background categories). In this set *comparative* properties would still be meaningful (IQ relative to other girls), however. But take away the set, for example, define the units as the only one of its type, and one is left with absolute properties only.

This will apply to the next level as well. In the first case, structural properties would no longer be meaningful, but one could still say something meaningful about the dispersion of female intelligence scores. Reduce the subunit set to a unit set, and the analytical properties lose most of their meaning. A nation may still be characterized as having an authoritarian prime minister, but this case of only one subunit may also be seen as an example of the missing category in the Table presenting the Lazarsfeld-Menzel terms. Here the basic idea is simply that of inclusion, and reference to a lower level is meaningless unless the subunit level has only one element.

In sociological work, there is a scarcity of analyses using the last three kinds of variables in the list, relative to the abundance of analyses based on the first two kinds, although the fifth kind can sometimes be seen as a special way of getting absolute properties. Insight in very complex processes can be obtained using the scheme. For instance, relational variables can be used to construct an analytical variable; and this can be used again as a contextual variable, – as when a *person* is characterized by the average number of intra-group friendships possessed by members of his group.

It should be emphasized, however, that the scheme represents a solution to the two problems posed at the beginning, but not necessarily to the general problem of finding suitable units of analysis. Thus, the third kind of variables, the relational variables, can probably be analyzed more satisfactorily *by dealing with the relations themselves as units.* Since relations in sociological analysis are usually binary, this means taking as units of analysis all the n^2 ordered pairs in a group of n members, or $n(n-1)$ pairs if the relation to be dealt with is irreflexive (e.g., 'having command over'), or $\frac{1}{2}n(n-1)$ if in addition it is symmetric (interaction relations). One can then start characterizing the *pairs* instead of the units and apply the whole Lazarsfeld-Menzel scheme to the pairs and sets of pairs. Conceptual difficulties enter when the question of structure is introduced: what kind of structure can there be to a set of pairs? Clearly, they can have the structure implied when they are compared, as when we say that relations between nations bordering on each other are more bellicose than those between nations not bordering on each other. But if the pair is not an empirical unit, it is difficult to see how a set of pairs can have a structure of its own. In the set of nations, this makes good sense however: much of balance of power thinking has to do with pairs relating themselves to other pairs, positively, negatively, or with indifference – and that is already the basis for imputing a structure to the set of pairs, or to the set of triples, etc., for that matter.

Thus, as units of analysis, units at different levels, as well as pairs of units, triples of units, etc., may serve; and they may be analyzed in terms of the five kinds of properties mentioned. The question is now whether this scheme can be applied, not only to the relation between an individual and its *super-*units, and various levels of superunits, but also to the relation between an individual and its possible *sub*units.

If we abstract away from the individual to his social personality, known in sociology as his status-set, this is a superunit with status as subunit. Let us apply the scheme of properties to this relationship to see how it works.

Obviously, an absolute property of a status is the number of statuses with which the individual has to interact – or the number of roles, as it is also called. Also obviously, the statuses can be ranked according to this characteristic. Further, an important relational characteristic of a status is its position in a salience hierarchy. A global characteristic would be relative frequency of the status-set (a comparative property at that level), an analytical characteristic the number of statuses in the status-set, or the dispersion (or average) in the distribution of number of roles. An important structural property is known as degree of 'integration' of the status-set, probably meaning degree of linearity in the hierarchy of the statuses according to salience. Properties referring to how well the individual is managing his status-conflict may also be used as global properties and be useful as contextual properties, whereby one might get information about how often status S is linked to other statuses in such a way that the individual is not able to manage properly the administration of his status-set.

This should now be related to the research models in 1.4. The most commonly found in sociological analysis is of type II, and it is easily seen how what has been developed here enters: *as a typology of possible background variables*. The common formula is the background as a context, a social context within which the overt and covert behavior of the individual unfolds itself. The context may be seen as a *set* and the relationship the unit has to the context merely as a question of *inclusion*. Since we work with three kinds of super systems when the units are individuals (tertiary, secondary and primary collectivities, respectively), we get three kinds of contextual variables. But, in addition, we may wish to include more information about the individual than the simple fact of membership. In general, we may want to say something about the social climate in which he is embedded. This brings us at once to the use of analytical, structural and global variables as contextual variables. Thus, we get as a typology of background variables:

Table 2.1.4. *A typology of background variables, for individuals*

Contextual variables

	Inclusion	Analytical	Structural	Global
Tertiary collectivity	(sex)	(average IQ)	impossible	impossible
Secondary collectivity	(pupil at school X)	(dispersion of final grades)	(sex-segregated)	(modern building)
Primary collectivity	(member of gang Y)	(number of members)	(steep power-pyramid)	(old, lasting group)

What this scheme amounts to is a way of *adhering to the use of individuals as research units, and still taking into account both levels and structures*. Thus, sociological analysis is considerably enriched.

But this does not preclude the importance of analysis at some other level in its own right: not to shed light on the level of individual interaction, but to understand a higher level better. Thus, in principle the research models in 1.4 can apply just as well to such units as nations, and the typology of background variables likewise. A 'secondary group' of nations may mean something more than a category (agricultural nations), yet someting less than a primary group with direct interaction in all pairs (Scandinavian countries). An example may be African states, and as a structural variable we may take some property of the directed graph obtained by representing every diplomatic mission from nation A to nation B by an arrow: A → B. The relation is in principle a symmetric one (the nations agree to exchange missions) but in practice it may often be asymmetric. Thus, the same richness in choice of variables should apply, in principle, to the study of international relations or to the study of the relations between intra-national groups. The study of international relations is nevertheless hampered by two trivial factors: the low number of national units that precludes many kinds of multivariate analysis (unless we use pairs of nations as units), and the low number of organizational levels. We have collectivities of the first order, but collectivities of the second order are likely to include the whole world, the whole international system. And, as Lazarsfeld and Menzel point out,[3] contextual properties are meaningless when there is only one collectivity involved, because all subunits of that collectivity would take on the same value since they are all members. Relative to other arguments voiced against extensive methods in international relations research, these arguments seem to carry considerable weight: not as arguments *against* using extensive methods where they can be applied, but as arguments *for* developing intensive methods.

Here we have actually only discussed two levels, the individual level and the level of a collectivity. But many more levels can be imagined. Elections can be studied, comparing nations, comparing provinces, comparing municipalities, and comparing individuals. Each comparison would be meaningful at its own level, but in addition would bring us closer to the individual and hence reduce (but not eliminated) the danger of sociological fallacies. There is a methodology inherent in this. The social scientist, according to the approach of the present book, proceeds by the method of comparison, and the more units and variables, the better, up to a certain point. To understand elections in a country, he has to look at distributions from units below the national level. He has to find a suitable level where units of analysis can be found, and then try to project his findings upwards and downwards, with care, afterwards. A full exploitation of analyses using a number of levels simultaneously has so far not been done, to our knowledge.

2.2. *The fallacy of the wrong level*

In general, the 'fallacy of the wrong level' consists not in making *inferences* from one level of analysis to another, but in making direct *translation of properties or relations* from one level to another, i.e., making too simple inferences. The fallacy can be committed working downwards, by projecting from groups or categories to individuals, or upwards, by projecting from individuals to higher units.

Thus, if one wants to prove that Negroes commit more crimes than whites, data based on census tracts are not sufficient. A high correlation between the percentage of Negroes and the crime-rate in a unit may serve as a basis for an hypothesis, but nothing more. If the crimes committed are lynchings of Negroes, and their frequency depends more on the availability of Negroes than on the number of whites to perform them – a hard core of whites is enough – the same correlation would obtain. In general, the reason may be that the more Negroes, the more marginal the whites. Correspondingly, a lack of correlation between democracy-autocracy and external bellicosity for nations does not imply that there is no relation between aggressiveness and authoritarianism on the individual level.[4] We also have the good example mentioned by Lazarsfeld and Menzel, that the indecision of a hung jury does not mean that the members are indecisive: on the contrary. Similarly, it is dangerous to take correlations between rates of juvenile delinquency and *dementia praecox* in cities, and apply them to individuals.

45

There are two aspects to these kinds of translation. One is related to a simplistic way of thinking about social phenomena, namely the idea that they somehow repeat themselves at different levels of organization. Here, there is also the danger of a semantic fallacy adding to the 'ecological fallacy' (as the fallacy of projecting downwards is often called, particularly when inferences are made from geographical units to individuals). Clearly, the word 'democratic' in 'democratic personality' and 'democratic form of government' means very different things, so inferences, if tenable, are indeed not trivial. The same word does not necessarily mean the same thing.

Secondly, there is the use of the lower level in proposing causal theories. To explain a correlation between collectivities, one may advance the hypothesis that the same relation holds for the individuals that are members of the collectivity. Thus, the correlation mentioned above is explained if one says that 'the members that are Negroes are also the ones who commit crimes'. But this is only an explanation as long as this statement is taken as unproblematic, not in need of further explanation. There are actually two problems here: first of all, the causal explanation using lower levels may be *completely* wrong, as in some of the examples above; and then it may be *partly* wrong, in which case interesting additional explanations may be lost – as in the case of Negro crime rates that may be explained partly as white crime rates.

The question is whether this way of thinking can also be applied to the relation between individuals and their subunits. Corresponding to the ecological fallacy one level above we would have this kind of fallacies:

A correlation is found between two variables applying to individuals. For analytical purposes the individual is seen as a boundary for subunits, such as psychological syndromes, role-behavior or status-behavior, time-slices in behavior sequences, etc. The ecological fallacy in general consists in this: *properties found to be correlated at the higher level are assumed correlated, i.e. found within the same unit, at the lower level.* Here, the fallacy would consist in believing that, because two behavioral elements are found within the same individual, they are also found within the same behavioral, temporal, spatial, or mental contexts we may choose to subdivide the individual into. And vice versa: if correlations are not found for the individuals, could it not be that they still may hold for the subunits?

To take a simple example with exactly the same structure as the Negro crime rate example: imagine it was found that in a set of individuals there was a high correlation between the two absolute properties of being cashiers and having incomes not accounted for by salaries. To deduce that cashiers embezzle would be to claim that the two properties are found within the same unit on the lower level too, i.e., within the cashier status. But alternative explanations may be given, e.g.: cashiers have incomes so low that they are forced to take extra jobs, i.e. add to their status-sets to add to their income. This alternative explanation (and others) would have to be ruled out and additional data obtained before settling for the first explanation. But how often is that done in cases with this structure?

The general idea is this: one cannot automatically infer that two or more behavioral or attitudinal patterns are located in the same role or status of a person because they are found within the same individual. Thus, one will not infer from a high correlation between wearing a tuxedo as opposed to a white dress in marriages and being a locomotive engineer (as opposed to not being one) that the latter wears a tuxedo at work, but rather that both properties seem to be monopolized by males. But other cases are more difficult: what about correlations between having some statuses and being classified as 'authoritarian'? Does this necessarily mean that one is authoritarian when acting in that particular status – clearly not. It may mean that there is self- or other-selection into the status of that kind of people, it may mean that the attitude is a result of occupying the status rather than vice versa – or it may mean that people with that status also tend to have other statuses where these kinds of relations apply. Any good analysis would take this into account to avoid this kind of contextual fallacy (a better term than 'ecological fallacy', which has a geographical connotation).

This leads to a general question of interpretation of behavioral or attitudinal elements and their correlation for individuals. Data should be obtained in such a way that we are able to say something about in which subunit they appear together. If the subunits are both analytically and empirically distinguishable, as is the case with statuses and roles (because of the identifiability of different status- and role-partners), then this should not be difficult. But often the subunits are only analytical and not empirical units, as in the case of psychological 'syndromes' or attitudinal clusters. Imagine that two attitudes are found to be closely correlated, say, aggressiveness in interpersonal and in international relations. Does this mean that they are manifestations of the same tendency towards aggressive attitudes? Or, could the former be a kind of spontaneous aggression and the latter the result of a long intellectual analysis with arguments for violent and non-violent means of conflict resolution and the scale finally tipping in favor of the former? One may argue that this is uninteresting, it is a case of two different kinds of aggression. And besides, since the scale tipped in favor of aggression, the outcome was aggression nevertheless. But even granting the objections, what remains is an important difference between the person who reacts to his total external world in terms of aggression, and the person who derives different aggressive conclusions from different layers of his psyche.

The most important conclusion to be drawn seems to be as follows: sometimes translation from one level to another may be *tenable in all* cases, sometimes it may be *untenable in all* cases, but very often it is likely to be a *mixture*. The translation selects one possible causal mechanism, and if this is the only one explored, the main dysfunction of the translation is more in making for poor theory than for wrong theory.[5]

Another way of formulating this problem is as follows: if we have a correlation (even a perfect one) between two variables at the individual level, can we infer that the mechanism linking the two variables is always the same? Of course not. In the cashier example, there may be one interpretation (read: mechanism) for one group, and a very different one for another group, etc. There may be one mechanism for each individual, even more than one, since they may interact within the individual. Nevertheless, sociological analysis usually treats individuals, and statistical analysis in general treats units, as if one could make the same inference from the general pattern to the individual case. It is easy to raise general criticism against sociology and statistical methods on this basis, because different mechanisms are lumped together, and on the basis of collective data, inferences may be made that are valid for all, some, or even none of the cases – only that the analyst does not know. One contra-argument is, of course, that statistical analysis serves to locate 'general patterns', whatever that may mean, if it applies to less than the majority of the units or even to none of them. A better argument is that statistisical data serve to see any tendency at all, to 'get it out'; and as a basis for the formulation of hypotheses that will have to be verified at the individual level. For, as will be pointed out later on, correlations are always collective and have no meaning for the individual case, whereas what we have vaguely called 'mechanisms' always work at the individual level and make no sense for sets of elements. Correlations serve as warning signals that 'there may be something interesting here at the individual level', but just as much as they may warn about nothing, they may also fail to warn when there is something.

2.3. *The problem of sampling*

In general, the problem of sampling can be stated as follows: Given (1) the set of units to be studied, (2) that the set has M elements, and (3) that for several reasons only m elements or units will be studied – how do we select the m units? If we have $m = M$ there is no problem. Only if for some reason, often expressed as lack of resources (energy, finances, time) $m < M$, does the problem of *selection* arise.

The set of units selected for study will then be a subset of the total set of possible units. It is customary to refer to this subset as a *sample S*, and to the total set as a *universe, U*. It should be noticed that in most cases there is no virtue, except that of saving resources, in having $m < M$. If the universe *can* be studied, that will as a rule be advisable. If not, the problem of sampling is how to choose among the $\binom{M}{m}$ possible samples of size m in such a way that the sample is useful for the researcher's purposes. If m is not fixed, we have a choice between 2^M possible samples, if we include the possibilities of taking no sample at all and of sampling the universe.

This leads to the trivial implication that the choice of a sample has to be made on the basis of the research purpose, a prescription which becomes less trivial in the light of the number of cases where standard recipes are followed just because they exist and are simple to follow. By far the most precise answers to the question of how to sample are given in statistical sampling theory. The question then arises of whether this kind of sampling is done for a purpose of interest to general social science analysis. In many cases, the answer to this is definitely in the negative. Thus, Cochran, in one of the best books on sampling techniques, uses this definition:[6]

The purpose of sampling theory is to make sampling more efficient. It attempts to develop methods of sample selection and of estimation that provide, at the lowest possible cost, estimates that are precise enough for our purpose. This principle of specified precision at minimum cost recurs repeatedly in the presentation of theory.

However, this definition does not focus on the fundamental aspects. Estimation is not without interest to social analysis, but it is hardly of central importance, except when the purpose is exact description.

A typology of sampling techniques, then, cannot be developed without a typology of research purposes; one must have a clear conception of the goal of research carried out on statistical units. It is to 'say something about the units', i.e. to state propositions about them. This can only be done in terms of their *properties,* or variables as we have called them: age, income, openness of mind, behavioral habits, attitudes. The propositions may take a number of different forms:

    (1) The units are all old.
    (2) The average age is 45 years.
    (3) The dispersion is 5 years.
    (4) The correlation between age and income is high.

(5) The higher the age, the more does income
    determine one's attitude to free enterprise.

In the first three, one variable (age) is involved; in the fourth proposition, there are two variables; and in the last one, three variables. For all five, the properties discussed belong to the units, even though the units have somehow disappeared: they are no longer needed when the relations have been established. The terms that do not refer to the variables, refer to the stastistical distribution, more or less precisely.

We now suggest that the general form of a proposition in social science is the following:

2.3.1 $$P(X_1, X_2, \ldots X_n)$$

where $X_1, X_2 \ldots X_n$ are the variables used in the proposition, and P is the relation that holds between them. (See also II, 4.1). P will often contain statistical terms (P may also be formulated as a mathematical equation, stochastic or not, but does not have to do so), as in propositions where we have translations involving frequency distributions:

1'. The units all have values for 'age' above the lower limit for 'old'.
5'. The correlation between income and attitude to free enterprise is higher for high age than for low age.

These translations are not quite unproblematic, however, as will be discussed later. It should be noticed that a proposition like 'men are more ... than women' involves two variables, one of them sex, even if it is stated as a comparison between two samples.

For some reason, two artificial distinctions are often made in social science and statistical methodology.

First of all, there is a tendency to say that a study is 'descriptive' if it results in propositions with only *one* variable ($n = 1$), and 'analytical' or 'theoretical' if it results in propositions with a higher number of variables. But even if it may be true in general that propositions with one variable are less interesting than more complex propositions – that simple predicates are less interesting from a theoretical point of view than relations – this distinction is not a distinction between description and theory or analysis. All propositions in the list above are descriptive with varying complexity; and they may all be theoretical statements or be used in a theory or an 'analytic study' if they can be included at some level in a theory, i.e. an interconnected set of propositions. Thus, the criterion of whether a proposition is 'descriptive' lies not in the number of variables it is based on, but in whether it is isolated or linked to other propositions.

Secondly, a distinction is made between 'estimation' and 'testing of statistical hypotheses'. Here, the division is not according to $n = 1$ or $n > 1$, for estimates are often made of correlation coefficients and hence of relations between two or more variables. Rather, the distinction has to do with degree of precision. When very precise inferences are made from a sample to a universe, one talks about estimation, as in propositions (2) and (3) [and (1)]; but if they are more qualitative, one often talks about 'testing hypotheses'. Abraham Wald has shown how these two can be conceived of as special cases of a general methodology of statistical decision-making.[7]

With this clarification of the goal, we can return to the problem of sampling. To repeat: if one can investigate the whole universe, this should be done, for the only thing obtained by sampling is reduced cost, where 'cost' is taken in a general sense (so as to include energy, manpower, talent, money, time, etc.). In general one can say this: *by sampling, one buys reduced 'cost' of data-collection, -processing and -analysis by using a lower N than the universe has, but at the expense*[8] *of adding one problem to the other problems offered by one's research: that of deciding whether propositions established for the sample can be generalized to the universe.* For we assume that the researcher is not really interested in the sample as such – for if he is, the sample is clearly a subuniverse of analytical interest in its own right.

From this follows that there are two conditions a sample must fulfill:

(1) It must be possible to test *substantive hypotheses* i.e. propositions about variables on the sample, and
(2) It must be possible to test *generalization hypotheses* from the sample to the universe, of the propositions established for the sample.

The first is a question of whether the sample can be used to test social science hypotheses, the latter of whether it can be used to test statistical hypotheses. Fortunately, these two requirements are generally compatible. Actually, they both lead in different terms to the requirement that *the sample shall somehow be a universe in miniature.*

To test a substantive hypothesis like the hypothesis that proposition (5) above is valid, one obviously needs a sample that includes the kind of units the proposition is about, i.e. young people and old people, people with high income and low income, people for and against free enterprise. Two catchwords often heard in this connection are 'heterogeneous' and 'representative'.

A sample is *heterogeneous* to the extent it contains units with high dispersion on the variables of interest, so this requirement is actually what we have already formulated. For instance, to test the proposition, a sample containing only low income people would not do, nor a sample containing only people in favor of free enterprise. Since the proposition uses 3 variables and we can conceive of them as dichotomies, we get 8 combinations. And this is where the word *representative* comes in: All eight *combinations* shall be 'represented' if they are present in the universe. A more strict interpretation of 'representative' would add: *shall be represented in the same proportions as in the universe.*

Thus, heterogeneity guarantees that the relevant values on each single variable will be represented; representativity, that the combinations will be represented, and if needed, in the right proportions. Since a sample is clearly heterogenous when it is representative (but not vice versa), the requirement about heterogeneity is only added for emphasis, unless it should be given a stronger interpretation: not only shall the extreme categories be represented, but they shall be overrepresented because they are of special analytical value. We are less interested in this interpretation.

The kind of sample we get by filling (proportionately) all combinations on certain selected variables is called a *quota-sample*. It is very good for testing substantive hypotheses, but unfortunately very bad for testing generalization hypotheses. Since we need samples that can be used for both purposes, this will not be discussed further, except by noting that what we have said so far includes nothing about *how* to get the required number in different cells, only *how many* or rather *what proportion* is needed.

Then, there is a second requirement in connection with sampling for testing substantive hypotheses. Almost all hypotheses that can be formulated can be verified on samples by selecting for the sample those and only those units that verify the relation posited by the hypothesis. Thus, verification may be built into the sampling procedure. A sample selected in such a way that it offers a higher degree of verification than the universe because of its composition is called (positively) *biased,* whether this is done on purpose or not. If this is not the case, the sample is called *unbiased.* This category may then be divided into the samples that are 'truly' unbiased, and samples that are negatively biased, in the sense that the sampling procedure makes it more difficult to verify the hypothesis on the sample than it would have been had the whole universe been taken. Thus, any degree of verification or falsification of an hypothesis about correlation between two attitudes can be obtained if this correlation varies with a background variable (e. g., social position) and samples are made consisting of different mixtures from the different values of that variable. The first requirement of any research is to work with *unbiased samples.* If the research has already led to the formulation of hypotheses, all that is needed is that the sample is unbiased relative to these hypotheses. But if it is explorative, the researcher must be on guard against bias with respect to any hypothesis, if he is not prepared to check his findings afterwards on other samples. We shall come back to this theme on several occasions.

The traditional way of guarding oneself against biased samples is to use samples, whether they are purposive or probability, where the proportions between main categories are at least roughly equal to the corresponding proportions in the universe. We have touched this problem before, in 1.4 in connection with the rejection of *le cas pur* methodology. As Hyman and Sheatsley point out in the critique of *The Authoritarian Personality*[9]:

We have not criticized them because their samples were unrepresentative. That is permissible and often wise – provided that the limitations of the sample are not ignored in drawing sweeping conclusions. – Particularly in exploratory research, where the primary aim is to develop hypotheses and investigate ideas, the use of rigorous sampling methods is usually unjustified. – But such studies, while quite proper for the purpose mentioned – the development of hypotheses – do not permit generalization, nor do they provide a *test* for the hypotheses. For a definitive test of the findings obtained from an unrepresentative sample, a similar study of a representative sample is required. (P. 67).

We agree, except for the expression 'definitive test'. It implies a kind of belief in the 'population' as the standard of everything, that we shall look into in II, 4.4. This comes out more clearly in another passage from the important article by Hyman and Sheatsley:

We are in agreement with the writers that one does not need a representative *number* of cases in each stratum or cell of a given population in order to demonstrate such conclusions and to generalize them to *that* population. We merely need enough cases from all cells, and it is inefficient to take a larger number of cases from a large cell, just to achieve over-all sampling representativeness when the aim is only to establish some correlation or difference. But the question of whether such relationships or differences extend beyond one population to some or all other populations is a thoroughly different matter. Correlation coefficients, just like means or percentages, fluctuate from sample to sample and may well vary in different populations. (P. 67).

Here the authors contradict themselves. Just because the parameters will fluctuate, of which there is no doubt, will our conclusions depend on the sampling method, and depend heavily on the amount of bias relative to the proportionate sample. A general warning should be issued against beliefs to the effect that 'whereas proportions may fluctuate with biased samples correlations can resist even strong biases'. This is simply not true, and it implies a general belief that 'single responses may fluctuate with background variables, patterns of responses not'. Although there may be some truth in this, in the sense that percentages will vary more than correlations, this grain of truth is magnified and perpetuated by adopting the belief mentioned.

Of the many possible examples of how correlations vary with background variables, we shall briefly mention two from our own studies.

In a study of how ideology was related to social position in a very backward region in Western Sicily[10] no correlation at all was found between traditionalism-modernism and social rank, or with economic sector. But a relatively strong and meaningful correlation was found between ideology and a combination of rank and sector: the villagers in the primary-low and tertiary-high sectors were 'modern' and the villagers in the primary-high and tertiary-low sectors were 'traditional'. The sample was simple random, and it required some analytic work to uncover the relationship. But if the sample had been biased, one could have obtained almost any correlation from, say, −.50 via 0 to +.50 (depending, of course, on the correlation measure used) by suitably mixing the sample from different social positions. Thus, one might easily be led into any conclusion about 'Sicilians'.

In another study, no correlation was found between being in favor of tough foreign policy and being in favor of soft foreign policy (e.g. NATO vs. technical assistance) *for the total sample*. But analysis showed that there was a strong positive correlation in the social periphery – people wanted both or nothing – and a strong negative correlation in the social center (they were seen as mutually exclusive).[11] Since these correlations actually varied systematically from +1 to −1 (Yule's Q), absolutely any correlation could be obtained: the machiavellian sociologist would only have to choose suitable proportions from the center and the periphery.

To test a *generalization* hypothesis, a remarkably well developed, although very recent, methodology is at our disposal. The methodology is so well developed that it is often, as will be argued later, confused with a methodology for testing the validity of the *substantive* hypothesis itself. There is one requirement: *the sample must be a probability sample*. The method of selection of the sample must be such that the probability of selecting a sample is different from 0 or 1, *and the probability of selecting the sample must be known*. Thus, the requirement does not focus on *which* elements have been selected, only on *how* they were selected. The requirements for testing *substantive* hypotheses did not fix the elements or units unambiguously either, only up to certain categories, but this requirement for testing generalization hypotheses goes further. For one type of sampling (simple random), it says that the sample shall be taken in such a way that all units have the same chance of being included; and this *may* lead to samples that are incompatible with the substantive requirement of representativity. One *may* get a completely random sample located in one of the cells. However, with even a moderate sample-size, the probability that a simple random sample will deviate much from being proportionate (i.e. a quota-sample) is very low, and can be made as low as one wants by increasing the sample size.

The reason for wanting a probability sample is as follows: guesses, even good guesses about the universe, can be made from quota-samples and other deterministic samples – for instance, the simple inductionist guess *as the sample, so the universe,* which is the major guess in statistical generalization theory. *But only with probability samples is it possible to give an evaluation of how good the guess is,* so that we can make statements of the type 'I am 95% certain that the mean of the universe is located between 35 years and 55 years', instead of the statement 'the mean of the universe is 45 years' or 'the mean of the universe is between 35 years and 55 years'. The last two statements can be made from any sample, but are of little value unless supplemented by a statement as to how certain the statement is. No such statements can be made from quota-samples, although these samples are very often treated as if this were possible.

Extensive comments on the different types of samples can be found in any textbook on statistics. We shall only give a genealogical tree of sampling procedures to show how they are interrelated. It should be noticed that for a sample to be a probability sample is neither a necessary, nor a sufficient condition for making generalizations, since methodologies are only explored and known for special types of probability samples. In principle, however, the mathematical statistician should be able to construct a test once the procedure for taking a probability sample is known. But we shall also see that meaningful techniques of evaluating how good generalizations are can also be developed for non-random samples.

It can be seen that a proportionate, stratified probability sample differs from a quota sample only in being random. This is precisely the difference that makes it possible to use it for *testing* generalization hypotheses statistically *and* evaluating them, not only formulating them. However, the researcher may well be interested only in *formulating* such hypotheses, e.g., in the more explorative stages of a research process; and since purposive samples are much easier to get, as a rule, they may be used for that purpose. That is, a substantive theory may be tested on them, but as to generalizability of the findings, one is left with the hypotheses until a probability sample has been drawn; or one may use replication techniques that are more difficult to evaluate. It should be noticed that a simple random sample (or a proportionate, stratified one) almost certainly will be representative and even a quota sample, so that one gets the best of both worlds. In addition,

Table 2.3.1. A diagram of different types of sampling

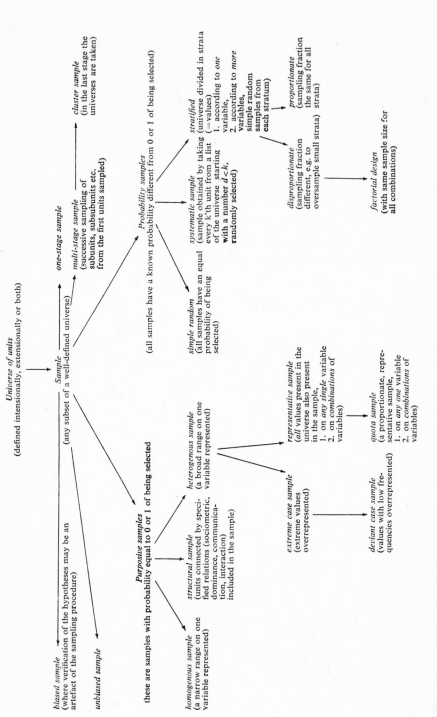

randomness is one way of avoiding a sample with built-in verification of the hypothesis, i.e. a biased sample. Another method would be to have somebody else draw the sample, to exclude one's own conscious or subconscious desires. But to leave the sampling to one's antagonist in a scientific dispute would not help much, however, since one might end up with a negatively biased instead of a positively biased sample. Finally, by means of randomization, one also controls the relevant conditions that may influence interaction between independent and dependent variables.

Obviously, when the diagram says 'more variables', this does not mean that the variables are taken one at a time; but that the combinations of two or more variables, the 'cells', are filled, proportionately or disproportionately. In the traditional 'factorial design', all cells get the same number of units, which in general means a disproportionate sample.

To repeat: by sampling, costs are reduced, the sampling fraction m/M indicating the gain. This is done, however, at the expense of involving ourselves in the additional problem of having to test generalization hypotheses, which can only be done on probability samples if we want to use the powerful techniques of statistical testing. In order to reduce costs, m must be low; in order to test substantive hypotheses and to generalize with reasonable certainty, m must be high: so a considerable part of the art of sampling consists in choosing the right m. This will be discussed subsequent to some remarks on the role of levels of units.

Since social relations unfold themselves at various levels, sampling procedures must be geared to a multiplicity of levels. Thus, for a comparative study of traditional societies one may start with a sample of nations, then take a sample of regions, then a sample of villages or other types of communities, and finally a sample of individuals. If these samples are taken independently of each other, in the sense that the units sampled at a lower level need not necessarily belong to units sampled at the level above (the villages may be from some other regions than the ones sampled, and even from other nations), we are only dealing with so many samples on different levels. But if the samples on one level are always taken from the units sampled at the level above, we talk about *multi-stage sampling*. If the lowest level sampling units are sampled directly, we talk about *one-stage sampling;* if they are sampled by first sampling villages, we have *two-stage sampling,* etc.

Multi-stage sampling is preferable to unrelated sampling at different levels, for two reasons. First of all, the lower level units will be located within the higher level units sampled, so that the dispersion will be less. This may be advantageous, both in terms of reduced costs during data-collection, and increased efficiency in estimation. Obviously, a gallup polling agency has an easier job obtaining data from 2000 respondents if they are subsampled from a sample of counties than if they are obtained by one-stage sampling from the central file of inhabitants. But secondly, and this has to do with testing substantive hypotheses: multi-stage sampling is the sampling counterpart of the idea of social analysis where different levels are related to each other. For each stage, a new set of units is sampled, so that absolute, comparative, and relational properties can be developed. These properties can then be transmitted to the units at the level *below* as contextual properties. Correspondingly, the lower level may be inspected for the properties of the distribution of the units, and the structure among them; and this information may be transmitted to the unit at the level *above* as analytical and structural properties.

A rich spectrum of possibilities now opens up for the researcher, and we have at present no good theory for choosing among all these possibilities. Imagine that the researcher has located three levels of analytical interest. For the reasons above, he decides to use a three-stage sample down to the level of the individuals. That means that for each stage he has to decide whether he should sample or take the whole universe; and in case he should sample, whether he should take a purposive or probability sample, etc. If the researcher decides to take the universes at the last level, the sample is called a *cluster sample*.

With the typology in Table 2.3.1, which is a simplification relative to the abundance of sampling methods in existence, there may be 12 possibilities offered, giving a total of 12^3 equal to 1728 combinations, or $12^2 = 144$ if there are only two levels, as is often the case. In addition to this, there is always the problem of sampling fraction to be decided for each new stage. The question is whether there are any principles available that can reduce this number, and particularly whether there is any typology of research purposes that can be matched with a typology of sampling procedures.

There is no simple formula: so, the entire richness is essentially at one's disposal. For instance, purposive samples may be used in the first stages, as when nations are picked for a comparative study because of the availability of social scientists who can cooperate; and in the last stage, as when organizations are sampled and the leadership hierarchy subsampled by means of sociometric techniques. One must only keep in mind exactly *at* what level probability sampling was applied, because only *to* that level does statistical testing of generalization hypotheses have any meaning.

Some rules may be formulated:

(1) If *generalization* is wanted at one level,
    (a) have a probability sample taken at this level

(b) have a sufficiently large N to permit generalization with a reasonable degree of precision.
(2) If *structural analysis* is wanted at some level, take a structural sample at that level and use the results as structural variables at the level above.
(3) If *contextual analysis* is wanted at some level, take a simple random sample or a representative sample at the level above, and a probability sample of the level below, and use the variables at the higher level as contextual variables at the lower level.

Some comments: The first condition for making a generalization, probability sampling, is indispensable if generalization is to be tested by statistical methods. But these are not the only methods for testing generalization hypotheses. For instance, if some correlations are found to hold for a heterogeneous sample of villages in Western Sicily, there will be a high degree of confirmation to the generalization hypothesis, even though this confirmation cannot be measured in the way statistical generalization hypotheses are measured (by means of confidence levels and significance levels). Consequently, purposive samples can also be used, provided they are heterogeneous enough, preferably even representative.

We then turn to the problem so far left out: how to decide on m, the number of units in the sample. This decision is crucial, insofar as it cannot be increased later on if found to be too low. The locality of data-collection may not be easily accessible, the first phase of data-collection may have destroyed it for later collection of the same kind of data, or the situation may simply have changed so much that new data would not be comparable. In practice, more important than all these theoretical reasons are often such simple considerations as economic and mental costs. The data-collection has a cost-curve that almost always shows decreasing additional costs with increasing m – provided the machinery for data-collection has already been set up. A new machinery costs more pr. data unit, and also costs in terms of mental energy. Few researchers will be willing to admit to themselves that they have to go into the field again. They are more likely to find all good reasons why the data they have are sufficient, provided they are not of the type who always prefer to escape into data-collection.

Since there are two kinds of hypotheses to be tested with samples, there will be two classes of requirements to m:

(1) Criteria arising from the needs to test the *substantive* hypothesis, and
(2) Criteria arising from the needs to test the *generalization* hypothesis.

We shall treat them in this order.

If we want to make use of one- and multi-variable frequency distributions to test the hypothesis that the proposition $P(X_1, X_2 \ldots X_n)$ is valid for the sample, then relatively definite answers can be given. Such distributions can be characterized for our purpose by

(a) the number of variables, n, in the distribution, and
(b) the number of values, r, on each variable.

If we have n variables and each variable is an r-chotomy, the n-dimensional table will obviously have r^n cells. As a rule of thumb, analysis is often difficult or meaningless if it has to be carried out with less than an average of ten cases per cell, and preferably there should be more than 20 for the tendencies to come out clearly. This gives the following Table:

Table 2.3.2. *Minimum number of units of analysis for an average of ten cases per cell* (twenty cases in parentheses)

		r: number of values per variable		
		2	3	4
	1	20 (40)	30 (60)	40 (80)
n: number of	2	40 (80)	90 (180)	160 (320)
variables per table	3	80 (160)	270 (540)	640 (1280)
	4	160 (320)	810 (1620)	2560 (5120)

Of course, there is no reason to assume that the variables forming a table will all have the same number of values, so many intermediate values for m can be found. For instance, if for some reason the analysis will be based on a dichotomy, a trichotomy and one variable with four values, it will yield a table with 24 cells and a sample size requirement of 240 (480). In general, we shall have to fill a table with $r_1 \cdot r_2 \cdot \ldots \cdot r_n$ cells. However, to these and all the other figures should be added a correction for attritions of two kinds. Only rarely will the researcher get relevant information for all units selected; he may fail to obtain *any* information for some of the units, and fail to get *some* information for other units (in surveys known as 'refusals' and 'NA').

In general the researcher should answer three questions before he decides on his sample size:

(1) How many variables does he want to analyze simultaneously?
(2) What is the minimum number of values that he wants to use per variable?
(3) Given his analytical techniques, what is the minimum average per cell that he needs?

Scientific analysis can be made on the basis of one variable, but not much insight can be obtained with n less than 2, and variables are meaningless for

r less than 2. With the minimum requirement of 10 per cell, this gives a minimum sample of 40 – which means 50 to correct for a 20% attrition. *But these are very minimal requirements,* that few would, or should, be willing to subscribe to. We shall later argue extensively for the use of trichotomies and at least three-variate analysis, which combined with the third requirement give corrected minimum sample sizes of 300 or 600.

It is difficult to give any rationale for the minimum average per cell, so this is very much up to the experience and inclination of the individual researcher. Two lines of argumentation can be presented, however.

In the first place, it may be argued that the number m shall be sufficient 'to get the variation out', to get some approximation to the shape of the distribution in the universe. Intuitively an average of 1 per cell would be too little, whereas 50 per cell would be fine, but hardly necessary. To get a good approximation means that the relative frequencies shall not deviate too far from the universe probabilities, or the absolute frequencies from the expected frequencies. For $n = 1$ and $r = 2$ the problem is simple, for we know that the standard deviation of the expected relative frequency is $\sqrt{\dfrac{pq}{m}}$, provided the sample is random. If we want one of these standard deviations to represent only a deviation of 0.10 or 10 percentage points, we get:

2.3.2 $$\sqrt{\frac{pq}{m}} \leqslant 0.10 \quad \text{or} \quad m \geqslant 100\,pq$$

For $p = q = \frac{1}{2}$ this yields $m > 25$ as a maximum value, since pq is a maximum for $p = q = \frac{1}{2}$. For p equal to 0.10 we get $m > 9$, so the values correspond fairly well to our rule of thumb. On the other hand, the requirement that the standard deviation should be less than 10% is equally arbitrary. For higher n and r, similar criteria may be developed, relating the rule of thumb to frequency distributions.

In the second place, we may want the percentages we usually make when we try to get out the information contained in a table not to be too subject to fluctuations with some small change in the absolute figures. For instance, it may be argued that if the change of one unit causes more difference than 5%, the analysis becomes very vulnerable, and this leads to an average base of 20. This is not the same as the minimum requirement per cell, however, since the percentaging will have to be done on the basis of one of the marginals. For $r = 2$ this leads to an average requirement of 10 per cell, since we need an average of 20 as a marginal base. But this will in turn lead to an average base in the marginals of 30 for $r = 3$, and hence to more than we need. Thus, this principle may lead us to be more lenient in our requirements if we are dealing with more than fourfold-tables. On the other hand, it should be remembered that we are dealing with averages, and the higher the r the more marginal bases can be far below the desirable minimum base of 20. To compensate for this, it may be worth-while to stick to the original requirement and fill the interior cells with a minimum of 10 units.

It should, of course, be emphasized that what is important here is not so much the exact figures arrived at, as the reasoning involved. What matters is to have an idea of the maximum table complexity we want to use, to be able to calculate its number of cells as the product $r_1 r_2 \ldots r_n$ of the number of values per variable, and have an idea of the average number of units necessary per cell – with or without an explicit rationale. Thus, there is a basis for arriving at a minimum sample size starting with the substantive hypotheses to be tested.

We can then turn to the second class of criteria: what is the minimum m necessary to test statistical generalization hypotheses? Here an abundant literature is available, and the general theory is perfectly clear. Once the problem is specified, i.e. once the type of proposition we want to test for generalizability and the sampling procedures are known, a test can be constructed provided certain conditions are met (such as independence, normality, homoscedasticity, etc.). The statistician can then ask what 'level of confidence and significance' is wanted, and calculate the minimum m necessary to obtain this. Thus, there will be two kinds of requirements:

(1) Requirements arising if we want to use a specified *test*.
(2) Requirements arising from the *level* of confidence or significance.

For instance, if we want to test the generalization hypothesis that two dichotomies are independent, m has to be so high as to permit a minimum theoretical frequency of 10, i.e. we must have

2.3.3 $$\mathrm{Min} \left(\frac{m_x m_y}{m}, \frac{m_{\bar{x}} m_y}{m}, \frac{m_x m_{\bar{y}}}{m}, \frac{m_{\bar{x}} m_{\bar{y}}}{m} \right) \geq 10;$$

where the frequencies in the numerators are the marginal frequencies – otherwise the chi square approximation to the multinominal distribution is not good enough. Moreover, if we want to generalize from a given size of correlation and a given level of significance or confidence, we can also indicate the minimum value of m. Thus, for correlation coefficients there are tables giving for each level of significance the minimum m needed to make the correlation 'significant', i.e. to make the proposition 'X and Y are correlated' generalizable. To solve such problems, we must have an idea of the size of the correlation in the universe, i.e. we must know what to expect.

62

When we do have an hypothesis, then the minimum m can be calculated from the methods used to test the generalization hypothesis and the level of confirmation wanted.

But very often we do not know what to expect, in fact the research is done precisely to find out. At the same time we want our findings to be generalizable. In this case the general form of the hypotheses to be generalized must be known, and the level of confidence or significance selected. Let us take a typical example, that of the significance of proportions. If the population proportion is p, and the sample proportion x/m, we get as condition of significance:

2.3.4
$$\left| \frac{x}{m} - p \right| > u \sqrt{\frac{pq}{m}}$$

Let us call $|x/m - p|$ d for difference, since that is what we are interested in in general; u is an approximately normally distributed variable. Let us set $u = 2$ so that we are working at approximately 5% level of significance (or 95% level of confidence). We then get

2.3.5
$$d > 2\sqrt{p(1-p)} \cdot \sqrt{\frac{1}{m}}$$

For $p = \frac{1}{2}$ we get

2.3.6
$$d > \sqrt{\frac{1}{m}}$$

The equation $d = \sqrt{1/m}$ has a property of general interest:

Table 2.3.3. *Corresponding values of sample size and significant difference*
$(u = 2, p = \frac{1}{2})$

m	1	4	9	16	25	36	49	64	81	100	121	144	169	225
d	1	0.5	0.33	0.25	0.20	0.17	0.14	0.12	0.11	0.10	0.09	0.08	0.08	0.07

What is evident from this Table is how little is gained by increasing the sample over a certain point. Thus, more than doubling a sample of size 100 will only make for a gain of 0.03 in terms of what can relatively safely be generalized. If we are interested in generalizing *any* difference, there is no limit to the size of sample needed. But *if for theoretical reasons* only differences down to a size d_{min} are interesting, the minimum m is easily found using equations 2.3.4-5. Obviously, the value of p must be taken into account.

However, there is another way of reasoning here. We may have no theoretical basis for assuming a minimum value of d, yet still not want a larger sample than 'necessary'. Since there is a clear tendency of diminishing return, a value of m may be found by asking: what is the 'significant decrement' wanted for a given 'sample size increment'? If we want at least a decrement of 0.02 from increasing the sample with 100 units, we must solve the difference equation:

2.3.7 $$d(m) - d(m+100) = 0.02$$

which gives m around 140 $[d(140) = 0.845$ and $d(240) = 0.645]$. Obviously, a difference and not a differential equation must be used since the distance between the argument values m and $m+100$ is substantial. (Equations of this kind are very conveniently solved numerically by using a slide-rule.) It may be objected that p seldom equals $\frac{1}{2}$. Hence, equation 2.3.7 should be conceived of as an equation in m and p:

2.3.8 $$2\sqrt{p(1-p)}\left[\sqrt{\frac{1}{m}} - \sqrt{\frac{1}{m+100}}\right] = 0.02$$

Solving for $m = m(p)$, we may find the maximum value of m when the range of p is known. That is usually obtainable from theory at least, so that the difficult tails (p less than 0.10 and higher than 0.90) can be excluded from consideration.

To illustrate further, suppose we want a decrease of at least 0.01 in d when doubling the sample. This leads to the equation:

2.3.9 $$2\sqrt{p(1-p)}\left[\sqrt{\frac{1}{m}} - \sqrt{\frac{1}{2m}}\right] = 0.01$$

which gives

2.3.10 $$m = 10^4 \cdot 4p(1-p)(3-\sqrt{2}) \approx 793 \cdot 4(p-p^2).$$

Here, $m = 793$ for $p = \frac{1}{2}$. This is the maximum value of m, so we will be safe with a sample size around 800. Obviously, what is important here is the general method.

Finally, after having considered functions and strategies of sampling and given some principles for the determination of sample sizes, let us turn to a problem often neglected in methodological and substantive analysis. Generally, we do sampling for two reasons: we cannot take *all* – that would be too costly – and we cannot manage with *one* – because of the difficulty of finding *le cas pur*. Hence, we take *some*, according to a more or less complex design. Thus, we take into consideration the possible influences of the different locations of the units in *space* where by 'space' we mean both physical and social space – and include these variations in contexts as variables to characterize the units. Essentially, the case against *le cas pur* is the case against preferring one context for the units at the expense of other contexts.

If we now try to translate these ideas from space to time we find a remarkable drop in sophistication of methodological thinking. Most studies are synchronic in the sense that they make a cut in time, and study a slice of social reality in space but not in time. Of course, there are both *panel* studies (same variables and same units, different cuts in time) and *trend* studies (same variables, different but 'comparable' units, different cuts in time) to be subsumed under the general category of *longitudinal* studies. But these studies should not be confused with sampling in time, for they are used to measure the effects of systematic changes that take place between the time-cuts. Just as for sampling in space, sampling in time can be argued on the basis of our lack of knowledge of the variability of the units. Of course, if we have a complete grasp of the variability in the sense that we can account for all of it by suitably specifying the conditions, then we may be able to specify the new conditions that develop when time passes on, so as to characterize sufficiently the changes in contexts over time. To take an example: much interviewing is done in the afternoons and early evening, after the subjects have returned home from work and before they have retired completely into the more private phases of family life. There is little reason to believe that hour of the day does not to some extent influence attitude. Thus, the respondent may be more conservative at home than at work, feeling more protected and less eager to reform. If interviewing time is randomized, one may control for this, but if it enters as a systematic variable it is more serious. Thus, it is easier to contact people who are their own employers during the working hours and less easy to contact them in their homes – their social status may provide them with too many other opportunities for spending their evening.

Correspondingly, what is the effect of the year cycle on people's attitudes? Probably not great, but it is not far-fetched to believe that more extreme attitudes of optimism and pessimism may develop in spring time corresponding to possible changes in moods during that season. But this is hardly ever taken into account, by sampling from different points in time. Nor is it customary to see specifications of the time-cut – there seems often to be an underlying doctrine of *uniformity of nature*. In other words, there seems to be a doctrine of *le cas pur* with regard to time: even if what applies to this unit does not apply to other units today, now, it applies to this unit tomorrow and next year unless there are some gross disturbances which we assume we know.

There are two obvious reasons for this lack of time-oriented sampling.

First of all, there are practical difficulties in sampling over time. Since we regard sampling here as a protection against unknown sources of variation, it will only be of any use if it can be done over an interval with no interferences from known sources of variation.

Secondly, this kind of study would often presuppose an organization of social research different from that we ordinarily have. Just as the transition from *le cas pur* to sampling presupposed a transition from individual to group research, division of work, etc., an extension from sampling in space to sampling in time would presuppose an additional 'postponement of gratification' – the researchers would have to wait even longer before they could start analyzing their data and promote their career by writing up the story.

In general, the remedy here as for insufficient sampling in space is *replication*. Formally, replication is like a multi-stage sample where the first stage consists in picking different contexts (space sampling) or different time-cuts (time sampling), and the subsequent stages can be developed in any way. The only difference between a replication and a multi-stage sample is terminological: a replication is done by means of a new data-collection process, whereas all the sampling in a multi-stage sample belongs to the same data-collection process. Thus, the difference is mainly one of administration – often the replication is even done by other people or institutions and as a part of a training process (thus, an M.A. thesis may be a replication of another's Ph.D. thesis; research in a country where sociology is new may consist partly in replication of research done in sociologically more advanced countries). The methodology of replication in sociology has never been quite clear, but it can safely be said that it serves both for testing substantive hypotheses and for testing generalization hypotheses.

Thus, we get essentially these four possibilities:

Table 2.3.3. *Outcomes of replications*

	little or no variation in the findings	variation in the findings
no known source of variation	(1)	(2)
known source of variation	(3)	(4)

In general, the conclusions to be drawn from these cases seem to be as follows:

66

Case (1): In this case one would argue *for generalizability*.
Case (2): In this case one would argue *against generalizability*.
Case (3): In this case one would probably blame the data-collection or the design for not being sensitive enough.
Case (4): This is the most important case in practice. If one feels that the known source of variation accounts adequately for the variation found, one will probably argue for generalizability. If one feels that the known source of variation can only account for part of the variation, one would argue against generalizability.

In principle, generalization from a set of replications offers no special difficulties if the replications can be seen as probability samples from a specified universe of possible replications. Replications are usually not carried out this way, however, so other principles of generalization must be found. One that offers itself readily is as follows: let the replications form a *representative* sample on the major dimensions which we have reasons to assume to be of importance, so that all combinations are represented (e. g., for investigations of attitudes to education among school children, pick schools in different social strata and in different ecological contexts – rural, small, medium-sized, and big towns). Then look for variations and try to account for them by means of these dimensions only. If there is similarity over and above what can be accounted for in this way, and the dimensions span the universe of possible replications adequately, it does not seem far-fetched to regard the generalization hypothesis as confirmed. At the same time, new insights will have been gained if the replications vary systematically with the dimensions.

2.4. *Content analysis*

The most important thing about content analysis is that there is nothing particular about it at all. Texts about content analysis are apt to present methodological principles of very general applicability as if these applied to content analysis alone, probably because they are texts with a relatively untrained target audience. But content analysis has its *units of analysis,* its *dimensions,* and its *values,* like other kinds of analysis. The definition Berelson uses of content analysis is the following:

Content analysis is a research technique for the objective, systematic, and quantitative description of the manifest content of communication.[12]

He actually introduces his essay on content analysis by stating that it refers to what is said in the 'classic sentence identifying the process of communication – *who* says *what* to *whom, how* with *what effect*'. Since general analysis of verbal responses also is concerned with the content of communication, the distinguishing feature about content analysis is not that it tries to describe what a communication consists of, but that it attempts to relate this to the communication itself, to the communicative act, the medium of communication, etc. Survey analysis would ordinarily concern itself with the relation between what a person has said and some other properties of the person; content analysis would relate what an editor has written in his editorial to the date of the paper, to other statements occurring in the editorial, to characteristics of the newspaper, etc. But even this borderline is not sharp – there is no principle excluding social background data about the editor. In practice, it looks as if the real characteristic of the data that content analysis makes use of is that the data are printed and not produced for the purpose of investigation only. In other words, content analysis is usually concerned with the analysis of communicative acts *post hoc,* with no arrangement other than that given by the communicators: in books, articles, in the press, radio, films, etc. – and, in open-ended interviews.

It should be added to this that communication need not be verbal to carry meaning. Analyses of bodily postures, facial expressions etc. are quite conceivable, and similar to the art historian's analysis of paintings. What is typical of content analysis, however, is the use of comparable data so as to have statistical material for the analysis. Here it encroaches on other human endeavours to analyse human communication: the political commentator, the historian, the philologist, etc.

Of course, the primary concern in choosing the unit of analysis is the theoretical or practical purpose of the study. The precise definition of the universe is as important here as everywhere else; sampling problems appear in exactly the same way. If the universe is 'everything written about something', it will usually have to be limited in four ways: precise indication of *where* (e. g., Norway), *when* (e. g., February to September 1959), what *medium* of communication (e. g., regular newspapers), and what *topic* (e. g., the invitation of Premier Khrushchev). Whether the whole universe should be taken or only a sample depends on the usual factors: size of the universe, precision needed, whether one can afford sampling errors in addition to other errors, etc. – content analysis is no different from other analyses in this regard.

As usual, the unit of analysis is that which one wants to characterize. There is no rule as to its level. It may be one single issue of a newspaper, it may be the paper *New York Times* as such in a given period, it may be editorials, it may be the headlines of editorials – it may be single movies or only scenes, it may be what is broadcast by a specific station, it may be a particular program, it may be the news and so on. Berelson makes a distinction:

First is the distinction between the recording unit and the context unit. The recording unit is 'the smallest body of content in which the appearance of a reference is counted' (a reference is a single occurrence of a content element). The context unit is 'the largest body content that may be examined in characterizing a recording unit'. (op. cit., p. 507).

This terminology is unnecessary, but the distinction is important. It all has to do with the *level of analysis,* and with the fact that units from different levels of analysis[13] may be included in each other. Just as data about the city in which a person lives may be used to characterize the person indirectly, data about the newspaper in which an editorial appears may be used to characterize, indirectly, that editorial. (These variables would then appear as contextual variables.) The analyst is free to use the same data for analysis on whatever level he pleases; he may analyse editorials, newspapers, or groups of newspapers, e.g., according to party color. There is only one warning which corresponds exactly to the rule of avoiding the contextual or ecological fallacy: only infer directly from smaller to larger units, never from larger to smaller units. If it can be shown that newspapers that argue for atomic weapons in Norwegian defense also argue for Norwegian membership in EEC, it does not follow that they do so in the same editorial – but if it can be shown that they do so in the same editorial it would also hold true for the newspapers as such. The danger of ecological fallacy is probably very high in content analysis, since the levels will look so alike.

Absolutely anything can be used as a dimension for the analysis of a piece of communication. (Berelson makes a useful distinction between 'what is said' and 'how it is said'.) Probably, new insights will mainly be obtained if somewhat unexpected dimensions are included – such as *length* (in inches or minutes) or *time order* (when it occurred). As to the *values* of the dimensions, they will very often be simple dichotomies of the present-absent type: the role of the dimensions is to single out phenomena for registration, special arguments, kinds of information, scenic effects, color contrasts – and it may be difficult to talk about degrees of presence. Since the task, or a part of the task, here as elsewhere is to get as intra- and intersubjectively good data as possible, it will probably be best to use quantitative measures, like number of lines or seconds or inches given to an argument or a theme – in addition to more subjective evaluation of how much or how strong the presence is.

To return to the definition given by Berelson: the word 'manifest' points to the problem of interpretation. Actually, the inclusion of the word 'manifest' in the definition does not preclude the experienced coder from adding to the code his own interpretation of what is communicated, for instance as to the communicator's intentions – and then comparing these face-value interpretations with interpretations obtained by means of statistical analysis. For instance, it may be useful to compare an interpretation of an editorial as being for or against an issue with a count of the relative number of pro and contra arguments to see what correspondence there is. But it should be clear what dimensions and values are directly observed and proved to be intersubjective – the *manifest content,* and what is inferred either directly or after analysis – the *latent intent.* The force of content analysis lies precisely in its possibilities as a technique for analysis of manifest content *before* one jumps to conclusions most people are willing to jump to right away.

This presents the investigator with a well-known problem, indicated in the diagram:

Diagram 2.4.1. *Relation between three variables of a content analysis*

What is coded:	latent intent	manifest content
Theoretical relevance:	high	low
Reliability (intra-subjective and inter-subjective):	low	high

The structure of the problem is simple enough: by coding the manifest symbols, e. g., the appearance of the term 'democracy' one may obtain excellent reliability coefficients,[14] but at the expense of entering the research with very low level data. By coding 'intentions', meanings, etc. one may get at more interesting conclusions, but this time at the expense of reliability.

The traditional answers to the problem are to argue for either of the extremes, with the well-known arguments of the historian and literary critic at one end and the statistically minded operationalist at the other. In general, we find either extreme fruitless and the debate relatively wasteful, since there are so many possible intermediate positions. One may codify editorials, as mentioned, in terms of whether they are 'for or against', even though they do not explicitly say where they stand, and obtain relatively high reliability by introducing a category of 'unclear'. It may well be that this trichotomy is fruitful, that what is unclear to the coders is also unclear to others, both readers and writers of editorials.[15] Thus we would opt for the middle range of the variables above, with some excursions into the extreme where manifest content is concerned – and some excursions into the extreme where latent intent is concerned in the interpretation.

There is, however, another answer to the problem of making inferences from the manifest and reliable – but trivial – to the latent and exciting – but less reliable. One can do for content analysis exactly the same as for opinion analysis with individuals as units: construct indices (see II, 3). The techniques and the arguments are the same; nevertheless, this is rarely done. All one has to do is to define a set of variables that can be shown to belong together, intensionally or extensionally, and use one of the standard techniques to construct indices.

Thus, we conclude as we started: the only difference between content analysis and standard opinion analysis is that the former is based on cultural artefacts, the latter on individuals. Formally, in terms of the data matrix and what can be done with it, they are completely equal. As a matter of fact, content analysis has one tremendous advantage: it is much easier to bring in the time dimension. One can get 365 editorials coded to watch changes over a period of one year, but hardly obtain interviews with the editor(s) 365 times. Thus, content analysis opens many new possibilities for a really dynamic social science, as North and his colleagues demonstrated in their pioneering analysis of documents that formed the basis of decision-making prior to the outbreak of the First World War in August 1914 and prior to the Cuban blocade in October 1962.[16]

However, in all the enthusiasm for content analysis, we should not forget that no inferences can be made either to the *intention* of the producer or to the *effect* on the consumer without additional theoretical insights and empirical data. Thus, content analysis runs the risk of being suspended between senders and receivers, never really bearing on the *social* system, only on the *cultural* system. Content analysis may often be better suited for a science of culturology or for all the humanistic sciences (e. g. literary criticism) than for a science of society; nevertheless, when linked to other kinds of data and theory, it can yield both insights and contributions. It seems safe to predict that it will change the features of the humanistic sciences in years to come; but precisely what impact it has had, has, and will have on the social sciences is more difficult to assay.

3. Variables

3.1. *Levels of analysis*

We now turn to the second dimension of the data matrix: the variables. As the theory of variables is, unfortunatly, less developed than the theory of units, we shall try to present it in a slightly new version, based on the theory of units. More precisely, we shall try to apply the most important concepts in the theory of units and see where this leads us in the basic problem of selection of variables.

We shall use the following definitions:

Given a set of units, then
a *value* is anything which can be predicated of a unit, and
a *variable* is a set of values that form a classification.

Thus, given the set of Latin-American nations, an illiteracy rate of 38% is a value, because it can be predicated a unit (Mexico, 1950); and the set of illiteracy rates from 0% to 100% is a variable, because (a) any unit can be predicated one of these values (exhaustive), (b) no unit can be predicated more than one of them (mutually exclusive), and (c) there is a *fundamentum divisionis* (the common meaning).[1] A value is any predicate of a unit, but a variable, according to the definition, is not any set of values: the set has to satisfy the conditions of a classification. Here the first and second conditions are indispensable, but the third condition, that the values shall have a common meaning, is less important. One may find that a set of units is divided exhaustively into mutually exclusive subsets and then impute a meaning to this division. In other words, the 'fundamentum divisionis' may come afterwards, not prior to the division, as when a social scientist looks at a list of occupational data, analyzes the distributions, and decides how to divide them into strata.

It should be noticed that the variable is defined with reference to an empirical set. Thus, the set of illiteracy rates (22, 57, 90) is a variable if it satisfies the conditions for three nations that form a set of units (the greater Antilles). The variable may then be extended when new units are encountered.[2]

The mathematical structure of the set of values that constitutes a variable is now of crucial importance. Usually this is expressed in terms of *levels of measurement,* which presupposes the idea of measurement. We shall use this definition:

Given a variable, then
measurement is the mapping of the values on a set of numbers.

Nothing more is required: just that to each value there is one and only one number. Thus, to measure a nation in terms of economic growth it may first be given a value, e.g. 'take-off stage' and then it may be measured by attributing the number 3 to this value.[3] Measurement of units is a two-stage process: first the value, then the number.

A set of numbers will always have a well-defined mathematical structure, depending on how many operations can be performed unrestrictedly within the set. Thus, in the set of natural numbers, addition and multiplication can be performed unrestrictedly, but not subtraction and division, because the latter may lead to negative numbers and to fractions. A great deal of importance is now attributed to the extent to which these operations or relations between the numbers can be interpreted empirically on the units, and the convention is to speak of higher levels of measurement, the more of the mathematical properties can be interpreted. More precisely, we may talk about:

nominal scale, N   if *equality and diversity* among the numbers can be interpreted as 'equivalence and non-equivalence' among the units

ordinal scale, O   if *greater or smaller* among the numbers can be interpreted as 'more than' or 'less than' among the units

interval scale, I   if *equal differences* among the numbers can be interpreted as 'equally distinct' among the units

ratio scale, R   if *equal ratios* among the units can be interpreted as 'equally distinct' among the units. A necessary condition for this is that a *zero* among the numbers can be interpreted as 'nothing' among the units

absolute scale, A   if 'one' among the numbers can be interpreted as 'the smallest unit' among the units, and the scale satisfies the condition of a ratio scale.

There is a considerable literature using this terminology[4] (except for the 'absolute' scale which is introduced here). In our definition all five scales constitute measurement, since mappings of units on numbers are made use of. But some authors exclude the nominal scale and call it 'classification' or 'attributes'; others exclude the ordinal scale, since neither addition nor subtraction can be performed; and in physics a tendency to regard only ratio scale measures as measurement may be found. The basic dimensions of physics, L(ength), M(ass), T(ime), and one of the electro-magnetic dimensions all satisfy the requirements of the ratio scale.

The point about these scales is how many of the mathematical properties of the numbers can be used. At the nominal level, numbers serve only to keep what is different apart and join together what is considered equivalent, as when football-players are given numbers from 1-11. At the ordinal level, numbers also serve to order the elements in terms of some relation that is transitive and asymmetric, and consequently isomorphic with the relations 'greater than' or 'smaller than' among numbers. But only at the level of the interval scale can operations be performed (with restrictions), for the famous condition of equidistance is satisfied. Imagine that it is not satisfied. For instance, we may have a variable consisting of the five values 'disagree strongly', 'disagree', 'uncertain', 'agree', and 'agree strongly', and map the values on the numbers -2, -1, 0, 1, 2. However, for some reason we may feel that it takes more to have an opinion at all than to make the step from -1 to -2 or from 1 to 2, and that it takes more to disagree than to agree. Imagine now that we have two persons who have answered 'strongly disagree', 'agree', and 'disagree', 'agree', respectively, to two questions, and that an expression for the average attitude is wanted. If the numbers are added and divided by 2 we will get some disagreement in the first case and uncertainty in the second, contrary to what we would get if the mapping on numbers were changed so as to reflect better the intuition about the structure of the scale, i.e. to -4, -3, 0, 2, 3. Since equal numerical differences in the simple -2, -1, 0, 1, 2 scale do not necessarily correspond to equal attitudinal differences, the operations of addition and subtraction are illegitimate.

The classical example used to illustrate the difference between interval scales and ratio scales is the difference between ordinary temperature scales (Centigrade, Fahrenheit, Reaumur) where addition and subtraction are meaningful because they correspond to adding and subtracting lengths of mercury columns (it is essentially a reduction of temperature to length, using mercury etc. as the mechanism of translation). It is customary to say the expression '20 °C is twice as hot as 10 °C' is meaningless because the zero-point is conventional. However, the much celebrated -273.15 °C is also conventional; it refers to certain aspects of our empirical world which are supposed to develop difficulties getting below that point. With reference to that theory, the expression above becomes simply wrong since we would have to talk about 293°K and 283°K.

One may accept the theoretical priority of the Kelvin scale to the Centigrade scale, particularly if one is working as a physicist. But a physiologist or psychologist might argue that 'twice as' also has a psychological meaning, and do experiments where a group of persons is exposed to one temperature, then to increasing temperatures until they say 'this is about twice as hot'. If there is a reasonable degree of consensus between the persons and for the same person when the experiment is repeated, this may be used as the basis for the construction of a ratio scale.

Thus, what is meaningful or not is highly conventional. It depends on a zero, for if there is no point more attractive than the others as a zero point, then 'X is twice as much as Y' may be true for any pair (X, Y) by using a scale where Y is half-way between what is called zero and X. But the selection of a zero-point must be made on the basis of some principle, and here the possibilities are numerous.

The best known, but often forgotten, scale is the scale of counting, i.e. the natural numbers and zero. It is nominal, because sets with the same cardinality (i.e., where a one-one relation can be established between the elements in the sets are given the same number; sets with different cardinality are given different numbers. It is ordinal, it is interval, and it is ratio – there is an *absolute zero* corresponding to empty sets. But in addition to this there is an *absolute unit,* the unit of counting. If we are counting cows, what is 'one cow' is not completely conventional.

We call this the absolute scale, because no change or transformation of it is permissible. For the ratio scale, all numbers can be multiplied with a constant k without changing the equality of ratios (because the k will cancel out); for the interval scale one may also add a constant b to all numbers (because it will be subtracted away if differences are to be compared); for ordinal scales any monotone transformation that preserves the order will do; and for the nominal scale any transformation where equal numbers are still equal numbers and different numbers are different is permissible. But no change whatsoever can be made with the absolute scale; if there are 32 students in a class, then that is adequately reflected by the number 32 (or its equivalents in other number systems, i.e. by 100000 in the binary system). The reason for this lies in the circumstance that numbers were originally introduced for counting purposes, i.e. for absolute scales, and only later extended to 'measurement', i.e. to weaker scales.

Level of measurement has to do with the structure of the variable, i.e. the structure of the set of values that constitutes the variable. We shall now show that these structures are cumulative, in the sense that one presupposes the other, or in other words that $A \to R \to I \to O \to N$. Since $P \to Q$ is equivalent to $\bar{Q} \to \bar{P}$, we shall use the latter form when that is easier, i.e. we shall show that if the conditions of one level are not fulfilled, then we cannot get the subsequent level of measurement either.

That $A \to R$ follows from the definitions. That $\bar{I} \to \bar{R}$, and hence $R \to I$, can be seen as follows. If we do not have an interval scale, then the units are not equidistant. But if the units are not equidistant, the numbers may be changed at will as long as the order is preserved (i.e. from 1, 2, 3, 4, 5 to -15, 23, 24, 517, 1063) and this process does not preserve ratios.

That $I \to O$ is easily seen. For if we have an interval scale then subtractions can be performed, and it can be decided whether the difference is positive, zero, or negative. Let us call a positive difference d. If we have $x - y = d$, then $y - x = -d$, or in other words: the relation is asymmetric, we cannot have both $x - y$ positive and $y - x$ positive. Similarly, the relation is transitive: if $x - y = d_1$ and $y - z = d_2$, then $x - z = d_1 + d_2$ (by adding the two equations). Thus, by using the simple rule that $x - y = d \to x > y$ one can always obtain an ordinal scale from an interval scale.

Finally, $O \to N$, for if we have an ordinal scale, we are supposed to be able to decide for each pair whether the relation 'equal', 'greater than' or 'smaller than' applies. The latter two are only a refinement of the cruder relation 'different from'. And that concludes the proof.

Earlier, in chapters 1 and 2, distinctions were made between variables that were

(1) *public* or *private*
(2) *permanent* or *temporary*
(3) *background, personality* or *elemental*
(4) *independent* or *dependent*
(5) *individual* or *collective*
(6) *absolute, relative* or *relational*
(7) *global, analytic* or *structural*
(8) *proper* or *contextual*

Here, different (9) *scales of measurement* has been distinguished. This means that we have used 'level' in two senses: as the level of the *units* to which the variable applies, and as the level of *measurement*. A variable that applies to nations may be said to be on a higher level than a variable that applies to individuals, and an interval scale variable is on higher level than a nominal scale variable. But in the former case, it is actually the *unit* that is of a higher level, not the variable; and in the latter, it is the *structure* of the variable as a set of values, not the variable itself.

We shall now introduce a third concept of level which refers to the variables themselves. To do this we must first indicate what could possibly be meant by a *universe of variables*.[5]

One possible definition would be as follows: given a set of units, the corresponding set of variables is the set of the sets of all values that can be attributed to the units. In other words: the set of variables associated with a set of units contains every thing that can be said about these units. The definition presupposes a set of units. This is usually legitimate, since a research project often, perhaps almost always, starts that way: one wants to know something about O, one finds out that O belongs to a more general class $\underline{O}$, and then looks for the attributes of the units in $\underline{O}$. But one could also start with a variable and generate a set of units the variable describes. However, we shall not try to go into the intricate problems this opposite way of thinking would lead us to.

Imagine now that such a universe has been more or less clearly delimited. We can call it $\underline{V}$; it consists of an unspecified number, n, of variables, V.

We now intersperse a level between $\underline{V}$ and V, between the universe and the single variable, of variables that somehow 'belong together', and call this the level of *dimensions* or *clusters* of variables. Thus, a dimension or a cluster is nothing but a subset of variables. The problem is how to delimit these subsets, and the possible subsubsets, the subdimensions and subclusters.

No clear line of reasoning exists here. In research on migration we might talk about 'motivation to leave' as a dimension of the problem and look for variables or sub-dimensions of that dimension. In survey research this will usually lead to a number of questions that should not be confused with the variables: the variables are the sets of mutually exclusive and exhaustive *answers*, the question is the stimulus we use to decide which value to apply to which unit. But how do we decide which variables belong to or 'tap' the dimension of 'motivation to migrate'?

There are two schools of thought here. Both are valuable, but they often lead to different results. We shall call them the *intensive* and *extensive* traditions, respectively.

The solution of this problem, *in intension,* lies in deciding, on the basis of the *meaning* of the variable, whether it belongs or not. This is usually done by means of some kind of a thought experiment. The variable is given and the investigator asks himself: would people who have different values on this variable also be different in, say, their degree of motivation to migrate? Answer: yes – perhaps – no, and then the variables for which the face value answer seems to be *no* are excluded. By this method, one would include in the cluster all variables thought by the investigator to belong to that cluster. This process can then be refined by his asking other investigators what they think, and he may decide to include in the cluster only variables about which there is a high degree of consensus (using a panel of judges).

The second solution of the problem, *in extension,* lies in deciding on the basis of how the units distribute. There are here a number of techniques at the disposal of the researcher, all with this much in common: the empirical distributions *of* the units *on* the variables are considered, especially the correlations between the variables, and a decision is made on the basis of these distributions. Obviously, the principle can never be to call a cluster everything that is correlated, for that would lump together with 'motivation to migrate' all kinds of background variables, etc. Somehow there must be a homogeneity in meaning, which is tantamount to saying that the extensive method is usually applied after a pre-selection made by means of the intensive method, which again is based on a simplified version of the extensive method taking place in the mind of the researcher rather than in the IBM machine.

If we look at social research as a kind of interaction between the researchers and the 'units', i.e. the individuals, the difference can be formulated as follows: the solution in intension, by the decision of the individual researcher is *autocratic;* the solution in intension by consensus within a group of competent researchers (i.e. group that considers itself competent) is *oligarchic*; and the solution in extension is *democratic.* The objections to the methods are very similar to the objections found in political life to these systems. Who is the researcher to decide? By his decisions, will he not perpetuate old theories and perspectives? And what about the 'democratic method', is it not rather a 'dictatorship of the proletariat'? If something happens to be correlated, any analyst knows there may be a vast variety of explanations, not all presupposing that the variables have a common content.

We shall emphasize the importance of the distinction by giving names to the variables according to their relationship to a dimension; distinguishing between (10) *items and indicators* where

an *item* is a variable that is included in a cluster by intensive criteria
an *indicator* is a variable that is included in a cluster by extensive criteria

This is a convenient usage of these words: the item is included because of its meaning, and the indicator because of its correlations. The problem is that the item may not be an indicator and the indicator not an item – there is some overlap, but never perfect overlapping. So, what do we do with the item that is not an indicator, or with the indicator that is not an item?

78

Here we shall merely formulate the problem, it will be taken up again in II, 3.7 in connection with index theory.

3.2. *The fallacy of the wrong level*

The universe of variables can be divided into clusters of variables that 'tap' the same dimension; the clusters divide into variables called items or indicators, depending on how they have been selected; and the variables divide into values that are attributes of units. Then, the units combine into collectivities, strata, classes, groups, or what they may be called; and these again combine into universes of units. This is the complexity with which we have to work:

Table 3.2.1. *Levels of units and levels of variables*

	unit side	variable side
universe	*universe of units*	*universe of variables*
cluster	*clusters of units* (collectivities)	*clusters of variables* (dimensions)
element	*units* (individuals)	*variables* (items, indicators)
	values	

Starting with the universe of units we go in two directions. The universe of variables can be defined as indicated in 3.1, and the universe of units can be subdivided as indicated in 2.3. Then we subdivide on both sides until we come to the level of the units and the variables. The two sides then meet in the values, where the values are classes of units (i. e. of the units that can be predicated the same value) and the variables are classes of values (i. e. values that are exhaustive and mutually exclusive). Thus, the logical structure is relatively clear. Obviously, there is no direct correspondence between a cluster of units and a cluster of variables, or between the single unit and the single variable.

The question is now whether there is a fallacy on the variable side, corresponding to what is variously called the ecological fallacy or the part-whole fallacy, or the contextual fallacy on the unit side. There seems to be such a fallacy, only that it is less noticed or appears under other headings in social science methodology. It consists in the following: to infer correlations between individual variables from correlations between dimensions or clusters of variables: in other words, exactly the same structure as the fallacy on the unit side.

More concretely, the fallacy will consist in believing that all variables that are items or indicators of two dimensions are correlated because the dimensions are correlated. This would be the fallacy downwards, but there is also a fallacy 'upwards': the belief that dimensions must be correlated because one indicator from each happens to be correlated, with each other. The fallacy may also take on an even simpler form. Imagine that a number of indicators designed to tap a dimension of militarism is developed, and that one of them has to do with attitudes to atomic weapons. In a complex picture taking a number of indicators into consideration, an indicator of that kind will be valuable; but considered alone, it is obvious that rejection of atomic weapons can take place without any rejection of pro-military attitudes in general. This is the problem touched upon in Table 1.2.2: why *that* question (indicator) rather than another?

The other problem, the fallacy downwards, will be commented on when more meaning has been given to the expression 'two dimensions are correlated' through the introduction of indices. Suffice it to say that one requirement of an index measuring a dimension must be precisely that it is sensitive to the problem of fallacy between levels. Thus, it seems reasonable to require that

(1) Indices must be correlated if all pairs of indicators from different dimensions show correlation, and
(2) The correlation between indices should be sensitive to variations in the correlation between indicators, and particularly be zero if all indicator-correlations are zero and negative if all indicator-correlations are negative.

We postpone further treatment of this problem to II, 3.7 and II, 5.4, since the intention here was only to emphasize the parallel between units and variables also where fallacies are concerned.

3.3. *The problem of selection*

In principle, there is no reason why we should not think about the selection of variables in the same way as we think about the selection of units: in terms of universes and samples. Theoretically, as mentioned, it is possible to delimit the universe by stipulating that it consists of all variables the the values of which can be attributed to the units we have selected for study. Just as we require of a variable that it shall serve as a classification – all units shall be given one and only one value, – we also use this as a principle for defining intensionally the universe of variables, as the set of everything that can be used to classify the units. Thus, the universe is defined relative to the universe of units. We could also proceed in the other direction: first defining a set of variables and then using this to specify the set of units to which the variables apply. In research practice, this corresponds to asking first 'what is the Problem', and next 'exactly to what kind of units does this apply'.

How, then, can we sample from such a universe of variables? We are confronted with the same problems as in the sampling of units, such as the problem of direct or multistage sampling. Usually, a two-stage or three-stage sample is used. First a set of subsets is picked, called 'problem-areas', or as we have done, 'dimensions' or 'clusters'. Then a subset is picked from each of these sets again. Here too a special terminology is often used: in the second stage of sampling we come to what is known as 'items', 'indicators', 'stimuli', etc. (A third stage, called subdimensions or sub-clusters, may come before this stage). Whatever the terminology, the structure of the final set of n variables is usually something like this:

Diagram 3.3.1. *The structure of selection of variables*

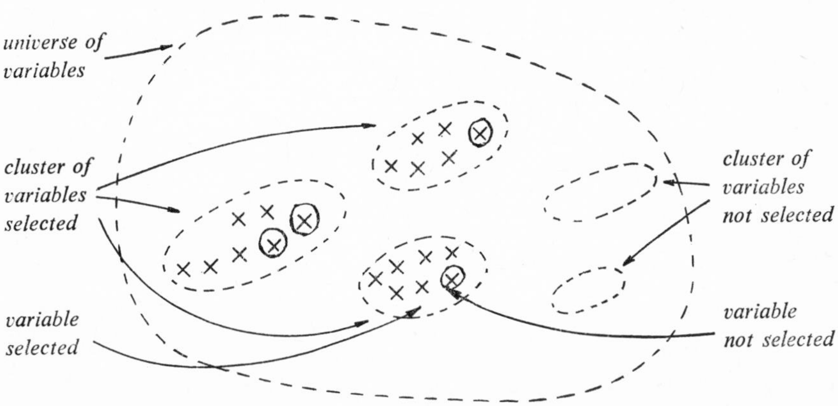

The lines delimiting universe and clusters are broken to symbolize the difficulties in establishing precise border lines.

The basic idea is not only that we group variables together if they seem to belong together, but that the way in which we develop our sets of variables for an investigation corresponds to what is known in unit-sampling as two-stage sampling.

Often one more stage enters in the beginning, in terms of 'independent', 'intervening' and 'dependent' variables. Just as for unit-sampling, what actually happens in a research process can best be described by reasoning the other way, from unit to cluster. Variables are somehow picked from the universe (which is defined in intension as above, and not in extension by actually listing all possible variables that can be used to describe the units) and then grouped together in sets, super-sets etc., as we start thinking about them or get information about how the units distribute relative to them.

The question then becomes: how is this sampling actually carried out? The immediate answer is that the researcher is generally guided by a Problem which serves as a first principle for the selection of variables. The Problem serves as the intension of a set defining what is known as relevant variables. It may, however, be argued that it serves only to designate the sets of variables to be included in the first stage of the sampling, the Problem is rarely specific enough to designate the variables themselves. If the Problem is that of getting insights into the conditions for an international expert to function adequately, a number of clusters of variables present themselves readily: background, institutional setting, travel experience, family pressures, etc. But since the possibility of further sub-division is almost unlimited, these are only sets of variables, dimensions. The question then becomes: when we have delimited the sets in the first stage more or less by a deductive process from the Problem, how do we sample in the second stage?

Usually what happens is that the researcher sits down to think, and then puts down the variables that come to mind, provided these variables (1) can be used to predicate something about the units, and (2) fall under the subsets selected. What then happens is not well known. It is probably in general a very complex mental process where the constraints known from the researcher's experiences with data-collection, data-processing, and data-analysis play a major role. Whatever happens, however, it is evident that the outcome in general cannot be characterized as a probability sample – even if no variables are excluded *a priori*, we can safely say that the probabilities of the possible samples of variables are not known. The question is whether this is consequential and that should be discussed under at least two headings: (1) the problem of generalizability, and (2) the problem of bias.

Essentially, this is the famous problem of discrepancy between on the one hand dimensions and the terms used for them; and on the other hand items/indicators. An important example is the dimension of 'fascism'. Imagine we have a well-defined set of items/indicators of that dimension; and let us for simplicity assume that all variables in that set are both items and indicators. Among these variables one subset will concern conservatism with regard to political-economic structure. Thus, it is reasonable to assume that most people who with any right can be said to have a 'fascist orientation' will be against industrial democracy, against efforts to engage in scientific precision planning of the economy of a country, and against reduction of military capacity. Another subset will concern radicalism or leftism with regard to political-economic structure: centralization of power, collectivism, emphasis on production, and technical achievement.

Imagine now one of these subsets selected as representative of the dimension. The result is obviously that in one case rightists and in the other case leftists will be classified as fascists, and the results probably used by the other camp for propaganda and by the same camp as proof of the fallacy of 'scientific sociology'. Obviously, the latter is correct. As a sample the subset is biased, and generalizations to the entire dimension, hence, illegitimate. Equally obvious is the remedy: to take a probability sample from the set and use that sample if it is not possible to use the whole universe. This method may be strengthened by taking more than one sample and by using the different samples as controls of each other. Further, we may stratify the set into subsets and take a proportionate, stratified sample as a guarantee against the possibility that even the random sample may be heavily biased. Thus, we may arrive at a cluster of variables that is representative to the extent the universe is representative.

Unfortunately, this last condition is rather problematic. A researcher may have a high understanding of what fascism is, and develop an extremely long list of items, yet his list will have three times as high a proportion of rightist items as the list developed by his colleague who happens to be rightist himself. Any proportionate sample will reflect this bias, random or not. The obvious remedy here is to make the construction of the list of variables a collective task, where the team consists of researchers with different orientation (in practice, this is difficult, because different orientation ideologically usually also means different orientation with regard to what is worth-while in social science). The rule for inclusion of an item in the list should then be (1) all consensual items, and (2) most dissensual items, provided they can be seen as efforts to balance bias. To adhere to the first rule only will often be tantamount to excluding interesting indicators.

If such a list exists, there are two policies to follow. It may be wise, if the set is found to be rather heterogeneous, to split it up into subsets that are so homogeneous that it does not seem to matter much which items are selected. The second possibility is to proceed as we have indicated and select a sample of variables that has no built-in bias and permits generalization. Such a sample does not have to be random. It can also be purposive, provided it is heterogeneous and, if possible, in some way representative. It should be emphasized that the psychometric tradition of having two parallel instruments, i.e. two samples of variables from the same subset, adds greatly to the weight of the evidence accumulated by means of the research.

At this point a distinction should be made between two formally similar, but actually very different strategies that both have their exact counterpart in unit theory. In unit theory, a distinction may be made between two kinds of replication

(1) On different sample, obtained the same way (duplication).
(2) On different sample, obtained in another way (replication).

In community studies, this may be the distinction between replicating the study on a new sample from the same village and replicating the study in another village. The first kind of replication is rarely done because it actually amounts to an increase in the size of the sample – if the two samples are not regarded as *time* samples. For that reason it should be referred to as duplication rather than replication. The second type of replication has a complex role as the provider of a higher degree of confirmation and a possible extension of the field of applicability of the hypothesis/proposition.

In variable theory the former corresponds to the parallel instrument of the test psychologist, whereas the latter corresponds to an additional instrument which is known not to be 'parallel', yet to be within the same general dimension. The latter is a true type of replication, which may extend the tenability of the findings from one sub-set to another sub-set within the dimension, and hence contribute to a high degree of confirmation for the dimension as a whole. All this will be developed in II, 3 and II, 5.4, and become more operational when various ways of measuring dimensions, i.e. of making composite measures from the variables in one dimension, have been discussed.

3.4. *Panel analysis and structural analysis*

Like content analysis, panel analysis is often announced as a unique method in social research. We have pointed out how content analysis differs from other methods only in the sense that the units are not individuals or collectivities, but some kind of socio-cultural artefacts, and that the whole manner of thinking in terms of levels of analysis and sampling applies equally well to this other kind of units. Similarly, panel analysis is easily seen to be a special method only in the sense that there is something particular about the variables: the variables are measured at least *twice*.

To see more clearly what this type of research implies let us compare it to other types of research involving repeated observation on the following crucial points: whether one uses the same sample or different samples whether different samples are obtained the same way or different ways, and whether the observations are made at the same time or at different points in time. We get this typology:

Table 3.4.1. *Different strategies for repeating observations*

sample of units	how it is obtained	points in time for observations	designation
1 same	same way	same	*intra-* or *inter-subjectivity* study
2 same	same way	different	*panel* (*replication* in *time*)
3 different	same way	same	*duplication*
4 different	same way	different	*trend* study
5 different	different ways	same	*replication* in *space*
6 different	different ways	different	*replication* in *time* and *space*

Thus, there are two 'same's in the panel study: the *same* units and the *same* variables, but the variables are observed for each unit at at least two points in time. In principle, they may be observed at any number of points in time, and it is customary in panel analysis to talk about each set of observations as a 'wave'. A panel variable, then, is a variable that is observed through all waves; but in addition there may be variables that are only observed in some of the waves. The most frequently found is the two-wave panel.

A panel study, defined above as a replication in time of the same observations on the same units, is clearly nothing exceptional for social science. The more or less controlled experiment in any science will have a before – after pattern of observations, where the unit is observed, exposed to a stimulus, and then observed again – with or without adequate control. The panel study is a translation into social science of this kind of thinking and represented a considerable improvement on the four other strategies listed above. The duplication brings in no time dimension and only a minor variation in space; the replication brings in variation in space but is also static; the trend study is exactly a trend study and does not permit inferences as to what happened to the individual unit – and the replication in time and space is a relatively undisciplined manner of obtaining data. The panel is dynamic, and at the same time permits analysis at the unit level as well as the collective level. In the trend analysis net changes are observed, in the panel analysis we get at the net changes as well as at what happens to every individual. The typical example is the post-election speculation: Party X has gained, party Y has lost. The speculation is that party Y has lost to party X. A panel analysis is needed to show that party Y may have lost to party Z who in turn has lost to party X, not to mention that the change observed is always a net change, the resultant of unequal flows in opposite directions.

For such technical problems as 'mortality' (loss of panel members from one wave to the other) and 're-interviewing bias' (the effects of being reinterviewed, whether it is as a drive towards consistency with earlier answers, a feeling that 'I have to say something different', an artificially high salience because of the impact of the repeated experience with the interviewers, etc.) and other topics see the excellent discussions by Zeisel.[6] For a more advanced discussion, see the publications by the Bureau of Applied Social Research, Columbia University, on panel analysis. Some of the problems of analysis of panel data will be taken up later (II, 2.3). They center on the problem of how to handle what one could call the analytical element of panel analysis, the first wave-second wave table:

Table 3.4.2. *The analytical element of panel analysis: the turnover table*

		First wave		
		Yes	No	
Second wave	Yes	a	b	$a+b$
	No	c	d	$c+d$
		$a+c$	$b+d$	N

N persons have been interviewed twice with the same question, so the two variables in the table are the same, only registered at different points in time. The question is how to measure the change that has taken place from first to second wave.

This general way of thinking, involving the *same* units and the same variables more than once, is, of course, not restricted to units that are individuals or to verbal methods to collect data. One of the most important extensions to behavioral data is made by using social rank as a variable and observing the rank of the unit individual more than once to measure his *intra*-generational mobility. The variation involved in measuring *inter*-generational mobility consists in extending the individual to comprise his father or his son (in a patrilineal society) and measuring this extended unit at two points in time. Any variable may be used for such purposes and yield growth (or decay) curves for individuals, with such famous examples as the curves for intelligence and creativity and sexual capacity.

And this can equally well be applied to collective units, only that data will usually be obtained from statistical yearbooks etc. Thus, one could measure all provinces of a country on a number of indicators of socioeconomic growth at two points using census data. The degree of change can then be measured through simple subtraction for each indicator (e. g. by subtracting percentages employed in the secondary sector of society or located in middle and high class positions) and as independent variables can be used the data from the first census supplemented with knowledge about what happened in the meantime. The same thing can be done with nations, comparing them with themselves – and with the others.

We turn from this problem to a presentation of what we have called general *structure analysis*. In this kind of analysis the point of departure is always a set O of actors (individuals, groups, nations). We then use them as their own stimuli, and get:

Table 3.4.3. *The analytical element of structural analysis: the structure matrix*

$$
\begin{array}{c|ccccc}
\rightarrow & O_1 & O_2 & \dots & O_j & \dots & O_m \\
\hline
O_1 & e_{11} & e_{12} & \dots & e_{1j} & \dots & e_{1m} \\
O_2 & e_{21} & e_{22} & \dots & e_{2j} & \dots & e_{2m} \\
\cdot & \cdot & \cdot & & \cdot & & \cdot \\
\cdot & \cdot & \cdot & & \cdot & & \cdot \\
O_i & e_{i1} & e_{i2} & \dots & e_{ij} & \dots & e_{im} \\
\cdot & \cdot & \cdot & & \cdot & & \cdot \\
\cdot & \cdot & \cdot & & \cdot & & \cdot \\
O_m & e_{m1} & e_{m2} & \dots & e_{mj} & \dots & e_{mn}
\end{array}
$$

This is nothing but a regular data matrix, except that the set of units functions both as units and as stimuli. One interpretation of e_{ij}, the general element in the *exchange matrix* as the structure matrix is often called in this context, is what O_j stimulates O_i to contribute to O_j. Correspondingly, e_{ji} is what O_j contributes to O_i. To make this clear, it is useful to add the arrow that indicates: *from* the elements to the *left, to* the elements *above* the matrix.

Three important interpretations of this general scheme:

Interpretation	Set of elements	Value exchanged
Sociometric analysis[7]	Individuals	Evaluations
Interaction process analysis[8]	Individuals, actors	Acts
Cross-run analysis[9]	Economic sectors	Economic value

All of these may be seen as special cases of a more general approach of *structural analysis*. A set of actors, preferably in a meaningful collectivity, are used as vertical and horizontal headings of a two-way table, and each cell in the table is used to characterize the relation between the elements, in other words to characterize pairs of elements.

Exchange analysis enters as a special case of structure analysis, where the relation can be interpreted in terms of some kind of exchange of value. Thus, depending on what relation we use, we get three important kinds of structure analysis:

Relation	Set of elements	Interpretation[10]
Interaction or not	Individuals or statuses	Social network analysis
Relative rank	Individuals or statuses	Hierarchy analysis
Relative power	Individuals or statuses	Dominance analysis

Since structural analysis is the more general, we have preferred to use this term for analysis where the data matrix is based on identical units and stimuli. One should be careful not to say 'identical units and variables', because the unit can never be a variable, i.e. a set of values.

What happens in sociometric analysis is only that each element is asked for verbal evaluation of the elements in the set; and in interaction process analysis that verbal and non-verbal action is observed for all pairs. This can be done in crude terms (there is or there is not interaction) as in the network analysis between individuals, and in more precise terms, as when the Bales category system is used. In cross-run analysis, e.g. between nations, economic flow in both directions is registered, and so on.

All these types of analysis are confronted with three basic problems that can profitably be discussed in this general framework:

(1) *The problem of the main diagonal.* The elements e_{ii} on the main diagonal differ from the other elements insofar as the word 'exchange' does not so easily apply. The case is well illustrated by sociometric analysis, where one sometimes permits the individuals to include themselves in the set to be evaluated, sometimes not. There is an obvious difference between 'with whom do you want to –' – which would leave the main diagonal empty, and 'who do you think should be the leader of –' – where the main diagonal enters like all other cells (except for such factors as

modesty). Interaction with oneself can sometimes be called intra-action, own sector enters in cross-run analysis as intra-regional trade, self-maintenance, etc. In hierarchy and dominance analyses it is customary to fill the main diagonal with zeros, indicating that an individual or status does not have higher rank or more power than itself.

If at all possible the empty diagonal should be avoided since it is likely to bring some difficulties into the analyses. On the other hand, it is better to leave the diagonal empty than to force something into the cells that it is not a natural interpretation intra-individually of what is put into the inter-individual cells.

(2) *The problem of symmetry.* From the very beginning it must be clear whether we have, in general, e_{ij} equal to e_{ji} or not. In most cases we do not. In sociometric analysis there is no reason why O_i should have the same evaluation of O_j as O_j has of O_i. This is also true in interaction process analysis, and in cross-run analysis. However, if we take a set of statuses and mark 1 if interaction is institutionalized for S_i to S_j, it seems artificial to work with concepts of interaction so that the matrix does not turn out symmetric. On the other hand, hierarchy matrices are clearly asymmetric and so are dominance matrices.

(3) *The structure of the variable.* The structure matrix is a special case of the data matrix in that there is not only vertical comparability but also horizontal comparability: all the stimuli are of the same kind. For this reason a number of analytic techniques are at the disposal of the analyst.[11] The structure of the variable is discussed in detail in the next chapter. Suffice it to say that for sociometric analysis for example, various possibilities are at the disposal of the investigator:

(a) *Choice*, i.e. put '1' for selection and '0' for indifference or rejection.
(b) *Rejection*, put '−1' for rejection, '0' for indifference or selection.
(c) *Evaluation*, put '1' and '−1' as above, '0' for indifference.
(d) *Ranking* – from 1 to m.
(e) *Picking and rating* – pick k, rate them as in methods (a), (b) or (c).
(f) *Picking and ranking* – pick k, rank them as in method (d).

All this has to be done with regard to a criterion, e.g. popularity, as leader, etc. Further, all of this can be done permitting or not permitting the inclusion of oneself, i.e. filling or leaving blank the main diagonal.

This type of structural analysis can now be combined with other kinds of analysis. Thus, a good three-stage sample might use a purposive selection of schools in a school district, for instance filling a factorial design as to socio-economic status; then draw a random sample of classes from each school; and then do structural analysis of evaluations or interactions for each class. But one may also study the structure of the inter-class or inter-school systems. In short, the possibilities are numerous indeed, and the researcher should have at his disposal the whole arsenal of combinations to select one that fits *his* problem.

4. Values

The idea of evaluation

The general line of thought in the preceding chapters has been to combine
all possible units of analysis with all possible stimuli or variables, and look
at the values that can be recorded as a result of the combination. We now
turn to these values.

A *variable* can be regarded as some kind of yardstick that gives us a basis
for the evaluation of the single unit of analysis. The dimension of marital
happiness is one example, national income another. It has already been
mentioned that the dimension must have at least two alternative values,
otherwise no information is yielded at all. We shall now argue that in most
cases we should actually have *r* equal to at least 3 in order to provide us with
a meaningful *evaluation;* as for instance when a respondent is evaluating a
car, or when a nation's level of religiousness is considered.

What, then do we mean by 'evaluation'? We are not particularly concerned with what goes on in the respondent's mind, only with how we can
conceive of the manifest result. In general, we define an *evaluation process as
a process where a set of elements are divided in three parts (trichotomized):
'positive', 'neutral or indifferent', and 'negative' elements.* This is what happens when a tourist makes up his mind about the places he visited during
his summer trip; this is what the art critic does; what everybody does when
he takes a stand for or against some slogan (or remains neutral or uncertain),
etc. But, of course, there is more to it than this.

First of all, the evaluation takes place according to some principle or
meaning, which has to do with what we have called a 'fundamentum divisionis'. When the prospective car-buyer divides the set of medium-priced
cars (his universe of interest) into three parts, this may be an all-over evaluation, but it may also be an evaluation with regard to some more specific
value, e.g., appearance, workmanship, etc. The relevant value gives us the
meaning or *intension* of the evaluation, whereas the division of the set in
three parts gives us the *extension* of the evaluation. Of course, one or more
of the three subsets may be empty: the car-buyer dislikes all cars, or is
neutral towards none of them – but in principle the set is divided in three
exhaustive and mutually exclusive subsets by the respondent.

Secondly, the evaluation seldom stops at the trichotomy, but often proceeds towards more refined gradations. There are shades of positive and negative – only the neutral category is commonly held to be indivisible. The result is a continuum of evaluations:

$$- \qquad 0 \qquad +$$

where the respondent can place any one of the objects according to how he evaluates it; or, to phrase it differently: for every single object, the respondents can be scattered according to how they evaluate that object. The assumption is that the continuum is somehow one-dimensional, which means that it carries only 'one meaning'; this again is of course a highly conventional notion.

Thus so far we have made an implicit distinction between *value* and *evaluation*. The latter is an *act,* observable in principle, and consists in the allocation of objects or stimuli of any kind to an element in a reference set with at least three elements, corresponding to 'good', 'neutral' and 'bad'. To evaluate is to sort and order stimuli. A value, however, is the *principle* according to which this sorting or ordering is done. A better term would perhaps be *value-standard.* Values or value-standards, hence, are identical with what we have referred to as the meaning or intension of the evaluation; the result of the evaluation is correspondingly the value in extension. The value expresses itself in the evaluations made, and from evaluations more or less valid inferences can be made about the values or value-standards of the respondents. In principle, then, we get:

Table 4.1.1. *Relation between objects, values and evaluations*

	Stimulus	Intervening variable	Response
Manifest level (phenotype)	*Psychological objects*		*Evaluations of objects*
Latent level (genotype)		*Values held by the respondent*	

An important special case is when the stimuli are *actions* or descriptions of actions. According to the general outline above, evaluations of actions may serve as a basis for the inference of values, *but these values are of the special kind called norms.* We can present a set of respondents with a set of actions to evaluate. The verbal symbols may be changed from 'good-bad' to 'right-wrong' in accordance with common usage, or the pair 'prescribed-proscribed' may be preferred, or we may use a five-point scale such as the following (where even some measure of intensity is included)[1]:

absolutely must not	preferably should not	may or may not	preferably should	absolutely must

There is another approach to attitude research which we shall also treat as a special case. We have discussed how values can be expressed through evaluations made by the respondent. For instance, the stimulus-object could be a car, and the respondent could be asked to evaluate its appearance as 'good', 'neutral', 'bad'. But if instead of appearance we took another attribute of the car, e.g., speed, the situation would be highly different. *If the top speed were known,* and printed under the picture, the respondent could be asked to evaluate it much as he evaluated the appearance, e.g. as 'too fast', 'OK', 'too slow'. But if it is not known, an encouragement to evaluate would confuse two things: *what he believes about the speed, and how he evaluates this cognition.* The result could very well be that two respondents evaluated the speed as bad, the first because he *believed* the car to be slow, which he dislikes; the second because he *knew* it to be a very 'hot' car, a fact which he evaluates negatively. It may be argued that this does not matter as long as they were both negative – but it is clear that the confusion of the two elements will limit the analysis considerably.

How do we deal with the registration of pure cognitions, with no evaluative components? The difference is the same as the difference between placing John Foster Dulles on a scale running from 'extremely good' to 'extremely bad' as a Secretary of State, and placing him on a scale running from 'very much pro' to 'very much contra' the Nasser regime in Egypt. The first yields an evaluation of JFD, the second a cognition about him. The two are not empirically unrelated – one of the most fascinating aspects of surveys is to find out how evaluations and cognitions are related – but they are logically of distinct types. In this example, the logical link would be a stimulus to evaluate the Nasser regime.

In complete analogy with figure 4.1.1 we get:

Figure 4.1.2. *Relation between objects, beliefs and cognitions*

	Stimulus	Intervening variable	Response
Manifest level (phenotype)	*Psychological objects*		*Cognitions about the objects*
Latent level (genotype)		*Beliefs held by the respondent*	

What do we mean, then, when we say that this is a special case of evaluation? To make the statement 'John Foster Dulles is very much contra the Nasser regime' is not in itself an evaluation of Dulles. However, if we change the focus a little and look at the statement in the preceding sentence *as the object to be evaluated,* we come closer to the meaning we have given to evaluation. Statements or propositions can be evaluated; the positive category when statements are evaluated is called 'true', the negative category is called 'false', and the neutral category for statements is called by various, not synonymous names, such as 'neither true, nor false', 'meaningless', etc. Just as for evaluations in general, a continuum of evaluations corresponding to degrees of truth and falsity may be conceived of, and the respondent can be given the statement above and presented with a choice between the following five evaluational categories (here called 'truth-values'):

completely false	somewhat false	neither true nor false	somewhat true	completely true

Thus, the cognitive task of expressing beliefs is subsumed under the general heading of evaluation of 'psychological objects'.

This does not mean that there are no differences. It may be said that our culture is biased in favor of cognitions, and treats evaluations more as a step-child, while there are many different units of cognition that enable us to make propositions of the kind: 'the speed of a car is 80 mph', we do not in the same sense have evaluational units: they are constructed *ad hoc.*

It may even be said that a dimension changes from evaluative to cognitive if units are introduced. To rate a person on a kindness scale is called 'evaluation', but if we had units of kindness this would be called 'measurement'.

On the other hand, consensual cognitive units exist mostly in the field of the natural sciences, and where *counting* is made use of as a measurement process. In these cases the manifest variables the respondents are instructed to use to indicate their belief (e. g., to the question: 'How many people do you think live in the Soviet Union to-day?') will be in existing units (e. g., in thousands or millions). But in other cases (e.g., to the question 'Do you think the group you participated in was efficient in solving the problem?') verbal, numerical, and graphical symbols very much like the ones indicated for attitude scales may be employed.

DK has a simpler meaning for beliefs than for attitudes, because only cognition is involved. NA, however, should have just the same interpretation as for attitude research. Except for what we have already mentioned, we assume that everything said about attitudes and evaluations applies to beliefs and cognitions as well. Note, however, that it may be impossible to draw a sharp borderline between a belief and an evaluation: statements as 'The group was a good discussion group' have cognitive and evaluational components, and it is difficult to say which ones dominate. In such cases, semantic clarification seems essential in order to know what the sentence meant to the respondents.

4.2. *The number of values*

Let us now imagine we have a data matrix like the one given in Table 1.1.3. According to our most general notions, the R_{ij} shall inform the reader of the matrix about which of the three sets O_i feels S_j belongs to – this is a minimum requirement. In addition, it may often be of analytic value if the R_{ij} could give more graded information as to *how* positive and *how* negative O_i's evaluation is. And finally, the intension of the evaluation should be given, but not in the matrix – that will only confuse. Usually, it is given in the heading of the table, like the row of S's in Table 1.1.3.

Imagine, now, that we have the set S and the set $\underline{O}$, that we are able to 'bring them together' so that the only thing to decide is what the set $\underline{R}$ shall look like. Of course, there is no reason why the set of possible values should be the same for all variables or stimuli, but there is a very good reason why it should be the same for all respondents or units confronted with the same variable: the principle of comparability. Focussing our attention on one stimulus, S_j, the first and simplest question we have to answer is this: *how many* values do we want in the corresponding set of values? This is the only *structural* variable at our disposal, all other choices depend on the nature of the sets S and $\underline{O}$. The higher r is, the more refined information we get. The choice is fundamental in the design of any study, and the outcome is usually a compromise based on factors such as:

(1) What is the *maximum* refinement we can get *about* the units of analysis, or *from* the units of analysis?
(2) What is the *minimum* refinement necessary for the analysis?

As a rule it is better to try to get too much than too little. If r is too high for the purpose of the analysis, a new set R^* can always be constructed, for instance by collapsing adjacent categories – but the opposite is not possible.

At this point we must make a distinction as to the values in R. One thing is what values are presented to the unit of analysis, another thing what values the analyst would like to work with. For instance, in an analysis of attitudes where the respondent is simply asked to say 'true' or 'false' to a number of statements, R consists of the two elements 'true' and 'false' for the respondent (with the possible addition of 'no answer'). But the analyst might like to work with figures and prefer to translate the two values by 1 and 2, or 1 and 0, or +1 and −1, etc. Similarly, the respondent may prefer the values 'disagree – uncertain – agree' where the analyst prefers '−1, 0, +1' and the IBM operator punches 0, 1, and 2. Obviously, there must be a one – one correspondence between all these possible ways of expressing R.

By definition, we would talk about the data-collection (i.e., the completion of the data matrix) as *measurement* if R is a set of *numbers*. However, if only the rules for a nominal scale are satisfied, we would say it is measurement at the lowest level.

When the number of symbols exceeds two, it is usually understood that *the symbols form at least an ordinal scale,* and that the respondent is instructed so as to understand fully the ordinal nature of the symbols he is to use to express his evaluation of the object. Further, it is generally felt that there shall be a certain symmetry between positive and negative symbols, which means:

(1) there shall be as many positive as negative symbols,
(2) they shall be symmetrically distributed, relative to the neutral point.

Otherwise the set of values is usually considered biased. *If* we accept a symbol for the set of neutral objects, these two rules imply that the number of symbols must be *uneven;* most common are 3, 5, 7, and 11. However, *two* symbols are also very often used for sake of simplicity. Let us briefly summarize the possibilities in Table 4.2.1 and adopt the convention of calling evaluation by means of n symbols an *n-point scale.*

The first rows of figures are intuitively most instructive, the second rows can often be of value in work with punched cards, etc.

Two-point scales. These contain less information than an evaluation in principle should, and hence are possible only when information is lost because one of the subsets (the neutral) is defined as empty, or two subsets are combined. The advantage lies in the data-processing: the simple dichotomy facilitates the construction of indices and scales tremendously. There are four possibilities:

(1) *The possibility of neutral objects is denied.* The choice is between 'agree' and 'disagree', 'good' or 'bad', 'like' or 'dislike', etc., and the respondents are instructed not to use neutral answers, and/or such answers are discarded.
(2) *Negative and neutral are combined* ('he who is not for me, is against me'). This is often done to reduce trichotomies to dichotomies, as well as
(3) *Positive and neutral are combined* ('he who is not against me, is for me')

(4) *Positive and negative are combined* so that the choice is between an evaluation in either direction or evaluation as neutral. This is done, for instance, when human beings are evaluated as 'interesting' or 'uninteresting'.

Table 4.2.1. *Different structures of the set of values*

r=No. of symbols in R	Total set of things S to be evaluated by or for each single 0. Three possibilities:		
	Negative evaluation	Neutral	Positive evaluation
$r=2$	$\begin{matrix}-1\\0\end{matrix}$		$\begin{matrix}+1\\1\end{matrix}$
$r=2$	$\begin{matrix}-1\\ \quad 0\end{matrix}$ (spanning)		$\begin{matrix}+1\\1\end{matrix}$
$r=2$	$\begin{matrix}-1\\0\end{matrix}$	$\begin{matrix}+1\\0\end{matrix}$ (spanning)	
$r=2$	1	0	1
$r=3$	$\begin{matrix}-1\\0\end{matrix}$	$\begin{matrix}0\\1\end{matrix}$	$\begin{matrix}+1\\2\end{matrix}$
$r=4$	$\begin{matrix}-2 & -1\\0 & 1\end{matrix}$		$\begin{matrix}+1 & +2\\2 & 3\end{matrix}$
$r=5$	$\begin{matrix}-2 & -1\\0 & 1\end{matrix}$	$\begin{matrix}0\\2\end{matrix}$	$\begin{matrix}+1 & +2\\3 & 4\end{matrix}$
$r=6$	$\begin{matrix}-3 & -2 & -1\\0 & 1 & 2\end{matrix}$		$\begin{matrix}+1 & +2 & +3\\3 & 4 & 5\end{matrix}$
$r=7$	$\begin{matrix}-3 & -2 & -1\\0 & 1 & 2\end{matrix}$	$\begin{matrix}0\\3\end{matrix}$	$\begin{matrix}+1 & +2 & +3\\4 & 5 & 6\end{matrix}$
$r=11$	$\begin{matrix}-5 & -4 & -3 & -2 & -1\\0 & 1 & 2 & 3 & 4\\A & B & C & D & E\end{matrix}$	$\begin{matrix}0\\5\\F\end{matrix}$	$\begin{matrix}+1 & +2 & +3 & +4 & +5\\6 & 7 & 8 & 9 & 10\\G & H & I & J & K\end{matrix}$
$r=\infty$			

Three-point scales. These correspond exactly to the basic idea of an evaluation, and the verbal symbols corresponding to the symbols in our list can be 'disagree', 'uncertain', 'agree', etc. Evidently, there cannot be any measure of intensity.

Five-point scales. These are more refined versions of the above, and are made use of in *Likert scales*[2] to evaluate statements. The verbal symbols

96

may be the symbols above, modified by words as 'strongly', 'slightly', etc. Quite often, the symbol for the neutral category is dropped, and the scale is reduced to a four-point scale.

Seven-point scales. These may be more refined versions of five-point scales, e. g., with the verbal symbols:
When the number of points is as high as seven, ambiguities may easily arise because of the verbal symbols chosen for the points – and *graphical scales* may be preferable, as the typical *Osgood scale*[3]:

:___:___:___:___:___:___:___:

which is easily grasped with the eye. Again the neutral symbol may be dropped, and we have a six-point scale.

Eleven-point scales. For one reason or another, nine-point scales are rarely made use of, but eleven-point scales were used in the first phase of the original *Thurstone scale.*[4] The symbols chosen were the letters *A* to *K*, and judges were asked to evaluate statements by means of these symbols. To find good verbal symbols here corresponding to five degrees of agreement or disagreement seems almost impossible. But graphic scales can be used, for instance in the slightly disguised form of a thermometer or a ladder:[5]

where the respondent can read off (or better: read *in*) his feelings towards the object, whether 'it leaves him cold', 'lukewarm', or what not.

Continuous scales. All the scales above are discrete scales, in the sense that the respondent must choose from a given finite set of symbols. If he is permitted to choose symbols freely between the given ones, a continuous scale will result, with the symbol set being e. g. the continuum of real numbers, a straight or any other countinuous line. The straight line is the simplest possibility. Here the respondent can indicate his evaluation with a stroke, if he is only given the orientation and the zero point of the line. And here it is important to distinguish between the structure of the *latent scale*, where latent, inferred properties of the respondents are mapped; and the *manifest scale,* where the manifestations of the values, the evaluations, are mapped. The latent scale is a purely theoretical construct, and leaves us relatively free as to which structure we want to endow it with.

But the structure of the *manifest* scale, i.e., the scales we have discussed above, is determined by the set of possible values. When the symbols are *numbers* (integers), or *strokes* on a straight line, the manifest scale is automatically given an interval structure (even a ratio structure). If the symbols are *letters* (Thurstone) or *verbal symbols* (Likert), the structure given to the scale by the symbols is only that of an ordinal scale. The alphabet tells us nothing about equality of distance between *D* and *E*, and *J* and *K* – but the *order* of the letters is defined. To argue that *on the symbolic level* there is just as much difference between 'strongly agree' and 'agree' as between 'disagree' and 'uncertain' seems completely devoid of meaning – and to argue that 'the distances are equal because they reflect equal distances on the latent level' is at best sheer speculation. If we look at the 'thermometer' under the eleven-point scales, it is the integers and their equi-distant spacing that makes this scale an interval scale – not any alleged relation to the latent scale. We *know,* for instance, that the so-called 'end-effects' (the tendency of some respondents to be attracted to or to be repelled from the extreme symbols) make the assumption of a directly corresponding, equidistant, latent scale very dubious – not to mention what we could call the 'zero-effect' (the tendency to be attracted to or repelled from the neutral category).

Briefly, our point is that in determining the structure of the manifest scale, we refrain from all speculations about *equal distances between attitudes,* and *look at the symbols we have made use of alone.* In the case of dichotomous scales, this is particularly simple, as there is no question of interval scale at all (except in the trivial sense that a dichotomy is always interval because there is only one difference which obviously is equal to itself). For the other scales, when figures or strokes are employed, an interval scale is immediately induced. But what relation this interval scale has to the scale we postulate for the latent attitude, is another (and difficult) question which usually leads to the rejection of the idea of an interval scale at the latent level.

4.3. *The role of the neutral category*

This is a very difficult question, because of the frequent practice of using the neutral category as a kind of dust-bin for DK, NA, and all kinds of vagaries. There are clearly at least two important dimensions here:

the *cognition* of the psychological objects, the stimuli, to what extent they exist at all to the respondent, and

the *evaluation* of the object (or of the cognition of the object) – where the object is placed somewhere along the scale (or in one of the three sets positive, neutral, negative).

In addition to this, we have all kinds of interview or observation difficulties – the question was not asked, the respondent forgot to answer, the answer was overheard or not put down, the instructions were misunderstood, the respondent refused to answer, data were not found for one of the nations in the comparative study, etc. We suggest that the symbol for all these defects of the data-collection should be NA, and that the number-code should be a blank, not a zero; or a 9 if there must be a punch in the column.

When the object *is* fully cognized but is evaluated as neither negative nor positive (because the respondent sees nothing negative or positive in the object, or because negative and positive attributes counterbalance) the object clearly belongs to the neutral category, and the number-code might be 0.

But what if the object is *not* fully cognized? First of all, this has nothing to do with the *intensity* of the evaluation – that is already taken care of when we have n-point scales, $n > 3$. We have this case when the statement the respondent is asked to evaluate (to indicate whether he favors or opposes it) has no or little meaning for the respondent, e. g., *Do you think John Foster Dulles is doing a good job?* when JFD is very vaguely cognized by the respondent. Or – *Do you think the new Ford Edsel is a very beautiful car?* when the Edsel has so far only appeared in ads. However, faulty cognitions, lack of knowledge, etc. has never been sufficient to prevent people from passing judgments, even extreme ones. On the other hand, people with substantial knowledge or 'depth of intention' where the psychological objects are concerned may very well express their tacit evaluation of the object as 'really I do not know what to say' – and be recorded as DK. The ideal would be, of course, to have some idea about *both* to what extent the object is cognized, *and* how it is evaluated.

More should be known about how these two variables are related. We can argue that the *less* a respondent knows, the more will he hesitate to evaluate, and the more likely will it be that he categorizes the object as 'neutral' – this argument will lead to a hypothetical U-curve (see Figure 4.3.1). But we can also argue that the *more* a person knows, the more aspects will the object have to him, and the more difficult will any extreme evaluation of the object be – and this will lead us to a hypothetical A-curve. What can safely be said is that the shape of the curve depends on both the sets $\underline{O}$ and S, and that we can get DK because of *too little* and *too much* knowledge.

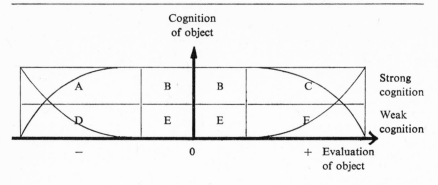

Figure 4.3.1. *The relations between strength of cognition and evaluation*

We have divided the plane in six fields to facilitate the discussion. There is no doubt about the coding of *A*, *B*, and *C* as negative, neutral, and positive evaluation respectively, even if a respondent with *strong* cognition verbalizes his evaluation of the object as neutral with a DK. But what about *D* and *F*? As mentioned above, the ideal is to be able to place the respondent some-where in the plane above by means of a double set of stimuli, testing both cognitions and evaluations, but where this is not done, small variations in the stimuli will probably make a DK out of an evaluation, and *vice versa*.

To summarize, a full discussion should include stimuli and analytic tools to make the following distinction:

(1) *The respondents for whom we lack information of one kind or another*: they should be classified as NA.
(2) *The respondents with weak cognitions*: they fall in three categories:
   (a) those who evaluate negatively,
   (b) those who evaluate positively, and
   (c) those who evaluate as neutral: they should be classified as DK.
(3) *The respondents with strong cognitions*: they fall in three categories:
   (a) those who evaluate negatively: they should be coded with negative or low numbers
   (b) those who evaluate positively: they should be coded with positive or high numbers
   (c) those who evaluate as neutral: they should be coded as 0, or as the middle number.

In practice, what we do with categories (1) and (2) above depends on our empirical or theoretical focus. From one point of view, the ideal would be to discard them; from another point of view (if we are interested in evaluations, however ill-founded) *D, E,* and *F* can be treated as *A, B,* and *C.* But to treat NA as neutral – because we know of no negative or positive evaluation – is very unsatisfactory. And it is almost equally unsatisfactory to collapse 'don't know' and neutral categories like 'indifferent', 'both-and', etc.

If these two points about the neutral category are satisfactorily clarified, the result will as mentioned be a set of evaluations forming an evaluation-pattern (more generally: a response-pattern) for each respondent and a set of such patterns for the entire set of respondents. The evaluations we elicit are *expressions* of values held by the respondent, they are not identical with the values. If we define a value as a trichotomy of a set of objects in three subsets: the 'good', the 'bad' and the 'neutral', it is immediately clear that a row in the matrix *M* for the individual respondent tells us exactly which objects he thinks belongs in which of the three categories of evaluation – and how much they belong there if $r > 3$. On the other hand, this gives us only how the values of the respondent *order* a set of stimuli, not what these values are in a deeper sense. We get at the extensions, but not the intensions of the respondent's values. The latter must be inferred, and here there will always be a variety of possibilities.

In conclusion, let us look at this important problem from a practical point of view. Imagine that a question is asked by means of a questionnaire or an interview, and that the respondent is supposed to emit some kind of response. Three conditions must be fulfilled before he can give a response that is either positive or negative:

(1) the respondent must understand the question, or internalize it, to use a better term;
(2) the respondent must understand the possible answers, and
(3) the respondent must feel attracted by a positive or negative answer.

If only the third condition is not fulfilled, it means that the respondent cannot give an answer in terms of good or bad, true or false, simply because he does not feel that way. If no other provision is made, the respondent may try to cope with the situation by saying or writing something like this: 'I do not know what to say –', which may be recorded as a 'don't know'. But this is what is called an 'evaluative don't know', where the true meaning is that the respondent understands questions and answers, but does not feel that he can make a choice. The way to distinguish this from 'cognitive don't knows' that will arise if conditions (2) or even (1) are not satisfied, is to provide a special answer category, such as 'depends', 'both-and', 'both true and false', 'neither true, nor false'. This category should catch the evaluative DK, and make the response 'don't know' more meaningful if it still appears. In addition to cognitive and evaluative 'don't know' comes evasive 'don't know' where the respondent escapes by saying 'don't know'. The remedy here lies in the interview technique.

The 'evaluative don't know' is more or less identical with what we have called the neutral category in evaluation. Hence, our conclusion is that ideally there should be at least four response categories to any question, as indicated in Table 4.3.2. But it may be wise to have more categories to lure the respondent away from neutral and DK answers.

Table 4.3.2. *The four response categories*

	negative category	neutral category	positive category	cognitive don't know
pure evaluation	bad	both good and bad	good	don't know
cognitive evaluation	false	both true and false	true	don't know

In addition to this comes the NA as an explicit, but hopefully very small category.

4.4. *Variety and constraint*

Having now presented all parts of the data matrix – the units, the variables, the values – we can look at the three as parts of a whole. For simplicity, let us reason with the *survey* as an illustration; where m respondents map n stimuli on r values, or on a different number of values for each stimulus, as the case may be. We shall now introduce a new perspective on this process.

When a respondent O_i evaluates S_j there are two possible cases:

(1) the evaluation may be *independent* of all other evaluations made in the data matrix,

(2) the evaluation may be *dependent* on one, some, or all other evaluation(s) made in the data matrix.

By dependence, here, we mean something different from the empirical correlations we find when the data-matrix is analyzed. We are here talking of a dependence *a priori*, given in the instructions or the way the data matrix is constructed or the data collected. Similarly, 'independence' does not necessarily mean absence of any correlation, only that there is no built-in constraint to make the choice of value for some respondent(s) evaluating some object(s) less than completely free.

Imagine one respondent has to evaluate three books, with a three-point scale at his disposal. In that case 'independence' would mean assigning any one of the three values to each book; possibly even the same value to all of them. Since the three books can all be given three values, there are 3^3 ways in which he may end up, which means 27 different response-patterns. This is often called *rating* of the objects.

One way of evaluating with 'dependence' would be to make use of *ranking*, as 'the best', 'no. 2' and 'no. 3'. Again, three symbols would be needed, but the choice of values for each object would no longer be free. For instance, he might start out deciding which book was best and which one poorest, but that would already determine completely the value for the last book as 'no. 2' – provided ranking with ties was ruled out in the instructions. In this case there would be 3! = 6 different response patterns, which is only $\frac{2}{9}$ of the number of possibilities given complete independence.

We shall refer to the number of possible response-patterns for each respondent as the *variety* of the response-pattern. In the case of independence, the variety is *complete*; this is usually referred to as the case of *rating*. In the case of dependence, there is less than complete variety, because there is some kind of function that relates the evaluations to each other (in the case of ranking without ties of n objects, the values are all different natural numbers, and their *sum* has to be $\frac{1}{2}n(n+1)$). In this case, we shall say that the evaluation takes place under *constraint*. Essentially, this means that the variety is less than it could have been with independent evaluation (rating) and the same number of value-symbols.

So far, what we have discussed can properly be called 'horizontal constraint', because the idea is some kind of functional dependence in the horizontal rows of the data matrix. In practice, this will be the most frequent case, but 'vertical constraint' is also conceivable. This means that one respondent's reaction to a stimulus is dependent on how others react to it. If this is built into the instructions it will certainly be unconventional in survey research, where it is always assumed that the respondents evaluate an object independently of each other. A more conventional kind of vertical constraint would obtain if the units were *nations* and the variable *size,* but the mapping had to be in terms of *ranks,* not in terms of absolute figures (of population, military or industrial manpower, GNP, industrial potential, total area, arable area, etc.). Combinations of horizontal and vertical constraint can also occur, and there may perhaps be cases where R_{ij} is dependent, not on the other $R_i.$'s or the other $R._j$'s – but on some R_{kl}. As horizontal constraint, however, is the rule, we return to that.

Both for rating and for ranking it is assumed that the symbols form an ordinal scale. But these two possibilities are by no means the only ones. If there are n objects and the number of symbols is r, there will be r possibilities for each object and *hence r^n possible response patterns for each respondent, provided there is no constraint in the mapping.* Thus, ten statements with the instruction to indicate 'agree' or 'disagree' would lead to 2^{10} response patterns. This would be rating of the simplest kind and a case of no constraint.

The maximum constraint (or minimum variety) is not ranking, but the situation where the respondent is instructed to map the objects on predetermined symbols. The typical case is the totalitarian state with an inclination towards at least a part of the democratic symbolism. Imagine an 'election' with n candidates from different parties, mapped (in principle) on the two symbols 'I vote for him' – 'I do not vote for him' – but with the instruction to vote for the candidates from Party X (and those only). The variety of 2^n (if the voter can vote for as many or as few candidates as he pleases) has thus shrunk to 1, only one response pattern or no variety at all.

The variety of response patterns with r values, as defined by the instructions, will lie between 1 and r^n. To give some more examples: If there are only two symbols (agree-disagree, vote-not vote, etc.) the instruction is very often to *pick one* object ('which of the statements below is closest to your own opinion', 'which of our n political parties is closest to your political conviction', etc.). The variety is of course n. If he can pick 2, the variety is $\binom{n}{2}$, etc., and if he can pick as many as he pleases, the variety is the sum of all the binomial coefficients, i.e., 2^n – as above.

And there are other possibilities.[6] He may be instructed to pick k objects and then order them $\left[\text{variety } k!\binom{n}{k}\right]$, which in the special case of ranking described above (with $k = n$) gives a variety of $n!$. By comparing the two functions r^n and $n!$ one can easily find out whether ranking or rating will give more variety, i.e. more 'information', if one assumes that the number of possible response patterns determines the amount of 'information'.

But there are still other possibilities of constraints. Thus, in a dichotomous choice situation the numerical symbols may be 0 and 1 (pick *one* statement, pick *one* party), and the constraint might be that the sum of the symbols given to the objects by each respondent had to be 1.

for O_i $\qquad\qquad R_{i1} + R_{i2} + \ldots + R_{ij} + \ldots + R_{in} = 1$

This can be generalized to the instruction

for O_i $\qquad\qquad R_{i1} + R_{i2} + \ldots + R_{ij} + \ldots + R_{in} = k$, or, more generally:
for O_i $\qquad\qquad f(R_{i1}, R_{i2}, \ldots R_{ij}, \ldots R_{in}) = 0.$

An example of the first is the American 'game' 'Distribute 10 points', where, for instance, 3 objects can be given symbols from 0 to 10, but so that the sum of the symbols given is always 10. The variety will shrink from 11^3 (the number of integer points in the cube inmost in the first octant in a three-dimensional cartesian system) to 66 (the number of integer points in the part of the plane $x+y+z = 10$ lying in the first octant). If ranking had been used instead, the variety would have been only $3! = 6$. But this is still far from the situation where there is no choice at all among response-patterns.

By a suitable variation of instructions and sets of objects, respondents and symbols, the desired variety can be obtained. This kind of reasoning is a highly important step in the whole research process, and should be analyzed more carefully than is usually the case.

We can for instance apply the most elementary concepts in information theory. The single respondent is the *sender* of information, and the investigator is the *receiver* of information. The *channel* may be a very complex one, such as: respondent-response-coding-punching-tabulation-investigator; or a shorter one, as when there is direct interviewing. In both cases, however, the concept of *noise* is highly applicable. If there is no constraint, the variety is r^n – and we assume that the channel can transmit this variety, if needed by transmitting one response at a time. Further, we assume that there is agreement between sender and receiver about the variety possible. If all the response patterns are equally probable, the amount of information contained in one pattern is simply:

(1) $$H_1 = \log (r^n) = n \cdot \log r$$

But if we have *a priori* reason to assume that each pattern has a probability of p_i, the information is by definition:

(2) $$H_2 = - \sum_{i=1}^{N} p_i \log p_i, \text{ where } N = r^n, \text{ and } \sum_{i=1}^{N} p_i = 1$$

which simplifies to (1) if all p_i are equal, i.e. $(\forall i): p_i = \dfrac{1}{N}$. If $(\exists i): p_i = 1$, that is, if one pattern is certain, H is of course 0, because there is no information given when there is no variety ($\lim p \log p = 0$, when p tends to 0). We receive maximum information in the equiprobable case, as is well known.

This was the case of *maximum* variety. Let us then introduce a constraint by going from rating to ranking. We assume that *n is equal to or less than r* so that we do not need new symbols to carry out the ranking, and get in the equiprobable case:

$$H_3 = \log n! = \sum_{i=1}^{n} \log i$$

Because of the assumption, $n! < r^n$ and we get $H_3 < H_1$. The information we lose is measured by $\triangle H = H_1 - H_3$, and as a suitable measure of the relative information we suggest a measure between 0 and 1:

$$I \text{ (relative information): } I = \frac{H_3}{H_1}$$

which can be easily calculated. The equiprobable case corresponds to the situation of being out on a 'fishing expedition'. That is, our lack of knowledge simply makes all response patterns equally probably *a priori*.

Let us now relax the condition on r and n and ask: when do rating and ranking yield the same amount of information? Clearly when

$$H_1 = H_3$$

$$n \cdot \log r = \sum_{i=1}^{n} \log i$$

$$r = 2^{1/n \sum_{i=1}^{n} \log i} = \left(2^{\sum_{i=1}^{n} \log i} \right)^{1/n} = \sqrt[n]{n!}$$

(which could be seen by comparing the two varieties in the equiprobable case). This number is, of course, less than n. The equation above is a diophantic equation, and we do not know whether it is solvable at all [i.e., whether integer solutions in r and n (apart from the trivial 1,1) exist]. The graph of the corresponding function in positive, real numbers $y = \sqrt[x]{x!}$ looks like:

Diagram 4.4.1. *Conditions for equi-variety between rating and ranking*

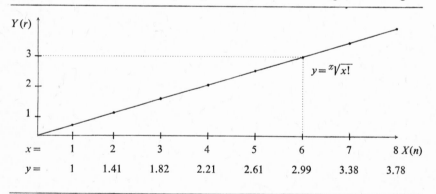

$x =$	1	2	3	4	5	6	7	8
$y =$	1	1.41	1.82	2.21	2.61	2.99	3.38	3.78

In this interval, the graph is for all practical purposes so close to the straight line $Y = \frac{2}{5}X + 0.6$ that we have used this line as an approximation. As we

106

see, ranking of six objects gives nearly the same information as rating the same objects on a three-point scale (in varieties: $729 \approx 720$).

It should be noticed that we have not found any exact equality by means of this method, except for the trivial case of zero information when we rank one object or rate it on a one-point scale. If we found a non-trivial, exact equality between two ways of eliciting responses from a respondent, *then these two forms should be translatable into one another by means of a suitable code* because they give the same amount of information. But their meaning (intension) may, of course, be different to us, even though their extensions are the same, *and the information measure in information theory is an extensional measure.*

The same method can in principle be applied to other ways of responding under constraint, and the measure of relative information is still applicable. If we have more information *a priori* about the probabilities of response patterns, the formulas will become more complicated, but the principles remain the same.

This kind of reasoning can be applied to *vertical* constraint as well. To take an example: imagine a kind of sociometric choice situation where all the pupils in a class are to select one other pupil, *but only one not yet selected.* If self-selection is possible, the first pupil has a choice of n, the second pupil of $n-1$, and so on down the list to the last one, who is left with no choice at all. The variety in the whole configuration is $n!$, because the problem is identical with the problem of ordering n pupils (the order being the order in which they are selected). The data matrix never has two 1's in the same horizontal or vertical row. If self-selection is impossible, the situation becomes more complicated. For $n = 3$, the variety shrinks from $3! = 6$ to 2, etc. But also here the problem may be raised: what kind of evaluation under constraint corresponds to ordinary, unconstrained rating? For instance, for which numbers r and n do we get the same or approximately the same amount of information by a rating using r values as by ranking the n objects? The answer is, of course, the same as the answer we have just discussed, since the two problems are formally identical.

Let us then look at all this from a more practical point of view. We have studied the relative merits of independent and dependent evaluation in terms of how much variety may be obtained, but there are clearly also some other arguments. A few of these will be discussed here.

In its simplest form, the problem presents itself as a choice the constructor of a questionnaire or interview-guide has to make quite often: given a set of items – objects, sentences, stimuli – that he wants the respondent to evalute, shall he ask the respondent to rate them, or to rank them? Table 4.4.2 presents a list of arguments:

Table 4.4.2. *Arguments for and against rating and ranking*

	Rating	Ranking
(1) The evaluation model:	corresponds exactly to evaluation, respondents can be asked to indicate for each object whether it is positive, neutral or negative	does not correspond to evaluation except in a relative sense: one object is said to rank higher than another, but one does not know for that reason whether it is positive, neutral or negative
(2) The problem of translation:	except for ties, a set of ratings can be translated into a set of rankings	can never be translated into ratings since the ranking gives no information about zero point or metric
(3) Presence of standard:	the standard is abstract, it refers to value standards in the mind of the respondent	the standard is concrete, for each element the other elements function as standards
(4) Resemblance to reality:	low, one is usually not asked to grade elements except in education and commerce, *absolute* utility is seldom important	high, one is constantly forced into choosing between objects, ranking them and picking in terms of *relative* utility

This is precisely the dilemma: rating is high on the first two, ranking on the last two; so one will have to decide on the basis of the nature of the problem what is most important. Does one want to map the respondent in an absolute sense or in a relative sense, and what are the real life implications of knowledge of one kind or the other?

Similar reasoning applies to special forms of ranking, such as paired comparison methods (where n elements are presented as $\binom{n}{2}$ pairs and the respondent is asked what he prefers for each pair), and to the 'pick k elements and order them' methods. Great caution should be exercised to ensure that the respondents are not asked to order too many elements at the same time. With rating they only have to 'order' one element, with ranking more elements have to be handled mentally simultaneously. According to some psychological research an upper limit is around 7 for most people, but in our experience it should be placed lower. One should not ask respondents to rank more than 5 elements at the time – otherwise intelligence becomes too important, and the respondents group the objects together, ranking the groups instead.[7]

5. Collection

5.1. *The main forms of data-collection*

We now turn to the main problem, how to obtain data. The scheme below does not apply to all kinds of units or elements of analysis, however. Instead, it is geared towards the needs of data-collection where the unit is a person who is exposed to *stimuli* and yields *responses,* these terms taken in the broader sense. But this covers a very broad class of cases of social science data collection.

By *systematic stimuli* we mean stimuli that are kept constant when the objects are changed, in the sense that *all* units are exposed to the same stimuli, systematically. If this is not the case, we shall say that the stimuli are *unsystematic,* as in more casual interviews where the interview-objects are asked the questions *they* are most likely to find meaningful. In this case, a data matrix cannot be constructed on the basis of the data.

By *systematic responses* we do not mean that the responses are kept constant; that would, of course, be meaningless, since it would yield no information. What is kept constant are the response *categories,* so that the responses of the objects to a stimulus S_j are recorded on a predetermined set of responses, R_j.

If this is not the case, we shall say that the responses are *unsystematic,* as in interviews where the answer is taken down, verbatim, with due regard to all possible individual variations.

These simple concepts yield a four-fold table:

Table 5.1.1. *The main settings for data-collection*

	unsystematic stimuli	systematic stimuli
unsystematic responses	informal	formal, unstructured
systematic responses	impossible	formal, structured

Clearly, if the stimuli are not kept constant, constancy in response categories would be rather meaningless, as the constancy would at most be extensional, never intensional. A 'strongly disagree' is not the same response if it is not a possible response to the same item. As to the other three cells, terms have been chosen that are widespread in the literature, and given a definition through their place in the Table.

Hence, three settings for the collection of data are defined: the informal, and the two forms of formal data-collection. We now turn to the aspects of the person-unit to which these settings can be applied.

By a response we mean, as mentioned, a state of the object. It should be emphasized that a state does not necessarily imply that any kind of *change* has taken place. Inaction or continued silence may be a very important response, more revealing than many responses involving change in the state of the object. Typically, however, we assume that all responses can be classified as *acts* (with inaction as a limiting case). For 'acts' we use the simple dichotomy into *non-verbal* and *verbal,* with the latter dichotomized into *oral* and *written.* By oral acts, then, we do not refer to all acts where the mouth is the executing organ – kissing and humming are excluded possibilities. The verbal acts are acts where verbal symbols are used to communicate, whereas nodding, shrugging of shoulders, etc. are regarded as non-verbal acts.

If we now combine the three settings for data-collection with the three kinds of manifest responses, we get a nine-fold table containing most known forms of data-collection in the social sciences. We could actually use the word 'all' instead of 'most', since we are dealing with two trichotomies. Another thing is that the categories certainly are not sufficiently refined to register the many variations known in the methodological literature.

Table 5.1.2. *The main forms of data-collection*
responses

		non-verbal acts	oral, verbal acts	written, verbal acts
s	*informal settings*	(participant) observation	conversations, use of informants	letters, articles biographies
t i m u	*formal, un- structured settings*	systematic observation	interviews, open-ended	questionnaire, open-ended
l i	*formal, structured settings*	experimental techniques	interviews, precoded	questionnaire, structured

In the cells, the most commonly used techniques corresponding to the headings are listed. However, the cells are thought of as expressing very general ideas that may also be used to generate other techniques. The advantage of the scheme lies in its generality. If we are able to present the pros and cons for the various headings, the arguments for the singular method follow, once we know in what cell it can be properly classified. Actually, the two trichotomies used as headings in the Table both stem from 2×2 tables (both with an empty cell), so that the arguments may be given relative to the four dichotomies nonverbal-verbal, oral-written, informal-formal, and unstructured-structured. The most important arguments will be given in the following sections.

5.2. *Non-verbal versus verbal responses*

Human beings are restricted to non-verbal acts for the first one or two years of their existence; then include oral, verbal acts if the external circumstances permit them to do so; and may later be able to include written, verbal acts in their repertoire if the social system in which they live permits this. This simple genetic sequence which it seems difficult to change may serve as a basis for explaining rankings of the three forms of acts.

From the point of view of cultural importance, the acts are probably ranked by most people in inverse order of their appearance in human life. As most social scientists should be regarded as cultured people, one should infer a certain preference for this ordering. They are mostly used to handling written, verbal acts, and this training may lead them to prefer data consisting of such acts. These acts have two very obvious advantages: they can yield an almost infinite variety of meaningful information, and they can easily be stored. In our culture, more differentiating capacity seem to be attribute to verbal than to non-verbal acts: we have no grammar or dictionary for the latter, even the rules of style are not many and not often codified – and do not even yield a good and fairly consensual typology for common use when data are collected.

There is an opposite ranking, however, of no less methodological importance: a ranking following the genetic order. Somehow, a tendency is often found in the literature to attribute more importance to the non-verbal than to the verbal. There is an asymmetry in the relationship: one thing is what a person *says* or *writes,* another thing is what he *does.* Probably linked to the genetic priority of the non-verbal act is the assumption that non-verbal acts in a sense are more *real,* more primordial, whereas the verbal acts are more to be regarded as epiphenomenal. If there is a discrepancy between what a person does and what he says he does, the interpretation is rather that the actor lies with his words than with his deeds.

In order to discuss this, let us first leave out the question of inference from past and present verbal acts to future non-verbal acts, as in the almost proverbial election prediction studies. That these inferences often are tenuous is true, but it is also true that we have little reason to believe in the complete impossibility of finding a set of verbal responses from which a satisfactory prediction of a future act can be made. This inference-problem, however, is not necessarily related to the problem of what kind of acts has the greatest share in 'reality'.

Let us further disregard a possible partial explanation of why social scientists may have come to regard verbal acts as somehow inferior: when sociologists, as the academic men and women they are, walk out of academic circles, perhaps they discover that non-verbal behavior plays a relatively much larger role – as anthropologists may do when working in the field. From this perception of differential relative presence may grow a feeling of differential importance, especially if illiterate peoples, and classes of non-professional people in literate societies are regarded consciously or unconsciously as incarnations of society in more 'pure' forms. We know of no empirical data to test this hypothesis, nor would it be of any relevance to the validity of the asymmetric argument.

What remains is first of all the undeniable statement that verbal reality and non-verbal reality are two different things, with no evaluation of relative importance. If a verbal stimulus elicits a certain verbal response, this is always of interest, as it may serve as a basis for the inference of, *at least, future verbal behavior*. If verbal behavior occupies a large proportion of total behavior, this is in itself no small gain. Without at all accepting that inference from verbal to non-verbal acts is not only difficult and tenuous but almost impossible, what we have so far said leaves us with the conclusion that verbal responses may be used and should be used for inferences about 'verbal reality', and non-verbal responses about 'non-verbal reality'.

Are non-verbal acts more consequential than verbal acts, and hence, do they constitute a more important part of the total social reality? It may be argued that since only non-verbal acts directly have physical consequences, they are more consequential. One can kill with a non-verbal act, but hardly with a verbal one. However, it may also be argued that verbal acts often precede or accompany dramatic non-verbal acts, so that a correspondence may be established between the two kinds of realities.

It may also be argued that verbal methods may be used to get at what people think, or at least what they think they think, but not at what they actually express in social situations. This is a methodological problem of constructing the data-collection situation so that valid information may be obtained. This methodological difficulty is not inescapable, at least not on technical grounds, but the researcher may certainly stumble on ethical problems if he tries to construct real-life situations.

Another problem lies in what one considers the subject matter of, for instance, sociology. It may be said that verbal responses are excellent if one is interested in ideology studies, as one may say that respondents can express their professed convictions better through verbal acts than through non-verbal acts. But the method may also be said to break down if one is interested in, for instance, communicative acts that are verbal acts but at the same time only parts of an interaction process. If sociology is considered as the science of inter*action*, this argument should be taken very seriously. However true a picture one may get of the ideology, the perceptions, cognitions and evaluations of the respondent, this may simply be said to be irrelevant to the field of sociology proper – and hence of value only if some solution is found to the inference problem.

Can a person lie with acts? It all depends on the definition of a lie. If we mean that there is an inconsistency between what the person knows and inferences people may legitimately draw from his overt behavior, then 'lie' applies equally well to the non-verbal sphere of human life. A may hate B, he may hypocritically affirm that he is fond of B (which probably is a lie), but he may also hypocritically act in what the culture defines as a way inconsistent with hatred. So what is the ultimate criterion?

We feel prone to say that the asymmetric conception of non-verbal as prior to verbal should yield to a symmetric conception of the two as manifest data in social research – to be used relatively safely for inferences within their own sphere, and with care for cross-sphere inferences.

Let us now approach this theme in more concrete terms, as a list of arguments for or against the two approaches.

(1) *Universality*. By and large, observation is more applicable: observing somebody presupposes less in terms of interaction than interviewing him, not to mention asking him to fill in a questionnaire. But precisely this argument may also be turned against observation, not for methodological but for ethical reasons. One may observe a person without his knowing it; it is more difficult to approach him verbally without his consent. Particularly important here have been the techniques of participant observation where insights have been bought at the expense of morality. If techniques of observation that do not presuppose the open or tacit consent of the observed are excluded, then observation becomes less universal and more similar to the other techniques.

(2) *Specificity*. One advantage of the verbal approach lies in the specificity of the verbal expressions mentioned above.[1] The number of words, ways of

combining them into sentences, and ways of combining these into human discourse is tremendous, especially in comparison with the crude distinctions we make for non-verbal behavior. Even if human non-verbal behavior has an infinite variety, in principle, our poor level of theoretization so far commands us to express this variety in words; and since we use only a small part of our vocabulary for this purpose, the variety will have to be smaller. If behavioral science were like physical science we would measure non-verbal behavior, smiles would be expressed in curvature of the lips and gesture in kinematical terms – and we would restore the variety. But so far no meaningful system of this kind has been developed.

(3) *Naturalness vs. artificiality.* As we have discussed this at some length above, there is no need to repeat the argument here. We shall only stress the importance of a symmetric point of view. However, there is little doubt that observation would be most 'natural' in many situations. One such class of situations can be characterized as follows: Many, perhaps most, actions human beings carry out are not easily verbalized, but easily observed. Hence, one can get meaningful data through observation only, when to press for verbalization would be painful and artificial. Thus, through observation a social process may be followed as it develops. Verbal techniques may give valuable reports, but *post hoc*, unless one is dealing with rather unusual respondents capable of acting and being interviewed at the same time. One can get at processes through observation, not only at the invariant structures that the individual can report on verbally because they have crystallized in his mind and are easily translated into linguistic structures.

(4) *Expense.* Which approach is more expensive, in terms of money, manpower, administration, etc.? It is difficult to tell, but verbal interaction seems to produce a large quantity of data elements per unit cost, so the discussion would have to introduce the problem of quality if one should decide in favor of observation. In general, however, verbal data will probably be cheaper, especially if the relative ease with which they can be processed and analyzed is considered.

(5) *Reliability.* It is customary to use this argument in favor of verbal techniques, and in general with good reason. The specificity of verbal categories, and particularly the possibility of varying the degree of specificity up and down as one wants, contribute to reliability. But this can also be obtained for non-verbal techniques, provided the setting for the data-collection is sufficiently formal and structured.[2] So far, however, there are few examples where this has been done successfully.

(6) *Validity.* This problem will be treated in a more general way in I, 5.6. In general, no answer can be given to the problem of which approach is more valid. It depends on the possibility of verbalization the respondents have. We have mentioned social processes, especially ongoing processes as more amenable to observation. Much emphasis should be put on the simple social fact that ability to verbalize varies strongly with social position; observation may be better at the social periphery, verbal approaches in the social center (that would also protest violently at the idea of being 'observed'). Also, in most cultures it is probably easier 'to lie with words' than 'to lie with acts', and this would turn the argument in favor of observation.[3]

114

In general, this leaves us with the conclusion 'it depends'. But the analysis also opens up the perspective of combining the two, to pool the strengths and avoid the weaknesses of either. Since these refer to different spheres of human activity we cannot solve the dilemma by a formula used later in this chapter: 'one of them for insight and interpretation, the other one for verification'. Rather, the two approaches should be seen as collateral and should be used for replication purposes, as we shall develop further in II, 5.4.

5.3. *Verbal responses: oral vs. written*

Much is known in pedagogical theory about types of perception, visual vs. auditive for instance, but little seems to be known about types of expression in the terms above: oral vs. written. However, much can be said in a list of arguments for or against the two forms of responses, since both of them imply certain social settings that a social scientist should be able to say something sensible about.

A word of caution should be inserted here. 'Oral vs. written responses' is not exactly the same as 'interview vs. questionnaire'. For instance, one could well imagine oral responses to written stimuli, where the responses are recorded on tape so that there is no interviewer-effect. Or, one could arrange interviews in much the way as in linguaphone records or language laboratories: the interviewer says something, and ample time is permitted for an answer to be recorded. Correspondingly, one might have written responses to oral stimuli, although it is hardly practical except in studies of people who are dumb but not deaf. These examples serve to emphasize the dilemma in a pure form; for all practical purposes, the two forms of data-collection to be compared are 'oral stimuli – oral responses' on the one hand, and 'written stimuli – written responses' on the other. We shall present some of the main problems.

(1) *Universality*. Basically, questionnaires presuppose a kind of training – literacy – that is not universally found and precludes the use of questionnaires in many countries and many social strata.[4] However, this is also a question of general acquaintance with forms, questionnaires, etc. in other contexts. Anybody who has had the opportunity, frustrating at times, to ask people from many nations to give information on a questionnaire will be acquainted with some of the national differences. As there are trigger-happy persons there are questionnaire-happy people. Probably, there is a component of training here, but there is also a strong component of orderliness. A questionnaire asks for information about facts and attitudes that

people with an efficient system of personal book-keeping will have no difficulties in giving, whereas others will perceive a questionnaire much as the librarian who gets a request for a book the day after an earthquake. Regardless of literacy, this personal trait is highly correlated with social position, thus making questionnaire methods less applicable in more peripheral strata. This will also apply to interviewing, but less so, for in the interaction process of the interview there are chances of modifying the question, of bargaining with the interviewer – whereas the written question permits no such bargain.

(2) *Standardization vs. flexibility.* This argument cuts both ways. First of all, there is the old problem of what is a 'constant stimulus'. If it is a stimulus that is kept constant, then the questionnaire method is an example; a printed or mimeographed questionnaire is as constant as anything can be. But if it is a stimulus that has a comparable effect, there are more possibilities with interviews. The questions can be adjusted to changing social position, levels of knowledge, frames of reference, etc. The dangers of too much flexibility are just as obvious as the truth in the argument that to give to everybody shoes of size 8 is to give the same thing to everybody, yet with different effect. However, with relatively homogenous samples, arguments in favor of the standardization offered by questionnaires are strong.

(3) *Follow-up.* This is a very strong argument in favor of interviewing. The questionnaire can contain all kinds of follow-ups too, there may be filter-questions, one after the other (if your answer was 'yes' above, proceed to Question 25: if it was 'no', to Question 26, etc.) – but with two shortcomings: (1) all these follow-ups have to be made *a priori*, and (2) they are the same for all respondents, or for all in a certain class. In the interviewing process, follow-ups can be improvised and adjusted to each individual respondent so as to get out of him all that is relevant. The questionnaire may be made quite sensitive, but never so sensitive as the human instruments of empathy and projection used in a good interview. Thus, the interviewer has a unique chance of correcting misunderstandings. And he can get much more out of the interview by recording the whole setting, including subtleties, non-verbal acts, etc.

(4) *Control of the setting.* The interviewer can control that nobody else is present to influence the respondent and that the work is done seriously. The respondent who receives his questionnaire through the mail or otherwise can fill it in by himself, but he can also make a good joke out of it in a circle of friends. This kind of excessive abuse is avoided with an interviewer present; it is also avoided if the questionnaire is filled in class or in the club or some other place where moderate supervision can be imposed.

But however well the interviewer is trained, there is one person's influence he cannot do much about: his own. There is an overwhelming literature on interviewer effect[5] that can only be controlled by the three classical methods of (1) keeping him *constant* (same interviewer, which is impossible even for what would today be moderate samples), (2) making him *irrelevant* (i.e. substituting for him a questionnaire), and (3) *randomization* (random matching of interviewers with respondents). This last method is satisfactory from the point of view of control, but not from other points of view, as will be developed in I, 6.3.

(5) *Temporal sequence.* In an interview the stimuli are presented in time, one after another like music; in a questionnaire the stimuli appear as in a painting, in space. Of course, the respondent may only read one question at the time but when he has done so, the stimuli exist simultaneously for him, he can choose where to start and where to be impressed by the stimuli.

This may be advantageous in some situations, disadvantageous in others. Thus, one may want the respondent to react to all stimuli in their context, so as to avoid what often happens in interviews: the frame of reference is changed by a question that comes later on and the respondent may want to change his response. Thus, the questionnaire permits simultaneous evaluation of the stimuli, and without any hurry since there is nobody present to ask for speedy reactions. But there are also situations where one may want an answer before the next stimulus is presented – in that case the interview is preferable, or questionnaires with as little as one stimulus on each page and instructions not to turn the page before it is completed (this presupposes some kind of supervision).

(6) *Naturalness vs. artificiality.* Neither method is natural, since most stimuli ask the respondent to telescope his existence, to issue general statements about actions and attitudes. Thus, in real life he may be exposed at a certain point in space and time to the choice between the completion of some work and arriving in time for a party – but stimuli are more general: 'what do you think you would do' – and then follows a general description of the dilemma. The respondent is supposed to look at some role-behavior he has, with all its irregularities, and communicate some general policy statement. The problem is which is more natural, oral or written communication.

Obviously, this depends, but in general a strong argument in favor of interviewing is that it is reminiscent of something in social life, i.e. conversations. Thus, to the extent that one records verbal behavior in order to predict verbal behavior, interviews seem to be better, unless one is doing research on people particularly devoted to written expression.

(7) *Expense.* There is little doubt that questionnaires are rather inexpensive and for that reason quite attractive. This is not merely a question of saving money, but also of saving administrative time and talent, e.g. by using the mail system instead of a costly *ad hoc* staff of interviewers. The condition is that such a mail system exists, as it does almost everywhere where such research methods would be considered at all. One special advantage lies in the simultaneity: if it is important to reach all respondents at the same time this is probably easier by means of questionnaires than interviews unless the ratio of interviewers to interviewees is close to 1. On the other hand, a skilled interviewer can always get the refusal rate down; in general he will have more persuasive power than the letter accompanying questionnaires, even including the follow-up letters.

(8) *Reliability.* In general, it is difficult to say. The interviewer is better trained to record than the respondent, but the respondent knows himself what he wants to answer and will get an immediate reinforcement and check when he circles or underlines an alternative. Thus, one extra human and fallible link is cut out, but even more important, we think, is the visual

check provided by the manual operation with the questionnnaire. There is nothing quite corresponding to this in interviewing. The interviewer may read aloud what he has written; but that will probably only lead to a lengthy argument, since the respondent did not possess the answer alternatives in advance, as he does for the questionnaire.[6]

(9) *Validity*. Again, it is difficult to say because of the problems mentioned under (2) above. The literature seems to favor questionnaires for many reasons, but the authors do not agree between themselves. Thus, there is argument to the effect that the flexibility provided by the interviewing permits more refinement, more nuances and thus more validity, and there is the argument that the skilled interviewer will have a number of soothing techniques for 'the embarrassing question' than can never quite be imitated in the questionnaire. We are inclined to say that 'it depends' but that in general questionnaires seem to be more valid.[7]

But this vague answer does not imply that the researcher is completely without a guide in the choice between the two methods, for it is rather obvious that the one does not exclude the other. Glancing through this list, we can easily muster arguments for a division in time, using the flexibility of the interview method in the beginning of a project and at the end, to get insight both for hypotheses and for interpretation; and using the standardization of the questionnaire technique in the middle phase for confirmation purposes. This is yet an example of the importance in social research of not being invidious, but rather finding the adequate method for the problem at hand or restructuring the problem so that methods can be fully exploited for their strong aspects.

5.4. *Informal vs. formal settings*

The two main dimensions of argumentation here are rather well-known:

(1) *Naturalness vs. artificiality*. The formal setting involves systematic stimuli, i.e. many units are exposed to the same stimulus. There is no reason why this should imply artificiality. Both nature and society very often expose individuals (or higher level units) to the same stimulus, such as earthquakes, wars, social policies, elections, etc. These natural experiments can be exploited, as they have been. Bur their occurrence does not necessarily coincide with research projects; sociologists often let obvious chances pass by because the structure of academic life and research grants, and a certain mental inertia, force them out of habits of improvisation. Besides, 'natural' experiments may provide for a common stimulus but not for control of relevant factors. Thus, a certain amount of artificiality is called for, and one can imagine a continuum where more and more of the setting is provided for by the social scientist and less and less by other parts of the environment of the respondent.[8]

118

There have been many misunderstandings in this debate because of a confusion between the two goals of *prediction* and *explanation* in social science. It may well be that the 'natural', unmanipulated, setting is better for prediction studies and the manipulated, formal setting better for explanatory studies. A partial reason for this is that systematic variation of stimuli may permit the researcher to see his unit from many angles and not only under the limited range of variation provided by the natural setting. The physicist does this, but also one thing more to learn more about his material: *expose it to the extremes of the range of variation*. The structure of a compound is revealed by such methods as extreme pressure, temperature, bombardment by various particles, etc. A car is tested not under natural conditions but under extreme and artificial conditions. Correspondingly, the social scientist can learn more about the structure of a society, its strong and weak points, by observing it under crisis. And here the systematic stimuli of the formal setting enter: they can be regarded as some kind of bombardment to make the individuals reveal what is ordinarily not revealed.

(2) *Comparability*. With more than one unit one can compare the units and use dispersion and covariation measures as analytical tools. There is little more to be said about that; the advantage of the formal setting is here rather undisputable, by definition. Actually, both the historian and the anthropologist, however anti-nomothetic and ideographic their ideology, use contrasts as their analytical tool, only that the contrasting cases are more likely to be mental constructs, and less likely to be systematic.

Again, the conclusion should never exclude one in favor of the other. Rather, the two combine dynamically into a combination that has proved to be very powerful in the research process. Most research will start at the informal end of the spectrum, during hypothesis-formation, then move towards the formal end in the phase of verification, and then again take excursions into the informal region during interpretation.

5.5. *Formal settings: unstructured vs. structured*

In this section, systematic stimuli are assumed. In practical terms we are either dealing with systematic observations or questionnaires/schedules where the responses are extracted orally or in writing. The problem is whether we should operate with pre-fixed categories of response or not. For the observations this would mean that a set of categories for recording behavior is made up prior to the observation, and that the observations are squeezed into these categories – the most famous example being the Bales system of observation. For written questionnaires it means that the response variable is spelt out for the respondent, so that all he has to do is to choose the value that comes closest to his response. This is the 'closed question', a misnomer since it is really a 'closed answer'.

For interviews, a distinction can be made between closed questions and closed answers. In the former, the respondent is given, orally, the answer alternatives: 'Which candidate do you favor, Allende, Frei or Durán?', which means that the response variable is spelt out for him as in the questionnaire. In the latter he is asked 'Which candidate do you favor?' The question is open, but the interviewer may have closed the answers by a precoding in his schedule. This, however, is only known to him and not to the respondent, and hence serves only administrative purposes like facilitation of coding. It does not structure the mind of the respondent. We can have closed answers without closing the question, but the closed question implies closed answers. This is the case we are most interested in. The problem is what we obtain and what we lose by structuring the mind of the respondent, but we shall also mention what we obtain and what we lose by structuring the mind of the social scientist. Some of the main dimensions of discussion are as follows; they are similar to the dimensions in I, 5.3.

(1) *Comparability*. The main advantage of the structured response is to facilitate comparability. The structured response, one hopes, will create a common frame of reference and by definition a common response variable, and hence complete comparability. Even if it is only structured for the social scientist as in the 'open question, closed answer' or systematic observation cases, the result will be at least formal comparability. Only in this case will the model of the data matrix which we have used extensively apply. 'Which car do you prefer' may elicit two answers, one in terms of craftsmanship – but the question 'Which car do you prefer, speedy but not so solid, or solid but not so speedy' makes for a more precise, and *known*, frame of reference. Thus, we get standardization, but possibly at the expense of

(2) *Flexibility*. One major advantage of the unstructured response is the freedom it permits. The respondent may choose his frame of reference himself and one may get at the context of the answers, extra perceptions or motivations, etc. On the other hand, comparability can be obtained to a certain extent by means of content analyses of the open answers, coding and checks for reliability of the coding. The advantage of structured responses is that they yield precise versions of the question; the advantage of the unstructured response is to be unprecise, that they permit the unexpected response.

(3) *Naturalness vs. artificiality*. Again, the argument seems to favor the unstructured technique, for the same reason as it favors the informal setting. But this presupposes that one is interested in prediction rather than explanation, and wants to infer from one 'natural setting' to another one. Explanatory studies can probably benefit by using techniques that permit more refined kinds of analyses.

(4) *Expense*. Anyone who has carried out research of both kinds will know how much this argument favors the structured technique. The amount

of work put into structuring the answers for the respondent and pre-coding them for the analyst is little compared with the job of doing all of it *a posteriori*. This applies to all phases of the project: structuring facilitates the data-collection enormously for both parties involved, it facilitates the data-processing and the analysis because of the comparability involved. In terms of money, administration time, and manpower, this may mean considerable savings particularly appreciable in low-budget centers of research.

(5) *Reliability*. The technique of structured responses permits a very high degree of reliability, whereas the differences in frames of reference and linguistic habits, etc., will make for lower reliability when the responses are unstructured. By this we do not mean 'constancy', i.e. the property of the *respondent* to give the same response when exposed to the same stimulus (very often confused with reliability in the literature); but *intra-subjectivity* (i.e. that the same social scientist codes the same response the same way) and *inter-subjectivity* (that various social scientists code the same response the same way). As to constancy, it is well known that a respondent can vary his response to the same stimulus even over rather short time intervals, for which reason it is so important to present him with a set of stimuli (see I, 1.2) and combine the responses into indices in such a way that the index value is not sensitive to unsystematic variations in the responses to the individual stimuli (see II, 3.2).[9]

(6) *Validity*. As usual, the requirement of reliability may conflict with the requirement of validity. The major accusation against the technique of structured responses would be that it makes for a certain quasi-validity: it looks as if the respondents are answering the same question because of the precise formulations provided by the structuring of the response, but there is always a good possibility of misinterpretation, misunderstanding, response-set, etc. The theory is often that less structuring will bring this out; but that is, of course, wrong, unless a considerable amount of probing is done that will almost by definition exclude the questionnnaire as an instrument. Moreover, empirical research seems to favor structuring.[10]

Again, the arguments make for no clear picture, and for the trivial conclusion of using both. But in which order? It is rather obvious, since the structuring of responses will have to come from somewhere, and if it shall not simply be decided upon by the researcher it will have to come from using unstructured techniques first. Hence: unstructured techniques for development of hypotheses and possibly for interpretation; structured techniques for verification.

5.6. *The problem of validity*

This is to a considerable extent an epistemological and philosophical problem, not simply a question of measurement. It has to do with the general problem discussed in this chapter: whether some forms of data-collection (referring to Table 5.1.2) give more valid information than others. The focus on validity presupposes an asymmetric perception of the forms of data-collection – if not, validity is reduced to a question of correlation (for instance, between verbal and non-verbal behavior).

But validity is more than a question of comparing cells in the table, using one cell as a criterion for the other. With regard to verbal data (oral or written), there is a particular skepticism which seems to have three dimensions:

(1) *Latent vs. manifest*: to what extent can we infer from the verbal expressions to a person's 'true' position on a dimension that gives his attitude?
(2) *Expressions vs. thoughts*: to what extent can we infer from what a person says to what he thinks?
(3) *Expressions vs. behavior*: to what extent can we infer from verbal expressions to a person's behavior?

As it is formulated here it appears as if we accept these requirements, i.e. that there should be an unambiguous relation connecting thoughts, expressions, and behavior, so that each such chain can be mapped on a latent dimension. However, we do not necessarily accept such a view.

Let us start with the problem of the latent vs. the manifest. This was briefly mentioned in I, 1.3 and will be taken up in some detail in II, 3.4-5. Broadly speaking, we feel the problem cannot be attacked in terms of *one* observation variable – as we shall develop at length in II, 3.8. In line with our reasoning in I, 3, the problem is solved by (1) *n* manifest indicators rather than one, (2) seeing to it that these *n* indicators are somehow sampled from a reasonably well defined set of possible indicators, and (3) combining these indicators into a summary measure by some kind of index formation, *or* using all of them separately (but never relying on only one, except when there is long experience supporting the belief in exactly that indicator). Following this procedure, the 'manifest vs. latent' is not a problem of validity, for the latent dimension is a construct that is given content by the manifest indicators. It is in no sense an independently existing dimension that can be used as a control of the manifest indicators. The 'validity' of the manifest indicators depends on how they correlate with other variables – as will be developed later.

The problem of expressions vs. thoughts is more interesting. Do people speak (or write) the truth when they are approached by interviewing or questionnaire procedures? If the 'truth' is defined as what they have in mind, obviously no absolute answer can be given. The degree of correspondence between a person's private thoughts and what he chooses to express depends on a cultural component and an individual component. We

122

have not seen good data on this, but all experience seems to indicate that 'veracity' in the sense of thought-speech correspondence is to a considerable extent a product of culture and *socialization*. No social scientist working in former colonial nations (whether they were or are political, economic, or cultural colonies) will have failed to get this 'advice' from residing *colons:* 'Do not trust what people say in interviews. They only say what they think you want to hear, not what they think themselves'. It is difficult to evaluate the degree of truth in a statement of this kind. It probably describes relatively well the kind of relationship that prevailed and prevails between the upper class (foreign or indigenous) in these parts of the world and their servants (whether working in their masters' houses or in restaurants, bars, as shoe-shiners, taxi-drivers, or in other service-positions). In a culture of servility and strong competition, there is a clear incentive for very scarce positions with access to the ruling class to please the master. One way of so advancing is obviously to have a rather pragmatic view on truth.

This does not mean that the same phenomenon automatically obtains in interviews – although it is likely to be true, the more similar the interview situation is to the master-servant situation. Thus, interviewing should probably be done by natives, not by the foreign social scientist (who should, however, carry out some interviews to get first-hand insight in how the process functions). Nevertheless, the problem will remain. The researcher may reduce it by maximizing trust in the interview situation; by asking so many questions so quickly that it becomes too complicated for the interviewee to work out a system of systematic distortion; by having a number of questions that refer to facts, to past and present actions, or pure knowledge, so as to induce in the interviewee a pattern of speaking the truth (especially if some of the facts are very easily verifiable), in the hope that there may be a carry-over effect from the factual part of the questionnaire to the value part. By such techniques the discrepancy can no doubt be reduced, if not cut down to zero.

However, it will always be difficult to confirm this: confirmation would lead to the famous problem of distortion hierarchies. To measure discrepancy between expressions and thoughts, we have to use other indicators of thoughts – since our ability to read thoughts directly is at best somewhat underdeveloped. Other indicators could be obtained by a new interview – and there is again the same problem. Or, they could be obtained by observing behavior or reading letters or diaries – and there is the problem, important for historical research, of whether there is any reason at all to believe more in behavior or written documents than spoken words as expression of thoughts. We have seen no theory or evidence to support this hypothesis, and would even be inclined to believe just as much the opposite.

But we can also approach this problem from a quite different angle, asking: is the correspondence between thoughts and words really important? Or is this just a transfer of a moral problem ('Thou shalt speak the truth and nothing but the truth') to the realm of methodology without a real analysis of the implications? For we may also reason as follows: in surveys, e. g. of how people react to certain policy measures, it may be socially much more important how people say they would react than how they 'really' (meaning when they are alone with themselves) do react. If the ordinary Frenchman polled says he is in favor of the *force de frappe,* then this is more important than his inner reservations. They may be important for a personal analysis, not for an analysis of attitudes here and now. The spoken word is a social act, the inner thought is not, and the sociologist has good reasons to be most interested and concerned with the former, the psychologist perhaps with the latter. But this only transforms the problem from the problem of correspondence between words and thoughts to the problem of how representative the interview situation is as social intercourse. Thus, the idea would be that the sociologist wants to know what kind of verbal expression the respondent, given certain stimuli, would present to others – and the interview should then be a copy of such situations rather than deep, fast and probing. For this purpose, interviewing in groups may quite possibly be better, since it may give a social setting more true to life. On the other hand, it also seems obvious that interviewing that aims more at inner psychological dynamics should give data closer to the mental pre-image of the person and be less concerned with what he chooses to present to others. In short: the problem of expressions vs. thoughts depends very much on the analytical purpose of the interviewing.

Then there is a third way of looking at the problem, which we shall just barely touch on: why presuppose a mental pre-image at all? Many questions fall on virgin soil, but that does not mean that they fall on barren soil. They are stimuli that create mental images and start mental processes, they do not tap pre-existing ideas. Hence, the idea of correspondence would be meaningless – unless we interpreted it as correspondence between words and mental *post*-images.

We turn to the basic problem of correspondence between words and deeds, between expressions and behavior. In I, 5.2 we have done some reasoning in favor of a symmetric point of view: that verbal and non-verbal data represent different spheres of behavior, and that data may be valid in their own right. Here we shall make some reflections on the relation between them.

First of all: there is also here the danger of a moralistic argument, that there shall be consistency between words and deeds. The degree of consistency will depend on a general cultural and a more specific individual component; there will be cultures inculcating norms about consistency and there are probably cultures that are more lenient in this respect, just as individuals differ. This is not simply a question of speaking the truth or not, but of conceiving of the two spheres as tighly coupled or not. Whereas to some people it seems obvious that if one expresses democratic values then one should also behave democratically in some specified way, to others this is less obvious. Words may be defined as being epiphenomenal, as belonging to a sphere of the ideal, whereas deeds are reality; and the two may belong to different regimes, so to speak ('Regimenten' in Luther's sense).

Secondly: we do not accept the idea that actions should always serve as a basis for validating words, we prefer a symmetric perspective. One may use words to validate actions as one does very often, for instance when one contrasts a person's happy-go-lucky face with his sad verbal reports about the poor health of some of his close relatives. In some cases we would say that he is lying with words ('he is not really concerned, as evidenced by the way he looks'), in other cases that he is lying with his non-verbal behavior ('he pretends he does not care', or 'he is taking it extremely well'). Which interpretation to choose depends on what other information we have; this should also be the case in social analysis, with no sweeping assumption as to what can be used as a criterion and what should be validated against that criterion.

Thirdly: whether we should require consistency or not depends, of course, on what expressions and what actions we have. Three important dimensions here are:

(1) *Descriptive vs. normative*, i.e. what did the person do, what is he doing, what is he going to do – as against what does he think he should do.
(2) *Specific vs. general*, i.e. what did you do yesterday at noon, as against what do you generally do in the middle of the day; what should one do when one's best friend spreads gossip behind one's back as against 'what do you think of gossip'.
(3) *The temporally close vs. the temporally distant*, i.e. 'what are you doing now' as against 'what did you do ten years ago' or 'what will you do in ten years'.

If a person describes his own behavior in specific terms, and the reference is to the present, or very recent past or close future, we should have good reasons to expect consistency. But if he expresses values in general terms, applying to the distant past or remote future, there are so many very acceptable reasons for inconsistency that a process of validation on that basis would be out of place. Surveys may be criticized if they do not predict correctly elections one week or one month prior to the event (provided, of course, that the sampling is adequate, that the results are not published so as to interfere with the events, and that no important external event appears on the scene in the meantime). But they should not be criticized if they refer to general values applying to choices that will be made some time in the future, and the 'predictions' do not come true. There simply is no reason to suppose consistency in this case, except as a moral dogma or an unwarranted methodological postulate.

Then, of course, it may be objected: what is the value of analyzing complex value-patterns if they do not serve as predictors of overt behavior? We have three answers to this important question. (1) They may predict *verbal* behavior, i.e. future value-assertions quite well, as shown by the relatively high degree of consistency over time in panel analyses (except when external events have changed the perceptual field of the respondent drastically). (2) They serve as signals from the depths of the person, giving us a synchronic cut in time both in the life of the person and the life of the system, valuable for the analysis of both (if not for the prediction) up till the date of the data-collection. And (3), even if the value-patterns do not predict behavior or outcomes in a general sense, this only serves to indicate that a simplified model of consistency fails, and should lead to an analysis of *why*, not to mention to the collection of behavioral data.

Thus, imagine two different villages are presented with the same stimulus to social change, e.g. in the form of a technical assistance project. Generally, economic development may be said to depend on three kinds of factors: material and capital resources (the approach often favored by economists), social structure (the approach often favored by anthropologists), and value patterns (the approach often favored by sociologists and psychologists). Let us assume the villages are equivalent on the first dimension, and get the same input from the technical assistance project; further, that village A has values that should favor utilization of the new resources more than village B, and that village B has an organizational structure that should favor acceptance more than village A. Which factor will dominate may be very difficult to predict, but let us imagine that the structural factor dominates. This does not mean that the value factor is not consistent with behavior, only that it has been overridden by another factor that works in the opposite direction. Nor does it mean in general that social structure is a better predictor than value patterns, for this is a question of degrees. Only one thing is obvious: if village A is favored both by value patterns and by social structure, then we would be rather surprised if our prediction did not come true.[11]

In short: the question of validity is complicated, and we prefer to treat it in the second part of the book. There are clear norms of how data-collection should be carried out, so as not do distort what is already there. But: (1) the social scientist should rather be pleased by the variety of techniques at his disposal and try to enlarge the number than try to reduce some of them to others that are seen as 'more basic', (2) he should use a variety of techniques to get data of different kinds rather than rely on one of them alone (this will be elaborated in II, 5.4), and (3) 'the proof of the pudding is in the eating', i.e. what can be explained and predicted from the data collected is the important thing, not how much 'consistency' there is between forms of data-collection with perhaps no theoretical reason for consistency at all between them.

Finally, let us make some comments on the literature in this field. While there is a vast general literature on the problems of reliability and validity,[12] we are concerned with more specific findings. Most of this literature goes to show that what people say is not what people do, and it is rather important for the social scientist to be well informed about this. We shall give some examples:

(1) Mosteller, Hyman, McCarthy, Marks and Truman[13] discuss the polls prior to the election of 1948 in the United States with a total sample of 14,696 persons. 65% said they would vote, but the participation in the election was actually only 52%. However, many discrepancies between forecasts and voting are explained by (1) use of quota-samples, (2) error in estimating who is really going to vote, (3) erroneous treatment of people who had not yet made up their minds, and (4) last-minute change of mind. Besides, there is the famous factor of self-denying prophecy, of people who stay at home because they feel confident after hearing the forecasts (in the famous words attributed to Elmor Roper: 'It was not the polls that went to the dogs, but the dogs that did not go to the polls').

(2) Parry and Crossly[14] discuss an experiment carried out in Denver by the Opinion Research Center. Data about how people said they had voted in 1944 were compared with election data. It appeared that 23% of the respondents said they had voted, but had not voted at all. Answers about 'Community Chest contributions' were also very inaccurate, but data about whether one had a valid library card, a driver's license, telephone, car, etc. were more accurate, but still with 5%–15% of invalid answers (some of it due to the interviewers).

(3) Katona in his celebrated *Psychological Analysis of Economic Behavior*[15] compares income distributions obtained from surveys and from the income tax authorities, and finds considerable discrepancies – but here the truth is likely to be located in-between.

(4) Middle[16] reports a study of readership. People known to read a certain magazine were asked which magazines they read, only 47.3% mentioned spontaneously the magazine. However, when the remaining 52.7% were asked directly whether they read the magazine, 91% said that they did so. This is indicative of the importance of structured answers for increased validity, but also that 'readership studies are largely measurements of mental images and impressions'.

(5) Cohen and Lipstein[17] in a study conclude differently; they find it quite possible to collect wage statistics validly and reliably by mail questionnaire. Again, this may be an argument for questionnaires as opposed to interviews.[18]

(6) Larsen and DeFleur[19] report from one of their leaflet studies where people were asked to mail a postage-paid reply card in response to a leaflet drop. 98% of those who said they had not mailed any card in fact had not done so, but only 53% of those who said they had done so were verified. People with valid verbal behavior differed from the others on age.

Many more examples could be given but we do not need more to make the basic point already made above: validity varies with the technique chosen, and by and large seems to increase when we move from the upper left corner in Table 5.1.2 to the lower right corner. At the same time, this transition is the transition from exploratory to confirmatory phases of a research project, which is fortunate.[20]

6. Surveys

6.1. *The first steps*

The survey method, if conceived of in very general terms, is nothing but the general method of filling data matrices. More narrowly, it is conceived of, vaguely, as another term for public opinion studies. The two definitions can be contrasted:

Table 6.1.1. *Definitions of survey methods*

	General definition	Special definition
Units	Any social or cultural unit	Individuals
Variables	Any variable that can be used to characterize the units	Attitudes and some background variables
Method of data-collection	Any method by which the matrix can be filled	Oral: the interview Written: the questionnaire

Even if the special definition is too narrow, as evidenced by such expressions as 'the UN survey of economic growth in developing countries' it may be objected that the first definition is too wide. It makes the survey coextensional with social research. However, it may still be distinguished from the experiment with controlled conditions, where, typically, the data would be presented as a set of data matrices – for instance, one for 'before' and one for 'after', or one for the experiment group and one for the control group. Such distinctions, however, are nothing more than just one more independent variable – there is nothing special about the before-after distinction relative to other variables.

However, there is no need for a precise delimitation. In the following, we shall mainly have the narrow definition in mind, but make some comments on the possible extensions of the principles. Strictly speaking, we should talk about survey methods rather than *the* survey method, and keep in mind how close these methods are to general methodology in social science when conceived of in the broader sense.

The beginning of any survey is a Problem. There is something the researcher wants to know about the world. He has certain preconceptions, however vague, which he wants to compare with the world. These preconceptions are his hypotheses, a concept which will be clarified in II, 4 when the necessary statistical apparatus has been developed. At this point we need only these two ideas: the problem or the hypotheses as a source generating ideas about units, variables, and methods of data-collection; and the idea that precision as to problem is no precondition for doing a survey. In II, 4.2 a number of dimensions of hypotheses will be developed, but they do not enter in the definition of a survey (although they may certainly enter among the conditions of a *good* survey). A researcher may decide by fiat that 'here are my units, my variables, and my methods' – provided they correspond to each other – 'fill the matrix for me!' To do this, we do not have to know where the set of units (in surveys called the *sample*), or the variables and data-collection (in surveys called the *instrument*), come from, as long as they are well defined.

To get information (i.e. values) about the units, variables are needed. But units and variables are not enough: also needed is an 'instrument' to reveal the value of the unit. The unit has a property, but something must be done with the unit to make it display the property so that it can be assigned to one of the values in the variable. An analogy that suggests itself is the measurement of temperature. A body has a property, 'hotness', but we cannot map the body directly on a temperature scale. A thermometer has to be applied to make the body manifest its hotness; a magnet has to be applied to make it manifest its magnetism, etc. And a set of questions or verbal stimuli or even non-verbal stimuli have to be applied to make an individual manifest its attitude so that it can be mapped on a set of values (i.e. a set of responses). We imagine the unit as having a certain disposition which is revealed fully or partially under the conditions provided by the instrument.[1]

Just as it is customary in physics to use the term 'instrument' for stimulus + variable (the thermometer includes the set of temperatures), it is customary in social science to use the term 'instrument' not only for the questions, but also for the set of possible responses. The variable is a set of exhaustive and mutually exclusive responses and should not be confused with the question, the card-presentation, or whatever technique is used to elicit this response. Thus, the instrument contains the variables, but is also part of

130

the method of data-collection. It may, for instance, be fruitful to consider the interviewer as part of the instrument.

As the literature on the development of instruments is considerable, there is no sense in trying to summarize all the advice given. Most of it is relatively obvious with a certain quality of the trivial when presented in standard recipe form. Besides, few investigators seem ever to have used such standard lists. For one reason or another, most social scientists develop their own style, possibly because this is the kind of technical know-how that has to be assimilated by experience more than by rote learning. We shall merely point out some stages in this process.

The construction of the instrument obviously derives from a Problem, however vague, which has normally been further developed by some kind of *pilot project*. Only the unexperienced or very experienced social scientist will sit down and devote much work to an instrument before he has acquainted himself with the units, the individuals, by means of field work. He must know at least something about how the Problem (or the common sense counterpart of the research problem) appears to the individuals he will be sampling. Unnecessary to say, in this phase the literature too enters. Any attempt to codify and establish rules for this phase seems to be doomed to failure both as descriptive and normative methodology: as normative methodology it may kill initiative, as descriptive methodology it must at least be made rather complex.

The selection of sample and instrument must be done with two questions constantly in mind: *is it relevant?* and *is it feasible?* and every single step should be defensible in these two terms. The relevance question is especially important in connection with the selection, and the feasibility question in connection with the data-collection, where sample and instrument shall be put together. Obviously, the sample and the instrument may be excellent *per se,* but not together; considerations of this type will lead to a constant adjustment of either – or of only one of them, if the researcher is set on keeping the other as it is. Usually the units are given and the instrument adapted to them; but there are many types of research where the problem dictates the variables, and the units are selected so as to obtain feasibility (this is how classes of psychology students often enter as subjects in social research). In general, feasibility includes considerations of *costs,* in terms of money, time, human resources, etc. to be invested in the research.

The selection of sample and the selection of variables have already been discussed in I, 2.3 and I, 3.3. Usually one starts with relatively amorphous ideas, which crystallize as ideas about subsamples of units and subuniverses or dimensions of variables. We shall not repeat the advantages and disadvantages of different kinds of sampling, or the importance of being able to generalize both on the unit and on the variable side. What is important is that the problem is translated into more or less specified sets of relations between dimensions, and that indicators/items are developed for each dimension. There is no sacred rule about the number of variables needed for each dimension. If the dimension is 'age', one variable is enough; if the dimension is 'authoritarianism', more variables are obviously needed. In our experience, most attitudinal variables are quite well covered by means of 5 to 10 variables. If one thinks of index formation (II, 3) it is very important that the variables possess a certain degree of symmetry:

(1) within the variables: that the values are equidistant
(2) between the variables: that the values correspond to each other, and
(3) between the variables: that they are roughly of the same kind so that they can be given about the same weight.

If these conditions are fulfilled, the simple and very powerful technique of additive index formation can be used.

However, the basic question in this phase of research is how to put the variables together to form a practicable instrument. Here, there are some very precise norms that can help the process of data collection, and save the investigator considerable amounts of time in the phases of processing and analysis. There is nothing sacred about the details of these rules either, but the general line of thinking should be taken into account.

(a) *To facilitate data collection.* We assume that the instrument is systematic and has the standard form of questions with answer categories provided. Whether it is to be used as an interview or as a questionnaire, there are two problems of major importance:
(1) to distinguish between the three types of text in the instrument: questions, answers and instructions, and
(2) the order of the variables.
The important thing is not exactly how the distinction between *stimuli* (questions), *responses* (answers), and *instructions* is made, but that some kind of distinction is made in a clear way. In practice, this is a question of typography, which can be solved by using different types or by spatial arrangement. In general we think one should rely on the former and, for instance, not use two columns in the questionnaire, since that can be a source of error. It is important that there is much open space for comments and to avoid confusion, but it is also important that the instrument does not become unnecessarily bulky. For one set of suggestions see Table 6.1.2. With these simple techniques it is immediately seen where the new question starts – this should also be emphasized with spacing between questions – and where the answer categories are. In general, the number of instructions should be kept as low as possible. The rule is that the instrument shall be

Table 6.1.2. *Typographical suggestions for instruments*

	Type-written/mimeographed instrument	Printed instrument
Stimulus (question)	CAPITAL LETTERS	**bold face type**
Response (answers)	small letters	ordinary type
Instructions	(in parentheses):	*italics*

easy to administer, so that the interviewer can make the interview more of a conversation, or the person who has to fill it in not be tired. It should be clear, evident, and self-administered.

The second problem, the problem of the order, is the problem of the dynamics of the data collection. Whether by the oral or the written method the data collection is an interaction process, even in the case of the questionnaire; for the imaginary role partner, the social scientist, will always be present in the mind of the subject. Without trying to be too sophisticated it is quite useful to assume the validity of the Parsons scheme of phases in a normal interaction process, i.e. the sequence adaptation, goal-achievement, integration and latency.[2] Let us interpret them in terms of survey research:

Table 6.1.3. *The Parsonian phase-system applied to questionnaires*

Phase no.	Term	General definition	In instrument terms
(1)	Adaptation	Exploring, searching, 'warming up'	Easy introductory questions
(2)	Goal-achievement	Doing the task itself, the main phase	The main, complicated, emotional questions
(3)	Integration	Tension release, 'cooling off'	Easy questions, opportunity to express sentiment
(4)	Latency	Interaction suspended	'Waiting for the next questionnaire'

If there is any validity to the Parsonian scheme for social relations in task-solution, and if the survey data collection can be considered a problem-solving kind of social interaction, then the conclusions that follow are of the type indicated in the last column. The instrument is introduced with some unproblematic questions, e.g. of the background type, and a gradual approach is made to the central problem area. By this method the subject is introduced not only to the problem, but also to the role as a subject exposed to an instrument. Then comes the bulk of the instrument with the more complex and/or more emotional questions (of which there will always be some, otherwise the instrument is almost certainly trivial) when the respondent is in a mood that corresponds to the nature of the stimuli. And then, at last, comes a third part of stimuli of an easier kind that can give both interviewer and interviewee a feeling of ease and easiness. For expression of sentiment it may be a good idea to include at the end questions about how the subject reacted to the process of data collection, since this is also of high importance methodologically as one among many indicators of how good the process was.

It may also be a good idea to set aside some general background questions for this part of the instrument, since thay are so easily answered, and use background questions with special reference to the subject matter of the investigation in the first phase. Thus, 'how long have you worked in this factory' would belong to the first phase, 'have you ever informed on any of your colleagues to the foreman?' to the second phase, and 'where was your father born' to the last phase. In a sense this is trivial, because it corresponds exactly to the implicit rules for daily conversation: first, approach the subject gradually, then launch the main topic, and when that has been exposed sufficiently, relax in more general talk for a short period before terminating the conversation. This is also the formula for the good party: the host warms up his guests gradually so that they do not exhaust themselves immediately, then there enters a phase of high pitch, and when the pitch of the party starts decreasing he brings it to a natural end. The good party should be suspended not too long after the maximum of involvement – few things are as boring as the party that drags on and on because nobody has the courage to kill it – and the interview/questionnaire should reach its end shortly after the most critical section has passed. However, it is equally wrong to suspend the activities at the maximum point of the curve. Even if one may have collected the information necessary or had a good time, it leaves interviewees (and guests) with no tension release, no natural termination of the process. Here the social scientist has a responsibility to his subjects, as well as to future social scientists who may want to use the same subjects. But there may be considerable cultural variations.

(b) *To facilitate data processing and analysis.* We assume that data processing is essentially a question of making the schedules so that they are easily transferred to punch cards. Here two considerations must be weighed against each other. On the one hand, the transfer should be as easy and as direct as possible. On the other hand, the schedule should not be overloaded with figures and symbols, partly because it makes the schedule more complicated and less surveyable, and partly because it may irritate the respondents, giving them a (correct) feeling that they are 'going to be treated like numbers'. Obviously, the latter consideration is of no importance when the instrument is used as an interview-guide which the interviewee is not supposed to see. Hence, the problem should be approached under these two headings:

Table 6.1.4. *Systems for precoding of instruments*

	Interview guide	Questionnaire
Column number	In the margin to the right of the question	Identical with question number
Punch number	Below or to the left of the answer category	Given by the position of the answer category by counting from the left and from above

In either case it is recommendable to let question numbers and column numbers coincide; two series of numbers is one source of error more. To accomplish this one may start with question/column no. 1 and have the ID (identification) at the end of the card, or start, for instance, with question/column no. 5, leaving four columns for the ID. The latter solution may look odd to the respondents if the instrument is used as a questionnaire, however. Further, if one should leave at least the last twenty columns of an IBM card blank (for transfers, recoding, index-construction, calculations etc.) one will have to restart the numbering after question/column 60. To avoid confusion roman numerals should be used for the different cards, so that one question may have number I/60 and the following question no. II/1. Evidently, II/1 should be at the top of a new page, and great care should be exercised not to divide between different cards a set of variables that belong together.

Thus, in the case of the interview guide, all that is necessary is to provide a margin to the right on every page, separated by a vertical line and repeat the question number with a dash after. For the punch number any system can be used, as long as it is clear. Thus, one question might look like this:

46. (if no): **On what occasion were you here earlier?**   46–

on another UN mission	on vacation, as a tourist	to visit relatives	I was working	I grew up here
(x)	(1)	(2)	(3)	(4)

To avoid doublepunching one may have the convention that the answer to the right is accepted (because it implies more involvement), except for the UN answer. Of course, much more simple is the following question:

59. **In general how satisfied are you with your own performance as an expert during this mission?**   59–

satisfied	fairly satisfied	both/and	fairly dissatisfied	dissatisfied
(1)	(2)	(3)	(4)	(5)

135

because the answer categories form a variable. All the interviewer has to do is to underline or circle the answer category chosen. In general we feel that this method is better than the use of small square boxes where interviewer or respondent is supposed to check the response, for underlining or circling gives a more direct contact with the answer, a more immediate reinforcement that may serve as an efficient control.

The point of departure for the coding of the questionnaire is the simple observation that both column number and punch number are actually redundant in the system above. If the column number is always the same as the question number, all one has to do is to look at the left hand side of the page; if the answer categories are always ordered so that the punch corresponds to the position of the answer, all one has to do is to count. In addition to that, one would need such simple rules as standard punches for DK, NA and DNA (does not apply) (e.g.: DK:0, NA:– and DNA:9, or, to avoid blanks, DK:0, NA8:, DNA:9). Thus, if the question is as follows:

28. And how were you recruited to *this* mission for the UN?

applied on a circular which described the mission and got it	applied on a circular describing another mission and got this one	forwarded a general application and was asked to take this job
UN or agency knew me and asked me directly to take this job	UN or agency asked me because I had been recommended by someone outside the UN	UN or agency asked me because I had been recommended by a present or former expert
I was asked by an organization in my own country to apply	I was asked by an organization in this country to apply	*other* (specify):

all one has to do is to count from the left to the right, and then from above. Thus, the answer 'I was asked by an organization in this country to apply' receives the punch 8 (not 6, as it would have been if the rule was to count from above and then from the left). In this case one would also have a margin, where column number (i.e. question number) and punch could be written: 28-8. Thus, the net result is the same with the two methods.

The question is now what to do with the margins. Three methods are immediately available:

(1) *To transfer from the margin to code-sheets, and punch from them.* By this method one also has a chance of checking the coding (especially if it is done by two persons, one who checks and dictates and a second person who writes on the code-sheets and repeats). Unfortunately, this is also an occasion for introducing new errors.

(2) *To detach the margins, collate and staple them together, and punch from them.* This is facilitated by perforating the dividing line beforehand so that all one has to do is to detach and staple. The method is recommend-

136

able when no check seems necessary and the person who punches is agreeable to the idea.

(3) *To punch directly from the instrument.* This means that the person who punches will have to turn the pages with one hand and punch with the other, which again means that a relatively skilled operator is needed. Also, the written text may be a source of distraction. An even more radical version of this is to punch straight from the page with no coding, so as to combine the operations of coding and punching. This probably introduces so many errors that it will have to be done twice – but since any punching operation will have to be verified, one will get a verification of the whole operation (see II, 1.2).

Which system to use depends so much on the capacity of the different persons working in the research team that no general rule can be given. What matters is only to know that there is a variety of possible techniques so that one may always choose the most suitable one.

All these details are technicalities, but there is one question involved that is of more than purely technical interest. We have presented a range of possibilities where precoding is concerned, from the 'tough' system recommended for interview-guides only to the 'soft' system recommended for sensitive respondents. But does this really matter? Unfortunately, we can only give impressions, not data; but they all go in the direction that it does matter. In some cultures, e.g. middle-class Mid-West USA, the population is so trained for social research, so well socialized as respondents, that it seems of no concern. But in other cultures, e.g. in the elite in developing countries, the difficulties in entering with social research are already considerable, and to add to them with excessive, and really unnecessary, precoding would be anti-methodological. There is also an ethical problem involved. Although the respondents are going 'to be treated like cards, like numbers' in the processing and in the analysis, they are not going to be treated as such in the (good) interpretation. To make visible the numbers involved in any data processing system is to make visible what to many appears as a kind of lack of respect for human dignity and integrity. One may laugh or sneer at this attitude, but that does not change it: besides, there is something highly laudable about it. Again, what is important is to know a range of possibilities that can be adapted to the occasion at hand, and we have presented some of them.

6.2. *The pretest*

Since there are few discussions in the literature of the general problem of what to do with a pretest, we shall try to develop some lines of analysis within the present framework of data collection.

First of all, it should be noticed that the pretest is never in any abstract sense only a test of the instrument, but a test of the entire process of data collection and even of the first steps of analysis. It is a test both of feasibility and of relevance, and should be designed so as to be an efficient test of all aspects of the process. For this purpose it is obviously unnecessary to have a statistically sophisticated probability sample, or a purposive quota sample – but what we have called a heterogeneous sample with extreme cases is indispensable. The instruments have to be tried on the whole range of possible subjects; the extremes, socially, attitudinally, or both, are most likely to lead to difficulties. The function of the pretest is to discover these difficulties and try to remedy them, not to avoid them.

Secondly, a test of the data collection is not only a test of the subjects, but also of the interviewers, or observers, or experimenters. Hence, these should also be chosen in a way that corresponds to the way the real data collection will be run. In practice, this means avoiding 'pretests' that consist in having the project director, who is probably more experienced than the others, try the instrument on some selected subjects. Preferable is a combination of all degrees of interviewer experience and interviewee difficulties likely to be met with in practice. At the same time this will prepare the interviewers for difficulties to come and may also serve as a training and screening process.

In general, what we do in a pretest analysis is to check whether the bridge between the Problem and Reality has been constructed. Concretely, the function of the pretest is to find out whether the variables developed theoretically, during the construction of the questionnaire, really correspond to something in the minds of the respondents. It may be useful to think in terms of 'richness': questions and answers may be too simple, too straightforward to tap the variety and richness existing; or they may be too complex, much more involved than the feelings the respondents can offer. Both are bad.

In the first case, we will never discover what there is to discover; in the second case, we will impose upon the respondents a complexity they do not have, a depth of intention which is not theirs – thus creating a false reality. Often the band we have to compromise on is quite narrow, and much skill and experience is needed. The variable has to be 'relevant': it must be an indicator of the dimension we are interested in. And the variable has to be 'feasible': it has to correspond to the reality of the respondent – not necessarily at a conscious, manifest level, but at some level. At exactly this point, open-ended questions are indispensable to permit Reality to impose itself on the Problem, not only vice versa. But most of this process cannot be codified, we feel.

There are, however, some simple codifiable techniques that can almost always be used with advantage.

We imagine that the data have been collected so that the data matrix is filled as well as possible, and proceed to some ideas for 'analysis'. Obviously, this will never be analysis in the sense of testing substantive hypotheses, but analysis in the sense of testing hypotheses about the data collection process. We suggest the following general scheme, consisting of three steps (the logic will be elaborated in II, 1.3).

(1) *DK, NA analysis*. The data matrix should be inspected for the distributions of DK and NA, and the number of DK's and NA's should be found for each unit and each variable simply by adding across the rows and down the columns. There are two dimensions of control here: *frequency* and *distribution*. A *random* pattern of DK or NA may be tolerated provided the total percentage does not exceed, for instance, 5%. Thus, in a matrix with 50 individuals and 60 questions one should not tolerate more than 150 DK–NA. The difficulty comes when the pattern is non-random, but tends to cluster (as it almost always does) in certain columns and certain rows. Thus, we get two sub-cases:

(a) *Concentration in certain columns*. If there is sufficient variation in interviewees and interviewers, this indicates a difficulty with the item, and may serve as an indication that it should be discarded from the instrument, or be reworded. Usually, a comparison of *variables* according to frequency of DK or NA gives important information as to what is wrong.

(b) *Concentration in certain rows*. If there is sufficient variation in the variables, this indicates difficulty in the data collection, which again may be rooted in the interviewee, in the interviewer, or both. There are a number of conclusions that can be drawn, depending on the merits of the case: retraining of the particular interviewer(s), exclusion of certain groups from the sample, or special instruments for those groups, etc. Usually, a comparison of *units* according to frequency of DK or NA gives important information as to what is wrong.

Analyses of the kinds indicated here can be facilitated if the frequency of DK or NA is computed for each column and for each row. This gives an immediate quantitative idea of where the difficulties are located in the process, and also an idea of how much can be gained if certain variables and certain units – those having the highest frequencies – are excluded from the analysis. This is also recommended for the analysis of the real data: an index of no. of DK–NA responses is made by counting for each individual, and the distribution is inspected. Often one can get rid of 50% of the total DK–NA by dropping relatively few individuals.

(2) *Response analysis*. The data matrix is now inspected for the real responses, let us for simplicity call them 'yes' and 'no'. Again, there are two kinds of analysis that should be done: vertical and horizontal.

(a) *Vertical response analysis*. This amounts to ordinary distribution analysis, where a question is analyzed in terms of the relative frequencies of the answers. The distinction is now made between *consensual* items where more than 85%–90% fall in one response category, and *dissensual* items where this is not the case (to indicate a limit). Again, it is useful to order all variables according to the frequency of the modal response. Very consensual items are usually discarded on the ground that they will have no function in the analysis, since analysis is based on *co*variation, and co-variation presupposes variation in both variables. Generally this is sound, provided one does not forget about the consensus, which may be a finding of high substantive importance. For that reason, important consensual variables should be retained to find out whether the finding holds up in the real sample. The variables that *discriminate* best are retained as potentially most useful for analysis, at the cost of a false impression of dissensus.

(b) *Horizontal response analysis.* This amounts to ordinary pattern analysis where a unit, an individual, is analyzed in terms of the relative frequency of certain response categories. This has nothing to do with index formation (II, 3), where one might, e.g., count the number of answers indicative of a certain attitude. Here, responses are considered at their face value, not for what they mean in terms of latent attitudes. Thus, a good procedure would be for each individual to count the number of times he has answered 'yes' or answered 'no', and to order the individuals according to this variable. For those who score very high there may be *response-set* present, i.e. the tendency to give a certain response regardless of stimulus. The condition for drawing this conclusion is that the questions have been worded so that one can distinguish between response-set and an attitudinal variable, e.g. by alternating between negative and positive wording.

The conclusions to be drawn from high response-set may be retraining of interviewers, reformulation of question – or exclusion of certain categories of respondents if response-set is systematically related to background variables (as it almost always is; more response-set with lower social position). This also depends on the response-set present. Some people are yes-sayers, others no-sayers, still others 'middle-men' – always choosing the category in the middle; and then there are the 'extremists' who prefer 'disagree very strongly' or 'agree very strongly' – regardless of the item. We cannot go into the intricate details of the response-set literature here,[3] but the following questions should be asked before one tries to remedy the difficulty:

(1) *What kind of response-set,* i.e. what kind of response is preferred regardless of item content?

(2) *How does it depend on the item,* e.g. is there a tendency for response-set in connection with certain formulations or words (does 'God' always elicit 'yes'), with authoritarian, political, religious, Biblical, especially learned slogans, etc.?

(3) *How does it depend on the interview situation,* e.g. is the response-set particularly pronounced when the rank-distance interviewer-interviewee is especially high (in terms of age, education, social position in general, race); does response-set disappear completely with rank-equivalence or even rank-inferiority of the interviewer; how does it depend on how directive the interviewing is, etc.?

(4) *How does it depend on the interviewee, which splits into two questions*:
(a) How is it related to his personality?
(b) How is it related to his social position?
The literature has many findings about either question, and the general tendency is an unflattering psychological and sociological characteriza-

tion of the people with response-set: they have weak ego-controls or reject external stimuli; and they are located in the periphery of society, etc.

(5) *Is the response-set an interview effect or could it happen in real-life situations as well?* If it is a finding restricted to the interview situation one would have to discard it as something artificial. But since most interview-situations are not too different from important situations in real life (e.g., conversations) the response-set may be an expression of a stable tendency and, as such, a finding in its own right.

Some of the more recent research in this field (see, for example, footnote 3) tends to see response-set less as a disturbing side-effect and more as an interesting personality variable, for instance called 'degree of acquiescence'. Clearly, what the researcher can do about it is not to refuse people their right to say 'yes' to every question they get, but (1) to arrange the interview so that this occurs less frequently, and (2) to introduce changes in the wording of the items so that a person who is high on some kind of response-set will not also be extreme on the dimension one wants to measure. The classical method is to formulate half of the indicators positively and the other half negatively. This way the yes-sayer and the no-sayer will both end up in the middle category if we use an additive index, and (3) to disperse the questions that are too similar so that they will not appear together.

(3) *Correlation analysis.* At this point the social researcher enters a very difficult field. He can, of course, legitimately do correlation analysis on the pretest data, provided he does not draw unwarranted conclusions. Usually, this is done to see 'whether the instrument works'. The question is what this 'works' means. If it means 'works as predicted' one is definitely very close to committing a serious error in scientific methodology. If a predicted correlation does not show up, the temptation may be to look for other indicators of the same variables and then to continue the search until a combination of indicators is found that yields correlations. By doing this, confirmation of hypotheses is not far from guaranteed. We have mentioned some of the principles for sampling variables from universes and sub-universes of variables earlier (I, 3.3) and the necessity of being on guard against too purposive sampling. Under the pretext of pretest analysis, the researcher would here be led into not only purposive sampling of indicators, but even guarantee that he has sampled the indicators he needs for confirmation, not only testing. In principle there is no difference between excluding *variables* that fail to give the wanted correlation and excluding *units* that fall in cells not predicted by the hypothesis.

For instance, imagine the hypothesis that there is some kind of difference between workers with a farm background and workers with a city background with regard to a dimension D, and that the researcher has developed a set of items, $X_1, X_2, \ldots X_n$, on that dimension. The pretest shows that some of them correlate (or 'discriminate' as it is often called in an effort to present this as pretest work, and not as substantive analysis), and some of them do not. He proceeds with the items that correlate, and later on the correlation is suddenly announced as a finding. If, however, he is reasonably certain as to the tenability of the hypothesis from other empirical work (not only theoretical!) the procedure is legitimate and may be used to pick the items that best represent what one is after. In that case, the correlation is used for a kind of validation, not for analysis.

In general, correlation analysis may be used to validate the whole data collection process by examining whether one can rediscover findings that already are well substantiated. Thus, imagine the hypothesis is that X and Y are correlated. We have suggested that if X and Y are not correlated in the pretest, this is no reason for discarding the method. But if X beforehand is *known* to be related to Z, and Y to W, and this does not show up in the pretest, we have legitimate reasons to doubt the validity of X and Y. But exactly where to draw the line between the permissible and the unpermissible in this delicate situation is a difficult question, and it may also be advantageous not to ask for too much precision as long as there is awareness of the problem as a problem. One so often hears about work that has been stopped because 'the instrument did not work', meaning it did not show what the researcher on a more or less firm basis wanted. Cutting the research process at this point is in reality obstructing scientific progress, by limiting it to small steps forward into the realm of the expected and predicted, instead of opening up for research into the unexpected, into the truly new combinations.

We have mentioned the two problems of relevance and feasibility. The function of the pretest is to check whether these problems have been so well solved that the investigation can proceed. Of the three techniques mentioned in this section for analysis of the pretest data matrix, the first one is a check on feasibility. A too high number of DK-NA responses or a non-random concentration of them are clear indications that the process does not work. In the second technique, both feasibility and relevance are checked. If items do not discriminate or there is response-set, this may be interpreted both as lack of relevance for the problem to be elucidated and as lack of feasibility. Finally, with the third method of correlation analysis, efforts are made to explore the relevance, or 'validity', of the variables.

6.3. *The data collection*

We assume that the sample has been drawn, the instrument prepared, and that the pretest has assured us of relevance as well as feasibility of the sample/instrument combination we are going to use. Data collection is then the task of filling the data matrix by confronting each unit with the instrument, and recording the values. Since this will have to be done with the conscious knowledge of the respondent (to do it without seems either technically or ethically impossible), this is only partly a technical question. Above all, it is a question of human interaction. Again, we shall not try to repeat or supplement the many manuals on this topic, but merely indicate some points that, in our experience, have been important. Below, then, is a list ranging from petty, clerical details to more grandiose principles.

(a) *How to approach the respondents*

Should the respondents be notified beforehand? We feel definitely yes. It is more difficult for a respondent to withdraw when the interviewer is already at the door, but it seems improper not to provide the respondent with a warning so that he may defend himself and withdraw from any contact if he so wants. The level of manipulation in the world is already so high the sociologist should not increase it even more. He has no self-evident right to take other people's time and make them expose themselves: rather, he should be grateful for each respondent he gets. This does not mean that he should not in his approach try to make the project as attractive as possible, as long as he does not exceed the limits of veracity. But he shall not impose himself.

(b) *Some technical details*

Whether by interview or questionnaire, the investigator will need the names of the respondents a number of times. More concretely, for a typical interview project he would need the following:

(1) Name and address on envelope with letter informing about interview, or with questionnaire to fill in,

(2) Name and address on extra envelope for second letter (asking again in case there is no response, reminding to send back filled-in questionnaire, etc.), and for final letter thanking for cooperation,

(3) Index card, one for each unit in the sample. If possible, there should be an extra set.

Many valuable hours are lost in writing the complete set of names and addresses three or four times when it can be done more simply. Thus, on most good office typewriters all three can be made at the same time with carbon paper (with the index card at the bottom). This can be done simultaneously with the drawing of the sample from registers. Thus, a systematic sample ('every k'th') can be entrusted to a secretary who at the same time does the typing. The net result is two sets of envelopes and a complete file for the sample.

Often more sets of names are needed, e.g. for more letters (letters expressing gratitude for cooperation, letters giving some of the findings of the study, etc.). For this purpose it may be worth-while from the beginning to write all the names and addresses on stencils or address plate systems so that all one has to do is to 'roll on' (mimeographing can also be done on paper that is glued and adequately perforated in advance).

(c) *The question of identification*

On the one hand there is the indispensable requirement that there be an identification on each schedule so that an IBM card may be traced back to its schedule for checks, more information, comments, etc. On the other hand there is the almost indispensable requirement of protecting the anonymity of the respondents. We say 'almost' because there may be occasions when the respondents do not insist on anonymity, with the enquete to well-known people as the extreme case: they would insist on identifiability, not the contrary. Thus, one has to distinguish between identifiability card-schedule, and identifiability schedule-respondent.

The first kind can easily be obtained, by numbering the schedules. Generally it is advisable to use the numbering as a source of information, for instance by numbering the filled-in mail questionnaires in the order they are returned so that one can use the numbers as a variable to do an analysis on the difference between early and late returners. This number is then coded on the card, and there is no problem of identification.

The second kind of identifiability may be desirable and obtainable without infringing on the wishes for anonymity. One may want this kind of identifiability for reinterviewing (e.g. in a panel study, or in a study of particularly important cases, or deviant cases) or to match with some other information (a questionnaire from the wife, income tax records, non-verbal observations, etc.).

To obtain this there are several methods. One may put the name of the respondent on the schedule or ask him to do so, and there will be no problem. In general this is not recommendable. The need for anonymity is precisely a desire that nobody shall know *who* have these responses, not what were the responses. Even with all guarantees that only the head investigator will ever see the questionnaires, this method should not be used, for the risk of leaks in the system and to remove anxieties in the respondent, anxieties that may interfere considerably with his answers.

Another, and very simple, method is to number the questionnaire before it is sent out and to number the interview-guide before the interview or after, when the name is still remembered. The number should of course be the same as numbers put on the sample file cards mentioned above, where the name of the respondent is written. The identifiability now rests with the file and only there, and this file is easily protected, locked into a safe, etc.

For interviews there should be no difficulties with this method, nor for directly obtained questionnaires. For mail quetionnaires the difficulty is that they arrive anonymously in the mail so that the numbering will have to be done beforehand. There are three difficulties with this. First of all, it may give the respondent a fear that his anonymity will not be respected, and this may distort his answers or make him refuse to cooperate. For that reason, a complete explanation should be given in the accompanying letter. Secondly, the respondent may for some reason or another exchange his questionnaire with that of another respondent. For a random national sample this is of course so improbable that it is a factor of no importance; for studies of small organizations it may be important. And thirdly, the respondent may erase the number – and nothing is gained. With the correct letter of explanation this should be avoided, but one must be prepared for these kinds of difficulties.

To avoid them it is tempting to introduce a system of hidden numbering. A small square with nine points has a variety of 2^9 or more than 500, which is sufficient for many survey samples. Thus, with small pencil dots on one of the pages the equivalent of numbering can be introduced. We will not recommend this, for the reasons indicated above: it is one more way of identifying social science with the science of hidden manipulators; and is ethically unjustifiable, however much it may be argued that 'what the respondents do not know does not worry them'.

(d) *The division of the sample among the interviewers*

If the number of interviewees is N and the number of interviewers is I, the ratio N/I gives the average amount of work to be done for each interviewer. There are many factors to consider when this ratio is decided:

Table 6.3.1. *Factors influencing the interviewee/interviewer ratio*

Increasing the ratio	Decreasing the ratio
to standardize the interviewing by using only a few interviewers who really know the instrument	to diversify the interviewing so that the data collection is not too dependent on the style of some very few interviewers
to reduce costs: fewer people have to be trained and paid, less administration	to reduce costs: less travel expenses because people can be interviewed by somebody from the same place
to reduce the risk of indiscretion and incidents: the fewer interviewers, the stronger the internal control	to do the job more quickly, there is a limit to how long one can do interviewing in a community before there is a contagion effect from people already interviewed, and a cumulation of incidents that may cause friction – the field work should be a 'short, sharp shock'

When the number of interviewers is decided on this is usually done in terms of simple factors of availability and cost more than in terms of design. Since most studies show that the properties of the interviewers are relevant for the responses given,[4] more sophisticated research would have to build this into the design.

The simplest way of building a relevant factor into a design is by making it irrelevant. In principle, this can be done in three ways:
(1) *by removing it*: e.g. by using questionnaire in lieu of interviews,
(2) *by keeping it constant*: e.g. by very thorough training so as to standardize the interviewers, or by selection of a very homogeneous group of interviewers (with regard to background, personality, and attitude towards the problem to be studied) or by having all the interviewing done by the same person,
(3) *by randomization*: e.g. by giving every k'th respondent to the same interviewer, or by drawing lots (or by using random numbers).
The third method is the least costly and has the advantage that for large samples it also gives some opportunities for factorial *post hoc* analysis. Thus, one can examine attitude distributions for all combinations of the

type age, sex, race of interviewer – age, sex, race of interviewee and all combinations of basic attitudes held by interviewers and by interviewee. This can, of course, also be built systematically into the data collection as mentioned.

The third method does, however, run contra to two important considerations, one practical and one more theoretical. In a community study, it is highly inconvenient to distribute individual respondents randomly to the interviewers. Rather, they should be given adjacent respondents, i.e. districts. This has two advantages: travel and walking distance is reduced enormously, and the interviewer gets to know a certain district. The allocation district-interviewer should of course be done randomly, since the allocation respondent-district is not random.

The second consideration is not against the district idea, or at least not very much so. Rather, it enters as a constraint on complete randomness in the allocation. Interviewing is an interaction between the local population and a team of interviewers. Both groups are stratified by rank, and the principle of rank equivalence in contact applies here as well as in other forms of human interaction. More concretely, the head of the team (who is probably also the oldest, the most experienced, the best-known, the one with most education) should have the district with most community leaders – and if they do not all live in the same district, some kind of adjustment after the general division has been made should be done, to achieve more rank-equivalence.

Essentially, this means renouncing on some of the control of the relevant condition in order to ease social interaction. It is difficult to develop a good theory for where the compromise should be, as long as this principle of rank congruence is more of a hunch than a demonstrated, empirical effect. But since interview, however well done, has elements both of the *examination* ('did I give the *true* answer?') and the *trial* ('did I give the *right* answer?') the interviewer will appear very much like the well-known authority roles of the teacher and the judge. If he is below the interviewee in some other rank (sex, race, education, etc.) this may cause difficulty, a certain uneasiness – according to our experience.

(e) *Some technicalities in the survey administration*

Indispensable for any survey is the best map available, if necessary by air photography (not too high altitude) and the systematic use of people who know the social geography of the community very well. The community has to be divided into districts, and each interviewer has to be equipped with
(1) general instructions about interviewing and special instructions for the interview-guide[5]
(2) empty schedules
(3) the file cards for 'his' respondents
(4) a general map of the community
(5) a special map of the district with exact location of each respondent. The obvious procedure is to make a route through the district and to write on the card all particulars about the efforts to contact the respondent (when first call was made, what happened, when second call was made, etc.). To

146

make sure that all such information is recorded it may be a good idea to have file cards especially prepared for the purpose, with the items printed on them. It is also useful to equip the cards with holes so they may be analyzed quickly by coding the information (see II, 1.1).

Each completed schedule is then given the ID number of the card and given to the head of the team with the card so that an exact count of the situation can be given at any moment. This is very important, since there is usually a limited time period available and one may have to rush the interviewing the last days. The interviewer only has to check his map, and he will know at each point how many, who, and where to interview.

A weekend is indispensable as a part of the period of data collection and should preferably be located at the end of the period. On weekends most people are more available, although this may differ from one district to the other, but some (the relatively well-off) may be less available – this one will have to find out during the first days of the data collection. Thus, the sensible thing to do is usually to call on all or almost all as quickly as possible and set up appointments, so as to have some idea about how the whole system works and what will remain of problems.

Since the percentage of interviews obtained is one of the most important determinants of the quality of the whole process, no effort short of irritating the respondent should be left untried to get as high a percentage as possible. Often the head of the team may get through where one of his students did not, and vice versa, so that the ideal lower limit, 90% of the sample, can be attained.[6] Substitutes should be avoided.

(f) *The problem of what to give in return for an interview*

To make a person accept to be interviewed is to exercise some kind of power over him, and if we accept that there are three ways of making people comply with our wishes – the normative, remunerative, and coercive,[7] – we have also three ways of obtaining interviews. The last one should not be analyzed in terms of force and violence, rather rare as methods of obtaining interviews, but in terms of captive audience techniques. It is not obvious that such methods are doomed to failure, nor is it obvious that they will succeed – the only thing that is obvious is that the captured interviewee who wants to take revenge and is skillfull enough to do it will have at his disposal a large array of techniques for counteracting the purpose of the interviewer completely. If he is clever enough to detect where the basic independent variable is, all he has to do is to give false information on this one variable – and he does not have to bother with the indicators of dependent variables.

Leaving that technique aside, we are left with a choice between normative and remunerative power. We may try to make the interviewee want the interview himself, or try to give him something in return for the favor of being exposed to the questions. The typical techniques of the first kind consist in efforts to subsume the interview under some recognized norm, e.g. 'for the sake of science', 'for the sake of this or that institution', or 'for the sake of the interviewer's dissertation'. Very often interviewees do not want to perceive the interview as potentially helpful for them or their organization, for that would put them in the position of needing help, which they have not asked for, and is a position rarely appreciated anyhow. Rather, they will accept being the helpers -- helping science or helping the interviewer to get his degree.

Remunerative power does not necessarily amount to giving the interviewee something concrete (a sum of money, for the time used; cigarettes or other utilities): it may just as well be some more abstract value. The most current case is probably by the interviewing itself: the interview is its own reward, by permitting the interviewee to participate in something relatively exciting, relative to the daily routine of household work, low status occupations, prison life, etc. All interviewers have experienced that it may be more problematic to stop an interview with an experience-starved interviewee than to make an experience-overfed interviewee talk. Obviously, this factor varies with social position; with the elite perceiving the interview itself as meager compensation and the lower layers being attracted to it (with the exception that the extreme periphery of a society may be frightened away).

For i.a. the elite, there is another kind of countervalue: giving them some of the results. This kind of exchange is especially attractive because it is equal in kind: the interviewee gives information about himself – so he receives in return information about the group interviewed. This may even be formulated as something close to an obligation: does one not owe at least one or two sheets giving the main results as quickly as possible to the people who have made the study feasible at all? It costs very little and establishes a reasonable basis of exchange between the two sides of the interview relation. Besides, it may be highly rewarding to the investigator as a kind of check on some of his findings; his respondents may point out weaknesses he is blind to.

What should be avoided, however, is to give such data only to selected subgroups (even if they are self-selected). For instance, data given to one side in a conflict should immediately be given to the other side as well.

At this point we end our brief discussion of this infinite field of descriptive and normative methodology, and turn to a final, more principal, discussion of the limitations of the survey method.

6.4. *Limitations of the survey method*

The survey method, in the more narrow sense, is characterized by the following:

(1) The data obtained are about individuals.
(2) The individuals and the variables used to characterize them are picked for the specific purpose of a research project.
(3) The values the individuals have on these variables are obtained by means of one or more of the verbal methods of data-collection:
    (a) in oral form: the interview.
    (b) in written form: the questionnaire.

(4) To obtain the values, the knowledge of the individual and even his cooperation are needed.

Nobody will today deny the usefulness and importance of this method for the development of sociology. However misleading it may be at times, especially in the hands of the less knowledgeable,[8] it has been indispensable in gaining information about the human condition and new insights in social theory. Important works in postwar social science, like *The Authoritarian Personality, Sexual Behavior in the Human Male and Female, The American Soldier, Union Democracy, The Academic Mind,* and the numerous voting studies, would have been inconceivable without the survey method. Such important theoretical concepts as 'relative deprivation', 'cross-pressure', etc., and techniques like context analysis would have been relatively empty, could they not be referred to empirical operations linked to the survey method.

The reasons for the success of the survey method seem to be two: (1) *theoretically relevant* data are obtained, (2) they are amenable to *statistical treatment,* which means (a) the use of the powerful tools of correlation analysis and multivariate analysis to test substantive relationships, and (b) the tools of statistical tests of hypotheses about generalizability from samples to universes. There has never been a shortage of *relevant* data in social science: everybody observes relevant social facts every day; but these facts are only rarely amenable to rigorous analytical treatment. Nor has there been any shortage of *statistical* data. Any elementary textbook in statistics has at least one example that refers to the heights and weights of conscripts; moreover, there are the censuses – but even though there may be much more to be gained than is usually realized, these data are rarely relevant for the problems of the social science of our generation. Survey analysis bridged the gap and gave social science the tool for its explosive development in the past decades. In fact this development has been so successful that it has led to exactly the situation that now forces us to pause and consider the limitations of the survey method.

Some problems of the survey method are very general, like the problem of verbal vs. non-verbal, and manifest vs. latent data, discussed in the preceding chapter. But there are other problems particularly linked to the problem of exporting sociology to other regions of the world, less industrially developed than the North Atlantic communities in which empirical sociology currently has its strongest foothold. These problems are often cast in the form of the 'ideological implications' of X, where X may be 'North American "yanquí", "gringo" sociology'; 'empirical sociology'; 'the statistical method'; 'too rigorous methods'; 'the survey method'. It is extremely difficult to find critiques of this kind that are not too uninformed and general and engaged in polemics rather than analysis.[9] But even if formulations may be unfortunate and the examples picked by the authors marginal, the problem is real enough and must be confronted. We shall present five such objections to the survey method and see to what extent they can be said to have 'ideological implications'.

(1) *The survey method is too individualistic.* Characteristic of the traditional survey is the tendency to treat the individual as the social unit. Only the individual can be interviewed and given questionnaires (even though he may express himself in the presence of others, as in the group interview).[10] This individualism is further emphasized by building a probability model into the sampling procedure, so that the individual is literally torn out of his social context and made to appear in the sample as a society of one person to be compared with other societies of one person. In very heterogeneous societies like Mexico, Colombia, India such samples quickly lose any meaning.

In the elementary analysis of surveys, individuals may then be grouped together on the basis of their attitudes and with a disregard for their formal and informal positions in the social structure. The extent to which individuals may suddenly act together in groups, because new groups are formed or old ones are reinforced, is easily lost sight of and predictions are made on the basis of so and so many percent of the sample having this or that attitude. One may say that this can be justified in societies where individuals are all by themselves; but not in societies (like any known society) where most individuals wait for some kind of group consensus in a group – small or big – which is salient for them, before attitude is translated into action.

Modern survey analysis can deal with this problem of excessive individualism in two ways. First of all, the sampling procedures can be revised in accordance with the advice of the Columbia tradition, i.e. more emphasis on purposive sampling where individuals are picked according to their position in the social structure, less on random procedures (tests of generalizability will then have to be done by means of replication methods). For instance, one may sample individuals together with some salient members of their role-set. And secondly, analysis can play down the importance of the manifest attitude and play up the importance of social position, especially in prediction studies – as when the vote of the wife is predicted better from the voting intention of her husband than from the voting intention she herself expresses. The latter is a question of including the crucial information about the social position of the respondents in relevant subsystems, which is usually rather different from the superficial knowledge gained through the traditional 'background questions'. Sociometric questions have been used here with some success, as has contextual analysis and all kinds of analysis where properties of collectivities are brought into the picture. Although much remains to be done, the social scientist is better equipped at this point than he was some years ago.

Which are now the ideological implications? In more precise terms, does the individualistic survey method yield results that can be said to reflect the conditions of one type of society better than other types of societies? We think this is not far-fetched. Imagine we classify societies according to two variables: degree of individual mobility (geographical, horizontal, vertical), and degree of inner-directedness (i.e. the degree to which one does not take one's cues for behavior from others). We think it can be argued that traditional survey analysis is a much better instrument for explanations and predictions in societies high on both, than in societies low on both. Characteristic of traditional survey analysis based on random samples from universes of individuals, is the effort to account for attitudes in terms of background variables and personality variables, or – preferably – in terms of the interaction between them. If individuals move, we can nevertheless predict what they will do (verbally or non-verbally) as long as we have a theory about the relative importance of social position and personality, and of how social position shapes personality. We do not need any knowledge about their 'significant others' and how they relate to them, since they are so inner-directed. Thus, if we are satisfied with this kind of impoverished sociologism or psychologism, then we get what we want; if not, the method clearly falls short of the desirable.

In the society low on both we would, by means of traditional survey analysis, be unable to account for the influence of significant others. This, however, might be of little importance if individuals were highly mobile and if the effects of mobility were of a greater magnitude than the impact of role-partners, etc. In that case one could still use social position as a basic predictor, with or without personality variables as intervening variables. But in a caste society with mainly other-directed individuals we would be unable to account for changes. It may be argued that there are not many changes either: norms, roles, and statuses are all well institutionalized, and external control is supported by other-directedness. But this is precisely the type of stereotyped image that fails to distinguish, for instance, between traditional and transitional societies, and thus excludes undercurrents that cannot be predicted, only be discovered *post hoc*. Hence, the need for a methodology richer in its conception of what constitues a social unit. Neither theoretically nor methodologically has modern social science come to grips with what might be termed collective attitudes, as opposed to the individual attitudes of which we know a lot.

(2) *The survey method is too democratic*. The real-life counterpart of the survey is the election in a democratic society, where everybody is asked, and there is always more than one answer alternative. Mixed with this model is the model of the oral or written examination and the court case. In a society where participation in the institutions of Education and Polity is (almost) universal and most people know of and identify (at least partly) with government, educators, and the judiciary, this similarity will probably lead to a transfer of emotions and role-playing. The respondent may feel a mixture of importance and responsibility, nervousness and some guilt, anticipating that some answers will not be 'right'. Regardless of interview technique, a certain residual of these feelings will remain – and probably conduce to, rather than deduct from, the validity of the responses.

But the difficulties of the practices of democracy, examinations in schools, and hearings in courts also become the difficulties of the survey method. The democratic principle is one person – one vote; the principle of statistical analysis is usually the same: one card – one count, where each individual has one punch card. Thus, a democratic bias is introduced. This may be valid in systems where individuals count about equally much or equally little, but not in systems with tremendous differences in the degree to which the properties of people count. Hence, individuals might be weighted.

It may be objected that the argument only applies to naive attempts to use a survey as a kind of a vote, not as an analytical instrument with complicated cross-runs and break-downs. This is certainly correct. In a study of attitudes towards disarmament, a gross percentage of people 'in favor' tells us little – except as a substitute for a referendum – but an analysis of how the attitude depends on social position may yield much material for explanation and prediction. Interest would focus on respondents high on social position, where one would run the risk of elite bias, but not of democratic bias.

There is yet another kind of democratic bias. The idea is that public opinion (in the sense of the opinion the individual makes public, not in the sense of the opinion of the public) can be used both as an indicator inward, to the individual; and outward, to the society. In other words, there is a tacit assumption that the culture is verbal, in the sense that there is a reasonable degree of correspondence between thought and word, and between word and action. Both of these assumptions play an important role in modern democracies: people shall express what they feel, and feel what they express; they shall act according to what they say, and report what they have done. In other words, they shall be predictable and accountable, both to themselves and to their environment.

Again, it may be said that this is geared to a certain type of culture; and that other cultures, where words may have a more expressive and less instrumental function, should be approached with other instruments than the survey. The survey may impose on the society an opinion-structure with neither explanatory nor predictive functions, and hence lead to a false image.

(3) *The survey method is too static.* A survey yields manifest verbal reactions at one point in time, nothing more. A panel study can, perhaps, be applied again already after one month – but the interval must be made longer and longer for each panel if one wants to avoid the effect of people's desire to be consistent. Thus, the survey is no good instrument to detect very swift changes. One may say that it is adjusted to a society that changes from one year to the next, but not much from one month to the following one. The survey presupposes some kind of verbal interaction, which cannot be made a continuous *process:* there must be intervals and even long intervals.

If we emphasize the word *manifest,* another factor that contributes to the static nature of the survey research becomes evident. If one is not to use some kind of depth-psychological interview technique (which would drastically cut down on the advantage of having statistical data by reducing number and comparability), attitudes will have to reach a relatively manifest level before they enter the data of the survey analyst. In a way, the survey can catch the individual in a phase between latent attitude and overt behavior. But with this kind of data one could never have predicted the tremendous change in Cuban public opinion in the first month of 1959.

This is partially connected with the individualism of the survey method, but also with what we are touching here: sometimes, in periods of rapid social change, behavior may come prior to the manifest attitude and even prior to the slightest trace of any attitude. Thus, to the extent one tries to catch social change with the survey method, it may be said that the model is a little bit like the classical model of democracy: society is like a philosophers' club, like the *peripatetikos,* with action (if any) always preceded by a phase where the attitudinal component of behavior is made manifest and even public. The sudden crystallization into behavior of an amorphous opinion structure is very hard to predict with a method based on an intermediate stage only, at least as long as we lack better theory.

Of course, survey analysis is not without methods to counteract this. The latent can be elicited by means of a number of indicators, indices of dispositions can be constructed. But even if there is no intrinsic and necessary relationship between the survey method and reliance on the face value of a

response, there may still be a tendency to adapt this model of correspondence between attitude and behavior. This makes the method particularly
inadequate in societies where there are sudden and gross changes, not preceded by anything like the public debate – formal and informal – known
in the societies where empirical sociology is strongest, and where the model
latent attitude $\rightarrow$ manifest attitude $\rightarrow$ action is more appropriate.

(4) *The survey method is restricted to a middle range of social position.*
The survey method presupposes some kind of verbal interaction, and consequently reaches into the corners of the social structure to the extent this
kind of verbal interaction is feasible. Many factors may work against its
applicability in particularly low and particularly high strata, or particularly
peripheral and particularly central social positions. By 'periphery', then, we
do not mean 'workers' or what is often called 'low class', but the real periphery: the illiterates, the aged, the non-participants, the destitute, the
vagabonds, the geographically-isolated periphery, etc. By 'center' we mean
the opposite of all this.

For the low strata in many countries complete or partial illiteracy may
exclude questionnaires. That still leaves interviews, in principle. In practice,
however, interviews may also encounter difficulties because of lack of training in manipulating symbols. Questions may have to be simplified to the
point where the great advantage of the survey – using the enormous variety
of human *verbal* interaction to get at exactly the variables needed – vanishes.
But more importantly: even if the verbal interaction is technically feasible,
the strata concerned may reject any kind of interaction with the team of
interviewers, who almost invariably will be middle class. This may be due
to fear, anxiety, hatred, suspicion, or simply to lack of general training in
human interaction outside a narrow peer group or social category.[11] Hence,
the survey method can always count on considerable constraint in the social
periphery, and with tremendous possibilities of error even if the process
works smoothly on the surface. In fact, smoothness may be an indicator of
submissiveness and excessive courtesy. Obviously, one remedy here is to
impart to the survey investigator some of the training anthropologists get
in dealing with culturally alien groups. And there are other remedies.[12]

The same applies to the social center, the elite; and explains to some extent why there are so few elite studies.[13] But here the reasons are different.
The elite is verbal, is trained in interaction over a considerable range of
social position, – at least as far down as to include most professional social
scientists – and very often feel that they are asked, not too much, but too
little about what they feel and think. The difficulty lies rather in the social
setting of the survey, in its combination of voting, examination, and trial.

154

As mentioned, the setting suggests that the interviewer has higher social rank than the interviewee, and for many definitions of 'elite' that will exclude the survey even if the head of the team himself takes care of all elite members, as suggested. Adding to this comes the fear of abuse. The elite is more exposed, by definition, more in the public light. The individual interviewee may fear that rules about anonymity will be broken, and the group as a whole may feel that the results of the study will be used as a basis for social criticism against them. The same fear, and equally justified, is often expressed in the social periphery – 'they only come to write bad things about us, how little we know, what silly ideas we have, how filthy we are –'.

There is another aspect to this. Whatever the intention of the sociologist, there has hardly ever been an analysis made that has not somehow alienated or infuriated some of the interviewees whose responses formed the basis of the analysis. To write about any group, to make any kind of analysis that is not self-analysis, can provoke conflicts between the analyst and the analyzed. The clinician defends himself against attacks from the analyzed by making them *pay* for a (promise of) *cure* (both inconsistent with attacks on him); the historian defends himself by analyzing groups long since deceased; the anthropologist by leaving the place of the field study and publishing in another language, on another continent; – and the sociologist defends himself by drawing amorphous, anonymous survey samples, which he then tears apart and puts together as it suits him, knowing that it is hardly likely that there will be any effort to expose him, from his 'victims'. By defining them as anonymous he also, in a sense, defines himself as anonymous. Here, of course, random sampling is a marvellous device, since it deprives the interviewees of any principle of knowing who the others are, and hence of any real basis for social organization. It is like *decimation* of troops.

It is more difficult when there are faces in the crowd, as in an elite sample. The sociologist may be in the elite himself, or close to it; he may know some members of his target elite groups personally, or depend on them for favors of different kinds (including general recognition of sociology as a profession, at which point he will also be under pressure from his colleagues). Thus, he runs risks, even personal risks that are easily avoided if he concentrates on more anonymous layers of the society. He may, for instance, run the risk of hurting one of his own friends.

Behind all this, however, is yet another factor: the fear the sociologist may feel when meeting somebody whose criticism of the whole survey is not only sarcastic, but valid. Most likely, this will be among the elite in the system he is investigating, and is a good reason why specially trained personnel should engage in the collection of such data to be able to counteract some of the criticism. Thus, we suggest that one good reason for the shortage of elite studies is simply the sociologists' fear of being revealed.

This should not be construed as a social inferiority or climbing complex in the sociologist or as excessive paranoia in center or periphery. The sociologist may feel socially clumsy when interviewing a cabinet member with his prepared schedule, feeling that he is playing the inquisitor upward instead of downward. However, he can avoid this rank incongruency by three simple techniques: the informal interview, the formal questionnaire, and content analysis. With the former the setting is rank congruent: it is more like the journalist with his informant, or the student who is informed by his professor. The elite member leads the conversation. Individual treatment is given, one is not implicitly suggesting what few elite members like: that 'you must not think you are so unique that we cannot use exactly the same questionnaire for you as we use for all the others'.[14]

With the formal questionnaire interaction is symbolic only; and even though the questionnaire will have to be very good not to arouse the anger of the elite, it probably involves the researcher in less direct pain. He will have the same difficulties when it comes to the consequences of publishing his conclusions, but not with the process of data collection as such. However, he must be aware that as the elite are more critical, the questionnaire must be eminently worth-while for them: it must present them with perspectives they do not consider trivial or irrelevant, and must reveal thorough knowledge.

The third way out may at times be excellent, at times less satisfactory. The social scientist can use data left by the elite but not solicited by him, such as speeches, articles, actions – all the traces an elite person will leave behind as he moves through life. Such data are often considered more true, they are not 'artificial', and there will be no difficulties with the elite itself during the data-collection if the data are public. Also, in a possible conflict following publication of an analysis of these data the social scientist does not have to defend himself against the charge of having exploited good-will: he has only used in his ways what is available to everybody. The debate, if any, will be an ordinary debate, possibly sharpened by the deeper penetration one should expect from a social scientist, but also mellowed by difficult terminology and complex thinking.

Thus, our prediction will be that the sociologist will approach contemporary elites with his techniques, ordered after decreasing frequency: content analysis (including all kinds of biographic data), formal questionnaires, informal interviews, and formal interviews. Obviously, there is ample space for methodological ingenuity to unfold itself.

This all suggests that there is a social center of gravity with relatively low dispersion in the choice of targets for social research, an hypothesis confirmed by a small investigation we made of three leading journals in the USA.[15] We suggest that the ideal respondent, from the point of view of the survey method, has the following characteristics: he is well socialized and disciplined, used to examinations, to listening, to answering honestly and clearly. He has a certain minimum of formal education, good enough to fill in a standard questionnaire. He is below the average social scientist in social rank, so that there will be no problem of congruency in rank relations, and unsolicited criticism (above the often hypocritical 'What do you think of this interview?' at the end of the schedule). Without too much protest he fits into the precoded answers. Finally, he expresses some joy at having had the favor of being included in this important study: he is grateful, not overly critical. Although the methods can tolerate much deviance from this ideal pattern, there are limits, and we have suggested that they are found in periphery and center. Hence, these are the least explored regions in the social structure.

This is consequential. To the extent social research is motivated by a social problem orientation, this means that the survey method will conduce to a conception of social problems as something found in the middle ranges of society. The periphery may be seen as being too much outside, as being *of* the society rather than *in* the society. The center may be perceived as so inaccessible that it is forgotten, or given scant and unsystematic attention. The social consequence of this is an abundance of studies of divorce, integration in sub-systems, work adjustment, family life, role of vocational training, public opinion; but very few systematic studies of the alienated, the old, the very young, the people who are outside (except for ideal-typical studies of a more anthropological nature); and a scarcity of studies of the elite – whether in business, politics, the military establishment, diplomacy, science. For this reason, social science may easily become a weapon of the elite against non-elite, as it may expose the problems of the latter, so that they can be more easily manipulated. And even though this may be less dangerous in countries with a good system for exchange between elite and non-elite, the social scientist will certainly fail in his mission as social investigator and social critic in other countries, if this limitation of an otherwise powerful tool makes him forget about the center of society.

For developing countries this seems to be particularly important. Regardless of what one's theory about social determinants of economic development might be, nobody will claim that these determinants are randomly distributed in society. Whether they are structural or in terms of value-orientations there is no theoretical justification known at present for the overwhelming concentration of research initiative on workers and farmers in the developing countries, and the almost total neglect (by social scientists) of the ruling elite, whose values and interaction pattern must be at the very least equally consequential. For instance, where is the good study of the function of the legal mind and training in jurisprudence among the decision-makers of, say, Latin-American countries?

It should be added that this tendency for sociology to be directed from above downwards is also found in other fields. Thus, there are hundreds of studies where whites are invited to express their sentiments towards all kinds of 'minorities' – and the studies are published with little regard for how these minorities may like to read about the feelings of the same whites. We suggest that there is a strong and well-institutionalized mechanism of defence that prevents studies of how the same minorities perceive the whites, from emerging in a sufficient number. For the same reason we shall probably have to wait for the first good empirical study of the image other people have of the social scientist.

(5) *The survey method works only across relatively narrow social distances.* In one sense, this is a generalization of what has already been said; in another sense, a specification. The survey method is for the ingroup, not for the outgroup; for your friend, not for your enemy; but not for your very best friends either – to do social science on them might impair the friendship. It presupposes verbal interaction that is friendly, or at least not hostile. In a social conflict with high degree of polarization this is denied your enemy – partly a special case of the norm against any kind of interaction, partly because the survey can be seen as a trick, a kind of espionage (which may be a quite realistic assessment). This explains to a considerable extent why there is so little good research done on social conflict – just as the third problem above (the static nature of survey research) contributes to the scarcity of systematic research on social change. And it does not depend on the researcher alone. Even though a social scientist belonging to group X may like to make a study of attitudes in group Y with which X is in bitter conflict, other members of group X may prevent him from doing so.

Of course, there are many ways, none of them quite satisfactory, of getting around this problem. One method would be to cooperate with social scientists in Y, establishing a kind of professional tie bridging the gap provoked by the conflict. Another is to use a social scientist from a neutral group if he can gain access to both sides. A third method is to use refugees, etc., from Y – as was done in a well-known project on the social structure of the Soviet Union.[16] But all methods will provoke suspicion during the data collection.

For instance, the second method – as experienced by the present author – will lead to the suspicion that the neutral person is not so neutral after all, that he is going to inform the other party, and so on.

The net result is not only the scarcity of the kind of studies one might like to have of society in conflict, but much more importantly: a social science based on surveys will tend, at present, to be a science where society is presented in a less discordant state than might be considered realistic. The method thus has its ideological implications in distorting the total image of society, because of the difficulties in doing research on both parties to a conflict. At times the topdog image is given, at times the underdog perception – but the total picture is biased away from social conflict. Two possible action consequences of this bias would be neglect of the grievances of the parties, so that a particular conflict might not be solved; and neglect of conflict in general, so that better ways and means of tackling conflicts might not be developed.

To summarize: the survey method favors a society with a slow rate of change and little internal conflict, highly individualistic, inner-directed and mobile, and with a high degree of correspondence between thought, word, and deed. Even within such a society, the survey method is more applicable downwards than upwards, and for that reason better as an instrument of control of underdogs than of topdogs. Obviously, we are not dealing here with absolute categories, but with degrees of applicability. And the frontiers of applicability for the survey method are constantly moved into new and relatively unexplored territory, by new techniques of data collection and data analysis. Some of these innovations have been mentioned. But it would be a great disfavor to empirical social research to pretend that the application of survey methods to social systems very different from the ideal case described above – for instance, most of the developing countries – is unproblematic.

On the other hand, it should be emphasized how segmental this limitation of social science techniques is. It does not exclude verbal methods as such, although it may at times exclude verbal methods used to collect systematic data that can be treated statistically. Nor does it exclude statistical data as such, which would mean the exclusion of rigorous methods of testing hypotheses (see the arguments in I, 1.2 for 'more than one unit', 'more than one variable'). Human interaction does not have to be projected to the level of verbal interaction found in the survey. There are countless other methods, often unhappily lumped together under the heading of 'content analysis'. The elite, as mentioned, usually leaves some traces of its existence. These traces can be studied systematically, whether in the form of studies of kinship patterns, interaction data obtained at first and second hand, content analysis of what the elite says or writes, content analysis of observed actions, or other forms; with a critical attitude to all these sources.

In a conflict situation, the interaction patterns observed in a number of similar conflicts may be a better basis for social theory than a high number of interviews. Thus, it may well be argued that the very success of the survey method has impeded the development of other rigorous methods. It may have forced the perspective of the social scientist too much away from the non-verbal towards the verbal, with an exaggerated belief in the usefulness of attitude studies and the uselessness of other studies as the result.

But this, again, does not mean that the search for the perfection of the survey method should not continue. Foremost in this search should be the young social scientists in the developing countries, for the five problems of survey analysis discussed here are their problems more than anybody else's. This is not only important for the development of methodology. It is also a way of opening the most remote corners of society, national or international, for the rest of that society, and a potential lever in the transformation of a closed society into an open one. And so, in the right hands, the frontiers of survey research are also some of the frontiers of a society that dares to do open research on itself – as a tool in the search for new and better human institutions, and for better and deeper insights.

APPENDIX A

An example of an interview guide

General instructions:

1. Be sure to keep your cards in a safe place. If they become illegible, check with the corresponding McBee-card (they are arranged numerically), and/or with the three directories: *City Directory, Telephone Book* and *University Directory*.
2. The quota is 5 pr. day, preferably more, but 5 is OK. Rather quality than quantity when you are sure you make 5 (the days of arrival and departure count as 1 day together). Generally it is wise to make as many telephone-calls as possible well in advance and have fixed dates with the respondents. All respondents have been 'warned' by mail, so there is no obligation to call them before you visit them – and telephone-calling may be unwise as it is easier to refuse over the telephone.
3. Be sure to write on your white card whether the respondent was

   | completely | partly | unwilling | impossible | absent, ill, |
   | interviewed | interviewed | | to locate | vacation, etc. |

4. Be sure to put on the schedule, upper right hand corner on the first page, the number of the respondent (the number of his card). This is our only means of identifying him; however, the schedules will be treated confidentially as promised. Put the number on *immediately after the interview*, so as not to make the respondent 'feel like a number'. Never put his name on the schedule anywhere.
5. When the interview is completed, fill in the questions about the interview, the last with your own initials; and put your initials on the white card. Keep all cards and schedules until all is over.
6. Do not tell the respondent that he probably will be reinterviewed.

General instructions for the interviewing:

1. Please remember that these people are under the strain of conflict, that the whole issue is very painful for them, so be as tactful as possible. Further, methodological ends do not warrent ethically dubious means. As a general attitude, be maximally *open-minded*, curious, receptive, without committing yourself to either camp. When asked what you mean and think, tell them you are here to learn, not to pass any judgement, that the situation is very complex, that the Northern and foreign press are biased, and that we are more interested in studying a community under *conflict* (but be careful with this word) than the race-issue.
2. *Introduce yourself something like this:* How do you do, my name is –, I am one of a team of interviewers under the direction of Professor N.N. – I think you got a letter from him some days ago –. Do you think I may have an interview with you? It does not last long, it is completely confidential, and not for any magazine or newspaper.

3. *Why do you do it then*? Well, this is a social science study, and we are interested in learning something about a community in the kind of situation X-ville is in right now.
   Why me? We picked some 300 people at random, and you happened to be one of them. You would do us a great favor –
   I don't know anything! Very few people know anything for certain in this situation, but we would very much like to hear your opinions.
   Do you get any money for this? *I never heard of anybody who did anything for nothing*! I just get my expenses covered (and barely that!) – but you are right insofar as I do not do it for nothing, I am very interested in the situation myself, and it is very good training for me as a student.
   And what is going to happen to this schedule? Well, it will all be put on small cards and analyzed to find out something about who think what.
4. As far as possible, know the questions by heart so you can have eye-contact with the respondent. Remember that each page is a unit in itself. Keep the schedule so the respondent does not see what you write, but not so that it looks like you try to hide it (difficult, training in front of a mirror is advisable). Do not turn pages too often. Check the correct category in a discrete way. Remember to write down something verbatim even though it is covered by the precoding just once in a while, otherwise the respondent feels badly about it. However, do not write too much, it takes time, and the respondent feels awkward, the flow of conversation stops.
5. As a rule, let the respondent lead, do not argue, but cut him short on some places if the 'story' becomes unnecessarily involved. However, some of these stories may be extremely valuable. Be sure you know where the questions are placed, so you can easily check as the respondent tosses around.
6. Make use of the background questions as a quick cooling-off. They should give both parties a feeling of being through, which is important.
7. If the respondent wants to see the schedule, tell him to wait till the interview is over. If he insists, give him a few questions as a sample. When the interview is completed, give him a blank schedule to look at, but tell him you must have it back as 'they are scarce'.
8. If a husband or wife is to be interviewed, the situation will often be problematic. Ideally, they should be interviewed alone, with nobody, especially not the wife or the husband, listening. To achieve this, two obvious techniques may be used:
   a. Get the husband on the job, e.g., during the lunch-break, or in connection with the lunch-break so as not to ruin it for him.
   b. Get the wife at home when the husband is working (but she may be afraid to let you in).
   If you meet the couple at home, proceed as follows:
   Talk to both of them if you meet them, just to introduce yourself, let the husband inspect you, and then say something like: 'Well, we drew a random sample, and it happened to be *Mr.* Smith (*Mrs.* Smith) in this family –', but say it with tact so that the implication is not too obvious. If this has no effect, say: 'So, do you think I may interview Mr. Smith

alone?' If this has no effect, or if the mate explicitly asks for permission to stay, try for the third and last time: 'According to my instructions, I should try to interview the person we selected alone –', but do not say it if the situation is already tense.

If you have to take 'both or none' (and in addition you may get one dog, two children, the laundry, and some in-laws who just dropped in) then make yourself comfortable and go ahead, addressing yourself to the respondent only. This may work all right. If it does not, you may have to decide whether what you are doing is

    a. Conducting two interviews at the same time, with two schedules (then take up another schedule, and say, 'if you do not object, I find that what you say is so interesting that I would like to put that down too').

    b. Conducting one interview with two persons at the same time, where they arrive at a common answer after some decision-making. This is the least preferable situation.

9. Do not forget to make compliments about X-ville if you feel they are justified (do not be a hypocrite, you are not a salesman). Further, it is very important to mention the good reception we have been given (and which we expect we shall get this time too) – this can mean quite a lot in establishing rapport.

10. When the interview is completed, and you have left the house and can no longer be seen, look the schedule over, add comments that are still fresh in your memory, make sure that your coding has been correct, etc. This will save all of us an enormous amount of work later on.

11. You will undoubtedly be told stories, some of them extremely interesting. Put them down on the back of a sheet in the schedule, and type it out as soon as possible so that you can get some of the flavor. Put the respondent's number on it, and append it to the schedule (preferably, take a copy of the story or whatever you find interesting).

APPENDIX B
Sampling in social research

To get an impression of sampling used in social research, two recent volumes of the *American Sociological Review* (1962 and 1963), the *American Journal of Sociology* (1960/61 and 1961/62) and the *Public Opinion Quarterly* (1963 and 1964) were analyzed for the kind of samples used in the research reported. In addition, the *American Sociological Review* for 1954 was examined to get a check on possible time trends. However, the differences were so insignificant (except for much shorter articles, so that more samples were brought into the public eye via articles per year than for later volumes) that we decided to concentrate on the volumes from the 'sixties'.

Some of the results were as follows[1]:

Table B.1. *Some properties of samples used in social research*

		ASR, 62 & 63	AJS, 60/61 & 61/62	POQ, 63 & 64
% with data		74 %	73 %	56 %[2]
% with census data, of articles with data		20 %	19 %	20 %
Percentage of	*students*	18 %	20 %	21 %
articles with data,	*deviants*	9 %	12 %	4 %
but not census	*workers*	12 %	7 %	4 %
data, based on	*elite,*			
	business geographical	16 %	18 %	4 %
	center geographical	12 %	12 %	14 %
	periphery	0 %	7 %	7 %

The proportion *with* data is quite high, corresponding to a very empirical orientation. At the same time about one fifth of the empirical work is based on census data, which means that extreme center and extreme periphery are to some extent brought in. But this is not sufficient: census methods do not get the kind of information extensive interviews can bring, nor do general samples, since the questionnaire or interview guide will have to be cut according to a least common denominator. And when it comes to bringing in special groups, it is immediately seen that the students, easiest to reach, are heavily oversampled. And what passes for 'elite' is (almost) never top elite, nor are the workers very marginal workers. The 'deviants' are usually institutionalized and do not represent the periphery of society as such; rather they are people from various layers of society with some kind of deviance in common. And where geography is concerned, the center is overrepresented and the periphery underrepresented.

But the basic point does not really emerge from the Table, nor shall we express it in quantitative form, since the empirical basis is so limited. It is the following: Even though 'elite', or 'center', and 'deviants', or 'periphery', appear, they are rarely complete versions of center and periphery. Rather, when top businessmen are interviewed, they have a tendency to be located away from the center of the nation, and when 'workers' appear, their lower social status is compensated for by higher geographical status. There are studies of lower class whites and of Negro professionals – but there is not much of the really low class, destitute Negro population, for instance in some isolated district in some peripherial state in the US South. And so on: the general impression is that to get into the design of a study, a certain minimum score on an index measuring total rank in the status-set of an individual is needed – provided the score keeps below a certain maximum.

We offer this as a suggestion for proof or disproof by further empirical research in descriptive methodology.

PART II

Data Analysis

1. Processing

1.1. *The structure and function of processing*

In Part I, 'Data Collection', the task was defined as follows: given an empty data matrix, with its units of analysis and its stimuli or variables, *fill it* with values! The task of data collection is completed when all entries (or almost all) are filled with the appropriate responses or values.

In the present part, 'Data Processing and Analysis', the task is to take the completed data matrix, which is amenable to processing, and do two things with it, in this order:

(1) *Processing*: to recast the matrix, concentrate and otherwise deal with it so that the data are as amenable to analysis as possible;
(2) *Analysis*: to see the data in the light of hypotheses and theories, and draw conclusions that are as amenable to theory formation as possible.

The first will be dealt with in chapters 1-3 of the present text, the second part in chapters 4 and 5. In the sixth chapter, 'Theory Formation', the last phase of the research process will be elaborated.

Relative to the phases of data collection and theory formation, data processing and data analysis are standard procedures. There exist fairly standard methods that have been tried again and again, and can be used once the data are available. Usually, this is not considered the part of a project that calls for most imagination, and large research outfits will often have a division of labor where data processing and routine analyses are left to 'coders', 'students', 'machine room people' and 'assistants'. Very often, however, this picture is misleading and may lower the quality of the work done. The idea that the sociologist can sit in his chair and write theories based on data collected, processed and analyzed by others neglects the importance both of direct contact with the 'units' during the data collection; and the role of the interplay between data-collection and the forms of processing that are *possible* on the one hand, and between theory formation and the kind of data analysis that is *necessary* on the other. A thorough knowledge of even the most tedious phases is indispensable if the researcher wants to know how well he can trust his own conclusions. But this is not the same as knowing all the technicalities in the field: what matters is having a broad view of the field.

Data processing is subject to the same requirements of intra-subjectivity and inter-subjectivity as data collection (I, 1.3). The results of a given procedure shall not depend on when, where and by whom it is carried out – these factors may only enter in the selection of a procedure for the processing. This means that the procedures must be unambiguously defined, and preferably be so well codified that only a few words or short sentences are needed when directives shall be given. Ideally, something of the same should apply to data analysis. As the borderline between data analysis and theory formation is unclear, however, it is obvious that non-codifiable elements of art and intuition enter and should enter on the fringes of the data analysis.

With the definition given of data processing it is also obvious that mechanical means are necessary. There is no practical limit to the number of ways in which we may 'recast' data, and in order to be able to use even very complicated ones, machine methods are today indispensable. This, then, introduces a new link between the units of analysis and the analyst: the transfer of the data to some kind of representation that a machine can work on. This relatively recent link, implying a certain division of labor, has contributed more than anything else to alienate the analyst from *all* phases his project goes through.

We shall use punched cards as an example, but similar principles are applied in other modern methods (paper tape, magnetic tape).

It also brings in a source of error by lengthening the distance the information from or about the units must pass. If we conceive of data collection and the parts of data processing as a channel of communication, this has consequences for the probabilities that information will pass unchanged through the entire channel. To study this, let us look at the stages the data go through.

We take as our point of departure Table I, 1.3.1, where the 'stimulus to datum'-sequence is indicated, and add to it a 'raw datum to processed datum'-sequence:

Table 1.1.1. *The raw datum to processed datum sequence*

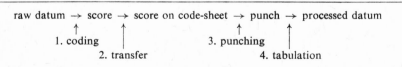

170

This way of presentation presupposes that the procedure is as follows:

(1) *coding*, where responses are given *scores* according to *coding-instructions* – for instance, done in the margin of the questionnaire or interview-guide,

(2) *transfer*, where the scores are transferred to a *code-sheet*, where they are presented in a form that makes it easy to punch them,

(3) *punching*, where data are transferred from the code-sheets to a representation of the data that can be used by the machines selected to do the mechanical job of 'recasting' the data, and

(4) *tabulation*, where the data are made to reappear in one form or another by the machines.

Although we shall not go into any detail,[1] we shall point out some characteristics of these procedures. The *coding* must be single-valued insofar as the same raw datum always must be given the same score, but it need not be one-one-valued. On the contrary, the coding will very often have the *grouping* of data as an important function, although this should be unnecessary in well pretested research: the grouping will already have been done during the recording.

The *transfer* is a purely clerical operation. Whereas the coding should be done as close to the raw data (e.g., in the observation protocols, on the questionnaires or the interview-guides, or on the publications to be content analyzed) as possible, in order to avoid errors, punching should also be done with the scores as easily accessible as possible. Another reason for the transfer is control of the coding; if the transfer is done by two people (one of them reading from the coded raw data, one writing on the code-sheets) an excellent opportunity for control is introduced.

The *punching* is a mechanical operation and like the transfer single-valued (relative to the transferred scores). Coding, transfer and punching are usually done in agreement with these rules:

Table 1.1.2. *Rules for the representation of data*

	Punched cards (e.g., IBM)	Keysort cards (e.g., McBee)
each *unit*	one *card*	one *card*
each *variable*	one *field*	one *field*
each *value*	one *punch-combination*	one *punch-combination*

When we say 'each unit–one card' we do not mean 'only one card' – this depends of course on the number of variables. But it simplifies never to have more than one unit on the same card. Similarly for the variables: it simplifies if we can give one column to each variable. By definition we give the variable a 'field' which is its own, but if one trichotomy has the range 1-2-3, a second the range 4-5-6 and so on in a column in an IBM card, then we save columns (and may also save much machine-work), but risk 1. increased confusion in all steps, with corresponding errors, and 2. that the cards break down because they become weakened by the multiple punches. Thus, it is in most cases better to let the field extend to the whole column, with the possible exception of the 11 and 12 punches – they may be useful for extra information.[2] On the other hand, it may sometimes be necessary to extend the field to more than one column because the variety in one column is not sufficient – e.g. if one wants an exact coding of the respondent's age.

For each value there should ideally be only one punch, and punch-*combinations* only when the field extends over more than one column. Thus, the simplest, most intuitive system is

each unit – its card   *each variable – its column*   *each value – its punch*

But deviations from this may be technically advisable in many cases. In the case of the key-sort cards, the problem is that they usually are equipped with only one hole, so that each 'column' has a variety of 2 only (hole closed – hole open). This suffices, e.g. for coding a set of answers to a true-false test, but in general more variety is needed. Two simple principles offer themselves:

the simplest method: for each variable take as many holes as there are possible values, use one hole for each value,
the cheapest method: for each variable, take so many holes (s) that the number of combinations (2^s) is greater or equal to the number of values (r), then use one combination for each value.

Thus, for a variable with seven values one would use seven holes with the first method, three holes with the second (since it yields eight combinations).

Evidently, a card in either system corresponds to a row in a data matrix: it gives all the information about the unit (we assume that one card is sufficient for this). Thus, if one lets each card correspond to a row, why could one not just as well let the card correspond to a column, i.e. have one card for each variable and code the value for unit 1 in column 1, for unit 2 in column 2, etc.? One may, *viz.*, in the case where there is what we have called horizontal comparability. One of the basic points about the cards is the idea of comparability, or more precisely that it makes sense to count the number of cards with the same punch-combination for a given field (the same punch in a given column). It makes sense when the rules in Table 1.1.2 are fol-

172

lowed. But if we interchange unit and variable in the rules, it makes sense only in special cases. In this case one could very easily get from the machines one individual's tendency to say 'yes', 'no', or 'don't know' – which makes sense, for instance in an analysis of response-set. This principle may also be useful in certain card operations, but in general the principles above are practical to follow.

It should also be mentioned that in surveys some 'values' are so standard that it is useful to have a standard code for them, such as:

don't know –	DK	0 (or 7)
no answer –	NA	8 (avoid blank columns)
does not apply –	DNA	9

where the latter is used for all the cases where a question is asked or not asked depending on the answer to the foregoing question (if 'yes': why did you do it?). If one does not code DNA one will have to go back to the preceding question (or have the machine go back to the preceding column/ field) to sort those with open columns or cards that did not answer although they should from those who did not answer because they should not answer. Blank columns may lead to confusion, for that reason the codes 8 and 9 above.

The *tabulation* process may consist in a simple listing of the data so that the data matrix reappears, this time printed by the machine. The machine will print one line for each card with all the information in the card, then go on to next card, etc.; until one has all cards listed. Such a listing is useful for checking purposes if m is not too high – checked against the raw data the whole chain in the processing is checked simultaneously.

Finally, some words should be said about *when* to use cards, with reference to the thinking in I, 1.2. Evidently, r has little or no importance here; the decision must be taken on the basis of m and n. The general rule is that it pays to put data on cards or other means of mechanical data-processing, even if the mechanical principle is that of the knitting-needle only. But there are some exceptions.

(1) *m low but n very high.* This is the case of the pilot project, where a lot is known about selected units. The analysis will typically proceed by mental manipulation of cluster of variables, 'gestalts', and not by the more piece-meal approach the machines lend themselves to. The researcher sitting in his armchair with half a dozen fat interview schedules, sifting out what seems to be valuable and insight-provoking is a better model for progress in this case than the man in the machine-room working with ten sets of cards, twelve cards in each.

(2) *m high but n very low.* In this case, the number of possible cross-runs will be so low that they can just as well be done by hand. If the cards exist, two people working with paper and pencil at a desk cannot beat a sorter-counter; but if the cards do not exist, they can very often beat the whole process needed to get to the point where the cards exist.

Thus, the general conclusion is not to use cards along the axes of Table I, 1.2.1. As to the choice between keysort cards and punched cards, it is obvious that the latter are suitable for higher $m \cdot n \cdot r$, but there is also another difference to be emphasized. The keysort cards are not simpler versions of punched cards, but elaborated versions of index cards; they can contain written information, and lend themselves to table making by storing some of that written information in the holes at the edges of the card.

Everything that has to do with data processing and the first phases of data analysis has strongly pronounced bureaucratic aspects. It resembles more the work of a business enterprise and an office in general than the stereotype of what happens within a scientific institution. For that reason one has to rationalize as much as possible by standardizing a number of operations. One step in that direction is the use of standard sheets for the different phases of data-processing, and Appendix C contains a complete set of suggestions.

1.2. *The information channel and the sources of noise*

If we now compare Tables I, 1.3.1 and II, 1.1.1 it becomes evident that the road from stimulus to processed datum is long, and the possibilities of error many. In this presentation, there are eight steps, but we shall omit the first one, assuming that the stimulus has been presented correctly. In many cases, we shall also have to omit the second one: the manifestation. A human being who is *interviewed* will have to yield or manifest a response which only then can be perceived, but if the human being is *observed,* for instance for its eye color, the problem is reduced to one of perception and subsequent recording. Imagine we are left with seven steps:

(1) manifestation
(2) perception
(3) recording
(4) coding
(5) transfer
(6) punching
(7) tabulation

and regard the road from the object or unit of analysis as a *channel of information,* where the object 'tries' to *send* some information that has to go

174

through all these seven steps before it is *received* as a processed datum. For sake of simplicity, let us imagine that the information consists of a dichotomous choice, either a 'yes' or a 'no' which shall pass through all seven steps. For any one step, for instance step (1), there is a certain matrix containing the probabilities that a sent 'yes' will be received as a 'no' when it has passed that step, etc.:

Table 1.2.1. *A transmission probability matrix in the information channel*

		received signal	
		yes	no
sent signal	yes	$1-p_i$	p_i
	no	q_i	$1-q_i$

$$\left.\begin{matrix} 1-p_i & p_i \\ q_i & 1-q_i \end{matrix}\right\} = M_i$$

The idea is, of course, that p_i and q_i should be as small as possible, preferably 0, which means perfect transmission. If we can make the reasonable assumption that transmission at one step is statistically independent of the transmission at any other step, we get this simple formula for the transmission probabilities in the total channel, i.e. from object to processed datum:

$$M = M_1M_2M_3M_4M_5M_6M_7 = \begin{Bmatrix} 1-p & p \\ q & 1-q \end{Bmatrix}$$

or simply the product of all matrices for the individual steps. For simplification, we assume all $p_i = q_i$, and hence $p = q$, in the rest of this section.

To give an idea of what this means in practice, let us consider the highly unrealistic case that all $p_i = 0.10$, i.e. each step has the same probability, $\frac{1}{10}$, corrupting a 'yes' into a 'no' and vice versa. We get:

$$M_i^2 = \begin{Bmatrix} 0.82 & 0.18 \\ 0.18 & 0.82 \end{Bmatrix} \quad M_i^3 = \begin{Bmatrix} 0.76 & 0.24 \\ 0.24 & 0.76 \end{Bmatrix} \quad M_i^4 = \begin{Bmatrix} 0.70 & 0.30 \\ 0.30 & 0.70 \end{Bmatrix} \quad M = M_i^7 = \begin{Bmatrix} 0.60 & 0.40 \\ 0.40 & 0.60 \end{Bmatrix}$$

which is the final transmission matrix. We have given some of the matrices in-between to indicate what can be saved by reducing the number of steps, *provided the probability of error is kept constant*. The latter is very often an unrealistic assumption, since one of the reasons for the relatively high number of steps is precisely to eliminate errors.

Let us base a very simple measure of how much distortion or 'noise' there is in this channel on p. $p = 0$ is the ideal case, but this does not mean that $p = q = 1$ is the worst one. On the contrary, if in that case we know that 'yes' means 'no' and vice versa, and know what has been received then, there is no difficulty in restoring the original message,[3] it is a question of translation. The worst possible case is the case of $p = q = \frac{1}{2}$, where there is absolutely no basis for inference about the state of the object. p is a function of n, the number of steps, and of all the p_i. Some calculation gives us this Table:

Table 1.2.2. *The amount of total noise as a function of the noise per step and the number of steps*

	Number of steps	1	2	3	4	5	6	7
	0.01	0.010	0.020	0.029	0.039	0.048	0.057	0.066
Noise	0.10	0.10	0.18	0.25	0.30	0.34	0.37	0.40
per step	0.30	0.30	0.42	0.47	0.49	0.49	0.50	0.50
	0.50	0.50	0.50	0.50	0.50	0.50	0.50	0.50

This Table serves to indicate how hazardous social science may be unless done carefully. It is a matter of taste how much noise one is willing to tolerate, but it seems at least unreasonable to tolerate more than $\frac{1}{10}$, which immediately rules out the better part of the Table.

Since there are two variables in the Table, there are two sources of cure: lower p_i without increase in the number of steps, and a lower number of steps without increase in the p_i. These two variables are logically but not empirically independent, as indicated, and either may be changed somewhat, but not too much before the other changes in the wrong direction. Let us briefly look at some of the possibilities.

*Lower p_i above all means *better control*. Since the last steps are easiest to control, the utmost should be done to insure that at least steps 4-7, viewed as a single step, have a lower total p than 0.01 or at least 0.05. One way of doing this is by listing the processed data and checking them directly with the recorded data. If the data matrix is of considerable size, say $m \cdot n = 10,000$, this may be unpracticable, and the p_i can be obtained by a suitable sampling method like the quality control methods used in commercial production. But it should be noticed that Table 1.2.2 shows the importance of checking *more than one step at a time*. Tabulation errors can be reduced by routine checks, mechanical control and maintenance; punching errors can be reduced by the process of verification; transfer errors can be reduced by doing it over again, and the same applies to coding errors – but even if the individual errors become reasonable, the total errors over all four steps may still be considerable.

176

In actual research we shall probably find that the most important sources of error are p_1, p_2 and p_3, in that order. It may be extremely difficult to arrange the stimulus so that what the object manifests is reasonably valid as an expression of more latent variables; and it may also require an extremely perceptive interviewer to know when and what to perceive. Again, there is a certain complementarity, this time between p_2 and p_3: to record a response correctly will often require something that may interfere with maximum perceptiveness; such as recording devices, even just paper and pencil or a mnemotechnic system. It may be possible to achieve a lot by training, but there are probably limits. The training may make the interviewer so artificial as a role-partner in the interviewing situation that a reduction of p_2 and p_3 are bought at the expense of a higher p_1.

Fewer steps above all means *rational procedures,* rationalization of the data-collection and processing. The methods can be classified according to how many steps are eliminated, but we exclude the first and last steps as candidates for elimination: they are indispensable if we want respondents, and if we want processed data. Elimination of *one step* at a time leads to these simplifications:[4]

(a) *Perception eliminated* – the best example is the self-administered questionnaire, where the respondent does the recording himself. This does not mean that the recording has been eliminated, however, only that the *respondent* is asked to do the job. In a certain sense it may also be argued that perception has not been eliminated either, because the respondent has to perceive what manifests itself on his inner screen, so to speak, but that is hair-splitting.

(b) *Recording eliminated* – use of movie-cameras and tape-recorders *may* be quoted as examples, but they are actually ways of postponing the recording: they must be watched and listened to later. To skip this step is to act counter to a basic scientific dictum: always preserve raw data that have not yet been processed in any way. To proceed immediately to coding is to lose information and probably also to try to do so many things at the same time that the probability of errors will increase.

(c) *Coding eliminated* – this can be achieved by means of a self-coding questionnaire or interview-guide, where respondent or interviewer marks the responses, which are pre-coded and supplied with appropriate numbers indicating coulmns and punches. The method works well for interview-guides, but is not to be recommended for questionnaires the respondents are supposed to fill in themselves: it may look too confusing and technical. If the IBM-numbers are put down very discretely, it may still work, however.

(d) *Transfer eliminated* – this can be achieved by various means, for instance by coding questionnaires in the right hand margin, which must have been perforated in advance, and then detach it after coding for punching. The whole step can also be dropped by punching directly from the coded data, or even by punching directly from the raw data.

12 *

(e) *Punching eliminated* – this is impossible if IBM-cards are wanted, but can be achieved by means of a method which also eliminates perception, coding and transfer: the respondent is given a questionnaire on a *mark-sensing card* of the same format as an IBM card, and records his responses by means of a pencil of a special kind. The marks made are electrically conducting and can be used for immediate transfer to standard IBM-cards. The method will hardly work with all respondents, however, it may upset them emotionally or technically or both; nor does it seem that errors are completely eliminated this way. But it is quite possible that this can be developed into a practicable method.[5]

We have actually mentioned implicitly some other methods that eliminate *more than one step* at the same time. Probably, what is required is a good deal of experimentation to find the best way of getting a low factor of distortion. In most cases nothing is done to estimate the values of the individual or total p. The result is that with $p_1 = 0.2$, very small errors for the remaining six steps will suffice to bring the total probability beyond one fifth, and this is a *very* tolerant level. Thus, extreme watchfulness and inventiveness is needed to achieve a useful result; too much distortion will make conclusions drawn from the data entirely fictitious.

The points mentioned in this section are very closely linked to the ideas put forward in I, 4.4 about the amount of information obtained under various degrees of constraint. When the data collection is planned, and a certain amount of information is settled for, it is wise to keep in mind that the amount of information that finally gets through depends on the capacity of the channel of information, and one should never try to collect more information than the channel can process.

1.3. *Variable-centered and unit-centered analysis*

The data-matrix is a two-way scheme, or table, and as such immediately lends itself to two distinct kinds of analysis:

(1) *variable-centered* analysis, or *vertical* analysis. Here the columns are analyzed separately for the information they give about the corresponding variables.
(2) *unit-centered* analysis, or *horizontal* analysis. Here the rows are analyzed separately for the information they give about the corresponding units.

In addition there is a third or combined type. We shall now spell out in more detail the differences and similarities between these ways of analyzing a data-matrix.

(1) *Variable-centered analysis.* We focus on one variable at the time, say v_j. The corresponding values of the units are all comparable, according to the

principle of comparability. Hence, the column can be expressed as a *distribution,* where for each possible *value* of the variable we give the number of units that had that value on the variable. If there are r values and m units the number of possible distribution is $\binom{m + r - 1}{r - 1}$. Out of this number the data produce *one* distribution, which is the one favored by the empirical circumstances. To express in a more concentrated way the essential characteristics of the distribution we use *parameters.* This will be discussed in detail in chapter 2.

(2) *Unit-centered analysis.* We focus on one unit at the time, say O_i. The corresponding values of the different variables are not comparable, for we have no principle of horizontal comparability (we do not require that 'zero' should mean the same when it represents incidence of smallpox and when it represents degree of literacy). Hence, the row can only be expressed as a *profile* or as a *pattern,* where for each *variable* we give the value for that unit. We cannot, in general, give the horizontal distribution by counting the number of occurrences of the 'same' value – when the values are not equivalent. If there are n variables with r_1, r_2 etc. values, then the number of possible patterns is $r_1 \cdot r_2 \cdot \ldots \cdot r_n$, or r^n if the number of values should happen to be the same on all variables. Out of this number the data produce *one* pattern, which is the one favored by the empirical circumstances. To express in a more concentrated way the essential characteristics of the pattern we use *indices.* This will be discussed in detail in chapter 3.

Thus, there is a fundamental parallel between the two procedures, but also the equally fundamental difference arising from the asymmetry in comparability. Imagine now that we do both kinds of analysis. Typical outcomes would be a set of parameter values, one for each variable, and a set of index-values, one for each unit. The moment one now starts comparing these parameter-values or index-values one jumps to the third kind of analysis, where both vertical and horizontal variation is taken into account.

(3) *Combined analysis.* Here, the possibilities are many, but a general theory does not really exist. The typical *bi*variate analysis found in almost all social research today consists in analysis of *two* columns at the time, or more if the analysis is *multi*-variate. What would correspond to this if the focus were on horizontal analysis? To analyze two rows would correspond to the typical profile comparison between two individuals – as when a psychologist compares two individuals with regard to their scores on different dimensions in an intelligence test.

Thus, the combined vertical and horizontal analysis may take many forms depending on how one proceeds. For instance, one may choose to start by means of some horizontal analysis, constructing indices based on some clusters of variables. From there some vertical analysis may be used, adding the index values as new columns to the data matrix, combining them with other variables, and so on. It is customary to say that only this type of combined analysis represents analysis proper, but for reasons expressed in I, 2.3 we will not single out this as a special case.

Patterns of combined analysis will be discussed in detail in chapter 5.

2. Distributions

2.1. *Statistical distributions*

In this chapter an introduction to descriptive statistics will be given. No claim is made to cover what texts in elementary statistics usually cover; rather, an attempt will be made to tie descriptive statistics in with the general perspective of this work. This means that the point of departure as usual is a completed data matrix and the task is that of gaining some insights into its structure. In a matrix where m and n have values higher than, say, 25, this is impossible without some means of concentrating the matrix – and descriptive statistics can well be defined as the techniques of giving concentrated descriptions of data matrices. For this purpose some simple terms should be defined.

By an *experiment* we mean a part of the empirical world that can be analyzed in terms of a set of *variables* (independent and dependent) and a set of *conditions* (relevant and irrelevant) that produce an *outcome* in terms of the dependent variable. By a *replicable* experiment we mean an experiment where the independent variables and the relevant conditions can be reproduced at different points in time. It should be noted that the *panta rei*-principle applies here: if we specify completely all conditions under which a specific experiment takes place, it is hardly possible that it can ever be repeated. But an experiment is defined in terms of a limited set of conditions, and is replicable insofar as the conditions are replicable. For instance, if the conditions are specified up till 'give a respondent from the sample S a stimulus in the form of the question Q' only, the experiment is replicable till the sample is exhausted as long as Q is asked of everyone. Thus, every row, horizontal or vertical, in the data matrix represents replications of certain experiments, where either the unit or the stimulus belongs to the conditions that are kept constant.

By a *determinate experiment* we mean an experiment where the relevant conditions are specified to the point that the outcome is known when the value of the independent variable is known. Thus, replications of a determinate experiment will yield constant outcomes if the independent variable is kept constant.

By a *stochastic experiment* we mean an experiment that is not determinate, i.e. an experiment where conditions are specified below the minimum required for perfect prediction. Thus, replications of stochastic experiments will yield different outcomes, at least if the number of replications is sufficiently high. In other words, when repeated, stochastic experiments yield *at least two* values of the dependent variable, whereas determinate experiments yield *only one*. The variables describing the outcome of these two types of experiments are called determinate or stochastic variables, respectively. The *degree* to which a variable is stochastic can be measured by measuring the dispersion of the distribution of outcomes. If the dispersion is zero, the variable is determinate.

By *statistics* we mean the science of stochastic experiments. Thus, statistics is a science that cuts across the ordinary dividing lines between sciences. In statistics, general propositions about stochastic experiments are put forward. In particular, statistics is concerned with what is constant when replications yield different values. There are several degrees of constancies or more or less apparent constancies – and correspondingly, several branches of statistical theory. The mathematical theory in the science of statistics is called *mathematical statistics,* and is a branch of mathematics.

The set of all possible outcomes of a single experiment is called the *outcome space.* In the outcome-space, every outcome of one experiment can be represented as a *point.* If the stochastic variable is one-dimensional (e. g., a five-point scale) the outcome-space is a line, and the outcome is represented as a point on that line. If the variable is two-dimensional (e. g., when two dice are tossed simultaneously, or the experiment consists in tossing the same dice twice) the outcome-space will be a plane, and the outcome will be represented as a 'point-cloud' or 'scatter-diagram' in that plane, etc.

By an *event* we mean any subset in the outcome-space. In a five-point scale the event 'agreement' may consist of the two points 'strongly agree' and 'agree'. The 'smallest' event is the single point or value, if we shall not count the 'zero event' that nothing has happened.

By a *frequency of an event* we mean the number of times that event has occurred under repetitions of the stochastic experiment. By the *relative frequency* of an event we mean the frequency divided by the number of performances of the experiment – which is the same as the size of the sample in the case of a survey.

By the *distribution* of the data we mean the set of pairs $(x_i; f_i)$ where x_i is the value of the stochastic variable and f_i is the corresponding frequency, i.e. the number of times that value has occurred. Thus, the distribution is completely specified when we know what the outcome-space is like, and how many times each possible outcome has occurred.

The distribution is the first step in the analysis of the data matrix, the first concentration of data. In horizontal analysis of a survey, for instance, we may simply be interested in knowing how often a respondent has answered 'yes', how often 'no', and how often 'don't know' – the first *may* give us a measure of his general tendency to acquiesce, the second his general tendency to disagree, and the third his general tendency not to know the answer to a question (or not to know what the question is about).

The distribution can be represented in different ways, depending on the purpose: as a *table*, or as a *diagram*. If it is represented as a diagram, there are several methods:

Table 2.1.1. *The basic forms of diagram representation*

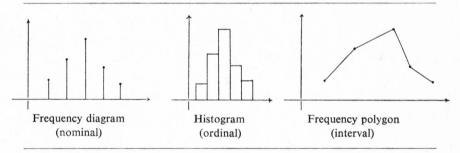

| Frequency diagram (nominal) | Histogram (ordinal) | Frequency polygon (interval) |

These forms should be chosen in accordance with the nature of the variable: the continuity of the polygon suggests a continuous variable at the interval level, the contiguity of the histogram suggests an ordinal scale, while the frequency diagram suggests a nominal level variable. Under no condition should a 'smooth' curve be fitted if it is supposed to represent an empirical distribution. The basic idea in graphic representation is to render as much of the information present in the distribution in as visible form as possible, without trying to convey more information or meaning than the data warrant. 'How to lie with graphs' would be a good title for a volume to accompany 'How to lie with statistics'.

The frequency distribution has been defined as the set of values with accompanying frequencies. From this as a basis, two other distributions may be deduced:

(1) *always*: the *relative* frequency distribution which is the set of all pairs $(x_i; f_i/N)$ where N is the size of the sample. This distribution has the ad-

vantage of being comparable with other distributions based on other sample sizes.

(2) *if the level of measurement is ordinal or above*: the *cumulative* distribution which is the set of all pairs $(x_i; F_i)$ where F_i is the frequency for x_i *and all values below* x_i. This distribution has only meaning if the word 'below' has meaning, which explains the condition given above. By dividing F_i with N, the *relative cumulative* frequency distribution can be obtained.

The three forms of diagrams are applicable to the relative frequency distribution and the cumulative frequency distribution under the same conditions as for the frequency distribution.

What has been said so far applies to distributions of *one* variable, X. If we have two variables, X and Y, the distribution is the set of pairs $[(x_i, y_j); f_{ij}]$ where (x_i, y_j) is a point in the outcome-space – which we here would have to represent by a two-dimensional plane. f_{ij} is the frequency at that point. Correspondingly, if we have n variables, the distribution is the pairing of each point in this n-dimensional outcome-space with a frequency. Again, we can divide by the size of the sample, N, and obtain the relative frequency distribution – and if the variables are both ordinal we can cumulate the (relative) frequencies and get the (relative) cumulative distribution.

For distributions with more than one variable, two special types of distributions can always be found when the multi-dimensional distribution is known:

(1) *marginal distributions*: these are distributions of one of the variables, *collapsing* the other variable(s).
(2) *conditional distributions*: these are distributions of one of the variables, *keeping constant* the other variable(s) by specifying its value.

Thus, if we have a two-dimensional distribution of one background variable (e.g. occupation in primary, secondary or tertiary sector) with one ideological variable (e.g. modernism vs. traditionalism), we get two marginal distributions (one on background, one on ideology) and five conditional distributions (one for each background variable value, and one for each ideological orientation).

Let us then give three definitions of the most important concept: *statistical independence*, in the case of two-dimensional distributions.

(1) Two variables are independent if knowledge of the value of one of them does not help us in *predicting* the value the unit has on the other variable.
(2) Two variables are independent if all *relative conditional distributions* of one variable keeping the other constant are *equal* (and equal to the relative marginal distribution of that variable).

184

(3) Two variables are independent if the relative *frequency of one pair of values is always equal to the product of the corresponding marginal, relative frequencies.*

If the variables are *not* statistically independent, then they are *dependent.*

Of these three definitions, the first one is rather imprecise, since 'help in predicting' is not defined. Nevertheless, the definition is important in linking the abstract definitions to substantive problems. If one should predict a person's height knowing only that he is a 'person', the best guess would perhaps be the average height in the population – since this is the prediction that would make for least error (in the 'least sum of squares' sense). In other words, one would have to use the marginal distribution. However, if in addition the weight is known, one could use the conditional distribution for that weight. But if the conditional distributions are the same as the marginal distribution this would not help us any – the predicted height would not be more precise. But if it is not the same and the averages are different, we would be better off using the average for the conditional distribution than for the total distribution. Thus, definitions (1) and (2) can be seen to be equivalent, if any property of the conditional distributions is relevant for the prediction. If only averages are used, then definition (2) implies definition (1) but not *vice versa,* for the averages may be equal without the conditional distributions being equal.

The equivalence of definitions (2) and (3) is well known from elementary probability calculus. Definition (3) is similar to the corresponding definition of independence in probability theory:

$$P(A \& B) = P(A) \cdot P(B)$$

If two events (boy, blue eyes) are independent, then the probability of both events is equal to the product of the probability of each of them. In relative frequencies this is translated as:

$$\frac{f_{ij}}{N} = \frac{f_i}{N} \cdot \frac{f_j}{N}$$

which is the same as:

$$f_{ij} = \frac{f_i f_j}{N}$$

Thus, we get the well-known calculation rule that when there is independence, then the frequency for any pair (x_i, y_j) can be calculated by multiplying the corresponding marginal frequencies and dividing by N, the sample size. *These are the frequencies corresponding to the case of independence.* They are often called 'theoretical frequencies', but this applies only to the situation where the theory is about independence. If we have no such theory they should rather be called 'independence frequencies' or something similar.

If the frequencies can be obtained in this way, the relative conditional distributions will have to be equal, and equal to the relative marginal distribution. Concretely, this means that we should get the same relative frequency for $Y = j$, whether the conditional distribution is given by $X = i_1$ or $X = i_2$. In other words, we have to prove that case (3) implies that

$$\frac{f_{i_1 j}}{f_{i_1}} \text{ and } \frac{f_{i_2 j}}{f_{i_2}} \text{ are equal.}$$

We insert the multiplicative expressions for $f_{i_1 j}$ and $f_{i_2 j}$, getting

$$\frac{\dfrac{f_{i_1} f_j}{N}}{f_{i_1}} \text{ and } \frac{\dfrac{f_{i_2} f_j}{N}}{f_{i_2}}$$

and they are both equal to f_j / N. Conversely, if the relative conditional distributions are equal we get the relative frequency at any point (i, j) by multiplying the corresponding relative, marginal frequencies, for $f_{ij} / f_i = f_j / N$ implies $f_{ij} = f_i f_j / N$.

The importance of these three definitions of statistical independence lies in their application as bases for the construction of various correlation coefficients (2.3).

Dependence is defined as *non-independence*. The three definitions of statistical independence give, then, three points of departure for evaluating dependence. Obviously, the more different the relative frequencies are from the product of the corresponding marginal frequencies, the more different the conditional distributions are from each other; and the better we are at predicting, the more statistically dependent are the two variables. The last idea is particularly important. If we use the value of one variable to predict the other, we may define the

regression-function of X on Y which gives for each value of X the value we predict of Y

The regression function (or 'prediction-function' or 'inference-function') does not only depend on the distribution, but also on the method of prediction. More precisely: for each value of X there is a conditional distribution on Y – which parameter do we use in this distribution as our best bet? Evidently, it will have to be some measure of central tendency. Two answers conventionally given to this problem are as follows:

if Y is interval scale: the *mean* of the conditional distribution
if Y is ordinal or nominal scale: the *mode* of the conditional distribution.

186

The median seems not to have been much used in this connection. Geometrically, this regression function will have some shape, and if it is

curved, the regression is called *curvilinear*; and the regression function, the *regression curve*

linear, the regression is called *linear*; and the regression function, the *regression line*.

For these concepts to have any meaning, they must be independent of the legitimate transformations at the level of measurement.

Obviously, this does not have any meaning if either or both of the variables are nominal – in that case, the values can be interchanged so as to produce the most different shapes of the regression function. On the other hand, it is clear that both concepts are meaningful if both variables are interval, since any legitimate (i.e. linear) transformation of the variables will not change the linear into curvilinear or the curvilinear into linear.

But what about the ordinal case? Obviously, if both variables are ordinal, only the order is constant – the numerical values can be changed; one can easily change a curvilinear relationship into a linear one, and vice versa. But this is not the practical problem, since we usually do not give numerical values to ordinal variables. Imagine one 'high-medium-low' variable is related to a 'positive-indifferent-negative' variable as in Table 2.1.2.

Table 2.1.2. *Linear vs. curvilinear correlation in the ordinal case*

	positive	indifferent	negative	positive	indifferent	negative
high	10	2	1	10	10	10
medium	2	10	1	2	3	10
low	1	2	10	1	2	10
		linear dependence			*curvilinear dependence*	

With these variables and distributions, nothing can change our judgment as to the shape of the regression function except one thing: new cuts for the values. If 'high', 'low', 'positive', and 'negative' are further divided, the shape may change drastically. But this has nothing to do with the level of measurement, and is equally true for the case of two interval variables. Hence, we conclude that the distinction between linear and curvilinear is valid for the ordinal case when the values of the variables have been chosen.

Let us then turn to the general frequency distribution of a sample of size N on an outcome-space with R points. If the outcome-space is one-dimensional, R is simply the number r of values of the variable; if it is two-dimensional,

R is equal to $r_1 \cdot r_2$ – the product of the number of values on the two variables, etc. The *distribution* now tells how the N elements distribute on the R points. This can take place in a number of different ways, known in mathematics as *the number of partitions of N in R parts*. For what we are interested in here is not *which* units are allocated to the different points, but *how many* units are allocated to which point – in other words, we distinguish between the R points but not between the N units.

Thus, if we have three units and shall distribute them in a space with $R = 2$, a simple dichotomy, we get these possible distributions or partitions of 3 in 2 parts:

$$(1) \; 3+0 = 3$$
$$(2) \; 2+1 = 3$$
$$(3) \; 1+2 = 3$$
$$(4) \; 0+3 = 3$$

To get some impression of the number of distributions for increasing N and R, this Table may serve:

Table 2.1.3. *The number of distributions of a sample of N on R points*

		size of outcome-space, R				
		1	2	3	4	5 ... 10
	0	1	1	1	1	1 .
	1	1	2	3	4	5 .
	2	1	3	6	10	15 .
size of	3	1	4	10	20	35 .
sample, N	4	1	5	15	35	70 .
	5	1	6	21	56	126 .
	.					
	10	.	.	.	.	. 92378

$$\text{General formula: } \binom{N+R-1}{R-1}$$

The number of distributions increases in both directions, not too quickly, but sufficiently to attain high levels even for only $N = R = 10$. Since N and R usually are given, the task of the social analyst is to distinguish between these distributions so that they have a bearing on the hypotheses developed. With samples running into the hundreds and outcome-spaces with thousands of points (see I, 2.3) the number of distributions becomes extremely high. Out of this variety the analyst is presented with *one,* selected for him by a combination of human and non-human nature and his own method of data-collection. The distribution to him is a means, not an end. It shall serve the purpose of understanding. To do this, a very simple and obvious principle is used: that the actual, empirical distribution should be judged against the logically possible distributions. If we assume that the data-collection is not biased, the distribution is 'nature's choice' or the 'social system's choice', depending on the kind of data we have. To evaluate this choice, we must know what *could* have been chosen. It may be that the actual distribution should only be compared with one or a class of potential distributions, and here the distributions that exhibit independence between the variables play an important and perhaps exaggerated role. The principle that a distribution is meaningless as a guide to understanding unless the empirically realized is compared with the logically possible does not imply comparison with *all* logically possible distributions, only that some kind of comparison is carried out.

One may say that this comparison is the task of data *analysis,* and that data *processing* is concerned with the problem of preparing the data matrix for the comparison. And here the most important tool is ordinary percentaging, to which we now turn.

2.2. *Frequencies and percentages*

The role of percentaging is to obtain *comparability*.[1] The idea is simply to correct for numerical inequality between categories; to obtain this, percentages are computed so that the categories can be compared as if they all had one hundred elements. Percentages do the same as relative frequencies; only the latter add up to 1, while percentages add up to 100.

When tables are presented with percentages, the numerical *bases* for the computation should always be given. It makes a great deal of difference whether the percentage is computed on the basis of 2000, 200 or 20, and it is hardly advisable to compute percentages based on figures smaller than 20. This is not to deny that 'two is fifty percent of four', only that *the law of large numbers,* which promises a certain stability of percentages and relative frequencies, is precisely a 'law of *large* numbers'. When we feel less confidence in '50%' based on 4 than '50%' based on 4000, it is because new data added, or replication of the entire data-collection, may lead to great fluctuations in the first percentage but rarely in the second, provided the relevant conditions defining the data-collection have been held constant.

A second point about percentaging lies in the presentation. It increases legibility if one makes it completely clear either how the percentages add up to 100, or that they are not meant to add up to 100. The latter can happen in many cases, for instance with multiple answers where some, but not all, respondents give more than one answer, or in cases where only the percentage in one category, e.g., the percentage of yes'es, is of interest. Some authors will also prefer to have graphic representations of the percentages in addition to the tables. If this really adds to comprehensibility it is of value, otherwise it is only a ritual (see II, 5.1).

Thirdly, how *accurately* should the percentages be computed? This must be decided on the basis of two factors: the *quality* of the data and the *purpose* for which they have been collected. Presentation of percentages with one or even two decimal places makes no sense unless:

(1) The *quality* of the collection is so good that it is meaningful to say that 70.1% and not 70.2% say 'yes', etc.
(2) The *purpose* of the data-collection is such that it makes a difference in interpretation whether 70.1% or 70.2% say 'yes', etc.

In general, we suggest that percentages should be given without any decimals, to avoid an often quite spurious impression of exactness. In most cases of sociological analysis, data are based on samples for which exact data are quite uninteresting; they are only used to yield information about trends in the 'underlying' universe. Sampling errors will make decimal places quite out of order as estimates of population figures, even if the sample size runs into a couple of thousands. And the sociological prose with which theories and insights shall be formulated is hardly so exact that it discriminates between differences in tenths of percentages. More often than not, a sociological hypothesis or theory is not even sensitive to differences in tens of percentages. In most cases, sociologists would for instance use these tables in the same way:

Table 2.2.1. *Three tables leading to same conclusion*

	males	females		males	females		males	females
yes	55%	45%	yes	75%	25%	yes	95%	5%
no	45%	55%	no	25%	75%	no	5%	95%
SUM	100%	100%	SUM	100%	100%	SUM	100%	100%
(N)	(200)	(300)	(N)	(200)	(300)	(N)	(200)	(300)

However, we should be aware of the danger in rounding off percentages. In a sample where a *two* percentage points difference is statistically significant, it should be remembered that the difference may stem from 70.50% rounded upwards and 69.49% rounded downwards; a difference of *one* percentage point. This can be corrected for by requiring a *three* percentage points difference where two would otherwise suffice, or by computing the percentages with more exactness (if this is warranted) in cases of doubt.

The main problem in connection with percentaging has to do with more fundamental matters, however. If we have a one-dimensional variable, percentaging is no problem, since there is only one meaningful basis: the sample size. With more than one variable, the situation becomes much more problematic. Looking at the case of two variables, we can illustrate our points by means of a fourfold-table:

Table 2.2.2. *Three ways of computing percentages in a fourfold-table*

	y	$\bar{y}$	
x	I a	II b	$a+b$
$\bar{x}$	III c	IV d	$c+d$
	$a+c$	$b+d$	N

Percentages with basis in	N	marginals for x	marginals for y
Cell I	$\dfrac{100a}{N}$	$\dfrac{100a}{a+b}$	$\dfrac{100a}{a+c}$
Cell II	$\dfrac{100b}{N}$	$\dfrac{100b}{a+b}$	$\dfrac{100b}{b+d}$
Comparison by means of percentage differences	$\dfrac{100(a-b)}{N}$	$\dfrac{100(a-b)}{a+b}$	$\dfrac{100(ad-bc)}{(a+c)(b+d)}$
Cell III	$\dfrac{100c}{N}$	$\dfrac{100c}{c+d}$	$\dfrac{100c}{a+c}$
Cell IV	$\dfrac{100d}{N}$	$\dfrac{100d}{c+d}$	$\dfrac{100d}{b+d}$
Comparison by means of percentage differences	$\dfrac{100(c-d)}{N}$	$\dfrac{100(c-d)}{c+d}$	$\dfrac{100(bc-ad)}{(a+c)(b+d)}$

We have given this lengthy Table to illustrate two points. First of all, *that the first two methods of percentaging are of no value in comparing all information in the two conditional distributions.*[2] This is seen most clearly for the second method, where *the percentaging is done in the same direction as the comparison* (both horizontally). The percentage differences do not take into account all the information in the Table. The expression $100(a-b)/(a+b)$ is independent of c and d, which means that it is the same regardless of how c and d vary. Essentially, this percentage difference is only a measure of the relative strength of a and b, with no regard to c and d at all.

In the first measure, c and d are taken into account in the sense that $N = a+b+c+d$. But this is of no interest: the addition of $c+d$ in the denominator will only serve to lower the percentages, and not to bring in the important fact: the relative strength of c and d, especially relative to the relative strength of a and b. Hence, we are left with the third method which can be described as follows: *always do the percentaging across the direction of comparison.* Only then can the two conditional distributions be compared.

The second point we can make is this: when the percentaging is done properly, across the direction of comparison, it is sufficient to do it for one pair of cells. If it is done for the other pair, the result will only be the same difference, with the opposite sign. This is good, because it means that the percentage difference can be used as a measure of the correlation (see II, 2.3). *But this is only true for fourfold-tables;* in a sixfold-table, for instance, there are more degrees of freedom for the frequencies, and percentage differences at the bottom can not be deduced from percentage differences at the top. *And, the percentage difference the other way in a fourfold-table will not be the same,* even when computed according to the same rule. Thus, comparison of cells I and II yields:

$$\frac{100\,(ad-bc)}{(a+c)(b+d)}$$

which is the same (except for the sign) as the difference between cells III and IV. But comparison between cells I and III yields:

$$\frac{100\,(ad-bc)}{(a+b)(c+d)}$$

The denominators are different, the difference being actually $[ab+cd-(ac+bd)]$. This difference *may* become 0 (e.g., for $a = b = c = d$), but is in general different from 0. Hence, the percentage difference is *not* symmetric with regard to basis of comparison, and should not be taken as a measure of the Table as a whole. Such a measure should rather be based on the factor in the numerator $(ad-bc)$ since it is the same regardless of direction of percentaging, and this factor reappears in most measures of the table as a whole (see next section). But the present measure is *asymmetric.*

This brings up the point that a choice must be made in most cases with regard to the direction of percentaging. Technically, it can be done in both directions as long as comparisons are done *across* the directions of percentaging, but in practice one direction is usually more interesting than the other because one variable "produces" the other, not vice versa,

The rule here is very simple: *always percentage with values of what is seen as the independent variable in the underlying model as bases.*[3] In sociological research, this means in most cases the following two things:

(1) Percentaging is done on the basis of values of indices (model I, I, 1.4).
(2) Percentaging is done on the basis of values of background variables model II, I, 1.4).

If the table is based on variables of *different* kinds in the list: *background variables – personality variables – behavioral elements* this means doing the percentaging with basis in the variable that comes first on this list. In these cases this is actually (in almost all cases) the only percentaging that makes sense, which means that there is only *one* percentage difference that becomes meaningful, and can be taken as a measure of the table (if it is fourfold only). But if the two variables defining the table are of the *same* kind, percentages can usually be computed equally well in both directions. In such cases it may be better to abstain from using percentage differences, using some other measure of covariation instead. That subject will be treated in the following section.

As an example of the role of how percentaging is done, some figures taken from a speech at the Plaza de la Revolución in Habana in September 1963 can be used. The speaker used numbers to prove that the Cuban Revolution had the support of all parts of the Cuban population, and more specifically made an analysis of the membership (said to be 1.5 million) of the 103,000 Committees for the Defence of the Revolution (CDR). The independent variable here would be social position, and the dependent would be the member/not-member dichotomy. Hence, the interesting thing would be percentages for each social category that are members, so that one could see which categories are over-represented and which are under-represented. But the data that were given were of this kind 'of the members, 35,000 are professionals, 700,000 are women, half a million are farmers, 550,000 are between 14 and 25 years old, and 750,000 are workers'. Hence, no conclusion can be drawn unless one knows the distribution of these categories in the population. Probably the most frequent error in amateur social research lies in ignoring this simple but important point.

It remains to be seen what role the direction of percentaging plays, not in terms of basic principles or the size of the percentage differences, but in terms of the conclusions that will be drawn. (To simplify, the common factor

100 has been cancelled from all percentages since it does not affect our computations.) For the case of the fourfold table this is simple enough. Imagine that we have one dichotomous background variable P and one other dichotomous variable, H:

Table 2.2.3. *A comparison of ways of percentaging: the fourfold table*

	H_1	H_2		H_1	H_2		H_1	H_2	Sum
P_1	a	b	P_1	p_{11}	p_{12}	P_1	q_{11}	q_{12}	1
P_2	c	d	P_2	p_{21}	p_{22}	P_2	q_{21}	q_{22}	1
			Sum	1	1				
	The original table			Percentaged vertically			Percentaged horizontally		

The question is whether P has an effect on H. In general, this depends on the relation between a, b, c, and d. If the hypothesis is that P_2 should produce a particularly high proportion of H_2 we would compare, as usual, across the direction of percentaging and get:

$$\text{Vertical percentaging} \qquad\qquad \text{Horizontal percentaging}$$

$$p_{22} > p_{21} \qquad\qquad\qquad q_{22} > q_{12}$$

$$\frac{d}{b+d} > \frac{c}{a+c} \qquad\qquad\qquad \frac{d}{c+d} > \frac{b}{a+b}$$

$$ad + dc > bc + dc \qquad\qquad ad + bd > bc + bd$$

$$ad - bc > 0 \qquad\qquad\qquad ad - bc > 0$$

which is the same condition. As long as we compare across the direction of percentaging (and if we do not, percentaging is of no use) we are led to the same conditions for the hypothesis to be valid for the case of the fourfold-table, regardless of what method we use.

But for the 2×3-table we are led into some interesting problems:

Table 2.2.4. *A comparison of ways of percentaging: the sixfold-table*

	H_1	H_2		H_1	H_2		H_1	H_2	Sum
P_1	a	b	P_1	p_{11}	p_{12}	P_1	q_{11}	q_{12}	1
P_2	c	d	P_2	p_{21}	p_{22}	P_2	q_{21}	q_{22}	1
P_3	e	f	P_3	p_{31}	p_{32}	P_3	q_{31}	q_{32}	1
			Sum	1	1				
	The original table			Percentaged vertically			Percentaged horizontally		

If the hypothesis is that P_3 should be particularly productive in terms of H_2, we would focus on f relative to its row or column and compare that ratio to some other ratio. If we do not require a trend $q_{12} < q_{22} < q_{32}$, we might collapse the rest of the table and form comparable ratios:

Vertical percentaging	*Horizontal percentaging*
$p_{32} > p_{31}$	$q_{32} > q_{12}$ and q_{22} collapsed
$\dfrac{f}{b+d+f} > \dfrac{e}{a+c+e}$	$\dfrac{f}{e+f} > \dfrac{b+d}{a+b+c+d}$
$f(a+c) > e(b+d)$	$f(a+c) > e(b+d)$

These are, of course, precisely the same conditions we would have obtained if we treated the table as a fourfold-table from the beginning, collapsing P_1 and P_2.

However, if P is an ordinal variable we would require more of the hypothesis; we would probably require a trend in the increase of the proportion of H_2 with increasing P from P_1 to P_3. That is, not only the formula above, but also the formula developed for the fourfold-table based on P_1, P_2, H_1, and H_2 would have to hold. In other words, we should have both:

$$ad > bc$$

and
$$f(a+c) > e(b+d)$$

which we add
$$ad+af+fc > bc+be+ed$$

and get
$$[a(d+f)+cf] - [b(c+e)+de] > 0$$

In other words, the hypothesis is valid to the extent this formula is valid. Important here is 'to the extent', because it asks: what is the maximum value possible for the expression? It is useful to think of the expression as the resultant of two 'forces': the first one pulling in the direction of the hypothesis, the second one in the opposite direction. If the two forces are equal, then the expression becomes zero, as it should; and if the second force exceeds the former, the hypothesis is not only not verified, but the opposite hypothesis will gradually gain in verification. In such cases it is always possible and even useful to 'norm' the expression by making it the numerator in a fraction where the denominator is the same expression with a plus sign:

$$\frac{[a(d+f)+cf] - [b(c+e)+de]}{[a(d+f)+cf] + [b(c+e)+de]}$$

This is Goodman-Kruskal's rightly celebrated gamma,[4] developed in a slightly new way. It can be generalized to tables of higher dimensions, but the logic is always the same: this measure of correlation is what we get when we *add* the conditions that an hypothesis of a relation between two ordinal variables shall hold *in a set of fourfold-tables* that can be formed from the original table, preserving the ordinal nature of the variables, and using proportions or percentages either way to express the conditions. Thus, gamma is really nothing more than a codification of the comparison of percentages. But it is 'weaker', since the conditions have been added together; a stronger condition would require all four-fold tables equations to hold simultaneously.

It only remains to characterize this set of fourfold-tables. The set can be conveniently described as follows. Starting with the lowest values on both variables and the direct fourfold-table found in that corner of the Table, one adds gradually more and more values of the two variables (but only for one variable at the time) and puts down the conditions for the hypothesis to be valid for the fourfold-tables arrived at this way. Finally, all these conditions are added. Thus, for the ninefold-table one gets:

Table 2.2.5. *Derivation of a measure of correlation: the ninefold-table*

	H_1	H_2	H_3	First	fourfold table	$ae > bd$
P_1	a	b	c	Second	' '	$f(a+b) > c(d+e)$
P_2	d	e	f	Third	' '	$h(a+d) > g(b+e)$
P_3	g	h	i	Fourth	' '	$i(a+b+d+e) > (g+h)(c+f)$

which by addition gives the numerator in Goodman-Kruskal's gamma.

This reasoning may be extended to give other correlation measures. Firstly, there are many other possible fourfold-tables in the ninefold-table for which conditions for *local* tenability of the hypothesis can be written down: why not include them? And secondly, why use addition, why not some other operation that preserves the inequalities, such as multiplication? The answer to both suggestions, after some experimentation, is that gamma is probably the simpler of these measures – but more research should be done on this.

Let us then return to the original line of reasoning: the role of the direction of percentaging for testing hypotheses. We have seen that it does not matter for the fourfold-table, nor for the 2×3 table, if it is treated as a fourfold-table. In general, direction of percentaging plays no role for any table treated as a set of fourfold-tables. But if we do not treat more complex tables as fourfold-tables, what then? For instance, if the hypothesis is 'increasing H with increasing P', does it or does it not matter which way we percentage in a ninefold-table? Using the letters in the Table above, this clearly refers to the question of comparing:

196

Vertical percentaging:

$$\frac{g}{a+d+g} < \frac{h}{b+e+h} < \frac{i}{c+f+i}$$

with

Horizontal percentaging:

$$\frac{c}{a+b+c} < \frac{f}{d+e+f} < \frac{i}{g+h+i}$$

Since the only constraint on the nine figures is that they add up to N there is no reason why the two sets of inequalities should, in general, imply each other. Another thing is that tables often lead to the same results because of the correlation present. But this cannot be counted on, so there is no way to avoid careful reasoning when selecting direction of percentaging.

One may object that looking at one row or one column of percentages is a poor way of analyzing a table in any case, since it only takes directly into account a portion of the data. In practice it will rarely be done this way either; the analyst will also look at the rows for P_1 and P_2 (or the columns for H_1 and H_2). If the row for P_3 shows a trend there must by necessity be a countertrend, since the percentages shall add up to 100 vertically – and the analyst will want to know whether the counter-trend is in the first or second row, or split between the two. Thus, the entire table is taken into account.

So far we have assumed that we are dealing with one sample that is representative of some universe, and have shown that we get the best picture of the relationship between the variables if we percentage using the values of the independent variable as a basis. We now take the case that we do not have one but several samples, or, in other words, that our sample is stratified. If the stratification is proportionate there is no difficulty, but if it is disproportionate a problem arises. If the sampling is done using the independent variable as a basis, percentaging can be done as usual and the special type of sampling will only be advantageous since the purpose usually is to avoid too small bases for percentaging. But if the sampling has used a dependent variable as a criterion, percentaging will produce strange results reflecting the relative proportion of the strata. Thus, a sample to study the relationship between age and position in an organization can be stratified on age or on position. Since most theoretical models would see age as producing position and not vice versa, stratification should be based on age since percentaging will have to be carried out with age as a basis. As has been shown above the conclusions will not necessarily be different, at least not for 2×2 tables, but the tables look strange and become more difficult to interpret. Thus, the percentage differences used as a basis for

Weber's famous theory about the protestant ethic and the spirit of capitalism become less impressive if the percentaging is carried out correctly (e. g., with a basis in religious affiliation and not in type of school attended or type of tax paid).[5]

We then turn to a more critical analysis of the use of percentage differences, this time presenting some reasons for *not* using them. The difficulty with percentage differences as measures of correlation does not appear when only one difference is computed, but when percentage differences are compared. Compare these three tables:

Table 2.2.6. *Comparison of percentage differences*

Table I				Table II				Table III			
	+	−	SUM		+	−	SUM		+	−	SUM
High	95	5	100	High	55	45	100	High	15	85	100
Low	85	15	100	Low	45	55	100	Low	5	95	100
Diff.	10	−10	0	Diff.	10	−10	0	Diff.	10	−10	0

'High' and 'low' may stand for class, ' + ' and ' − ' may stand for positive vs. negative attitudes to three *new* foreign policy measures. Since the tables have to do with the acceptance of something new, we have consistently given the highest percentages to the 'high' group, and the percentaging is, of course, in the direction of the background variable. The percentage *differences* are all the same, yet it seems improper to classify the tables as showing the same degree of *differential* in acceptance.

In all cases the percentage differences tell us that in the group of 'high's' the percentages are ten points higher than in the group of 'low's' – but in table I this means 19/17 or about 1.12 as many among the high's, in table II there are about 1.22 as many among the high's, but in table III there are 3 times as many among the high's as among the low's. Although the absolute acceptance is much lower in table III, the relative acceptance is undoubtedly much higher among the high's there. If percentages are measures of acceptance at all (it may be objected that they have built-in the 'democratic bias' in methodology, that everybody counts equally), then there is little doubt that foreign policy measure no. III has been more readily accepted among the highs, whereas the other two are more similar. Both causally and consequentially table III seems to indicate more acceptance, relatively speaking, and this becomes clear if we use the percentage *ratio* instead of the percentage *difference*.

198

What, then, would be the best measure if the table has the general form:

$$\begin{array}{lccc} & + & - & \text{SUM} \\ \text{High} & a & c & 100 \\ \text{Low} & b & d & 100 \end{array}$$

where a, b, c and d are percentages? If $a-b$ has serious shortcomings what should we use instead of it? What would we accept as equal differentials between percentages if differences are unacceptable?

To get a better perspective, let us see in detail how $a-b$ behaves:

Table 2.2.7. *The absolute percentage difference $(a-b)$ as a measure of correlation*

$a\backslash b$	0 %	10 %	20 %	30 %	40 %	50 %	60 %	70 %	80 %	90 %	100 %
0 %	0	-10	-20	-30	-40	-50	-60	-70	-80	-90	-100
10 %	10	0	-10	-20	-30	-40	-50	-60	-70	-80	-90
20 %	20	10	0	-10	-20	-30	-40	-50	-60	-70	-80
30 %	30	20	10	0	-10	-20	-30	-40	-50	-60	-70
40 %	40	30	20	10	0	-10	-20	-30	-40	-50	-60
50 %	50	40	30	20	10	0	-10	-20	-30	-40	-50
60 %	60	50	40	30	20	10	0	-10	-20	-30	-40
70 %	70	60	50	40	30	20	10	0	-10	-20	-30
80 %	80	70	60	50	40	30	20	10	0	-10	-20
90 %	90	80	70	60	50	40	30	20	10	0	-10
100 %	100	90	80	70	60	50	40	30	20	10	0

Characteristic here is the linearity of the *iso-differential curves:* they are, in fact, all parallel to the main diagonal. But if we follow the reasoning based on Table 2.2.6 the differential should depend on the marginals, or – in other words – on where the percentages are located; but the percentage difference does not take this into account at all.

What about the *statistical significance* of percentage differences? In this case the iso-differential curves are neither linear, nor parallel. This is seen when we compare the two functions for:

iso-percentage difference

$$p_1 - p_2 = k$$

iso-significance for percentage difference

$$\frac{p_1 - p_2}{\sqrt{\dfrac{n_1 p_1 + n_2 p_2}{n_1 n_2} \left(1 - \dfrac{n_1 p_1 + n_2 p_2}{n_1 + n_2}\right)}} = k$$

The first is linear with slope 1 as shown in Table 2.2.7, and the second is a curve of the second degree, which intersects the main diagonal at its two extremes. And the question that can now, perhaps, be decided on an intuitive basis is *which class of iso-differential curves we want.* Below are given four types:

Table 2.2.8. *Some major types of iso-differential curves*

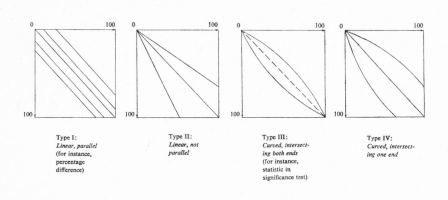

Type I:	Type II:	Type III:	Type IV:
Linear, parallel (for instance, percentage difference)	*Linear, not parallel*	*Curved, intersecting both ends* (for instance, statistic in significance test)	*Curved, intersecting one end*

Since we do not accept percentage differences as measures of the differentials, we must make a choice between the other three. Evidently, type III must also be excluded. It would make no sense to require smaller differences closer to the top of the percentage scale, since this is precisely where small differences have least impact. The choice is between types II and IV, where ''pe II might be preferred for the simple reason that it is linear and hence more intuitive. To get the type II case we need a function F of a and b which is constructed in such a way that $F = k$ defines a linear relation between a and b. We would also require F itself to be a *simple* function of a and b.

Since F is a measure of correlation, it is customary to require that it shall be *normed,* which means that it shall satisfy some requirements such as being zero when there is no correlation, $+1$ when there is a maximum of positive correlation, and -1 when there is a maximum of negative correlation. The first is obviously the case when $a = b$, the second when b is zero, and the third when a is zero (but in the last two cases it may also be required that the other two percentages equal 100). Another trivial requirement would be that it be *defined* (which in practice means not having a zero in the denominator) for all pairs (a, b) – except, possibly, for the pair $(0, 0)$ which means

200

that the category is empty. But the most important criteria are of another nature, and they become clear if we study the percentage ratio more closely.

Let us start with the two critical questions: Are we always willing to accept as *similar* tables with the same percentage ratio? Are we always willing to accept the *ordering* the percentage ratio induces? We have applied the *similarity criterion* to the percentage difference and found it wanting. Likewise, if we apply the *ordering criterion* to the percentage differences 95-65, 45-25 and 15-5 we find that they order the tables in that succession (differences 30, 20 and 10), whereas percentage ratios would order them in the *opposite* way (ratio 1.46, 1.8 and 3). Without necessarily accepting either, there is much to be said for the latter and little in favor of the former, except simplicity. It is arithmetically convenient, but may still be socially meaningless, perhaps even harmful, for the last difference may mean much more – there are three times as many people to propagate new ideas, for instance.

Let us now examine some more percentage ratios. Are we willing to accept these as similar: $100:50$, $40:20$ and $2:1$? The ratio is the same, so the 'differential in impact potential' is similar if we are interested in that phenomenon. It may be objected that this measure does not take into account the fact that 100%, *everybody*, is for at one place, or the fact that almost *nobody* was for (2%, 1%) at some other places in the tables, but neither does the percentage difference. Actually, this is completely outside the scope of a correlation measure; its role is to measure covariation. However, it may be objected that the percentage ratio is too sensitive to even small changes when it is based on very low percentages – provided the data are sampled and the sample is not very big. But this is a problem of sampling reliability, and may lead to the rejection of the measure for very small percentages.

However, there is also another way out, a way of getting the best of both worlds. Percentage differences are less sensitive to changes in the data, and if we introduce this *stability criterion* in addition to the other two, we get a new constraint on our choice. Percentage differences are relatively stable, but according to what we said they must somehow be evaluated relative to *where* on the percentage scale from 0% to 100% the difference is located. The problem is how to measure this 'where', and here there are three possibilities based on the higher of the two percentages, the lower of the two, or on both. The latter seems most reasonable in order to introduce symmetry in the measure. One possibility would be to use the average, $\frac{1}{2}(a+b)$, but the simple sum $a+b$ has the advantage that the measure $(a-b)/(a+b)$ is well normed and can be calculated for (almost) all values of a and b.

Let us now compare all measures suggested, relative to the six criteria mentioned:

Table 2.2.9. *A comparison of percentage measures of correlation criteria*

measure	simplicity	norm	defined for whole range	similarity	ordering	stability
$a-b$	+	−	+	−	−	+
a/b	+	−	− (not for $b = 0$)	+	+	−
$(a-b)/a$	−	+	− (not for $a = 0$)	+	+	+
$(a-b)/(a+b)$	−	+	+ (except $a = b = 0$)	+	+	+

We decide in favor of the latter to the extent we feel it orders the tables the way we want them ordered and defines tables as similar when they look similar for our purpose, and because of the other built-in properties. It is not so simple as the others, but a table can easily be made. The behavior of the measure can actually be seen from Table 2.2.10 below, which is a simplified version giving every tenth percentage only:

Table 2.2.10. *The relative percentage difference as a measure of correlation*

$a\backslash b$	0 %	10 %	20 %	30 %	40 %	50 %	60 %	70 %	80 %	90 %	100 %
0 %	?	−1	−1	−1	−1	−1	−1	−1	−1	−1	−1
10 %	1	0	−.33	−.50	−.60	−.66	−.71	−.75	−.78	−.80	−.82
20 %	1	.33	0	−.20	−.33	−.43	−.50	−.56	−.60	−.64	−.66
30 %	1	.50	.20	0	−.14	−.25	−.33	−.40	−.45	−.50	−.54
40 %	1	.60	.33	.14	0	−.11	−.20	−.28	−.33	−.38	−.43
50 %	1	.66	.43	.25	.11	0	−.09	−.17	−.23	−.29	−.33
60 %	1	.71	.50	.33	.20	.09	0	−.08	−.14	−.20	−.25
70 %	1	.75	.56	.40	.28	.17	.08	0	−.07	−.12	−.18
80 %	1	.78	.60	.45	.33	.23	.14	.07	0	−.06	−.11
90 %	1	.80	.64	.50	.38	.29	.20	.12	.06	0	−.05
100 %	1	.82	.66	.54	.43	.33	.25	.18	.11	.05	0

In this way we have achieved what we initially wanted: a measure that runs from −1 through 0 to +1, is relatively stable, and takes into account what we wanted, viz., the dependence of the difference on the marginals. As can be seen from the Table, the iso-differentials are linear, which is obvious since their equations are $a = (1+k)/(1-k)b$, and as we wanted of type II in Table 2.2.8.

But still, there is a feeling of arbitrariness. Let us control that the measure selected not only satisfies our more intuitive criteria of similarity and ordering, but also satisfies them in the same way as such simple competitors as, the measures a/b and $(a-b)/a$:

Table 2.2.11. *The relation between the measures*
a/b, $(a-b)/a$, $(a-b)/(a+b)$

control measures \ measures	$\dfrac{a}{b} = k, a > b$	$\dfrac{a-b}{a} = 1 - \dfrac{b}{a} = k, a > b$
range for k	$k > 0$	$0 < k < 1$
to express $\dfrac{a-b}{a+b}$ in terms of k we change it a little	$\dfrac{\dfrac{a}{b} - 1}{\dfrac{a}{b} + 1}$	$\dfrac{a-b}{1 + \dfrac{b}{a}}$
and then we substitute k	$\dfrac{k-1}{k+1}$	$\dfrac{k}{2-k}$
which can be written	$1 - \dfrac{2}{k+1}$	$\dfrac{2}{2-k} - 1$
and then we find the derivative (to test whether the function is monotone)	$\dfrac{2}{(k+1)^2} > 0$	$\dfrac{2}{(2-k)^2} > 0$

From this Table two important findings emerge. First of all $(a-b)/(a+b)$ can be expressed as a function of k alone, both when $k = a/b$ and when $k = (a-b)/(a)$, which means that it is constant when k is constant and changes when k changes – which in turn means that *the three measures define the same tables as similar*. Secondly, as can be seen from the last or next to the last lines, when k increases, so does $(a-b)/(a+b)$ – within the range for k. This means that the two measures order the tables in the same way as our selected measure does (this also applies to the other two measures between themselves). In fact, if a/b equals k, then $(a-b)/a$ equals $1-1/k$ and $(a-b)/(a+b)$ equals $1-2/(k+1)$, and they are all increasing together, constant together, and decreasing together, regardless of the absolute sizes of a and b. Since we are not interested in the absolute values of our measure but only in a way of ordering tables, this concludes the investigation of similarity and ordering properties.

It should be noticed, however, that what we have done here does not really answer the question of *validity*. What we have shown is only that the three measures classify and order the tables *in the same way*, which is a kind of inter-measure reliability. We have not shown in any concrete instance that this way of classifying and ordering is more fruitful than what can be obtained by other means, such as for instance the percentage difference. But we have argued in favor of such a position by means of one simple line of thought: if we compare social categories in terms of their differences with regard to an attribute, then the *relative* difference should count more than the *absolute* difference. For the relative difference, expressed as a/b, tells us how much more probable it is to find a person with the attribute in the first category than in the second category, whereas the absolute difference only says how many more there are in the first category. There may be cases where the latter is sociologically more relevant; but if one is relating, for instance, values to social background data and one is interested in evaluating the impact of the difference, then the relative measure seems much better. If the groups or categories are of sizes N_1 and N_2 and x_1 and x_2 have the attributes, we might expect the impact of the attribute to be proportional to x_1/N_1 and to x_2/N_2:

$$I_1 = k_1 \cdot x_1/N_1 \quad I_2 = k_2 \cdot x_2/N_2$$

If x_1 or x_2 is zero, there can be no impact; hence, there is no constant to be added to these expressions. Imagine now that we want to compare the two impacts. Would we use $I_1 - I_2$ or I_1/I_2? There are good reasons to choose I_1/I_2, since there is a zero-point and hence the conditions for a ratio scale. If the groups are so similar that we feel we can set k_1 equal to k_2 the ratio of the impacts would be the ratio of the percentages, and we can say that 'the impact is twice as great' in the first as in the second category if we have 20% in the former and 10% in the latter.

We offer this not so much as a concrete suggestion that social scientists use percentage ratios instead of percentage differences, as an indication of the kind of methodology that is useful when measures shall be introduced. It is common-sense to say that measures should be selected according to their substantive usefulness and not according to tradition or computational ease, but in practice the choice may depend on rather complex reasoning.

2.3. *Parameters*

As this subject is treated in every textbook on elementary statistics, we shall only give it a very cursory treatment, pointing out what to us seems to be essential, bringing together what is often kept apart by different textbook traditions.

Parameters are numerical characteristics of statistical distributions. Their function is to give, in a concentrated way, an expression of what the distribution is like. Preferably, they should be simple to calculate, and meaningful, easy to interpret. But this is not always easily obtained. Two factors must be pointed out.

Firstly, it should be noticed that one parameter cannot and should not characterize all aspects of a statistical distribution at the same time. A statistical distribution for income may be centered around N.kr. 20,000 or N.kr. 50,000 depending on whether one is examining a sample of fishermen or a sample of professionals; it may be very closely located around the value N.kr. 30,000 or have a distribution which goes far above and far below depending on whether one is studying high-school teachers or business men. In other words, aspects of general interest of statistical distributions must be defined, and this Table gives an idea of the distribution properties most frequently used:

Table 2.3.1. *Properties of statistical distributions*

	Frequently used	Less frequently used
One-dimensional variables	*Central tendency* *Dispersion*	*Skewness* *Kurtosis*
Two-dimensional variables	*Covariation*	*Agreement*

'Central tendency' is the value of the variable which the stochastic experiment somehow seems to favor; 'dispersion' is the tendency the experiment has to give values that are far from what seems to be the central tendency; skewness is the tendency of the experiment to yield values that do not distribute themselves symmetrically around the central tendency; and 'kurtosis' has to do with whether the distribution is more or less peaked than the normal distribution.

For two-dimensional variables, there are two properties of interest: 'covariation', which is the extent to which knowledge of the value on one of the variables increases one's ability to predict the value of the other variable; and 'agreement', which is the extent to which knowledge of the value on one of the variables increases one's ability to predict, not only the value of the other variable, but that the other variable takes on exactly the same value ('agreement' has only meaning when the two variables are the same). Thus, when there is much 'agreement' there is also much 'covariation', but not vice versa as can be seen from these two Figures:

Figure 2.3.2. *An illustration of the difference between covariation and agreement*

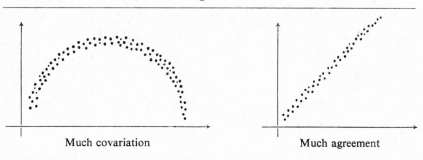

Much covariation   Much agreement

In an analysis where statistical data are used, one must make sure that these frequently used aspects of distributions really correspond to what one wants to examine. For instance, imagine the distribution has to do with some property of iron bars. If we want *one* number that can characterize, in a general way, the *quality* of a batch of bars, some measure of central tendency seems to be a good choice. But it is not entirely obvious; it may well be argued that the upper or lower extremes are better measures, the upper because it indicates the heights the production can achieve, the lower because it gives a warning about what may happen. The latter two are very optimistic or very pessimistic measures, respectively, whereas the central tendency may be a more realistic one.

Correspondingly, if a measure of *standardization* is wanted, it seems reasonable to use a measure of dispersion to get at how much variety there is in the production. But this does not determine the measure unambiguously: the necessity for *some* measure of central tendency and *some* measure of dispersion does not by itself lead to an exact *formula*. Further, one must never be so hypnotized by these old war-horses in statistics and social analysis as to believe that there cannot be other aspects of distributions worthy of a parameter or two. Just to mention one example: it may be argued that production cannot be evaluated in terms of quality or standardization alone; both are needed to give a fair picture. High central tendency obtained at the expense of much dispersion will not satisfy the customers. Hence, it may be said that a valid measure must be some monotone function of the average quality, Q, and the degree of standardization, S^{-1} (S being a measure of dispersion.) In other words:

$$M = f(Q, S^{-1}) \text{ (for instance } M = QS^{-1})$$

where M never decreases when Q and S^{-1} increase. It should be emphasized that our speculations do not lead to the last formula, only to the first one. The latter may be a good choice and it may not, that is a question of validation.

Secondly, a good parameter should make use of as much of the information contained in the statistical distribution as possible. Since its function is to concentrate and in a simple way, it is obvious that something must get lost; but the more information the parameter can give, the better. Since a distribution is defined as a set of pairs of values and frequencies, the problem is to utilize as much as possible. This brings in the question of *what the values stand for,* which again is a question of what level of measurement the variable is located on. If we want to calculate the central tendency of a distribution defined as:

$$(1; 5), \ (2; 10), \ (3; 15), \ (4; 20), \ (5; 5)$$

it must make some difference whether the values 1, 2, 3, 4, and 5 refer to a nominal, ordinal, or interval scale.

If we now combine the two criteria of *aspect* on the one hand and what the values stand for, i.e. *level of measurement* on the other, we get the following chart (Table 2.3.3, p. 208). It might be objected that more can be added, but since most of the coefficients in the chart already have severe disadvantages it would be better to look critically at them first. This can only be done by developing criteria for the evaluation of parameters, i.e. for the mapping of a set of distributions on a one-dimensional continuum.

It is easy to list a number of such criteria for picking a parameter, less easy to justify all of them theoretically, and least easy to develop parameters in agreement with all these principles. We shall give the criteria in two groups, relating to parameters in general, and to the problem of measuring correlation in particular. (Six of these $10+6$ criteria have already been used in the discussion in II, 2.2, see Table 2.2.9.)

I. *Criteria for parameters in general*

(1) *The parameter should be defined for all possible distributions.* In other words, for all distributions with the characteristic (m, n, r) there shall be one and only one value of the parameter. Mathematically this usually means that parameters with denominators that can take on the value 0 should

Table 2.3.3. *A classification of parameters*

	Nominal	Ordinal	Interval
Central tendency	Mode	Median	Mean
Dispersion	% in the mode 'information', H	Percentile differences $Q = P_{75} - P_{25}$ Gini index	Standard deviation Variance Gini index
Co-variation	Goodman-Kruskal's lambda Chi-square and its derivatives φ coefficient Yule's Q Percentage differences	Spearman's rho Kendall's tau Goodman-Kruskal's gamma Somers' d_{yx} Yule's Q Percentage differences	Correlation ratio Correlation coefficient Point biserial coefficient Biserial coefficient Phi coefficient Tetrachoric coefficient
Agreement	Scott's measure	Kendall's tau	Robinson's measure

not be used (e.g. the ratio between two percentages). Parameters like the median and the mode can also present difficulties, the latter, for instance, in uniform (rectangular) distributions.

(2) *The parameter should give as much information as possible.* This does not mean that all information, i.e. *everything* about the distribution, should be reflected in the parameter, for that would be contrary to its function; nor does it mean that the value of the parameter shall be sensitive to any small change in the distribution – only that the whole distribution is needed to get the value of the parameter. A parameter based on one half of the sample would not do, in general.

(3) *The parameter should be stable.* Although the parameter should be sensitive in the sense of changing values with changes in the distribution, it should not be sensitive to small changes, such as the transfer of one unit from one cell to an other.

(4) *The parameter should be simple.* Obviously, if the choice is between different parameters satisfying the same criteria, the simpler one, i.e. the one that can be computed most quickly, should be preferred. Today 'simplicity' would have to be defined relative to desk calculators, electronic calculators, etc., as well as relative to the human brain.

(5) *The parameter should depend on the number of variables in the distribution.* By this we mean simply that parameters must be picked according to whether the distribution is one-dimensional, two-dimensional, etc. This is logically trivial but not empirically so, since one can still find in the

literature 'analyses' made of two-dimensional distributions by means of means and variances of the marginal distributions.

(6) *The parameter should permit comparisons.* The idea of the parameter is to evaluate a distribution with regard to some aspect in order to know where the distribution stands relative to other distributions. The least we can require is comparability with regard to other distributions with the same N and r – this is actually covered by the first point above. We add these requirements:

(a) *The parameter should be 'N-free' – independent of number of unit.* This does not mean that N may not enter in the formula, but may for instance be interpreted to mean that if all frequencies in the distribution are doubled then the parameter should remain about the same. The function of this requirement is to permit comparisons between distributions involving different numbers of units.

(b) *The parameter should be 'r-free' – independent of number of values.* This does not mean that r may not enter in the formula, but may, for instance, be interpreted to mean that if all pairs of adjacent values are collapsed, the parameter should remain about the same. This permits comparisons between distributions involving different numbers of values of the variable(s).

(7) *The parameter should be independent of legitimate transformations of the values of the variable(s).* By 'legitimate' we mean 'legitimate' at the level of measurement intended. Thus, the mode will have to be independent of any permutations of the values; the traditional correlation coefficient will have to be independent of any linear transformation of the variables, etc. If this invariance, required at the intended level of measurement is absent, the parameter may vary much in value depending on which set of permissible values we have chosen to express the measurement. A parameter should always be examined for the kind of transformation of the values it permits, and be assigned to the

interval level – if it permits only linear transformations,
ordinal level – if it permits monotone transformations, and
nominal level – if it permits any permutation.

If the parameter is based on distributions of more than one variable, the lowest level variable determines what is permissible. But what is valid at a lower level of measurement is also valid for the higher level(s).

(8) *The parameter should have a known sampling distribution*, to permit testing of generalization hypotheses. The danger with this criterion is that it may impede the development of parameters that do not have the classical distributions (normal, t, chi-square, F) but may be far better on other criteria in this list. On the other hand, this requirement is as valid as the requirement of checking findings for generalizability in general. Often it leads to mathematically quite difficult work, as when it took Goodman-Kruskal almost ten years between the first publication of their important coefficient gamma and the publication of the sampling distribution. It is obvious that the ideal is to know the sampling distribution for all values of the universe parameter, but knowledge for especially important values (such as zero correlation in the universe) comes as a good second best.

(9) *The parameter should be valid as a measure.* The parameter measures a property of the elements in the set of distributions. In most cases (except mode, median and percentile ranges), the parameter is expressed as a figure, and in all cases, by definition, as a value. The set of possible distributions gives rise to a set of possible parameter values, and the structure of this set should be *examined for its measurement properties.*

Thus, parameters may be equal or different; greater or smaller than each other; or the difference between two parameters may be smaller, equal to, or greater than the difference between two other parameters, etc. This is obvious to the extent parameters are numbers. The question is whether the numerical structure of the set of possible parameters can be interpreted in the set of possible distributions. In other words, *when we use the numbers to decide that the*

> *parameters are equal or different* – do we accept that the corresponding distributions are equivalent or not equivalent for our purpose?

> *parameters can be strongly ordered* – do we accept that the corresponding distributions can be ordered the same way, for our purpose?

> *differences between pairs of parameters are equal* – do we accept that the differences between the corresponding distributions are equal?

That is to say, the question of validity is the question of whether the parameters *classify the distributions* (nominal scale), *order the distributions* (ordinal scale), or *measure the distributions* (interval scale). The last is perhaps neither necessary nor attainable, but the parameters should be valid at the ordinal level. In many cases, however, parameters are used although they do not even classify the distributions as one would want them to. Per capita income (a special name for arithmetic mean) is a good example, where a highly *U*-shaped and a highly *A*-shaped income distribution may be classified as 'equivalent' because the means happen to be the same. Whether this is acceptable can only be decided on the basis of substantive theory.

(10) *The parameter should be interpretable.* The parameter should have a 'meaning' over and above being a measure of 'central tendency', etc. Two meanings have been given to the question of 'meaning' here: the statistical and the substantive. Thus, the measures called 'variance' and 'product-moment correlation coefficient' are based on such mathematical entities as sums of squares; and arithmetic means and regression curves are justified because they 'minimize sums of squares'. However interesting and useful such properties are mathematically, they do not by themselves add to social science insight unless the sums of squares can be given a direct social science interpretation – which so far has not been done.

The ideal from a social science point of view would be a measure that appeared as a parameter in a mathematical model, as a 'coefficient of cohesion', 'index of criss-cross', 'degree of equilibration in status-set', etc., and then was used to characterize distributions. This has so far only been done to a very limited extent. The tendency is to use the parameters that can be given an interpretation on a statistical-mathematical basis, without requiring a substantive interpretation as well; detached from social theory.

II. *Criteria for parameters measuring covariation and agreement*

(1) *The parameter should be zero when the variables are independent.*

(a) *Condition sufficient.* The parameter should be zero only if the variables are independent. The value 0 is meaningful when the parameter is seen as a measure of dependence, since it means 'zero dependence'.

(b) *Condition necessary.* The parameter should be zero only if the variables are independent – and under no other condition. Since independence is unambiguously defined, this together with condition (a) would make the zero-value a *criterion* of independence.

(2) *The parameter should be maximum when the variables are maximally dependent.*

(a) *Condition sufficient.* The parameter should be maximum if the variables are maximally dependent.

(b) *Condition necessary.* The parameter should be maximum only if the variables are maximally dependent. If both (a) and (b) are satisfied the parameter can be used as a criterion of maximal dependence.

This condition is less strict than condition (1) above, since maximum dependence is less well defined. One may use the criterion as a definition and say 'maximum dependence is found in the distribution that yields maximum value of the parameter'. However, one may also use the prediction criterion for defining independence and say that 'two variables are maximally dependent when knowledge of the value of one of them enables us to predict with certainty the value of the other variable'. The difficulty is that only two-dimensional distributions with the same number of values on each variable can ever attain maximum dependence. For, e.g., with $r_1 = 3$ and $r_2 = 2$ we get distributions like this

Y_1	0	0	c
Y_2	d	e	0
	X_1	X_2	X_3

where we can predict unambiguously from all X-values but not from Y_2.

(3) *The parameter should tell the direction of dependence.* Direction of dependence has no meaning unless both variables are at least ordinal, but there is no condition on the number of values. Both variables must permit a consensual definition of what constitutes a 'higher' value and what constitutes a 'lower' value, since positive (negative) dependence is defined as the general tendency for the other variable to increase (decrease) when the first variable increases. Thus, there will be no difficulty in deciding on the direction of dependence if degrees of time perspective and space perspective are compared. It is more difficult if time perspective is related to an ideological variable where the values are 'traditional', 'medium', 'modern', unless there is a consensus on the direction of this variable, too. Conventionally,

the parameter is given a positive value if the dependence is positive, and a negative value if the dependence is negative.

(4) *The parameter should be normed.* Usually, the parameter is normed so that it is bound to vary in the range -1 to $+1$, these extreme values representing maximum negative and positive dependence respectively. The function of this requirement is to permit comparisons between distributions involving different maximum values of the parameters.

If the parameter varies from $P_{ind} = 0$ to P_{max}, comparability is obtained simply by using as a new parameter

$$P^* = P/P_{max}.$$

Here $P^* = 0.8$ means that the parameter is 80% of the maximum value, etc. If P_{ind} is different from 0 one has to take care of that too. The technique generally used is to define a linear transformation

$$P^* = aP + b$$

so that these two conditions are satisfied

$$P = P_{ind} \rightarrow P^* = 0$$
$$P = P_{max} \rightarrow P^* = 1$$

which leads to the equations

$$aP_{ind} + b = 0$$
$$aP_{max} + b = 1$$

and to the expression

$$P^* = \frac{P - P_{ind}}{P_{max} - P_{ind}}$$

which is easily seen to range within the unit interval. The expression can be supplied with $+$ or $-$, depending on whether inspection of the distribution leads us to conclude that the dependence is positive or negative. The expression measures the excess of the parameter over its independence value relative to the maximum excess possible. Since the zero point is fixed here, we actually give the parameter the structure of a ratio scale.

Often, however, we may want the parameter to vary from -1 when P has a value P_{min} to $+1$ if it has the value P_{max}. This gives another system of equations:

$$P^{**} = aP + b$$
$$P = P_{max} \rightarrow P^{**} = +1 \quad aP_{max} + b = +1$$
$$P = P_{min} \rightarrow P^{**} = -1 \quad aP_{min} + b = -1$$

and we get

$$P^{**} = 1 - 2\frac{P_{max} - P}{P_{max} - P_{min}}.$$

Ideally, we should also have $P^{**}_{ind} = 0$, but this presupposes that $P_{ind} = \frac{1}{2}(P_{min} + P_{max})$, which is usually, but not necessarlily, the case.

(5) *The parameter should be asymmetric if necessary.* In general one wants the parameter to be symmetric in the sense of treating the two variables symmetrically. Since *independence* is a symmetric relation (if X is indepen-

dent of Y then Y is independent of X), this is usually the best way of looking at a correlation coefficient. But if we use the prediction definition of dependence, we have seen that it may be possible to predict unambiguously in one direction but not in the other. Coefficients based on this definition should be asymmetric, reflecting the difference in predictive power of one variable with regard to the other. And in general, if the variables are of different class (I, 1.4), a symmetric measure may be out of order.

(6) *The parameter should be sensitive to the difference between linear and curvilinear dependence, if necessary.* This leads to two kinds of correlation coefficients, one that can take on maximum value for any reasonable kind of regression function, and one that can only take on maximum value if the regression function is linear. It would not make much sense to have a correlation measure that could only take on maximum value for curvilinear regression. Thus, one has measures of general dependence, and measures of linear dependence, but this distinction has no meaning if one or both of the variables is nominal.

This concludes the list. We now proceed to a discussion of the parameters currently found in the light of these criteria. This will mainly be a discussion of the correlation coefficients. While the other parameters are found in any textbook, the literature on correlation useful for the social scientist is very scattered.

In passing, only a few comments on percentages and the nominal measures of *dispersion*. It is highly trivial but easily forgotten that a percentage represents nothing new as a parameter; it is an arithmetic mean based on a dichotomy (those elements that have and those that do not have a given attribute) where the values are called 0 and 1, and then multiplied by 100.

Finding a nominal measure of dispersion long troubled analysts, but the problem is actually easily solved. Since the values of the variables can be permuted in any way the values as such cannot serve as a basis. What is invariant is only the relative size of the frequencies, so a measure must be based on that. Obviously, the dispersion is minimum (concentration maximum) when all units have the same value, and the dispersion is maximum (concentration minimum) when the units are uniformly distributed. A very simple measure is as follows:

$$d = \frac{1 - p_M}{1 - \dfrac{1}{r}} = \frac{r - r p_M}{r - 1}$$

where r is the number of values and p_M is the modal proportion. Since the minimum of p_M is $1/r$ – in the case of the uniform distribution – the measure attains unity in that case (and only in that case) and is 0 when all units are concentrated on one value ($p_M = 1$). The measure tells what is missing in modal concentration relative to the maximum possible.

The measure is not ideal, since it is not sensitive to the other values; it only compares the mode with the rest. A measure suggested here is the measure of *information* in information theory:

$$H = - \sum_{i=1}^{r} p_i \log_2 p_i$$

It is 0 if all units are concentrated on one value (for $\log_2 1 = 0$). For the case of the uniform distribution we get:

$$H = - \sum_{i=1}^{r} \frac{1}{r} \log_2 \frac{1}{r} = \frac{1}{r} \sum_{i=1}^{r} \log_2 r = \log_2 r$$

which can be used to norm the measure if we want, so as to make it vary between 0 and 1. The measure is sensitive, not quite simple, but has the virtue of having an interpretation: it measures the amount of 'uncertainty', and hence of 'information' in the distribution. Obviously, the uncertainty is zero when only one value is present, and maximum when all values are used equally much. The social science interpretation of this would be in terms of predictability: the more uncertainty (the higher the dispersion), the less can an outsider predict the value of a given unit.

Measures can also be constructed by treating the distribution of frequencies as a regular distribution, where the variable (the frequency) is interval scale. In the case of uniformity, this dispersion would be zero (all r frequencies are the same), but the maximum value is less clear. In general we would recommend d above, or H if more sensitivity is needed.

There is no limit, seemingly, to the number of coefficients of *correlation* that have been, and will be, proposed. First of all, there is the necessity of working out coefficients for all three levels of measurement. Secondly, coefficients can be based on different definitions of independence. Even though these definitions are equivalent, the coefficients may be different, emphasizing different aspects of the case of independence. In addition to this, a coefficient may take as a point of departure the definition of dependence rather than independence. Finally, coefficients may differ to the extent they satisfy or fail to satisfy the 10 plus 6 criteria listed above for such parameters – so possibilities are legion. The most important coefficients for social scientists are given in the 'genealogical chart' at the end of this section (p. 232), which we shall now comment on.

I. *The interval scale family*

The standard correlation coefficient and its generalization, the correlation ratio, are based on a very simple idea: the regression curve or regression line as a means of prediction. If we want to predict from X to Y, and the total variance of the latter is s_y^2, the fundamental equation in (large-sample) regression theory can be written as follows:

$$s_y^2 = s_{dep}^2 + s_{res}^2$$

or

$$s_{total}^2 = s_{between}^2 + s_{within}^2$$

The total variance is equal to the sum of two variances; the variance due to the covariation between X and Y – due to Y's dependence on X – and a residual variance. This statement, of course, is a tautology, it is true by definition. The question is whether one is willing to accept the standard interpretation of these variances in terms of 'between means of conditional distributions' and 'within conditional distributions'. If one accepts this, the rest is simple. The obvious correlation measure is the variance explained by the dependence, s_{dep}^2. It only has to be normed, and since its maximum value is s_y^2, one gets:

$$e^2 = \frac{s_{dep}^2}{s_y^2} \text{, or in the linear case } r^2 = \frac{s_{dep}^2}{s_y^2}$$

which varies between 0 and 1 (the square root may be extracted to make it comply with requirement 4). In practice, it is easier to calculate the residual variance, so one generally writes:

$$e^2 \text{ (or } r^2) = 1 - \frac{s_{res}^2}{s_y^2} \text{ which gives } r = \frac{\Sigma (x - \bar{x}) (y - \bar{y})}{\sqrt{\Sigma (x - \bar{x})^2 \cdot \Sigma (y - \bar{y})^2}}.$$

Thus, one has the familiar interpretation of r^2 (and e^2) as the fraction of the total *variance* that can be ascribed to the dependence on the independent variable. Similarly, r (and e) can be interpreted as the fraction of the total *standard deviation* that can be similarly ascribed. But the latter is mathematically less convenient, although it is difficult to say that s^2 represents the general idea of 'variation' better than s.[6]

These correlation measures measure the gain in precision by fitting a regression curve (line) through the distribution. Thus, they are equal to zero if nothing is gained, and to unity if complete precision is gained. The question is what this means in terms of the other definitions of independence.

There is no residual variance when all conditional distributions consist of points only – so that the variance around these points is zero – i.e. when the distribution falls entirely on the regression curve. This corresponds well to what we have called *maximum* dependence. But does a zero coefficient imply *minimum* dependence, i.e. independence?

It implies that the residual variance is equal to the total variance which is true if and only if the regression curve is a line parallel to the X-axis. *But this is a necessary and not a sufficient condition for statistical independence,* as can be seen from this simple distribution:

Y			
2	0	0	15
1	0	10	0
0	5	0	0
-1	0	10	0
-2	0	0	15
	1	2	3

which is a clear case of linear and horizontal regression, but also a clear case of dependence, although of a peculiar kind. Thus, the correlation ratio as well as the correlation coefficient infracts requirement II, (16) above.

As to the correlation *coefficient*, it is also contrary to criterion I, (1), p. 207, since it is only applicable to distributions with linear regression, 'applicable' in the sense of being interpretable. Further, it cannot be said to be 'simple'. But it is N-free, relatively r-free, and one of its great virtues is its invariance with regard to linear transformations of the variables. With most statistical coefficients it shares the problem of lacking social science interpretation, and, consequently, validity at higher levels. It is symmetric (but e is not; it depends on which regression curve one is using).

A major problem of the correlation coefficient is the general problem of the interval scale in social science. Imagine that we have made a standard questionnaire investigation and are interested in the association between the answers to two questions, where the answers are given as:

	strongly disagree	disagree a little	uncertain indifferent	agree a little	strongly agree
with codes	-2	-1	0	$+1$	$+2$
or	0	1	2	3	4
or	1	2	3	4	5

The first code is most 'intuitive' because of the correspondence between numbers and meaning, but cannot be used directly as punches in IBM-cards. The second and third can. All three differ only in their location of the zero point. Thus, the transformations from one code to another are linear, and correlation coefficients will not depend on which scale is used. Also, one may use different scales for the two variables without affecting the correlation coefficient.

But these transformations, however useful for IBM purposes, do not touch the problem. The problem is that it is highly arbitrary which numbers we assign to the answer categories. As long as the arbitrariness is within the group of linear transformations, there is no danger to the value of the correlation coefficient. When it moves outside this range, however, the correlation coefficient may vary; and if we have no good *a priori* reason for excluding transformations that are non-linear, the value of the correlation coefficient may become rather meaningless.

Thus, in the case above we might argue that there is a 'side effect' in the sense that it is much more difficult to be *for* (agree) than *against* (disagree)– for that reason one should not use the code $-2, -1, 0, 1, 2$ but, say, $-2, -1, 0, 2, 4$. Or one might argue that there is a 'tail effect' – that to agree or disagree a little is easily done, while it is more difficult to take extreme points of view (code $-3, -1, 0, 1, 3$). Or one may argue in favor of an 'opinion effect' – the difficulty consists in having a point of view at all (code $-3, -2, 0, 2, 3$).

To explore the effect of these changes a distribution was used as an example and all correlation coefficients were computed:

+3	+3	+4	+2	strongly agree	0	0	1	3	1
+2	+1	+2	+1	agree a little	0	5	7	5	3
0	0	0	0	uncertain	1	7	9	7	1
−2	−1	−1	−1	disagree a little	3	5	7	5	0
−3	−3	−2	−2	strongly disagree	1	3	1	0	0

	strongly disagree	disagree a little	uncertain	agree a little	strongly agree
'normal'	−2	−1	0	+1	+2
'side'	−2	−1	0	+2	+4
'tail'	−3	−1	0	+1	+3
'opinion'	−3	−2	0	+2	+3

We get these coefficients of correlation using the different scales:

	'normal'	'side'	'tail'	'opinion'
'normal'	.40	.41	.41	.38
'side'	.41	.38	.40	.37
'tail'	.41	.40	.41	.40
'opinion'	.38	.37	.40	.36

The table is, of course, symmetric since r is a symmetric coefficient. Also, it shows that the transformations *change* the coefficient, since they are not linear. Finally, the changes are not very great.

The biggest change is for the 'opinion' transformation, because it affects the center of gravity of the distribution. Thus, if instead of $-3, -2, 0, 2, 3$ we use $-5, -4, 0, 4, 5$ to express the idea of the opinion effect, and use this for both variables, we get a coefficient as low as .32. Clearly, if we want to decide whether a correlation coefficient is statistically significant or not such variations may be crucial, and for more drastic transformations and some of the rather irregular types of distributions often found in survey research the range of variation may be considerable. The range may decrease if the transformations can be limited by theory or empirical research or (preferably) both, but as long as we feel there are good reasons for some of the transformations above, the range of variation may still be considerable, particularly if we consider r^2 instead of r.

Thus, the correlation coefficient has serious drawbacks in social research. And its offspring is not of much importance, except the phi coefficient. The point biserial coefficient is only what we get applying r to a two-dimensional distribution where one variable has the values 0,1; and the biserial and tetrachoric coefficients involve assumptions about underlying continua with normal distributions and dichotomous splits that are rarely fulfilled in practice. The phi coefficient for a fourfold-table, however, is useful. It is zero if and only if $ad = bc$, which is if and only if the conditional distributions are equal, as it should be. If one diagonal is empty the coefficient is -1 or $+1$; this is also a necessary condition by the argument above for r in general.[7]

II. *The ordinal scale family*

Some years ago the only coefficients used for the ordinal case were Spearman's rho and Kendall's tau,[8] but in the last decade the development has been very rapid, mainly due to the work by Goodman-Kruskal[9] and Somers.[10] Some of the more important features of these coefficients will be pointed out.

Spearman's rho has serious shortcomings that should be mentioned. First of all, it is at variance with principle (7) in the general list. It is not invariant under legitimate transformations at the ordinal level, for if the values given to the elements are not the ranks from 1 to n, we will change the value of the differences, and hence of the coefficient. Thus, if we have five elements and two rankings:

	A	B	C	D	E	SUM
1st ranking	1	2	3	4	5	15
2nd ranking	2	4	1	3	5	15
differences	−1	−2	2	1	0	0
squared	1	4	4	1	0	10

we get rho = 0.5. If we now make a monotone transformation of the numbers, for instance to the first five prime numbers, we get:

	A	B	C	D	E	SUM
1st ranking	1	3	5	7	11	27
2nd ranking	3	7	1	5	11	27
differences	−2	−4	4	2	0	0
squared	4	16	16	4	0	40

and the result becomes 0.66 since the new maximum sum is 232. Rho is invariant under linear transformations only, as it should be, since it is derived from the linear correlation coefficient of Pearson. But the general monotone transformation will change it. Hence, the coefficient is precisely what it says: a rank correlation coefficient, and it assumes that one is willing to define rank as an interval scale, and not as ordinal.

But the coefficient has another weakness. It attains its maximum and minimum values for the cases of perfect concordance or discordance in the ranking, but there are difficulties with the zero value. By the prediction criterion we should have independence when knowledge of one rank does not give any basis for inferring the other rank. Imagine an extreme special case of this, where two judges are ranking the same objects, one of them from 1 to n, but the other is unable to discriminate so that he gives them all the same rank, which by the usual convention will be the arithmetic mean of the ranks he should have distributed, i.e. $\frac{1}{2}(n+1)$. For instance, one might have:

Judge 1:	1	2	3	4	5	6	7
Judge 2:	4	4	4	4	4	4	4
d	−3	−2	−1	0	+1	+2	+3
d^2	9	4	1	0	1	4	9

and $\varrho = 1 - \dfrac{6.28}{7 \cdot 6 \cdot 8} = \frac{1}{2}$ and not zero. It is easily seen that this holds in the general case, for:

$$\sum_{i=1}^{N} \left(i - \frac{N+1}{2}\right)^2 = \frac{1}{12} N(N+1)(N-1)$$

which inserted into the formula gives $\varrho = \frac{1}{2}$. One may say, however, that this is because the general practice of using arithmetic means in case of ties is wrong and one may ask: what is the value k that should have been used instead of $\frac{1}{2}(n+1)$ so that one may still get the coefficient equal to zero in this case? But this leads to:

$$k = \frac{3(N+1) \pm \sqrt{3(N^2+1)}}{6}$$

which is hardly acceptable as a formula. Thus, $\varrho = 0$ is difficult to interpret.

All the other measures are based on another idea, which takes the ordinal nature of the data much more into account. Rho compares for *each unit* the *two values* given to it, but this assumes that the two values are comparable. The other measures compare *two units* to see whether the two variables order them in the same or the opposite direction. Thus, in principle all pairs are inspected; and if they are concordant, i.e. ordered in the same direction, this is recorded as $+1$, if they are discordant, ordered in different directions by the two measures, this is recorded as -1. It should be noticed that this presupposes not only ordinal scale but also direction. Since the latter is not always unambiguous (which is 'more', modern or traditional?) a minimum requirement of these measures is that they only differ by sign if we change the direction.

Since the number of pairs of N elements is $\frac{1}{2}N(N-1)$ the maximum concordance is this number and the maximum discordance $-\frac{1}{2}N(N-1)$. If we call the number of concordant pairs P and the number of discordant pairs Q, we get Kendall's tau:

$$\mathrm{Tau}_a = \frac{P-Q}{\binom{N}{2}}$$

This can be applied to two rank orders as below:

		First ranking				
		1	2	3	4	5
	1			x		
Second	2	x				
ranking	3				x	
	4		x			
	5					x

When written like this we get P by counting for each unit the number of units to the *right* and *below* and adding – since these are concordant relative to that unit. Then we get Q by counting for each unit the number of units to the *left* and *below* and adding – since they are discordant relative to that unit. This gives tau $= 0.4$, in the example (as against rho $= 0.5$.)

It is clear that tau does not have the two weaknesses mentioned in the case of rho. Here we talk only about relative order, so we can undertake any monotone transformation we want. And if the second ranking results in ties only, e. g. to the value 3, we get P and Q equal to zero and tau equal to zero as we should.

Since many two-dimensional distributions in social science will have more than one unit per cell the measure is not very applicable as it stands. In the 2×2 and 3×3 tables below:

a	b
c	d

$|N$

a	b	c
d	e	f
g	h	i

$|N$

we would get

$$\text{tau}_a = \frac{ad-bc}{\binom{N}{2}}$$

and $\text{tau}_a =$

$$\frac{a(e+f+h+i)+b(f+i)+d(h+i)+ei-c(d+e+g+h)-b(d+g)-f(h+g)-eg}{\binom{N}{2}}$$

respectively.

The difficulty is that they can never attain unity, since only untied pairs are counted in the numerator. Imagine that the distribution was concentrated on the main diagonal and equally divided between the diagonal cells. The tau-value would be $\dfrac{N}{2(N-1)}$ in the 2×2 case and $\dfrac{2N}{3(N-1)}$ in the 3×3 case, while the concordance is maximal and we ought to get unity.

Kendall suggests, to correct for ties[11]:

$$\text{tau}_b = \frac{P-Q}{\sqrt{\underset{i<j}{\Sigma} N_i. N_j. \times \underset{i<j}{\Sigma} N_{.i} N_{.j}}}$$

In our case we would get:

$$\frac{\dfrac{N}{2} \cdot \dfrac{N}{2} - 0}{\sqrt{\left(\dfrac{N}{2} \cdot \dfrac{N}{2}\right) \times \left(\dfrac{N}{2} \cdot \dfrac{N}{2}\right)}} = 1 \text{ and } \frac{\dfrac{N}{3}\left(\dfrac{N}{3} + \dfrac{N}{3}\right) + \dfrac{N}{3} \cdot \dfrac{N}{3} - 0}{\sqrt{3\left(\dfrac{N}{3} \cdot \dfrac{N}{3}\right) \times 3\left(\dfrac{N}{3} \cdot \dfrac{N}{3}\right)}} = 1 .$$

The difficulty with this measure is, as pointed out above, that it cannot attain unity unless the table has the same number of columns and rows. Hence a third measure is suggested:[12]

$$tau_c = \frac{P-Q}{\frac{1}{2}N^2 \frac{\min (r_1, r_2) - 1}{\min (r_1, r_2)}}$$

where r_1 and r_2 are the number of values for the two variables. But this measure does not correct for ties, so we would also have to apply the corrections in tau_b. Obviously, this brings us at variance with the pragmatic but very important rule about simplicity. Before leaving these measures it should be noticed that for 2×2 tables we get:

$$tau_b = \frac{ad-bc}{\sqrt{(a+b)(c+d)(a+c)(b+d)}} \text{ and } tau_c = \frac{ad-bc}{\frac{1}{4}N^2}.$$

Tau_b is the same as the phi coefficient, which is the same as the interval scale correlation coefficient for two dichotomies given the values 0 and 1. Tau_c can attain its maximum value, unity, when there is diagonal concentration *and* uniform distribution.

At this point the measure suggested by Goodman and Kruskal is a great simplification.[13] The basis is still $P-Q$ as a measure of the excess of concordance over discordance. The ideal would be to norm it so that we had:

	discordance	independence	concordance
definition	$P = 0$	$P = Q$	$Q = 0$
$d = P-Q =$	$-Q$	0	P
normed measure	-1	0	$+1$

We introduce $\gamma = xd+y$, which leads to

$$1 = Px+y$$
$$-1 = -Qx+y$$

and
$$\gamma = \frac{P-Q}{P+Q}$$

which for the 2×2 table is equal to the measure introduced by Yule, $Q = \frac{ad-bc}{ad+bc}$, as pointed out by Goodman and Kruskal.

The measure is extremely simple and generally applicable to all two-dimensional distributions of ordinal variables. It is invariant of legitimate (i.e. ordinal) transformations like tau, and is zero in the case of statistical independence (as is easily proved by writing each row in the 3×3 table as a product of the first row).

222

If $P+Q$ is equal to the number of all pairs, i.e. equal to $\frac{1}{2}N(N-1)$, then we get gamma equal to tau_a; but this presupposes no ties. The difference between gamma and tau_b is that tau_b incorporates ties in the formula, whereas gamma leaves them out from the very beginning. Thus the simplicity of gamma is bought at a certain cost: neither condition ($1b$) nor condition ($2b$) in the general list of criteria of correlation coefficients is satisfied. Gamma can be zero even if there is not statistical independence, and it can be maximum even if there is not maximum predictability:

m	0	m
0	m	0
m	0	m

Gamma equal to zero,
but not statistical independence

m	m	m
0	0	m
0	0	m

Gamma equal to unity,
but not maximum dependence

In the first case, $P = Q = 3m^2$, and gamma is equal to zero. In the second case there are no discordant pairs, hence the conclusion, gamma equal to unity. Both are based upon the fact that concordance and discordance exclude each other, but they are not exhaustive: there is also the possibility of a tie. (Actually, tau is also permissive when it comes to attaining the zero value, but tau_b is very restrictive as to its maximum value). But this, which may look as a disadvantage, can be turned into an advantage if we want a more generous measure of correlation that can attain its maximum also in the case of curvilinear dependence ('corner', not 'diagonal' correlation).

Thus, we get the following Table:

Table 2.3.4. *A classification of ordinal correlation coefficients*

	Linear regression	Curvilinear regression
3 < 3 *tables*, etc	τ_b	γ
	$\downarrow$	$\downarrow$
2 × 2 *tables*	φ	Q

The arrows indicate that simple mathematical deduction is possible.

All these measures are symmetric. But Somers has also introduced some interesting asymmetric measures that can be seen as generalizations of the percentage differences. The measures are:

$$\frac{P-Q}{\underset{i<j}{\Sigma}N_i.N_j.} \quad \text{and} \quad \frac{P-Q}{\underset{i<j}{\Sigma}N_{.i}N_{.j}}$$

For fourfold-tables these reduce to:

$$\frac{ad-bc}{(a+b)(c+d)} \quad \text{and} \quad \frac{ad-bc}{(a+c)(b+d)}$$

or the percentage differences (II, 2.2) divided by 100. It remains to be seen how useful they are in practice.

III. *The nominal scale family*

Since the values are completely arbitrary for the nominal scale there is no way in which they can be used to define coefficients. Hence all coefficients have to be based on a comparison of frequencies with the frequencies that correspond to independence. Chi square makes use of this, but in order to calculate frequencies that correspond to independence, the marginal distributions will have to be known. If only the total number of units is known, the number of two-dimensional distributions showing independence becomes too high.

The peculiar form of chi square is determined by other criteria than the ones in the list, above all by the criterion of arriving at a known sampling distribution. The four efforts to discipline it so as to make it N-free, r-free, and normed are not entirely successful and of minor importance in practical work, with the possible exception of φ which is less artificial than the others. φ also has the important advantage of reducing to r_φ in the 2×2 case – which makes this coefficient the legitimate offspring of all three families of correlation. This is, by the way, the only point where they could meet, since only in the case of the dichotomy is a nominal scale also (although in a trivial sense) an ordinal scale and an interval scale.

The advantage of the chi-square is that it satisfies condition (1) for correlation measures entirely, and that it has an approximate sampling distribution. The difficulties as to the extreme value are important but much more important is another issue. Like e^2 and r^2, chi square measures deviations from the case of independence. To do this, all three have to construct a case of independence, and e^2 and r^2 define it by linear *and* horizontal regression through the mean of the marginal distribution. Thus r^2 and e^2 compare the distribution with all other distributions that have the same s_y^2. And chi-square compares the empirical distribution to all other distributions that have the same set of frequencies corresponding to statistical independence – since these frequencies are the basis of comparison used by the measure. Its concept of independence is determined by its marginals. But why should

224

it? There are other bases of comparison, for instance the completely uniform distribution that would lead to the formula:

$$\Sigma \frac{\left(N_{ij} - \dfrac{N}{r_1 \cdot r_2}\right)^2}{\dfrac{N}{r_1 \cdot r_2}}$$

measuring the deviation from a completely chance distribution. Obviously, the chi square should only be used if one really feels that the marginal frequencies matter. Its form is highly artificial in any case, however, and only justifiable as an approximation to the multinomial distribution.

There is only one innovation in the field of nominal correlation, that also reported by Goodman and Kruskal.[14] They use the idea of gain in predictability if the value is known.

Essentially this is a kind of correlation ratio, based on the nominal regression function consisting of the set of modal values. Evidently, we have correlation to the extent we make less errors using the modal values of the conditional distributions than the modal value of the marginal distribution. Imagine we have N units; that the modal value of the marginal distribution for Y is M; and that the modal value for the conditional distribution defined by $X = X_1$ is M_1. Further let $\#(M)$ represent the number of units with value M. If we should predict the value of Y *not knowing* the value of X we would choose the mode, and be right in $\dfrac{\#(M)}{N}$ of the predictions. If we should predict the value *knowing* the value of X_1 we would choose the mode in the corresponding conditional distribution.

Thus, if we knew the value to be X_1, we would be right in $\dfrac{\#(M_1)}{N}$ of the predictions, and so on. To get at the average proportion of correct predictions, we use the weighted average:

$$\frac{N_1}{N} \cdot \frac{\#(M_1)}{N_1} + \frac{N_2}{N} \cdot \frac{\#(M_2)}{N_2} + \ldots + \frac{N_a}{N} \cdot \frac{\#(M_a)}{N_a} = \frac{1}{N} \sum_{i=1}^{a} \#(M_i)$$

Or, the average proportion of right answers is obtained by summing the number of modal units in the conditional distributions and dividing by the total number of units. Obviously, the maximum of this fraction is 1, corresponding to the situation where all units are in the modi.

Its minimum is $\dfrac{\#(M)}{N}$, as can easily be shown. For if all the conditional distributions have the same modal value, then obviously:

$$\#(M_1) + \#(M_2) + \ldots + \#(M_a) = \#(M)$$

If the modal values differ, then $\#(M)$ is a sum of frequencies – *not all of them modal*, and thus:

$$\#(M_1) + \#(M_2) + \ldots + \#(M_a) > \#(M)$$

We have both the maximum and the minimum; in agreement with the general formula for norming to the unit interval we get:

$$\lambda = \frac{\dfrac{1}{N} \Sigma \#(M_i) - \dfrac{1}{N} \#(M)}{1 - \dfrac{1}{N} \cdot \#(M)} = \frac{\Sigma \#(M_i) - \#(M)}{N - \#(M)}$$

The most immediate interpretation we can make of this is as 'the gain in number of times the prediction is correct, knowing the value of X, relative to the maximum gain possible'. It should be noticed that the measure is minimum when there is independence (for when there is independence, the conditional distributions are equal and the modi located at the same value) but not only under this condition. Just as for the ordinary correlation coefficient, we have the possibility of 'horizontal' regression function, without statistical independence.

Let us round off this survey of statistical parameters with some of the most important parameters that measure *agreement;* viz., *Scott*'s measure in the nominal case, *Kendall*'s tau in the ordinal case, and *Robinson*'s measure in the interval case. But first of all, some words about the kinds of problems that should be solved by means of agreement coefficients rather than correlation coefficients. That agreement implies correlation, but not vice versa, has already been pointed out.

Thus, if we are interested in the problems mentioned in I, 1.3, i.e. the problems of reliability (both intra-subjectively and inter-subjectively) and validity, then agreement analysis must be used. Inter-subjectivity is a question of whether two observers report the same in a situation of observation, interviewing, coding etc. Thus, if one observer has a personal equation relative to the other which reads $Y = X + 5$ (he is consistently five units higher) the correlation is perfect (and even rectilinear) but the agreement is low – in fact zero, since no unit has been given the same values. Another example of more theoretical interest is the case to be dealt with at the end of the section: if rank-equilibrium is a question of having the same rank on different dimensions, then the word 'same' again points towards agreement analysis.

In the *nominal* case the problem of developing a suitable measure has been relatively well solved by Scott. The basis is the two-dimensional table, but the measure can easily be generalized to more dimensions. In this table the main diagonal and the main diagonal only represents complete agreement, for we assume that, even though the order of the values is arbitrary in the nominal case, the values have the same order on the axes. As a first and primitive measure of agreement, then, could be used the proportion of pairs of observation on the main diagonal, which is often done. However, argues Scott, this is less than satisfactory, since a relatively high proportion can often be produced simply by chance. His suggestion is to measure not the proportion in the main diagonal, p_a, but the excess of this proportion over the chance proportion p_{ch} relative to the maximum possible excess $1-p_{ch}$. The measure is

$$\pi = \frac{p_a - p_{ch}}{1 - p_{ch}}$$

In this measure factual agreement between two observers (or between two rank dimensions) is measured relative to the agreement one would get 'by chance'. And the measure of what one would get 'by chance', p_{ch}, is what is known in contingency statistics as 'expected or theoretical relative frequency', p_e. Thus, in this little table we get:

first observer

	11	9	20
	7	3	10
	4	6	10
	11	9	second observer

$$p_a = \frac{7+6}{20} = 0.65$$

$$p_e = \frac{11 \cdot 10 + 9 \cdot 10}{20^2} = 0.50$$

$$\pi = \frac{0.65 - 0.50}{1 - 0.50} = \frac{0.15}{0.50} = 0.30$$

which is considerably less than p_a. Often, however, the reduction is less considerable, as in this case:

first observer

	15	5	20
	14	1	15
	1	4	5
			second observer

$$p_a = \frac{14+4}{20} = 0.90$$

$$p_e = \frac{15 \cdot 15 + 5 \cdot 5}{20^2} = 0.63$$

$$\pi = \frac{0.90 - 0.63}{1 - 0.63} = \frac{0.27}{0.37} = 0.73$$

As to *ordinal* and *interval* cases, the problem is to measure what above has been called 'diagonal correlation only'. Thus, gamma-based measures are quite unsuitable, and Kendall's tau$_b$ should be used in the ordinal case, but with care, since it is also unity when the data are on a parallel to the diagonal.

For the interval case the reader is referred to the articles by Robinson where a simple, correlation-like measure is suggested.[15]

It should be noticed that $1 - A$, where A is a measure of agreement, is a measure of change that can be used in the analysis of panel data. But, as the matter is complicated, the reader is referred to the specialized literature.

A survey of correlation parameters is given on page. 232–33. This is a highly simplified chart, giving only the most important coefficients and the relations between them, where the arrow stands for deducibility:

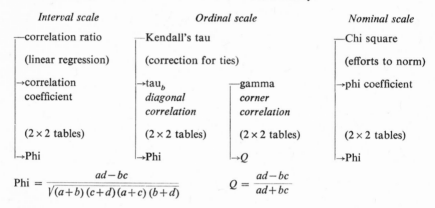

Interval scale	*Ordinal scale*		*Nominal scale*
─correlation ratio	─Kendall's tau		─Chi square
(linear regression)	(correction for ties)		(efforts to norm)
→correlation coefficient	→tau$_b$ *diagonal correlation*	─gamma *corner correlation*	→phi coefficient
(2×2 tables)	(2×2 tables)	(2×2 tables)	(2×2 tables)
└→Phi	└→Phi	└→Q	└→Phi

$$\text{Phi} = \frac{ad - bc}{\sqrt{(a+b)(c+d)(a+c)(b+d)}} \qquad Q = \frac{ad - bc}{ad + bc}$$

With this arsenal the social scientist should be rather well equipped.

*   *   *

In this section and in other sections the importance of constructing parameters with substantive interpretation rather than using mechanically standard parameters has been stressed. To pursue this point further we would like, in conclusion, to give a concrete realization of this principle.[16]

Imagine that we have two rank-dimensions (e.g., political and economic status) in a simple society with N members, and the individuals are divided as follows:

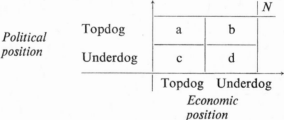

			Topdog	Underdog	N
Political position	Topdog		a	b	
	Underdog		c	d	

Topdog   Underdog
Economic position

Two problems that have been treated relatively extensively by sociologists in connection with such tables are the problems of 'criss-cross' and 'rank-equilibration'. The former has to do with the extent to which there are individuals in the society who can serve as bridges in case of conflicts (and thus possibly prevent intense conflicts). Thus, in a classical conflict between the TT and the UU in the table above, there will be no bridges in the society if b and c are equal to zero. The more people are allocated to cells b and c, the better, in terms of criss-cross, until we come to the point where a and d decrease towards zero and there are no bridges between the combinations TU and UT.

A person in cell b can help preventing conflicts between TT and UU in two ways:

(1) by serving as a *link of communication* between a and d,
(2) by refusing to take sides in the conflict because of *multiple loyalties*.

In terms of conflict theory, we can say that cells b and c represent a bulwark against complete polarization, because they keep the chain of communication or interaction in general open between a and d and serve as a reservoir of neutrals (who, for instance, can be used to keep the social machinery going in periods of conflict). Both factors are due to one common circumstance: that they share statuses with both conflict groups – and the underlying assumption is that interaction between status equals is conflict-dampening rather than conflict-inciting. Between individuals in cells a and d there is no such opportunity of meeting as status equals.

For the group as a whole, it is obvious that the criss-cross effect is greater, the higher the number of such links. This is not only a question of how many individuals are placed in b and c, however. The potency of an individual in cell b as a conflict-preventing link is proportionate to the number of individuals in a and d that he can act as a bridge between, in other words:

$$C_i' = k_i(a+d)$$

where C_i' is the criss-cross contribution by individual i, k_i is a parameter giving the capacity of that individual as an interaction link (he may be more or less 'gregarious' in general, he may dislike interaction with status equals, etc.). The total contribution from cell b becomes:

$$C_b' = (k_1+k_2+ \ldots +k_b)(a+d)$$

However, since this parameter can only use the information present in the distribution (which does not include any individual characteristic), we can as well set all the personal coefficients equal to unity, and get:

$$C_b' = b(a+d)$$

Correspondingly we get:

$$C_c' = c(a+d)$$

and the total criss-cross effect proportionate to:

$$C' = C_b' + C_c' = (b+c)(a+d)$$

If the conflict were between TU and UT we would get exactly the same expression. We then have to see if the expression behaves properly.

Since the frequencies a, b, c and d have to be non-negative and add up to N, C' itself has to be non-negative, and we can write:

$$C' = [N-(a+d)](a+d)$$

Obviously, C' is zero if and only if one or both of the diagonal sums is equal to zero. We discard the case 'both equal to zero', since it would mean N equal to zero, hence no society, no conflict and no criss-cross. For either of the diagonal sums to be equal to zero both of the cells must be empty – and this corresponds exactly to the theory: no criss-cross if and only if all individuals are grouped in status sets that permit no interaction as status equals.

The last expression for C' has the form $p(N-p)$ which has a maximum when the two factors are equal, i.e. when $N/2$ of the individuals are placed on either diagonal. Hence, the maximum value of C' is $N^2/4$, which we use to norm the parameter, so that we get:

$$C = \frac{(a+d)(b+c)}{N^2/4} \quad \text{or} \quad C = \tfrac{1}{4}(p_{11}+p_{22})(p_{12}+p_{21})$$

if we want to express it as relative frequencies. The parameter varies from 0 (no criss-cross) to 1 (maximum criss-cross), deals symmetrically with TT–UU conflicts and UT–TU conflicts, and is valid up to ratio scale since it gives the *number* of links relative to the maximum possible. Thus it is a measure of a very particular kind of correlation.

Let us then turn to the much easier task of devising an index of rank-equilibration. We repeat the structure matrix and fill in not only the number of individuals allocated, but also the degree of rank-disequilibration:

		Topdog	Underdog	N
Political position	Topdog	0 (a)	1 (b)	
	Underdog	1 (c)	0 (d)	
		Topdog	Underdog	

Economic position

To measure the degree of rank-disequilibration in the society all we have to do is to sum the frequencies weighted with their degree of disequilibrium (i.e. the rank-distance between the statuses in the status-set), getting:

$$D = a \cdot 0 + b \cdot 1 + c \cdot 1 + d \cdot 0 = b + c$$

We now want a measure R that has these properties:

$$D = 0 \rightarrow R = 1$$
$$D = D_{max} \rightarrow R = -1$$
$$D = \tfrac{1}{2}D_{max} \rightarrow R = 0$$

We get this by means of:

$$R = 1 - \frac{2D}{N} = 1 - \frac{2(b+c)}{N} = \frac{(a+d)-(b+c)}{N} = (p_{11}+p_{22})-(p_{12}+p_{21})$$

since D_{max} is obviously N. Thus R is the difference between the proportion that have equilibrated status-sets and the proportion that have disequilibrated status-sets. Again, the measure is valid to the level of ratio scale because it expresses exactly what sociological theory so far has made out of the idea of rank-equilibration.

It is now easily seen that the two parameters introduced are related to each other as follows:

$$C = 1 - R^2$$

In physics the degree to which parameters and variables relate to each other in a simple and meaningful way has been an important guide to the development of that science, and this should also be a principle in sociology.

2.4. Curve shape analysis

The parameters traditionally used in statistical analysis have a long and venerable history, but the social scientist who wants to use them in data processing and analysis will often become disenchanted, for two reasons. First of all, they do not nearly always measure what he is really interested in having measured, and he may well feel that his theoretical concerns are redefined almost unperceptibly to fit into the formulas of the parameters (or, he does not even see that this is what happens). And, secondly, they will often involve him in a lot of laborious and tedious work to produce figures according to formulas that give more precise results than he can make use of in his analysis. For that reason, two highly simplified systems of curve shape analysis will be suggested here, particularly applicable in classifying quickly a large number of distributions. (There is no necessity in actually drawing curves, the shapes can readily be seen from sets of (relative) frequencies.)

Coefficients of two-dimensional correlation I

I Interval scale

(1) *Correlation ratio, e*

$$e^2 = \frac{s^2_{\text{dep}}}{s^2_y} = 1 - \frac{s^2_{\text{res}}}{s^2_y}$$

linear regression $\rightarrow$ ranks as measure

(2) *Correlation coefficient, r*

$$r^2 = 1 - \frac{s^2_{\text{res}}}{s^2_y}, \quad r = \frac{\Sigma (x-\bar{x})(y-\bar{y})}{\sqrt{\Sigma (x-\bar{x})^2 \, \Sigma (y-\bar{y})^2}}$$

introducing dichotomies $\rightarrow$

(3)

	Dichotomies genuine	Underlying continuum and normal distribution
One variable dichotomous	Point biserial coefficient, r_{pb}	Biserial coefficient, r_b
Both variables dichotomous	Phi coefficient, r_φ	Tetrachoric coefficient, r_t

$$r_\varphi = \frac{ad-bc}{\sqrt{(a+b)(c+d)(a+c)(b+d)}}$$

II Ordinal scale

(1) *Spearman's* ϱ

$$\varrho = 1 - \frac{6 \, \Sigma \, d^2}{N^3 - N}$$

(2) *Kendall's* τ

$$\tau_a = \frac{P-Q}{\frac{1}{2}N(N-1)}$$

$$\tau_b = \frac{P-Q}{\sqrt{\underset{i<j}{\Sigma} N_{i\cdot}N_{j\cdot} \cdot \underset{i<j}{\Sigma} N_{\cdot i}N_{\cdot j}}} \;\rightarrow\; \frac{ad-bc}{\sqrt{(a+b)(c+d)(a+c)(b+d)}}$$

$$\tau_c = \frac{P-Q}{\frac{1}{2}N^2 \dfrac{\min(r_1,r_2)-1}{\min(r_1,r_2)}} \;\rightarrow\; \frac{ad-bc}{\frac{1}{4}N^2}$$

(3) *Goodman-Kruskal's* γ — *Yule's Q*

$$\gamma = \frac{P-Q}{P+Q} \;\rightarrow\; Q = \frac{ad-bc}{ad+bc}$$

(4) *Somer's* d_{yx} — *Percentage difference, d%*

$$d = \frac{P-Q}{\underset{i<j}{\Sigma} N_{i\cdot}N_{j\cdot}} \;\rightarrow\; d\% = \frac{100\,(ad-bc)}{(a+c)(b+d)}$$

Coefficients of two-dimensional correlation II

III Nominal scale

(1) *Goodman-Kruskal's λ*

$$= \frac{\sum\limits_{j} \max\limits_{i} N_{ij} - \max\limits_{j} N_{\cdot j}}{N - \max\limits_{j} N_{\cdot j}}$$

(2) *Chi-square, χ^2*

$$= \sum \frac{\left(N_{ij} - \dfrac{N_{i\cdot} \times N_{\cdot j}}{N} \right)^2}{\dfrac{N_{i\cdot} \times N_{\cdot j}}{N}} \rightarrow \text{fourfold table} \rightarrow \frac{N(ad-bc)^2}{(a+b)(c+d)(a+c)(b+d)}$$

Efforts to norm χ^2

(a) *Contingency coefficient, C* $= \sqrt{\dfrac{\chi^2}{N + \chi^2}}$

(b) *Tschuprow's coefficient, T* $= \dfrac{\chi^2}{N\sqrt{(r_1-1)(r_2-1)}}$

(c) *Cramer's coefficient, C_r* $= \dfrac{\chi^2}{N(\min(r_1, r_2)-1)}$

(d) *φ coefficient, φ* $= \sqrt{\dfrac{\chi^2}{N}} \rightarrow \text{fourfold table} \rightarrow \varphi = \dfrac{ad-bc}{\sqrt{(a+b)(c+d)(a+c)(b+d)}}$

Note how the formulas for r_φ, τ_b and φ are the same.

Essentially, these are systems for classifying one-dimensional curves, according to shapes. The first system, the AJUS-system, takes shape very explicitly into account, whereas the second system, the ISD-system is merely concerned with increase vs. stability vs. decrease.

(1) *The AJUS-system*

For one-dimensional variables central tendency, dispersion, skewness, flatness, and modality (how many 'modi' or tops the distribution has) are the traditional means of classifying distributions. If we are willing to disregard dispersion, we can get a very rough classification that takes some other properties into consideration as well by means of this system:

Table 2.4.1. *The AJUS curve shapes*

		pos. skew +	symmetric 0	neg. skew −
unimodal	A			
	J			
bimodal	U			
	S			

The letters are intended to characterize the shapes, although J_0 and S_0 may be said to be misnomers from this point of view. A- and J-curves are unimodal, U- and S-curves bimodal. If they are symmetric (or nearly so) a footscript zero can be used, otherwise + or − will indicate whether the distribution is skewed to the left or to the right, in accordance with usual terminology.

Imagine now that a large number of distributions over the same, say, five-point variable shall be classified – they may be about attitudes to the same object for a high number of sub-samples. In that case, an A_0, J_0, U_0, and S_0 may well be given the same arithmetic mean and perhaps even the same dispersion and skewness (the latter equal or close to 0) – but not the same kurtosis. The calculation of the latter is very time-consuming and hardly necessary, since the theoretically relevant information in most cases will be contained in our simple scheme of four classes. The first case, A_0, is the case of a central climate of opinion clustered in one homogeneous camp (the degree of homogeneity should then be measured by the dispersion);

234

the second case is the case of no school of thought, equivalent to answers at random; the third case is the story of two highly polarized camps; and the fourth case is really a combination of the first and the third. Generally speaking, the S-curves can be seen as a superimposition of an A-curve on a U-curve. Sociologically these are very different cases that can only too easily be obscured through the indiscriminate use of parameters.

If these curves serve as points of departure, then the skewed curves can be seen as deviations that favor one or the other extreme. Thus, a U is a distribution of the sample in two camps with the leftist one stronger in number, etc. If a subsample consistently gets this distribution for a class of variables, there is good reason to suspect that it may reflect a partition of the subsample in two meaningful sub-subsamples that will yield J-curves if analyzed separately. Thus, the U-curve can be seen as the juxtaposition of two J-curves, which may be a point of departure for utilizing the many J- and U-curve hypotheses in social psychology and political science.[17]

If the distribution is actually two-dimensional, as when the curves show the proportion answering 'yes' to a dichotomous question for each value of the variable, the curves may be more meaningful. A J_0 curve is a necessary and sufficient condition for no correlation between the variables. A correlation coefficient of any kind might here lump together as having the same amount of correlation A-, U- and S-curves that are quite different in meaning, and that should be avoided. For instance, if the underlying variable is age and the question has to do with a foreign policy attitude, it may make a tremendous difference for the analysis of causes and consequences whether the middle-aged, or the younger *and* older people support an aggressive measure.

Just as for the purely one-dimensional case, skewed curves may at the same time give information about the central tendency. If one subsample is A_0 and a comparable subsample is A-, there is usually no reason to demonstrate by means of averages that the latter subsample has an attitude more to the right. There is one condition, however: that all distributions have a tendency to fill the available scale. Otherwise, one might well get an A_0 curve located at the right, in the middle or at the left – because the zero refers only to symmetry, not to central tendency. The point is only that if a quick general view is needed, then asymmetric curves will almost always be curves with averages deviating from the average of the averages, *and vice versa.*

When the underlying variable is an index, that is really a disguised multidimensional variable, much can be learnt about the intercorrelations of the items in the index. If items are strongly correlated and they are used to make up an additive index, the result will be one of the U-distributions, depending on the marginal distributions.[18] Correspondingly, if the items are correlated 'in one end, but not the other' we would get skew U-distributions or J-distributions. Low or no correlations, not to mention negative correlations, would lead to A shapes. Thus, important properties of indices can be ascertained at a glance. This point will be developed in II, 3.2.

(2) The ISD-system

The point of departure here is a trichotomized variable, whereas there is no such restriction for the AJUS-system (exept that the variable should preferably have more than three values and under no condition less for the shapes to manifest themselves). Thus, continuous variables must be made into three-point discrete variables, and discrete variables must be collapsed until a meaningful trichotomy is obtained. While this may sound extremely restrictive, it is compensated for in practice by the high analytic utility of trichotomies. The distributions may, however, be of any of the three kinds we have discussed above: pure one-dimensional, two-dimensional, and index-distributions.

The idea is now simply to compare the (relative) frequency for one value with the relative frequency for the next value. Criteria must be established for deciding whether they are 'different' or 'the same' (the latter meaning within the range of sampling and other errors, such as measurement and rounding errors). If they are 'different' there should be no problem in deciding whether it is 'increase' or 'decrease' since the only thing needed is a decision as to the orientation of the basic variable. Since a trichotomy permits two transitions from one value to the next, and since there are three possibilities at either transition point (increase, stability, decrease), we get $3^2 = 9$ possible curve shapes, given below:

Table 2.4.2. *The ISD curve shapes*

Second transition point

First transition point		increase	stability	decrease
	increase	I	II	III
	stability	IV	V	VI
	decrease	VII	VIII	IX

There are no other possibilities within this system, and it is very quickly administered.

The curve types are indicated by Roman numerals for reference. Types II, IV, VI and VIII – that all admit stability – are not found in the AJUS-system. As the terms 'increase', 'stability' and 'decrease' indicate, the system is particularly meaningful if the basic variable is *time*. Thus, in a study of student careers, type III might be suspected to represent the rate of student association activity, type VII the amount of activity outside the university system, etc. – not forgetting type V which means that the variable is un-affected by student career. Mean values, dispersions, etc., would in most cases be quite out of order here.

There are also many other uses the system can be put to. If the variable is a measure of social rank and the rate has to do with some kind of social participation each curve shape tells its special story. Type V says that social rank does not matter, types I and IX that it does matter in a uniform and simple way, whereas types III and VII in most cases would interest the analyst most because there is more to explain. A typical problem, for in-stance, would be whether the sample could possibly be split into two sub-samples with different curve shapes that add up to the shape for the total sample. Curves II and VI may under certain conditions of relative size of the groups and the sub-samples combine to yield a curve of type III.

In collection with both systems, a basic problem is that of deciding whether the (relative) frequencies are different or not. 'Shape' is a concept entirely dependent on two factors: that the basic variable is at least ordinal and that two adjacent (adjacency has meaning only when ordinality can be as-sumed) percentages or frequencies can be compared so that it can be decided whether they are the 'same' or 'different'. Under these two conditions the shapes in the two systems can be found.

The problem boils down to that of comparing pairs of adjacent percent-ages. The model is that each value of the variable generates its own percent-ages independently of the other values, so that the decision as to difference or constancy when moving from one value to the next should be taken un-prejudiced by the other sections of the curve. Comparison of two percent-ages for this purpose must be done with some standards in mind, standards which will depend on the purpose for which the comparison is made. If the percentages are based on samples and the sole purpose is to find out whether differences are big enough to be attributable to the universe from which the sample is drawn, then tests of statistical significance based on the standard deviation for differences between percentages would probably be the best standard. Similarly, if we prefer to deal with the problem in absolute frequencies a test for differences in a fourfold-table would be recommendable. The results are given below; we shall only anticipate two objections that will be dealt with more fully in II, 4.4. First of all, even if the differences are found to be reliable (that is, even if sampling and measurement errors can be disregarded), we do not necessarily find the differences sufficient to make sense theoretically. This can be decided only on the basis of some theoretical standard. And secondly, the statistical criteria are meaningful only when the data can legitimately be regarded as random samples from a universe. If the data are themselves the universe, no statistical standards will be of any value in this connection, and only theoretical considerations can help in deciding what is enough to constitute a difference, a 'dip' on a curve, etc.

But in case the data form a random sample and the study is rather exploratory, statistical standards should be used, for nothing should be called 'different' unless it is statistically significant – this is a necessary if not sufficient condition for difference in a more theoretical sense. If the two adjacent values of the variable have a total of n_1 and n_2 cases respectively, we get:

Table 2.4.3. *Survey of formulas for testing differences*

	relative frequencies			*absolute frequencies*		
	p_1 $\quad$ p_2 $\quad$ $p_1 - p_2$			a $\qquad$ b $\quad$ $a+b$		
	q_1 $\quad$ q_2 $\quad$ $q_1 - q_2$			c $\qquad$ d $\quad$ $c+d$		
	n_1 $\quad$ n_2			$a+c = n_1$ $\;$ $b+d = n_2$ $\,\big|\, n_1 + n_2 = N$		
Statistics	$\dfrac{p_1 - p_2}{\sqrt{\dfrac{n_1 p_1 + n_2 p_2}{n_1 n_2}\left(1 - \dfrac{n_1 p_1 + n_2 p_2}{n_1 + n_2}\right)}}$			$\dfrac{N(ad - bc)^2}{(a+c)(b+d)(a+b)(c+d)}$		
are distributed approximately	standard normal provided theoretical frequencies exceed 5, preferably 10			chi-square, 1 d.f. provided theoretical frequencies exceed 5 preferably 10		
If we can assume $n_1 = n_2 = n$ we get	$\dfrac{p_1 - p_2}{\sqrt{\dfrac{(p_1 + p_2)(2 - (p_1 + p_2))}{2n}}}$			$\dfrac{2(a(n-b) - b(n-a))^2}{n(a+b)(2n - (a+b))}$		

If we substitute $a = np_1$ etc. in the second formula, we get the square of the first formula (as we should, since chi square for one degree of freedom is distributed as the square of a standard normal variable). The two methods lead, of course, to exactly the same result; the choice of formula will depend on the form of the data and computational possibilities. It should be noticed

238

how greatly the formula for percentage differences simplifies if the basic frequencies can be assumed to be equal. This is actually a good argument for the use of equal cells when a big number of curves are to be compared.

With these formulas, *ad hoc* tables can easily be made, so that the decision can be made at once when the percentages are known and a significance level is chosen. A simple way of doing this is to calculate the distance from one of the percentages necessary to get statistical significance. Thus if in the formula:

$$\frac{p_1 - p_2}{\sqrt{\dfrac{(p_1 + p_2)\,[2 - (p_1 + p_2)]}{2n}}} = k$$

we set $p_1 - p_1 = d$ and $p_1 = p$, we get:

$$d = \frac{k^2(2p - 1) \pm k\sqrt{k^2 + 8np - 8np^2}}{2n + k^2}$$

where k and n are constants. If we choose $p = p_1$ the higher of the two, then $d > 0$, which will correspond to the $+$ sign.

In choosing k, some reflections are necessary. In most cases, the interest will focus on curves of the types I, III, VII or IX; in other words, the curves that show changes at both transition points. Types I and IX, the patterns of linear change, will be particularly important, if not necessarily so theoretically exciting. In such distributions the total shape matters, not only the individual break. Therefore, it seems reasonable to choose a *total* significance level of 5% (corresponding to no changes at all), which gives a level of $\sqrt{5} = 2.23\%$ to the single comparison. Since the test is two-sided, this means 1.12% in either tail and $k = 1.22$.[19]

3. Patterns

3.1. *Patterns and indices*

In II, 1.3 patterns and indices are defined as the horizontal analysis counterparts of distributions and parameters in vertical analysis. Since the whole topic of patterns and their variety under different degrees of constraint have been dealt with relatively extensively in I, 4 and the general parameter theory has been given in II, 2, we should now be able to reap the harvest, conceptually speaking.

We can approach index theory in two ways, both leading to the same result.[1] On the one hand we have the idea given in I, 1.3 of being able to characterize patterns, not only distributions. On the other hand we have the equally important idea, arising from the concept of multi-stage sampling of variables (I, 3.3), of being able to handle not only variables, but clusters of variables. We may want to do an analysis not on the level of the individual variables, but on the level of the clusters. Formally, this corresponds to contextual analysis of units. The problem is how to deal with clusters of variables at the same time. Whether we come to this problem because we want to characterize the units in more comprehensive terms, or because we want an analytical instrument at a higher level of abstraction, the problem is the same: how to reduce the n-dimensional space given by n variables to one master-variable or index.

If the n variables have $r_1, r_2, \ldots r_n$ values respectively, the number of possible patterns is as usual:

$$R = r_1 \cdot r_2 \cdot \ldots \cdot r_n$$

We conceive of these patterns as forming a space $\underline{V}$ with n dimensions, and define: *By an index we mean a one-dimensional variable, $\underline{I}$, with r values, formed by a single-valued mapping of $\underline{V}$ on $\underline{I}$.* There may also be two-dimensional indices, etc. but we shall be concerned only with the simplest case. Obviously, the problem of index-formation is the same as the problem of parameter-construction: how to reduce the variety as much as possible without losing essential information. To achieve this aim the ten general requirements we make of parameters are very valuable, *mutatis mutandis*. We give them here with some changes from the version given in II, 2.3.

(1) *The index should be defined for all possible patterns.* To every pattern there should be one and only one index value.

(2) *The index should give as much information as possible.* This means that the index should be explicitly based on all variables in the cluster, but also only on those, and that we should be able to infer as much as possible about the pattern from the index value.

(3) *The index should be stable.* Although the index should be sensitive, it should not be sensitive to very small changes in the pattern. This principle actually means there may be some changes in the values of the variables that enter in the index and yet the index should be relatively stable. But this means, with reference to the basic trichotomy of variables in I, 1.4, that the index should be a 'private, but permanent' variable. This point will be spelt out later.

(4) *The index should be simple.* Obviously, the simpler of two otherwise equal indices will always be preferred.

(5) *The index should depend on the number of units that have the pattern.* Since we are usually interested in patterns for one unit, (not, for instance, for pairs of units), this is easy enough. But we may also be interested in indices for units that are pairs of individuals or nations, for instance to measure degree of friendliness in the pair, or total rank of the dyad.

(6) *The index should permit comparisons.* The idea of the index is to evaluate a pattern with regard to some aspect, in order to know where the pattern stands relative to other patterns. The least we can require is comparability with regard to all other patterns with the same *n* (number of variables this time) and *R* – this is actually covered by the first point above. We then add these requirements:

(a) *The index should be 'n-free' – independent of number of variables.*

(b) *The index should be 'R-free' – independent of number of values.*

(7) *The index should be independent of legitimate transformation of the values of the variables.* This principle, spelt out in II, 2.3, is as important in connection with indices as in connection with parameters.

(8) *The index should have a known sampling distribution.* In principle there will always be a sampling distribution, but it should preferably be simple and be known.

(9) *The index should be valid as a measure.* In other words, when we use the index values to decide that the

indices are equal or different – do we accept that the corresponding patterns are equivalent or not equivalent for our purpose?

indices can be strongly ordered – do we accept that the corresponding patterns can be ordered the same way, for our purpose?

differences between pairs of indices are equal – do we accept that the differences between the corresponding patterns are equal?

16 *

Depending on whether we can answer these questions in the affirmative, we get an index at the nominal, ordinal or interval level respectively. The latter is rarely obtained, however.

(10) *The index should be interpretable.* The index should have a meaning over and above that given to it by its mathematical definition. Preferably, it should be derived from social theory so as to reflect in a precise manner some aspect of social thought.

We shall now look at the general problem of index-construction in the light of these ten requirements, and explore some of the requirements further.

It should be noticed that it is always possible to arrive at a one-dimensional representation of the space V simply by having the number of values of I, r, equal to R and letting each value correspond to one pattern. Thus, an index of illiteracy could be as follows:

	does write	does not write
does not read	1	3
does read	0	2

With this kind of 'index' no information is lost and the variability is exactly the same as before. Since we cannot have $r > r_1 r_2 \ldots r_n$ (for that would be against the requirement that the mapping should be single-valued) this is the extreme case where there is no gain in terms of reducing the number of values, nor is there any loss of information. Clearly, this is an improper index. Thus, by a *proper* index we shall mean an index where we have:

$$r < r_1 r_2 \ldots r_n, r \geqslant 2.$$

As usual, it clarifies to ask: how many proper indices can we associate with a given cluster of variables according to the definition? Since an index is a question of mapping V on I, where V has R elements and I has r elements, the answer is simply r^R for a given r. But since r may vary from 2 to $R-1$, we get the sum $2^R + 3^R + \ldots + (R-1)^R$. This, however, is too much again. It disregards the little but very meaningful word in the definition: mapping of V on I. In other words, *all* values of I shall be used in the definition of the mapping. For $r = 2$ this means we do not permit the two mappings that leave one of the index-values empty, so the total number for $r = 2$ becomes $2^R - 2$. For $r = 3$ we get correspondingly 3^R minus all the mappings with empty index-values, etc.[2]

It should be noticed our assumption means that to *each* index-value there shall correspond at least one logical combination of values – we do not

242

assume that there also corresponds an empirical pattern. In other words, we are willing to accept indices with empirical distributions 'that touch the axis', i.e. have no units for one or more index-values.

As mentioned, the general problem of index-formation consists in balancing against each other:

The requirement of preservation of information: as much as possible, one should be able to restore the original distribution from the index-distribution. *The requirement of simplification*: r should not only be less, but preferably much less than $r_1 r_2 \ldots r_n$.

(These requirements are specifications of requirements (2) and (4) above.)

The lower r relative to the number of combinations, R, the more information is lost, in general. To get a quantitative expression for this, the problem can be phrased as follows: The mapping used is single-valued; but only if it is also single-valued the other way, i.e. from $\underline{I}$ to $\underline{V}$, can we infer the original combination of values from the index-value of a given unit.

Thus, the following index of illiteracy:

does not read	1	2
does read	0	1
	does write	does not write

is single-valued but not one-one; to the index value '1' correspond two elements in $\underline{V}$.

Instead of just talking about preservation of information and simplification we want to measure them, however crudely it will have to be done at this level of generality. To preserve information is to be able to restore the data matrix from the index values. Since there are m units and n variables in the index there are always $m \cdot n$ values to be inferred. Imagine that we are only able to infer v of them, so we get:

$$\textit{degree of preservation of information}: I = \frac{v}{m \cdot n}$$

For each unit, then, an inference will have to be made on the basis of the index value about the pattern of that unit. Some inferences may be entirely correct, some entirely wrong: the measure above gives an average for all units and all variables as to how often we are right, relative to how often we should be right in the ideal case. If only one pattern is mapped on each index value, we obviously get $I = 1$; but the moment different patterns may be mapped on the same index value, we are bound to make errors.

As to the other crucial dimension of index formation we get:

$$\text{degree of simplification}: S = 1 - \frac{r}{r_1 r_2 \ldots r_n} = 1 - \frac{r}{R}$$

which is equal to zero when $r = R$, which means that the index is improper. It can never attain unity because of the condition $r \geqslant 2$; for that reason one might use $1 - \frac{r-2}{R-2}$ as a measure. This measure should not let one lose sight of the most essential aspect of the simplification, which is not the reduction in number of values, but the reduction from n-dimensional patterns to values of one-dimensional variables.

In general, the problem of obtaining simplification with no loss of information is insoluble. But the empirical distribution may open possibilities of simplification without losing much information. Thus, one way of constructing indices would be as follows.

First, obtain information about the n-dimensional distribution of the m units. Disregard all empirically empty patterns; they do not have to be mapped on the index, since they are not represented. Then, collapse patterns with very low frequencies and retain patterns with high frequencies. The final step would consist in allocating numbers (index-values) to the combinations thus arrived at. For the case where patterns have been combined, one may rule that the index value corresponds to the pattern with the highest of the low frequencies, thus reducing the loss of information. In the example given above, there are probably few people who write but cannot read, so we can lay down the rule that index-value '1' should be mapped on 'read, but does not write'. Thus, our inverse mapping will be right 100% of the time for respondents with index-values 0 and 2, and perhaps 80% of the time for the rest.

A serious shortcoming of this method is that it is limited to relatively few variables. To arrive at the n-dimensional distribution is easily said but in practice not so easily done for n exceeding 5, since it involves the analyst with very complicated tables. Another method that yields similar results would be graphical pattern analysis. In principle, this method is very simple. It takes as its point of departure neither the data matrix nor the cartesian product of the variables, but a simple chart where the horizontal axis has a point for each variable and the vertical axis or axes give the values. Each unit has one value on each variable and, hence, is represented by a set of points (incidentally, this is exactly what an IBM cards looks like). To make the patterns stand out more clearly it is customary to connect these points with a line, and if one wants to distinguish between different kinds of units these lines may be given different appearance and colors, etc. Thus, a typical chart for pattern analysis would look as follows:

Table 3.1.1. *Format for pattern analysis charts*

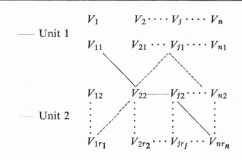

The chart is rectangular only when the number of values is the same for all variables, $r_1 = r_2 = r_j = r_n$. Obviously it is advantageous if not only the number of values is the same but one also has some kind of comparability between the values in the same row. One way of obtaining this is by transforming the values to percentiles, e.g. by setting $r_1 = r_2 = \ldots = r_n = 4$ so that v_{11} to v_{n1} would be the first quartile of the distributions on the variables and v_{14} to v_{n4} the last quartile. A horizontal pattern would then correspond to some kind of equivalence, a very erratic pattern to a high degree of disequilibrium, etc. Evidently, there is no limit on m, n, or r with this method, although the chart becomes somewhat unsurveyable for high m.

The chart can then be inspected for possible clusters of patterns. Depending on the theoretical focus one may choose either or both of the criteria of *adjacence* and *parallelism*. For adjacence one would require the patterns to be not more than x units apart for any variable, for parallelism one would require the patterns never to diverge more than a certain angle. Both criteria have their theoretical interpretation, and it is easy to develop systematic principles for grouping of patterns. Thus, one may choose a principle on theoretical grounds; then choose a pattern and look for all the other patterns that can be classified together with it; go on till all patterns have been grouped together; and then do it over again with another pattern as a 'starter' until the criteria have been adjusted to lead to approximately the same grouping, regardless of where one starts in the set of patterns. The final step would be to identify each bundle of patterns with a number (nominal scale) and preferably so that the numbering reflects an assumed underlying dimension (ordinal scale).

By these two methods, if there are many empty cells/patterns, one may obtain considerable simplification without loss of information. The objection to the procedures is their *ad hoc* nature and their lack of general applicability: what if there are no empty or almost no empty cells in the table and the patterns exhibit no pattern?

The requirement of nominal scale is a requirement of equivalence classes: the patterns given the same value by the index shall be equivalent for the purpose at hand. This is only problematic where simplification involves loss of information. One often hears the objection to index-formation that 'it lumps together what is essentially different and hence should be kept apart'. This is a misunderstanding of the function of index-formation, which is carried out precisely because the analyst believes that patterns can be combined to grosser equivalence-classes for specific purposes (but he may be unjustified in specific cases, of course). Thus, in the example above it makes good sense to lump together what is mapped on index-value '1' and call it 'semi-literate' if for analytical purposes it is considered sufficient to work with the three groups of 'literates', 'semi-literates' and 'illiterates'.

Thus, we have two essentially different procedures for index-construction. One is as described above, where all patterns are classified according to their *frequencies*. The other procedure would disregard the distribution, but classify the patterns according to their *meaning*. We shall as usual call them *extensional* and *intensional* procedures respectively. Here too, it seems wise not to be invidious, but rather try to devise principles of index-formation that combine both. The extensional procedures can also be called statistical, distributional, empirical, or *a posteriori;* the intensional procedures can be called semantical, meaningful, logical, or *a priori*.

Usually we will not be satisfied with an index that forms a nominal scale, but will require an ordinal scale for analytical purposes. Actually, this is one major rationale of index-construction: *where the original patterns do not constitute a strong order, the classes of patterns may*. Statuses can be distributed in a socio-economic space according to social and economic rank:

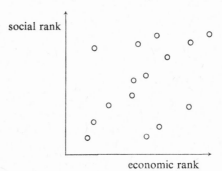

Even if there is a relatively high correlation between the two types of rank, it is rarely perfect. We have an order relation which says that 'S_1 has higher total rank or 'SES' (socio-economic status) than S_2 if it is higher than S_2 on at least one and not lower on any dimension'. This relation is irreflexive, asymmetric, and transitive as it should be, *but not connected:* if S_1 is higher socially but lower economically, or vice versa, than S_2, then the relation does not hold in either direction. Hence we have only a partial, not a linear order. To get a linear order we may try to make the two dimensions comparable, which is tantamount to deciding for each point on one dimension which point it corresponds to on the other dimension. But this is rarely feasible.

Hence, we shall stick to the strategy of *combining* patterns. Imagine we have a simple case with $n = 2$, both variables ordinal level, and lay down the following rule: 'an order relation is said to hold between two *classes* if it holds for all pairs of elements, one from either class'. The interesting thing about this rule is that it also gives us a good guide for deciding what constitutes an equivalence class: elements that are all 'lower' than all elements in the next class and all 'higher' than all elements in the preceding class. We shall see that this simple principle limits the number of possible indices drastically, in fact so much that it will have to be abandoned.

	low	medium	high
high	d	g	i
medium	b	e	h
low	a	c	f

The order relation defined above induces this partial order on the value-combinations:

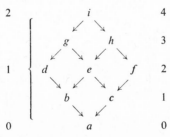

The problem is that of collapsing this partial order to a linear order by suitably grouping together some of the patterns. We *may* use the very common procedure, indicated in the column to the right, of grouping together elements that appear at the same level in this graph (which is a lattice). It is immediately seen that this corresponds to simple addition of the variables where for 'low, medium, high' we substitute '0, 1, 2':

2	2	3	4
1	1	2	3
0	0	1	2
	0	1	2

But this procedure would infract the rule of class-order. For instance, we would have b in a lower class than f in spite of the fact that they are not comparable. Of course, we are free to follow the rule given by the simple, additive index above, but it is worth-while looking into the conditions for constructing an index such that class-order would imply element-order.

It is easily seen that the simple index indicated to the *left* of the lattice satisfies the rule. But can we get more indices than this one? The rule is adhered to when we, for every new element included in a given class, also bring in all the elements with which the element does not compare. The question is whether this brings us anything new. Thus, if we include g in the same class as i, we have to bring in h and f, but with h we have to take d, and with d (and f) we have to include e. Further, f brings in b, while d brings in c; the whole process giving one index-value based on a and one based on all the other cells. This index is clearly just a collapsed version of the first one.

We shall now prove the general case: *with two ordered variables we can get an ordinal index but only with three values if we want class-order to imply element-order*. Clearly, this is always possible if we map the combination of the lowest values on the lowest index value, the combination of the highest values on the highest index value, and all the other combinations on the middle value. We now prove that we cannot split the middle class. For imagine we did split it in two non-empty subclasses. All elements in one subclass would have to be comparable with all elements in the other subclass, and order them the same way. The two corner elements 'low-high' and 'high-low' will have to belong to the same class since they are not comparable. But if they belong, so must all elements that are 'more than low' on the first variable, provided they are not also high on the second (because they are incomparable with the first corner element), and all elements that are 'more than low' on the second variable, provided they are not high on the first (because they are incomparable with the second element). It is easily seen that this means *all* elements except the other two corner elements.

248

Since there is nothing in the reasoning to limit the number of values on the two variables, the point is proved. Actually it can be extended to any number of variables, e.g. to n variables. In this case, we would get 2^n corners representing all possible combinations of extremes. The lowest index value would be low-low- ... -low and the highest high-high- ... -high. The medium value would cover the rest, and would have to do so as can be seen by starting with the inclusion of all the other $2^n - 2$ corner cells.

We have dealt so extensively with this for one particular reason: to motivate the *exclusion* of the principle 'class-order shall imply element-order' from our list of principles. If we include it, index-formation would be seriously limited to trichotomies (and of course, to the two dichotomies we can obtain by collapsing the middle group to either of the extremes) and moreover: to trichotomies where very often one or both extremes would be empirically empty.[3] Hence, we shall have to accept a weaker principle of ordinal ordering, and suggest the following: *class-order shall exclude element-order in the opposite direction.* In other words, class-order implies either element-order or else incomparability, but never order in the opposite direction. This opens up a great number of possibilities in our example above. For instance, we can now accept the index from 0 to 4 to the right of the lattice, or an index where we give one variable the weight '1' and the other variable the weight '0' – in other words, an index where we use only one of the variables. In what follows we shall use this as a precisation of the ordinal requirement for indices.

We have now elaborated some of the ten requirements. Let us list in a diagrammatic form the problems to be confronted in any index-construction:

Table 3.1.2. *A survey of the dimensions of index-formation*

	Variables	Index
(1) *Which?*	$X_1, X_2, \ldots X_n$; elements in a cluster of variables	I, the index for the cluster
(2) *How many?*	n	1
(3) *Values?*	$r_1, r_2, \ldots r_n$	$2 \leqslant r < r_1 r_2 \ldots r_n = R$
(4) *Distributions?*	$D_1, D_2, \ldots D_n$	D
(5) *Correlations?*	$\binom{n}{2}$ intercorrelations	n correlations with index (a) with variable included (b) without variable included
(6) *Definition of index?*	$I = I(X_1, X_2, \ldots X_n)$	

In this Table everything on the left hand side is given, once we have chosen the variables, and know the empirical distribution. If, in addition, the mapping I is defined, everything on the right hand side will also be fixed. But the way to reason is more like this: ten principles have been given for index-construction; the index shall be related to a cluster and be one-dimensional: choose the rest in accordance with this.

Our point of departure has been the mapping of patterns. In practice, the problem is often handled by direct reference to the variables, as in the formula $I = I(X_1, X_2, \ldots X_n)$. This by no means reduces the generality, since any unit will have to enter the formula in terms of its value-combination, i.e. its pattern. We now make this simple typology:

Table 3.1.3. *A typology of index-functions*

	I is additive in the variables (additive index)	I is not additive in the variables (not additive index)
The variables enter symmetrically (equal weights)	(1)	(2)
The variables do not enter symmetrically (not equal weights)	(3)	(4)

In practice, the additive index is by far the most important one, and we now turn to the symmetric version of that case, case (1).

3.2. *Additive indices*

So far we have made no assumption that the values of the variables or the index shall be expressed in terms of numbers. This will now have to be done, otherwise addition makes no sense; and addition is a highly practical and simple, although not unproblematic, tool in index-construction.

The first problem is immediate: since addition presupposes interval scale, how can we impose numerical values on the variables if they do not have that structure? The answer is simple: *by restricting the number of values of the variables to two and three, in other words by constructing indices on the basis of dichotomies and trichotomies only.*

The reasoning behind this is clear. We can represent a dichotomy by the numbers 0 and 1 without making any assumption above the level of the nominal scale, and still get what we need for addition. A trichotomy can be represented by the numbers -1, 0, and 1, or – what comes to exactly the same, since it is only a linear transformation – 0, 1, and 2. For the trichotomy we make the assumption of ordinal scale: there are extremes and one middle value. But we also make the assumption that the two extremes are equidistant from the middle. Consequently, trichotomies should only be used when this can be reasonably justified; otherwise, dichotomies should be chosen. Obviously, the numbers are assigned so that the variables all 'go in the same direction' whether this is decided according to meaning (intension) or according to distribution (extension).

However, it may often not be advisable to stick to dichotomies for reasons given in I, 4. There will almost always be cases of NA, DK, DNA, or middle answers that call for at least one category of their own, since there may be no good rationale available for classifying them with the clear answers to either side. With a trichotomy there will be a direct isomorphism between the variable and the structure of the data: all middle answers can be given the middle value and the clear answers the extreme values. This means that the middle value will serve as a dust bin; the unclear cases are thrown in the middle on the assumption that this is where they do least harm. We then must see to it that this assumption is followed up. It should also be noticed that the most important assumption is that clear answers are about equally distant from the middle, e.g. that it does not 'take more' to disagree than to agree, etc. If there are serious doubts here, the trichotomy should be reduced to a dichotomy.

Variables with *more* than three values should be avoided; even if they may be good for data-collection and for showing distributions they are not necessarily good for index-formation. If variables with five values are used, for instance, the consequence may easily be that a number of 'strongly agree' will balance twice that number of 'agree', even though there may be good reasons to believe that the important difference is between indifference and opinion, not between shades of opinion. This throws out Likert Scales.

We shall now argue that one should have $r_1 = r_2 = \ldots = r_n$, i.e., either all equal to 2 or all equal to 3. The reason for this is evident. Imagine we add one dichotomy coded 0,1 to a trichotomy coded 0, 1, 2. Index-values 0 and 3 would have a clear, symmetric meaning, and would refer to one value-combination each. But index-value 2, for instance, could be interpreted as 'disagree + agree' or as 'agree + middle answer'. That there are two different interpretations of the same value need not concern us, that lies in the nature of any index. What is more troublesome is that they seem so different in meaning; the first pattern looks like 'zero' and the second one like '+', to put it that way. By means of two trichotomies we get much more equal combinations in the same class:

agree	2	2	3	4
middle	1	1	2	3
disagree	0	0	1	2
		0: disagree	1: middle	2: agree

When we use one trichotomy and one dichotomy, we give an 'agree' in the trichotomy twice as much weight as an 'agree' in the dichotomy. This can, of course, be corrected for by coding the dichotomy 0, 2, which means that we make space for an empirically empty middle category, but then we could just as well have coded it as a trichotomy or reduced the trichotomy to a dichotomy.

We have now cut down the variety in Table 3.1.1 considerably by requesting that the variables be recast so as to have the same number of values, but also that this number should be equal to 2 or equal to 3. We shall now simplify even further by saying that not only should the *number* of the values be equal, the values themselves should also be equal. This means that the variables enter symmetrically, for instance with the values 0, 1, and 2 in the formula. Imagine, however, that one variable was given the values 0, 2, and 4. Obviously, this would be tantamount to giving it a double weight. If this is desired, it should rather be done in terms of explicit weights than implicitly in connection with the values. But we will also argue that weights should not be given in these indices, for the following reasons:

(1) it makes the index-construction more complex,
(2) it is doubtful that comparability between the variables is really arrived at, since assumptions become rather complex – not only the assumptions linked to the additivity, but also the idea that a 'yes' on one variable equals not one other yes but *two* other yes'es on less heavily weighted variables, and
(3) if weighting seems necessary it is highly probable that the variables are not only quantitatively but also qualitatively different so that they really belong to different clusters and should enter different indices. Thus, if all variables are perceived as equal, except one which one would like to give double weight, it will probably be much better to leave it out of the index and make a separate analysis with that variable.

In the following we assume that all variables that shall be included in the index have the values 0, 1, and 2.

The next problem is the distribution of the variables in the index. The distribution is given by the data, but we can change it by collapsing the values to make trichotomous variables. One general recommendation would run as follows:

(1) Make the new values according to *meaning*, so that they combine the old values in a meaningful way. If this does not determine the cuts unambiguously, then
(2) make the new values so that the distribution on the variable is as nearly *uniform* as possible, for three reasons
    (a) to avoid the introduction of a bias, deliberate or not, in the index by means of a 'mechanical' principle,
    (b) to permit a good dispersion of the units on the index, and
    (c) it is the only distribution that suggests itself – all other distributions would be artificial.

In practice the division of the index is often given when the distribution is inspected. As will be shown later, an index based on trichotomous items (and this is what we have recommended in general) will, provided the items are well intercorrelated, show a W-shaped distribution. To trichotomize a W is simple enough, even if this does not lead to an exactly uniform distribution. One should try to include the index value n in the middle group since it corresponds to the 'central' pattern $11 \ldots 1$. That index-values 0 and $2n$ fall in the first and third groups is evident.

In general it is obvious that the rules for the cutting points are so *ad hoc* that the skilled analyst often can prove the most diverse things. For this reason it is recommended, for important findings, to show that they are invariant of changes in the cutting points, a point which will be elaborated in II, 5.4.

If we now proceed to the index construction, it will be done according to this format:

Table 3.2.1. *Format for the construction of additive indices*

Variables	Values		
	0	1	2
X_1	v_{10}	v_{11}	v_{12}
X_2	v_{20}	v_{21}	v_{22}
.	.	.	.
.	.	.	.
.	.	.	.
X_n	v_{n0}	v_{n1}	v_{n2}

The Table only tells which are the values on the n variables that are given the numerical values 0, 1, and 2 respectively. The index-value of a *pattern* is then simply the sum of the numerical values of all the n values that enter in the pattern. If M is the data matrix of the m units by the n variables, we get this simple expression for the index-values:

$$I = MU$$

where U is the column vector with n 1's. I will come out as a column vector too. Thus, imagine that we have $m = n = 3$ and this simple data matrix:

$$M = \begin{Bmatrix} 0 & 0 & 2 \\ 1 & 2 & 0 \\ 0 & 1 & 1 \end{Bmatrix}$$

Multiplication by U gives:

$$I = \begin{Bmatrix} 2 \\ 3 \\ 2 \end{Bmatrix}$$

because postmultiplication by U is tantamount to adding up the rows.

The formula $I = MU$ is easily generalized. Thus, we can introduce weights by substituting for U the column vector k, which has the w_i in its position no. i corresponding to the weight w_i being given to variable no. i.[3] U can then be seen as the special case where all weights are equal and for simplicity set equal to 1. Correspondingly, we may permit a greater range than 0 to 2 inside the matrix, i.e. from 0 to 4, but still use U – and we get the 'Likert scale'. If we combine these two ideas, we may arrive at a combined Thurstone-Likert scale, where the scores on the individual variables are given according to the Likert system but the weights according to the Thurstone system. But a researcher who suggests a method of index-construction as cumbersome as this also has the burden of proving that he really gains something that could not be more easily obtained by the simpler means discussed above, and without infracting the conditions for adding variables.

The classical Thurstone method can be seen in the perspective of what has been said so far. As is well known, it consists in two steps, one cognitive and the other evaluative. First of all, a panel of judges is asked to score a number of stimuli (e.g. sentences presumably tapping the same attitudinal dimension) on an 11-point scale, where the values are called A to K according to how favorable or unfavorable they are on the underlying dimension. This yields a data matrix, and for each column two *parameters* are calculated: the median and the dispersion (e.g., P_{75}-P_{25}). Only variables or items with less than a conventionally established dispersion are accepted – the others are considered too dissensual to be useful. For the acceptable items the median value (translating A to K as 1 to 11) is then used as its *weight*.

In the second stage relatively consensual items are handed out to respondents, who are supposed to express their own attitude on a two-point scale – by checking the items with which they agree. The median of the weights of the items checked is then used as the index of the individual attitude.

We agree with the criticism, raised against Thurstone's original work, that there is no built-in guarantee for an interval scale at any point here – hence ordinal parameters ($P_{75} - P_{25}$ for dispersion and P_{50} for central tendency) are used.[4] With interval scale parameters, all becomes more elegant, however. Let us call the cognitive data matrix M_c, the evaluative data matrix M_e (both based on the acceptable items only), and the number of judges m_c. We then get the final values of the weighted, additive index:

$$I = M_e \cdot \left(\frac{1}{m_c} U' M_c \right)'$$

To the right we have a column vector containing all the means of the distributions in the cognitive matrix (originally we get it as a row vector, so it has to be transposed). This is then postmultiplied with the evaluative matrix to give the index vector, where each element is a weighted sum of the values on the variables. This formula also illustrates the meaning of premultiplication with the row vector: it gives us an additive parameter (the mean, when divided by the number of units) just as postmultiplication gives us an index (an additive index, that is).

We next turn to the *distribution* of the index. It depends on the distributions of the items, *and* on the relations between the items. The simplest possible case, the index based on the sum of two dichotomous items, may serve as an introduction.

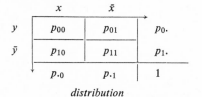

distribution   index

The probabilities are not conditional but total probabilities; and the subscripts are so as to identify them relative to the index: *the sum of the footscripts is the index value.* We may now compare these two distributions:

Index value:	0	1	2
Empirical distribution	p_{00}	$p_{01} + p_{10}$	p_{11}
Distribution in the case of independent variables	$p_{0 \cdot} p_{\cdot 0}$	$p_{1 \cdot} p_{\cdot 0} + p_{0 \cdot} p_{\cdot 1}$	$p_{1 \cdot} p_{\cdot 1}$

Imagine that all the marginal frequencies are equal to $\frac{1}{2}$. In this case the index distribution corresponding to independence is $(\frac{1}{4}, \frac{1}{2}, \frac{1}{4})$; which illustrates the important point that the case of independence relative to this distibution corresponding to independence, yields a relatively peaked distribution of the index. Evidently,

when the correlation is positive, the empirical distribution is higher at the extremes, and
when the correlation is negative, the empirical distribution is higher in the middle.

With the distribution corresponding to independence as a standard, very quick judgments as to the degree of correlation between the variables can be arrived at. But the relation is not quite simple.

Thus, one may have coincidence between the two marginal distributions without independence, as in the case below:

$\frac{1}{4}$	$\frac{1}{2}$
0	$\frac{1}{4}$

since the middle values of the index only ask for *sums* of probabilities. Further, one may have 'positive correlation to the left only', as in this case:

$\frac{1}{3}$	$\frac{1}{4}$
$\frac{1}{4}$	$\frac{1}{6}$

or positive correlation to the right only. All these cases where the data are concentrated in the corners correspond to high values of Yule's Q – and a comparison of the index distributions shows us *which* of the cases we have. To summarize:

Table 3.2.2. *Location of empirical index distribution relative to distribution corresponding to independence (2×2 case)*

	Data concentrated in	
	upper corner	lower corner
left hand corner	above to the left	above in the middle
right hand corner	above in the middle	above to the right

We may now ask the opposite question: given a shape of the distribution, what level of correlation corresponds to it? The only shape that will be studied is the straight line, i.e. the uniform distribution of the index. The distribution is uniform if and only if:

$$p_{00} = p_{01}+p_{10} = p_{11} = \tfrac{1}{3}$$

This does not determine the distribution unambiguously, since we still have the ambiguity in the bidiagonal. If we divide the third evenly between the two cells, we get the minimum value of Q compatible with the requirement of the straight line, $Q = 0.6$ (the maximum value is unity).

We now turn to the more general theory.

(1) *The case of n dichotomies.* In this case, the index value runs from 0 to n, and we may divide the index by n to make it comparable to other indices. The number of cells with the index value i is given by the binomial coefficient $\binom{n}{i}$: only one combination has the pattern $0, 0, 0, \ldots$; n combinations have one 1, and so on, till the single pattern $1, 1, 1, \ldots$.

This can be represented in Pascal's number pyramid:

Table 3.2.3. *The numbers of patterns with the same index values*
(dichotomous items)

No. of dichotomies							index value	No. of patterns
				0				
				0				
					1			
1				1		1		$2^1=2$
							2	
2				1	2		1	$2^2=4$
							3	
3			1	3		3	1	$2^3=8$
							4	
4		1	4	6		4	1	$2^4=16$
							5	
5	1	5	10	10		5	1	$2^5=32$

The distribution corresponding to independence is given by expanding (where the superscripts stand for variables 1 to n):

$$(p_0^1+p_1^1)(p_0^2+p_1^2) \ldots (p_0^n+p_1^n)$$

and collecting terms with the same sums of the subscripts: in other words, simply by multiplying the marginal sums. For the empirical distribution to be above in the left end, the frequencies with many zeros in the footscripts must be particularly high; if it is to be above in the middle, the frequencies with a medium number of zeros must be high; and finally, to be above at the right hand end, the frequencies with very few zeros must be high. This corresponds exactly to the cases outlined on p. 254.

In the case of perfect *positive* correlation only two of the 2^n patterns are empirically present: the patterns with index values 0 and n, respectively. This means that the distribution is concentrated in the extreme points. And in the case of perfect *negative* correlation there will be a peak corresponding to $\frac{1}{2}n$ or the closest integer, or rather, this may be what we define as 'perfect negative correlation' when we have more than two variables.

(2) *The case of n trichotomies.* In this case the index value runs from 0 to $2n$, and we may divide the index by $2n$ to make it comparable to other indices. Let us call the number of patterns with index value i, C_i^n. The following relation holds:

$$C_i^n = C_{i-2}^{n-1} + C_{i-1}^{n-1} + C_i^{n-1}, \text{ provided we define } C_i^n = 0 \text{ for } i > 2n.$$

For imagine we have $n-1$ trichotomies and add a new one. We can now get patterns with index value i in three and only three ways: by combining the 0 of the new trichotomy with the value i in the old combination, or the 1 in the new trichotomy with the value $i-1$ in the old combination, or finally the 2 of the new trichotomy with the value $i-2$ of the old combination. This leads to the pyramid:

Table 3.2.4. *The numbers of patterns with the same index values*
(for trichotomous items)

No. of trichotomies	*index value* 0	1	2	3	4	5	6	7	8	9	10	No. of patterns
1	1	1	1									$3^1 = 3$
2	1	2	3	2	1							$3^2 = 9$
3	1	3	6	7	6	3	1					$3^3 = 27$
4	1	4	10	16	19	16	10	4	1			$3^4 = 81$
5	1	5	15	30	45	51	45	30	15	5	1	$3^5 = 243$

The sum of each row in the pyramid is equal to the total number of patterns. The pyramid can easily be developed starting with the case of one trichotomy where the numbers of 'patterns' with the three possible values is 1, 1, 1; just as Pascal's pyramid for the binomial coefficients is developed starting with 1,1 (but locating the next level *between* the numbers in the level above – for the binomial coefficients are the sums of only *two* terms at the preceding level).

The distribution corresponding to independence is obtained by expanding:

$$(p_0^1 + p_1^1 + p_2^1)(p_0^2 + p_1^2 + p_2^2) \ldots (p_0^n + p_1^n + p_2^n)$$

and collecting terms with the same sums of the subscripts. The pyramid in Table 3.2.2 gives us the relative size of the frequencies in the case where all marginals are uniform.[5]

In the case of perfect *positive* correlation we do *not* get a U-shaped, but a W-shaped, distribution with three peaks. The first peak will be located at index value 0 and correspond to the pattern 0, 0 ... 0; the second peak will be located at index value n and correspond to pattern 1, 1, ... 1; and the third peak will be located at index value $2n$ and correspond to pattern 2, 2, 2, ... 2. Likewise, if the variables tend to be correlated negatively, there will be a peak corresponding to one middle index value. In this case, the index is of no value for the simple reason that it does not discriminate between the units.

The problem of how to divide the index distribution should be mentioned. Only rarely will one use the entire range of value: from 0 to n or $2n$. For analytical purposes a trichotomized index is probably most useful, and there are two obvious alternatives: to trichotomize the *index scale* in three equal parts, or to trichotomize the *index distribution* in three equal parts. If the distribution happens to be uniform, which generally means a relatively high positive correlation, then the two principles will lead to the same result. If not, we shall have to choose, and the recommendation will be to choose the latter. To cut the *scale* in three equal parts does not tell us much, but with the *distribution* in three equal parts we still have an intersubjective basis for the cuts and at the same time a distribution that can stand up against the splits brought in by multi-variate analysis.

The ideal case is the case where the correlation is so high that we get about one third in either of the extremes, and the rest in the middle. This is actually close to the case mentioned in II, 3.1 where class order implies element order – but the condition is very strong and very rarely fulfilled in practice. Or rather, if it is fulfilled it may be argued that too similar items have been used. The problem is to find dissimilar items tapping the same dimension so as to yield an index with sufficient dispersion to be useful. For this to happen, independence is not enough – that also yields a peaked distribution. Positive intercorrelations are needed, and they must be relatively high if one wants the index distribution to beat the uniform distribution. But to fix limits for *how* high seems to us quite futile.

Let us then look at the additive index in the light of the ten criteria put forward in II, 3.1 for the evaluation of indices in general. The additive index is defined for all possible patterns, since addition of the values in the pattern is everywhere possible. How much information an index value gives, however, depends on the distributions. And here it is obvious that the additive index is far from ideal, in general. But this topic is so important that it will be discussed in the next section.

We then proceed to the question of *stability*, the third requirement on the list in II, 3.1. One of the major reasons for the usefulness of the additive index is its stability, a property it has by definition: it always obtains and is not subject to evaluation like the *degree* of preservation of information, for it is built into the definition of the index. To show this, imagine that a respondent is asked a set of questions one day, that the pattern is recorded, and that the same set of questions is asked some other day. For both patterns the additive index value is computed. In general, there will be fluctuations in the responses; the respondent will not be able to repeat his own performance completely. We can now distinguish between two cases:

(1) *The fluctuations are random* – some of them are in one direction, some in the other. In this case we would require of the index that it yield (almost) the same value.
(2) *The fluctuations are not random* – they are systematic or have a systematic component over and above the random component; which means that the individual has changed his attitude. In this case we would require of the index that it yield a different value.

It is easily seen that the additive index fulfills both of these requirements; for in the first case the value lost on one variable (e.g. from '2' to '1') is gained on the other variable (e.g. from '0' to '1'), and the sum is constant. This is a strong argument for the additive index, and gives it analytical status as what we have called a 'personality variable', because values are permanent.

It is easily seen that a *multiplicative* index does not satisfy (1) in general. Imagine we work with trichotomies and give them the values 1, 2, and 3 to avoid the difficulties with 0. A change from '3' to '2' on one variable would then reduce the index value by one third, but this would be more than compensated for by a change from '1' to '2' on the other variable – which would double the index value so that we would end up with $2\frac{2}{3}I = \frac{4}{3}I$. This can be corrected for by giving the three values numbers that have equal ratios instead of equal differences, e. g. 1, 2, and 4, however, which would make the multiplicative index equivalent to the additive one.

Thus, with the additive index the mathematical conditions for stability are satisfied, except for one problem. If the index is based on six trichotomies, for instance, and the interval from 0 to 12 is divided in three ('high', 'medium', and 'low'), one-step differences will be registered for individuals who change a little close to the divisions, but not for individuals well inside the divisions. This is arbitrary and gives us one reason more for some variation in the way an index is divided, for trying several alternatives.

Thus, the additive index combines stability with sensitivity: it registers even a one-step change in one variable, but is stable with regard to random changes. It does quite well on the next requirement too, *simplicity;* both in the sense that the index is conceptually simple and in the sense that it is simple to calculate. With the data matrix written out, the index is calculated immediately by summing the rows.

There are also simple IBM methods. The index may be made from the deck of cards in two ways, depending on the kind of machinery available. The first thing to do is obviously to recode the variables and repunch them, as 0,1 or 0,1,2. If a calculator is available, the machine can be asked to sum the content of the columns specified and punch the sum in an empty column. But this can also be done by means of a sorter if one has a sorting shelf and equipment for gang-punching. The sorting shelf is very simple. It has two levels and, say, 21 positions on each level, numbered from 0 to 20 so that a maximum of ten trichotomous indices can be handled (more than this is not practical). The shelf is placed on the wall above the sorter. One then starts by sorting on the first variable, and, in case of an index based on trichotomies, gets three decks of cards, representing '0', '1', and '2'. These three decks are then placed in the corresponding rooms on the lower level of the shelf. Then the 0-deck is sorted on the second variable and put in the corresponding rooms, 0, 1, and 2 on the upper level. But when the 1-deck is sorted on the second variable the three decks that will normally result from this are not placed in 0, 1, and 2 on the upper level, but on 1, 2, and 3 – because they already have '1' from the first variable. Similarly, when the 2-deck is sorted, the decks are placed in 2, 3, and 4. Thus, the position a card has in the sorting shelf tells the operator, at any moment in this process, what index value the card has *so far*. One then continues sorting on all the variables, moving the cards up and down, and zero, one, or two steps to the right depending on the outcome of the last sorting. One ends up with all the cards distributed according to index value, which can then be gang-punched in an empty column. Also, one may get the distribution of the index from the cards as they are in the shelf, and combine adjacent values before punching.

As to *comparability* of indices a very simple procedure is available: dividing the index value with the maximum value, i. e. by n for dichotomous indices and $2n$ for trichotomous indices. The index distribution does not change with this linear transformation, and comparability is obtained as long as we can claim additivity, i.e. as long as the items and the values are 'symmetric'. In other words: as long as the variables can be said to count equally and the values are comparable, we can assume additivity, and consequently comparability when we only divide with the maximum index value. In this way we can compare indices with different content, different n, and different r.

As to *transformations* of the variables the additive index is independent of linear transformations only, and only if the same transformation is applied to all variables. But this is built into the symmetry conditions that define the additive index: we are not supposed to change the numerical values given to the variables as we want. Whether we call them 0, 1, 2; 1, 2, 3; or 4, 7, 10 is only a puestion of convenience – but 0, 2, 1 or 0, 1, 3 are both illegitimate, changing the order of the units or the distance between them. Only linear transformations, not monotone transformations or permutations, are permitted.

The *sampling distribution* presents us with a relatively knotty problem. As pointed out, the central limit theorem guarantees relatively rapid approximation to the normal distribution when dependence is weak or absent and n (not m) is high. This gives a base line for evaluation of the often very strangely shaped distributions to be found in practice, particularly when trichotomized items are used. In general, some kind of non-parametric, ordinal statistical test seems to be recommendable, since we cannot assume interval scale.

The *validity as a measure* is less complicated, for here nothing, not even nominal scale level, can be claimed from the mathematical properties of the index. If the index is cumulative (see next section), then the difference between one value and the next is by definition that one more item has been 'endorsed', 'accepted', or whatever one prefers to call it. But this also applies to the non-cumulative additive index if it is based on dichotomies: an index of total social rank would count the number of topdog statuses a person has, an index of test achievement may count the number of correct answers, etc. The difference between a general additive index and a cumulative index is in the interpretation of one unit more on the index: in the first case, it means that the number of endorsed items is higher by one; in the second case, that the same items have been endorsed, and one more. Thus, in the second case not only nominal but also ordinal scale is guaranteed since there is only one pattern per value, and one more item is added for each additional step in index value. But in general the results of the additive scale in an analysis would be such that we would be quite willing to grant it the same ordinal status. And here the distinction between an index for descriptive and for analytic work should be noticed.

Of the *analytic* index we would not require that all pairs of individuals be 'correctly' ordered (on the underlying dimension) as long as the index can be used as an analytic tool, i.e. to reveal patterns of relations with other variables, because the ordering is correct *grosso modo*. For the *descriptive* index we would require correct ordering also within each single pair. A good example is the ordering of applicants to a vacancy or fellowship. If one wanted to test hypotheses about them, an index that orders them fairly well is sufficient to get at significant correlations. But this is rather insufficient if what they apply for is scarce and a decisive cut has to be introduced somewhere. For Norwegians this is known as the *artium* grade problem.

To claim interval scale properties seems unwarranted with the high number of assumptions that have been made. Both symmetry conditions will have to be fulfilled within and between the variables, and that claim is at any rate meaningless if it cannot be validated, as will be discussed in II, 3.4. The *interpretability* will depend on the selection of variables and the outcome of the analysis – topics to be discussed in II, 3.7 and in II, 5.

Since this section on additive indices constitutes an important link in our general methodology, let us conclude with some practical remarks.

First of all, when variables are selected for inclusion in the index it is highly important that they are 'of the same kind'. Thus, one should not mix behavioral and attitudinal variables in the same index, nor combine cognitive and evaluative stimuli. Imagine the task is to construct an index measuring localism-cosmopolitanism. One index may be based on travel experience, another index on knowledge, and a third index on evaluation of the 'How would you like to live at X, Y, Z', where X, Y, and Z form a distance scale from where the respondent actually lives. These three indices tap different sub-dimensions and should be kept separate at least in the initial stages of the analysis; otherwise it is difficult to argue that the variables should count equally much, as they do in the additive index. Another matter is the possibility of combining these three indices in one super-index after more knowledge about them is obtained.

Secondly, one should see to it that the variables are structurally as similar as possible. In the cases above this is easily obtained. One may ask five times 'Have you ever been to –' with answers 'never, once, more than once' and five times 'how would you like to live at –' with answers 'like, indifferent, dislike, DK', and two indices can be constructed with five items coded 0, 1, 2 in each. The indices, hence, will range from 0 to 10. The only difficulty here is that five very similar questions with identical answer categories very easily will produce a response-set. To avoid this, the method of changing the wording for one half of the items from positive to negative should not be used, since it introduces a difference between variables to be combined in the same index. Rather, one should try to disperse the variables in the same index to different parts of the questionnaire, even at the risk that the questionnaire will look less tidy.

Thirdly, the arguments for trichotomous items (more flexibility; DK and neutral answers can be put in middle category) should be weighed against the arguments for dichotomous items (additivity more permissible since one is really only counting true answers, or topdog statuses, or positive responses). Dichotomous items are preferable, since the requirements of additivity are better satisfied; hence, one should try to eliminate evasive answers by forcing the respondents to answer clearly (or by eliminating items that cause difficulties). In any case, high index value is indicative of response consistency.

Fourthly, a distinction should be made between two kinds of additive indices. In some indices the theoretical zero point in both variables and index will be in the middle, in other cases the zero point will be at the (left hand) end. The two examples of answer alternatives given above can serve as an illustration. In either case the code of the answers should be 0, 1, 2; but in the first case '0' will refer to 'never', which is also the theoretical zero point, since it registers travel experience; and in the second case, '0' will correspond to 'like', where 'indifferent' is the theoretical zero point. The theoretical zero point will usually be in the middle when a dimension is explored by means of the technique of 'paired comparisons' where alternatives are presented pairwise,[7] as in this case:

Imagine your country was attacked by an enemy and the choice was between the following alternatives, which one would you prefer:

atomic war	or	conventional war
occupation	or	atomic war
conventional war	or	occupation

If the respondents make clear choices, a three-variable index may be constructed based on dichotomous items coded '0' for the 'softer' alternative and '1' for the 'tougher' alternative. If DK or 'both terrible' or similar answers are frequent, trichotomous items must be used, and the neutral or zero points of the variables and the index would be in the middle. In practice the two kinds of indices can be handled in the same way, as long as one remembers that the middle category is usually contaminated since it serves as a dustbin, to some extent – and that the middle category has different substantive interpretations depending on where the zero point is located.

3.3. *Cumulative indices*

As mentioned, the question of loss of information in additive indices is important, although its importance may often have been exaggerated. To get an impression of the nature of the problem, imagine that we have an index based on six dichotomous items, so that the index runs from 0 to 6. We get:

Table 3.3.1. *A comparison of number of patterns in the general case and when no information is lost*

Index value	No. of possible patterns	No. of empirical patterns when no information is lost
0	1	1
1	6	1
2	15	1
3	20	1
4	15	1
5	6	1
6	1	1
SUM	64	7

Only in the case where there is one and only one pattern corresponding to each of the $n+1$ index values do we lose no information: for only in this case is the mapping of V on I not only single-valued, but one-one; so that one can infer the whole pattern from the index value. In general, the pattern variety has to be reduced from 2^n down to $n+1$ to permit complete restorability, which is rather demanding on the distributions. On the other hand there is a case of an additive index that satisfies this requirement or at least almost satisfies it: the famous Guttman scale, or cumulative scale.[8]

To evaluate to what extent an additive index forms a cumulative scale there are several procedures; the simplest and most 'objective' one seems to be that suggested by Goodenough.[9] One starts with the data matrix, but with two important changes:

units are ordered in terms of additive index value, with the highest at the top; variables are ordered in terms of distribution of positive responses, with the highest to the left.

Thus, a perfect Guttman scale or cumulative scale might have this data matrix:

Table 3.3.2. *The data matrix of a cumulative scale*

| Indi- | Variables | | | | Index | Cumulative | | | |
viduals	1	2	3	4	value	pattern			
1	1	1	1	1	4	1	1	1	1
2	1	1	1	0					
3	1	1	1	0	3	1	1	1	0
4	1	1	0	0					
5	1	1	0	0	2	1	1	0	0
6	1	1	0	0					
7	1	0	0	0					
8	1	0	0	0	1	1	0	0	0
9	0	0	0	0					
10	0	0	0	0	0	0	0	0	0
proportion of positive response	.8	.6	.3	.1					

For each index value there is only one pattern, and that pattern is given very simply by the imposed order of the variables. The variables are ordered according to frequencies of 1's. Hence, for each drop in index value as we go down the list, one more variable changes from 1 to 0. The scale is said to be *cumulative* because increasing index value means not only *more* responses that are positive, but that the original ones remain and *more are added*. It should be noticed that this implies a one-one correspondence between pattern and index – *but* the converse is not true. One can have 'each index value – one pattern' without having a cumulative scale, as in Table 3.3.3.

In this case index value 1 corresponds to one and only one pattern, but this is not the pattern we should have according to the principle of cumulative variables. Thus there are two kinds of deviations from the perfect scale: more than one pattern corresponds to the same index value, and patterns appear that do not belong to the cumulative scale. Both can be defined as *errors*, as deviations from the perfect.

The famous *coefficient of reproducibility* is a measure of the degree to which the empirical data matrix, arranged according to the two rules above corresponds to the data matrix of a cumulative scale. This is done simply by counting the number of errors we would commit if we predicted for index

266

Table 3.3.3. *The data matrix of a non-cumulative scale with perfect corre-spondence between index and pattern*

Indi-viduals	Variables				Index value	Cumulative pattern			
	1	2	3	4					
1	1	1	1	1	4	1	1	1	1
2	1	1	1	0	3	1	1	1	0
3	1	1	1	0					
4	1	1	0	0	2	1	1	0	0
5	0	0	0	1	1	0	0	0	1
6	0	0	0	0	0	0	0	0	0
proportion of positive response	$\frac{2}{3}$	$\frac{2}{3}$	$\frac{1}{2}$	$\frac{1}{3}$					

value i always the pattern with i 1's and $(n-i)$ 0's – as we have done above. Thus, for respondent no. 5 above we would predict 1000 (knowing that he has index value 1) whereas his pattern actually is 0001 – consequently we would commit two errors. Since the *number* of 1's is correct, the error is always in *where* they are placed; so if there is a 1 where there should be a 0, there will have to be a zero where there should be a 1 – consequently the number of errors will have to be even. The maximum number of errors one can make is obviously $m \cdot n$ – predicting all variables incorrectly for all individuals, so one (naive) coefficient of reproducibility would be

$$R = 1 - \frac{e}{m \cdot n}$$

If we write it as $\dfrac{m \cdot n - e}{m \cdot n}$ we see that $R = I$, the measure of information defined in 3.1.

When no errors are made in the prediction from the perfect cumulative scale, then $R = 1$. But from this it does not follow that the minimum value of R is zero. By the method described it is impossible to make *only* wrong predictions, in the general case. For each additive index value, i, the pre-dicted pattern:

$$\underbrace{11 \ldots 1}_{i \text{ times}} \underbrace{00 \ldots 0}_{n-i \text{ times}}$$

is to be compared with the empirical patterns, of which there are $\binom{n}{i}$ differ-ent kinds (depending on *where* the 1's are located). For $i = 0$ we cannot

267

make mistakes in the prediction, as there is only one pattern that corresponds to this index value. The same applies to the case of $i = n$. For $i = 1$ we either make no error or 2 errors: either the 1 is located where it should be and there is no mistake, or it is not and there are two mistakes in the prediction. For $i = 2$ there are three possibilities: both 1's are where they should be (no error), one of them is located wrongly (2 errors), or both of them are located wrongly (4 errors). Thus, for index value i we get a maximum of $2i$ errors when all the i 1's are placed where they should not be. However, this is only true as long as $i \leqslant n/2$, and must also distinguish between n even and n uneven so as to get this Table:

Table 3.3.4. *Maximum errors in a cumulative scale*

Index value	n even	n uneven
$i = 0$	0	0
$i = 1$	2	2
$i = 2$	4	4
.	.	.
.	.	.
.	.	.
$i = \dfrac{n-1}{2}$	–	$n-1$
$i = \dfrac{n}{2}$	n	–
$i = \dfrac{n+1}{2}$	–	$n-1$
.	.	.
.	.	.
.	.	.
$i = n-2$	4	4
$i = n-1$	2	2
$i = n$	0	0

In the case of n even the maximum number of errors is n – which means all values erroneously predicted – but this occurs only if two conditions are satisfied: (1) index value $i = n/2$, and (2) all 1's where there should be zeros and all zeros where there should be 1's. For n uneven this is impossible, for the simple reason that the number of 1's and zeros will always be different. One value will have to be correct when one cannot interchange everything, and the result is not n, but $n-1$ errors.

From this reasoning alone nothing can be said about the maximum error unless we know the distribution of the m units on the index variable. If m_i

units have index value i, we get these formulas for the maximum number of errors:

n even: $\quad 2 \sum\limits_{i=0}^{n/2-1} i(m_i+m_{n-i})+n \cdot m_{n/2}$

n uneven: $2 \sum\limits_{i=0}^{n-1} i(m_i+m_{n-i})$

or to spell it out:

n even: $\quad 0 \cdot m_0+2 \cdot m_1+4 \cdot m_2+ \ldots +n \cdot m_{n/2}+ \ldots +4m_{n-2}$
$$+2m_{n-1}+0m_n$$

n uneven: $0 \cdot m_0+2 \cdot m_1+4 \cdot m_2+ \ldots +(n-1)m_{(n-1)/2}+(n-1)m_{(n+1)/2}+ \ldots$
$$+4m_{n-2}+2m_{n-1}+0m_n$$

Worse one cannot do, and this is much better than having everything wrong, which would correspond to $m \cdot n$ errors. Thus, imagine that we have two cases, one with 6 variables and the other with 7, and in either case one unit for each index value (which means 7 units in the first case, 8 in the second). It is easily verified that the maximum number of errors is 18 in the first case and 24 in the second, and not 42 and 56 as one might be led to believe. This means that the minimum reproducibility is

$$1-\frac{18}{42} = = 0.57 \quad \text{and} \quad 1-\frac{24}{56} = 0.57$$

The general formulas for the minimum reproducibility in this case of uniform index distribution are

n even: $\quad 1-\dfrac{4 \cdot \frac{1}{2}\left(\dfrac{n}{2}-1\right)\dfrac{n}{2}+n}{n(n+1)} = 1-\frac{1}{2}\frac{n}{n+1} = 1-\frac{1}{2}\left(1-\frac{1}{n}+\frac{1}{n^2}- \cdot \cdot\right)$

n uneven: $\quad 1-\dfrac{4 \cdot \frac{1}{2}\dfrac{n-1}{2} \cdot \dfrac{n+1}{2}}{n(n+1)} = 1-\frac{1}{2}\left(1-\frac{1}{n}\right)$

The two are very similar, as they should be. For increasing n they tend to the value $R_{min} = 0.50$. But with a peaked index distribution we get much lower values of R_{min}, and for n even and $m_{n/2} = m$ we get $R_{min} = 0$. However, with this calculation we have not taken into account the rule for ordering items, only the rule for ordering units, so in practice R_{min} would be high. Obviously, R should be evaluated relative to R_{min} to be meaningful, e.g. by means of:

$$\frac{R-R_{\min}}{1-R_{\min}}$$

To get an estimate of the coefficient of reproducibility or preservation of information, the obvious method is to take *a sample* of units and rearrange the data matrix for them. By suitable exclusion and inclusion of items and introduction of new cutting points, a high coefficient can almost always be obtained, but these *ad hoc* changes will have to be well justified.

In conclusion, it should be pointed out what it *means* when an additive index satisfies this condition of being cumulative. It does *not* mean that the index variable suddenly becomes interval or anything similar. It *does* mean that precise inferences can be made about the pattern, although the importance of this seems to have been exaggerated considerably. What is wanted in social science analysis is not knowledge about the individual's response pattern in concentrated form, but a simple and fruitful way of ordering the individuals according to how much they have of some latent attribute; and for that purpose an additive index even with very low reproducibility coefficient may be just as good.

There is, however, another meaning that can be given to the cumulative scale which is of considerable importance. Imagine an investigation is made of the inhabitants in, say, a Moroccan village. Six dichotomies that have to do with 'modernism – traditionalism' may be used for the villagers, e. g. whether they use shoes or 'babouches', European clothes (shirt and trousers) or 'djellaba', how much French they speak, what kind of food they eat, how much they travel, and what they listen to on the radio. With six items we get seven scale types, and 57 non-scale, among them two extreme types – provided the variables are cumulative. Whether they are or not, probably means very little in terms of the *analytical* conclusions we could draw based on the relation between such variables and background or attitudinal data. But the very fact that the combination of units and items is such as to produce a cumulative scale is an important empirical fact in itself. One interpretation of this is in terms of accessibility of modern attributes: such data would give insight into the *process* of modernization, not only the *degree* of modernization. Similarly, if the items in a mental test are cumulative, the standard interpretation in terms of degree of *difficulty* is probably correct.[10]

To summarize: a high coefficient of reproducibility does not change the structure of the index variable, e. g. to interval. But it does represent an important empirical fact which may or may not have an interesting interpretation.[11]

3.4. *Comparative indices*

In I, 4 the general problem of how to present variables or objects for evaluation was treated as a problem of degree of constraint. The distinction was made between, on one hand, evaluation of each item/variable/object by it-self, one at a time, and on the other hand, an evaluation of each item relative to a set of items. The latter is evaluation under constraint and leads to a certain loss of variety under comparable conditions. The question confronting us here is then: data obtained under constraint also form patterns. How do we find one-dimensional expressions, how do we project from the set of possible patterns to an index, with loss of variety but gains in simplicity?

We shall only consider some simple, but important forms of data obtained under constraint. Imagine n items are given and the individual is asked to pick k of them (thus, he is not asked to reject any). Let us first imagine that he is *not* also asked to order them. This would differ from evaluation without constraint with $r = 2$ (agree – do not agree) in one significant way: the number of agreements is laid down in the instructions to be equal to k (this is the constraint). Thus, if all variables are indicators of the same dimension, an additive index would give the value k to all individuals who have followed the instructions correctly, and consequently not differentiate at all, which makes it useless.

There are two ways out of this dilemma, where the first may be used alone, and the second presupposes the first. The individual, the *unit,* is constant, so nothing can be done with him/it. But we can introduce differentiation in the *variables* and in the *values.* For the variables we may introduce *weights,* and instead of the two values (pick – not pick) that serve as a minimum to select the k items we may use as many values as necessary to discriminate between n items, i.e. n, or a trichotomy of the type: pick k_1, reject k_2, where $k_1 + k_2 < n$.

The first method, giving weights to the items, depends on how much discrimination is needed. The simplest is a system with two weights, 0 and 1. Thus, the respondent may have been asked to pick three reasons from a set of six of why he is for the Common Market. The reasons may then have been prearranged so that three of them are indicative of nationalistic orientation and the other three of a regional orientation. If we are interested in an index of regional orientation we would give '1' to those items and '0' to the other items. The index would run from 0 to 3, depending on how many 'regionalistic' choices there are in the pattern. The total number of patterns is $\binom{6}{3}$, out of which, say, index-value '2' is produced by $\binom{3}{2}\binom{3}{1}$ patterns (2 regional and 1 national choice).

In general, n items are divided into two groups (for simplicity we make them equal in size). The individual is asked to pick k, which may be equal to $n/2$. The number of patterns is $\binom{n}{k}$ and the number of index values $k+1$. Thus, in general, a considerable simplification is obtained. Of the patterns $\binom{n/2}{p}\binom{n/2}{n/2-p}$ yield index value p.

We may also permit more variety in the weights given to the items; but, for reasons discussed many times, more than three weights (reject, leave or pick; 0, 1, 2) should not be used unless there is an independent validation of them.[12] Since the method essentially yields an additive index, we have no more reason to assume interval scale for the weights given to the *variables* here than we had for assuming interval scale for the *values* given to the responses in II, 3.2, in the discussion of additive indices. In the construction of an ordinary additive index the items are usually not given weights, and the individual may be given a score '2' because of his response. In the kind of comparative index we discuss here the responses are not given weights, but the individual may receive a score '2' because of the item he picked. Although we know of no research to substantiate this, it is hard to believe that the two methods should make much difference as to how they classify individuals.

The second method, then, consists in introducing a measure of the *degree* to which an item is picked, not only 'accept' – 'reject'. If one first picks k items and then evaluates each of them independently one has a basis for an ordinary additive index. But we assume that the instruction is to evaluate them relative to each other, i.e. *to order them*. In this case we get 'pick k and order them', which results in $k! \cdot \binom{n}{k}$ patterns. For the case $k = n$ the instruction amounts to simple ranking of all items, for $k = 1$ it makes no sense, and for k much higher than 5 it probably does not make too much sense either, since it requests too much of the individuals, at least of a sample without special training in mental manipulation of many items.

On the basis of k ranks no index can be formed, since the sum of the k ranks will always be $\frac{1}{2}k(k+1)$ for all patterns (provided ties are averaged in the standard way). But it makes good sense to combine this with the 0,1 weight system for the items. Thus, what matters is not how many items of the type given weight '1' the individual picks, but what rank order he gives to these items relative to the items of weight '0' he has picked. (Scores would then be given in the reverse order of the ranking, k for the first rank, etc.) Imagine there are $n/2$ of either kind of items and that the individual has to pick and rank order $k \leqslant n/2$. The index will vary from 0 to $\frac{1}{2}k(k+1)$, and he can compensate for items he does not pick from the '1' group by

272

giving high rank to the ones he picks. To discriminate further, *three* weights may be given to the items. This very simple method is illustrated in:

Table 3.4.1. *Examples of comparative index-formation, $n = 6$, $k = 3$*

	Weights 0,1								Weights 0,1,2						
	0	0	0	1	1	1	Index		0	0	1	1	2	2	Index
I_1	1	2	3	0	0	0	0	I_1	1	2	3	0	0	0	3
I_2	0	0	1	2	3	0	5	I_2	0	1	2	3	0	0	5
I_3	0	0	0	1	2	3	6	I_3	0	0	0	1	2	3	11

scores = inverted ranks

For the same reason as it seems fictitious to have a system with more than three weights, it seems fictitious to use $k > 3$ in this method. Even with k equal to 3 we in fact equalize patterns that are very different. The person who picks one item with weight 1 (and the others with weight 0) and gives it the first rank receives the same score for this as the person who picks one item with weight 0 (and the others with weight 1) and gives that the first rank (left half of Table 3.4.1, both get the total score of 3). This is not essentially different from the problems of additive indices in general, but the fictitiousness will increase very rapidly with more elaborate systems, – if we still want to use some kind of product-sum index process.

A variation of this scheme occurs if we use the 'distribute k points' method mentioned in I, 4.4. If the k points are to be distributed on n items, the number of patterns is the number of partitions of the number k in n parts, in other words $\binom{k+n-1}{n-1}$ patterns. But on this basis alone no additive index can be made, for the constraint operates in this case so as to make the sum of all scores equal to k. To discriminate, we have to give weights to the items, and the only difference between this technique and the one discussed above is the greater variety of values given to the scores. In this there is a pretense of interval scale which actually may be closely approximated, because the instruction forces the respondent to make exactly the type of judgments pertinent for interval scales, i.e. comparisons of differences.

Comparative indices can now be analyzed in terms of the same dimensions we have applied in II, 3.2 and II, 3.3 above, i.e. in terms of relations between intercorrelation pattern and shape of index distribution, and in

18 *

terms of whether the items are cumulative. We leave this to the motivated reader, however.

A much more refined technique for dealing with comparative data has been developed by Coombs, viz., the unfolding technique.[13] However, the method seems to be much too refined. Torgerson gives an excellent review of the technique,[14] but concludes that 'few if any sets of data have been found that fit the model exactly'.[15] He also feels that 'the unfolding procedure will likely remain of more theoretical than practical interest',[16] because there is no process for evaluating degree of approximation of model to data, and no probability models. The techniques developed by Coombs, like the ones developed by Guttman and Lazarsfeld, are models insofar as they require something of the data. But the additive index as such is not a model (the additive index with U-shaped or W-shaped distribution is) – whether based on absolute or comparative data its usefulness depends on whether one can rediscover the known, and discover the unknown.

3.5. *Manifest vs. latent*

We assume in the following that data have been obtained for m units on n variables by means of r-point scales. Thus, if we concentrate on *one* variable only, the distribution of values over the r-point discrete variable is given. This is *the manifest variable*. For some reasons, however, social scientists seem not to be content with this variable, but talk about 'underlying psychological continuum', 'true values', 'latent variables', etc. We shall now examine this position more closely, and follow Lazarsfeld in calling this variable *the latent variable* (see I, 1.3).

First of all some definitory characteristics of the two kinds of variables:

Table 3.5.1. *Some characteristics of manifest and latent variables*

	What is mapped on the variable:	Mathematical properties:
Manifest variables M (observed)	*Responses*, i.e. expressions of evaluations or beliefs re some object	*Discrete, r-point, more complex* for response *patterns*
Latent variables L (inferred)	*Respondents*, i.e. attitudes or cognitions held by persons re some object	*Continuous, interval scale*, or *discrete, interval scale*

If, on a Likert-scale a '3' is expressed, this is a response. The question is: *what attitude corresponds to this response,* i.e., how do we get from this

274

response to the respondent? If two respondents have given the responses 3, does this imply that they have the same attitude? Or if two responses are 4 and 3, and two others are 2 and 1, so that the response pairs are equidistant – does this imply that the respondents are equidistant? Psychometricians often talk about the 'true' value of a response, and we suggest that this is conceptually the same as the value we ought to give to the respondent because of his response.

The general problem can be formulated as follows: *given the two variables M and L, what is the transformation T that maps M on L, or vice versa?* If we know this transformation, the transition from the *response* to the *respondent* (or more correctly to his attitude or his belief) is in principle an easy one. And that may be said to be the object of 'true' measurement.

However, one distinction must be made at once. Transformations may be *single-valued* or *many-valued.* In the latter case, we must at least have a probability distribution that gives the probabilities of the transforms (if there are more than one transform). In either case, the transformation can be represented as a *function* or *probability distribution;* as a *mapping* (by means of a matrix), or as a *graph* or *scatter diagram.* The cases are illustrated below for a 5-point scale (and two very simple transformations):

Table 3.5.2. *Some representations of the relation between manifest and latent variables*

	Function	Mapping	Graph
Deterministic transformation $L = T(M)$	$L = M$	$\begin{array}{c|ccccc} & 1 & 2 & 3 & 4 & 5 \\ 1 & 1 & 0 & 0 & 0 & 0 \\ 2 & 0 & 1 & 0 & 0 & 0 \\ 3 & 0 & 0 & 1 & 0 & 0 \\ 4 & 0 & 0 & 0 & 1 & 0 \\ 5 & 0 & 0 & 0 & 0 & 1 \end{array}$	
Stochastic transformation $p = f(L,M)$	$P(L,M) = P_{ij}$	$\begin{array}{c|ccccc} & 1 & 2 & 3 & 4 & 5 \\ 1 & \frac{1}{2} & \frac{1}{4} & 0 & 0 & 0 \\ 2 & \frac{1}{4} & \frac{1}{2} & \frac{1}{4} & 0 & 0 \\ 3 & \frac{1}{4} & \frac{1}{4} & \frac{1}{2} & \frac{1}{4} & \frac{1}{4} \\ 4 & 0 & 0 & \frac{1}{4} & \frac{1}{2} & \frac{1}{4} \\ 5 & 0 & 0 & 0 & \frac{1}{4} & \frac{1}{2} \end{array}$	

All the forms presented have their advantages and disadvantages, depending on the purpose. The diagrammatic form renders the idea very well, but the other forms are better for calculations, except that the matrix form cannot be used for L continuous.

The deterministic transformation given in the example is what we may call the Likert transform, and it certainly represents the least sophisticated model. One can argue against it on two bases: firstly because the straight line is *too simple* a transform (when so much is known about end-effects and mid-effects, and the subjective difference between interval-widths) and secondly because it is *deterministic*.[17] The case for a stochastic transformation is so strong that we need not repeat the arguments except one: when we know how high the *number of relevant conditions* that are extremely difficult to control for is, in most social science investigations, it seems strange that one can believe in single-valued correspondence between responses and respondents. We know, for instance, that the same respondent rarely repeats himself completely when asked the same questions – yet it may be artificial to claim that the respondent is not the 'same'.

But the first objection can be met by introducing a more complex function as a transformation. Another straight line would not take care of the difficulties mentioned, but a more complex function (e.g., the logistic curve, or any ogive curve) may. However, the class of eligible functions is limited. If we cling to the deterministic case, a logical implication is (in addition to the definitory belief that 'same response corresponds to same attitude') that, of two persons, the one with the 'highest' response should be mapped on the 'highest' attitude. This leads to the *class of monotone functions as possible transformations.*

If we assume that the transformation preferably should be of the stochastic kind, some of the terminology from bivariate statistics is immediately applicable. We start by introducing the notion of the bivariate probability (density) distribution $p = f(M, L)$ which gives us the probability that a unit has the response M *and* the attitude L, and the corresponding cumulative distribution $P = F(M, L)$. From this follow the usual definitions (Table 3.5.3).

Of course, nothing except a general view is gained by listing these formulas. The depressing point of departure is that of these eight functions *only two are always known: $f_1(M)$ and $F_1(M)$* – because they are simply the frequency and cumulative distribution of the response variable, which are known as soon as the data are collected. All the rest is by definition unknown, because they all depend on the empirically unobservable variable, L.

Hence, if we shall be able to determine this system and realize the goal of making inferences from the responses or response-patterns to the respondent, i.e., from the manifest to the latent, we must make assumptions. This is the same as constructing models, and criteria should, at least ideally, be established to test the adequacy of the model. From what has been said above, the model can take as its point of departure any part of the relation

Table 3.5.3. *The distribution functions for the mapping*

Variable	Marginal frequency distribution	Marginal cumulative distribution	Conditional frequency distribution	Regression curves
M	$f_1(M) = \int\limits_{-\infty}^{+\infty} f dL$	$F_1(M) = \int\limits_{-\infty}^{+\infty} F dL$	$f_L(M) = \dfrac{f(M,L)}{f_2(L)}$	$L = R_1(M) =$ $= \int\limits_{-\infty}^{+\infty} L f_M(L) dL$
L	$f_2(L) = \int\limits_{-\infty}^{+\infty} f dM$	$F_2(L) = \int\limits_{-\infty}^{+\infty} F dM$	$f_M(L) = \dfrac{f(M,L)}{f_1(M)}$	$M = R_2(L) =$ $= \int\limits_{-\infty}^{+\infty} M f_L(M) dM$

between L and M where L enters. This gives us essentially four possibilities:

    (1) the bivariate distribution of M and L,
    (2) the marginal distribution of L,
    (3) the conditional distributions, or
    (4) the regression curves.

We shall examine some consequences of making assumptions about these four aspects of the relation between M and L.

(1) *Assumptions about the bivariate distribution.* A bivariate distribution can be hypothesized such that it corresponds to the empirically given marginal distribution. This would completely specify the model, but seems in general to be too restrictive as an assumption.

(2) *Assumptions about the latent marginal distribution.* A common assumption here is that this distribution is *normal* (see below) – and that the difference between the manifest and the 'true' latent scale is that the latter has been distorted by the empirical process so as to produce response distributions other than normal. With A-shaped response distributions this way of thinking is not in itself unreasonable, but experience shows that *J*-, *U*-, *S*- and curves of other shapes occur quite frequently, and it is not easily seen how they can be conceived of as 'distorted' normal distributions. Besides, if the distribution shall be 'normal' in the statistical sense, the sample should perhaps also be 'normal' in some substantive sense, and this kind of normality may be difficult to define. Of course, there are other distributions that also may be conceived of as idealizations of the observed distribution, but then they should be justified by good substantive theory.[18]

(3) *Assumptions about the conditional distributions or trace curves.* The most useful here would be the conditional distribution that gives us – *for a*

given value of the response variable M – the probability (density) that L will have any value l, i.e. $f_M(L)$.

If this function were known for all values of M, our problem would in a sense have been solved, for M is what we get from our data and L is what we want. There would still be the problem of picking a specific value of L or at least an interval on the basis of the conditional distribution; this is discussed under 4 below. But there are two reasons why it is still better to turn the problem around and ask: *for a given value of the latent variable L, what is the probability of a specific manifest value, M = m?* First of all, this gives a better, more intuitive basis for the construction of models: we reason *from* a respondent and ask 'how will he express his attitudes in terms of responses'? And secondly, we can endow the latent variable with mathematically desirable properties by definition. As the models relating M and L will have to be mathematical in order to be precise, this is of tremendous importance.

From Table 3.5.3 we get the conditional frequency distribution for M given L:

$$f_L(M) = \frac{f(M, L)}{f_2(L)}$$

If we now focus on one particular value of the manifest variable, the response $M = m$, we get the function called the trace curve for the value $M = m$:

$$Tr_m(L) = \frac{f(M = m, L)}{f_2(L)}$$

The important fact about this function is that it is a function of L alone.

Clearly, for a given $L = l$, the response must be one out of the set $1, 2, \ldots r$, so that the sum of these probabilities over all possible responses must be 1, as evidenced by:

$$\sum_{m=1}^{r} Tr_m(L) = \frac{\sum_{m=1}^{r} f(M = m, L)}{f_2(L)} = \frac{f_2(L)}{f_2(L)} = 1$$

With an r-point scale, the number of independent trace curves for a 'psychological object' is $r - 1$. If $r = 2$, only one trace curve is needed; and in this case of dichotomous choice, it is usually called the *tracecurve of endorsement*. In test-psychology, the tracecurve is often called 'operating characteristic'.

The advantage of this curve or line over the conditional distributions is the immediate interpretation it can be given as the 'propensity' to give a certain response (m) for different values of the latent variable. It should be noticed that although the formula given for the trace curve resembles the formula given for the conditional frequency distribution $f_L(M)$, they are completely different: the former is a function of L, and the latter a function of M. It should be noticed that we get $f_1(M = m) = p_m$ if we integrate $Tr_m(L) \cdot f_2(L)$ over L.

Assumptions can now be made about the shape of the tracecurve. On quite intuitive grounds, we would expect in very many cases the tracecurves to go through the succession J_-, A_-, A_0, A_+, J_+ as M increases from 1 to r ($M = 1$ will be given mostly by those very low on the latent continuum ($M = r$ to those very high on the latent continuum). For a dichotomous item, this means that the only trace curve we need will be a J_+ or a never decreasing function. However, this will of course not always be the case.

(4) *Assumptions about the regression curves.* Imagine that the bivariate distribution is known, and that we want to infer from M to L. For a given value of M the distribution for L is given by $f_m(L)$. Clearly, we have a choice between saying that there to $M = m$ corresponds an *interval* or a *point* for L, and the most satisfactory choice is the latter (though, for instance the interval between P_{25} and P_{75} also may be a possibility). But which point should be chosen – mode, median, or mean? The *mode* would be the maximum likelihood solution, and is attractive for that reason. The *mean* will immediately be given by the regression curve $L = R_1(M)$. The *median* too could easily be calculated. It seems that at the moment we lack a good criterion to make a choice between these possibilities, so the choice we make will necessarily be *ad hoc*. Unless substantive theory is used one shall not pretend that this is not the case.

If we choose the mean, an assumption about the regression curve may be helpful. But if this is the only assumption made, what we have done is just to reduce the case to the deterministic case.

Let us then consider the example of deterministic transformation alluded to above. The transformation is based on $F_1(M)$ which is empirically given and $F_2(L)$ (the cumulative distribution of the respondents on the latent variable), which is defined to be, e.g., normal. One possible transformation rule is simply:

$$F_2(L) = F_1(M) \quad \text{or} \quad L = F_2^{-1} F_1(M)$$

which means that to the response-value m corresponds the respondent-value l, which is such that the proportion of respondents below or equal to l under the normal distribution is the same as the empirically given proportion of responses below or equal to m. Geometrically, this can be done very easily, as shown in the accompanying Figure 3.5.4.

The coordinate system has four quadrants as usual, and the end result of the process is in quadrant I – the graph connecting M and L. In quadrant

279

Diagram 3.5.4. *A transformation procedure*

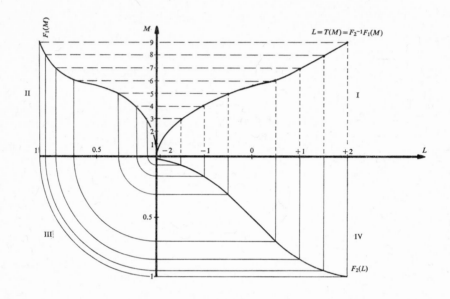

II is the empirical cumulative distribution of the responses, in quadrant IV the theoretical, cumulative distribution of the respondents. If we start with any value of M, say $m = 5$, we first use quadrant II to find the corresponding value of $F_1(M)$ (about 0.3), then use quadrant III to draw a circle with center in the origin and find the corresponding point on $F_2(L)$, then the corresponding value of L (about -0.6). Since the purpose is to find the value of L for any value of M this actually solves the problem – but it is useful to complete the process by plotting some points of correspondence in quadrant I and then fitting a curve through these points. If the curve is good enough, the whole procedure boils down to using that curve. Of course, we can only get approximate values, but with the assumptions we make nothing more seems to be warranted.

Essentially, we have made two assumptions:

(1) that the respondents or the traits we are interested in are *normally distributed* on the latent variable,
(2) the principle of *cumulative correspondence*.

The main danger here lies in claiming unwarranted theoretical bases for this. For what is actually the structure of the L-scale? Evidently, it is at most interval – as there is nothing to guide us about the choice of origin or unit of measurement – and we choose as usual the origin in the mean and the unit as the standard deviation so that the distribution becomes $N(0,1)$. Other possibilities frequently encountered are $N(100,15)$ and $N(50,10)$. But in what sense of the word is this scale interval at all? Even if we take for granted that the 'real distribution' is the normal distribution? Do we actually feel more insured about the equality of intervals for the L-scale than for the M-scale? And if not, what significance has the transformation got at all? All experience from physics shows that a cumbersome transformation from ordinal scale to interval and from there to ratio is only justified insofar as it helps us formulate laws and theories that are simpler and/or embrace more phenomena. It seems, however, that validations of this kind have rarely been attempted in the social sciences.

To summarize, let us try and make some final points about the transformations from manifest to latent variables and *vice versa*.

First of all, it should be pointed out that one of the main values of this distinction between manifest and latent is on the conceptual level, forcing us to make a distinction between the measurement of responses and the measurement of respondents (or aspects of respondents or 'units', to use the general term). It is as important as it is perhaps trivial that the variable fit for measuring responses is not *ipso facto* fit for measuring respondents.

Secondly, if a transformation from a response or response pattern to a value for the unit is attempted, there should exist at least some rule-of-thumb criteria to test the adequacy of the transformation. In short, the transformation *should be based on a model which it is conceivably and empirically possible to falsify*.

Thirdly, even if there is a model and it is not falsified, this is not in itself a guarantee that the transformation can give us any further insight. That it is possible to infer a latent variable 'temperature' from indicators like gas-, alcohol- and mercury thermometers is not in itself a guarantee that temperature or a measure of temperature is theoretically fruitful. Where the first problem is concerned, that of the fruitfulness of the concepts measured, there should be no great occasion for worry. If the psychological objects responded to are in some sense linked together, if they display 'functional unity' and there is good association between the latent variable and the responses to some objects selected *a priori,* the investigator should be fairly able to select the conceptual dimensions he deems to be fruitful. *But,* this together with a satisfactory model that regenerates the manifest data is not sufficient to warrant fruitfulness of the measures. To take the definitory characteristics of the three main types of scales:

Nominal: what *more* can be said about two respondents with the same latent score (or different latent score) than just that their *scores are the same (different)*?

Ordinal: what *more* can be said about the relation between two respondents, the score of the one being higher than the score of the other, than just this relation?

Interval: what *more* can be said about two pairs of respondents with equal distances on the latent variable than just this equidistance?

In short, we want the latent variable to serve as a bridge from the manifest data to other empirical and theoretical results *that could not just as easily be attained by means of some simple untransformed variable, like additive indices etc.* The ordering and spacing of the respondents on the latent variable will not necessarily yield this. Since it is usually a cumbersome process, we must require that it be worth the trouble.

These two requirements (to any transformation from manifest to latent variables) of *falsifiability* and *fruitfulness* seem to us indispensable, although difficult to satisfy. The conclusion of all this, however, is not an attack on the usefulness of the distinction between the manifest and latent levels. This way of thinking seems to be indispensable, but the fictitious idea that a latent scale can be endowed with any desirable mathematical property is dangerous. On the manifest level, where the responses have been recorded as, say, 1, 2, 3, 4, and 5, the numbers form an interval scale *per se,* but this manifest interval scale has no empirical meaning in most cases. And in most cases there is no gain in meaning by transformation either, and absolutely not by the kind of transformations exemplified in Figure 3.5.4.

3.6. *Latent structure analysis*

We now turn to the most audacious attempt to link the manifest with the latent: Lazarsfeld's latent structure analysis. Because of the excellent presentations in print[19] we content ourselves with presenting just enough to get an image of the epistemological status of the theory.

Latent structure analysis takes as its point of departure three elements: the latent space, the manifest space, and the function connecting them – just as we did in Table 3.5.2. The dimensions of latent structure analysis, hence, are presented in Table 3.6.1.

The Table gives in highly summarized form the essentials about the components of latent structure analysis. In the general case, a latent space of

Table 3.6.1. *Dimensions of latent structure analysis*

		General case	Special case
(I)	Latent space, X		
	(1) no. of dimensions	$n*$	1
	(2) structure, level of measurement	any	interval
	(3) distribution of units	any, $\varphi(x)$	any, $\varphi(x)$
	(a) continuous	latent structure model	
	(b) discrete	latent class model	
(II)	Manifest space, Y		
	(1) no. of dimensions or items	n	n
	(2) structure, no. of values on each item	r	2
	(3) distribution of units	empirically given	
(III)	Trace function	$P(X, Y)$	
	(1) horizontal, uniform – item does not discriminate		
	(2) non-horizontal – item does discriminate		
	(a) non-monotone – 'point-item'		
	(b) monotone		
	(1) curvilinear		
	(2) linear	$P\left(\begin{array}{c}\text{positive}\\\text{response}\end{array}\right) = a_i + b_i x$	

any number of dimensions with any kind of mathematical structure may be conceived of. For each point, X, in latent space, there is a probability for each point, Y, in manifest space, viz., the probability that a respondent thus located in latent space shall exhibit such and such a manifest response. Thus, if manifest space consists of eight dichotomies, and hence has 256 points, for *each* latent point in X there will be 256 probabilities adding to unity.

This is the general case. It is, however, much too general, and completely tautological: because it specifies nothing, it says nothing. To get from this general thought-model to a model about the relationship between the latent and the manifest we have to (1) simplify, (2) assume something, and (3) postulate some axioms. This will be done as indicated in the special case in the right-hand column of Table 3.6.1.

The simplifications require no comment. With only one latent dimension there will be no intricate problems as to the relation between two or more dimensions, the metric in n-dimensional space, etc. With only two values of the manifest variable, i.e. dichotomies, one of them can be called 'positive', viz., the value that indicates most of the property measured by the

(I) *Simplifications*
    (1) no. of dimensions in latent space: 1 (one-dimensional)
    (2) no. of values of manifest variables: 2 (dichotomy)

(II) *Assumptions*
    (1) about the trace function: $P\begin{pmatrix}\text{positive}\\\text{response}\end{pmatrix} = a_i + b_i x$ (linearity)

    (2) about the items: that they are representative for the dimension, and have nothing else in common

(III) *Axioms*
    (1) the latent dimension is interval
    (2) *the axiom of local independence*

latent dimension. The trace function thus becomes particularly simple. For each value x of the one-dimensional latent variable, we have only to give the probability of the positive response, $P(x)$, and the probability of the negative response is given by $1 - P(x)$. But if the items are trichotomies, we need two probabilities (obtaining the third by subtraction).

While these *simplifications* make it mathematically possible to manage this system, they are not as fundamental as they may look. Variables can always be reduced to dichotomies, latent spaces can always be made unidimensional – at least by definition. But the *assumptions* are more problematic, and so are the *axioms*.

Since the trace function is a mental construct with no immediate empirical counterpart, we are deplorably free in our choice. Theory may guide us somewhat, as when we decide that the trace function of the item 'the Negro is mentally inferior, but should be helped to a better position' must be non-monotone;[20] it will be endorsed neither by integrationists (because of the first clause) nor by segregationists (because of the second clause). We may have the general idea that the probability of a positive response will increase and can argue for linear trace-lines on this basis: the straight line embodies the idea of the monotone relationship and nothing more, *hence we do not have to assume more than the minimum necessary*. It is like setting the probability of an event equal to $\frac{1}{2}$ when nothing is known: it is certainly not satisfactory, but one may argue that all other choices would be even less satisfactory and more difficult to justify.

It should be noticed that these trace-lines do *not* give us the probabilities of response *patterns,* only the probabilities of responses on one item at the time. But the axiom of local independence will give us the link we need here, as will be shown below.

The assumption about the items is the same for latent structure analysis as for any other method of index formation. It is needed for several reasons.

First of all, a high index value may be produced not because of a high value on the latent dimension, but because of a high value on some other latent dimension which the items are also 'tapping'. A typical example is the use of knowledge questions, where 'knowledge about X' is used as an indicator of 'concern about X', without controlling for the effect of education. Secondly, the items may constitute a highly biased sample from the universe of variables, as discussed in I, 3.3. Thus, if only items about attitude towards atomic weapons are used in a study of attitudes towards military defense, the results may easily be misleading; if only attitudes towards whites are used in a study of race relations, the study should be given a special title, and so on.

The axioms are true by definition. The task of latent structure analysis is to get hold of that variable which is (1) interval and (2) satisfies the condition of 'local independence'. Lazarsfeld has argued very convincingly for this axiom.[21] The idea is simply this: *if* there are differences between units with regard to the latent variable, *and* the manifest variables have positively monotone tracelines, *then* some units will have higher probability of accepting *both* and some units will have lower probability for *both;* the result is correlation between the manifest variables. This is true for any interval of the latent variable: as soon as there is an interval and the trace-lines increase together, there will be a concentration along the main diagonal in any fourfold table constructed on the basis of the manifest variables. The axiom of local independence is now simply the logical consequence of this: if we reduce the interval to a point (in other words, if we take units with the same amount of the latent attribute), then there shall be no probability differential within the group and hence no correlation. And if one of the trace-lines is horizontal, there will be no correlation either, because there will be no *co*variation.

The way Lazarsfeld approaches this axiom is as follows:[22] he has ten 5-point items and uses eight of them in an additive index with range 0-32. The index is then divided in five intervals; for each interval, the correlations between the remaining two items are calculated. The correlation between these two items is also calculated for the total sample, and he shows that with the splitting the correlations are practically reduced to zero. Thus, the additive index is a good approximation to the latent variable, it 'takes out' practically all the correlation. But it cannot always be trusted, so the task is to construct the latent variable *so that it is not only an approximation but a realization of the ideal that all inter-correlation between the manifest variables shall be due to their common content in terms of the latent variable.* The weak point in this, of course, is the lack of congruity between this very precise ideal and rigorous mathematics on the one hand, and the more intuitive selection of indicators on the other. But that this is adequately done belongs to our list of assumptions.

We may now compute any joint probability we want. Thus, imagine that in the example in the beginning, with eight manifest dichotomies, we want to know, for $X = x$, the probability of accepting the first item, rejecting the second, accepting the third and fourth, and rejecting the fifth – nothing said about the attitude to items 6, 7, and 8. We get by simple multiplication:

$$(a_1+b_1x)\,[1-(a_2+b_2x)]\,(a_3+b_3x)\,(a_4+b_4x)\,[1-(a_5+b_5x)] = P_{1\bar{2}34\bar{5}}$$

This is for $X = x$. If we want the probability for the whole sample, this must be multiplied with the probability density and summated (integrated) over the whole range:

$$\int P_{1\bar{2}34\bar{5}}\,\varphi(x)dx$$

Thus, from the trace-lines for the single items we can find all the joint probabilities of any order we want. This simplification is precisely what makes LSA manageable.

From now on everything is mathematics and even very simple mathematics. Everything *manifest* is known, all kinds of simple and joint frequencies, but the *latent* distribution as well as the trace-lines are unknown. We now reason from the latent to the manifest, asking: given the trace-lines and the latent distribution, what is the manifest distribution we would expect. We then use this to estimate the trace-lines and the distribution. We shall use a combination of Lazarsfeld's and Torgerson's presentations in the following.

In latent structure analysis the latent distribution, $\varphi(x)$, is characterized by means of its moments, where the k'th moment is:

3.6:1. $$M_k = \int x^k \varphi(x)dx$$

By definition of a 'distribution' we have:

3.6:2: $$M_0 = \int \varphi(x)dx = 1$$

We now, by convention, fix the zero point and the unit of the latent variable so that:

3.6:3. $$M_1 = \int x\varphi(x)dx = \bar{x} = 0$$

and

3.6:4. $$M_2 = \int x^2 \varphi(x)dx = 1$$

from which follows:

3.6:5. $$s^2 = M_2 - M_1^2 = 1 - 0^2 = 1$$

In other words, we 'standardize' the distribution. This is a linear transformation, and legitimate, since we assume that the variable is interval. No information is lost by this, while we gain greatly in simplification.

We can now present the model of how any first order probability of a manifest response is produced. p_i, the manifest probability, is the sum of all the probabilities under the corresponding trace-line $(a_i + b_i x)$ weighted with the probability (density) that an individual is located at the value x:

3.6:6. $\qquad p_i = \int (a_i + b_i x) \varphi(x) dx = a_i \int \varphi(x) dx + b_i \int x \varphi(x) dx = a_i$

by virtue of 3.6: 3-4.

The solution is simple: The probability of a positive response is equal to the probability axis intercept, *provided* this axis passes through the mean of the distribution. In a sense this is obvious. p_i is the average probability for the whole sample, regardless of where the individual is located on the latent variable – and a_i is also the average probability since it is the probability in the average.

Obtaining b_i is more complicated. We start with the expression for p_{ij}, the joint probability of two positive responses, which can be obtained by multiplying for each value x the probability of each single response (according to the axiom of local independence) and weighting with the distribution of units:

3.6:7. $\quad p_{ij} = \int (a_i + b_i x)(a_j + b_j x) \, \varphi(x) dx =$
$\qquad a_i a_j \int \varphi(x) dx + (a_i b_j + a_j b_i) \int x \varphi(x) dx + b_i b_j \int x^2 \varphi(x) dx = a_i a_j + b_i b_j$

and hence:

3.6:8. $\qquad\qquad\qquad b_i b_j = p_{ij} - p_i p_j$

The term to the right is the excess a joint probability has over the product of the marginal probabilities – in other words, a measure of correlation. In standard fourfold table terms it translates into:

3.6:9. $\qquad p_{ij} - p_i p_j = \dfrac{a}{N} - \dfrac{a+c}{N} \cdot \dfrac{a+b}{N} = \dfrac{ad - bc}{N^2}$

This is the *covariance* between items i and j, and easily calculated from the manifest data. If we call it c_{ij}, we get:

3.6:10. $\qquad b_i b_j = c_{ij}, \; b_i b_k = c_{ik} \quad \text{and} \quad b_j b_k = c_{jk}$

Multiplying the first two and dividing by the third we get:

3.6:11. $\qquad\qquad\qquad b_i = \sqrt{\dfrac{c_{ij} \, c_{ik}}{c_{jk}}}$

Thus, to calculate the slope of the trace-line of *one* item, the covariance of that item with *two* other items is needed. This means that there will be $\binom{n-1}{2}$ different estimates of b_i according to 3.6:11, so some averaging procedure is needed. For $n = 3$, $\binom{n-1}{2}$ is equal to 1, which means that the equations will be identically fulfilled. *Hence, the number of items must be 4 or more.*

Thus, the trace-lines are determined. One measure of how good the model is can be obtained by comparing the covariances c_{ij} (as calculated from manifest data) with the products $b_i b_j$ (the theoretical covariances) to see to what extent we are able to reproduce the covariances. If the procedure involving the $\binom{n-1}{2}$ different estimates of b_i leads to results that are too discrepant, the residuals may be considerable. In general, it is hardly advisable to use a model with residuals exceeding 10% – but even this figure is rather arbitrary. If the fit is good, it means that we have obtained precisely what we should: all of the covariance is accounted for by means of the latent variable.[23]

Before proceeding, something should be said about equation 3.6:8, which says that the product of two slopes is equal to the covariance. When both slopes are positive (or negative), the correlation is positive; when either or both are zero, the correlation is also zero, precisely because there is no covariation; and when the slopes have different sign, the correlation is, of course, negative. In other words: 3.6:8 mirrors very well the relationship between slopes and correlation as originally posited.

The formula for the k'th moment is[24]

3.6:12.
$$M_k = \frac{c_{123 \, \cdots \, k}}{_1 b b_2 b_3 \cdots b_k}$$

Since it is based on any group of k items (with the k-dimensional covariance in the numerator and the product of the corresponding slopes in the denominator) we have to make an average between the $\binom{n}{k}$ different estimates. But in principle the distribution can be approximated as well as we want by means of expressions based on moments.[25] A simple procedure would consist in a comparison with the standard normal distribution which has $M_1 = 0$, $M_2 = 1$, $M_3 = 0$ and $M_4 = 3$.

With these inferences about distribution and trace-lines in latent space we can now do the following:

(1) *Find the trace function of any response pattern.* Because of the local independence all we have to do is to multiply the trace-lines that correspond to the items. Thus, if the pattern is $+ + + - -$ the trace function is

$$(a_1 + b_1 x)(a_2 + b_2 x)(a_3 + b_3 x)[1 - (a_4 + b_4 x)][1 - (a_5 + b_5 x)].$$

We can then put this expression equal to, say, 0.5 to find how far out, in terms of standard deviations, we have to go to get a 'fifty-fifty chance' of obtaining that pattern. This is particularly important for the pattern $+ + + + +$ which corresponds to the additive index value of 5. If the answer is $x = 4$, it means that the pattern is rather extreme. Of course, answers of this type can be obtained with an additive index too, using its distribution – but the index variable does not have the property of local independence (although it may approximate it).

(2) *Find an order among the units and among the response patterns.* Since an individual can come from any value of the variable with trace function for his response pattern different from zero, we have to *choose* a point, or an interval. To find such a point we cannot use the trace function of the the response pattern, since that gives for each value of the latent variable the probability of having that response pattern. What is needed is the inverse probability: given the response pattern, what is the probability that the individual comes from x? This is what Lazarsfeld calls the 'recruitment probability', and the distribution is given by:

3.6:13.
$$\frac{f_g(x)\, \varphi(x)}{p_g}$$

where p_g is the manifest probability of the pattern, $f_g(x)$ is its trace-function, and $\varphi(x)$ the latent distribution.[26]

The most logical thing would be to find the mode of this distribution by calculating the derivative, but since $\varphi(x)$ is unknown this may be problematic. Another method, given by Lazarsfeld, is to compute the mean of the recruitment distribution, since this is given by:

3.6:14.
$$\frac{1}{p_g} \int x f_g(x)\, \varphi(x)\, dx$$

Since $f_g(x)$ is a polynomial this integration involves us in a sum of moments that can be found by means of 3.6:12. Thus, one value of x can be given to each response pattern and, hence, to each unit, which means that they are ordered uni-dimensionally.

(3) *Find an order among the items.* The advantage of the cumulative scale or Guttman scale is that it orders not only response-patterns and units, but also variables or items, and gives information about the process involved. This is also true for latent structure analysis, although less unambiguously so. If we have a set of pairs (a_i, b_i) we get a lot of useful information. Thus, the lower a_i, including negative values, the higher must x be before item i gets a positive probability *when b_i is constant*. But we have to take into account *both* parameters. Latent structure analysis gives more information about how the items enter into the total pattern, at the expense, of course, of added complexity. On the other hand, it is a far more realistic

19 *

289

way of handling the relation between latent and manifest than the cumulative scale.

The question is now whether this is worth all the trouble even in this, the simplest of all cases. The answer is not obvious, particularly because so much of the same can be obtained by the much simpler means of the additive index based on dichotomous items, as pointed out by Torgerson:[27]

'If the stimuli are all sensed in the same direction, which in the present case means that they are sensed so that the slopes of the trace lines are all positive, then the expected number of positive responses is monotonically related to the scale value on the underlying continuum. Hence, if a respectable number of items is used, the total number of positive responses given by a subject would be highly correlated with the scale values assigned by more elaborate procedures'.

If the ordering of the respondents is about the same and the distribution not too different, the question is whether the two undoubtedly elegant properties of the latent variable by definition, i.e. local independence and interval scale, are sufficient as arguments. As to the latter, our answer is no. As pointed out in 3.5: to have the structure of interval scale by definition is not enough, we must show that this structure translates into an empirically demonstrable relation of equality of differences, and this has so far not been done in latent structure analysis.

The argument for local independence is better, since it leads, in principle, to a pure scale, viz., the scale that reduces local correlation between the indicators to zero. Indeed, this seems to be a valuable criterion for the evaluation of any index, and should be introduced in the theory of additive indices. That is, one should show that the inter-item correlation is very low for each separate index level. But additive indices may be rather close to this criterion, and also give information about how the variables combine to produce a pattern when the coefficient of reproducibility is not too low. Hence, little remains except a feeling of having produced a more pure scale, without analytical victories that cannot also be obtained by other and simpler means. This, however, is not the case when the trace curves are curvilinear so that they give more information about the relation between an item and the latent variable.[28]

In conclusion, let us give an example of a latent structure analysis.[29] A gallup sample of the Norwegian population ($N = 1859$, $t =$ January 1961) was asked a number of questions about attitudes to military defense in the atomic age. The questions are shown on the next page.

We then assumed one latent dimension, dichotomized the items (there were actually four alternatives for each) as indicated above, and found the

Question:	Positive response:	p_i:
Everything considered, do you think it would be an advantage to have atomic weapons in Norway or do you think it would be an advantage not to have atomic weapons in Norway?	advantage to have atomic weapons	0.112
What would you prefer, disarmament and use of the money for international cooperation, or the kind of defense we have now, or defense with atomic weapons (disarmament even unilaterally)?	conventional defense or atomic defense	0.330
In case Norway was attacked by an enemy and the choice was between occupation of Norway or an atomic war in Norway, what would you prefer?	prefer atomic war	0.130
Everything taken into consideration, do you consider it an advantage for Norway to be a member of NATO, or would it be an advantage if Norway were not a member of NATO?	advantage to be a member of NATO	0.458

equations of the trace-lines according to the method outlined above. We got:

$$P_1(x) = 0.112 + 0.171x \qquad P_3(x) = 0.130 + 0.195x$$
$$P_2(x) = 0.330 + 0.257x \qquad P_4(x) = 0.458 + 0.277x$$

Clearly, the trace-lines are of two kinds. In one group we have $P_2(x)$ and $P_4(x)$, and in the other $P_1(x)$ and $P_3(x)$; the first two have both higher intercepts and higher slopes. Inspection of the items reveals the significance of this: the first items tap attitudes to conventional defense or any defense in military terms, the second group has to do with atomic defense. That the intercepts of the former are higher is not strange: conventional weapons are more accepted than atomic weapons and the relationship is largely cumulative. The interesting point brought out by the LSA is the relative size of the slopes. One interpretation is as follows: the conventional defense items discriminate more (have higher slopes) because they are more integrated into the whole syndrome of attitudes related to defense. Below these, atomic weapons are accepted and rejected according to other principles: the attitude is not yet brought firmly in line with the general attitude to military defense. Thus, we had actually expected lower intercepts but steeper slopes for the atomic items, because we knew relatively few were in favor, but believed they would be concentrated in a hard core. Instead they show up as more evenly distributed. It would be interesting to know more about the changes of these parameters over time, for they are obviously subject to such changes. Increasing polarization and integration of the atomic items would increase the slopes of the trace-lines of these items.

This is, substantively speaking, an important finding and can only be relied upon if the residuals are moderate. Since we have four variables, we have $\binom{4}{2}$ or 6 covariances, and can use them to check the model. We calculated them from the empirical data and from the products of the slopes, got the residuals by subtraction, and calculated the percentage the residuals made of the empirical covariances. These percentages were 7.1%, -10.0%, -0.6%, -0.2%, -6.2%, and 6.3%, so there are no residuals exceeding 10%. We also calculated the four trivariate frequencies empirically and theoretically, getting 4.5%, -3.9%, -4.9%, and 5.6% – all quite satisfactory. However, what we do not know is whether we could not have obtained approximately the same residuals with even considerable changes in the model, e.g. by using curved trace-lines. In general, a model should be evaluated not only in terms of its fit with the data, but also in terms of alternative models; and that is not built into latent structure analysis.

The third and fourth moments were found to be 1.110 and 1.804 respectively, which means that the distribution is positively skewed – i.e. skewed away from the increasing slope-lines (this explains the low total frequencies). Further, it is flatter than the normal curve (which has fourth moment equal to 3). We made use of this to order the response patterns, finally finding the intercept of the trace-curve for positive responses on all four items with the line $P = 0.5$ to be above 3 sigma (this is best found graphically). Thus, the completely positive respondent with regard to military defense in the nuclear age was a relatively rare individual.

3.7. *Items vs. indicators*

We are now in a position to attack the general problem of selection of indicators on the basis of general variable theory, correlation theory, and index theory. The point of departure is a set of items, selected intensionally and the problem that of selecting a set of indicators of the dimension we are interested in.

In principle, the problem is not difficult. Imagine we were able to measure the dimension directly. In latent structure theory this would amount to being able to place the units on the latent dimension by means of one observation – which by definition is impossible, since the latent would then be manifest – but it is a useful idea heuristically. We would then, for each indicator ask the following question: *to what extent does it classify the units the same way as the dimension it is supposed to be an indicator of?* If the indicator classifies the units exactly the same way, then it can be used as a *criterion,* instead of the dimension itself. Such indicators are rarely found, however, except as trivial cases. Thus, voice may be used as an indicator of sex (for people talking from the other side of a wall) – and perfect correspondence in classification be obtained. But the accent of a Spanish-speaking Latin American is not a perfect indicator of his nationality – except, perhaps, for extremely well-trained specialists.

Given this point of departure, the problems of indicator theory are three:

(1) How do we measure the extent to which the classifications coincide?
(2) What do we do when the dimension is not observable?
(3) What consequences follow from the measures of coincidence of classifications?

The first problem is a general problem in measurement and correlation theory. We have a dimension D with values $D_1, D_2, \ldots D_{r_D}$, an indicator I with values $I_1, I_2, \ldots I_{r_I}$, and a two-dimensional distribution $P(I, D)$ of the m units. We shall accept no restrictions as to the distribution, or about the marginal distributions (such as the assumption that $P(D)$ – the distribution on the dimension itself – is normal), since such assumptions have the tendency discussed in 3.5 to introduce an element of fictitiousness in methodological theory. The problem is now clearly a problem of measuring the correlation in $P(I, D)$.

However, the problem is complicated by the factor discussed in II, 2.3: *perfect coincidence in classification implies perfect correlation, but perfect correlation does not imply perfect coincidence in classification.* For perfect coincidence means two things: D and I are isomorphic; and all m units are classified in corresponding classes in D and I.

What the first condition above says is this: (a) $r_I = r_D$ – there is the same number of classes in D and I; (b) there is a pre-established one-one correspondence between them, in the sense that it is known which D-class corresponds to any given I-class and vice versa, and (c) the relations between the classes – known as the rules of measurement – are the same. If, in addition to this, the m units distribute as they should, we clearly have a perfect indicator of the dimension. In this case, the best measure of coincidence is *not* one of the measures of correlation but one of the measures of agreement, for coincidence means exactly that the classification given by the indicator 'agrees with' the classification given by the dimension.

This strong condition of isomorphism is rarely fulfilled in practice. Typically, the dimension is more specified than the indicator. This means that we have $r_I < r_D$. Thus, if we identify the dimension with an additive index, cumulative or not, the index may be based on n trichotomies, so that we have $r_D = 2n + 1$ and all the $r_I = 3$. However, this problem is easily overcome by renouncing on the variety in the index. In fact, trichotomization of the index is also recommended on other grounds, and this would re-establish the first condition of isomorphism: one-one correspondence (but at the expense of variety).

If, now, both D and I are at least ordinal, $r_I = r_D = r$ will imply the fulfilment of condition b above (for if the number and order of the classes are the same there is no doubt as to which class corresponds to which. In the nominal case, however, there are $r!$ possible translations from I to D. If one is measuring the extent of agreement or coincidence in classification, one of these translations will have to be picked *a priori*. In the case of guessing nationalities from accents, the judge may be wrong not only because of low correlations, but also because of wrong identification, i.e. because he has picked a wrong translation. He may, however, maximize his correlation by picking that rule of correspondence *a posteriori* that gives highest correlation. This is not necessarily 'wrong'. In some situations one may have the intuition that I is an indicator of D without knowing in detail how the correspondence is. If this is acceptable, correlation is all we ask for, not agreement, and correlation coefficients may be used.

The relation between levels of measurement for D and I is of importance. With three possibilities for either (nominal, ordinal, interval), only five of the nine combinations are meaningful; for from an indicator on the nominal level we cannot infer to a dimension on the ordinal or interval levels, nor from an ordinal or interval indicator to a nominal dimension. However, it makes sense to infer from an interval indicator to an ordinal dimension – as when age is used as an indicator of life-cycle – and from an ordinal indicator to an interval dimension. But in the measurement of correlation or agreement, the rule is invariably that the lowest level determines what coefficient to use, which means that we only have to distinguish between the nominal, ordinal, and interval cases as usual.

The problem of measuring coincidence has now been split into two subcases depending on whether we have isomorphism between I and D or not. The measures suggested follow from the development in II, 2.3 where the agreement measures are discussed towards the end (Table 3.7.1.)

In selecting the measure we must keep in mind exactly what we want to measure: the extent to which we can predict the value on the D-variable from the value of the I-variable. If r_I is much less than r_D, the result will usually be a loss of correlation, since the units will be likely to distribute on more than one value of D for each value of I. We may still obtain high

Table 3.7.1. *Measures of coincidence between indicator and dimension*

Measurement-levels	Degree of correlation	Degree of agreement
lowest level nominal	lambda$_{ID}$	nominal agreement measure[30]
lowest level ordinal	tau$_b$, d_{ID}	ordinal agreement measure[31]
lowest level interval	r_{ID}	interval agreement measure[32]

correlation by cutting down on r_D, and this loss in specificity is not accounted for by the formulas. It is obvious, however, that we would *ceteris paribus* prefer high specificity to low specificity (see 4.2).

The coefficients for degree of correlation all measure degree of predictability. Guttman's lambda gives us exactly what we gain in predictability knowing I. The ordinal measures are both based on the difference between concordance and discordance; they inform us to what extent we can predict the order correctly. So does gamma, but gamma cannot be used here since it is too permissive – the measure should attain its maximum value only for some kind of diagonal concentration, not for 'corner correlation'. Somers' measure d_{ID} is probably better than Kendall's tau since it is asymmetric, as is the relation between I and D. For the interval level the traditional correlation coefficient r_{ID} will do a good job since it measures precision of prediction.

A simplification of all this, known as Likert's 'discriminatory power', DP, is often used. The important thing according to that measure is not that I and D classify all units in the same way. What matters is that I is able to keep units apart that should be kept apart, viz., units that fall in some particular D-groups. For the ordinal and interval cases, this usually translates into a problem of whether the indicator discriminates well between the extreme groups. For the nominal case, there may be two groups we are particularly interested in, even though 'extreme' makes no sense.

Thus, two D-groups are picked, and the conditional distributions on the indicator are examined. The measure of central tendency for the conditional distributions are found and compared; and the idea is simply that the more different they are, the better does the indicator 'discriminate'. If the indicator is nominal level, one would require the two conditional distributions to have different modes. If the indicator is ordinal level, one would require the medians to be different; and if the indicator is at the interval level, one would require the two means to be different. Let us call the two D-groups D_1 and D_2. The formulas are then given as shown in Table 3.7.2.

As D_1 and D_2 groups in the ordinal and interval cases one may take the extreme quartiles.[33]

Table 3.7.2. *Measures of discriminatory power, DP*

	DP	Range
Nominal level	$\mathrm{Mod}_{D_1}-\mathrm{Mod}_{D_2}$	0 if they are equal, 1 otherwise
Ordinal level	$\mathrm{Med}_{D_1}-\mathrm{Med}_{D_2}$	from 0 to range of 1
Interval level	$\mathrm{Mean}_{D_1}-\mathrm{Mean}_{D_2}$	from 0 to range of 1

The statistical meaning of *DP* is simple. *It is not a measure of correlation but a simplified measure of regression:*

Diagram 3.7.3. *The interpretation of discriminatory power, DP*

The two measures of central tendency (*CT*) for the two conditional distributions are given, and *DP* is calculated as the difference between them. Since the geometrical locus of all the central tendencies of the conditional distributions is known as the regression curve, *DP* is simply the difference between two points on that curve.

The measure has a high number of weaknesses. Thus, *it does not give the range of the regression curve* (for some other intermediate *D*-group might have a lower or higher *CT*-value). *It says something, but not much, about the shape of the regression curve* [for the tacit assumption that it is (close to) linear between the two points measured is not necessarily tenable]. *It says something, but not much, about the degree of correlation between I and D.* Thus, if there is independence between *I* and *D*, the regression curve will (by implication of the definition of independence) be a horizontal line and *DP* = 0. But *DP* = 0 does not imply independence, for the regression curve may (theoretically) make all kinds of moves between the two points fixed by the method. And even if *DP* is high, there may nevertheless be a considerable scatter in the *I, D* distribution. To control for all these difficulties we would have to compute the *CT*'s for the other *D*-values, and even to inspect the scatter of the *I, D* pairs – and then we might as well compute a correlation- or agreement-coefficient.

296

The measure establishes a rank order, even linear, between the indicators according to the rule 'the higher DP, the better'. This rank order has only two classes in the nominal case, however, according to whether the two conditional distributions have the same or different modes. But a more refined measure can easily be constructed. To compare two nominal level distributions to see how different they are, all we have to do is to add the absolute differences between all corresponding percentages and divide by 200, which is the maximum possible. Or we may do the same, discounting all values of I except the two modes of the two conditional distributions.

In spite of all weaknesses, the measure may give valuable indication under reasonable conditions (relatively high I, D correlation, and relatively linear correlation) of how well an indicator coincides in classification with the dimension. And if we are interested only in D_1 and D_2 this measure becomes even more valuable since it is based on these two groups – but we are usually so interested in a high number of units that the other groups in the sample also are included.[34]

Let us now turn to the second problem: what to do when the dimension, D, is not observable. The answer is simply: use what comes closest to it according to accumulated theory/data. In index theory this means using the index as the closest approximation we have to the dimension. In other words, we accept the index as at least closely correlated to the dimension – of course only after having validated it carefully – and then proceed as above.

The distinction must now be made between two cases. There is no problem involved if we use the index as a basis for ranking indicators that are *not* used in the index. In this case the index only functions as the closest approximation we can get to the dimension itself, and the indicators are ranked according to their approximation to the index. The problem is whether the index also can be used as a basis for evaluating indicators that *are* included in the index.

Since the indicator correlates with itself perfectly, we will obviously get a component of auto-correlation in the correlation between I and D, which will increase 'artificially' the degree of agreement between I and D. There are two ways from here: we may correlate each item I with $D-I$; or we may accept the correlations with D uncorrected. We shall prefer the latter, for two reasons. The first method actually means a comparison of the different items with *different* dimensions, I_1 with $D_1 = D-I_1$, I_2 with $D_2 = D-I_2$, etc., even if they may all be assumed to be close approximations to the latent dimension. And the second method, even though it involves autocorrelation, and more so the lower the number of constituent items, is nevertheless useful in *ranking* the indicators in terms of their capacity to classify in the same

·way as the dimension itself. All correlations are too high, but we may assume that this is a distortion of the zero point, and not a distortion of the internal order between the items, generally speaking.

We shall mention also a third argument which may be illegitimate because it 'only' involves costs that are of less importance in the age of computers. With the second method n correlations have to be studied, one for each item with D; but in the first method, we in addition have to construct a new index for each item. Although this can be done with the assistance of computers, it is not inviting as a method; moreover, it seems unnecessary. This is *a fortiori* true if there is a theoretical rationale behind the complete index which is lost when items are taken out of it.

What we do, then, is to study the correlations of all items with the dimension and use this to rank the items on a scale from $+1$ to -1. For the negative correlations, the items and the signs are reversed, so the result is a listing of the items in terms of their degree of agreement with D, from $+1$ to 0. The question is now what this list actually means, and what should be the consequences that follow from a high, medium, or low position of an item in the list. This is the third problem.

The answer depends on the kind of index we use as dimension approximation. The main results are given in Table 3.7.4. (next page).

The value of cumulative indices and latent structure is evident from the Table, since they are both built around the idea of the correlation of the item with the dimension. But Lazarsfeld's technique is much more tolerant than Guttman's: where the latter in principle only accepts items with very high level of agreement, the former in practice accepts any level of agreement, getting the ranking of the items in terms of the agreement with the latent dimension as a by-product of the construction of the latent structure. Thus, in linear *LSA* the ranking can be done in terms of the slopes of the trace-lines; the steeper the line, the higher the correlation.

Imagine now that the items are ordered in terms of agreement with the dimension, in three groups 'high', 'medium' and 'low'. The conclusions to be drawn for an indicator differ from one group to the other.

If the agreement is very *high,* e.g. close to unity, and the number of values is the same on I and D, the conclusion should be to *reject the index* as an approximation of the dimension and use the indicator instead. For if nothing is gained by the index, it should not be used to the exclusion of a simpler method; and if the agreement is (almost) perfect nothing can be gained (what is meant by 'gain' will be discussed below). If the agreement is perfect but $r_D > r_I$, we may still prefer D for reasons to be developed in II, 5.4: D will give more refined results. Thus, even if the person judging

Table 3.7.4. *Cases of low and high indicator correlation*

D-approximation	D, I correlation low (zero)	high (unity)
Additive indices (dichotomous or trichotomous)	the value of the indicator does not depend (much) on the value of D. If the item is dichotomous, the percentage accepting the item will be (about) the same regardless of D	the values of the indicator depend (very) much on D. The percentages accepting a dichotomous item will be a steadily increasing function of D
Cumulative indices (dichotomous items)	this will show up as a random scatter for the item after the matrix has been rearranged according to the principles in II, 3.3	by definition, any item that scales perfectly has a correlation of $+1$ with the index dichotomized. All items are perfect criteria, except that $r_I = 2$ and $r_D = n+1$
Comparative indices (based on product-sums)	as for additive indices	as for additive indices
Latent structure (dichotomous items)	the item will have a horizontal traceline, since the probability does not depend on the value of D	the item will have a vertical trace-line since the probability will change from 0 to 1 for a value of D (this, then, is a cumulative item)

Latin Americans by their accents draws a perfect line between the countries bordering on the Caribbean and the countries further to the South, his dichotomy does not serve as a substitute for the 18 nation variable.

If the agreement is very *low,* e.g. close to zero, the conclusion should be to *reject the item* as a possible indicator. It may be objected that it does not necessarily do much harm, which in a sense may be true. But the single individual may be grossly misclassified by an item that does not belong, and for that reason the dimension should be approximated by an index purified for the contamination from the items that give low correlations. Often this is expressed by saying that the items 'tap' different dimensions.

What is sometimes forgotten, however, is that the process does not terminate by a decision to take out items with low correlation. One then has to construct a new index composed of the remaining items and do the same kind of analysis for the new index. If there still are items that yield unsatisfactory correlations, they will have to be eliminated, a new index will have to be constructed, and so on, until all correlations are reasonably high. Theoretically, one may risk ending up with one item, but in practice the process is likely to stop much before that, because the correlations remain reasonably high.

What then does all this actually *mean?* Essentially this: if an index is based on items that all correlate highly with the index, then there is a kind of *internal consistency* present giving a certain guarantee that whatever use one makes of the index, the conclusions can be drawn in terms of *one* dimension, the one expressed by the index. That is all. *This has nothing to do with validity,* for an index may have maximum internal consistency, yet measure something quite different from what the researcher believes it measures. Nor does it guarantee that the index will be a *fruitful* instrument in analytical work.

Since internal consistency is a relation that may or may not hold between the items when they are compared one at a time with the index we may ask: why not just as well use all the correlations between the items themselves? With n items this leads to an intercorrelation matrix with $\binom{n}{2}$ different correlations. We then add columns or rows in the correlation matrix (since the matrix is symmetric, this yields the same result) and rank the items in terms of average inter-correlation (this presupposes additivity of correlations, an assumption which will be discussed in section II, 3.8). The item with the highest average inter-correlation may be said to be the item that passes most centrally through the set of variables, and one should exclude variables that are too distant from this item – i.e. exclude variables that have low average inter-correlations.

In general this method will yield the same or almost the same result as the methods described above, based on correlation with the index (provided the same measures of correlation are used). Thus, in a study we found perfect rank correlation when eight items were ranked (1) according to correlation with an additive index, (2) according to average inter-correlation. The method has the additional advantage that an inter-correlation matrix is a tool that can be used for other purposes as well, whereas correlations with the index have no other uses of importance. However, whereas the first method implies n correlations, $\binom{n}{2}$ correlations will have to be calculated for the second method.

By means of the methods discussed here we may exclude from the items the variables that are not indicators – because they correlate too badly with the dimension or the approximation to the dimension. In other words, items accepted as such because they look as if they belong are excluded because of extensional criteria of the type presented in this section. But what about the opposite case, where the variable is an indicator by virtue of its ability to classify the units in the same way as the dimension itself, but without satisfying the intensional criterion of meaningful belongingness, of being theoretically derived as an item belonging to the dimension? In this case we shall still speak of indicators, even though the variable is not an item. The correlation between the variable and the dimension in this case is simply a finding, an empirical fact that may be more or less perfect, more or less interesting. But it may also lead to a revision of our concept of the dimension, that we 'see' that this or that aspect also belongs meaningfully. Just as we may be wrong and include items that are not indicators, we may also forget variables and get indicators that have not yet been classified as items. Thus, the result of an empirical analysis of the type indicated will invariably be an adjustment of the set of items to the set of indicators, but with a surplus on either side: items that are not indicators because we suspect the operational process is not good enough, and indicators that are not items (with correlations that represent *bona fide* empirical findings).

In conclusion, the distinction between *consistency, validity,* and *empirical finding* should be emphasized once again. They have this much in common: the adequate measure is some measure of correlation or agreement. But they are very different as to meaning. Consistency is the property a set of variables has if all intercorrelations are high, or all correlations with a measure of the dimension they are supposed to tap are high (the two criteria are equivalent if this measure is an additive index based on the variables). Validity is the property an indicator has of indicating what it says it indicates; it is a question of correlation with a criterion. In other words, it is the extent to which the indicator (which may be an index) *rediscovers something already known.* This is different from the empirical finding, which is a *discovery of something unknown so far.* The validation condition is a normative condition and is not rejected if the correlations are low; *the variable is rejected as an indicator.* But when we are testing an empirical hypothesis we should be able to trust the variable and consequently reject the hypotheses if the correlations do not turn out as predicted. In practice many cases will be mixtures of the two, however.

3.8. *Graph, cluster, and factor analysis*

The point of departure in this section is the following: we assume agreement/correlation to be a measure of some kind of proximity in a set of variables; the higher the correlation, the closer the variables. Given a set of n variables one can always construct the matrix of intercorrelations, which will be symmetric (if the coefficients are symmetric), with $\binom{n}{2}$ different correlations (although they need not be numerically different) and fill the main diagonal with 1's, reliability coefficients, 'communalities', or simply leave it open. The question is what to do with this analytical tool, when the variables do not necessarily belong to the same dimension. This is a generalization of the problem discussed in the preceding section, and the idea is to develop and present methods with which we can handle sets of variables from different dimensions.

First of all, it should be emphasized that what can be done on the basis of the matrix alone is very limited. The correlations are bivariate and do not by themselves provide for any kind of multivariate analysis, which is probably the most forceful instrument of social science analysis (II, 5.3). And since the matrix does not imply any theory, only a set of purely extensional findings, we can never *by means of the matrix alone* get beyond a division of the set of n variables in subsets that can be said to belong to the same dimension/cluster/factor by some criterion. Intercorrelation analysis can be compared to an analysis of a matrix of the distances between n cities. By inspection of the matrix, we can divide the set of cities in subsets of cities with reasonable proximity. But we cannot develop a theory of *why* the distances are as they are: that will have to be derived from additional sources. Correspondingly, we can use the intercorrelations to measure inter-variable distance and, under certain conditions, use this to subdivide the variables. For this reason the topic is treated here and not in the chapter on analysis, because the techniques are essentially pre-analytical.

Secondly, an important problem often completely by-passed in discussions of techniques for analyzing correlation matrices is this: *what type of correlations?* In II, 2.3 we have presented and discussed more than twenty measures of correlation, all with their special advantages and disadvantages. We may now take either of two stands: a technique for analyzing correlation matrices should lead to the same subdivision of the set of variables regardless of what measure of correlation is used; or we have to admit that different measures classify variables differently, and try to explain it on the basis of the difference between the correlation measures. Thus, we might conclude something like this: 'With regard to the kind of correlation measured by r, we get subdivision S_r; with regard to the kind of correlation measured by tau, we get subdivision S_{tau}; and with regard to the kind of correlation measured by gamma, we get subdivision S_{gamma}. They are different because the measures are different, and the relation is as follows – – –'. Since the first position seems untenable we shall take the second stand. We believe that there is no inherent difficulty once we accept the rather obvious point that correlation is not an unambiguous concept.

Let us now turn to three techniques that can be used, starting with the simplest of them.

(1) *Graph analysis*

Graph theory can handle some simple systems of interrelations between elements. The immediate application can have great heuristic value: we simply make a dot on a sheet of paper for each variable, and draw all possible lines between them (this works at least for n up to 10, for higher values of n it may confuse more than clarify because of the high number of lines). On each line we write the magnitude of the correlation, disregarding the sign (since a high negative correlation can be changed into a high positive one simply by changing the order of values in one variable).

There are now several possible approaches to the problem of grouping together variables that belong together. We may express the magnitude of the correlation as the length of the line between two variables: the higher the correlation, the shorter the line, and the greater the proximity. The convention may be '100 mm for a correlation of zero' and '0 for a correlation of unity'. A correlation of 0.46 will be rendered by a line 54 mm long. The difficulty is that this is only guaranteed to work for three variables (they form a triangle, although the triangle may be degenerate; $r_{xy} = 0.5$, $r_{xz} = r_{yz} = 0.8$); for more variables, more dimensions than offered by the two-dimensional sheet of paper are needed to represent the inter-correlations. Nevertheless, the method can be quite useful as a first approximation. Variables with high inter-correlations cluster visually together and can be circled off – variables with low intercorrelation are kept apart by physical distance on the sheet of paper.

Another and more systematic approach would start with an inspection of the distribution of the correlations. The $\binom{n}{2}$ correlations can distribute on the interval $(0,1)$ in almost any manner, yielding all kinds of curve shapes discussed in II, 2.4.

If the curve is heavily skewed towards 1 (which is the special case of consistency discussed in preceding section) the conclusion will be that the variables all belong to the same dimension; if it is heavily skewed towards 0, that they belong to many different dimensions. This is trivial, the interesting cases are the symmetric distributions, i.e. the cases of U-shaped, uniform, and A-shaped distributions (we shall not discuss more complex cases).

(a) *U-shaped distributions.* In this case, the correlations divide into two groups: high and low; and the graph can be traced with two kinds of lines: solid for 'high' and broken for 'low'. There are now many possibilities, the simplest being: *the variables divide into two groups so that all correlations within the groups are 'high' and all correlations between the groups are 'low'.*[35] In that case two dimensions have been delimited.[36] In practice, however, this case occurs only rarely. What happens is very often an approximation with one or two 'high's *between* the clusters and some 'low's *within*.

Actually, the lines for the 'low' correlations are superfluous, and a graph based on the 'high' correlations alone can be constructed. The graph is then inspected for *connected subgraphs*, and these subgraphs again are inspected to see whether they possibly are *strongly connected*. To the extent they are, a set of variables belonging to the same dimension has been detected, one for each subgraph.

In other words, what we do is simply to circle the groups of variables that are not connected to other variables, and then see whether these groups are completely connected within, i.e. whether the correlation is 'high' for all possible pairs *within* the groups (it must be low *between* groups, otherwise they would be connected). Thus, in the first case below we may say that there are two groups of variables that belong together, but not in the second case, because one of the groups is not completely connected:

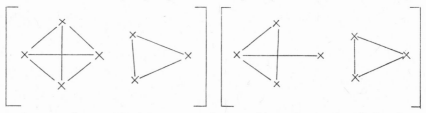

As a rough, quantitative measure, degree of 'togetherness' or 'belonging-ness' in a group of variables can be measured as the ratio of the number of high correlations to the maximum possible. The advantage of this method lies in how quickly it can be carried out; the disadvantage is mainly that it is very crude. However, for a rapid sorting out of variables it may nevertheless be valuable.

(b) *Uniform distributions.* In this case the correlations are dispersed over the entire continuum with no pronounced clustering. Hence, there is no immediate basis for a simplification in terms of 'high' and 'low' correlations. Nevertheless, there are at least two attempts that can be made.

We may try to trichotomize the correlations in 'low', 'medium', and 'high' and redraw the graph in these terms. It may be that a pattern emerges of the 'high vs. medium-low' or 'high-medium vs. low' kinds, and we are essentially back to case (a). There is also the possibility that the medium correlations are found within a limited subset of variables, and that this subset is linked to other sets with low correlations only.

The second attempt tries to change the uniform distribution into a U-shaped distribution by eliminating medium-sized correlations. To eliminate one correlation we have to eliminate at least one variable, and the problem is whether we can get rid of all the medium-sized correlations with a minimum elimination of variables. Since p variables can produce a maximum of $\binom{p}{2}$ 'medium' inter-correlations, these are the figures to keep in mind. Thus, imagine we have 10 correlations that are 'medium'. They can be found between not less than 5 variables, (which then would be completely connected by the correlations) and between not more than 20 variables (two for each correlation). In the first case, we get rid of the correlations by eliminating 5 variables, in the latter case by eliminating 10 (one for each correlation). Technically, we proceed by counting for each variable how many 'medium' correlations it is engaged in, and then start by eliminating from above. If this cannot be done except by considerably exceeding the minimum, the method makes no sense. If it can be done at (close to) the minimum level, we can proceed with the remaining variables as for case (a) above.

(c) *A-shaped distributions*. In this case, the correlations are all of the medium type, so there is no clear indication either of belongingness, nor of separateness. We would recommend not to try the graph method in this case, which is quite frequent in practice. However, case (c) is also a finding, even if it is not a particularly interesting one.

(2) *Cluster analysis*

Cluster analysis, developed by Tryon and Holzinger-Harman, is relatively easily applied in practice.[37] In this method the correlation coefficients are used as interval scale, continuous measures of belonging-together-ness. This assumption may be disputed (which rarely happens), but it is indispensable since the coefficients are added together and an arithmetic mean calculated.

To assume that the difference between a correlation of 1.0 and 0.9 is the same as the difference between a correlation of 0.5 and 0.4 is meaningful only if a criterion is available. This we have in 'variance accounted for', which contradicts the assumption, since we would have to square the correlations, and $1.00 - 0.81 = 0.19$ is not equal to $0.25 - 0.16 = 0.09$. This result would also correspond to the more intuitive idea that it is 'more difficult' to achieve the last step in correlation, from 0.9 to 1.0, than the step from 0.4 to 0.5. However, we shall accept the assumption of additivity for the sake of presentation, but will argue for the same kind of analysis based on the squares of the coefficients.

The method, essentially a quantitative refinement of the graph method, arranges the variables in groups (clusters) with high within and low between correlation. The highest correlation in the matrix is found by inspection. By definition, the two variables in the correlation form a cluster (the correlation must be above a stipulated minimum level). The technical instrument is now the *B*-coefficient (for 'belongingness') and the definition, as given by Fruchter, is simply: 'The B-coefficient gives the ratio of the average intercorrelations of the variables in the cluster to their average correlation with the variables not included in the cluster'.[38] Obviously, the higher B, the more do the variables set themselves off against the rest of the variables.

To calculate B, three steps are needed:

(1) The within-cluster correlations are found, added, and divided by the number of correlations (i.e. $\binom{k}{2}$ in a cluster of k variables).
(2) For all variables in the cluster the correlations with variables outside the cluster are found, added, and averaged [i.e. divided by $k(n-k)$].
(3) The result of the first operation is divided by the result of the second operation.

When this is done, the question is whether it is possible to add more variables to the cluster. The obvious first candidate would be the variable with the highest average correlation with the two variables already in the cluster – and that variable is easily found by inspection. Exactly the same operation is then carried out, and the new B-coefficient is compared to the old. If it is significantly lower, the new variable is rejected; if not, it is retained, and we continue until (and if) the series of B-coefficients suffers a significant drop. Exactly what constitutes a 'significant drop' will have to be decided by inspection and on the basis of experience. Characteristically, the drop should appear when a variable is included that does not have higher average correlation with the variables inside than outside the cluster. As a good standard, we should accept B-coefficients of the magnitude 2 and above, signifying that the average correlation inside is twice the correlation outside the cluster.

Thus, by means of cluster analysis we can arrive at dichotomous judgments to the effect that a variable either belongs or does not belong to a cluster. The basis is, precisely as for graph analysis, that correlations *within* clusters are higher than correlations *between* clusters, but there is this important difference: With graph analysis, it is decided in advance what constitutes 'high' and what constitutes 'low' correlations, and the correlation matrix or correlation graph is inspected to see whether the 'high' and 'low' correlations between variables distribute according to a certain pattern. In cluster analysis, correlations within and between are compared *in an average sense,* which means that there may be high correlations between and low correlations within, as long as the averages are sufficiently different. This has one important consequence. In a strongly connected dimension arrived at by graph analysis, there is transitivity between correlations in the following sense: if there is high correlation between X and Y and between Y and Z, and all three belong to the same dimension, then there is also high correla-

306

tion between X and Z (for if there were low correlation between X and Z, then it would not be permitted according to the criterion of strong connectedness). But in a cluster arrived at by the method of cluster analysis, there is no built-in transitivity, since the only requirement is that the cluster distinguish itself in an average sense.

Finally, some words about the parsimony of the methods. If we use r^2 instead of r in cluster analysis, the correlations will be ordered in the same way, since r^2 is a monotone function of r. For that reason, graph analysis will yield the same result, since the cut between 'high' and 'low' correlations will be at the same place. For the cluster analysis to yield the same result, successive B-coefficients have to be ordered more or less the same way, regardless of whether we use r or r^2 to calculate them. However, it is quite possible for B to increase when it is based on r^2 and decrease when based on r,[39] which makes it unreliable even though it may yield the same result in special cases. This is not necessarily an objection, since we can always add to the definition of the cluster 'as measured by r', 'as measured by r^2' etc., but it reduces the utility of the method somewhat.

(3) *Factor analysis*

To give a full presentation of factor analysis would obviously fall outside the scope of this book, as the field is highly technical and there are many excellent texts available. We shall only try to place factor analysis on the map of social science methodology.

In principle what the method does is to place variables in groups, here referred to as factors. It should not be confused with theory-formation: it does not answer any 'why?', but only informs the analyst that the manifold of variables made use of can be reduced to a much lower number, called factors; and that the correlations observed between the variables can be accounted for in terms of the *loadings* each variable has on each factor. The basic equation of factor analysis (for independent factors) is $R = FF'$; where R is the matrix of intercorrelations ($n \cdot n$ since there are n variables) and F is the matrix of factor loadings ($n \cdot f$, yielding for each variable its component for each one of the f factors). Thus, not only variables but also units can be characterized in terms of these factors.

The tremendous advantage of factor analysis relative to the two preceding methods is that it is quantitative, not qualitative. It does not end with the obviously too simplistic decision that 'this variable belongs completely to dimension/cluster D_i and not at all to any other dimension/cluster', but with conclusions of this type 'this variable has a loading of .8 on factor F_1,

.4 of factor F_2, .3 on factor F_3 and no loading on factor F_4'. Thus, variables are apportioned to factors in degrees, and not in terms of either-or, yielding a much more realistic picture of the topography of variables used in an investigation.

But this precision is bought at a considerable price, and with the data typical of social science probably often at too high a price. Thus, the equations of factor analysis are based on interval scale measures of correlation, principally on r. The conditions for calculating r also become, to a considerable extent, conditions for using factor analysis, since the outcome may be quite different if other coefficients are fed into the machinery. (This is of course no argument for not using factor analysis when the conditions are satisfied, as they often are with census data, with data where the variables are frequencies, proportions, percentages, etc.) Moreover, it is difficult to be convinced that there is nothing rather arbitrary both in the decision 'when to stop factoring' and in the decision as to what subroutine to use when it comes to rotation, assumptions about the relation between the factors, and so on. But the final word about factor analysis has certainly not been said, and we can only refer readers to the many excellent texts in the field,[40] as well as to fascinating investigations.[41]

*

         *   *

In conclusion, let us point out how this section ties in with the problems touched in I, chapters 2 and 3. As mentioned there, a good sampling theory exists for units, but not for variables. On the other hand, a relatively good methodology exists for the measurement of inter-variable distances. This can be used in a cumulative way to solve the sampling problem for variables.

First, an intensional methodology is used whereby variables are selected because they are felt to belong to a universe of variables. Better than relying on the judgment of one social scientist only is to rely on a panel of judges: they are asked independently of each other to volunteer suggestions until there is a clear pattern of diminishing returns in terms of new ideas. These variables are then used to collect data, and a correlation matrix is calculated on the basis of the data matrix. From this correlation matrix extensional methods are used to decide how the universe of variables can be split into sub-universes – and for these subuniverses intensional methods are used again. The final result should be relatively firm definitions of the universes of variables – although we would certainty not claim that this problem is solved.

308

4. Hypotheses

4.1. *Definition of 'hypothesis'*

For many purposes vague statements like 'propositions are about how the world is, hypotheses about how we expect it to be' or 'a proposition is a confirmed hypothesis' may be sufficient. But they do not provide us with tools for an analysis of the types of problems we have to confront if we want to work with hypotheses and propositions. In the following we shall try an approach to hypotheses and propositions that is more useful in locating such problems. In this process we shall use 'hypothesis' as the more general of the two, and define 'proposition' later, as a special case of 'hypothesis'.

It is probably fruitless to discuss whether statements are primarily about things or about their properties. 'This house is red' and 'It will rain to-morrow' are hypotheses, and whether they attribute 'redness' to 'house', 'rainy weather' to 'tomorrow', or 'houseness' to 'red' and 'to-morrowness' to 'rain' is perhaps only a question of linguistic conventions. What is essential in our terms is that a unit ('house', 'to-morrow') is assigned a predicate, attribute, or value ('red', 'rain'), not which is the unit and which is the predicate. For our scheme, as pointed out many times, is completely open to a symmetric view of the relation between units and variables. It may be objected that there are no variables present in the propositions, but that is only because the propositions can be said to be incomplete. They state only what is or is believed to be, not what is not or is not believed to be. Thus, one may add to the above 'This house is not not-red' and 'I believe it will not not-rain to-morrow' to see more clearly the composition of the variables.

Thus, in the data matrix language the hypotheses above have the following form: a *unit* is given (house, to-morrow), a *variable* is given (color, meteorological states), and the variable has a set of *values* (red, not-red; rainy, not-rainy). The unit is then assigned a value of the variable: an hypothesis/proposition assigns a *value* of a *variable* to a *unit*.

We shall now generalize this formula in three directions.

First of all, an hypothesis can be about sets of units with *more than one element*. 'All human beings are mortals' is an hypothesis that distributes the set of 'beings' in a two-dimensional space made by the dichotomies 'human, not-human', 'mortal, not-mortal' leaving the category 'human, not-mortal' empty. We shall call this set S, and as usual assume that it can have any number, m, of elements.

Secondly, an hypothesis can be about *more than one attribute of the unit* – 'this house is red and old' – which corresponds to locating the unit in a two-dimensional space, based on color and age. This can then be extended to any number, n, of dimensions, X_1, X_2, ... X_n that form a space $X = X_1 \times X_2 \times X_3 \times \ldots \times X_n$.

Thirdly, the distribution of units in the n-dimensional space of the variables does not have to be of the 'all units in one cell, all other cells empty' type. Instead we can assign *probabilities* to each of the $r_1 r_2 \ldots r_n$ cells so that they add up to unity. We may say that we have a total mass of unity to be distributed over the cells. We shall call this distribution P, and it is in principle an ordinary (relative) frequency or probability distribution.

Thus, we arrive at the following definition:

An *hypothesis* is a statement about how a set of units, S, is distributed in a space of variables X_1, X_2, ... X_n, or

An *hypothesis* is a statement specifying $P_S(X_1, X_2, \ldots X_n)$.

We claim that an hypothesis can always be given this form; and if something cannot, it is because it is not an hypothesis. On the other hand, we are quite willing to accept a statement like 'God is infinitely good' as an hypothesis, since it has the required form (it places S = God with $P = 1$ at the extreme point of a variable indicating goodness).

The word 'specifying' has been left vague. Obviously, the completely specified hypothesis would be given when all $r_1 r_2 \ldots r_n$ probabilities are given. But that is unnecessarily restrictive. Thus, 'with increasing rank-disequilibration, increasing radicalism' only specifies the two-dimensional distribution insofar as it postulates a positive correlation. This delimits a fairly large class among the many distributions possible when m units are to be distributed in X (see II, 2.1).

An hypothesis presupposes a set of units and a set of variables, and then says something about how the units distribute on the variables. This should not be confused with a statement about what the data matrix looks like; since the hypothesis only specifies distributions, not *which* elements have which properties. But S and X have to be specified completely, and P at least to some extent for the hypothesis to make sense.

The definition given is general mainly because it is given a probabilistic form usually not found in symbolic logic. This form has the deterministic case as a special case; thus 'this book is boring' is a proposition about S =

this book, that assigns probability 1, certainty, to the value 'boring' on a variable X describing the entertainment value of books.

This, then, is our point of departure. In the next section the definition will be justified in terms of its power to locate problems of hypothesis-formation and -confirmation. We shall now point out two alternative definitions that are more useful in practice, although they are less general and not so useful heuristically for a general discussion.

The first alternative definition starts with a set of m units and n variables and sees the hypothesis as a *relation between the variables,* in terms of how the distribution of the units ties the variables together. Just as a theory may be defined as a set of interrelated hypotheses (see 6.1), an hypothesis may be defined as a set of interrelated variables. The problem is only that whereas the language of statistical distributions has maximum generality, the language of 'relations' has generality only in principle. In practice, the language is quite poor.

Thus, we may say that X and Y are 'positively related' or 'negatively related', or 'not related at all'. In this case we have $n = 2$, $M = m$ and P is left relatively unspecified. To operationalize the hypotheses we would have to use some measures of correlation, so as to distinguish three classes of probability distributions: correlation positive, negative or zero. The language can then be enriched (i.e., be made more discriminating) by specifying the magnitude of correlation, not only the sign. But even with a specification of, say, $C = 0.5$, the number of distributions even for moderate values of m will still be considerable.

On the other hand, this relative poverty in the specification of P is realistic, reflecting the relatively undiscriminating vernacular of social theory. What can be deduced from a theory is very often of the 'X will increase with Y' type, where only the sign of the correlation is indicated, and with the implicit assumption that the correlation will have to be above a certain magnitude (often confused with level of significance, see II, 4.4). The distribution language is too precise relative to social theory, a (cor)relation language is more realistic.

For that reason we want to spell out this simplified language of hypotheses, and to do so some symbols are needed. For correlation between two variables we shall not use r, but $C(X, Y)$, in order not to tie the idea to any particular correlation coefficient and to symbolize adequately that correlation can be conceived of as a relation between the variables. Thus, $C^-(X, Y)$ is the hypothesis of negative correlation, $C^0(X, Y)$ the hypothesis of independence, $C^{0.5}(X, Y)$ the hypothesis of a positive correlation of $+0.5$, and so on. This represents a major simplification relative to efforts to specify

$P(X, Y)$, the distribution itself. With some extra symbolism, partial and multiple correlations of any order can be handled, but there is no need to go into detail here.

However, we need symbols of the $C^+(X; C(Y, Z))$ type, which means that 'there is a positive correlation between X and the correlation between Y and Z''. Or in other words: the higher X, the more strongly are Y and Z related. Thus, a famous condition that the correlation between X and Y is not 'spurious', e.g. due to a third variable T, can be expressed as $C^0(T; C(X, Y))$. Further, if we want to study $C(X, Y; C(Z, W))$ what we do is obviously to find out how the correlation between Z and W depends on the values given to both X and Y. All this is known as multivariate analysis, and will be discussed in detail in II, 5.3. There, the scheme will be complicated somewhat by using the distinction from II, 2.3 between symmetric and asymmetric correlation.

The second alternative definition of 'proposition' or 'hypothesis' is as follows[1]:

An *hypothesis/proposition* is a trichotomy of an event-set, or

An *hypothesis/proposition* is a single-valued mapping of an event-set on a set with three elements,

where the three subsets, or the three elements, are called, e.g.,

true	undecided	false
correspondence	undecided	non-correspondence
confirmed	undecided	disconfirmed
+	0	−

How does this definition, which has certain advantages because it reflects research practice (an observation is read off against a standard, and the standard is the hypothesis), square with the definition given?

The term 'event-set' corresponds to the frame given by the cartesian product of the variables: it is the set in which the 'event', i.e. the unit, is supposed to be located. The definition then says that this set is divided into three parts: a true-set where the unit is supposed to appear according to the hypothesis, a false-set where the unit is not supposed to appear at all, and an undecidable-set where we may permit the unit to appear without for that reason rejecting the hypothesis, but rather postpone decision. The definition does not exclude the possibility of more than one unit in the event-set, so it incorporates the first two generalizations discussed above. But the probability distribution is in terms of one subset given the probability 1 and an other the probability 0. Thus, the definition is less general.

By means of a little trick, however, it can be made equivalent to the other definition, and this is important for the last sections of this chapter. In the

$(X_1, X_2, \ldots X_n)$ space each point corresponds to *one* unit (or event in the event-set). This space can be meaningfully divided into two parts, true-set and false-set if our hypothesis is deterministic [as we divide the (distance, time) space for bodies falling in vacuum in two regions, the true-set described by the parabola $s = \frac{1}{2}gt^2$ and the false-set which is the rest – perhaps admitting for a small undecidable-set].

If the hypothesis is probabilistic as in the general case we can nevertheless proceed as follows.

We want to simplify the distribution, to make it deterministic. But this can only be done at the expense of complicating at some other point; and since the number, m, of units is constant, we have to introduce more axes. If we let each unit have its own set of axes, then the whole set of observations will be represented as a point in this $m \cdot n$-dimensional space. But this does not solve our problem, for we would still have to distribute probabilities in this monstrous space in order to specify the hypothesis. Thus, if we toss a coin twice (or two coins once) and the variable is simply head-tail, we can use either of these representations:

Diagram 4.1.1. *Probabilistic representations of hypothesis*
with $m = 2, n = 1, r = 2$

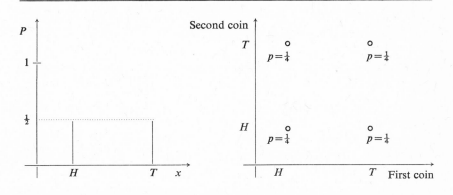

To the right there is one point for each possible set of observations, but the hypothesis is still not given a deterministic form.

To obtain this we have to admit the probabilities as axes. In general, we need $r_1 r_2 \ldots r_n - 1$ such axes since the space has $r_1 r_2 \ldots r_n$ points or cells, but the probabilities add up to 1 so we can do without one of the axes (the number of degrees of freedom, in general, is $r_1 r_2 \ldots r_n - 1$). In the case above, the formula gives one axis, viz. the probability of getting (say) heads, and for this probability axis the hypothesis can be given a deterministic formulation:

Diagram 4.1.2. *Deterministic representation of hypothesis*
with $m = 2$, $n = 1$, $r = 2$

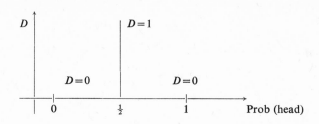

The true-set here is the point $P = \frac{1}{2}$, and the false-set consists of the other two points. This form is equivalent to the forms above and the definition in its most general form. The advantage of talking in terms of true-sets, false-sets, etc. will be evident in 4.2.

However, the form has the disadvantage of being too general. The number of axes becomes very high even for quite simple problems. For that reason, simpler ways of characterizing the probability distribution in all-or-none terms should be found. And this brings in the first alternative definition above, in terms of correlation coefficients. In a case where we have $m = 100$, $n = 2$, $r_1 = r_2 = 5$, we would need a two dimensional space to represent an hypothesis according to the general definition; a two-hundred dimensional space, if we want to represent the set of observations as one point; a 24-dimensional space, if we want one axis for each degree of freedom and a simple representation in terms of true-set and false-set (in all three cases we might add one axis for the probabilities of the hypothesis) – but we can do with one simple axis if the hypothesis can be expressed in terms of correlation coefficients, for instance:

Diagram 4.1.3. *Deterministic representation of correlation hypothesis*

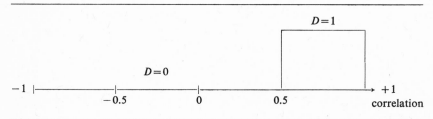

The hypothesis is simply that the correlation is 0.5 or above, and this region, then, is the true-set.

One may also use two-dimensional parameter-spaces, and an hypothesis may look like this:

Diagram 4.1.4. *Hypothesis in two-dimensional parameter-space*

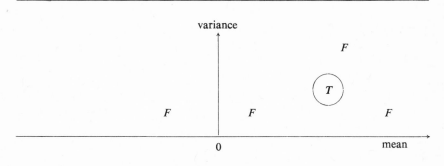

where *T* stands for the true-set and *F* for the false-set. Clearly, all these forms represent great simplifications relative to the original definition and the representation in terms of $r_1 r_2 \ldots \cdot r_n - 1$ axes. This will be discussed in detail in next section, especially in the paragraph on specificity.

4.2. *Dimensions of hypotheses*

By means of the general definition, an hypothesis can be recognized on formal criteria alone, since it can be put on the form $P_S(X_1, X_2, \ldots X_n)$. The variety of hypotheses is enormous, however. In this section, hypotheses will be discussed in terms of ten dimensions. All of them imply important methodological and epistemological problems, and all are rank-dimensions in the sense that they can be used to evaluate hypotheses. For easy reference the ten dimensions are

  (1) Generality
  (2) Complexity

  (3) Specificity
  (4) Determinacy

  (5) Falsifiability
  (6) Testability

  (7) Communicability
  (8) Reproducibility

  (9) Predictability
  (10) Tenability

They are presented as five pairs, since there is a certain similarity between the dimensions in the same pair. This grouping will also facilitate the discussion.

The procedure will be as follows: The dimension will be introduced by means of some examples, and its use as rank-dimension, as a standard for *evaluation* of hypotheses will be discussed. Then it may be split into sub-dimensions, and efforts will be made to operationalize the dimension(s) by means of simple measures. In this process any dichotomous conception of the dimension will be replaced by a polytomous or even continuous presentation of it. All this will then be seen in the light of some currently predominant canons of scientific research, and efforts to specify criteria for ranking hypotheses will be presented. The symbol '>' will be used as a preference relation between hypotheses.

Throughout the presentation, the relation between the dimensions will be explored, since it will rapidly be clear that efforts to maximize at the same time almost any pair of dimensions leads to difficulties that should be explored.

(1) *Generality*

Science is generalizing, although it may elaborate special cases, as is done in the ideographic sciences. The hypothesis is about the units in the set S, which we shall call the *intended field of tenability* (when it is confirmed, we drop the word 'intended'). *To specify this set is to specify the conditions under which the hypothesis is assumed to be valid.* A cardinal sin in social science research is precisely the failure to specify the conditions of assumed validity. Propositions are presented with sweeping generality, as valid for mankind from eternity to eternity, where a specification might read 'at least as far as students in the Psychology 1 course at X college, located in Mid-West, U.S.A., spring of 1959, are concerned'. Since the problem of specifying is intimately linked to the problem of sampling, and through that to the *cas pur* problematics, this touches on very general problems in social science methodology. Since most hypotheses are probably tenable under *some* conditions, instead of saying: 'given the set of conditions C, show me a tenable hypothesis, H' we may say 'given an hypothesis H, show me the set of conditions C under which it is tenable'. The continous adjustment of hypotheses and conditions of tenability to each other is at the root of any scientific activity.

Imagine now that we have two hypotheses, H_1, and H_2, with intended fields of tenability S, and S_2. We then get, simply:

> *Ceteris paribus*, we have $H_2 > H_1$ if $S_2 \supset S_1$.

That is, we prefer an hypothesis to another if its field of tenability includes the field of tenability of the other hypothesis. This definition is trite, but it is difficult to say more than this. Thus, if the condition above is satisfied, we also have $m_2 > m_1$. But $m_2 > m_1$ also obtains under a number of other conditions. S_1 and S_2 may overlap so that both hypotheses cover the intersection and specialize in the excess on either side. Which hypothesis to prefer in this case cannot be decided on the basis of numbers alone, but possibly on the basis of some criteria to be discussed in 6.2. Obviously, we are here very close to a discussion of theory construction, since a theory is an effort to join together hypotheses.

Imagine now that we have an hypothesis/proposition and want to generalize it. The point of attack is the set of conditions, C. The set of conditions is always a point or a region in a product-space, where time, space, and social background often are the most important variables. An effort to generalize, then, is an effort to try out the hypothesis for other points or regions in the condition-space. In principle either of two outcomes is possible. The hypothesis may be confirmed for this new value of one or more of the condition variables, and we have a clear case of generalization. What was valid in Norway or for middle class people was also valid in Italy or for lower class people. And the hypothesis may be disconfirmed: what was valid for U.S. was not valid for Latin America. In this case, which is the more interesting one, we have to increase the complexity of the hypothesis by working the condition variable into the hypothesis. This will be elaborated in the next paragraph.

(2) *Complexity*

We then pass on to the second element in the definition of 'hypothesis': the set of variables used to span the event-space. Structurally, this set has two properties of importance here, viz., the number, n, of variables that are used to form the productspace, and the number, r, of values on these variables. We shall discuss the first of these properties here, and the second under point (3).

By the 'complexity' of an hypothesis we simply mean n. An hypothesis at level 1 is an hypothesis involving one variable; at level 2 two variables are involved, and so on. This dimension, crucial in social analyses, will be explored more thoroughly in the discussion of multivariate analysis. The relation is very simple:

Ceteris paribus, we have $H_2 > H_1$ if $n_2 > n_1$.

Thus, we conceive of science as an activity that tries to integrate a maximum number of variables in its hypotheses/propositions, whether they pass under the headings of 'independent', 'intervening', 'dependent', 'parameters', 'relevant conditions', 'irrelevant conditions', or what not.

We shall cut through this elaborate terminology with only one distinction: dependence vs. independence between variables. Imagine we have an hypothesis/proposition about a relation between two variables, X and Y. In the condition-set, C, is the variable T, value t_1. This means that we have so far only tested the relationship between X and Y for $T = t_1$, and we go on to see what happens if $T = t_2$. It may be useful to classify the possible outcomes as follows:

(1) The relation between X and Y is unchanged, i.e. it does not depend on T. The hypothesis/proposition is generalized to $T = t_2$.
(2) The relation between X and Y is changed, i.e. it does depend on T. There are two subcases:
   (a) T appears as a *parameter* so as to change some secondary characteristic of the relationship between X and Y, (e.g. the regression coefficient).
   (b) T appears in the *functional relationship* so as to change some primary characteristic of the relationship between X and Y, (e.g. from linear to curvilinear correlation).

In the second case, for both subcases, the hypothesis has changed from the second to the third level of complexity, in such a way that *the original hypothesis can be deduced from the new one by specifying the value of T*. Obviously, *the first hypothesis was not wrong, only incomplete* (tenable only for $T = t_1$).

But in the first case above, the level has also changed from the second to the third, only this is very often forgotten. Independence is not trivial, even though we may be conditioned to give it less attention. Thus, increases in complexity are tantamount to generalizations if the new variables are independent of the old, and tantamount to completion if there is dependence.

If the relation between X and Y can be shown to be or is supposed to be independent of T, then the proposition/hypothesis is three-dimensional – but if no mention is made of T it is only two-dimensional.

The idea of complexity can now be used to shed some light on the problem of how to increase generality. Gains in generality can often be made by simple extensions of S, but sooner rather than later we arrive at a point where there is a sharp dip in tenability with extension. This can be seen as a signal that further gains in generality can only be made by increasing the complexity of the hypothesis, adding at least one variable that specifies the difference between S and what is outside S.

318

(3) Specificity

We now move to the second aspect of X: number of values. There are two kinds of specificity that arise immediately from the general definition: the specificity of the variables, and the specificity of the distribution. By this we mean simply the number of potential discriminations that can be made. Thus, we shall prefer an hypothesis based on a trichotomy to one based on a dichotomy, and prefer polytomies of higher order to trichotomies, both in the variables and in the discriminations made between the probabilities. But the dimension is more complex than this.

We shall define the specificity, E, of an hypothesis as the number of discriminations that can be made in the empirical outcomes for the given combinations of X and S. If X has R cells (n-tuples, combinations of valves) and S has N elements, the specificity is given as the number of distributions, i.e.

$$E = \binom{N+R-1}{R-1}$$

Thus, the specificity depends on the number of cells, i.e. on the number of values on each variable and on the number of units. But this kind of specificity presupposes that we are interested in the total set of distributions.

If the hypothesis is deterministic we get:

$$E = 2^R$$

for R is the number of elements in X and the total number of subsets is 2^R, each of them representing one possible deterministic hypothesis. [Two of them, however, will have to be ruled out on some other basis (see point 6), because they are contradiction and tautology, respectively.]

This formula corresponds precisely to the idea of dividing the event-space into two subsets (we disregard, as usual, the undecidable-set). Thus, if we have 4 units and the hypothesis is about their distribution on a set of two dichotomies, we get a specificity of 35 in the general and a specificity of 16 in the deterministic case. Specificity, thus, is nothing but the variety in the set of possible distributions, which in this case is less if we restrict ourselves to deterministic hypotheses. This does not hold always, however, as is evident from Table 4.2.1. (p. 318).

Thus, for low N/R ratios we get more specificity out of a deterministic than a probabilistic hypothesis. The reason is simple enough: in the deterministic hypothesis we do not ask for the distribution of the elements within the true-region or false-region, only for how many possible true-regions we can define. But if N is equal to R or higher (except for the case $R = 2$), we get more variety or specificity out of the probabilistic hypothesis.

Table 4.2.1. *Specificity ratios between deterministic and probabilistic hypotheses,* $2^R : \begin{pmatrix} N+R-1 \\ R-1 \end{pmatrix}$

		Number of value-combinations, R			
		2	3	4	5
	1	2.0	2.7	4.0	6.4
Number of units, N	2	1.3	1.3	1.6	2.1
	3	1.0	0.8	0.8	0.9
	4	0.8	0.5	0.5	0.5
	5	0.7	0.4	0.3	0.3

We can now take the other presentations of hypotheses in II, 4.1 and for each case find out how many discriminations are actually made. For instance, we can construct the space with one axis for all except one of the probabilities ($R-1$ axes) and divide this space into a true-set and a false-set. The variety of this space will depend on how fine discriminations we are willing to make for the probabilities (and this will depend on m since the probability will be approximated by a fraction). If they are measured to one decimal place, there will be 11 possibilities for each axis (.0, .1, .2, ... 1.0) and the variety will be $2^{11^{R-1}}$ which soon becomes very high. In the case of diagram 4.1.2. this reduces to $2^{3^1} = 8$ from which we might deduct the two extremes (the contradiction and the tautology).

The types of representations given in diagram 4.1.3-4, however, are more realistic. If in diagram 4.1.3 we only have seven levels of correlations (negative: high, medium, and low; zero; positive: low, medium, and high) the specificity is 7. With discriminations as for probabilities the variety would be 2^{21}. But this would be unrealistically high, since nobody will be likely to put forward the hypothesis that 'the correlation is $-.9$, or 0, or .4'. And the specificity refers to the outcome, where one correlation excludes the other – so the specificity would be 21 (-1.0, -0.9, -0.8, ..., $+0.9$, 1.0).

If we use the curve shape system given in II, 2.4, based on increase, decrease, and stability, nine curve-shapes are distinguished and the specificity is 9 (since they are exhaustive and mutually exclusive). The other curve shape system may have specificity 12 (AJUS, by positive, symmetric, negative). In other words: all depends as mentioned in the definition on the number of mutually exclusive discriminations that can be made.

And this should not be confused with the number of possible hypotheses. As pointed out in 4.1, an hypothesis may be more or less specified. It cannot be made more specific than down to the level of one distribution, but it can be made less specific, comprising more distributions than the empirical techniques, in fact, permit one to discriminate between. One logical consequence of this is to adjust the level of specificity to the level of discrimination we actually want to make when we test the hypotheses; in other words, to adjust the empirical specificity to the theoretical specificity. If the hypothesis is in terms of 'high' or 'low' correlations, it is not necessary to have discriminations at the level of two decimal places, for instance. On the other hand we then lose the possibility of refining the hypothesis in the light of the data.

(4) *Determinacy*

In general, the deterministic hypothesis is preferable to the probabilistic hypothesis. The goal is to be able to specify the conditions so well (i.e. arrive at a high level of complexity) that the units can be said with certainty to fall in one region (the true-set) and not in another (the false-set). In other words, there should be a firm border-line between true-set and false-set, not blurred by shades of probability. Let us call determinacy D, so as to be able to write:

Ceteris paribus, we have $H_2 > H_1$ when $D_2 > D_1$.

The question is how to operationalize D. The ideal would be a measure that takes on its extreme values, 0 and 1, for the maximally probabilistic and maximally deterministic hypothesis, respectively. Further, the measure should be based on the same idea for hypotheses of any level of complexity. Finally, measures should be developed for the main levels of measurement.

A one-dimensional hypothesis specifies the distribution on one variable. Clearly, the more the mass of the distribution is concentrated on one value or a set of values, the higher the determinacy. Similarly, a two-dimensional hypothesis specifies a distribution on two variables. The more the mass of the distribution is concentrated on a region or a set of regions in that space, the higher the determinacy. Thus, determinacy is high when dispersion is low, and vice versa. The question is only which measure of dispersion to use.

For one-dimensional hypotheses, the percentage in the modal category, $\%_M$, is completely sufficient as a basis. It varies from $\dfrac{100}{r}\%$ to 100%; the former if the distribution is uniform, the latter if it is concentrated in the modal category. Thus, we get:

$$D^* = \frac{\%_M \cdot r - 100}{100r - 100}$$

which has the desired properties. It is applicable at all levels of measurement, since all levels are intrinsically nominal. The question is whether it can be extended to hypotheses with two variables. Obviously, the standard correlation coefficients at the ordinal and interval levels will not do the job. For instance, for tau$_b$ or r to be high the distribution has to be concentrated on a regression line. But an hypothesis that says that the outcomes will fall with certainty in a number of non-contiguous regions with considerable dispersion is deterministic; and so is an hypothesis that excludes almost nothing but talks with certainty about the region singled out as the true-set.

In other words, it is not a question of the dispersion of the observations but of the dispersion of the probabilities that constitute the hypothesis. In general, there are $R = r_1 r_2 \ldots r_n$ probabilities that make up the hypothesis. It is now easily seen what constitutes the case of maximum determinacy and what corresponds to minimum determinacy. We have maximum determinacy when one probability is 1 and the others are 0, and minimum determinacy when all probabilities are equal, i.e. equal to $1/R$. For in the former case the hypothesis is completely deterministic with no shades of probability, and in the latter case the hypothesis indicates no preference for anything, just an even dispersion of the outcomes.

From information theory there is a well-known measure of information, or indeterminacy given by:

$$H = - \sum_1^R p_i \log_2 p_i$$

This measure is zero in the determinate case and takes on its maximum value, $\log_2 R$ if and only if all R probabilities are equal. Thus, an excellent measure of determinacy would be:

$$D = 1 - \frac{H}{\log_2 R}$$

which varies as it should from 0 to 1. It works on all levels of measurement, for all levels of complexity and generality, and expresses an important characteristic of any probability distribution. Finally, it has the important advantage of being linked to the whole theory of information.

Determinacy is obviously related to specificity. By decreasing the specificity we can always obtain almost any level of determinacy simply by making the cells so gross that one of the probabilities approaches unity. Correspondingly, we can increase specificity, but usually at the expense of a serious loss in determinacy. The ideal, obviously, is to get both – as in the often quoted $s = \frac{1}{2}gt^2$ case where very fine discriminations are made in the measurements of t and s, without losing the forceful determinacy. But this is rarely obtained

322

in social science. The social science hypothesis is often based on a fourfold-table and 'positive correlation', and both determinacy and specificity are low.

(5) *Falsifiability*

We now assume that the hypothesis is presented in such a way (see 4.1) that the true-set, undecidable-set, and false-set are clearly delimited (i.e. for probabilistic hypotheses we choose one of the representations where the sample appears as a point). If we then call the false-set of an hypothesis H_i for F_i, we get this simple and forceful principle of falsifiability:

Ceteris paribus, we have $H_2 > H_1$ when $F_2 \supset F_1$.

Thus, we shall prefer the hypothesis with the most inclusive class of falsifiers.[2] This formula has the same general form as the corresponding formula for generality; we are equally unhappy about it, since it obviously does not say much. Thus, hypotheses are only comparable according to this formula if they are defined over the same outcome-space.

To get some steps further we have to assume that a value can be given to each falsifying outcome so that they can be compared. The goal is to construct a measure of falsifiability, F, composed of the falsification-values of each single, falsifying outcome. The simplest point of departure here is obviously to assume all E distributions equally probable *a priori* and then simply define falsifiability as:

$$F = \frac{n_F}{E}$$

or the ratio of falsifying outcomes to the total number of possible outcomes. The measure varies between 0 and 1 and has a number of other advantages. Thus, one can define the relative falsifiability of two hypotheses as:

$$F_r = \frac{n_{F_1}}{n_{F_2}}$$

in the case of the two hypotheses being defined over the same outcome-space or in general with the same degree of specificity; and as:

$$F_r = \frac{n_{F_1}}{n_{F_2}} \cdot \frac{E_2}{E_1}$$

in all other cases. The measure cannot be much simpler, and is very useful in the kind of reasoning that will be given in 5.3 and particularly in 5.4.

We shall not try to refine this measure, only indicate how it might be done. First of all, the measure is based on the assumption of equal probability *a priori*. This assumption must somehow be justified; otherwise, any degree of falsifiability can be obtained by increasing the degree of specificity in the false-set, maintaining the degree of specificity in the true-set. Nor can the basis for the justification be an equally distributed degree of rational belief in all outcomes, for if the degree of rational belief were equally distributed, the hypothesis would have to be about a uniform probability distribution. This, by the way, is not the same as a tautology (which is a uniform distribution giving probability 1 to the total outcome-set as a true-set); the hypothesis 'head: $\frac{1}{2}$, tail: $\frac{1}{2}$' is a specified hypothesis, and no tautology. The reasoning is rather that 'Nature should be given a fair chance', and one way of obtaining this is probably precisely by giving the same level of specificity to distributions in the false-set as to the distributions in the true-set. The act of testing the hypothesis is then seen as a competition with 'Nature's equiprobability hypothesis'.

The question is whether or not we should take into account prior knowledge. The basis would be that all distributions are only equally probable *a priori* in a state of no knowledge (and assuming equi-specificity); and that this state of ignorance is rare, since most hypotheses are probably based on (however badly founded and however incomplete) induction. Thus, we might say that the falsifiability of an hypothesis decreases with increasing confirmation, and that to keep the level of falsifiability constant (keep the risk of being wrong constant, that is) we should gradually reduce the true-set. However, this quickly becomes very complex, and we will have to make assumptions that are no longer on the purely formal level we have used so far, e.g. about the empirical level of knowledge of the investigator. Thus, this kind of falsifiability would be a pragmatic relation between hypothesizer and hypothesis, not a formal property of the hypothesis alone.

If we keep it that way, the simple interpretation of degree of falsifiability as defined above is as follows: it is the probability of being wrong, or disconfirmation, if Nature is producing outcomes according to chance, or 'by chance only' as it is often said. While the simplest interpretation of 'by chance only' is equiprobability, there are also other, more limiting interpretations.[3] But we shall stick to simplicity, and assume that we obtain this by keeping uniform the level of *a priori* probability. In other words, we do not think that all distributions are equiprobable, but want to know how much chance of disconfirmation there would be if they were equiprobable.

(6) *Testability*

An hypothesis is testable or possesses testability to the extent a conclusion in terms of true/confirmed *or* false/disconfirmed can be arrived at when the

324

hypothesis is compared with the empirical distribution. Degree of testability, T, is a formal characteristic of the *a priori* distribution of possible outcomes on the true-set, undecidable-set and false-set. Since the total number of possible outcomes is equal to the specificity, E, this is a question of how E is partitioned into three parts. We call the numbers n_T, n_U, and n_F, with the basic equation:

$$E = n_T + n_U + n_F$$

The problem is to construct a function:

$$T = f(n_T, n_U, n_F) \quad \text{or} \quad T = f(n_T, n_F)$$

(since n_U is given by subtracting $n_T + n_F$ from E), which gives the degree of testability as a function of the formal properties *a priori* of the system on which the hypothesis is based. We shall proceed by trying to fix the conditions for T to attain its minimum and maximum values.

The conditions for a minimum value of T, which we may fix to be 0, follow immediately from the definition of testability given above, i.e. testability as not only decidability, but as a built-in possibility of a *choice* between confirmation and disconfirmation. There are five conditions under which no such *a priori* choice exists:

Table 4.2.2. *The conditions for zero testability* $(T = 0)$

Case	Name	Characterization
(1)	Tautology	$n_T = E \; n_F = 0 \; n_U = 0$
(2)	Contradiction	$n_T = 0 \; n_F = E \; n_U = 0$
(3)	Indecision	$n_T = 0 \; n_F = 0 \; n_U = E$
(4)	Non-verificability	$n_T = 0 \; n_F \neq 0 \; n_U \neq 0$
(5)	Non-falsifiability	$n_T \neq 0 \; n_F = 0 \; n_U \neq 0$

One algebraic function that fulfills these conditions is obviously:

$$T = (n_T n_F)/E^2$$

It takes on the value 0 if and only if one or more of the five conditions above are satisfied. All of them are well known from any standard treatise on methodology. An hypothesis that admits all possible distributions in its true-set excludes nothing, there is no 'state of the world' (read: distribution) that can disconfirm it; hence it says nothing, and so on, down the list. It may be disputed whether cases (4) and (5) are equal to cases (1), (2), and (3) since they actually permit shades. But according to the definition they do not permit testing. Thus, in case (5) the choice is between confirmation and indecision, with no built-in possibility of disconfirmation.

We can now make a diagram of the testability as a function of n_T and n_F, the numbers of outcomes in the true-regions and false-regions, respectively:

Diagram 4.2.3. *The testability function (numbers refer to cases in Table* 4.2.2)

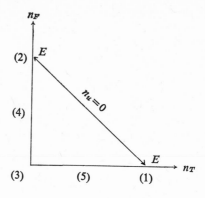

The formula expresses the five conditions perfectly well, but that does not mean that we have to accept the formula when this *Randbedingung* ($T = 0$) is not satisfied. According to the formula we have equitestability on curves of the type $T = k$, where k varies from 0 to $\frac{1}{4}$. The critical test of the formula lies in under what condition(s) it attains its maximum value. The maximum is $\frac{1}{4}$ for $n_T = n_F = E/2$. But do we accept this as maximum testability on other grounds?

Since the metric of testability has never been made very clear, only the conditions for non-testability, it is difficult to tell. We can accept it provided we introduce a precization of the definition given above of testability. We could try 'testability is the a priori probability of confirming or disconfirming the hypothesis'. This would give us:

$$T^* = \frac{n_T + n_F}{E}$$

It would attain maximum for any point on the diagonal line in diagram 4.2.3, which corresponds to $n_U = 0$, but it would not attain the value zero as it should (as a matter of fact, only for the case of indecision). Since we have to have $T = 0$ along the coordinate axes,[4] we can certainly argue that it does not make sense to accept a jump in T from minimum to maximum when we move from points 1 or 2 in the diagram to a neighbor point on the diagonal. And how could we justify this on epistemological grounds?

326

Let us compare the case $n_T = 0.10$ and $n_F = 0.90$ with the case $n_T = n_F = 0.50$. It should be remembered that testability is completely symmetric; it does not favor confirmation to disconfirmation. In the first case one is gambling on a higher *a priori* probability of disconfirmation, while in the latter the indication of symmetris is reflected in an equal split. We can *define* this case as the case of maximum testability if we see testing as a kind of game against Nature where we do not know Nature's cards, and for lack of knowledge assume that they may as well favor the true-set as the false-set.

What, then, is the ideal hypothesis, according to what has been said about falsificability and testability? It should satisfy three criteria:

    (1) Minimize the *true-set*, but not to the zero-set
    (2) Minimize the *undecidable-set*, if possible to the zero-set
    (3) Maximize the *false-set*, but not to the universal set.

In practice this means that the hypothesis should be located as close as possible to the diagonal in diagram 4.2.3, preferably *on* the diagonal. Moreover, it should be located close to the upper left corner, where n_T is very low and n_F is very high – without coinciding with the contradiction in point 2. Thus, the requirements specified so far delimit our choice considerably, to a small subset, in the total set of possibilities bordered by the triangle in the diagram.

From these formal considerations we now turn to more practical problems: under which conditions do we, in practice, get a testability of zero? This problem can be attacked at three points. The kind of testing we are talking about has to do with a confrontation of an hypothesis with data. Hence, the lack of testability may be due to the hypothesis itself, to the problem of defining data that can be confronted with the hypothesis, and to the problem of getting these data. Many other bases of systematization are possible, but this gives us what we need.

The first question, then, is whether the hypothesis as a verbal statement is such that there are world-states that can change its degree of confirmation at all. If the hypothesis derives its truth-value on the basis of its form alone, it is customary to call it an analytic proposition – if it is true it is called positively analytic, if it is false it is called negatively analytic. Thus, no state of the world can change the degree of confirmation given to the hypothesis 'with increasing rank-disequilibration we get more, less, or the same degree of radicalism', or to the hypothesis 'rank-disequilibration leads to both more and the same and less radicalism'. Thus, the positively analytic proposition is a special case of the tautology, and the negatively analytic proposition a special case of the contradiction. Both are derived on the basis of the hypothesis alone, with no reference at all to the data problem, since no data can be imagined that can confirm or disconfirm.

Analyticity is a question of form. But there are non-analytical hypotheses for which no known or imagined world-states would lead to confirmation or disconfirmation. In this case, where no world-states can be defined as verifiers or falsifiers (as falling in the truth-set or false-set of the hypothesis, respectively) we have $n_U = E$, which is the case (3), perfect indecision. 'God is infinitely good' is one case which is certainly not analytic (its truth-value cannot be decided on the basis of form alone), yet so far no intersubjectively agreed upon falsifiers or verifiers have been found.

The third point of attack lies in the methodology applied. As pointed out In I, 2.3 and I, 3.3, selection of units and of variables can favor or disfavor an hypothesis – there may be a built-in tendency to (dis)confirm the hypothesis over and above the tendency given in the system when it is not touched by any methodology. Thus, it is easy to compose a sample so as to arrive at (almost) any degree of correlation, and the same applies to variables. In II, 5.4 methods to avoid this will be developed. Here the point is only that in extreme cases there will be so much built-in tendency that we may arrive at non-verificability or non-falsifiability. One such case, of some practical importance for the investigator, lies in developing two indices with an overlap in items, and then showing that they are correlated. In this case of (almost) non-falsifiability, the degree of confirmation is actually negative [see (10) below], even though there is a perfect correspondence.

(7) *Predictability*

This dimension of an hypothesis, as well as the following two dimensions, differ from the first six in that these are not formal properties of how an hypothesis is defined, nor are they (for that reason) as explicit or subject to operationalization as the preceding dimensions.

The point of departure for a discussion of the role of predictability is the ordering in time of three events: the formation of the hypothesis, the states of the world to which the data refer, and the knowledge of the data (by the investigator, the same person who formed or is going to form the hypothesis). For simplicity, let us imagine that the three events can be ordered, i.e. that there is no coincidence in time between them. Since the states of the world, or the phenomena, will have to take place before the data about them can be known, we get three cases, depending on where the formation of the hypothesis is located. These are shown in Table 4.2.4.

The first case is the clear prediction, it is *pre dicere* both relative to the phenomenon and to the knowledge of the data about it. In the second case,

Table 4.2.4. *The role of time in the formation of hypotheses*

(1) Prediction	formation of hypothesis	→	relevant world states	→	knowledge of data
(2) Postdiction	relevant world states	→	formation of hypothesis	→	knowledge of data
(3) Description, Explanation, 'Accounting for'	relevant world states	→	knowledge of data	→	formation of hypothesis

the postdiction, there is *post dicere,* but only relative to the phenomenon, not relative to the knowledge of the data. This, for instance, will be the historian's kind of prediction. The world-states he refers to will necessarily precede his formation of hypothesis. But the data about them may be unknown to him – an excavation, a new inscription, a new collection of letters, archives that can be opened for the first time. In either case the hypothesis is what most people probably associate with the word, i.e. a kind of educated guess, without looking into the cards.

In the third case, the cards are looked into and even fully known. Nature's deal of cards is read off, so to say, and the hypothesis is formed accordingly. There are several more or less current ways of expressing this: the data are *accounted for* by the hypothesis, the phenomenon is *described,* or the phenomenon is *explained,* but it is certainly not predicted. The distinction between the last two seems to be mainly a question of linguistic habits as to the use of such key words as 'how' (description) and 'why' (explanation). Instead of invoking these words we shall prefer the following basis for regulating the usage of the words description and explanation: a phenomenon is *explained* if it can be deduced from a theory. This will be elaborated in 6.1. Hence, we shall not use the word 'explained' in the present context.

The question is now to what extent the order (1), (2), (3) in Table 4.2.4 is also a rank order in the domain of hypotheses. Whatever the conclusion may be as to case (3) it does not seem reasonable to prefer case (1) to case (2), however. For if we did, knowledge obtained by the hypothetical-deductive method about the past would forever have a scientifically inferior status. We may argue that this is the case if for no other reason because of the uncertainty involved, but that should show up in a lower degree of confirmation, because of fewer indicators and less control over relevant conditions than for future phenomena. Hence, the basic distinction is between hypothesis-formation *before* and *after* the *data* are known – *ex ante* and *ex post.* The distinction between prediction and postdiction is important, but not in this context.

This being said, it is obvious that any sharp distinction between *ex ante* and *ex post* will have to yield to a continuum that can be envisaged as follows. If we change from the unrealistic view of 'formation of hypothesis' and 'knowledge of data' as events located at *points* in time, to envisage them as processes in *intervals* of time, we arrive at all kinds of overlaps between the two. The hypothesis formation may precede or may be subsequent to the data process – but these are extremes that hardly occur very often in practice. The question is rather 'how much knowledge of the data at what stage in the formation of the hypothesis' without necessarily accepting what actually happens in scientific practice as a norm for what should happen. Thus, there is a basis for a measure of the degree of predictability in the hypothesis, i.e. the degree to which the hypothesis-formation precedes the knowledge of the data.

There are many ways in which this overlap comes about in practice. The most famous one is probably the *principle of finite induction* where the first m observations of a specified kind of units serve as a basis for a 'prediction' about other units of the same kind. These units may or may not have come into being when the hypothesis was formed, leading to a prediction or a postdiction respectively.

Another form is the typical *ex post facto* analysis known to any social scientist who has worked with surveys. One looks at some variables in the data with or without an explicit hypothesis in mind. Inspired by the data, new hypotheses are formed, which are then tested on other parts of the data, provided such virgin parts exist. For instance, they may be tested on other variables, or on other subgroups within the data (for a discussion of this, see II, 5.4). Here a full scale can be imagined, from one extreme where one does not look at the data at all but enters them with a fullfledged, ready-made hypothesis, via stages where a part of the data matrix is used *ex post* and another part *ex ante,* to the other extreme where the whole data matrix with its statistical implications is known before the final hypothesis is formulated.

Allocating relative ranks to these types of scientific strategies is complicated. Let us phrase it in terms of *predicting vs. accounting* for the data. If we conceive of confirmation in terms of a correspondence theory of truth, i.e. as the consonance (correspondence) between hypothesis and data, then obviously an hypothesis *ex post* can be fully confirmed. In general, it should be confirmable to a higher degree, since knowledge of the data does not reduce the degree of consonance – at worst it remains constant.

It is easy on pragmatic grounds to argue in favor of one and against the other. To formulate the hypothesis *ex ante* has very often the serious con-

330

sequence that the researcher becomes a slave of his hypothesis, looking only for what his hypothesis tells him to. He confirms or disconfirms, but he enters his data with a mental bias that makes him less open to other aspects of the data, less analytically inventive. This may even have the undesirable consequence that he forces his hypothesis on the data by means of analytical tricks, instead of letting the data impress their 'story' on him.

To formulate the hypothesis *ex post* has a corresponding disadvantage, also of a pragmatic nature. Here, the researcher is not led by theory towards new, possible insights. He becomes a slave of the data. What they tell him is what he is able to receive, nothing more; he does not stimulate the data sufficiently to arrive at more interesting stories. Moreover, since he is not oriented towards a specific goal, his whole data collection procedure, including sampling of units and variables, is probably incomplete. Thus, he will discover in his analysis that he is left with very incomplete data, without possibilities of really following up hunches and intuitions.

In a situation of this kind, standards are needed to evaluate the relative merits of the two approaches. We shall discuss four such standards, which we shall call the *richness-argument,* the *utility-argument,* the *sportmanship-argument* and the *falsifiability argument.*

The *richness-argument* runs as follows. Nature may be richer than our imagination in terms of variety of world-states and their interrelations, or our imagination may be richer than Nature – that is not the question. But we do not accept a symmetric view between Nature and investigator. The task of the investigator is to extract from Nature its distributions of units under a given set of conditions. The question of *ex ante* vs. *ex post* is a question of which is the better strategy, in other words an empirical question. Without data to demonstrate this, we would argue in favor of *ex post,* along the following lines. The analytically trained investigator willing to listen to the full richness of his data and equipped to let the data display their richness will, we feel, get more out of them than the investigator who enters with a prediction only. It is the difference between forming the hypothesis according to the data, and arranging the data according to the hypothesis. It should be emphasized that either party needs theory to guide them in hypothesis-formation, so that is not the difference. The question is, *ceteris paribus,* who gets more out of the data? We feel the investigator with the *ex post* approach does, because he enters with a more open mind.

The *utility-argument* favors the *ex ante* approach. It is based on the usefulness of science as an instrument of control, and prediction as a necessary condition for controlling the future. At this point, a crucial independence between prediction and explanation should be pointed out. A prediction does not presuppose an explanation or a good theory. As has often been pointed out, one may predict that 'Man eats bread' applying the syllogism *barbara:*

P1. All stones are bread
P2. Man eats stones

C. Man eats bread

Or, to take another example: to predict distance from time elapsed for a freely falling body one may use a section of a fourth degree curve as well as an ordinary second degree parabola. Prediction does not ask for understanding, only for coincidence between hypothesis and future observations.

Similarly a very thorough understanding may yield low predictive power. Thus, the understanding may be at a micro level but the prediction only at the macro level. An example is the kinetic theory of gases from which the basic equation relating volume, pressure, and temperature of a gas can be deduced. Examples from sociological theories may be found in the theories relating rank disequilibrium and social change; they may be very wrong in their prediction of the single individual, yet be correct in their prediction of societal phenomena. Even though we shall not go as far as to assert that explanation may be easier than prediction the two tasks are clearly different. And obviously: to predict the data serves better the goal of prediction than merely to account for them *ex post.*

We now turn to the *sportmanship argument.* No one will argue against the pleasure that derives from having arrived *ex ante* at a subtle hypothesis with a high degree of falsifiability *a priori,* and then getting it confirmed. The question is whether this feeling of delight at one's own cleverness adds to science, defined as the body of confirmed hypotheses, interrelated in terms of deducibility. We will argue against the argument as a standard and proceed by way of an illustration. In survey research there is a technique frequently described as the 'fishing expedition', where one 'runs everything against everything else' and starts investigation the highest correlation to see 'whether there is anything in it'. As is evident from the above we see nothing wrong in this, provided the investigator is sufficiently equipped with theory and analytical techniques to know how to do it (which he very often is not, because if he were his strategy would probably be more to the *ex ante* end of the scale). Opposed to this is the *ex ante* approach, where the data are presented, by means of multivariate analysis, so as to be comparable to the hypothesis.

To use the analogy from fishing techniques: the former is evidently a kind of trawling with a net designed to catch everything, the latter is fishing with the sportsman's rod, placing the fly with a masterly throw at the right point above the fish to tempt it, without scaring it. The sportsman gets more pride out of his 2 lbs trout than the trawler team from their 2 ton catch. But the trawler gets both more fish and more money. Industrial fishing gains in efficiency what it loses in charm. It is interesting to notice that this is at times considered unfair to the fish – 'the fish is not given a fair chance'. Correspondingly, we wonder whether 'industrial science-making' – like feeding all data into an IBM 1401 or 7090, asking the machine to scan all possible combinations up to fifth level analysis and produce the findings in order of decreasing correlation – may not be resented on somewhat similar grounds. In the game between Nature and the Investigator, the game called Science, the old norm always was to dip down in the data at a preassigned point, to catch the golden fish; not to surround it with a net so fine that it cannot escape.

In short: delight derived from being a good guesser of Nature's ways is not to be scoffed at, but it is outside the field of discourse. In a different culture it might just as well have been otherwise, with prediction seen as trivial and the complex explanation as the real thing. We feel the trend is moving in this direction, particularly since modern electronic calculators make it possible to design analytical techniques that give us a net with sufficiently fine meshes to catch the more refined findings, not only the crude and evident and trivial.

The sportsmanship argument is rejected on the basis of irrelevance: it refers to feelings held by or towards the investigator and does not have epistemological validity. But the same can be said about the richness and utility arguments. The utility argument has a pragmatic rather than epistemological basis: it is concerned with control of Nature, not with arriving at propositions about it. And the richness argument is a question of strategy. It falls in the same category as arguments of the sociology of knowledge kind: do investigators produce more and better science when they work in teams than when they work alone; is the good scientist the one who reads very much extensively, or very little intensively; etc. For the administrator of science these arguments are important, but not for the philosopher of science.

We then turn to the final and most important argument, about *falsifiability*. This is used to reject the *ex post* approach as follows: if the hypothesis is formed after the data are known, there is no risk involved. The distribution is known, and the hypothesis is tailor-made to the distribution. Thus, Nature is not given any chance to falsify the hypothesis, for Nature's distribution is already given. Thus, with this approach one will always (1) get a maximum degree of confirmation by fitting hypotheses to the data, and (2) get a minimum falsifiability by fitting the hypothesis to the data.

The first argument above is compelling, but should be analyzed further. *If the hypothesis fits, then it fits;* and if the degree of confirmation is maximum, then so much the better. *But,* the consonance/correspondence may be an effect of the particular combination of units-variables-values-data collection used, so we would have to replicate the investigation. And the hypothesis will probably have to be rejected or modified on some other ground, e.g. that it cannot be fitted into a known body of hypotheses (called a theory). Thus, while there is ample room for improvement, we do not for that reason have to deny the validity of the hypothesis relative to that body of data. Actually, we then come to the paradoxical situation that when we use the hypothesis to predict what will happen with replications, the degree of confirmation will probably decrease (see II, 5.4), while our degree of belief in the hypothesis increases.

We feel the second argument, about falsifiability, rests on a misunderstanding. Our falsifiability concept refers to falsifiability *a priori* and is a question of what would happen *if* Nature gave equal probability to each possible outcome. What Nature in fact does is irrelevant in this context: it is what Nature could have done that counts.

That concludes our argument. There are good reasons for making predictions, but they are not, in our opinion, essential to the progress of science. We increase the degree of confirmation by getting more data that correspond to a pre-existing hypothesis – but also by fitting the hypothesis to already known data. In practice, then, we do both, constantly modifying the hypothesis until new replications give no further gains in degree of confirmation. In principle there is *no* end to this process, nor is there any beginning. It can be seen as a chain of *ex ante* and *ex post* strategies where what matters are the final results, the published book or article. And that again is only the beginning of a new chain or set of chains.

(8) *Communicability*

An hypothesis is communicable to the extent its meaning can be transmitted to others. By this we mean that communicator (sender) and communicand (receiver) can develop the same images of what the hypothesis is about. However, there is more to cummunicability than this. It is not only a question of sharing the meaning of the hypothesis as a statement with the investigator, but also a question of sharing his evaluation of the degree of confirmation. Thus, communicability is a question of three factors:

    (1) communication of the *hypothesis*
    (2) communication of the *data* (including method)
    (3) communication of the *evaluation* of the relation between them.

334

This sharing is the public aspect of scientific research, and is known as publication, usually in written form. The tripartite division above corresponds more or less to the disposition of most scientific treatises.

Communicability, thus, is a question of transmission of meaning, not of acceptance – that will be treated under point (9), 'reproducibility'. This, again, is a question of semantics, of interpretation and preciseness, and should be treated as such. The conditions under which it is highly probable that the receiver will interpret the text as intended by the sender are only partly known. The role of a technical language is obvious, but it is also obvious that the technical language shuts out people who do not have the required training. For that reason, communicability is only intended within a certain field, a *competence group* known as 'colleagues'.

Communicability is a partial guarantee against idiosyncracy, against the tendency to develop systems of hypotheses and data that cannot even be communicated to others. The principle serves to rule out types of 'mystical' experiences that cannot even be communicated, that are not 'intersubjectively communicable'. This is, indeed, a *partial* guarantee only, for at least two simple reasons.

First of all, there is the idea of the 'competence group'. By suitably limiting the membership of the group so as to make it coextensional with not only 'colleagues' but 'disciples' communicability may be ensured, but its value as a check limited. It is the communicability across borders of scientific discourse and disagreement that should count – and here the philosopher of science should cooperate with specialists in semantics and sociology of conflict to develop better criteria.

Secondly, just as communicability is not a sufficient condition in its crude from, it is not a necessary condition either. The genius in science does not 'communicate' to his contemporaries but to his successors and imitators – his contemporaries do not understand, or will not understand. Again, it is difficult to make the criterion more precise.

(9) *Reproducibility*

An hypothesis, or rather, a scientific process, is reproducible to the extent it can be repeated with the same conclusion. This definition immediately raises two questions: repetition of what? and repetition by whom? The last question is easily answered in terms of 'same' vs. 'different' investigators. The first question can, in agreement with Table 4.2.4, be answered in terms of 'phenomena' vs. 'data', so that we get the typology shown in Table 4.2.5.

The interest should focus on reproducibility type (4) in the Table, for two reasons. First of all, intra-subjective reproducibility is so embedded in all

Table 4.2.5. *A typology of reproducibility*

		Reproduction of		
		phenomena, world-states	data, analysis	
by whom	by the same investigator	(1)	(2)	*intra*-subjectivity
	by different investigators	(3)	(4)	*inter*-subjectivity

parts of scientific methodology: the investigator should at all points be able to retrace his own steps so as to convince at least himself of consistency. In the field of data-collection this is known as reliability, in the field of data-analysis this is known as checking, control. And, when it comes to reproduction of the phenomenon itself, obtaining or using *new* data (not only going over the old), this is better known as *replication* – and will be treated extensively in II, 5.4.

Secondly, the reproduction of the phenomena is not really required, although it is considered desirable. What is indispensable is that other investigators should be able to go through the same data and not only *understand* the process as intended by the first investigator, but also accept it. Then, and only then is the finding not only *intersubjectively communicable,* but also *intersubjectively reproducible.* In earlier periods the word 'objective' was often used, but it seems difficult or impossible to find a basis for the effort to rule out the purely subjective finding, true for one person only, except on the basis given when the acceptance is *shared. Objectivity is intersubjectivity,* nothing more, nothing less, according to this way of thinking.

This immediately raises the question of the conditions for spread of acceptance, a phenomenon studied by sociologists and social psychologists as a branch of the sociology of knowledge. That other factors than detached intellectual reasoning are at work here, too, is obvious – we need only think of such factors as those studied in sociology under the heading of conflict polarization,[5] and by social psychologists as the Asch effect.[6] However important this principle is, we have yet to see a good theory relating sociology of knowledge to epistemology so as to understand the dimension better.

(10) *Tenability*

We now come to the final and in a sense most important of all the dimensions: tenability. The *raison d'être* of the hypothesis is not to remain an hypothesis but to be confronted with data, and this confrontation leads to an evaluation of the hypothesis where terms like the following are used:

Diagram 4.2.6. *Evaluations of hypotheses*

-1		0		$+1$
falsification,	disconfirmation	*undecidable*	confirmation	verification,
'false', falsified	*untenable*		*tenable*	'true', verified

d. of c.

The line stands for 'degree of confirmation': a concept we shall try to explicate. We have called the extreme points verified (true) and falsified (false) and the zero point undecidable. The extreme points should be conceived of as abstractions, as useful fictions, since we cannot imagine a synthetic hypothesis that we cannot also imagine being confirmed to an even higher degree, or even more disconfirmed.[7] For that reason we talk of an hypothesis as *tenable* when it has received a satisfactory degree of confirmation, and about *confirmation* as the process that leads to tenability. The word 'true' will not be used, nor 'verified'; correspondingly on the negative side of the scale. These terms will only be used about analytic statements, for which no data will change the degree of confirmation or disconfirmation. We then introduce the symbol DC for degree of confirmation and get the obvious:

Ceteris paribus, $H_2 > H_1$ if $DC_2 > DC_1$.

The only non-triviality in this are the words 'ceteris paribus'. They indicate, as we think is justified, that we may be willing to 'trade' a drop in degree of confirmation for some compensation on some other dimension, e.g. degree of falsifiability or determinacy. This will be elaborated later. Obviously, we also have:

A *proposition* is a tenable hypothesis.

But all this is only an allocation of key terms to key positions. It all rests on how we evaluate degree of confirmation, and at what point the undecidable shades over in the tenable. Unfortunately, there are no good answers available to either question.

The first, and naive, approach to degree of confirmation would consist in computing the frequency of outcomes in the true-set of the hypothesis – regardless of form of presentation (II, 4.1) – to the total number of replications of the set of relevant conditions. Thus, if out of 100 falling bodies 90 follow the laws of motion, we may say we have a degree of confirmation equal to 90%. A more refined measure might perhaps give a weight of 1 to the true-set, 0 to the undecidable-set and -1 to the false-set. For simplicity, however, let us disregard the undecidable-set, give a weight of 1 to an observation in the true-set and of 0 to an observation in the false-set, and call this 'the naive degree of confirmation-measure', DC^*.

The measure is naive because it does not take into account the *a priori* probability of confirming the hypothesis. Clearly, if this probability is very high, i.e. if the hypothesis is 'almost' a tautology, a high DC should count less, since it could have been produced by Nature playing a chance game with the investigator. The higher the degree of falsifiability, defined as $F = n_F/E$ where E is the specificity, the higher DC for the same DC^*. But it would be equally naive to identify degree of confirmation with falsifiability. DC^* counts, of course, since this is a measure of how the data go.

A simple measure that combines the two points of view (relative frequency in the true-set, and *a priori* falsifiability) is:

$$DC' = \frac{DC^*-(1-F)}{1-(1-F)} = 1 - \frac{1-DC^*}{F}$$

The first expression gives the logic of the measure, but the second expression is better for a discussion.

Degree of confirmation is defined here as the excess the relative frequency in the true-set has over the *a priori* probability of confirmation $(1-F)$, relative to the maximum excess, which obtains when we have $DC^* = 1$. In that case, the measure takes on its maximum value, $DC' = 1$. It is zero when and only when $DC^* = 1-F$, i.e. equal to the expected frequency in the true-set. For DC^* less than that, it is negative as it should be; and when $DC^* = 0$, it is equal to $1-1/F$, which is always negative, and more so the lower F is.

From the second expression, it can be seen that both increasing F and increasing DC^* will increase DC' by reducing the term to be subtracted from unity. Thus, for constant DC^* we can increase DC' by increasing the risk of being wrong *a priori*, viz., by extending the false-set. There is no compelling reason against even doing this *a posteriori:* we observe a distribution and adjust the hypothesis so as to get an optimum combination of falsifiability and relative frequency of correctly predicted events. In practice one may have to be traded for the other – as is true in most realms of life.

The question is now how the other dimensions enter into the picture of degree of confirmation. Generality, complexity, determinacy, and specificity are obviously *desiderata,* but not necessary conditions for confirmation. They may be varied; and since they all will affect F and DC^* they will affect DC', but only indirectly. Falsifiability enters directly. Testability enters indirectly, as a condition for obtaining DC^* and F different from zero. For if the hypothesis is not testable, we have either $F = 0$ [Table 4.2.2 cases (1) and (5)] or $DC^* = 0$ [cases (2) and (4)] or both [case (3)], and we get negative or zero values of DC'.

For the remaining three dimensions we shall regard communicability and reproducibility, at least at an unspecified minimum level, as necessary conditions for a proposition to be established. In other words, if the field of acceptability cannot be extended beyond the original investigator, the hypothesis is out – at least until the investigator finds some way of persuading others of the acceptability of his ideas. As to predictability, we shall not deny that DC' should increase with successful reproduction, but that can only be done *a posteriori;* and that in turn means that the total mass of data is bigger. *The measures of DC^* and F that enter in the formula above are based on all data available,* whether the hypothesis was wholly, partly, or not at all formulated prior to the knowledge of any part of the data, and regardless of whether the findings were reproduced by the same or different researchers. Thus, predictability in the sense that the hypothesis is *supposed to* hold for future data does not add to the degree of confirmation. But successful prediction does, because of added DC^* and possibly also because of added F. That concludes our discussion of degree of confirmation.

*　　　*　　　*

If we now disregard the three pragmatic dimensions (7), (8), and (9) and concentrate on the six formal dimensions and the last one, we obtain a relatively comprehensive picture of the situation facing the scientist. With good justification we can talk about a scientific strategy just as we talk about a political strategy, meaning a realistic assessment of the ways to achieve an optimum. Striving for a maximum on all variables at the same time is illusory, since they cannot be maximized simultaneously.

To take some examples: imagine we increase specificity. This may enable us to encircle the true set more precisely, so that we increase falsifiability. But there will be an immediate price to pay in terms of determinacy and testability. With increasing specificity the outcomes become less distinguishable, more similar to each other in a sense. This implies an ordering of the outcomes that approximates a continuum: for any pair of outcomes there will, if we only increase the specificity enough, always be a third outcome that can be fitted in between the two. With this continuum a sudden jump from a probability of 0 to a probability of 1 becomes less defendable, and we will have to substitute a probability model for the deterministic one. Or, we may prefer to simplify by delimiting the true-set and false-set, with their probabilities of 0 and 1, and lump all outcomes with intermediate probabilities together in an undecidable-set. This means a loss in testability.

A second example: imagine we increase falsifiability. This can always be done simply by extending the false-set. But if this extension is done as far as to comprise the total set, testability becomes zero (because a contradiction is arrived at). Thus, testability has priority to falsifiability as a requirement. Falsifiability, however, seems to us more important than determinacy – it is the risk-taking that is the mark of good science, not avoidance of probability statements.

A third example: imagine we want to increase degree of confirmation. The dilemma is clearly expressed in the formula for DC': if we increase the true-set, the catch in terms of outcomes may increase, but at the expense of a loss in falsifiability. The problem, then, is to adjust the true-set so as to get the maximum 'catch' of outcomes at the minimum expense in falsifiability – and the formula for DC' is *one* suggestion as to how pairs (DC^*, F) can be ranked so that we can judge whether the degree of confirmation has actually been increased.

In conclusion let us just point out where we stand. Ten requirements have been specified, which can be used to characterize propositions by giving them scores according to how many requirements they satisfy – in the manner of the additive index. The index would range from 0 to 10. All values are attainable, although we have just shown that it is highly difficult to obtain a full score. The requirements quite often work against each other. But if all ten are satisfied the proposition obviously has a tremendous power, and it is probably in line with common usage of the term to refer to it as a 'law of nature' in that case. It is also probably true that the natural sciences on the average produce propositions that score higher than the social sciences on this index, and that the social sciences in turn score higher than the humanities – but then, the requirements have been modeled, implicitly, after the pattern set by the natural sciences and imitated by the social sciences. Nevertheless, in spite of a certain arbitrariness, the model of the additive index as an index of position in a hierarchy of propositions may be useful; and we offer it for what it is: an effort to systematize and operationalize some current concepts in general methodology.

4.3. *Statistical hypotheses*

With the publication of Sidney Siegel's *Nonparametric Statistics for the Behavioral Sciences* in 1956, a major reorientation in statistical thinking in behavioral science was a fact. The bulk of classical statistics developed by such brilliant members of the English school as Galton, Pearson, Gosset,

Yule, Kendall and above all by Fisher, was to a considerable extent based on two assumptions: interval scale variables, and normally distributed universes. On these two assumptions an impressive and highly coherent structure of mathematical statistics could be founded, using classical mathematics and applying it to sciences in an intermediate position on the hard-soft scale, such as the biological sciences (especially agriculture). With the weak position of quantitative, probabilistic social science in England (anthropology being qualitative and economics deterministic in the English variants), no major motivation existed to serve more adequately the needs of the behavioral sciences. More ample perspectives were needed, permitting parameters that did not presuppose the strong requirements of the interval scale (the term 'nonparametric' is indeed a misnomer for 'non-interval scale parametric') and universes that were not normally distributed (and here the term 'distribution-free' is often a misnomer for 'non-normal distribution'). The field of non-parametric and/or distribution-free statistics has expanded rapidly, and although there are still white spots on the map one is at least not tied to the implicit assumptions of the past.

We made a distinction in I, 2.3 between the *substantive hypothesis* which is about social reality and to be tested by means of the data, and the *generalization hypothesis* which is about the data. As mentioned in I, 2.3 we often have to test hypotheses on a sample, because the whole universe is not available and the problem is whether the finding can be 'generalized' to the universe. Another way of saying the same is as follows: since we have a sample, the data are *imperfect;* they may be subject to sampling fluctuations. What we have found in the data may have been an accident which may happen when a sample less than the universe is made use of – as one may get thirteen spades playing bridge. But this immediately leads to a question: what about all the other sources of imperfection that data suffer from? Low validity, low intra- and inter-subjectivity, errors of measurement, coding errors, punching errors, reading errors, typing errors, and what-not? Why be so particularly concerned about sampling error? One simple reason is probably that we can *do* something about it by means of well-founded statistical techniques.

Nevertheless, the apparatus developed to check on sampling errors is disproportionate relative to what is usually done with the other kinds of error – but this is certainly no argument against statistics, but rather a reflection on a sad state of affairs. However, the tool of statistics can also be meaningfully applied to other sources of imperfection of data, such as errors of measurement (under certain conditions), but we shall limit ourselves to the testing of generalization hypotheses.

341

Without going into any detail, let us focus on the essential aspects of statistical inference:

Table 4.3.1. *Elements of statistical inference*

Data	Model
Sample distribution	*Universe* specification
Sampling procedure	*Sampling* specification

Thus, what we have is to the left: a sample (S) with its one-, two-, or many-dimensional distribution (or several samples) *and* knowledge about how the sample(s) was actually obtained. To the right is the model (M) which has two parts: a universe U and a sampling process, both specified wholly or partly. Thus, the universe is *completely specified* when its distribution is given, but it can also be specified by means of a parameter-space (for instance with two dimensions: one for a measure of central tendency, and one for a measure of dispersion) where the universe is given as a point (a point-hypothesis) or a region. In general terms, the parameter-space or any other space where the universe may be represented as a point can be divided into any number of regions corresponding to sets of universes. But in standard procedures it is divided into only two regions, and two hypotheses are formulated:

The null hypothesis: H_0:   'S is a sample from U, generated by the specified sampling process'; or simply 'S is generated by the model M'.
Alternative hypothesis: H_1: 'S is not generated by the model M'.

The distribution of samples of the same size as S drawn under the conditions of M is then simulated, usually by the techniques of mathematical statistics, but also empirically or by computer simulation. S is then compared with this sampling distribution and evaluated in terms of how rare an event it represents, as seen from the point of view of M. In what is now classical theory of statistical testing, a *critical region* is chosen so as to conform to two principles: (1) the probability for the sample of being registered in the critical region when H_0 is true (probability of error of type I) shall be equal to an *a priori* selected level of significance (usually 5%, 1% or 0.1%) and (2) the probability for the sample of not being registered in the critical region when H_1 is true (probability of error of type II) shall be at a minimum (the power of the test at a maximum). When the sample, then, is registered in the critical region of the test, H_0 is rejected, and H_1 is accepted; and

342

when it is not, H_0 is not rejected, which does not mean that it is accepted. Thus knowledge is gained, eventually, by excluding alternatives.

In this sense, *theoretical statistics* (as distinct from *descriptive statistics,* which is presented in I, 2 and II, 2 and results in the distribution of the sample obtained by a known sampling procedure; and as distinct from *mathematical statistics,* which is a branch of pure mathematics) proceeds essentially like any science. Data are collected and compared with a model to see whether the model 'implies' the data. But there is the major difference between this and ordinary theory-formation (see chapter 6) that the procedure is not by compatibility but by incompatibility. In theory-formation, hypotheses are derived and tested by examining to what extent they are compatible with data; when statistical hypotheses are tested, sampling distributions are derived from the model and compared with the sample to see whether the sample is incompatible. The goal is to use the data to reject the model; and if the model is not rejected, it is not necessarily accepted.

Actually, this distinction is less sharp than we have presented it here, for a simple reason. Imagine that we have a model defined by a set of properties $(P: P_1, P_2, \ldots P_n)$, such as (universe normal, mean 0, standard deviation 1, sample size N, sampling process simple random) – to quote the property-set of a classical model. Also imagine that we accept the dichotomization introduced by the statistical test; that we either reject or do not reject the model on the basis of the sample obtained; either conclude with incompatibility or with compatibility. At this point the classical canons of research pronounced by J. S. Mill can be used, to arrive at the principle alluded to: in general we can only make specific conclusions if the model is satisfied for all properties in P except one.

For imagine we conclude with incompatibility between model and data. This is a very general conclusion, and can only be reduced to a specific conclusion in terms of *one* property in P if the $n-1$ other properties are known to be satisfied. Thus, if the universe in the example is normal, the standard deviation is 1, the sample size is N, and the sample is registered in the critical region, we cannot say that this is due to differences in means unless we also know that the sample was in fact obtained in a random way. And similarly if we conclude with compatibility: unless we know that all properties but one are satisfied, we cannot say anything specific, for there is also the possibility that two properties that are not satisfied have cancelled each other so as to lead to compatibility (unnecessary to say, compatibility is not the same as acceptability).

This means that the property-set P associated with the model M will have to be divided into two disjoint parts: P_c, which specifies the conditions;

and P_h, which specifies the hypothesis we really are interested in. P_h can consist of any number of properties (for instance refer to a parameter-space of any number of dimensions), but we can make conclusions in terms of P_h only if the conditions in P_c are satisfied. One such condition behind most statistical work done by behavioral scientists is the design of simple random sampling, which is not easily satisfied in practice. But, as mentioned, the conditions of interval scale variables and normally distributed universe are gradually being eliminated from P_c except, of course, when they are appropriate, by 'non-parametric' and 'distribution-free' methods.

We could now proceed to choose a variety of P, divide them into P_c and P_h, and say something about sampling distributions and critical regions, but this can be found in any textbook in statistics. Usually one starts with the condition of interval scale and normal distribution, and derives (or simply informs the reader) that the sample mean $\bar{x}$ is normally distributed $N\left(m, \dfrac{\sigma}{\sqrt{N}}\right)$. Since the universe dispersion is usually unknown, one is also informed that $t = \dfrac{\bar{x}-m}{s} \sqrt{N-1}$ has a t distribution with $N-1$ degrees of freedom, which makes it more difficult to reject the hypothesis that the sample comes from a universe with mean m. Around this theme a number of variations appear: even if the universe is not normally distributed, the sample mean has a distribution that is approximated by $N\left(m, \dfrac{\sigma}{\sqrt{N}}\right)$, and a number of formulas can be developed involving differences between means, etc. However, since the conditions of all these tests are relatively strong, they receive attention disproportionate to their utility in social research.

What is valid is the approach in terms of parameters,[10] only that they should be other parameters than the interval scale parameters. In principle, there should be a test for each parameter mentioned in II, 2 where P_h has the form 'the value of the parameter in the universe is p' and P_c has a number of forms. At one extreme is the case where no conditions at all are specified with regard to the distribution of the universe, only with regard to the sampling process (usually simple random) and to the variable (it must satisfy the conditions for calculating the parameter). From that point on we may include more and more properties in the set P_c. Generally this has two consequences:

(1) the power of the test increases,
(2) the test becomes less applicable.

Thus, we have on the one hand the test that is highly applicable but less powerful; and on the other hand the test that applies to more specified models only, but is more powerful. The ideal situation would be to have for each P_h a complete array of tests involving all important combinations where specifications of universe and sampling procedures are concerned. This, generally, is more a remote goal than reality – and it is perhaps unlikely that it will be attained with the present piecemeal methodology in statistical research. Sometime in the future a major breakthrough will probably come where all these problems will be considered from a more general vantage point. The ideal would be some kind of simple multi-purpose test which the researcher himself could specify and make more powerful by bringing in the conditions that he knows to be satisfied in his particular case, and where he could also specify the hypothesis exactly the way he wants it to be. Thus, we may often want to test the hypothesis that the value of a correlation coefficient C is c, not only that it is 0 (that the variables are independent).

But in order not to make the best the enemy of the good we shall present here what in our experience is a *minimum* of knowledge about statistical tests. This minimum falls considerably below what Siegel presents, although it contains some other elements of importance for the social scientist in practice. In so doing we shall omit the case of interval scale variables because it is infrequent and because it is covered in any textbook. We shall also omit what is usually referred to as the case of 'dependent samples' since we have not treated experimental data at all. Moreover, we shall limit ourselves to a maximum of two samples with two variables, and k samples with one variable, thus not entering the k sample and n variable cases which are considerably more complicated.

We start with nominal variables. In this case the values of the variable have no significance, so everything must be based on frequencies. For that reason this case is usually referred to as *frequency statistics,* and the major models are determined by the complexity of our data. It is customary in this field to characterize the data in terms of k, the number of samples (1, 2, or k); n, the number of variables (1 or 2) and r, the number of values (2 or r). If we spell out some of the possible combinations we arrive at the ten cases given in Table 4.3.2, they should be sufficient for most purposes.[11] We shall now comment on them in detail:

Case (1): *One sample, one variable, two values*

In this case the sample of size N has the frequencies f_1 and f_2 and the universe is specified by means of the corresponding probabilities p_1 and p_2, or corresponding 'theoretical' (better term: hypothetical) frequencies $t_1 = Np_1$ and

$t_2 = Np_2$. If we set $f_1 = x$, $p_1 = p$, and $p_1 = q$ the exact distribution can be expressed by means of the familiar formula for the *binomial* distribution:

$$4.3:1. \qquad P(x) = \binom{N}{x} p^x q^{(N-x)} = \frac{N!}{f_1! f_2!} (p_1{}^{f_1} p_2{}^{f_2}) = P(f_1, f_2)$$

Under conditions expressed in different terms by various authors (both t_i at least 5, preferably 10, but if p_1 is very different from p_2 then Np_1p_2 should at least be equal to 9) the following expressions have a *standard normal* distribution:

$$4.3:2. \qquad u = \frac{x - Np}{\sqrt{Npq}} = \frac{f_1 - t_1}{\sqrt{Np_1p_2}} = \frac{\frac{x}{N} - p}{\sqrt{\frac{pq}{N}}} = \frac{\frac{f_1}{N} - p_1}{\sqrt{\frac{p_1p_2}{N}}}$$

Here and in the following we assume Yate's correction to be known: all approximations will improve if the absolute values of the differences between the empirical and the theoretical frequencies $f_i - t_i$, are diminished by 0.5.

Case (2): *One sample, one variable, r values*

In this case we get the exact distribution, which is the *multinomial* distribution:

$$4.3:3. \qquad P(f_1, f_2, \ldots f_r) = \frac{N!}{f_1! f_2! \ldots f_r!} p_1{}^{f_1} p_2{}^{f_2} \ldots p_r{}^{f_r}.$$

Under the condition that all t_i are at least 5 (or Cochran's weaker condition that no t_i is smaller than 1 and not more than 20% of them are smaller than 5) the following expression will have a chi-square distribution with $r - 1$ degrees of freedom:

$$4.3:4. \qquad \chi^2 = \sum_1^r \frac{(f_i - t_i)^2}{t_i}$$

Here the t_i may be of any kind and be derived from any theoretical assumption as long as they add to N and satisfy the conditions mentioned; and r may have any value compatible with this (thus, categories may be combined so as to obtain satisfactory values for t_i).

Since the case $r = 2$ has been treated above as case 1 it is important to verify that we get the same results by means of 4.3:4 as by means of 4.3:2. We transform 4.3:4 for $r = 2$:

$$4.3:5. \qquad \chi^2 = \frac{(f_1 - t_1)^2}{t_1} + \frac{(f_2 - t_2)^2}{t_2} = \frac{(f_1 - t_1)^2}{t_1} + \frac{(t_1 - f_1)^2}{N - t_1}$$
$$= \frac{N(f_1 - t_1)^2}{t_1 t_2} = u^2.$$

Table 4.3.2. *A survey of tests for frequency distributions, nominal case*

Case no.	Character k	n	r	Conditions	Test	Exact method	Approximate method	Conditions
(1)	1	1	2	total N constant	distribution	*binomial*	normal, chi-square 1 d.f.	$t_i \geqslant 5$
(2)	1	1	r	total N constant	distribution	*multinomial*	chi-square, $r-1$ d.f.	$t_i \geqslant 5$; or at least 80 % of them, and no $t_i < 1$
(3)	2	1	2	marginals constant	same universe	*hypergeometric* (Fishers exact test)	(1) chi-square 1 d.f. (2) diff. between prop.	$t_i \geqslant 5$
(4)	2	1	r	marginals constant	same universe		chi-square $r-1$ d.f.	$t_i \geqslant 5$
(5)	1	2	2×2	marginals constant	independence	*hypergeometric* (Fishers' exact test)	(1) chi-square 1 d.f. (2) diff. between prop.	$t_i \geqslant 5$
(6)	1	2	2×r	marginals constant	independence		chi-square $r-1$ d.f.	$t_i \geqslant 5$
(7)	1	2	q×r	marginals constant	independence		chi-square $(q-1)(r-1)$ d.f.	$t_i \geqslant 5$
(8)	2	2	2×2	marginals constant	universe with same association		(1) diff. between diff. (2) diff. between Q	$t_i \geqslant 5$
(9)	1	3	2×2×2	marginals constant	no interaction		(1) diff. between diff. (2) diff. between Q	
(10)	k	1	r	marginals constant	same universe		chi-square, $(k-1)(r-1)$ d.f.	$t_i \geqslant 5$

Since chi-square with one degree of freedom is distributed like the square of a standard normal variable this means that we get exactly the same results with u as with chi-square.

Very often the researcher will encounter problems where a great number of tests of significance will have to be carried out. This can become both time-consuming and expensive. The following is an example of a procedure of rationalization for the case of a chi-square test with two degrees of freedom.

We have a list of adjectives, a list of items the adjectives may be attributed to, and a sample of respondents. The sample may consist of N college students, the list of items may be 'owner of a Ford', 'owner of a Chevrolet', and 'owner of a Plymouth', and the list of adjectives may contain words such as masculine, fat, daring, funny, etc.[12] Let us further assume that the respondent shall check one and only one item for each adjective – viz., the item that corresponds best to the adjective in his opinion.

We want
(1) to test the hypothesis that the adjectives are not randomly distributed among the items,
(2) to make lists of the adjectives that are significantly often or significantly seldom used for each item, for further analysis.

It is clear that once problem (1) is solved, problem (2) is not difficult. Once we have ascertained that an adjective is used by the sample in a discriminating way, we can always, by inspection of the numbers, find out for which items it is used more often or more seldom than chance.

Let us take one adjective as an example, 'masculine'. For each respondent, there are three possibilities:

Item	Ford	Chevrolet	Plymouth	SUM
masculine	x	y	$N-x-y$	N

The instructions guarantee that the choices will be exhaustive and exclusive. The probability of the combination above is

$$4.3\!:\!6. \qquad P(x,y) = \frac{N!}{x!\,y!\,(N-x-y)!}\, p_2^x\, p_1^y\, p_3^{N-x-y}$$

where p_1, p_2, and p_3 are the probabilities that the choice will be Ford, Chevrolet, or Plymouth respectively, and the sum of them is 1. The obvious null-hypothesis is

$$4.3\!:\!7. \qquad H_0\!: p_1 = p_2 = p_3 = p = \tfrac{1}{3}$$

The exact test could be constructed by use of the multinomial distribution and the likelihood ratio technique. However, if $Np_i = t_i$ exceed 10 (in the research referred to, $N = 100$, so $t = 33.3$) the chi-square approximation to the multinomial distribution can safely be used. The problem is to find an easy way of testing the hypothesis so that we do not have to compute the chi-square for each adjective – of which there are 108 in the list.

The chi-square for the test of the hypothesis is

4.3:8. $$\chi^2 = \frac{(x-t)^2}{t} + \frac{(y-t)^2}{t} + \frac{(N-x-y-t)^2}{t} \qquad \text{d.f.} = 2$$

which has its maximum in the points $(0, N)$ and $(N, 0)$, and minimum in (t, t). If the chi-square corresponding to a preassigned level of significance is k, the borderline between the acceptance and rejection region in the x,y-plane is given by:

4.3:9. $$\chi^2 = k$$

This gives a conic (ellipse):

4.3:10. $$F(x,y) = x^2+xy+y^2-Nx-Ny = \frac{tk-3t^2+2Nt-N^2}{2} = Q$$

where the right hand member is called Q. The equation can be plotted directly – but it is better to use a linear transformation to get rid of the product term. We rotate the coordinate system an angle φ, given by $tg\varphi = \frac{1 \cdot 1}{1} = 1$ which gives $\varphi = 45°$. It is, anyhow, obvious from the symmetry of x and y in F, that the conic must be symmetric about the line $y = x$. The transformation becomes:

4.3:11. $$\begin{Bmatrix} x \\ y \end{Bmatrix} = \begin{Bmatrix} \cos\varphi & -\sin\varphi \\ \sin\varphi & \cos\varphi \end{Bmatrix} \begin{Bmatrix} x' \\ y' \end{Bmatrix} = \tfrac{1}{2} \begin{Bmatrix} \sqrt{2} & -\sqrt{2} \\ \sqrt{2} & \sqrt{2} \end{Bmatrix} \begin{Bmatrix} x' \\ y' \end{Bmatrix} = T \cdot \begin{Bmatrix} x' \\ y' \end{Bmatrix}$$

where T is an orthogonal matrix. (10) and (11) give

4.3:12. $$\tfrac{3}{2}x'^2+\tfrac{1}{2}y'^2-N\sqrt{2}\,x' = Q, \text{ or}$$

$$Q + \frac{N^2}{3} = Q',$$

this can be written as:

4.3:13. $$\frac{\left(x' - \dfrac{N}{3}\sqrt{2}\right)^2}{\dfrac{2Q'}{\sqrt{3}}} + \frac{y'^2}{2Q'} = 1$$

substituting $t = \dfrac{N}{3}$ in Q' gives

4.3:14. $$Q' = \frac{Nk}{3}$$

In our case, $N = 100$, $t = \dfrac{100}{3}$, k_1 (5% level – twotailed test) $= 5.99$ and k_2 (1% level – two-tailed test) $= 9.21$.
We get
$$Q_1' = 99.83, \quad Q_2' = 153.5$$
and the ellipses:

4.3:15. $$5\%\text{-level}: \frac{(x'-47.1)^2}{8.2^2} + \frac{y'^2}{14.1^2} = 1$$

349

4.3:16. $\qquad$ 1%-level: $\dfrac{x'-(47.1)^2}{10.1^2} + \dfrac{y'^2}{17.5^2} = 1$

The formulas we have given can be used for all cases involving two degrees of freedom and the null-hypothesis 4.3:7. However, the latter restriction is not essential. The same method can be used for all point-hypotheses – but $F(x,y)$ will no longer be symmetric in x and y, and be somewhat more complicated. To simplify the equation of the ellipse, we have to rotate the coordinate-axes by an angle given by

4.3:17. $\qquad\qquad\qquad\qquad tg\varphi = \dfrac{AC}{B}$

where A, B, and C are the coefficients of the x^2, xy, and y^2 terms respectively. This will, however, be a far less time-consuming procedure than the computation of a high number of chi-squares – and it has the advantage of giving us an idea of how strongly significant a difference is just by looking at the position the adjective is given in the x, y-plane. Of course, there may still be borderline cases where this visual method will break down.

Unfortunately, the procedure is not generalizable to d.f. > 2, because the plane where we plot the ellipses has only two degrees of freedom.

Case (3): *Two samples, one variable, two values*

In this case we have four frequencies that correspond to two values of the variable and two samples:

Variable X

	x_1	x_2	
Sample (1)	f_{11}	f_{12}	$f_{11}+f_{12} = N_1.$
Sample (2)	f_{21}	f_{22}	$f_{21}+f_{22} = N_2.$
	$f_{11}+f_{21}$	$f_{12}+f_{22}$	N
	$N._1$	$N._2$	

Fisher's reasoning in deriving his exact test is based on the assumption that all four marginals are constant. The problem is then: given these marginals, what is the probability of that particular distribution of frequencies? This can be solved by finding how many samples of size $N_1 = f_{11}+f_{12}$ have f_{11} units from the total of $f_{11}+f_{21}$ with value x_1 and, consequently f_{12} from the total of $f_{12}+f_{22}$ with value x_2. Elementary probability calculus yields:

4.3:18. $\quad P(f_{11},f_{12},f_{21},f_{22}) = \dfrac{\dbinom{f_{11}+f_{21}}{f_{11}} \dbinom{f_{12}+f_{22}}{f_{12}}}{\dbinom{N}{f_{11}+f_{12}}}$

$\qquad\qquad\qquad = \dfrac{N_1.!\,N_2.!\,N._1!\,N._2!}{N!f_{11}!f_{12}!f_{21}!f_{22}!} = \dfrac{(a+b)!(c+d)!(a+c)!(b+d)!}{N!a!b!c!d!}$

350

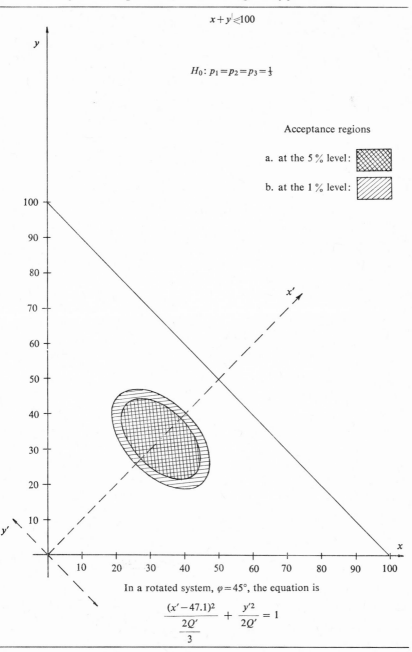

$x + y' \leqslant 100$

$H_0: p_1 = p_2 = p_3 = \frac{1}{3}$

Acceptance regions

a. at the 5 % level:

b. at the 1 % level:

In a rotated system, $\varphi = 45°$, the equation is

$$\frac{(x' - 47.1)^2}{\dfrac{2Q'}{3}} + \frac{y'^2}{2Q'} = 1$$

if we use a, b, c, d as symbols for the frequencies. Provided one accepts the condition that the data, the Table with the two samples, shall only be compared with other Tables with the same marginals, then this formula gives the basis for Tables that can be used to test the hypothesis that the two samples come from the same universe. For further details, see Siegel (pp. 96 ff.).

This problem can also be approached by means of two other methods that are approximate, but have reasonable validity provided no t_i is smaller than 5. The t_i will have to be calculated according to the hypothesis which states that the two samples come from the same universe with the same probability p_1 of getting x_1 and p_2 of getting x_2. However, the proportion of x_1's in sample 1 and sample 2 are $\dfrac{a}{a+b}$ and $\dfrac{c}{c+d}$ respectively, so that we can calculate the difference d between the two proportions. This difference is normally distributed under the conditions of approximation. Under the condition of the hypothesis its mean is 0 and its variance equal to the sum of the variances of the two proportions, in other words:

4.3:19.
$$\sigma_d^2 = \frac{p_1 p_2}{N_1} + \frac{p_1 p_2}{N_2}$$

In general this proportion p_1, common to both samples according to the hypothesis, will be unknown. The best estimate is obtained by collapsing the two samples, which gives us $\bar{p}_1 = \dfrac{a+c}{N}$ and $\bar{p}_2 = \dfrac{b+d}{N}$.

Combining all this we find that the following quantity has the *standard normal* distribution:

4.3:20. $u = \dfrac{\dfrac{a}{a+b} - \dfrac{c}{c+d}}{\sqrt{\dfrac{(a+c)(b+d)}{N^2(a+b)} + \dfrac{(a+c)(b+d)}{N^2(c+d)}}} = \dfrac{\sqrt{N}\,(ad-bc)}{\sqrt{(a+b)(c+d)(a+c)(b+d)}}$

A third way of approach, under the conditions of approximate distributions, is by means of chi-square techniques. All we have to do is to calculate four frequencies t_{ij} that reflect the null hypothesis of a common universe, and insert them. The frequencies below are proportionate and add to N, hence are the ones we need:

4.3:21.
$$t_{11} = \frac{N_1 . N_{.1}}{N}, \; t_{12} = \frac{N_1 . N_{.2}}{N}, \; t_{21} = \frac{N_2 . N_{.1}}{N}, \; t_{22} = \frac{N_2 . N_{.2}}{N}$$

Inserting and simplifying, we get:

4.3:22.
$$\chi^2 = \frac{N(f_{11}f_{22} - f_{12}f_{21})^2}{N_1 . N_2 . N_{.1} N_{.2}} = \frac{N(ad-bc)^2}{(a+b)(c+d)(a+c)(b+d)}$$

which has a chi-square distribution with one degree of freedom, since thers is only one frequency that can be chosen freely when all the marginals are constant. By comparing 4.3:20 and 4.3:22 we see that the two methode will give exactly the same result – just as for case (2) and case (1).

Case (4): *Two samples, one variable, r values*

In this case the chi-square distribution is used, based on formula 4.3:4, with theoretical frequencies calculated analogous to 4.3:21 (products of marginals divided by total). The distribution has $r-1$ degrees of freedom since this is the number of frequencies that can be chosen freely.

Case (5): *One sample, two variables, both dichotomies*

In this case one can proceed exactly as in case (3), because 'independence' between the two variables is equivalent to equality between conditional distributions, which was tested in case (3) under the heading of 'samples coming from the same universe'. The procedure for finding the frequencies according to 4.3:21 can then be seen as an application of the formula in II, 2.3.

Case (6): *One sample, two variables, one dichotomy, one polytomy*

In this case we would proceed exactly as in case (4), for the reasons mentioned in case (5).

Case (7): *One sample, two variables, both polytomies*

In this case we would proceed as in case (6) with the only difference that we would have to calculate more theoretical frequencies and that the number of degrees of freedom would be $(q-1)(r-1)$.

Case (8): *Two samples, two variables, both dichotomies*

In this case we are dealing with two fourfold-tables that are to be compared, a very frequent case in social research. We shall follow the methodology outlined by Leo Goodman[13] and by Costner and Wager[14] – bearing in mind what was done in case (3) with two dichotomies but only one sample. Evidently, we have two options available, one based on proportions (or percentage differences) and the other based on chi-square. The data are as follows (Table 4.3.3., next page):

Empirically we may evaluate the difference between the associations in the two samples by means of $d_1 - d_2$ (the differences between differences between proportions) or $Q_1 - Q_2$ (the difference between the Q's) or R_1/R_2 (the ratio

Table 4.3.3. *Comparisons of two fourfold-tables*

Sample (1)	Sample (2)	Hypothesis:

a	b	$\dfrac{a}{a+b}$	a'	b'	$\dfrac{a'}{a'+b'}$	
c	d	$\dfrac{c}{c+d}$	c'	d'	$\dfrac{c'}{c'+d'}$	

$$d_1 = \frac{a}{a+b} - \frac{c}{c+d} \qquad d_2 = \frac{a'}{a'+b'} - \frac{c'}{c'+d'} \qquad d_1 = d_2$$

$$Q_1 = \frac{ad-bc}{ad+bc} \qquad Q_2 = \frac{a'd'-b'c'}{a'd'+b'c'} \qquad Q_1 = Q_2$$

$$R_1 = \frac{ad}{bc} \qquad R_2 = \frac{a'd'}{b'c'} \qquad R_1 = R_2$$

between the ratio between cross-products). The differences are evaluated, then, relative to 0 and the ratio relative to 1 – and these are the conditions that express the null hypothesis that the samples come from universes with the *same* association. This must not be confused with the hypothesis that the samples come from universes with *no* association, because this hypothesis specifies the association in each universe and, hence, can be tested separately for each sample [case (5), with the methodology of case (3)].

The estimate suggested for the variance of the difference between the differences is:

4.3:23.
$$\hat{\sigma}^2_{d_1-d_2} = \frac{\dfrac{a}{a+b} \cdot \dfrac{b}{a+b}}{a+b} + \frac{\dfrac{c}{c+d} \cdot \dfrac{d}{c+p}}{c+d}$$
$$+ \frac{\dfrac{a'}{a'+b'} \cdot \dfrac{b'}{a'+b'}}{a'+b'} + \frac{\dfrac{c'}{c'+d'} \cdot \dfrac{d'}{c'+d'}}{c'+d'}$$

which means that the following quantity has an approximately *standard normal* distribution:

4.3:24.
$$u = \frac{d_1-d_2}{\sqrt{\hat{\sigma}^2_{d_1-d_2}}}$$

This should be compared to the estimate given in 4.3:19. In that case we collapsed the two samples, because the null hypothesis was that the two samples had come from the same universe. In this case there is also a null hypothesis about two samples but not to the effect that the two differences are zero: rather, to the effect that they are the same. Moreover, since the variance of $d_1 - d_2$ is the sum of the variances of d_1 and d_2, we have to calculate these variances. That has to be done within each sample, which means within each four-fold-table. But within each fourfold-table there is no assumption that the proportions are equal (difference is zero), which means that we have to estimate the variance of each proportion separately.

If, instead of using the difference between differences between proportions, we use the ratio between the ratios of cross-products, the null hypothesis would be that this ratio is equal to 1. This is, of course, a different test, since $d_1 - d_2 = 0$ and $R_1/R_2 = 1$ are not equivalent conditions. We are reminded of the type of discussion in II, 2.2 as to the relative virtues of percentage differences and percentage ratios. This becomes particularly clear if we make use of the relation Goodman[15] points out, that

4.3:25. $R_1 = R_2 \rightarrow Q_1 = Q_2$ where Q is Yule's Q.

Costner and Wager point out that the ratio test is 'nothing other than a test of the null nypothesis of equal Q's for any pair of 2×2 tables'.[16] But the statistical test uses the ratio condition and a highly complicated procedure to fill the cells of the two tables with theoretical frequencies. (The reader is referred to the article for details.) It should be noted that since the ratio test is equivalent to a test of the difference between the Q's being 0, it is essentially a test of differences in degrees of 'corner' correlation (since Q can attain its maximum value also when only one cell is empty). The difference test, however, is a test based on proportion differences and relates to 'diagonal' correlation (since d can attain its maximum value only when two cells are empty). Thus, we would expect the difference test to yield results similar to the test of differences between two phi coefficients, since they also measure 'diagonal' correlation.[17]

Case (9): *One sample, three variables, all dichotomies*

This case stands in the same relation to case (8) as case (5) to case (3). Instead of conceiving of the two tables in Table 4.3.2 as coming from two samples, we can define the sampling itself as a variable, and even as a dichotomy. We now have a three-variable case. As this case has been presented in case (8), two correlation measures are compared to see to what extent they are different, the correlation measures being proportion differences or Q's. In multivariate analysis (II, 5.3) this will be known as analysis of type 3.1 (three variables, one independent and two dependent). But in the case of three variables we may also be interested in phrasing the problem differently, in terms of two independent and one dependent variable (analysis of type 3.2). The problem is whether we can use the same procedures in that case.

This will be explored systematically in 5.3, here we shall only show how the correspondence with case (8) is made. In the case of multivariate analysis of type 3.2 data can be presented as follows:

Table 4.3.3. *The three-variable case, analysis of type* 3.2

$$
\begin{array}{c|ccc}
y_2 & p_{12} \, p_{22} & p_{22} - p_{12} = d_2 \\
y_1 & p_{11} \, p_{21} & p_{21} - p_{11} = d_1 \\
\hline
& x_1 \quad x_2
\end{array}
$$

The proportions in the Table are the proportions for each combination of X and Y that have the value, say, z_2 of the third variable Z. Thus, y_1 corresponds to sample (1) in Table 4.3.2 and y_2 to sample (2); and Z and X are the two variables. Since it makes very good sense to call $d_1 - d_2$ the *interaction* between X and Y, the test of the null hypothesis that the difference between the differences is 0, becomes a test of the hypothesis that there is no interaction. This can then easily be generalized to a test of the hypothesis that there is no second-order interaction, by using four dichotomies and calculating the difference between the difference between the differences between the proportions. Since this would involve eight proportions, the variance of this difference would have eight terms, but be quite similar to the variance in 4.3:23.

Case (10): *k samples, one variable, r values*

This stands in the same relation to case (7) as case (6) to case (4): since it is essentially an hypothesis to the effect that k conditional distributions are equal (the condition being the sample they come from) all one has to do is to compute the theoretical frequencies and calculate the chi-square which will have $(k-1)(r-1)$ degrees of freedom.

That concludes our survey of frequency statistics. The tools are powerful and flexible, as the list of situations in which they can be used shows. Much more actually exists, but for this the reader is referred to the literature; we have only wanted to present the minimum that is necessary, and for most purposes also sufficient.

356

A frequent error is to use these tests when both variables are not nominal. In all such cases, frequency test procedures do not reflect information that could be included among the conditions, which makes the test less powerful (higher probability of committing errors of type II) than it might have been.

Using frequency statistics as a kind of model, it is easy to see what is needed for each parameter presented in II, 2. For various sets of conditions one should have distributions for sample parameters in these two cases:

One sample: the universe parameter has a given value (weaker requirement for correlation measures: value equal to 0).

Two samples: the universe parameters have given values (weaker requirement: difference equal to 0 or ratio equal to 1).

For the interval scale parameters ($\bar{x}$, s^2, r) this is completely solved, although the conditions involved are often quite restrictive. For the case of r the tests gain vastly in simplicity if one is satisfied with the two weaker requirements; zero correlation in the universe for the one-sample case, and zero difference between the universe correlations for the two-sample case. In general these two modifications make the list of demands above more realistic from the point of view of the mathematical statistician.

For the ordinal scale parameters there are, as far as we know, still holes to be filled, because it is easier to invent a correlation measure than to find its sampling distribution under various null hypotheses and conditions. The reader is referred to the literature.[18] As to the nominal scale parameters, much has been indicated under the presentation of frequency statistics above. The tests can easily be extended to the more general case that the difference, or the difference between the differences, has a given value in the universe, by subtracting that value in the numerator. Since d is the most important measure of correlation, this is already an important gain. And since proportions in a sense correspond to arithmetic means (on a variable with two values, 0 and 1) and proportions can be tested relative to any universe value given by the null hypothesis by means of formula 4.3:2, we have what we need here too.

But much is still missing, and, as mentioned in the beginning of this section: we have a feeling that the whole field will undergo a discontinuous change in the near future, when a sufficient number of disparate and ad hoc statistical tests have been accumulated. Although the field of frequency statistics has a certain unity, and interval scale statistics possesses the unity given to it by classical statistics, the field of ordinal scale statistics is in wild disorder – and since this is by far the most important field for the social scientist (who typically can develop ordinal measures, but rarely interval scale measures) the total situation is far from satisfactory. On top of this come various problems about the total function of statistics in social science – and perhaps in science in general – but these will be treated in the next section.

4.4. *On the use of statistical tests*

(1) *Introduction*

'In this book, no statistical tests of significance have been used. This may seem unaccountable, particularly in view of the numerous quantitative comparisons which constitute much of the analysis. Can it be defended, and if so how? It can be defended, and we shall defend it at length because there seems to be no good statement of our position in print'. (J.S.Coleman in *Union Democracy*, p.427).

'Although the arguments for the omission of significance tests are well stated in the appendix, it is difficult to countenance the use of raw percentage differences according to the whims of the authors, as occurred on a few occasions when a percentage difference in one instance is considered important while in another the same difference is considered unimportant'. (Harold Guetzkow, reviewing *Union Democracy*).

'The reader will find that no traditional significance tests have been reported in connection with the statistical results in this volume. This is intentional policy rather than accidental oversight. It is a policy, furthermore, which the Bureau of Applied Social Research has always adhered to in reporting the results of exploratory studies such as are presented in this volume'. (P.L.Kendall in *The Student Physician*, p.301).

'At first glance, we note the trademark of this school – the absence of significance tests – and, as in other recent Bureau publications, an appendix purporting to justify their exclusion. While some of the argument is trenchant (---) and some of it plain foolish (---), it is our opinion that it is not the absence of significance tests but the absence of *any formal criterion* for arriving at a conclusion which typifies this approach. – The net result is art, not science'. (J.A.Davis, reviewing *The Student Physician*).

These four quotations may serve as an introduction to the debate about the use and misuse of significance tests which attracted considerable attention during the last decade among American social scientists. Symptomatic for the importance attributed to the controversy is the fact that the American Sociological Association devoted one session of its 1959 convention to the question, and the list of references to the debate itself is already extensive (see bibliography at the end of the section).

Here we shall review the main arguments in the debate, adding to them some arguments and ways of analysis that seem so far to have been neglected. For this purpose, some principal points of view on the subject of hypothesis-testing will be presented in the next sub-section, while in the three following

358

sub-sections more specific arguments will be examined. The final sub-section is an effort to answer the *où en sommes-nous?* question arising from the debate.

Due to the usual polarization phenomenon in human conflicts, of which academic debates form a particular case where the value at stake is that of being 'right', the controversy has sometimes gotten an unfortunate flavor of the 'are-you-for-or-against-statistics' type. In a sense this is natural, because more than mere attitudes towards the use of significance tests is at stake. By means of this hypothesis from the sociology of knowledge – 'Most scholars will try to define or perceive a field of academic inquiry in such a way that their own training achieves maximum importance and the importance of the kind of training they do not possess is minimized, and they will try to inculcate in their students the same beliefs' – a sociological basis for the *prediction* of the controversy is available. 'Trained capacity' will be posited against 'trained incapacity'.

This hypothesis seems particularly valid when the kind of training at issue is difficult and the insight it gives inaccessible to the layman. Cochran, Mosteller, and Tukey write in their critique of the Kinsey report[19] how serious the need for adequate statistical assistance is for a study of that kind, and add: 'Unfortunately the sort of assistance which might resolve some of their most complex problems would require understanding, background, and techniques that perhaps not more than twenty statisticians in the world possess'. This statement, presumably written by three of the twenty, indicates how expensive a *tool* statistics is. At the same time, most social scientists working in the field of empirical study with data amenable to statistical treatment beyond mere description will know both the almost insurmountable difficulties they encounter when they try to make data meet the statistical requirements, and the not-too-appreciative comments of their statistical colleagues.

Hence, the great temptation to do without statistical tests is understandable on this basis alone, as is the temptation to justify the stand by arguments of the kind we are going to discuss. The situation may become even more obscured when this controversy serves as a reminder of the eternal struggle between adherents of 'Verstehen' vs. 'Erklären' or phenomenological vs. positivistic approaches to the subject matter of social science, with the deep emotions attached to these and similar symbols. However, our focus will be on the arguments themselves, not on their psychological or sociological determinants. Nor are we concerned with *ad hominem* arguments of the 'statistical-tests-are-a-ritual-that-serves-as-a-substitute-for-hard-substantive-thinking' type or some version of the 'science-is-measurement' argument.

T. D. Sterling has analyzed 'outcomes of tests of significance for four psychology research journals' (16, esp. p. 31).[20] He gives his analysis an interesting twist by turning it from the field of statistical methodology to sociology of knowledge: as 81% of the articles made use of tests of significance, and out of these only slightly less than 3% did not report significant results, and the 'number of research reports that are replications of previously published experiments' is zero – conclusions as to the publication policy of the journals can be drawn. And this has consequences for the Type I error of the reader of a journal which prints nothing but the articles that report statistically significant results: 'Before the reader can make an intelligent decision he must have some information concerning the distribution of outcomes of similar experiments or at least the assurance that a similar experiment has never been performed. Since the latter information is unobtainable, he is in a dilemma. One thing is clear, however. The risk stated by the author cannot be accepted at its face value once the author's conclusions appear in print' (16, p. 34).

In sociology, the use of significance tests is considerably less extensive. The 1959 volume of three leading journals, two of them American and one European, were examined. The results are summarized in Table 4.4.1. (the classification was checked for intersubjectivity, and the disagreement did not exceed 5%). Evidently, either statistical tests are less frequently used by social scientists, or editorial policies differ.[21]

The remarkable homogeneity in content of the two American journals as well as the different nature of the one European journal are easily seen from the Table. No article was found where no significance was obtained, but 4 of the 29 articles where significance tests were used reported many nonsignificant findings. We found 31 articles with empirical content, and more or less hypothesis-directed, but making no use of statistical tests at all. From this, however, we can only direct attention to other tests of hypotheses than statistical ones, and they were of different kinds: comparisons of percentage differences, theoretical substantiation, etc. *None of the articles* could meaningfully be called replications of previous research. This is interesting, as *replicability* is mentioned among the *desiderata* of a research report in a report given by the Committee on Research of the American Sociological Association.[23] But the fruits of this virtue are either not easily found, or not easily published.

Significance tests, hence, play a role in social science research; but social science work is not considered without value if they are not used. This is what we want to explore; and we turn now to a discussion of the significance of significance tests.

Table 4.4.1. *A classification of articles in three leading sociological journals,* [22] *1959*

	Metho-dolo-gical	Theoret-ical	Empirical				Total
				With units of enumeration			
			Without units of enumer-ation	Without statistical tests	With statistical tests		
					Signifi-cance obtained	Signifi-cance not obtained	
American Sociological Review	2	10	2	15	15	0	44
American Journal of Sociology	5	12	6	11	13	0	47
British Journal of Sociology	0	9	0	5	1	0	15
Total	7	31	8	31	29	0(4)	106

(2) *What do we test when we test statistical hypotheses?*

Undoubtedly, what we do has something to do with 'tenability' of an hypothesis, but the problem is what kind of hypothesis and what kind of tenability. To explore this we shall again make use of the distinction made in I, 2.3 between *substantive hypotheses* and *generalization hypotheses,* that may both be tenable or untenable.

To test the substantive part of the hypothesis some kind *of empirical unit* is needed, – a lump of sulphur, an individual, a sample of members of a party, an epoch in a nation's history – for further scrutiny about its 'state of affairs'. To test the generalizing part of the hypothesis some kind of *universe of interest* is needed – sulphur in general, all individuals with a specific configuration of muscle tensions, all members affiliated to a party, corresponding epochs in the history of all comparable nations – to see whether the same 'state of affairs' is found. In the physical sciences these two steps merge because of what we might call 'pure case' methodology, where what holds true for one lump of 'pure' sulphur is taken to hold true for all of sulphurdom. In the social sciences, as mentioned in I, 1.2, the belief in the possibility of finding pure empirical units that permit immediate generalization is very low at the time being. Thus, a social scientist has to face the distinctness of the substantive hypothesis and the generalization hypothesis. We shall examine this idea closer by means of an example.

Imagine we have a country divided into constituencies, and an election where two parties, Left and Right, approximately with the same following, compete for political power; and that from each constituency one MP is chosen by the majority rule. To study the constituency, we can adopt two points of view: either regard the constituency as our universe of interest, or as an empirical unit where the findings will be subjected to tests of generalization. We shall adopt the first point of view, and look at the outcome of the electron as given by the percentage p of votes cast for the Left, $0\% \leqslant p \leqslant 100\%$.

There are three outcomes of primary importance: a draw ($p = \frac{1}{2}$), a Left candidate ($p > \frac{1}{2}$), and a Right candidate ($p < \frac{1}{2}$). We get this exhaustive set of mutually exclusive hypotheses:

H_0: In the constituency $p = \frac{1}{2}$,
H_1: Left wins the election,
H_2: Right wins the election.

A priori, a simple sample space consisting of a straight line representing the possible outcomes between 0% and 100% may be prepared. For the sake of the argument, let us imagine (which is unrealistic for the case of a constituency, but not for the case of a national assembly) that the electorate first wants to know whether there is a draw or not, secondly who is the winner if there is no draw. Clearly, H_0 will be accepted if $p = \frac{1}{2}$, rejected in all other cases. When the outcome is known and it shows up that $p = .61$, there is no doubt that H_0 has to be rejected and H_1 chosen between the rest.

This is clearly a *substantive hypothesis with no generalization component* as the result is interesting enough in its own right. Actually, there was no need for p to be .61: it could be .51 or even closer to the middle, and still the conclusions concerning the hypotheses and the political implications would be the same. No one would talk about sampling distributions and tests of significance to see whether the difference between the two parties was 'valid', 'real', 'reliable', or 'significant'; it would be sufficient to know that H_0 was rejected and H_1 accepted. Actually, the political implications are not needed except to illustrate the point that results from empirical units may be interesting in their own right.

362

But this is a very extreme case in its textbook-like clarity. In very many empirical cases in the social sciences the data would not permit such a clear cut between the region of acceptance and the region of rejection, relative to the hypothesis H_0. When all the votes have been cast, counted, and controlled, we have what may be called *perfect knowledge* relevant to H_0. But the cases of *imperfect knowledge* are numerous. A case at hand is the situation after the first count of votes, before the control count; another case is that of knowledge through hear-say; a third is that of knowledge based on expert opinion prior to the election, or based on pre-election surveys.

A good typology of 'imperfect knowledge' has not been developed, as far as we know. Distinctions can be made between imperfection due to errors of observation or other shortcomings of otherwise relevant (valid) data, and imperfection due to different degrees of irrelevance (invalidity) of data. And a very important special case of the first category is incomplete data, based on samples. But sampling is certainly not the only or most important source of error.

Thus, we have implicitly distinguished between four cases:

(1) *The case of perfect data about a universe*: where by 'universe' we actually mean an empirical unit which is of substantive interest to us in its own right. In this case substantive hypotheses can be tested directly on the data; tests of statistical hypotheses are out of order, since there is nothing to generalize.

(2) *The case of imperfect data about a universe*: where we must know the nature of imperfection. If it is similar to sampling fluctuations and several conditions pertaining to the model used are satisfied, tests of statistical hypotheses are applicable to ascertain whether one can generalize from the data or not. In very many cases, however, they are not applicable (even cases where sampling may be said to be involved); and methodological research in the direction of establishing canons of generalization from imperfect data should be undertaken.

(3) *The case of perfect data about a sample*: where substantive hypotheses can be tested directly on the data, but will be of less interest, since a 'sample' by definition is not of substantive interest to us in its own right. Hence only hypotheses that are not only substantively tenable but also significant or generalizable are of real substantive interest because they may tell us something about the universe in which we are interested.

(4) *The case of imperfect data about a sample*: which, of course, is a rather unhappy case, but a most common one in sociological research, for instance in the case of samples with attrition due to 'not-at-home', 'refusals', 'panel mortality' etc. Analytically, the case primarily calls for a perfection of data, secondly generalization of the perfected data, if possible.

Case (3) above is only a special case of (2). What is pointed out is the distinction between substantive hypotheses and generalization hypotheses, and the use of statistical thinking when data are imperfect; particularly in the case where information is based on a sample. It should also be pointed out that testing generalization hypotheses is neither more nor less important than testing substantive hypotheses – it is simply an analytically distinct process which takes on a superior value when we have data based on a sample with no intrinsic value *per se*.

Thus, our main thesis is that statistical tests are out of order if we do not have a sample. As this is a much debated point, the thesis has to be defended. Even though there may be agreement that statistical tests are more appropriate to test generalization hypotheses for samples, many investigators feel there are exceptions, where tests nevertheless are appropriate for universes as well. We shall explore some of these possible cases.

(1) *The data form a universe, but are imperfect.* This is case (2) on the list above. There is no doubt that techniques of statistical inference *may* be appropriate, but the condition for using them is that in turn the data can be conceived of as a sample generated from a universe, by a more or less specified model. The idea would be that measurement or observation techniques are such as to produce a number of possible and different data matrices, out of which we have obtained one; and that this one data matrix can be meaningfully compared with a distribution of possible data matrices, under the hypothesis that differences, etc. found in the data are due to measurement or observation errors only. But there is no reason *a priori* to assume that models that may function well for sampling fluctuations also function well for observation fluctuations. Thus, it is much more easy to obtain independence between units in sampling than to obtain independence between observations – because of certain inertia phenomena in human minds. Hence, if a model for the generation of observation and measurement errors exists, and a reasonable number of the conditions are satisfied, then statistical inference techniques should be used to test the null hypothesis that findings are due to imperfection; but uncritical borrowing from models appropriate for sampling fluctuations is illegitimate. And we doubt that good models, comparable to the classical gaussian error curves in physical measurement or the 'personal equations' of astronomical observations, exist in social science research so far. The bias is hard to catch.

(2) *The data form a universe, but the universe can be conceived of as a sample from a super-universe.* This is the most common line of defense when significance tests are used on data that form a universe, and there seem to be three subcases that should be considered separately.

(a) *The sample is a sub-universe in space.* The typical case consists in selecting one unit which is a collectivity and taking a sample of all individuals

364

in that unit – and then trying to generalize to all collectivities of the same kind. Thus, we may interview all workers in a factory and use this as the basis for a study of 'workers' – meaning *all* (industrial, qualified) workers. Or we may sample all municipalities in a province and try to use this as a basis for a theory of the municipalities in the nation; or all provinces in one nation and use that as a basis for a study of provinces in Latin America, or in the world for that matter. The error is obvious. As a study of that factory, that province, that nation, the data are perfect to the extent the observations or measurements are perfect. As a study of factories in general, provinces in general, and nations in general, it is a two-stage sample where the *first* contains *one* unit only (selected at random or intentionally), and the *second* stage contains *all* units (which then may be called a sub-universe). Although we can say everything we want about the sub-universe, a sample of one unit is insufficient for inferences about the super-universe, unless we can legitimately assume homogeneity between sub-universes. If this is not justified explicitly, inferences beyond the limits set by the sub-universe are illegitimate – and it usually is unjustified, precisely because of the objections against *cas pur* thinking in social science. This should then be reflected in the author's choice of title: he may of course title the book or article with reference to a general phenomenon, but then he should add in the subtitle an indication of the limitations set by the sample (see the discussion of the relation between generality and complexity in II, 4.2).

In order to generalize to the super-universe the first stage sample must contain more units, a design which is usually referred to as 'comparative', 'external replication'. If the first stage sample is a probability sample, then statistical tests may be used (provided conditions are fulfilled); if not, techniques of systematic replication should be used – and they will be discussed in II, 5.3.

(b) *The sample is a sub-universe in time.* The typical case consists in selecting all units of a certain kind at a certain point or interval in time, often referred to as a 'time-chunk'. Thus, we may select all prisoners present in a prison and claim that this is a sample from the total universe of prisoners. In this case the universe is defined in intension and not in extension: not as a list of elements in the universe (from which a sample can be drawn), but as a set of criteria to be satisfied for something to be an element. The universe is *open* since new elements can be generated and enter as time passes so in that sense the sample selected is a sub-universe and inferences can be made to that sub-universe or to the universe for all points in time. But to make inferences to this super-universe, we will have to remedy the same defects of the two-stage sample with one unit only in the first stage (one time-chunk). We can do so either by justifying an assumption of homo-geneity *(cas pur)*, or by more extensive first-stage sampling. This design is comparative over time (whether the time-points or time-intervals are chosen at random or intentionally) and is sometimes referred to by the term 're-visited'. If the second sample is carried out not only after some time has elapsed, but also by another person, changes through time and low inter-subjectivity will probably both contribute to quite different results from the first study.[24] Unfortunately, it is less likely that the same person will study the same phenomenon in a pattern that is comparative over time for two simple reasons: it means deferred gratification in terms of what may accrue to him after publication (promotion, etc.), and he may become tired of the problem. Neither reason is methodologically satisfactory. To the extent such deficiencies in the academic structure interfere with the validity of scientific research, something should be done to change them, so as to make replica-tion in time at least as fashionable as replication in space.

At any rate, universes that are time-samples do not constitute a basis for statistical inference techniques. As a sub-universe, they are a sample of size 1 only, which gives too wide limits for inferences. As a sample they have m units, but that sample is not a probability sample from the total universe, since elements outside the time-interval have a probability of 0 of being included in the sample. Thus a book may be titled, *The Prison Community,* but then the subtitle should be *A Norwegian Prison in the 'Fifties.*

The comments about choice of title and how to obtain data that can be used for generalization made above are applicable *mutatis mutandis.*

(c) *The samples comes from a hypothetical universe.* This is the most dif-ficult case to analyze. It says this: if there is no empirical universe, because the sample is identical with the universe, let us nevertheless assume that one exists and call it an hypothetical universe. Thus, suppose we have data about the national holidays of most nations in the world, and we are test-ing the hypothesis that such holidays have a tendency to cluster in the spring and summer. Should we apply statistical tests?[25] If we disregard the irrelevant circumstance that it was impossible to get information on some nations and assume that we have data about all, we would say *no.* The hypothesis is about the nations of this world as they exist today; and the data show that more than 70% of the holidays are found in spring and summer. To us this is case (1) in the list above; we see no sense in invoking an hypothetical universe except that of trying to legitimize the use of tech-niques that may look convincing although they are irrelevant. Thus, the statistical significance would depend on the number of nations; and it would be higher for the same percentage difference, the higher the number of nations. This means that the tenability of our hypothesis about national holidays for all nations in the world would depend on the political structure of the world – whether the international system favors a division into many small or a few big nations. We find this unreasonable when we have the universe in our data, and since we are studying *this particular* world.

To this it may be objected that our degree of confirmation in a finding should depend on the number of observations, whether the observations are based on a sample or a universe. Although we may present a finding about Latin American nations that shows a sizeable correlation, our degree of rational belief in the finding would be higher if there were 200 such nations and not 20, and considerably lower if there were only 2 such nations. This should not be confused with the problem of increasing degree of a confirmation through replication, as when Galileo's laws of motion are continuously reconfirmed; for in that case we have an *open* universe. In this case the universe is *closed* (or we may so assume, for if more Latin American nations were formed, this would not merely add to but also change the existing nations).

The objection can be rejected by simply saying that 'these 20 nations are my universe and there is nothing beyond that I am interested in – a finding based on them is the final answer'. While we would be tempted to accept this reasoning, let us nevertheless assume that there is something to the objection. First of all, however, from that admission it would not follow that statistical inference techniques provide the answer to the problem of how to evaluate the degree of confirmation. There is nothing that corresponds to the sampling model or the error model in the data. Maybe some other answer exists, in inductive logic or elsewhere. For instance, we might use the classical $\frac{m+1}{m+2}$ as a measure of the degree of confirmation, where m is the number of successful replication. But significance levels seem quite out of order, since there is no operational interpretation of the level of significance. And even if there were, it is not obvious that degree of confirmation must be given a probability interpretation if other interpretations are available

But secondly, if we accept the objection we take a rather strong stand on the problem of whether firm knowledge can ever be obtained. Since an 'hypothetical universe' can always be constructed in the minds of a researcher with a minimum of imagination this means that all data, in principle, should be subject to statistical testing. Data with a sufficient number of units will stand up against this test. But all data can be considered as samples on not only one but at least two levels, and as a sample of only one unit in the first stage. Thus, data about all human beings in the world may show any level of statistical significance, but it may always be objected that this world is a sample of one from an 'hypothetical' universe consisting of all possible *(imaginable?)* worlds. And samples of only one unit may of course be significant; but they also may not, in which case we would end up with a number of unrejected null hypotheses. We feel, on the contrary, that it is necessary to fix an upper limit and say that 'this is the level at which I accept my data' and then see to it that it really is possible to generalize to that level from the data (and that the samples do not cluster in space or in time, for instance, as in cases (a) and (b) above).

Thirdly, if we are free to construct hypothetical universes, we are also free to construct several hypothetical super-universes for each universe we have data about. We cannot see how these universes will avoid difficulties discussed under points (a) and (b) above, since it seems that any hypothetical universe will also have to be stretched out in time and space, in our imagination. What is the universe of all possible Latin American nations if we do not imagine that the twenty nations presently existing do not represent a sample in space, time, or both, from that universe? For if we do not, we must be thinking in terms of the 'idea' of a Latin American nation which has twenty manifestations with the idea existing *in rebus* but also *ante rem,* or if not 'ante' at least 'outside' in some unspecified sense that does not involve time explicity.[26]

At this point the defender of the hypothetical universe will say that this is exactly what is done in experimental research. An experiment is defined in terms of relevant conditions (to be controlled), independent variables (to be varied), and dependent variables (to be measured, observed); and a set of experiments is performed, perhaps only one experiment, or 'run'. When this has been done, the results are evaluated by means of techniques of statistical inference, because the experiment is regarded as a sample from the hypothetical universe one would obtain if the experiment could be repeated (controlling for the same conditions). This seems legitimate, so why not apply the same reasoning to data produced by societies as to data produced by nature, and construct stochastic models?

There are two objections to this reasoning.

First of all, for the experiment, an operational procedure exists, whereby we may approximate the hypothetical universe by repeating the experiment under constant control of relevant conditions. By means of this an empirical check on the model is possible. But we cannot turn back to 1810 and start generating Latin American nations again, a circumstance that makes the hypothetical universe not only hypothetical but operationally empty.

Secondly, for the experiment the data obtained represent one set of data among many possible. But for the Latin American nations the data obtained concern precisely the nations that interest us – we are interested in this particular configuration and nothing else.

Then it may be objected that this reasoning could be applied to any sample too: one might defend not using statistics by arguing 'this is precisely the sample that interests me'. If the sample exhausts a theoretical category this would be valid, but if not the implication is that there is a universe 'behind' which is our real target. Statistical tests are then used to evaluate our degree of confidence in rejecting the null hypothesis and, consequently, accepting the alternative hypothesis. But it should be admitted that there are gradations here: universes may, perhaps, be replicable to some extent; and they may be close to, but perhaps not represent, our ultimate interest.

On the other hand, if we want to accept the interpretation of the universe as a sample, there is still one problem: how is the sample obtained, what is the hypothetical sampling model from the hypothetical universe? Most investigators would, perhaps, say 'simple random'. But why? Because it is, in a sense, the simplest design? Why not a three-stage sample with built-in clustering effects at all levels? And since the significance level depends not only on the size of the sample and the universe, but also on the sampling method, this would affect the significance level. We have to ask: which one of the many sampling models harbors the idea of hypothetical sampling, *and why?* And could we test both the sampling model and the null hypothesis?

Thus, to summarize: we think the idea of the hypothetical universe with the hypothetical sampling is misplaced, when we already have data about the universe we want – at least as long as no one has presented a good case for an operational definition. And that concludes our discussion of the application of statistical tests to universes: such use of statistics makes sense, but only in some cases and only when some conditions are fulfilled.

Since we are not discussing fluctuations due to errors, only sampling fluctuations, this leaves us with case (3) as the candidate for the application of statistical tests. But this does not mean that case (3) is unproblematic. In the next three sections we shall deal with difficulties the working social scientist encounters when he tries to test his *generalization* hypothesis; when he has statistical data, and wants to apply significance tests. At the same time the debate we have already alluded to will be reviewed. Tentatively, the 'difficulties' have been grouped under three headings: *technical, pragmatic,* and *principal* difficulties. By 'technical difficulties' we mean those connected with assumptions we have to make to assure the validity of the statistical tests and that are defined within statistics itself (in the sense that it is within the intended goal of statistics to solve them). By 'pragmatic difficulties' we mean those arising from misuse or misunderstandings or thought habits one easily falls into by using statistical tests and 'statistical thinking'. And by 'principal difficulties' we mean difficulties outside statistics itself (in the sense that statistics, properly understood, does not pretend to solve them) but not due to any misunderstanding. It should be pointed out that those who blame 'statistics' for not solving the pragmatic and principal difficulties only betray their own ignorance of the field – whereas statisticians certainly should be encouraged to work on the technical problems and students of general methodology to cooperate with statisticians on the other two categories of difficulties.

(3) *Technical difficulties with statistical tests.* While textbooks vary in their ability to emphasize conditions that should be satisfied for statistical tests to have validity, recent texts are usually the more critical. We shall not try to make any exhaustive survey of these difficulties, only list a few. In so doing the rationale is simply that the basis for inference about the null-hypothesis is that the conditions are fulfilled; the technical difficulties are concerned with the fulfilment of these conditions. The conditions can be divided into two parts according to Table 4.3.1: (1) relating to the universe, (2) relating to the sample. Table 4.4.2 gives a highly concentrated survey.

This simple list alone should serve as a warning, not to give up statistical testing but to be careful, especially in using the simplest models (based on normality and simple random sampling). The excellent articles by Kish (7,8), the texts by Stephan-McCarthy and by Cochran earlier referred to (in I, 2.3), and the works by Hansen, Hurwitz, and Madow[28] give valuable analysis and advice on what to do in the case of sampling difficulties, and most recent texts contain material on what to do about difficulties with the universe conditions. We shall only look into one case, the case of deterministic sampling, where we have said that statistical tests are inappropriate.

The case can be presented in textbook fashion as follows: In order to develop a model, or sampling distribution, the statistician must have known probability factors somewhere. This means that not only must the sample be a probability sample, but its elements must also have known probabilities of being selected, and these are only necessary, not sufficient conditions. What the statistician then does is to compare the empirical sample with a model of all possible samples selected with the same probabilities. To reject the null hypothesis, the sampling specifications in the model must reflect the sampling method used; otherwise, we cannot be sure on which basis

Table 4.4.2. *A survey of conditions for statistical tests*

(I) *Conditions relating to the universe*	Remedy:
(1) Interval or ratio scale measurement	'non-parametric tests'
(2) Normal distribution	'distribution-free tests'
(3) Homoscedasticity ⎤ (4) Independence ⎦	correlation analysis and analysis of variance/covariance not too vulnerable
(5) Linear regression	use correlation ratios

(II) *Difficulties relating to the sampling*[27]	Remedy:
(1) Sample not probabilistic	statistical tests inappropriate
(2) Sample probabilistic but probabilities unknown	impossible to construct models
(3) Sample not simple random, but stratified random	correct for that (less variance than with SR sampling)
(4) Sample not one-stage, but multi-stage	correct for that
(5) Sample with clusters	correct for that (more variance than with SR sampling)
(6) Sample from finite population without replacement	finite population correction or sampling with replacement
(7) DK, NA	correct for that

we reject: the conditions of the null hypothesis, or the unsatisfied conditions of the sampling specifications.

But then it may be argued, as for the tests for universes: could we not proceed under the assumption of *as if,* saying that 'if this had been a probability sample selected in such and such a manner, then the level of significance of this finding (difference, correlation) would have been such and such'? Nobody can be prevented from saying this, but it is difficult to see that it makes sense to use terms from a language defined for certain situations when these situations are not present. To say about a person performing the twist that if he had been a dog the performance would have been rather splendid, or even significant, may be fine as an insult but nevertheless inadequate as a basis of comparison. The fact is that with intentional samples *any* discrepancy can be obtained at will when we have some *a priori* insights that tell us how to select. And here we are actually touching on the argument in the preceding section about statistical tests relative to universes. An intentional sample will be like a sub-universe limited to a specific time or space region, only that the principle of selection may be less obvious (and for that reason more dangerous), and lead to any amount of bias.

We can now imagine a continuum from the SR sample to the intentional sample with increasing degree of bias in favor of some types of elements and in disfavor of other elements. Along this continuum are such manageable situations as the disproportionate stratified sample, for which a methodology exists. At the extreme end is the deterministic sample, for which we claim that statistical tests are inappropriate. However, what if the deterministic sample is biased according to some variable of selection, but nevertheless representative according to some other variable? For instance, what about the systematic sample where every k'th element on the list is selected?

But the systematic sample is not a deterministic sample unless the list has a periodicity of k for some relevant property, so statistical tests are highly meaningful.[29] And as to representative, deterministic samples, of which the quota samples used in the gallup methodology are the most famous, no sampling distribution is known, so to speak of significance levels would be not only meaningless but misleading. This does not mean that the result cannot be highly generalizable and the findings reliable, only that we cannot use the very precise tools of statistical inference to arrive at a measure of *how* generalizable and reliable. And as mentioned in I, 2.3, such samples may also be very good for multivariate analysis if the size is decided according to the necessities of multivariate breakdowns rather than precision of statistical estimates.

(4) *Pragmatic difficulties with statistical tests*

We now turn to the difficulties that are only indirectly rooted in statistics, in the sense that its use may lead to unfortunate habits or patterns of thought. The first two of these are much commented upon in the literature we refer to, so we shall only give some of the main arguments.

(a) *Confusion of statistical significance with theoretical significance.*[30] This confusion is partly a semantic one. If 'tests of significance' were called 'tests of generalizability', as we think they should, there would be no confusion because one would talk about tenability of the substantive hypothesis and tenability of the generalization hypothesis as two separate phenomena (referred to in the heading as 'theoretical significance' and 'statistical significance', respectively, because these terms are often used in the literature). The problem lies precisely in the logical independence of these concepts, as illustrated in Table 4.4.3:

Table 4.4.3. *The relation between statistical and theoretical significance*

	The finding in the data is	
	theoretically significant	theoretically insignificant
statistically significant	(1)	(2)
statistically insignificant	(3)	(4)

In case (1) both hypotheses are confirmed or found tenable, in cases (2) and (3) one but not the other, in case (4) neither. Cases (2) and (3) are the interesting ones, since they pinpoint the distinction between the substantive hypothesis and the generalization hypothesis.

Case (2) is the well-known case where a finding is significant for the simple reason that it is (semi-) tautologous, or trivial for other reasons, or because the sample size is so high that almost any discernible finding becomes statistically significant (which is as it should be; the larger the sample the smaller differences between percentages or correlations etc. should be required for generalization if the whole design permits it).[31] Thus, many findings may be declared statistically significant without confirming substantive hypotheses, whether they are derived from theories or not. If the hypothesis is that the correlation should be 0.7, then it does not help that the significance level is very high for a correlation of only 0.5. A person may get significantly more votes than his adversary, yet that does not help him if he needs a two-thirds majority and has only 60%.

Case (3) is less trivial. A substantive hypothesis is confirmed, but the finding is not statistically significant; the null-hypothesis is not rejected. What, then, about the substantive hypothesis – would it have to fall, together with the generalization hypothesis? The most extreme case would be the case where we have a sample that is a sub-universe, and the substantive hypothesis is rejected because the finding is not 'significant'. This all investigators who apply statistical tests to universes must be willing to do, as one obviously cannot apply a test only if one has looked at the data in advance and been guaranteed significance. But we shall disregard this case and assume that the sample is a sample. Would it not be better, then, to disregard a finding that might have been due to sampling fluctuations alone? Often yes, at least if the finding is highly insignificant ($p = 0.50$ for instance). But there are at least two important arguments against so doing.

First, let us imagine that the finding is isolated in the sense that it cannot be related to any other finding. In that case, the argument may be phrased in terms of the probability of committing an error of type II. This probability is often quite high, especially for the low-powered tests likely to be used in the social sciences because of the many conditions that cannot be fulfilled. Moreover, the probability is often unknown since the tests are chosen with reference to significance level and not to the other error probability. Thus, rejection may mean rejecting something with substance, something which might have led to important insights.

Secondly, let us imagine that the finding is not isolated, but can be related (theoretically) to other findings. In that case, as has often been emphasized in the literature,[32] we should consider theoretically related findings, jointly. Here we get into the difficulty that the related findings are not based on independent samples, but often based on the same sample. Hence it becomes difficult to compute the significance level of the joint finding (we cannot just multiply the significance levels), nor does it seem feasible to compute nontrivial upper or lower limits for the joint finding.[33] It should be noted that this is a technical difficulty which more advanced statistical techniques than exist today may be able to solve.

In this context one illegitimate technique should be exposed as particularly dangerous. Imagine a number of indicators of the same dimension exists for the same individuals, obtained by very slight variation in the wording; and that these indicators all show a slight correlation with a background variable, s, such as sex. Any technique based on calculation of 'joint significance' that gives higher significance levels the more items that are correlated (as would be the only reasonable relation) will have to meet with the objection that not only are the samples dependent, but the indicators are also dependent. If any level of dependence between the indicators were permitted, then any level of significance could be obtained by including a sufficient number of such indicators (for instance forty questions of the type 'have you travelled to X, Y, Z' etc.).

We shall return to this problem later in this section and in II, 5.4. As anyone would agree, a better, although not always feasible, policy would be to obtain a larger sample (or more samples) to see whether the finding still holds up; or to see whether the same finding also holds for independent subsamples. The latter would be 'internal replication', the former 'external replication';[34] whereas the hunt for other findings to which one could relate the first finding theoretically may be referred to as 'theoretical replication'. We reject the latter because we feel it is only a function of the level of imagination of the researcher: any imaginative researcher will be able to find some principle that unites any set of non-contradictory findings, at least while the number is as low as two or three – provided the findings are not in direct contradiction. To say 'I believe in my sample because my findings are so consistent, they make sense to me' is illegitimate – it may reflect a high level of imagination in the researcher or that he is consistently making the same errors so that his samples always make sense for the same wrong reason. Besides, why should perfectly obtained samples necessarily make theoretical sense?

Of course, statistical significance and theoretical significance *may* coincide, but this coincidence is accidental and empirical, and not logical. If one, nevertheless believes in the logical equivalence between the two – a kind of pragmatic equivalence where the substantive hypothesis is abandoned when there is no statistical significance, whereas all statistically significant findings are elaborated on – then it is obvious which two mistakes are easily committed: to reject what is interesting and to elaborate the trivial. It is not correct, however, to equate throwing out nonsignificant substantive findings with errors of type II in the statistical sense; this error is committed when a *generalizable* finding (substantively important or not, but satisfying the alternative hypothesis) is overlooked because it does not attain statistical significance.

But one problem nevertheless remains: how to test the substantive hypothesis if we cannot automatically make use of the decision criteria implicit in statistical testing. That will to some extent be answered in the following.[35]

(b) *Confusion of level of significance with size of association.*[36] Since significance level depends on sampling procedure and size of sample, it can obviously not be used, in general, as a measure of association, if for no other reason because comparisons cannot be made (the measure is not N-free, compare the list of desiderata in II, 2.3). But what if we have two samples of the same size obtained in the same way – could we not use the significance levels as measures of association in these cases? Of course, the significance level can be used to order the samples and will order them the same way as the correlation coefficient, since significance level is a monotonous function of the size of association when the measure of association is used to test the hypothesis of zero correlation. *But,* this is like arguing that one could measure a man's height by measuring the length of his shadow: why not rather measure the man himself? Level of significance has its very precise interpretation which refers to sampling distributions, and measures of association have their interpretations, which refer to the definition of statistical independence, and these are two quite distinct matters. Hence, *this* is the main reason for rejecting level of significance, not that it is not N-free.

Thus, substantive hypotheses can be formulated in terms of the level of association, *as measured by a specified coefficient,* and generalization hypotheses in terms of level of significance *relative to a specified test.* If we object that it is arbitrary which level of association will be accepted as confirmation of the substantive hypothesis, we may answer that which level of significance will be accepted for the rejection of the null hypothesis (and consequently for the acceptance of the alternative generalization hypothesis) is arbitrary too. But this is, of course, no answer, for two wrongs do not make one right; it merely emphasises the parallelism between the two kinds of hypothesis. And that brings us to the major pragmatic point: the abuse of statistical tests to test the substantive hypotheses has, we feel, conduced to a much too low acceptance level where degree of association is concerned. Correlation coefficients are accepted just because they are statistically significant, which means that a methodology invented to guard against too low differences and associations has led to exactly the opposite of what was intended, with the sample sizes modern researchers usually have at their disposal. Complex theories are constructed on the basis of rather small percentage differences just because they are 'significant' – and so on. But the remedy here, theories refined enough to permit the derivation of propositions about a specified level of association, not only 'association' in general, is still for the future. This will be discussed further in II, 5.3 and II, 6.

(c) *Statistical tests focus on isolated findings, not on patterns.* We have already touched this point in 4.1. This is due to the technical difficulty in arriving at an evaluation of the significance level for joint findings when there is dependence both on the unit and variable side. Maybe empirical techniques for deriving sampling distributions would be useful here, but in the absence of any methodology the temptation will be to stick to the feasible; and the feasible is to test each table separately, and to evaluate it separately. This methodology is highly compatible with a theoretically unguided empiricism but not with theoretization *a priori:* it will, for that reason, conduce to inductive rather than deductive social science, resulting in very flat theoretical pyramids. We see nothing inherently wrong in inductive social science, but it represents only one of two possibilities; and to the extent a methodology that relies highly on statistical tests favors one more than the other, a bias is introduced that may be harmful.

(d) *Statistical tests focus on differences, not on similarities.*[37] When the constituency example was given in II, 4.4 (2), it had to be constructed in an artificial way so that the substantive and generalization hypotheses should have an apparent similarity and yet be fundamentally different. This artificiality, however, can be traced back to the way in which statistical tests work:

by exclusion. The possible universes are outlined in an hypothesis-space, and the null-hypothesis (hopefully to be excluded) is defined by a subset in this space. Usually, however, this subset has lower dimensionality than the space itself, as in the very frequent case of the point-hypothesis (e. g., for differences between means or percentages) or the hypothesis given in II, 4.4 (2). This, however, is quite fortunate, as it corresponds to modern views on theory formation, where theories are discarded or excluded if they do not work, and kept as working hypotheses until they can be either discarded or made more precise so that some interpretations of them can be eliminated. The point is that the statistical null-hypotheses usually are about some kind of similarity (in means, in percentages, in dispersions, in correlations, in entire distributions). Hence, as 'significance' means the exclusion of these hypotheses, 'statistical significance' in most cases means some kind of difference.

One simple reason for this is that we are dealing with distributions, and that there is a basic asymmetry between 'similarity' and 'difference'. The former is a point (or of lower dimensionality in the hypothesis-space in general), whereas the latter is all the rest. This means that if we reject a null hypothesis about similarity, we will have a multitude of difference-hypotheses to choose between; but the rejection of one specific difference-hypothesis (e. g. that the correlation in the universe is 1) will not imply the acceptance of the similarity hypothesis (e. g. that the correlation in the universe is 0) but to the acceptance of that similarity hypothesis together with a multitude of difference-hypotheses. Thus, by means of confidence intervals, we may see which universes are compatible with the sample,[38] but the uncorrelated universe, if it appears at all, will be together with a number of correlated universes.

The result, as has often been pointed out, is to regard similarities as uninteresting (whereas multivariate analysis can make them the most interesting of all findings) and focus on differences; it is forgotten that similarities may be equally problematic and worthy of theoretical exploration. We know of only one exception, where the tendency is to accept similarities and not differences as *bona fide* findings: that is research on the correlates of background characteristics such as sex and race, when the ideological climate commands that all differences shall be 'explained' (away).

Regardless of whether statistical tests are used or not, there are probably some fundamental characteristics of our perception and cognition which favor contrasts at the expense of uniformity. If, in addition, dissimilarities are to be explained in terms of dissimilarities, and similarities in terms of similarities, then this predilection for dissimilarities will feed on itself, with or without statistics. Nevertheless, it might be interesting to know whether there is a socialization effect here, in the sense that statistical training accentuates this disregard for similarities, and contributes to the image of dissensus.

(e) *Statistical testing implies a discontinuity between generalizability and non-generalizability.* The word 'implies' should not be interpreted in its logical sense, because there is nothing in statistical theory against the idea that 'generalizability' is a continuum, not a dichotomy. However, there is also the idea that we have to draw the line somewhere, and that applies to H_0: we either reject H_0 (and accept H_1) or not (just as a defendant is either found guilty or not). The importance of drawing this line *a priori* (i.e., before the tables have been inspected, at least not too thoroughly) by choosing the level of significance at an early stage in the research process is often pointed out. If this line is adhered to rigorously, however, the practical consequence is that a dichotomy *is* enforced on the generalizability continuum, e.g., at the 5% level. As an alternative, let us consider this procedure: rank all the findings according to level of significance or generalizability and list the levels so that the reader himself may draw the borderline where he wants to. By this procedure, contiguous findings can be grouped in classes with different levels of generalizability, and decreasing degrees of tenability can be attached to the generalization hypotheses with decreasing levels of significance. Thus, we could work with any number of classes, not only with two (reject-nonreject). 'Critical level' reasoning is an implementation of this.

Dichotomous thinking has the psychological advantage of providing an escape from ambiguity by disregarding borderline or ambiguous cases by definition. For decision-makers (it is interesting that Abraham Wald provided a common framework for the classical statistical disciplines of estimation theory and testing of hypotheses under the name of 'statistical decision theory') dichotomies are in a sense the easy way out, because they then escape the difficulties of fine gradations (as judicial bodies do when they pass the verdict *guilty* vs. *not guilty,* or an academic body when they make the first evaluation of the candidate in terms of *pass* or *fail*). But usually it soon becomes apparent that important nuances are lost – and many researchers have undoubtedly felt that they are playing a cruel game when one of their favorite findings disappears because it fails to attain significance by a small fraction. More important is perhaps the perspective of the continuum which may be lost, and the possibly interesting conclusions which may be drawn when one starts talking about *levels* of generalizability. Thus, we would argue in favor of at least three levels instead of two, in favor of at least trichotomous thinking: generalizable, dubious, and not generalizable findings. Nor are we so convinced that the borderlines will have to be established *a priori* – in many cases important ideas about what is generalizable and what is not can be obtained by inspecting *a posteriori* the ranking list referred to above (for there may be 'jumps' in the list).

(b) *Statistical tests lead to the acceptance of unvalidated parameters and tests of doubtful relevance.* We have made the point many times in this text – that parameters should be subject to the same kind of rigorous testing for validity as indices – if for no other reason because of the symmetry we have emphasized between vertical and horizontal analysis. The circumstance that a parameter exists is a necessary but certainly not sufficient condition for its application. That it serves well as a measure of yield (arithmetic mean), homogeneity (variance), and association (product-moment correlation) in one science (for instance, in agriculture) is not convincing proof that it will serve the purposes of a social science. Statistics is the science of stochastic (probabilistic) phenomena; and since such phenomena can be found in all other sciences, statistics cuts across traditional borderlines. But this versatility has made many investigators believe that its parameters also, necessarily, have cross-disciplinary validity (for an example to the contrary, see the discussion of the criss-cross measure at the end of II, 2.3).

Thus, parameters are accepted because sampling distributions for them exist and can be used to test generalization hypotheses, not because they are valid. The blame for this certainly does not fall on the statisticians, but on the social scientists themselves for not working out their own tools with proper care. Basically, this is a problem of institutionalization. The tendency will be particularly pronounced if statisticians and social scientists never meet, and if the courses given by the former in the faculties dominated by the latter are uncoordinated with social science research. The situation will probably continue to improve in the years to come, and lead to parameters that reflect adequately the concepts to be measured, and to statistical tests that reflect adequately the theories, however.

(5) Principal difficulties with statistical tests

The difficulties to be described below are of a more principal nature since they refer to important problems statistics does not solve. We have listed them here since they are very real difficulties, not minor technical problems or just patterns that may lead to unfortunate habits.

(a) *The choice of level of significance is arbitrary.* The more one insists on a dichotomous choice, the more important a rationale for the choice of a cutting point. The ideal would be to proceed as in sequential testing by choosing the two probabilities of errors of type I and type II and construct the test on that basis.[39] However, the choice would still be arbitrary. A rational basis for choice can only come from specific substantive insights. Thus, the obvious procedure would be to explore the consequences of the two types of error and try to evaluate them in terms of gain and loss, and then arrive at some basis for a choice.[40] It may be objected that this only pushes the problem one step further away, from an arbitrary choice of level of significance (and, ideally, also the level of the other probability) to an arbitrary choice of what represents a tolerable loss. But that objection is irrelevant because (1) a choice has to be made somewhere anyhow and (2) the new choice is located in the substantive field of interest and not in general statistics. And the latter means that levels of significance may be arrived at that corresponds to something in social science theory, which in turn means that the level may vary from one investigation to the other.

More specifically, constant levels imply:

(1) *inter-hypotheses constancy* in fixing the limits,
(2) *inter-individual constancy* in fixing the limits, and
(3) *intra-individual constancy* in fixing the limits,

so that a decision concerning the hypothesis is not overly dependent on irrelevant aspects of the hypothesis, such as *who* tests it, and *when* it is tested by the same person; thus adding to the universality of the finding.

In a sense this problem has the same structure as the problem discussed in (4) (f) above. What to many appear as a strength, the versatility of statistical parameters and the universality of the level of significance, should rather lead to suspicion. Just as it is unreasonable to believe that the same parameter should function equally well across all scientific borders, it is unreasonable to believe that the 'same' level of significance is in fact the 'same', regardless of the consequences of the errors. In legal justice a parallel problem exists: the error of type I would be to declare guilty a person who is not, the error of type II to declare not-guilty a person who is guilty. The norm is to attach more importance to error of type I than to errors of type II, but this obviously varies with the legal culture. And to fix a legal procedure so that the probabilities relate to each other as 1:10 would be to let one legal culture prevail over others, regardles of the merits of the case.

The unique function of 'same-ness' that can be claimed for the level of significance is that it can be kept constant throughout one particular investigation. In other words, the investigator will avoid the difficulty referred to by Guetzkow in the beginning of II, 4.4. But, although this constancy is a virtue, it becomes less impressive if the level of probability of errors of type II is not equally constant, in other words if the tests used do not have the same power. And if one wants to avoid the difficulty referred to under

(4) (c) above, a constant level of significance becomes a vice because it forces one into non-rejection of some null-hypotheses where the finding might contribute greatly to the theory if combined with other findings.

(b) *The decision as to one-tailed vs. two-tailed test is often arbitrary.* This difficulty is logically similar to the one above. It is connected with the quite frequent practice of saving generalizability for one's pet findings by adding, after a failure to obtain significance, 'with a one-tailed test, however, the difference becomes significant' or a similar comment. This may be legitimate if there existed *a priori* an explicit principle according to which there was every reason to predict that the outcomes would only be distributed on a subset of the space (usually one half of the space). If such a principle does not exist, then two-tailed tests should be used. Thus, if we are testing the significance of means, the null hypothesis for a two-tailed test is typically H_0: $m = m_0$, and for a one-tailed test H_0: $m \gtrless m_0$.

In principle this sounds easy enough, but in practice the borderline is not so sharp. All hinges on the expressions '*a priori*' and 'principle'. How much *a priori* does it have to be? For instance, can we start out with no assumption as to which side the sample will be located on, apply a two-tailed test to establish significance if there is any, and on replications make use of one-tailed tests to the side where the significance was found? Or is this only legitimate on completely new data? At any rate, the idea about a two-tailed test will have to come from somewhere. It may come from theory, but at one point or another some data must have been used to suggest, or to lead to suggestions about, one-tailed tests. Again, can we use parts of the data to suggest a principle of prediction and other parts to test the principle by means of a one-tailed test? How independent will the data have to be? Or is the point rather that the suggestion may arise from the same data, but not within the mind of the same researcher?

And what about the 'principle' – is not this one more of those dichotomous concepts that corresponds badly with scientific reality? If a person is completely convinced, or if the only alternative hypothesis he is interested in is to the effect that the sample will be registered on one side of a point representing the null-hypothesis, then the one-tailed test seems appropriate. But if he is only 90% sure? Should he then divide the critical region between the two tails proportionately to his subjective belief? Or must he be 50% sure about one side and 50% about the other before the discontinuous transition from one-tailed to two-tailed tests takes place? And if we admit that this is unfortunate, then how do we measure degree of *a priorism* and degree of *belief* in the principle so as to correct for this in the construction of the critical region?

We suggest that this is not a statistical problem either, but essentially a problem in general methodology, and as such an unsolved problem.

(c) *Analysis interferes with the level of significance.* Imagine we have an ideal situation with a probability sample from a universe that satisfies all conditions of the universe of the model; and we want to test a finding for level of significance. Anyone informed about statistical inference knows that the conditions of the test are violated if a number of tables is inspected and the most promising ones are selected for statistical testing. For imagine the null hypothesis is correct. In that case, up to 5% of the tables, if that is the level of significance, will show significance. If we have 1000 independent comparisons to make between men and women with our data, as many as 50 of them may be significant, even when no differences exist. This means that if we inspect all tables and select the 50 most extreme ones we shall reach very gratifying conclusions if we are looking for differences.[41] But if we have just one table and no basis for comparison so that we cannot say whether it is extreme or not, then no rule is violated. Hence it might make sense to request an increasingly higher level of significance, the more knowledge is gained about the data.

Obviously, if we have a random sample of the adult population of a nation, then the subsample consisting of males with high income and high education living in cities will also be a random sample from the universe with the same specifications. Hence, any subsample is still a random sample, so statistical tests applied to the subsamples produced by multivariate analysis are not invalid for lack of randomness.

But these subsamples are not selected according to some probability model from the set of all possible subsamples. Rather they are selected precisely because the investigator suspects that findings will appear in the subsamples. Even if he is not guided by *a posteriori* selection of the 'best' tables, he is nevertheless guided by some knowledge of the data that has led him towards that particular type of multivariate analysis. In II, 5.3 the goal of maximizing variation will be emphasized, so the difference between what happens in any good analysis of statistical data in social science and the *a posteriori* selection mentioned above is one of degree, not of kind.

Thus, we are in a peculiar situation. If the sample can be tested by one inclusive, sweeping test, then there is no problem – but this condition is completely unrealistic in connection with survey research, although it may be well approximated by experimental research. If the researcher knows nothing about his data, the first table he encounters in his explorations can be subjected to statistical testing; but if he uses that information when he tests his next table, he is already in difficulty. He can proceed by testing all possible tables simultaneously – and he is in a number of difficulties: some of them will be significant when the null-hypothesis is true, he will have no chance to see one table in the light of the other, and the burden of work will be unsurmountable with the size of contemporary surveys, even with the most modern computers (the number of tables in a survey with 500 variables is $2^{500} - 1$).

Finally, he can do as is usually done – he proceeds step by step. But then the significance level should somehow increase in a monotone way as a function of the number of steps in order to give any meaning to the idea of constancy in level of significance: it can remain constant only by changing.

But which monotone function should be chosen? If the original significance level is p, should he choose, for instance, p/n where n is the number of steps? It looks arbitrary, for some of the steps may be explorations in other corners of the data that do not contribute to insights before they have been brought to bear on prior steps. In other words, the function is probably discontinuous and monotone, and besides more dependent on what goes on in the researcher's mind than on the number, n, of steps he has taken. This subjective element is at best difficult to measure; at worst it may make us suspect that there is something wrong with this entire way of thinking. For we cannot answer by blaming survey data and the *ex post facto* experiment where the 'experiment' is performed on punched cards instead of on social units. Both for technical and ethical reasons it is difficult in social science to obtain data according to an experimental design *ex ante*.

Hence, it looks as if we have to be satisfied with the answer that statistical testing is most meaningful (the significance level closest to what it claims to be) if (1) isolated findings are inspected and (2) the study is exploratory with insights obtained from sources outside the data. This does not mean that we should not proceed with multivariate analysis, only that the role of statistical testing in these *ex post facto* experiments is dubious, to say the least, so that we will have to look for other ways of testing the generalization hypotheses.

(d) *Statistical reasoning alone is not sufficient to test a causal hypothesis.* While the nature of causality will remain a matter of discussion for a long time to come, there is one thing that can be pointed out here. Statistical reasoning in the testing of causal relationships has concentrated on different expressions of partial correlations, whether on the nominal, ordinal, or interval levels of measurement. That is, a total correlation is not taken at its face value, but interpreted as neither a necessary nor a sufficient condition for a causal relation to exist. To uncover spuriousness or masking effects (II, 5.3) statistical techniques are indispensable. However, at least three elements of a non-statistical nature will usually enter in any discussion of causality: the *time-relation* between the variables, the theory needed to '*see a mechanism working*' between the variables, and the subjective feeling that the relation has been tested for a *sufficient number of relevant variables* in a sufficient number of combinations. This additional kind of insight required is not better or poorer, only different; statistics alone is not sufficient. This is a commonplace, but should nevertheless be pointed out to reduce the belief in statistics as a procedure that can be used to obtain almost anything.

(e) *Statistical reasoning alone is not sufficient to test a theory*. The reasoning here is as above: whereas an invariance-hypothesis (e.g., hypotheses about one-dimensional or multi-dimensional distributions) can be tested statistically, there is a non-statistical residual left where theory-hypotheses are concerned. By a 'theory', then, we mean a set of propositions (axioms) from which preferably qualitatively quite different invariance-hypotheses can be derived. To take an example: imagine that we study a co-educational college for adults with a considerable age-span and a highly universalistic ideology that everybody shall be evaluated on the basis of academic merits alone, regardless of age or sex. Imagine further that we assume a general ranking in the surrounding society with 'old males' at the top, 'young females' at the bottom and 'young males' and 'old females' in-between. The theory is then, stated in simple terms, that various kinds of behavior at school will be a function of the discrepancy between present experience in that universalistic community and past and present experience with the ranking in the surrounding society. From this theory a lot of quite different consequences can be derived: old males will show a general tendency to overestimate their own achievement, young females to underestimate it; old males will externalize the school to achieve balance by reference to the priority of outside commitments and by seating themselves in the background of the class, young females will do vice versa – but in highly 'expressive' subjects with a reputation for being 'feminine', like 'music appreciation', everything said may be reversed, etc.

Thus, a number of consequences may be derived, as from any theory. At the present stage in social science theory it appears rather impossible to express the theory as an axiomatic system in the strict sense of this term, including a procedure so that we can decide for any proposition formulated with the terms of the theory whether it can be derived from the theory or not (see II, 6.2). This means that we cannot formulate the multi-dimensional hypothesis to include *all* derivations from the theory, and subject it to a global statistical test. But what about the empirical consequences we *do* derive, can they be tested?

In order to test them simultaneously we have to overcome the difficulty mentioned under (4) (a) above in testing a set of related tables, a problem that has by no means been solved. But even if we accept that this is only a technical difficulty, there still remains one problem of a non-statistical nature.

We want to test the theory as such, not only isolated propositions. Is this the same as testing the set of propositions derived from the theory? If it were, then this would amount to saying that a theory is the equivalent of its set of derived propositions, or at least that the residual is of no significance for the evaluation of the theory. But, in general, several theories (in the sense of sets of axioms) will be compatible with the same set of propositions (see II, 6.1). Nevertheless, we make choices between such theories, too, for instance in terms of the properties discussed in II, 6.2. And these properties do not enter in the statistical test. Thus, one such property will refer to the relative weight or emphasis placed on the propositions derived; according to theory T_1, proposition P_1 may be more important than P_2 – according to T_2, vice versa. Since this judgment at best is not yet operationalized, and at worst not even operationalizable because of the complexity and lack of explicitness at this level of scientific operation, it is difficult to see how it could enter into the statistical procedure. But, as we added at the end of (5) (d) above: statistics should not be held responsible for what it does not claim to solve, we should only emphasize the areas of non-statistical reasoning in a methodology that is already highly statistically oriented.

(f) *Statistical reasoning makes the universe the criterion of truth.* This problem could have been listed as a pragmatic difficulty, but it also has more principal components, as we shall try to show. The good thing about statistical testing is that it emphasizes scepticism towards the sample; our point here is that that particular scepticism is often bought at the price of accepting the universe from which the sample is drawn. No-one will deny today that science advanced greatly when sampling theory and randomisation were introduced and researchers in the softer sciences were trained to regard their samples with suspicion. The harder and more established sciences like physics and chemistry had not had the same sampling problem, but rather a problem of idealization or purification: of providing the experimenter with as perfect isolation, as friction-free balls, as airtight tubes, or as purified a lump of sulphur as possible – and generalization was made on the *cas pur* assumption. And this was perhaps to some extent taken over by biology (and by early sociology), so that one giant comes out against another giant with this conclusion: 'The one flaw in Darwin's procedure was the absence of randomisation'.[42]

However this emphasis on sampling merely places the problem at another level. Most obvious is the case of the (relatively) perfect sample from the imperfect universe, found in two of the major works of the post-war period, *The Kinsey Reports* and the Berkeley study on *The Authoritarian Personality*, with a sample from a universe around the San Francisco Bay in the latter, and one from a universe heavily concentrated in the state of Indiana for the former. It is easy for us to criticise on such a basis if we ourselves are not confronted with an unlimited scientific problem and highly limited means to explore the problem, however. Besides, our point is not that a solid basis for inferences about sexual behavior or authoritarian personality would be obtained simply by extending the universe to the total US population at the end of the 1940's. This is also a sub-universe in space and time and has no monopoly as the final arbiter about what is true and what is not in the fields of sex and authoritarianism. Thus, the whole discussion about super-universe and sub-universe becomes relevant.

The problem is that propositions are even more dependent on the universe than on the sample, for which reason it may be better to have a biased sample (provided the type of bias is known) from a relevant universe, than to have a perfect sample from an irrelevant universe. We certainly cannot base a social science on propositions that vary from sample to sample, but neither can we base it on propositions that are highly vulnerable to choice of universe, unless we can include the choice of universe among our variables. For that reason it is fruitful to regard any sampling as at least at two-stage sample: first the universe is selected (and usually there is only one universe, which is selected with a probability of 1), and then the sample is selected.

But there is another sense in which the universe may be a problematic criterion. Some of this has been discussed in I, 2.2 and more will be taken up in II, 6.3. It is the general problem of to what extent inferences about intra-individual processes can be made from data based on inter-individual comparisons. Since this will be discussed extensively in II, 6.3 we shall only point to one fundamental mistake that seems particularly frequent: that of accepting a universe that represents several individuals at one point in time, and using this as a substitute for a universe that represents one individual at several points in time. This is not an attack against the idea of using universes as criteria of truth, but against the use of inappropriate universes. In the future, perhaps, social science methodology may be more successful in developing something that corresponds to *cas pur* methodology, but in the meantime, at least the same care has to be exercised in the choice of universes as in the choice of samples.

(6) *Conclusion*

There is no doubt that statistical tests should be used to test the generalization hypotheses when they are appropriate, which means (1) the data form a probability sample with known probabilities from a specified universe (regardless of whether these also are super-universes), where the universe may be empirical or hypothetical (in the latter case an operational procedure for generating it should exist); (2) the findings to be tested are (a) isolated, (b) generated from the data by random or at least not too systematic procedures. For if *all* findings are tested, then we shall frequently commit errors of type I, and if the findings are generated by a systematic search procedure that takes prior findings into account the level of significance will not generally be constant.

This considerably limits the applicability of statistical tests to survey data, whether they are about individuals or collectivities; and it raises the problem of a search for alternative ways of testing the generalization hypothesis. The alternative suggested by the Columbia school has, as mentioned, been in terms of replication on *independent* samples, whether this is done on sub-samples (internal replication) or additional samples (external replication). In addition there are the methodologies of 'theoretical consistency' which we have rejected, and replication on other variables. The following typology may be useful:

Table 4.4.4. *Types of replication*

		Samples	
		same	*different*
Variables	*same*	(1)	(2)
	different	(3)	(4)

In case (1) there is no replication at all, to test generalizability we have to use statistical tests if they are appropriate. In case (2) more than one sample is involved, whether it is by internal or external replication. If we can assume that the samples are mutually independent (not only that they do not contain the same units, but also that they have been obtained independently, that information from one sample has not interfered with the composition of the next sample, for instance), then the total level of significance can be meaningfully computed by multiplying the levels of significance obtained for the individual samples. By means of the binomial distribution we can easily compute the probability of obtaining k samples that are significant at the 5% level among a total of n tables. This probability is simply

$\binom{n}{k}(0.05)^k(0.95)^{n-k}$, as usual under the condition of the null hypothesis.[43]

Obviously, the conditions for statistical tests to be used must still obtain in each individual case – this is not a way of circumventing the conditions, but a way of testing a set of tables. There are also other methods.

In case (3) the same hypothesis is tested on the same sample, but with different variables. Obviously, since the sample is the same and the variables are not independent (if they were, they would not have been accepted as indicators of the same dimension), we cannot evaluate the degree of generalization obtained if the finding holds up by multiplying significance levels. And if the variables are not indicators of the same dimension, but independent, it may be important and interesting that the finding is as expected with the new variable too, but that is a development of the theory we are testing, not a case of generalization.

At this point, an objection against mechanical use of the procedures listed under cases (3) and (4) should be repeated: somehow the degree of generalization obtained should depend not only on the significance level of each separate table and the number of tables (whether for different samples) or different variables – but also on the difference between the samples and between the variables. The binomial formula above takes care of individual significance levels and their number, but it is blind to whether the samples are trivial copies of each other or span an important dimension. Thus, we might have a sample of the population and find that a correlation holds up for the subsample of the 21-year-olds, the 22-year-olds, ... the 78-year-olds, and so on (internal replication). We only suggest that this is not the same as being able to replicate the finding for all villages in a province, for instance. And correspondingly for variables: to replicate a finding on variables that have very high inter-correlations is trivial. But we postpone further discussion of this to II, 5.4, where some suggestions will be made.

Finally there is case (4) where both dimensions of replication are used simultaneously. Case (4) should only be used in connection with cases (2) and (3), to guarantee against the obvious source of error that both kinds of extension (to new samples and to new variables) lead to findings completely different from the original one when applied one at the time; but that these discrepancies cancel out each other when they are both applied, so that we may end up with an impression of replication. When case (4) is added to cases (2) and (3) the total amount of replication becomes considerable, if the finding is extended to samples and variables that are sufficiently different from the sample and variable at the point of departure. But, as this shades over into multivariate analysis, we prefer to treat it there.

BIBLIOGRAPHY

1. Beshers, James M.: 'On "A Critique of Tests of Significance in Survey Research"', *ASR*, 1958, p.199.

2. Coleman, James S.: 'Statistical Problems', Appendix I-B in Seymour M. Lipset, Martin Trow, and James S. Coleman: *Union Democracy* (Glencoe: The Free Press, 1956), pp.427-432.

3. Davis, James A.: Review of *The Student Physician, AJS*, 1958, p.445f.

4. Guetzkow, Harold: Review of *Union Democracy, ASR*, 1957, p.245.

5. Gold: 'Comment on "A Critique of Tests of Significance"', *ASR*, 1958, pp.85f.

6. Kendall, Patricia L.: 'Note on Significance Tests', Appendix C in Robert K. Merton, George G. Reader, and Patricia L. Kendall (eds.): *The Student Physician* (Cambridge Harvard University Press, 1957), pp.301-305.

7. Kish, Leslie: 'Some Statistical Problems in Research Design', *ASR*, 1959, pp. 328-338.

8. Kish, Leslie: 'Confidence Intervals for Clustered Sampling', *ASR*, 1957, pp.154-165.

9. McGinnis, Robert: 'Randomization and Inference in Sociological Research', *ASR*, 1958, pp.408-414.

10. Selvin, Hanan: 'A Critique of Tests of Significance in Survey Research', *ASR*, 1957, pp.519-527.

11. Selvin, Hanan: 'Reply to Gold's Comment', *ASR*, 1958, p.86.

12. Selvin, Hanan: 'Reply to Beshers', *ASR*, 1958, pp.199f.

13. Selvin, Hanan: 'Durkheim's Suicide and Problems of Empirical Research', *AJS*, 1958, pp.607-619.

14. Selvin, Hanan: 'Statistical Significance and Sociological Theory', paper read at the annual meeting of the American Sociological Association, Chicago, 1959.

15. Selvin, Hanan: 'Appendix C', in *The Effects of Leadership* (Glencoe: The Free Press, 1960).

16. Sterling, T.D.: 'Publication Decisions and Their Possible Effects on Inference Drawn from Tests of Significance', *Journal of the American Statistical Association*, 1959, pp.30-34.

5. Analysis

The first steps

With data recorded and processed in a way that makes them amenable to analysis, the first steps will depend on the amount of specified hypotheses the analyst has. If there exists an elaborate network of hypotheses geared to the kind of data in possession, each hypothesis can be seen as a norm prescribing a certain action to be taken with the data. The more specific the hypothesis, the more specific the action. In this case, the analysis is an almost completely mechanical procedure: a question of getting the appropriate combinations of data and reading them off against the instructions for verification and falsification of the hypotheses. This, however, is a relatively rare case.

In most cases, data are collected more according to hunches than to hypotheses, and analyzed inductively more than deductively, by means of procedures discovered and invented during the process, not by means of a prescribed set of rules. Of the many ways of proceding, one way of starting is indicated here:

The point of departure is the selection of a *principal variable*. By this we mean a variable that is *theoretically important* as independent variable or dependent variable, or as both. In almost all cases, the variable will be what we have called a 'permanent variable', because it should be consensual, valid, and reliable, but it may be public or private. In some cases, background variables may do, as when the ideas is 'to run everything against sex to see what is in the data'. Another idea is to make use of an index that has been validated, whether it is an index based on public or private variables. The main requirement is that the variable shall be fundamental and interesting and worth-while as a point of departure. Psychologically, there is a good chance that the findings made with this variable will dominate one's focus for the rest of the analysis, so one has to be careful in the selection.

The next step is to see to it that the variable has a suitable number of values. In general, as mentioned in I, 4 and II, 3, *a good rule is to settle for three values,* 'high', 'medium', 'low' or something corresponding to this. This rule is based on the following lines of reasoning:

Arguments against only two values: First of all, with two values only, it is impossible to know whether a positive correlation between x and y is of the first, second, or third of the following types:

Table 5.1.1. *Three different interpretations of positive correlation*

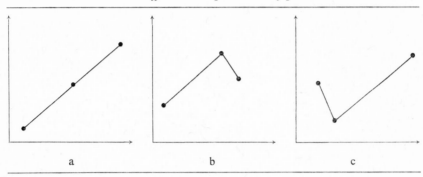

a   b   c

There may be a tremendous difference in interpretation, as can be seen by this simple example: the horizontal axis represents how far one has come in his studies at a university, the vertical axis represents satisfaction with own performance. Dichotomies would have blurred the differences between these diagrams completely.

Secondly, as has been shown in II, 2.2, percentage differences are the same (only with opposite sign) in a fourfold-table, but this is not true in general for a sixfold- or ninefold-table. This means that the latter tables yield much more information, because 'upper' and 'lower' percentage differences can be computed, compared, and the difference between them interpreted.

Arguments against more than three values: Of course, if there are more than three values, what has been said above is *a fortiori* true, because many more nuances can be caught. In general, this may be of value, but the present state of social science theory sets a limit for how valuable it actually is. Social science thinking can discriminate between the three curves shown in Table 5.1.1, but only rarely between all the different shapes that can emerge from an analysis based on more than three values of the variables. More work will be involved, and very often with rather quickly diminishing returns. The same applies to the argument about percentaging. But these ar-

391

guments are not arguments against more than three values in all cases or in general, only against more than three values when the first explorations of data are about to be done. Later on more discriminations may be necessary.

The data, thus, should be trichotomized and if possible in three parts of approximately the same size, to facilitate analysis. This is the most rational way of handling the data, since we do not in general know how the correlations will come out, and hence must be on guard in all directions against too small frequencies. Moreover, there is the need for a simple and parsimonious principle that does not tempt us to fix the cutting points so that higher correlations are obtained. There is also a third reason which will be discussed in 5.3.

As mentioned, this principal variable should be chosen so as to be located clearly at the left hand side of an imagined continuum of the variables in the study arranged from the most independent variables to the most dependent ones. This continuum enters at five points in the first phase of the analysis:

Table 5.1.2. *Some consequences of the independent-dependent distinction*

	Independent variable	Dependent variable
For ordering tables from the tabulator	write first the independent variable	then the dependent variable
For 'running' tables	sort first on independent variable	then on the dependent variable
For presenting tables	put the values of the independent variable horizontally	put the values of the dependent variable vertically
For percentaging tables	percentage vertically, with basis in the values of the independent variable	read off horizontally, from the values of the dependent variable
For making diagrams	put the values of the independent variable along the horizontal axis	put the frequency along the vertical axis, make one curve for each dependent value of any interest

The Table above is for the case of two variables, in other words for a low level kind of analysis. Of course, the rules are only meant as a guide line for routinizing work, to save the analyst time and extra work. However, they should not be taken too seriously. Thus, if the independent variable has more values than the dependent variable, it would be unwise not to sort first on the variable with fewer values, because this will involve fewer operations. Standard IBM machines will often present tables with the principal variable to the left, vertically.

We recommend presenting the independent variable horizontally for three reasons: it corresponds to the general pattern of 'X-axis-horizontal-independent; Y-axis-vertical-dependent' used in mathematics and statistics; it makes it possible to combine diagrammatic and tabular presentation; and the SUM 100% will come out at the bottom of the table, which is advantageous for control because it is easier to add numbers vertically than horizontally, and easier to read them horizontally.

Thus, the distinction between independent and dependent according to the hypotheses developed is crucial. For the first runs to be economical and efficient, the principal variable should be independent relative to as great a number of the other variables as possible without being trivial (thus there is little to be gained in general from runs against sex and age). If this is the case, we can have percentages calculated at once much more easily, because the basis for the percentaging will be the same through the whole set of variables. However, this saving is not so important that it should be obtained at the expense of introducing trivial combinations of variables.

The rules in Table 5.1.2 are easily adjusted to the case of more than two variables, provided it is possible to order the variables completely in terms of degrees of independence and dependence. Thus, imagine we have three variables, X, Y and Z in that order of independence (e. g., social class, authoritarianism, a foreign policy attitude). For *ordering tables* we simply would write:

Keep constant	Run from	Run to
X	Y	Z

or the same expressed in technical terms (majors and minors). This means asking the machine to produce one table for each value of X, each table showing the relation between Y and Z. In general, the runs should then be executed in this order as well, and the tables will look as follows (for the case of dichotomous variables):

Table 5.1.3. *Format for tables with three variables*

	$X = x_1$			$X = x_2$	
	$Y = y_1$	$Y = y_2$		$Y = y_1$	$Y = y_2$
$Z = z_1$			$Z = z_1$		
$Z = z_2$			$Z = z_2$		

The importance of this is only that percentaging is now carried out within each table as if it were a bivariate table, and all kinds of comparisons of corresponding percentages and of percentage differences can be performed. Thus, we can keep X constant and compare the effects Y has on Z for different levels of X, or we can keep Y constant and compare the effects X has on Z for different levels of Y. For the latter purpose, however, the tendencies are seen more clearly if X and Y change positions in the table. Thus, comparison of percentage differences becomes an important analytic tool in the tri- and generally multi-variate case, as will be mentioned in 4.5.3.

For the diagrammatic representation there is an important point to be made. With *three* variables and the frequency variable we actually have four variables, which shall all somehow be pressed onto the two-dimensional page. Obviously, something will have to be sacrificed. In the *two*-dimensional case what we do is to use the horizontal axis for the independent variable and the vertical axis as a frequency axis. We may then pick one value of the dependent variable and trace the percentage variation for each value of the independent variable. In the three-dimensional case we should do exactly the same, only with the addition of making one curve for each value of the *most* independent variable. Thus,

one value is picked, e.g. 'yes', of the *dependent variable*
the horizontal axis is used for the *intervening variable*
one curve is made for each value of the *independent variable*

For instance, we could make one curve for each of three social classes, each curve showing for each level of authoritarianism the percentage favoring nuclear weapons. Essentially the three-dimensional diagram has exactly the same relation to the two-dimensional diagram as the three-dimensional table to the two-dimensional table: it consists of as many two-dimensional diagrams as there are values of the most independent variable. Obviously, the curves will have to be distinguished from each other by the standard techniques of unbroken lines, broken lines and dots.

With four variables the matter becomes more complicated since there are actually five variables if we count the frequency variable. One idea would be to make as many tables of the kind described for three-variable analysis as there are values of the fourth variable. Another method would be to collapse two of the independent variables and make separate curves for, say, 'young males', 'old males', 'young females' and 'old females'. Still another method, hardly recommendable in general, is to try perspective drawing. Or, finally, what is probably the best, would be to superimpose the diagrams for various values of the fourth variable on each other so as to arrive at the

394

same type of diagram as described for three-various analysis, with the caution that one has to be very careful comparing the curves.

Thus, an enormous amount of information can be made quickly available to the analyst in standard formats that do not require any major mental effort. In this process, a combination of horizontal and vertical analysis, a kind of come-and-go process between the two major orientations, is recommendable. Often it may be preferable to start with horizontal analysis, study some patterns and develop indices, and then look at the distributions and develop parameters. But we may also look at the distributions to see how the items inter-correlate, and then develop indices. Only with a skillful interplay between horizontal and vertical analysis can we hope to extract from the data matrix the information it harbors, so as to get a basis for theory-formation.

And here the first steps will usually be of either or both of two kinds. First, by using one (or few) independent variables to see how they affect all dependent variables. And secondly, by doing the same on the dependent variable side: select one important variable and see how it relates to all independent variables. All this would involve bi-variate analysis only and will always be of importance in the first phases of an analysis. It should be emphasized that there is nothing wrong in these procedures, only that they are incomplete and if the analysis stops at that point, with the *consequences of one independent variable* and/or by exploring the *conditions for one dependent variable* then what one can safely say is that the data have not been fully utilized.

In this entire process the analytic element is always co-variation and the analytic atom, if one may use that expression, is the 2×2-table. In chapter 2 a number of principles have been given for the proper choice of tool to measure co-variation. The first steps of an analysis of a data matrix, then, should be directed towards a kind of inventory of the correlations in the data. We now turn to this topic.

5.2. *Covariation as analytical tool*

It can safely be said that the main analytical tool in social science investigations is *covariation*. Presence or absence of correlation between two variables, and the degree of presence, are the points of departure for most analyses beyond mere descriptions, and for these purposes the parameters discussed in II, 2.3 and the tests of the generalization hypotheses discussed in II, 4.4 are at the disposal of the analyst. As already mentioned in the preceding section, a mapping of correlations will always be among the first steps in an analysis.

There are two important points that should be kept in mind in connection with any analysis based on covariation techniques.

First of all, analysts must try to overcome the bias in favor of correlations and the neglect of zero correlations. There is a tendency to see only correlations as problematic and worthy of being 'explained' and to see absence of correlations as absence of 'findings', and hence as unproblematical. If there is no correlation between, say, sex and attitude to an important issue, an explanation is required just as much as when there is a correlation. If there is a correlation, differences in e.g. the percentage of yes'es may often be explained by invoking some differences in the roles of men and women, which is an example of the standard canon of research that differences are explained by means of other differences. But if there is no correlation, the general difference between men and women still remains and it is absolutely necessary to explain why it has not found an expression in that particular table. One cannot invoke a principle of explanation one moment, and forget about it when it no longer fits.

This is a general danger in social research and accentuated by the procedures for selecting questions and variables in general. Social research often gives an artificially dramatic and dissensual image of society, because variables that do not 'discriminate' are rejected.

Secondly, correlations may be present in various degrees. If the generalization hypothesis is found to be tenable there is still the question of how much the correlation means in terms of the theory. A correlation of five percentage points may be statistically significant, but theoretically without any real relevance. The point here is not the distinction made in II, 4.3 between the two kinds of hypotheses, however, but to avoid the frequent error of interpreting differences of five, fifty and ninety-five percentage points equally much as 'trends in the expected direction', with no effort to discriminate between strong and socially important correberations of an hypothesis and weak, socially uninteresting correlations. What social science analysis lacks most at the moment, is a language in which *degrees* of correlations can be expressed; a language which is stronger than ordinary prose, yet weaker than interval scale mathematics of functional relationships. But even if this language is presently lacking, care should be exercised not to try to make as much out of a table showing five percentage points as of one showing fifty percentage points, if they are otherwise similar.

With these two warnings, the question becomes which variables to select for correlation analysis. Since most analyses of this kind are done with individuals as units, one may use the simple typology of variables introduced in I, 1.4, but a similar typology was also developed for nations. The question is which pairs of variables we can combine with the hope of achieving anything at all – a question which can only be answered knowing the specific hypotheses the research is designed to explore. However, some ideas can be gained from this Table, which gives a new twist to the research models in I, 1.4:

Table 5.2.1. *Some possibilities for covariation analysis*

Dependent variable

		Background variable	Personality variable	Behavior elements
Independent variable	Background variable	(Social structure)	(Social psychology)	(Sociology)
	Personality variable		(Personality structure)	(Psychology)
	Behavior elements			(Structure of behavior elements)

In this nine-fold table three cells indicate impossible combinations. As already mentioned, there is usually a basic model underlying any analysis, and models that operate with for instance attitudes as independent and background data as dependent variables are rare, to say the least. This probably says more about how the terms 'independent' and 'dependent' are used, however, than about substantive matters.

In the other cells are put some terms that indicate where these types of analysis are typically found, with many reservations as to the validity of this scheme. But like most other schemes, it is more often right than wrong. The Table reveals the fundamental and unfortunate division of labor between sociologists and psychologists when it comes to analysing attitudes and behavior elements: the psychologists will typically study them in the light of personality variables, the sociologist in the light of structural or background variables, and account in different ways for the same variation. In a more integrated future social science, interdisciplinary work will probably consist not only in doing both, but of achieving some kind of unity in the schemes of analysis, that uses a combination of personality and structural variables and takes into account the interaction between them.

Along the main diagonal are shown combinations that yield the 'structure', i.e. the set of relations *within* a set of variables. Typically, one would get such results as how income is related to education, how intelligence is related to authoritarianism and how answers to two different questions in an interview are related. It should be noticed that there is a dangerous source of error here: one may get at *personality* structure by interrelating individual properties, but does one also get at *social* structure by interrelating individual characteristics? What about the kind of findings one would get by interrelating a number of variables describing total societies? We shall prefer to call that *society structure,* in analogy with the term personality structure, and use the term *social structure* for the structure of *a* society, as described by using the properties of the individuals in that society.[1]

The covariation techniques for main-diagonal and off-diagonal cells in Table 5.2.1 are somewhat different. When, for instance, a set of behavior elements, like the speech-reactions given in interviews, are correlated with each other, techniques like *factor analysis* can be used. Such techniques are meaningless unless they are based on a set of correlations of variables with themselves. For off-diagonal cells less forceful methods like the use of percentage differences may be useful. This leads to the question of which way the percentaging should be done, and the answer is given in II, 2.2.

Finally, let us point out an important source of error in covariation analysis: the confusion between *propensity* and *preponderance*. Imagine that a study of the desire to leave a community gives the following result:

Table 5.2.2. *The difference between propensity and preponderance*

	upper class	lower class	Total	Percentage difference
want to stay	40 %	60 %	58 %	−20 %
want to leave	60 %	40 %	42 %	+20 %
SUM	100 %	100 %	100 %	0 %
(N)	(30)	(300)	(330)	(330)

First of all, there is a correlation, and the direction is unmistakable. People in the upper classes have a stronger propensity to leave; many more than in the total sample want to leave. But the local observer, who does not have this Table, and does not know how to interpret, will protest and say: but *most* people who leave are low class people who do not have jobs! He is right, because he is referring to 120 low class people as against 18 potential movers in the upper classes. But the sociologist is also right when he says

398

that local conditions are such that the total effect yields more of an urge to leave in the upper classes than in the lower. He is talking about propensity, the local observer about preponderance in what he can observe daily. We suggest that this is a structure behind much misunderstanding between social scientists and laymen, and that the former should take great care in his presentation to avoid statements that can lead to this confusion.

In a sense, the problem of layman confusion of propensity with preponderance is also the problem of observational methods with no systematic data-collection in general. The sociologist who is a participant observer will also be exposed to sense-impressions, and simple counting of frequencies, consciously or unconsciously, will play a tremendous role. But he will not so easily 'see' correlations. It may be very difficult for him to correct for the feeling that preponderance must also imply some kind of propensity above what is average for the system he studies, and it is difficult to see how this can be corrected for except by means of systematic data, i.e. statistical data.

5.3. *Multivariate analysis*

The level of analysis, the depth of insights, and the subtlety of results in a survey analysis is above all a function of how many variables the analyst is able to handle simultaneously. Generally, we can distinguish between levels of analysis depending on how many variables are used at the time:

1st level: marginal distributions only – most useful if the purpose is estimation and simple description, not if the purpose is analysis.

2nd level: 'crossruns' only – indispensable for analysis, but usually insufficient if the goal is to find substantially new insights, not only rediscover old ones.

3rd level: a third variable is introduced and relations between two variables at the time are studied in the light of this variable; or one variable is studied as a function of the relation between the other two.

4th level: a fourth variable is introduced to study relations developed on the third level; or one pair of variables is used to study how another pair is interrelated, etc.

5th level: a fifth level is introduced to study relations developed on the fourth level, etc.

It is customary to call analysis on any level beyond the second level for 'multivariate analysis'. It is a good term because it points out that variables are treated together: subtlety is not obtained by means of many-variable analysis, one at a time, but possibly by means of multivariate analysis.[2]

The standard treatment of this important topic is rightly dominated by the important contributions of the Lazarsfeld school.[3] The basic consideration in this tradition are two simple points of departure from second level analysis:

(1) When two variables are correlated, it may nevertheless happen that the introduction of a third variable leads to the disappearance of this correlation.
(2) When two variables are uncorrelated, it may nevertheless happen that the introduction of a third variable leads to the appearance of correlations.

With the usual bias of the researcher in favor of correlations, the first experience is often a disappointing one, whereas the second experience ('elaboration of zero relationships') may be very pleasant. The reason why most of this analysis is carried out is usually to be able to talk about *causal* relations instead of only *probabilistic* relations. The difficulty is that we can infer nothing from bivariate analysis. In the Table:

Table 5.3.1. *Combinations of causal and probabilistic relations*

	Causal independence	Causal dependence
Stochastic independence	I *trivial*	II Nowak: TBC and mortality. Poverty and migration
Stochastic dependence	III numerous examples, e.g., storks and babies	IV *trivial*

all four combinations are possible. Quadrant II contains cases where two variables are clearly related, e.g. extreme poverty and a desire to leave, to migrate – but with a third variable intervening – e.g., space perspective: the extremely poor may be very low on space perspective, and hence deprived of a psychological condition for migration. Thus, a clear causal relationship (for most usages of the term 'causal') is masked by this third variable, which produces little or no correlation, in the final table.

Correspondingly, in quadrant III we have the cases where the correlation is due to something different from causal dependence. These bivariate correlations are often called 'spurious' which is a misnomer, because it indicates that causal relations are somehow 'finer' than stochastic relations. The Table shows that the two concepts are at least not related in any simple way. In addition, most analyses of causality endow the concept of 'causality' with many additional connotations (in addition to stochastic dependence under

400

certain 'ideal' conditions, e.g. when there is nothing 'masking' the relation) that are not easily satisfied in ordinary research. As Nowak points out,[4] even Lazarsfeld-Kendall's definition where stochastic dependence can only be accepted as indicative of a causal relation if it holds 'for all possible relevant test factors as third variables', is too wide. The relation must also hold for all *combinations* of test factors, for instance. The amount of work this implies is hardly conducive to the full acceptance of the definition. Thus, it may well be that the concept of 'causality' is on its way out in social analysis and will be replaced by statements indicating functional relationships 'when X increases, so does Y', and theories relating such statements. (see II, 6.3)

But multivariate analysis should not be given the narrow definition of being a step on the difficult road from statement about stochastic relations to statements about causal relations. We have already indicated more fruitful ways of conceiving of it, and turn now to the problem of a complete survey of multivariate research strategies.

Here, the distinction between symmetric and asymmetric models for the relationship between the variables is crucial. If we have a set of n variables, we may want to regard a cluster of k of them as independent and look at how the $n-k$ remaining variables depend on them. Thus, we may be interested in how the correlation between behavioral and attitudinal integration in university life depends on sex and phase in the studies (whether the student is in the beginning, the middle or the end of his studies). In this case $n = 4$ and $k = 2$. The distinction is best known in the case of $n = 2$, $k = 1$ – which is the case discussed throughout the literature – but we shall extend this basis.

The complete list is shown in Table 5.3.2.

A simple notation may be introduced for these strategies. Thus, 4 stands for level 4, 4.2 for level 4 with two variables kept constant, and 4.2.1 for level four with two variables kept constant and one variable kept constant among the remaining two.

The logic behind this scheme is as follows.

At the first level all that can be done is 'distribution analysis', i.e. calculation of proportions, means, etc. But at the second level there are already two models at one's disposal: the symmetric where no variable is singled out as independent, and the asymmetric. In the symmetric case, regular correlation analysis with suitable coefficients of correlation is carried out. In the asymmetric case, one also does covariation analysis, i.e. finds out how the values of one variable depends on the other. But the measures are asymmetric, e.g. percentage differences. These three types belonging to the first and second levels have all been treated extensively in II, 2.

Table 5.3.2. *Multivariate research strategies*

Total number of variables (level of analysis)		No. of variables kept constant	To be done with the other variables	Type
1	(1st level)	0	distribution analysis	1.0
2	(2nd level)	0	correlation analysis	2.0
		1	first level analysis	2.1
3	(3rd level)	0	correlation analysis	3.0
		1	second level analysis	3.1
		2	first level analysis	3.2
4	(4th level)	0	correlation analysis	4.0
		1	third level analysis	4.1
		2	second level analysis	4.2
		3	first level analysis	4.3
5	(5th level)	0	correlation analysis	5.0
		1	fourth level analysis	5.1
		2	third level analysis	5.2
		3	second level analysis	5.3
		4	first level analysis	5.4

With the third level, multi-variate analysis proper begins, and the first possibility is trivariate analysis based on total, multiple, and partial correlation as known from textbooks in general statistics. Characteristic of this analysis, which can be repeated at any level, is that *no variable is kept constant*. A partial correlation coefficient between x and y 'with z constant' is a weighted average of the correlations between x and y for $z = z_1$, $z = z_2$, etc. *But even though this information is useful, it is usually too crude for social science analysis.* It is interesting to know that the obvious relation between a modern attitude and the tendency to favor few children per family decreases when 'age is kept constant', but much more interesting to know that the correlation only disappears for the young age groups, not for the older. To arrive at this type of result one has to use strategy 3.1 – really keeping one variable constant and seeing how the other two behave as a function of that variable. This can be done according to either of the two models at the second level; what matters is that the covariation between them is studied explicitly as a function of the variable kept constant – not implicitly as in the techniques of partial correlation.

The difference between strategies 3.1 and 3.0 is actually the same as between strategy 2.1 and 2.0. In 2.1 one of the variables is kept constant and the distribution of the other is studied, then these distributions are compared (often by subtracting percentages). In 2.0 such a comparison is also carried out and presented as a correlation coefficient; this gives the total picture but masks the details of the variation from one value of the constant variable to the other. The parallel actually goes further: we have shown (II, 2.2) how a correlation coefficient like Goodman-Kruskal's gamma can be seen as a kind of average of a number of percentage differences.

Finally, at the third level, one may keep two variables constant and for each combination study the distribution of the third level variable, i.e. do first level analysis of the third variable. This is what is done when acceptance of technical assistance is seen as a function of degree of development *and* international allegiance, etc.

At the fourth level the first strategy is correlation analysis of the traditional kind. Then follows the strategy where one variable is kept constant, and with the remaining three variables any one of the third level strategies may be used. More frequent types of fourth level analyses are probably found in strategy 4.2: the covariation between two variables is seen as a function of two other variables. As strategy 4.3, then, one has the case of distribution analysis in a framework provided by three variables kept constant.

The fifth level is rarely used, but the logic is the same.

To get an image of what all this means in practice, let us calculate the number of strategies with n variables, $N(n)$. Table 5.3.2 yields:

$$N(n) = N(1) + N(2) + \ldots + N(n-1) + 1, N(1) = 1$$

This means that

$$N(n) = N(n-1) + [N(1) + N(2) + \ldots N(n-2) + 1] = 2N(n-1)$$

or simply (but some of them will differ only in emphasis):

$$N(n) = 1 + 2 + \ldots + 2^{n-2} + 1 = 2^{n-1}$$

Thus, at level 4 there are eight strategies (one of the type 4.0, one 4.3, two 4.2 and 4 of the type 4.1), and at level 5 sixteen strategies.

But this number is only a small beginning. The total number of strategies up to and including level n is

$$S(n) = \sum_{i=1}^{n} N(n) = \sum_{i=1}^{n} 2^{n-1} = 2^n - 1$$

Thus, with four variables there are fifteen strategies. Then, for each strategy there are several possibilities, depending on which of the n variables are given the different roles prescribed by the strategy. Thus, in an analysis at the fourth level, strategy 4.1, X may appear as one of the variables to be kept constant, or in the dependent part in three possible roles. Finally, add to this (or rather multiply) that in surveys there is usually a quite high number of variables: hence, the number of groups of four variables that can be selected for analyses up to and including the fourth level is considerable. There is no sense in trying to calculate this number, however, since a number of combinations will have to be excluded because of rules of what is considered independent and what is considered dependent.

Obviously, the variables chosen to be kept constant will, relatively speaking, be on the independent side. But this does not mean that there will not be independent variables among the remaining ones. Thus, in strategy 4.2.1 one first sets aside two relatively independent variables, and then, among the other two, makes use of a remaining asymmetry. If one is interested in where students sit in class as a function of perceived integration one has analysis of type 2.1; if this again is seen as a function of sex and phase the analysis obviously is of type 4.2.1.

To repeat and clarify:

In the Table we have analyzed research strategies in terms of independent and dependent parts; in other words: in terms of studying 'how something depends on something else'. As 'independent part' is always taken either one variable or a combination of variables. By the latter we simply mean the cartesian product space of two, three, or four variables, as when we operate with the four categories 'young males', 'young females', 'old males' and 'old females'. It should be noticed that product spaces are very often reduced to a one-dimensional variable by means of an index, but an index based on five items or indicators is *one* variable, not five.

As dependent parts in the Table are taken single variables or correlations. When we say that we want to study 'one variable' as a function of the combination of the other two, what we mean is actually that we want to study the *distribution* on this variable as a function of the other two. If this single variable is dichotomous, the whole problem may consist in comparing the percentages of yes's for all combinations of the other two variables, which is a very standard procedure.

When we have more variables at our disposal, however, we may want to go one step further, and see how they correlate – and these correlations may be taken as functions of combinations of one, two or three of the other variables. Thus, we can always add new dimensions to our research, and possibly new insights, provided it is skillfully done. Of the techniques listed in the Table the *last* technique mentioned for each level is very commonly found, with the elaboration on the independent side. Many of the other techniques are not so often found, especially techniques involving correlations as dependent parts in the analysis. There is one exception to this though:

strategies of the kind 3.1, 4.2, 5.3 − n. n−2 which are the classical procedures in the Lazarsfeld tradition. If Nowak's advice should be taken really seriously, this should lead to a high number of analyses where the dependent part consists of the correlations between two variables, and the independent part consists of all combinations of two, three etc. other variables; to test for spuriousness. And that would bring in the remaining strategies.

Multi-variate analysis with more than five variables is hardly practicable − it is found in the literature, but the intricacies very easily exceed what the human mind can follow without the guidance of tools like mathematics, symbolic logic and computers.

To study this more closely, let us take the simplest of all cases of multi-variate analysis (3.1); where we have three variables, all dichotomies, and study how the relation between two of them (x and y) vary when we introduce the third, t. We call the two values of t t_1 and t_2 and get:

Table 5.3.3. *Third level multi-variate analysis* (strategy 3.1)
Third variable (test factor)

$$
\begin{array}{ccc}
 & t_1 & t_2 \\
x_1\ x_2 & x_1\ x_2 & x_1\ x_2
\end{array}
$$

$$
\begin{array}{c}
y_1 \\
y_2
\end{array}
\begin{pmatrix} a & b \\ c & d \end{pmatrix}
=
\begin{pmatrix} a_1 & b_1 \\ c_1 & d_1 \end{pmatrix}
+
\begin{pmatrix} a_2 & b_2 \\ c_2 & d_2 \end{pmatrix}
$$

$$
(N) \quad = \quad (N_1) \quad + \quad (N_2)
$$

For instance, x may be social class, y may be incidence of illness and t one of the most favored test-factors: age (e. g., to test the hypothesis that class is important for illness at low age, but not later; when the first more exposed years have passed class differences may disappear).

From this Table we may reconstruct the relationship between x and t and between y and t:

$$
\begin{array}{c}
t_1 \\
t_2
\end{array}
\begin{array}{cc}
x_1 & x_2 \\
\left(a_1+c_1 \right. & \left. b_1+d_1 \right) \\
\left(a_2+c_2 \right. & \left. b_2+d_2 \right)
\end{array}
\qquad
\begin{array}{c}
t_1 \\
t_2
\end{array}
\begin{array}{cc}
y_1 & y_2 \\
\left(a_1+b_1 \right. & \left. c_1+d_1 \right) \\
\left(a_2+b_2 \right. & \left. c_2+d_2 \right)
\end{array}
$$

We shall then see what happens to the correlation between x and y when the third factor is introduced. The difficulty lies in the choice between measures of correlation (see II, 2.3) for fourfold tables:

0. δ: $\qquad \dfrac{ad-bc}{N}$

1. τ_a:
$$\frac{ad-bc}{\binom{N}{2}}$$

2. $\tau_b = \varphi = r_\varphi$:
$$\frac{ad-bc}{\sqrt{(a+b)(c+d)(a+c)(b+d)}}$$

3. τ_c:
$$\frac{ad-bc}{\frac{N^2}{4}}$$

4. $\gamma = Q$:
$$\frac{ad-bc}{ad+bc}$$

5. $d_\%$:
$$\frac{ad-bc}{(a+c)(b+d)}$$

The simplest of all these expressions is the δ, so we shall follow the tradition and find the relation in terms of this measure. Actually, the simple cross-product with no denominator is even simpler, but there is no reason to believe that a simple relation should exist between all the cross-products since they are so dependent on the N.

We get:

$$\delta = a - \frac{(a+b)(a+c)}{N} \; ; \; \delta_1 = a_1 - \frac{(a_1+b_1)(a_1+c_1)}{N_1} \; ;$$

$$\delta_2 = a_2 - \frac{(a_2+b_2)(a_2+c_2)}{N_2}$$

for the total and the partials, and for the marginals:

$$\delta_{xt} = (a_1+c_1) - \frac{(a+c)N_1}{N}, \; \delta_{yt} = (a_1+b_1) - \frac{(a+b)N_1}{N}$$

We shall now give the formula developed by Yule and Kendall for the relation between the δ's, but shall try to motivate the steps. The task is to find the simplest possible relationship between these five quantities, using the high number of simple additive relationships that exist between the frequencies. Since four of them are given in terms of the total and the first partial and the numbers from the second partial only appear in δ_2 the first task is to write δ_2 in terms of the first partial. This is best done in the following way:

$$\delta_1+\delta_2 = (a_1+a_2) - \frac{1}{N_1N_2}[(N-N_1)(a_1+b_1)(a_1+c_1)$$
$$+ N_1((a+b)-(a_1+b_1))((a+c)-(a_1+c_1))]$$

Inside the parenthesis two terms cancel, and we get:

406

$$\delta_1 + \delta_2 = a - \frac{N}{N_1 N_2} \left[(a_1 + b_1)(a_1 + c_1) - \frac{N_1(a+b)(a_1+c_1)}{N} \right.$$
$$\left. - \frac{N_1(a+c)(a_1+b_1)}{N} + \frac{N_1(a+b)(a+c)}{N} \right]$$

If we now compare what is inside the square brackets with the product of δ_{xt} and δ_{yt} we see that we are already very close. The first three terms are 'correct', but the last ought to be $N_1^2/N^2(a+b)(a+c)$. By adding the expression:

$$\frac{N(a+b)(a+c)}{N^2} - \frac{N_1(a+b)(a+c)}{N} \cdot \frac{N}{N} = - \frac{N_1 N_2(a+b)(a+c)}{N^2}$$

inside the brackets and subtracting it $\left(\text{multiplied by the factor} - \dfrac{N}{N_1 N_2}\right)$ outside, we get:

$$\delta_1 + \delta_2 = a - \frac{(a+b)(a+c)}{N} - \frac{N}{N_1 N_2} \left[\left((a_1 + c_1) \right. \right.$$
$$\left. \left. - \frac{(a+c)N_1}{N} \right) \left((a_1 + b_1) - \frac{(a+b)N_1}{N} \right) \right]$$

which, not quite by coincidence, reduces to:

$$\delta_1 + \delta_2 = \delta - \frac{N}{N_1 N_2} \delta_{xt} \cdot \delta_{yt}$$

or

$$\delta = \delta_1 + \delta_2 + \frac{N}{N_1 N_2} \delta_{xt} \cdot \delta_{yt}$$

The total is here expressed as a sum of the partials and the product of the marginals, multiplied by a simple factor.

Given this relationship, which Lazarsfeld has made famous among sociologists, it is easy to get the corresponding relationships among the other measures of correlation. Some of them are given below:

(1) $\tau_a = \dfrac{\delta}{\dfrac{N-1}{2}} = \dfrac{N_1 - 1}{N-1} \tau_{a1} + \dfrac{N_2 - 1}{N-1} \tau_{a2} + \dfrac{N(N-1)}{2 \cdot N_1 N_2} \tau_{axt} \cdot \tau_{ayt}$

(2) $\tau_b = \dfrac{N \cdot \delta}{\sqrt{(a+b)(c+d)(a+c)(b+d)}}$

(3) $\tau_c = \dfrac{\delta}{\dfrac{N}{4}} = \dfrac{N_1}{N} \tau_{c1} + \dfrac{N_2}{N} \tau_{c2} + \dfrac{N^2}{4 N_1 N_2} \tau_{cxt} \cdot \tau_{cyt}$

(4) $\quad Q = \dfrac{N\delta}{ad+bc}$

(5) $\quad d_\% = \dfrac{N\delta}{(a+c)(b+d)} = \dfrac{N}{N_1}\,\dfrac{(a_1+c_1)(b_1+d_1)}{(a+c)(b+d)}\,d_{\%1}$

$$+ \dfrac{N}{N_2}\,\dfrac{(a_2+c_2)(b_2+d_2)}{(a+c)(b+d)}\,d_{\%2} + d_{\%tx}\cdot d_{\%yt}$$

or, as the last term $\dfrac{N_1 N_2}{(a+c)(b+d)}\,d_{\%xt}\cdot d_{\%yt}$

depending on the order in which we put t; as intervening or as antecedent to both x and y. The simplest formulas are obtained for the coefficients that are least useful in analytical work, the τ_a and the τ_c. Actually, another simple formula is the formula for the covariance:

$$C = \frac{\delta}{N} = \frac{\tau_c}{4}$$

$$C_{xy} = \frac{N_1}{N}\,C_{xy1} + \frac{N_2}{N}\,C_{xy2} + \frac{N_1 N_2}{N^2}\,C_{xt}\cdot C_{yt}$$

where the total covariance is the sum of the weighted average of the partial covariances and a weighted product of the marginal covariances. However, the covariance is not a correlation coefficient, but the equation is nevertheless useful since it tells us everything about the signs of the correlations.

The formulas for $d_\%$, tau_b and Q become quite complex for calculation. There is a difference between them, however. The formulas for the percentage difference and for tau_b can be discussed since the coefficients are constant if the marginals of the five distributions are constant. If they vary, a systematic discussion becomes very complex. For Q, however, the situation is more difficult for the coefficients involve expressions of the form $ad+bc$. One cannot require this to be constant and still discuss the relationship between Q, Q_1, Q_2, Q_{xt} and Q_{yt} since the variation that makes this discussion worth while will also alter the coefficients.

The formula for the percentage difference is actually the least vulnerable one of the three, for only eight marginals are involved (we assume in the formula that x is more independent than y and t more independent than either, otherwise the formulas will have to be changed to account for the direction of percentaging). We count this as an additional advantage of the percentage difference. The formula actually becomes very symmetric if we multiply with $(a+c)(b+d)$ on both sides.

Before we proceed discussing these formulas it may be worth while to verify that they work, and for that purpose a very simple example will be studied (Table 5.3.4).

408

Table 5.3.4. *Testing formulas for relations between correlation measures*

		$x_1\ x_2$		$x_1\ x_2$		$x_1\ x_2$		$x_1\ x_2$		$t_1\ t_2$
Data	y_1	$\begin{pmatrix} 8 & 3 \\ 2 & 7 \end{pmatrix}$	$=$	$\begin{pmatrix} 5 & 2 \\ 1 & 3 \end{pmatrix}$	$+$	$\begin{pmatrix} 3 & 1 \\ 1 & 4 \end{pmatrix}$	t_1	6 5	y_1	7 4
	y_2						t_2	4 5	y_2	4 5
				$t = t_1$		$t = t_2$				

	Total	*Partials*		*Marginals*	
(N)	(20)	(11)	(9)	(20)	(20)
% difference	50	43	55	10 (x indep.) 11 (t indep.)	20 (t indep.)
Cross-product	50	13	11	10	19
$\delta = \dfrac{ad - bc}{N}$	2.5	1.18	1.22	0.5	0.95
$C = \dfrac{\delta}{N}$	0.125	0.107	0.136	0.025	0.0475
$\tau_c = \dfrac{\dfrac{\delta}{N}}{4} = 4C$	0.5	0.429	0.542	0.100	0.1900

$$\delta = 1.18 + 1.22 + \frac{20}{11.9}\, 0.5 \cdot 0.95 \approx 2.5$$

$$C = \frac{11}{20}\, 0.107 + \frac{9}{20}\, 0.136 + \frac{20^2}{11.9}\, 0.025 \cdot 0.0475 \approx 0.125$$

$$\tau_c = \frac{11}{20}\, 0.432 + \frac{9}{20}\, 0.544 + \frac{20^2}{4.11.9}\, 0.1 \cdot 0.19 \approx 0.5$$

$$d_{\%} = \frac{20}{11}\ \frac{6.5}{10.10}\, 0.44 + \frac{20}{9}\ \frac{4.5}{10.10}\, 0.55 + 0.10 \cdot 0.20 \approx 0.50$$

$$d_{\%} = \frac{20}{11} \cdot \frac{6.5}{10.10}\, 0.44 + \frac{20}{9}\ \frac{4.5}{10.10}\, 5.50 + \frac{11.9}{10.10}\, 0.11 \cdot 0.20 \approx 0.50$$

For percentage differences we have used both formulas, depending on whether we percentage with basis in x or in t in the first marginal.

All these formulas have the same form. The parameter for the total distribution is expressed as a sum with two components; the first component is the (weighted) *sum* of the parameters for the two *partials,* the second component is the (weighted) *product* of the parameters for the two *marginals.* Since all weights include frequencies they have to be positive, which means that one can discuss the signs entirely in terms of the parameters. If we say

409

that the 'Total is the Sum of Partials plus the Product of Marginals' then we capture the essential content of the equations. Here, the total, the sum and the product may be 0, positive or negative which gives a total of 27 combinations. Out of these combinations only 13 are possible, however. Thus, if the total is 0, then there are only three possibilities: both the sum and the product must be 0, or one of them must be positive and the other negative. When the total is positive there are five possibilities: One of them may be positive and the other one any of the three; and correspondingly for the case when the total is negative. However, with 13 combinations possible there is still considerable variety.

The reader is referred to the discussions by Lazarsfeld and Hyman for analyses of the interdependence between these quantities. We are less concerned with that type of discussion (1) because this is only one out of the many types of multivariate analysis (type 3.1), (2) because the concern with causation, we feel, is exaggerated for reasons to be made more explicit in 6.3 and (3) because in practical analysis the marginals will be analysed apart, according to types 2.0 or 2.1, and the analysis of type 3.1 will be focussed on how the covariation depends on the independent variable, in other words on how the partials vary with t more than on how the covariation is caught by the marginals. But before we proceed it should be noticed how the relative importance of the partials and the marginals depends on how N is divided into N_1 and N_2: the product $N_1 N_2$ attains its maximum value when $N_1 = N_2$ which means that under equipartition the relative contribution of the marginals to δ will be least.

The combinations of interest in standard analysis of the 3.1 type are found in Table 5.3.5 (we do not consider time relations).

Table 5.3.5. *Theoretical combinations in type 3.1 analysis*

		Partial correlations		
		same		different
		0	not 0	
Total correlation	0	'correlation *not masked* by third factor'	'correlation *masked* by third factor'	'*elaboration* of zero relationship'
	not 0	'*detection* of spurious relationship'	'correlation *maintained*, not spurious'	'*specification* of relationship'

In the Table some speech habits are indicated, mainly from Hyman and Lazarsfeld, but they should be used with some caution. The Table would have been much simpler if it were possible to rule out some combinations, but this is not possible. Thus, the sum of partials can be positive and the total be zero, because, as indicated above, the product of marginals may be negative. And if the sum of partials is positive, they *may* also, by some coincidence of all the frequencies, be equal. Correspondingly, the partials may be different from 0 even when the total is equal to zero. The six cases correspond to the discussion in the beginning of this section.

It should be noted that it is very rare indeed that the introduction of a 'test factor' leads to partials that are the same for the values of the test factor – whether this 'same' is 0 or not 0. In general the partials will be different and the practical possibilities are whether (1) the partials are all less in absolute value than the total, in which case we may say that the correlation has not been maintained and that there is indication of spuriousness (with respect to that test factor) or (2) some partials are greater than the total or no partials are smaller, in which case the correlation has been maintained and there is no indication of spuriousness (again, with respect to that test factor). In both cases it may be worth-while to see whether the partials increase, decrease, or remain constant with increasing values of the test factor – and to see this the test factor should at least be a trichotomy. Thus, in practice we get these combinations:

Table 5.3.6. *Practical combinations in type 3.1 analysis*

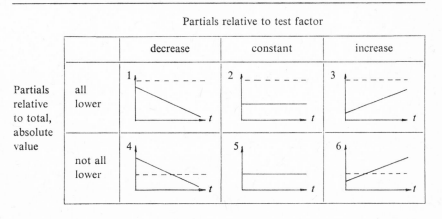

In all these cases the three-variate analysis has in a sense been reduced to bivariate analysis: the independent variable is *t* and the dependent variable is the covariation between x and y. In addition there is a point of reference (the broken line), the covariation between x and y for the total, regardless of the value of t. In the upper line diagrams the partials are below the point of reference, in the lower row not all partials are below. Of course, one may also have all partials above.

The trouble is that we now are close to talking about spuriousness in two senses: a theoretical one which usually only obtains with contrived data where all partials are equal to zero, and a more practical case where the only requirement is that they should be lower in absolute value – that the correlation is not maintained, in other words. But instead of trying to reconcile these two concepts we prefer to say that the analyst will have to take both dimensions in Table 5.3.6 into account. Both the trend in the partials and their size relative to the total are of interest and should be considered. The traditional scheme of analysis has a tendency to focus the attention on cases 2 and 5 only, whereas the cases where the correlation between the two dependent variables show a consistent trend as a function of the independent variable are perhaps even more rewarding. Particulary dramatic is the case where the partials change sign with t.[5]

Let us then look at a subcase of type 3.1, type 3.1.1. In this case there is still only one independent variable. But the two dependent variables no longer satisfy the conditions for an analysis of type 2.0 with symmetric measures of associations or covariation. One variable is less dependent than the other, and may perhaps be referred to as intervening. Thus, imagine the three variables are age, education, and degree of modernism. If 'education' means some kind of self-training like courses of correspondence the individual has engaged in out of his own initiative, then it may perhaps best be classified as dependent variable, and an appropriate type of analysis would be 3.1. If education means basic schooling in the sense known in the developed countries, then it may safely be put down as an independent variable together with age, and the type of analysis would be 3.2. And finally, if it means some kind of basic schooling but is highly age-dependent, it may be better to regard it as an intervening variable.

In this case we would analyse how modernism depends on education, which is an analysis of type 2.1 with asymmetric association measures, usually percentage differences and their generalization. But in addition to that we would study how this measure of association depends on the independent variable, age. Since the association measure used is a percentage difference, this amounts to a study of how a set of percentage differences varies with the independent variable – which brings us back to the formulas developed and Tables 5.3.5 and 5.3.6. Thus, the only difference between analysis of type 3.1.1 and of type 3.1 is that, in the former, asymmetric measures of association are used; in the latter, symmetric measures. Actually, percentage differences can also be used in the symmetric cases, especially if the two dependent variables are dichotomies. And one may, of course, also use symmetric measures in asymmetric cases although it is hardly recommendable – the symmetric measures yield so little information.

We now turn to a considerably less explored case, the type of analysis which here is referred to as type 3.2. In this case two variables are used to provide a space of combinations, and the distribution on the third variable is seen as a function of the points in that two-dimensional space. To get a concentrated expression the distribution on the third variable should be reduced to one single parameter. One possibility is the percentage who have given a specific answer or have some specific characteristic. Another possibility is some measure of the central tendency, still another possibility is one of the many measures of dispersion. Whatever measure is used it must be comparable for all points in the twodimensional space provided by the two independent variables. Thus, frequencies cannot be used, but proportions or percentages or arithmetic means or any measure that does not reflect (or has been corrected for) differences in the total number for each combination of the independent variables can be used (but with care, since there are upper limits of 1 and 100%).

What we get is:

Table 5.3.7. *Formats for type 3.2 analysis*

	First independent variable, X						
	1	2	... r_1				
	1 z_{11} z_{21} ... z_{r_11}				x	$\bar{x}$	Difference
	2 z_{12} z_{22} ... z_{r_12}			y	a	b	$a-b$
Second independent variable, Y	. . .		.	$\bar{y}$	c	d	$c-d$
	. . .		.				
	. . .		.	Differ-	$a-c$	$b-d$	$(a+d)-(b+c)$
	r_2 z_{1r_2} z_{2r_2} ... $z_{r_1r_2}$			ence			

The first Table is the general format, the second Table is for the special case where the two independent variables are dichotomies.

The general reflection of anyone with some training in elementary statistics is that this Table should lend itself to *analysis of variance* techniques. In general, analysis of variance is used when there is one dependent variable and any number of independent variables, which would be the case for all multi-variate analyses of the type *n. n−1*; 3.2, 4.3, 5.4 etc. (Similarly, analysis of covariance would be appropriate for types $n \cdot n - 2$). But analysis of variance is actually based on five assumptions:

(1) *the dependent variable is interval scale* (the independent variables can have any level of measurement)
(2) *arithmetic means are accepted as measures of average effect, and variances as measures of variation in effect* (for instance for each column or each row in the left hand table in table 5.3.7)
(3) *replications of the table would yield distributions in the z_{ij}* that would
    (a) be *normal*
    (b) be mutually *independent*
    (c) be *homoscedastic* (have the same dispersion).

For the testing of generalization hypotheses the conditions under (3) should be satisfied for the statistic to have the F-distribution, but research also indicates that the conditions may be relatively far from satisfied and the distribution will nevertheless (under the conditions of the null hypothesis) be satisfactorily close to F. However, this is not our concern. Neither is point no. (1), since proportions, percentages or arithmetic means all are interval scale. We are more worried about condition no. (2) which seems to be unquestioningly accepted by most researchers applying this methodology. There are many measures of dispersion and they all reflect different aspects of the distribution – hence we feel any use of analysis of variance techniques in this case should be theoretically justified on the grounds that variance is the measure that best reflects the variation or dispersion in the data. If this can be done and the other conditions are satisfied, the analysis of variance is an extremely powerful technique that is the logical answer to type 3.2 analysis in particular, and type $n \cdot n - 1$ analysis in general.[6]

However, it may be worth-while looking into some other procedures. Thus, in the highly simplified right hand part of Table 5.3.6 imagine that a, b, c, and d stand for percentages, means, or dispersions, and hence are an expression of what that particular combination of variables X and Y is able to produce of effect in terms of the third and dependent variable. As indicated, four differences may be computed measuring the effect of one of the variables, keeping the other constant. Thus, if we accept a, b, c, and d as good measures of the effect, and they have interval scale properties, then we should also accept the difference as a measure of variation in effect – whereas the square of the difference relative to the mean would introduce considerable artificiality.

We can then compute the difference between the differences, which would be a measure of how variation in one independent variable affects the effect the other independent variable has on the dependent variable. And we get

414

the same expression for the difference between the differences regardless of which differences we compare: the expression is the sum of the main diagonal minus the sum of the bidiagonal. The difference between the differences is a measure of how the two independent variables interact in producing changes in the dependent variable. Thus, if it is equal to zero, then the effect of one variable does not depend on the value of the second variable, which means that there is no interaction between the two independent variables. And this relation is symmetric: if X does not change Y's effect on Z, neither does Y change X's effect on Z.

But this is not the only possible measure of interaction between two independent variables. One might also reason as follows. When X and Y are not present, then the result is d; if X occurs the result is c, if Y occurs the result is b, if both occur the result is a. The problem is whether both together contribute more than one would have predicted from the joint effects of either, but taken one at the time; and *how* to predict the effects.

Using addition and multiplication there are now two ways of proceeding if one wants to build up a from d, using the effects of the variables, but one at the time: one may use an additive model or a multiplicative model.

Table 5.3.8. *The study of interaction effects in type 3.2 analysis*

	Additive model	Multiplicative model
effect of X	$c-d$	$\dfrac{c}{d}$
effect of Y	$b-d$	$\dfrac{b}{d}$
'predicted joint value' for both X and Y, a'	$d + (c-d) + (b-d) = a'$	$d\,\dfrac{cb}{dd} = a'$
Interaction	$a-a' = (a+d) - (b+c)$	$a:a' = \dfrac{ad}{bc}$

In the first case we get the difference between the differences as developed above; in the second case we get the cross-product ratio. Both of them have a certain standing as interaction measures.

The difference between interaction and association (co-variation) between X and Y should be noted. The former is meaningful only if there is a third variable, for the latter no third variable is needed. Moreover, we can have interaction between X and Y in their effects on Z whether X and Y are associated or not, and X and Y may be correlated and yet not interact in their effect on Z. Also, it should be noted that we do not assume a, b, c, and d to be measures of central tendency. They may be other parameters of one-dimensional distributions, such as dispersion. If all four dispersions are equal we have a case of *homoscedasticity,* if they are not equal we have *heteroscedasticity* – and analysis of type 3.2 is excellent for the analysis of these properties (that also can be analyzed in type 2.1).

When is the additive model appropriate and when the multiplicative model? That can only be decided knowing the nature of the variables, but the discussion is the same as the discussion about the relative virtues of per-centage differences and percentage ratios in II, 2.2. We have stuck to the additive model and used percentage differences rather than percentage ra-tios, but for no other reason than (1) they are simpler, (2) most researchers use them. Admittedly, this is a very weak rationale.

What would happen if one changed models during the race, so to speak? It would not make much sense, but if, for instance, in the right hand column instead of calculating a/a' one used $a - a'$ as an expression of to what extent X and Y together produce something different from what one would get if one took their effects one at the time, then one would get $(ad - bc)/d$; a cross-product divided by the point of departure, d.

One could also speculate that the effect of one of the variables should be measured not by means of one column alone but by means of the marginals. Thus, the effect of X may be put equal to $(a + c)/(b + d)$ and the effect of Y equal to $(a + b)/(c + d)$ and if the multiplicative model is used for this ex-pression, then one gets $[a(b + d)(c + d)]/[d(a + b)(a + c)]$. If the additive model is used, one would get $[(d - a)(ad - bc)]/[(b + d)(c + d)]$. Here the cross-product is appearing again and the expression reminds one of percentage differences. However, the two measures in Table 5.3.8 are more attractive, partly be-cause they are simpler, partly because they are based on the same model throughout, and partly because they do not confound the effects of X present and X absent or the effect of Y present and Y absent by using marginals.

The difficulty is only that the formulas do not apply in the general case in Table 5.3.7. More complicated tables can of course be reduced to four-fold-tables by collapsing values or discounting all but the two extreme values on both variables. This may be of great help, but the lack of generality is deplorable. In such cases analysis of variance will be helpful, if one is willing to accept its assumptions.

However, the formulas may be generalized. And there is also another way out that probably corresponds just as well to the practice of most data analysts: the graphic representation, which will be useful in any case and

416

particularly if one of the variables is still a dichotomy. According to the rules on p.392 one would use the horizontal axis for X (which we, for simplicity, assume is a trichotomy – but this is no necessity), the vertical axis for Z and then make one curve for each value of Y, which we imagine is a dichotomy ($r_2 = 2$ in Table 5.3.7). Table 5.3.9 shows possible outcomes.

These cases all have one unrealistic assumption in common: that the curves representing the variation in the dependent variable for all values of X and one value of Y are straight lines. For that reason these cases are ideal types to show the principles. And the assumption becomes less unrealistic when one realizes that for analysis the differences are more important than the z's. Obviously, there is interaction between X and Y only in cases V and VI, because these are the only cases where the variation of one independent variable influences the effect the second independent variable has on the dependent variable: the differences vary. Actually, case VI is only a subcase under case V, but a rather dramatic subcase since the differences vary from positive to negative (or vice versa – we could of course have reversed the inequality signs and the slopes of the lines).

In the first case neither variable has any effect on Z, in the second case only Y and in the third case only X. In the fourth case both have effects, but there is no interaction. In the fifth case both have effects and there is interaction – and case VI is a subcase. It should be noted that if only one of the variables has any effect on Z then there can be no interaction. Intuitively this is obvious, but it should be demonstrated. Imagine Y has no effect. In that case the two curves would coincide and the differences would all be equal to 0. If X has no effect, both curves would be lines parallel to the X-axis, and all differences would again be equal.

Thus, we get essentially three cases: the differences are equal to 0, the differences are equal but different from 0, and the differences are not equal. In the latter case we get two subcases: the differences are increasing (never decreasing) with X, or decreasing (never increasing) with X – and the differences show no clear pattern (no monotonous relationship). All these cases are theoretically very meaningful. Most fascinating is perhaps case VI where there is interaction in the sense that the effect of Y not only varies with X but even reverses itself with the value of X. This case is usually an analyst's delight, because a rich theoretical content can be extracted from it. But that should not make one disregard the simpler cases in Table 5.3.9. Thus, even case I will have to be explained: if X and Y are important independent variables, then it is certainly not trivial that they have no effect on Z.

If the differences show no clear monotonous relationship with X (or some simple curvilinear relationship of the A- or U-types), this may be taken as

Table 5.3.9. *The main outcomes in type 3.2 analysis**

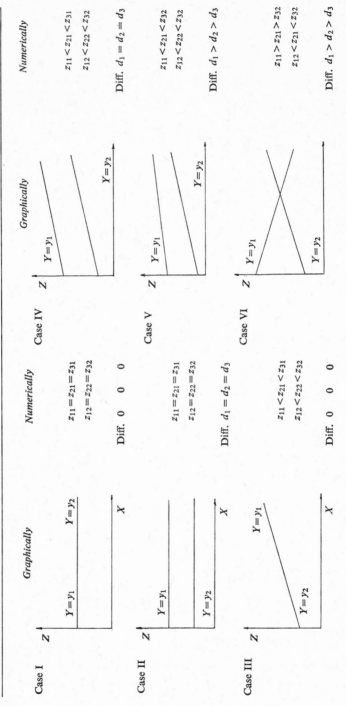

* In a stimulating article, 'A Technique for Analyzing the effects of Group Composition', by James A. Davies, Joe L. Spaeth, and Carolyn Hudson (*ASR*, 1961, 215–225) a similar typology is made for the special case when one of the independent variables is contextual.

an indication that one should try other variables instead of X, to see whether more clear patterns emerge. At any rate, one should not try to make too much out of a confused pattern, particularly not at the present level of social science theory where little more than monotonous relationships are ever expressed in the propositions.

Obviously all that has been said so far can be generalized to any number of values for X; the six cases would still be quite meaningful (but the assumption of linearity even less realistic). But what about generalization to more values of Y? In the Tables this would mean more rows, in the diagrams more lines. There are now a number of possible ways of analyzing the data. The simplest method, as mentioned, is to disregard all but the two extreme values of Y, which would correspond to the inspection of two lines and two rows only. In this case the lines for the other values of Y should be located between the lines for the extreme values so that this kind of simplified analysis would catch, in some sense, the total variation in the data.

By this method one will loose much information but one may also capture the most important aspects of the relationship. The diagrams can then be inspected for details, but it would be much better if these 'details' could somehow be worked into the analysis. What is actually needed is a measure of the total degree of 'parallelism' in the set of curves or lines when there are more than two of them. We shall now develop such a measure, using as simple mathematics as possible in order to introduce as few assumptions as possible.

The answer for the case of two dichotomies (right hand part of Table 5.3.7) is simple: the difference between the differences, $d_1 - d_2$. Let us first then generalize this to the case of three values for X, the case of Table 5.3.9. We get three differences d_1, d_2 and d_3 that may be positive, zero or negative. For any pair of differences the distance between the differences can be calculated: $|d_1 - d_2|$, $|d_1 - d_3|$ and $|d_2 - d_3|$. Each such difference is a measure of interaction, but for specified intervals of X only. If we now add these distances between the differences we get a measure of the total amount of disarray in the data.

Since all numbers are non-negative this measure is zero when and only when there is no interaction present in the data. The more the differences vary with X, the higher will the value of the measure be. Obviously it is 0 in cases I-IV in Table 5.3.9, as it should be. It almost reduces to the measure already introduced in Table 5.3.7 with the difference that here absolute value is used, $|d_1 - d_2|$, whereas in Table 5.3.7 the algebraic value is used, $d_1 - d_2$. The reason why is that if we did not use absolute value we might run the risk that two differences between differences cancel and yield a measure of 0 – even in a case where there is interaction. Thus, consider this example:

Table 5.3.10. *A case with sum of differences 0, sum of distances not 0*

	x_1	x_2	x_3
y_1	100	50	100
y_2	50	50	50
Difference	50	0	50
Difference between differences	50	-50	
		0	

Here the sum of differences is $50+(-50)+0 = 0$ and the sum of distances $50+50+0 = 100$. In the case of two dichotomies this does not matter since there is only one difference between differences – and the difference yields more information than the distance because of its sign. Hence one should use the difference between differences in that case.

We can now generalize to the case where also Y is a trichotomy. Since there are three lines they may be compared for parallelism two at the time, and for each pair of lines the process outlined above may be carried out. Thus, for two trichotomies and with obvious symbols, where $d_{1,2\text{-}3}$ means the difference for x_1 between the z values for y_2 and y_3 (in other words, $z_{12}\text{-}z_{13}$), we get:

Table 5.3.11. *A measure of non-parallelism for two trichotomies, type 3.2*

Original table			Difference table		
x_1	x_2	x_3	x_1	x_2	x_3
y_1 z_{11} z_{21} z_{31}			y_1-y_2 $d_{1,1\text{-}2}$ $d_{2,1\text{-}2}$ $d_{3,1\text{-}2}$		
y_2 z_{12} z_{22} z_{32}			y_1-y_3 $d_{1,1\text{-}3}$ $d_{2,1\text{-}3}$ $d_{3,1\text{-}3}$		
y_3 z_{13} z_{23} z_{33}			y_2-y_3 $d_{1,2\text{-}3}$ $d_{2,2\text{-}3}$ $d_{3,2\text{-}3}$		

and the measure

$$M = |d_{1,1\text{-}2} - d_{2,1\text{-}2}| + |d_{2,1\text{-}2} - d_{3,1\text{-}2}| + |d_{1,2\text{-}3} - d_{2,2\text{-}3}| + |d_{2,2\text{-}3} - d_{3,2\text{-}3}|$$

We do not need more than these four because of the interdependence. Thus, if all lines are parallel all differences in the same row will be equal, which means that all distances between them will be 0 and the measure will be zero. Correspondingly, if the measure M is zero all 4 *distances* will have to be 0, which means that the *differences* are equal two and two. But if $d_1 = d_2$ and $d_2 = d_3$ then $d_1 = d_3$ regardless of whether we are comparing the lines for

y_1 and y_2 or for y_2 and y_3. Graphically, this means that the first and the second lines are parallel, and that the second and the third lines are parallel – which again implies that the first and the third lines are parallel. Thus, because of the transitivity of the equality and parallelity relations we need no more than four of the nine distances in the measure M (for this is the number of degrees of freedom in the 3×3 table).

Actually this measure is computed very quickly and much more quickly than the corresponding measure in analysis of variance. All one needs are the tables given in Table 5.3.11, and since we have, in general, warned against independent variables with more than three values, M as given above is quite sufficient. Besides, the differences will usually have to be computed at any rate, and from there the step to the sum of distances is very short. The measure may then be normed by dividing it by its maximum value which will depend on the range of variation one wishes to take into account.

Let us now look at analyses of level 4. There are four main types: 4.0, 4.1, 4.2, and 4.3. We disregard the first two since they involve correlations of order three and four, and proceed to types 4.2 and 4.3.

Type 4.2 is simple in principle. The two independent variables provide a two-dimensional setting for the study of the variation of the covariation between the two dependent variables. Since we assume that they stand in a symmetric relationship a correlation coefficient will have been calculated as an indicator of the covariation, and this means that the format for type 4.2 analysis is actually exactly the same as for type 3.2 analysis, only that the z's in Table 5.3.7 are parameters of two-dimensional distributions, correlation coefficients (or agreement coefficients), and not parameters of one-dimensional distributions (means, proportions, percentages, dispersions, etc.). The analysis of the distribution can then proceed exactly as has been outlined for type 3.2, only that the interpretation will be more difficult. Thus, it will take some training and theoretical insight to capture the meaning of interaction between the two independent variables when it comes to producing correlations between the two dependent variables. Particularly rewarding would, as usual, be a combination that corresponds to case VI in Table 5.3.9 since this means that the correlation increases with increasing X for one value of Y and decreases with increasing X for another value of Y. Thus, if the correlation is a measure of polarization between two attitudes, X is age and Y is sex, then this means, say, that polarization increases with age for men and decreases with age for women. A finding at that level of complexity could yield much valuable insight.

Type 4.2, like all multivariate analyses of types $n. n-2$ is also a test of spuriousness of correlation only that this time the correlation is studied as a function of the variation of *two* independent variables simultaneously. For the information contained in cases I-III, analysis of type 3.1 would have been sufficient, but for the information contained in cases IV-VI, analysis of type 4.2 is indispensable.

Type 4.3 represents a complication of Table 5.3.7 insofar as there will have to be one such Table for each value of the third independent variable. Thus, if the three independent variables are all dichotomies we get the scheme of analysis given in Table 5.1.3, only that in each cell one would not put frequencies, but some parameter of the one-dimensional distribution of the dependent variable:

Table 5.3.12. *Format for type* 4.3 *analysis, independent variables dichotomies*

	$X = x_1$			$X = x_2$	
	$Y = y_1$	$Y = y_2$		$Y = y_1$	$Y = y_2$
$Z = z_1$	a	b	$Z = z_1$	e	f
$Z = z_1$	c	d	$Z = z_2$	g	h

Instead of u_{111} to u_{222} for the dependent variable U we have used the letters *a-h*. In more general cases we would have to be more systematic, but we shall only look at this special case since the principles will become quite clear. For each Table, analysis of type 3.2 can be carried out, which means that for each Table we can arrive at a classification, roughly, into cases I to VI. The important characteristic is the measure of interaction, and we will get one for each Table. This means that we can also compare these interactions to see 'whether X has any influence on the way Y and Z influence each other in their way of influencing U'. Thus, we get two measures of second order interaction (provided we do not mix the models):

Second order interaction, additive model: $[(a+d)-(b+c)]-[(e+h)-(g+f)]$

Second order interaction, multiplicative model: $\dfrac{ad}{bc} \Big/ \dfrac{eh}{gf}$

The first one is the difference between the first order interactions or 'the difference between the difference between the differences', and the second one is the ratio between the first order interactions, or 'the ratio between the ratios between the ratios'; but in the formulas we have simplified somewhat. It should be noted that these expressions are independent of the order in which we consider the independent variables.

422

For the additive model the question is whether the expression is greater, equal to, or less than 0; for the multiplicative model, whether it is greater, equal to, or less than 1. These expressions can then be generalized in line with what we have suggested in connection with analyses of type 3.2 – but the formulas quickly become rather tedious. Besides, the general strategy is obvious and can be followed in any particular case. Moreover, we doubt that many social scientists are able to infuse much theoretical content in third order interactions. But in principle this solves the problem of analysis of type 4.3.

Finally, some words on analysis at the fifth level. If we consider only analysis of types 5.3 and 5.4, the procedures to be followed are relatively obvious in principle, although they may be tedious in practice. Thus, in type 5.3 the correlation between the two dependent variables is studied as a function of three independent variables. The appropriate format for the analysis is of the type given in Table 5.3.12, but with the difference that a to h now are correlations and not parameters of one-dimensional distributions. Thus, one may study the second order interaction between the three independent variables in producing variations among the correlations between the two dependent variables.

In type 5.4 analysis we would have to add to Table 5.3.12 two more four-fold-tables, calculate the second order interaction for those two tables, and then proceed with an analysis of the third order interaction, measured according to the additive or the multiplicative model. Again, we feel that this is close to or beyond the limit of what contemporary social science theory can digest, regardless of the technical circumstance that in the age of the computers all these parameters can easily be calculated.

In conclusion, let us try to summarize the main points in a multivariate analysis, synthesizing much of what has been said in preceding chapters, particularly in I, 1.4, II, 2.3, and II, 5.1. These are the main points, when a set of variables and their multi-variate distribution is given.

(1) *Tentative classification of the variables* in independent, intervening and dependent, according to the division into 'permanent-temporary', 'public-private', or some other scheme.
(2) *Draw a tentative arrow-diagram* to indicate how the variables may be related, to have an image of 'how the processes run'. Like the classification of the variables, this is not an unambiguous operation.
(3) *If there are n variables, k independent variables, and l intervening variables, then the analysis should be of type n.k.l.* Thus, the general procedure is as follows:
    (a) Find the distribution of the $n-k$ remaining variables for each possible combination of the values of the k independent variables. This amounts to a set of tables, one for each such combination.

(b) For each such table proceed as follows, depending on the circumstances:
  (1) There are no intervening variables, $l = 0$.
    1.1. There is only one dependent variable. Calculate a parameter of theoretical interest for the one-dimensional distribution on the dependent variable, and study its variation as a function of the independent variables.
      1.1.1. There is only one independent variable. In this case (2.1) there can be no interaction effects.
      1.1.2. There are k independent variables, $k > 1$. In this case interaction effects up to order $k-1$ can be studied. The basic case is 3.2.
    1.2. There is more than one dependent variable. Calculate a parameter of theoretical interest, usually a correlation coefficient, and study its variation as a function of the independent variables.
      1.2.1. There is only one independent variable. In this case (3.1) there can be no interaction effects.
      1.2.2. There are k independent variables, $k > 1$. In this case interaction effects up to the order $k-1$ can be studied. The basic case is 4.2.
  (2) There are intervening variables, $l > 0$. In this case the intervening variables are actually included among the dependent variables, but instead of symmetric covariation measures asymmetric covariation measures are used. Predominant are percentage differences and their generalizations, but especially percentage differences because they give more detailed information.
(4) To interpret the results of an n-variate analysis it is usually indispensable to carry out some analyses with the same data but on lower levels. Thus, the three-variate analysis should be understood in terms of the two-variate analysis, etc. But whether one proceeds from higher to lower levels or vice versa may be a matter of taste – although most analysts probably will get more insight out of the data if they gradually increase the complexity.
(5) Distributions should be presented both as tables and as diagrams and according to the rules, in order to use visual impressions as an aid in the interpretations. Tables and diagrams should be self-explanatory, and the text should never be a repetition in words of what is already in the tables.

The major value of this system of multi-variate analysis, we feel, lies in its tremendous flexibility, particularly when percentage differences are used. One can approach a problem in many different ways and adjust the specific style of analysis to the problem. Thus, complex propositions in the sense of involving many variables can be established, and to the experienced social scientist they will almost invariably lead to a variety of interpretations of theoretical interest. Thus, given a set of independent variables I and dependent variables D the possibilities are many, and for any given set at least one of the types indicated in the systematic outline above should yield interesting results.

However, although all this is relatively clear in principle, there nevertheless remain three problems of considerable importance:

(1) How does one measure the extent to which one independent variable 'accounts for the variation' in one dependent variable?
(2) How does one measure the relative contribution of several independent variables on one dependent variable?
(3) When does one declare that a multivariate analysis is completed?

These three problems are highly related. Although no entirely satisfactory answer will be given, and none exists in the literature to our knowledge, we shall at least explore the questions.

The key to all three problems lies in the expression 'I accounts for the variation in D'. If the 'variation' in D is measured by means of the variance of D and the association between I and D by means of the product-moment correlation coefficient, then we may use the standard interpretation of r^2 as the proportion of the variance of D that is accounted for by I (the word 'explained' must not be used here since it has to do with derivation from higher order propositions, in other words with theory formation). This interpretation is only valid provided:

(1) interval scale measures exist both for I and D,
(2) the regression curve for D is linear.

If condition (2) is not satisfied, e^2, where e is the correlation ratio, can be used to yield the same interpretation. Thus, when e^2, or r^2 in the special case, is equal to 1, then we may say that I accounts completely for D; and this may be interpreted as one signal to stop the analysis (but one may still be interested in exploring how D relates to other independent variables). Moreover, e_i^2 (or r_i^2) for variable I_i can be used to establish a hierarchy of independent variables in terms of how much of the variance in D they account for, *one at the time*. Thus, in this case, problems (1) and (3) are solved in principle, and we shall return to problem (2) below in connection with some remarks on multiple regression analysis.

Heavy criticism can be raised against this procedure. It is of limited value because of the infrequency with which interval scale measures are found in social research. Secondly, and perhaps more importantly: the lack of rationale (except pure mathematical convenience) for using variance as a measure of variation and correlation ratios or coefficients as measures of association.[7] If one is satisfied with these measures, then they should be used, provided the conditions are fulfilled – if not, something else should be developed that corresponds better to the nature of the data of social research. For this purpose it is suggested to work with *percentage differences* as measures of the variation of D as well as of the association between I and D.

To explore this we shall start with the simplest possible case: one variable I and one variable D, both dichotomies, and then generalize so as to cover these cases:

1. *One independent variable, I*
   1.1. *D* dichotomy
      1.1.1. *I* dichotomy (case 1)
      1.1.2. *I* trichotomy (case 2)
   1.2. *D* trichotomy
      1.2.1. *I* dichotomy (case 3)
      1.2.2. *I* trichotomy (case 4)

2. *Two independent variables, I_1 and I_2*
   2.1. Both dichotomies   (case 5)
   2.2. Both trichotomies   (case 6)

This is quite sufficient for our purpose, and we prefer to proceed step by step to make sure that problems are not concealed by too general formulations.

Case 1. *The 2×2 table*

In this case there is only one percentage difference (there are two, but they differ only in sign) which means that this percentage difference can be used as a measure of the extent to which I accounts for D. The measure varies from 0 (no association) to 100 (complete association, I accounts completely for D), so we can divide it by 100 to keep it between 0 and 1. It is rarely 1, except for tautologies and other trivial cases (I may be sex, D whether the person has a male or female name); one usually has to go deeper into data to account completely for the variation in D.

The 2×2 table with maximum association has two characteristics:

(1) The percentage differences vary through the maximum range -100 to 100 with variation in D, or, equivalently:
   The percentages vary through the maximum range 0 to 100 with variation in I.
(2) There is perfect predictability from I to D – given the value of I the value of D can be inferred with certainty.

We shall refer to these two conditions as the conditions of 'maximum range of variation' and 'homogenous classes, or perfect predictability' respectively. They are not equivalent, as can be seen from these two cases:

	$d\%$					$d\%$		
D_2	0	100	-100		D_2	100	100	0
D_1	100	0	100		D_1	0	0	0
	I_1	I_2	0			I_1	I_2	0

maximum range,   perfect predictability,
perfect predictability   minimum range

However, if we stipulate that both variables shall use both values, the conditions will be equivalent in this case.

Case 2. *The 3×2 table*

Below are some examples of 3×2 tables:

		$d\%$					$d\%$						$d\%$
I accounts	0	30	100	-100		0	100	100	-100		0	0	100	-100
completely	100	70	0	100		100	0	0	100		100	100	0	100
for D	100	100	100	0		100	100	100	0		100	100	100	0

		$d\%$					$d\%$					$d\%$
I does not												
account	10	30	80	-70		20	90	70		40	40	40	0
completely	90	70	20	70		80	10	30		60	60	60	0
for D	100	100	100	0		100	100	100		100	100	100	0

If we want to stick to percentage differences two problems will have to be resolved. First of all, a difference is defined for two numbers at the time, which means it can be computed for any pair of columns. One might in fact compute the differences for all pairs of columns, but this is unnecessary since our purpose is to see to what extent the variation in D is maximum when the variation in I is maximum. Thus, it is suggested only to compute the percentage differences for the columns that correspond to the extreme values of I. But then one should lay down as a rule that this is only permissible when, for each row, the 'internal' percentage is not above or below the two percentages that correspond to the extreme values of I. This rules out one of the tables above, where the differences have not been computed; but one may collapse two adjacent values so as to reduce it to the 2×2 case, which will offer no problem.

The second problem is how to define 'accounts completely for'. In the first row of tables above, the percentages in each row vary from 0 to 100 (or vice versa), and the percentage differences correspondingly from -100 to 100. In the last two tables, the condition of predictability or homogeneity is also satisfied. But it seems unreasonable to require this in general, since it would make the case where 'I accounts completely for D' empirically so infrequent as to be uninteresting. Thus, from now on we adopt the maximum range definition, and that solves the 3×2 case. This case can then immediately be generalized to the $r \times 2$ case by calculating the percentage differences for the two extreme columns, with the condition that the other percentages are not located below or above. But we do not require that they are 'never decreasing' or 'never increasing': we can permit some internal irregularity, and refer to this condition as 'semimonotonicity'.

Case 3. *The 2×3 table*

Below are some examples of 2×3 tables:

		$d\%$			$d\%$			$d\%$			$d\%$
0	100	-100	10	80	-70	10	80	-70	0	100	-100
0	0	0	20	10	10	70	10	60	100	0	100
100	0	100	70	10	60	20	10	10	0	0	0
100	100	0	100	100	0	100	100	0	100	100	0

All percentage differences can be calculated, since only two columns are involved. But if the percentage differences shall have the maximum range from -100 to 100, then one value of D will have to be empty, which means that it should be combined with an adjacent value so as to reduce the table to the 2×2 case. For the first table this should be done, since no information will be lost. In the second table there is no problem, but in the third table the difficulty occurs that the percentage differences do not form a regular (monotonous) series but jump up and down when D varies. If we now add together the absolute values of the percentage differences in the second and the third tables to get a measure of the total variation we would get the same result. But it seems unreasonable to say that I accounts for as much of the variation in D in the third as in the second case, because of the irregularity. For this reason, we lay down as a rule that the percentage differences will have to be monotone before their absolute values are added, and if they are not monotone adjacent values of D (this time) will have to

428

be combined until that is obtained – eventually ending in the 2×2 case. Thus, the fourth table will also have to be reduced to a 2×2 table.

But then let us look at these three tables that all satisfy the condition and have the same sum of absolute values of the percentage differences:

	$d\%$			$d\%$			$d\%$	
10	60	-50	10	60	-50	10	60	-50
0	0	0	20	10	10	40	20	20
90	40	50	70	30	40	50	20	30
100	100	0	100	100	0	100	100	0

Intuitively it seems reasonable to say that I accounts for most variation in D in the first table, then for less in the second table, and for least in the third table, because of the decrease in the bottom percentage difference 50-40-30. This means, essentially, that only the extreme rows for D would count, just as we only used the extreme columns for I in case 2. But then the same condition should be laid down, that the intermediate percentage differences should not exceed the percentage differences for the extreme values of D. In the 2×3 table this is identical with the condition of monotonicity formulated above, but in the more general $2 \times s$ case some internal irregularity would be permitted as long as the 'internal' percentage differences are not located above or below the differences for the extreme values (semi-monotonicity).

Case 4. *The 3×3 table*

Everything has now actually been said and we can lay down this set of rules with reference to the table below:

D_3	p_{13}	p_{23}	p_{33}	d_3	$p_{13} - p_{33}$
D_2	p_{12}	p_{22}	p_{32}	d_2	$p_{12} - p_{32}$
D_1	p_{11}	p_{21}	p_{31}	d_1	$p_{11} - p_{31}$
	100	100	100		0
	I_1	I_2	I_3		

(1) Focus on the four corner cells.
(2) Calculate d_1 and d_3 only if p_{21} is between p_{11} and p_{31} and p_{23} between p_{13} and p_{33}, calculate d_2 in any case.
(3) Calculate $D = |d_1| + |d_3|$, the sum of the two absolute values of the percentage differences for the extreme values of D, provided d_2 is between d_1 or d_3.

(4) If the conditions are not satisfied, collapse the table until they are satisfied, then do the corresponding calculations.

(5) Divide D by the maximum possible, which is 200, which we then call the *coefficient of accountability*, A:

$$A = \frac{D}{200}$$

A is equal to 0 in the case of no association, but it is also equal to 0 under a wider class of conditions since it is mainly sensitive to the distribution in the corners of the Table. But we find it quite reasonable to say that I does not account for any variation in D when $A = 0$, because this means that both d_1 and d_3 are 0 (and hence also d_2), and whatever association there is, is of minor importance.

A is equal to 1 when and only when d_1 and d_3 are both equal to 100. This is the case when and only when the Table is reduced to either of these two forms:

		$d\%$				$d\%$	
0	p_{23}	100	−100	100	p_{23}	0	100
0	p_{22}	0	0	0	p_{22}	0	0
100	p_{21}	0	100	0	p_{21}	100	−100
100	100	100	0	100	100	100	0

That this is sufficient is seen immediately: but it is also a necessary condition. For $d_1 + d_3$ will have to be equal to 0, not to 200 (which is also compatible with the condition), since $d_1 + d_2 + d_3 = 0$ by the standard equation for percentage differences. But this means that one of them is equal to −100 and the other one to 100, which means that the corner cells have to be as in the Tables. That also determines p_{12} and p_{32}; they have to be 0, otherwise the percentages cannot add up to 100. Thus, A is equal to 1 under a family of conditions (depending on the middle column), but they all seem compatible with a more intuitive impression of what 'fully accounts for' should mean.

Moreover, the rules mentioned above can immediately be generalized to an $r \times s$ Table, only that more internal 'disorder' would be permissible. The maximum value of the sum of the absolute values of the percentage differences will always be equal to 200, so the formula is valid for any case. It reduces to the formula for the 2×2 case; for, if we add the absolute values of the two percentage differences, d and $-d$, equal to $2d$, and divide by 200, we get the same as d divided by 100. It should also be noted that the two cases compatible with the condition of $A = 1$ are also in agreement with the maximum range conditions formulated under case 1; there is maximum variation in percentage differences as well as in percentages – but the latter only for the extreme values of D, and the percentage differences are calculated only for the extreme values of I. Obviously, the higher the values of r and s the more unsatisfactory will it be to take only the corner cells into account. For that reason one should perhaps add the absolute values of all percentage differences for tables above 4×4.

Thus, the bivariate case is completely solved if one accepts the definitions formulated above. This means that in the traditional study where one dependent variable D is 'run against' a set of independent variables $\underline{I}$ an order relation can be introduced in the set $\underline{I}$ ranking the independent variables according to the degree to which they account for the variation in D. It also makes good sense to say that I_1 accounts for twice as much as I_2 because $A_1 = 2A_2$. Of course, this means that the same variation is accounted for partly or wholly, again and again – but that is not the issue here. This ranking is nevertheless useful, because it can give a first impression of the extent to which D is related to the various variables. Essentially, it is little more than the percentage difference, but in a simplified form that is applicable to tables of bigger formats than the 2×2 table.[8]

Case 5 and 6

The problem now is what to do in the much more complicated case where there are two independent variables I_1 and I_2. In this case we do not ask whether D is a dichotomy or a trichotomy or something else since we in principle will accept any comparable measure of how D varies with variations in I_1 and I_2 – for instance the percentage with value D_i, the arithmetic mean or anything else. Thus, we are again discussing the case in Table 5.3.7:

Table 5.3.13. *The relative effect of two independent variables on D*

		$m_1.$	$m_2.$	m
I_{22}		m_{12}	m_{22}	$m._2$
I_{21}		m_{11}	m_{21}	$m._1$
		I_{11}	I_{12}	

The total or *joint* effect of I_1 and I_2 is best measured by $m_{22} - m_{11}$, and we shall say that I_1 & I_2 account completely for the variation in D if $m_{22} - m_{11}$ is maximum, which means that m_{11} is minimum and m_{22} is maximum, or vice versa. This corresponds completely to the definition in the bivariate case where the percentages were supposed to vary through the maximum range (but we do not assume here that the m's are percentages).

We then express this difference as follows:

$$m_{22} - m_{11} = (m_{21} - m_{11}) + (m_{12} - m_{11}) + [(m_{11} + m_{22}) - (m_{12} + m_{21})]$$

joint effect of $I_1 \& I_2$	effect of I_1 alone	effect of I_2 alone	effect of *interaction* between $I_1 \& I_2$
(*total*)	(*partial I_1*)	(*partial I_2*)	

Now, $m_{22} - m_{11}$ is either maximum or not, and the interaction is either zero or not so we get four cases to discuss. If the interaction is zero then there should be no problem with these simple measures:

$$R_1 = \frac{m_{21} - m_{11}}{m_{22} - m_{11}} \qquad \text{the } relative \text{ effect of } I_1$$

$$R_2 = \frac{m_{12} - m_{11}}{m_{22} - m_{11}} \qquad \text{the } relative \text{ effect of } I_2$$

where we have $R_1 + R_2 = 1$. Thus, in the tables below,

		d				d	
	50	70	−20		30	100	−70
	20	40	−20		0	70	−70
d	30	30		d	30	30	

where the interaction is 0, the relative effect of I_1 is 40% and of I_2 60% in the first case, of I_1 70% and of I_2 30% in the second case. In the second case, one also finds that I_1 & I_2 accounts completely for the variation in D. This case is unproblematic, since the effects are additive. But this raises two problems: what is the relation between these measures and the measures used in the bivariate case, and what to do in the case of non-additivity or interaction?

As to the first problem, it should be noted that what we have done corresponds to the inspection of one row of percentages only in the bivariate case, to see whether the percentages run through the maximum range from 100 to 0 or 0 to 100. We have, so to speak, neglected the rest of the Table. This will yield the same result in the case where I accounts completely for D and when D has two values only (for in terms of absolute values there will only be one percentage difference). But it may also be satisfactory in other

432

cases: we may only be interested in one value of D, because that value represents the attribute of theoretical interest (voting for one particular party as opposed to all the rest, having made efforts to migrate as opposed to having thought of it but not done anything or not even thought of it, etc.).

This means that we may measure the effect of I_1 alone by means of $m_2. - m_1.$ and the effect of I_2 alone by means of $m_{.2} - m_{.1}$, simply by using the marginals and not the 'inside' of the Table. In the case of no interaction we have:

$$m_{22} - m_{12} = m_{21} - m_{11}$$

and

$$m_{22} - m_{21} = m_{12} - m_{11}$$

But these differences are not necessarily equal to the corresponding marginal differences. For imagine that all the m's are relative frequencies (expressed as proportions or percentages), of the form f/n. In that case we get:

Table 5.3.14. *The partial and total effects of I_1 and I_2 on D*

	$\dfrac{f_{11} + f_{12}}{n_{11} + n_{12}}$	$\dfrac{f_{21} + f_{22}}{n_{21} + n_{22}}$	$\dfrac{f}{n}$
I_{22}	$\dfrac{f_{12}}{n_{12}}$	$\dfrac{f_{22}}{n_{22}}$	$\dfrac{f_{12} + f_{22}}{n_{12} + n_{22}}$
I_{21}	$\dfrac{f_{11}}{n_{11}}$	$\dfrac{f_{21}}{n_{21}}$	$\dfrac{f_{11} + f_{21}}{n_{11} + n_{21}}$
	I_{11}	I_{12}	

The marginal relative frequencies will have to be located between the two corresponding relative frequencies, which is easily proved. But only under special and relatively uninteresting conditions, such as when there is the same number of cases for each combination of the values of the two independent variables, will marginal differences be equal to internal differences, in the case of non-interaction. In a sense this is obvious, since the two measures are measuring different things: $m_2. - m_1.$ is a measure of the *total* effect of I_1, whereas $m_{21} - m_{11}$ and $m_{22} - m_{12}$ are measures of *partial* effects, keeping I_2 constant. In the case of non-interaction, the partial effect is constant and we can also calculate the *relative* effect according to the formulas for R_1 and R_2 above.

In the case of interaction, one simple measure of the partial effect is the average of the absolute values of the differences, so that we get for the partials:

$$P_1 = \frac{|m_{21} - m_{11}| + |m_{22} - m_{12}|}{2}$$

$$P_2 = \frac{|m_{12} - m_{11}| + |m_{22} - m_{21}|}{2}$$

In our experience, these measures function relatively well and may also be used to calculate relative effects by dividing them with each other. Also, they are easily generalizable to case 6 where I_1 and I_2 are trichotomies: all one has to do is to focus on the extreme rows and columns, under the condition of monotonicity:

Table 5.3.15. *The relative effect of two independent variables on D,* *the case of trichotomies*

	$m_1.$	$m_2.$	$m_3.$	m
I_{23}	m_{13}	m_{23}	m_{33}	$m._3$
I_{22}	m_{12}	m_{22}	m_{32}	$m._2$
I_{21}	m_{11}	m_{21}	m_{31}	$m._1$
	I_{11}	I_{12}	I_{13}	

Although we have introduced earlier in this section much more satisfactory and complete measures of the total degree of disorder or non-parallelism present in the array, we think a simple measure based on the average of the absolute values of the differences between the extreme values in the same row should be quite useful:

$$P_1 = \frac{|m_{31} - m_{11}| + |m_{32} - m_{12}| + |m_{33} - m_{13}|}{3}$$

$$P_2 = \frac{|m_{13} - m_{11}| + |m_{23} - m_{21}| + |m_{33} - m_{31}|}{3}$$

But the conditions for doing this must be that the middle row and the middle column are located between the extreme rows and columns where magnitude of the m's is concerned. If this is not the case, then adjacent columns and rows should be collapsed until the condition is satisfied. Implicitly, this also solves the problem of the $r \times r$ table, with the condition that the magnitude of all m's is between the corresponding m's in the extreme rows and columns. But just as for the bivariate case some internal disorder should be permitted, in other words, one should not require complete monotonicity both ways.

Thus, a rough idea of the relative partial effect can be obtained, and in a way that we feel corresponds fairly well to what most data analysts are doing less explicitly when they are rapidly surveying their Tables to see 'whether there is anything in them'. Again if the format of the Table exceeds 4×4 these techniques may be too rough.

The case of the $r \times s$ Table merits some special consideration. The technique can be used there too, but the variable with more values will be at an advantage for the simple reason that the effect may be more pronounced towards the extreme of the variable. Thus, one should require that $r = s$, and preferably also that the marginal distributions are uniform, so that the values are medians, terciles, quartiles, quintiles, deciles, etc. Under these conditions comparisons are very meaningful.

All of this should not be confused with the problem of accounting for the variation in D in terms of the joint variation in I_1 and I_2; this is done by means of $m_{33} - m_{11}$ which is evaluated relative to the maximum variation possible – but only calculated if m_{11} and m_{33} are the extreme magnitudes of m. If this is not the case one of the variables may be reversed, and if this does not help either the Table may perhaps be collapsed. But it should be noted that collapsing the Table to comply with the conditions will tend to reduce the differences since the variables will have fewer values and hence less chance to elicit maximum variation in D.

Thus, the three problems announced have been solved in the sense that:

(1) a measure has been developed in the general case of the *total* effect one independent variable has on one dependent variable, and this measure can be used to order the independent variables.
(2) in the case of more than one independent variable, measures have been developed
   (a) of the *total* effect of the two independent variables jointly,
   (b) of the *partial* effect of the two independent variables, one at the time, keeping the other constant,
   (c) of the *relative* effect of the two independent variables in producing the total effect – but this is only meaningful when there is no interaction.
(3) a meaning has been given to a 'completed multi-variate analysis': the dependent variable has been fully accounted for.

Thus, a goal in multi-variate analysis is to try, by means of the independent variables, to account completely for the variation in the dependent variables. We use the plural also on the dependent side, for one exciting problem in multivariate analysis of type 4.2 is to use two independent variables to account completely for the variation in the association between the two dependent variables – for instance by producing conditions under which the correlation varies from 0 to 1, or perhaps even from -1 to 1. Obviously, the lower the number of variables used to account for the dependent variable, the better. But even with both these formal criteria satisfied the multivariate analysis may nevertheless be completely uninteresting; 'fully accounted for' is not the same as 'meaningfully accounted for'. Since meaning can only be derived from some kind of theory this still leaves us where any scientific methodology has to be located: in a compromise between criteria of analysis and criteria of theory-formation. Once in a while 'accounting for all variation in terms of few independent variables' may also represent an extremely meaningful, theoretically fruitful finding – but more often than not, we feel, will there be a tendency for the analytically perfect to be the theoretically less interesting while the theoretically interesting lies in propositions that may be complex in the sense of involving many variables, but not satisfactory in the sense of completely accounting for the variation.

In conclusion, some words about *multiple regression analysis (MRA)*. We are probably in a period where this kind of analysis as well as the related canonical analysis is competing more with multivariate analysis (MVA) for the attention of the social scientist, and the argumentation for and against either will possibly be as polarized as in a political debate. We feel that with the tremendous flexibility of MVA and with techniques of the kind indicated here to measure the total effects of variables singly and jointly as well as their partial effects, there is relatively little MRA has to offer. MRA has solved the problem of measuring the relative effect of the independent variables because it can produce statements of the kind '$p_1\%$ of the variance of D is due to its association with I_1, $p_2\%$ due to its association with I_2 and so forth', where the percentages add up to 100%. But just as for simple regression analysis there are the two conditions:

(1) interval scale measures exist both for I and D
(2) the regression surface for D is a hyper-plane (linearity);
and also
(3) there is no interaction between the independent variables.

In addition to this there is the difficulty in accepting the measures used – what was said in connection with simple regression analysis applies *a fortiori* here (which should not be confused with the purely technical problem of calculating all these regression and correlation coefficients, which of course is easily done with computers). For statistical testing there would also be the problems of non-normality and heteroscedasticity.

But even if we restrict ourselves to the limitations given in the three points above, it is difficult to see how these limitations can be circumvented with-

436

out dubious assumptions or further complications. On the other hand, when the conditions are satisfied, then MRA is a magnificent tool that certainly should be used in data analysis. And there is little doubt that new techniques will be developed that perhaps presuppose less than MRA and somewhat more than the kind of MVA we have presented here – without being unrealistically restrictive. In the meantime – and probably for a considerable future – social scientists will have a marvellous tool in multi-variate analysis if it is combined with ingenuity as to what can be considered units of social research.[9]

5.4. *Methods of replication*

The function of the analysis is to establish propositions, whether it takes the form of testing hypotheses developed *ex ante* or the form of accounting for data *ex post*. Basic in this process are efforts to increase the degree of confirmation of the propositions. Under the present heading of 'replication' we shall discuss efforts to *increase* the degree of confirmation by *decreasing* the tenability of the argument that the findings are artefacts of the method. The obvious way of doing this is to show that they are invariant of variations in the method, at least within a reasonable range. We shall give a typology of such methods, and point out some of the important methodological and epistemological problems involved.

Returning to the first part of this treatise on methodology, there are clearly four points of attack:

> the units (I,2)
> the variables (I,3)
> the values (I,4)
> the data-collection (I,5)

since these are the sources of variation we have at our disposal in the process of acquiring data to shed light on some problem.

Schematically, the problem can then be formulated as follows: Given a set of units, a set of variables, a set of values (for each variable) and a method of data-collection, which can be represented by one point in a four-dimensional space. If our hypotheses/propositions are explicitly linked to this point – then there is nothing more to do. If it is confirmed, then it is confirmed. But we assume that this is only very rarely the case. Generally, the hypotheses apply to a non-specified region in the space mentioned, while the method used confirms it for only one point in that region. The mental test here would run something like this: given that the hypothesis is confirmed for this particular point, how far out would you have to go in the four-dimensional

437

space before a disconfirmation can reasonably be written off as covering a different phenomenon?

This clearly depends on what is 'reasonable'. To simplify to two dimensions, units and variables, let us imagine that we have applied a set of questions (an 'instrument') to a sample by means of a standard survey method. Then, we draw a new sample and develop another instrument, presumably tapping the same dimension(s). In other words, we have this situation:

Table 5.4.1. *Examples of replication/generalization*

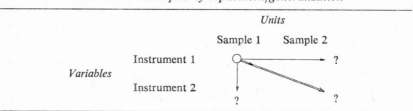

The question is what the arrows actually represent. On the one hand, the method is changed by definition, since the method is given as a point in this space. On the other hand, we are very close to what has been defined as generalization, which is, precisely, an effort to extend the field of tenability of an hypothesis/proposition to other units and also to other variables. We need a border-line between replication and generalization, and suggest the following (with reference to I, Table 3.2.1):

Table 5.4.2. *The difference between replication and generalization*

	On the unit side	*On the variable side*
Replication	on units from the same group of units	with variables from the same group of variables
Generalization	on units from other groups of units	with variables from other groups of variables

This definition is as unclear as is the delimitation of the 'groups' of units and variables in each single case, and that again depends on the amount of accumulated theory and data at hand. *One replicates within a group and generalizes outside.* The definition has the advantage of tying what we are now developing to the general theory of variables, but has the disadvantage of sharing the weaknesses of that theory.

We now proceed on the assumption that we are talking about replication; that this is one method of defence against the idiosyncrasies of the method-

438

ology chosen; and that generalization, hence, consists in linking together a set of, preferably replicated, methodologies.

1. *Replication on the unit side*
We shall start by distinguishing between *horizontal* and *vertical* replication. Horizontal replication is simply replication on units of the same kind, so far not brought into the analysis. Vertical replication is also on other units, belonging to the same group, but lower down or higher up in the hierarchy of units. Thus, imagine one is working on provinces in a country, e.g. correlating level of development and level of educational opportunity. A horizontal replication would include other provinces, and a vertical replication would try out the hypothesis on higher or lower level units, e.g. regions or municipalities. Again, these lower level units must somehow be 'of the same kind' for the replication to remain replication and not turn into generalization.

The standard method is horizontal replication, and is particularly commendable if one initially thought of working only with one unit, e.g. one country, one nation, one newspaper. Three subcases should be distinguished:

(1) One may work the replication *into the design from the very beginning*, by doing the work on three villages instead of one, on five nations instead of one, and proceed with parallel analyses simultaneously.

(2) One may work the replication *into the design from the very beginning, but do the analysis on one part of the data, the replication on other parts.* That is, one sets aside enough data to have what is needed for a replication. If one thinks it is important not to use the same data for developing and testing hypotheses (a point of view we only partly would share) this is one solution. It has the advantage that the data-collection is kept constant, since we probably can assume that the method is homogeneous enough to permit a partition of the data for replication in terms of units, with data-collection constant.

(3) *One may do the replication afterwards, by getting additional sample(s).* This has the advantage of being a real test, especially if the analyses of the first wave of data has already been made public (so that there is no possibility for the analyst of 'adjusting' the findings to each other). It has the disadvantage that not only the sample but also other factors will probably have changed, such as some features of the data-collection. Thus, this method would actually imply a replication to a new sample and to a (slightly) new method.

Method (1) is the cheapest one, not only in terms of data-collection, but also in terms of analysis (the punch card analyses can be done simultaneously). Method (3) is the most extensive form of replication. Nevertheless, we would recommend (1) if it is combined with complete willingness on the part of the analyst to reveal the differences he uncovers.

There is also a third dimension of unit replication that should be mentioned. The new units in a horizontal replication should, according to the definition, be chosen within a given group of units. But there will always be some differences between the possible units; and the question is, should one sample as homogeneously or as heterogeneously as possible within the group? The ideal would be to sample until the limit of tenability of one's propositions is found. The best strategy for this purpose is *not* to start close to the original sample of units, but rather to start far out and see whether the findings still hold. If they do, one may stop the process if one is satisfied with the extension of the replication. But if one had started very close to the base, replication of findings would be more trivial. For that reason, replication should not be done by split-half techniques, i.e. by splitting the sample in two parts (purposively, systematically or randomly), and hiding one for future analysis or proceeding simultaneously on both. The value of a replicated finding can be measured in terms of the span of heterogeneity it bridges. Thus, a survey of public opinion in Western Europa, using Norway as a base, should not be replicated on Sweden, but on, say, Italy.

The ideal would now be to have a measure of what one gains in degree of confirmation by unit replication. If we focus on horizontal replication, the problem involved is easily appreciated. Imagine one introduced a measure proportionate to the number of replications. One could then obtain, virtually, as high degree of confirmation as one wants simply by replicating on perfectly equivalent samples. Clearly, the gain will have to be measured not only in terms of how many times, but also in terms of heterogeneity span bridged by the replication. The extreme case is 'replicating' the finding on the original sample, where the replication distance is zero and the gain in confirmation value also zero. As we move gradually away from the original unit(s), we would attach more value to the gain in degree of confirmation, until we reach the borderline of the group of units, and replication shades into generalization. At the same time, we might get a decrease in degree of confirmation for each new sample of unit(s). Thus, a measure might possibly be constructed as a weighted sum of the separate degrees of confirmation, weighted by some measure of the distance from the base sample. But since we have no measure of the distance between samples, a measure of the kind suggested is of more heuristic than practical value.

2. *Replication on the variable side*

Just as for units, the distinction should be made between horizontal and vertical replication. Horizontal replication would bring in other variables from the same group, vertical replication would make use of sub-variables, i.e. lower level indicators from the same group, or super-variables. And just as for the case of units one gets these three subcases of horizontal replication:

(1) One may work the replication *into the design from the very beginning*, by having a twin for every variables (or for some of the variables) and proceed with parallel *analyses simultaneously*. In fact, this is quite often done in the design of questionnaires. However, it is not so often done at a level where it may be even more useful: for index-formation. Very often the work is based on one index for each fundamental dimension where one might at least have two indices. Thus, if one is interested in modern vs. traditional attitudes as a dimension, it is clear that this dimension comprises a number of sub-dimensions depending on what interpretation, what aspect one is interested in. For that reason a set of parallel indices should be included in the design.

(2) One may work the replication *into the design from the very beginning, but not use the method of parallel analysis*. One would use one set of variables to develop hypotheses, the other set(s) to test or replicate them. The data-collection is kept constant, and one has essentially only kept a second set of data in storage for later use.

(3) *One may do the replication afterwards*, by getting new data. This should perhaps preferably be done with the same method of data-collection and on the same sample, so that one is not trying to test too many kinds of replication at the same time – unless one is fairly certain that the hypotheses will stand up against such a test (there is also the danger one may replicate the finding, because the discrepancies in unit-replication and variable-replication cancel each other).

The basic problem for horizontal replication of variables is the same as for units: should one try to sample the variables for replication as close to, or as far from (within the given group of variables) the original set as possible? Within the limits set by the dimension, we would argue for heterogeneous sampling. And here the problem of measuring distance is solved. To measure the degree of homogeneity between variables one has to use some measure of their correlation (3.7); so our argument essentially says: *do horizontal replication by means of variables that do not have too high correlation*. A summary of the argument is given in Table 5.4.3.

The defense against the suspicion that one's findings are artefacts of the variables chosen does not consist in replicating the finding with other variables that correlate so highly that they classify the units (almost) the same way. When one is able to obtain the same findings by means of a new variable that classifies the units differently (medium level correlation), yet produces more or less the same correlation with a third variable, the hypothesis that the proposition is invariant of variations in method (here choice of variables) is more tenable. The danger lies in going so far towards the hetereogeneity

441

Table 5.4.3. *Criteria for picking replication variables*

Case:	Correlation *low*	Correlation *medium*	Correlation *high*
Suggested range	(0.0–0.6)	(0.7–0.8)	(0.9–1.0)
Advice:	*unsuitable*	*suitable*	*unsuitable*
	the two variables have too low correlation to belong to the same dimension	the variables may belong to the same dimension, yet replication of finding is not trivial	the correlation is so high that replication of finding is trivial

end of the scale that one is, in reality, experimenting with a new dimension, or with a very high degree of contamination.

Empirically this kind of replication quite often works, and especially if there is a good theory to guide one in the choice of variables. Interchangeability of variables is an empirical fact. If it were not, social science would be worth considerably less because of the arbitrariness prevailing in the choice of variables from one and the same dimension. Lazarsfeld has called this empirical phenomenon the principle of 'interchangeability of indices',[10] but it does, of course, apply not only to indices (that are unidimensional representations of clusters of variables), but also to lower-level variables.

It should be possible to obtain a measure of the degree of confirmation we would get by horizontal variable replication. The problem involved is exactly the same as for horizontal unit replication. Three factors are involved: degree of confirmation for each replication, distance for each new variable from the base variable, and number of replications. At the extreme is 'replication' by means of the same variable, which would add nothing to the general degree of confirmation because of the zero distance. If distance is not taken into account, the careless researcher could add as much as he wants to his degree of confirmation simply by replicating on a set of variables that correlate perfectly with the original variable, as mentioned.[11]

The measure of distance between variables introduced in 3.7 should be applicable here, too, i.e. $d_{ij} = 1 - r_{ij}$. It takes on its maximum value (different from unity) for the minimum correlation we would permit, yet feel reasonably certain that we are within the same dimension. Imagine we make p replications, and that we get a degree of confirmation dc_i for replication i, on a variable located at a distance d_i from the base variable. One could then argue for this measure of total degree of confirmation, DC, where dc is the original degree of confirmation, to illustrate the reasoning:

$$DC = \frac{dc + \sum_{1}^{p} d_i \cdot dc_i}{1 + \sum_{1}^{p} d_i}$$

Without replications ($p = 0$) we get the original measure. With replications on the same variable ($d_i = 0$) we also get the original measure. If all the separate degrees of confirmation are unity, then we get $DC = 1$; if $dc = 1$. If all $dc_i = dc$, then $DC = dc$; if only one of them is less (and the rest equal) we get a decrease in degree of confirmation; and if one of them is higher (and the rest equal) we get an increase. Thus, the measure does not register replications as gains in degree of confirmation unless they are better than the original. This, we feel, reflects well the often unwarranted belief in results obtained by means of one indicator only, where p indicators would lead to a more realistic (i.e. lower) estimate.

The main virtue of the measure lies in its emphasis on distance: if a degree of confirmation is lower than the base this may to some extent be compensated for by high distance from the base. Similarly, a high degree of confirmation close to the base counts less, and a low degree of confirmation close to the base will result in a very low contribution to the sum in the numerator. The measure might also be used for unit replication.

Vertical replication on the variable side is of much more importance than on the unit side, for one particular reason. On the variable side the higher level variable is a construct, based on lower level variables that are combined together by some process into an index. On the unit side the higher level unit has an existence in its own right, as the case of the nation relative to its subdivisions. On both sides vertical replication is the obvious technique to avoid the contextual fallacy (the fallacy of inferring from higher level relations to lower level relations). But on the variable side comes, in addition to this, vertical replication as a reality check of the higher level finding, because of the artificiality of indices.

If, in general, one has two indices and correlates them, the vertical replication would consist in correlating all indicators of the first index with all indicators of the second index. From one single Table of index correlation one would get $a \cdot b$ Tables of indicator correlations if the first index is based on a and the second on b indicators. This has many advantages[12] but we shall only explore one of them.

Correlations in all indicator Tables is obviously a sufficient but not necessary condition for correlation between the indices. The relation between indicator correlation and index correlation is complicated and depends, among other factors, on the method of index-construction and the kind of correlation measure made use of. To take one simple example: $a = b = 2$, both indices additive, and as measure of correlation the product moment correlation coefficient. We get:

$$X = X_1 + X_2, \quad Y = Y_1 + Y_2$$

$$r_{xy} = \frac{\Sigma (x_1 + x_2)(y_1 + y_2) - \dfrac{\Sigma (x_1 + x_2)\, \Sigma (y_1 + y_2)}{N}}{\sqrt{\left[\Sigma (x_1 + x_2)^2 - \dfrac{[\Sigma (x_1 + x_2)]^2}{N}\right]\left[\Sigma (y_1 + y_2)^2 - \dfrac{[\Sigma (y_1 + y_2)]^2}{N}\right]}}$$

which can be written on this form:

$$r_{xy} = \frac{\operatorname{cov}(x_1, y_1) + \operatorname{cov}(x_1, y_2) + \operatorname{cov}(x_2, y_1) + \operatorname{cov}(x_2, y_2)}{\sqrt{[\operatorname{var} x_1 + 2\operatorname{cov}(x_1, x_2) + \operatorname{var} x_2]\,[\operatorname{var} y_1 + 2\operatorname{cov}(y_1, y_2) + \operatorname{var} y_2]}}$$

Since the two X-indicators are indicators of the same dimension they will have to be positively correlated, and the same for the two Y-indicators – so all terms in the denominator will be positive, since we assume that all indicators discriminate, i.e. have a non-zero variance. In the numerator there is a sum of four terms, so for r_{xy} to be positive it is only necessary that one of the four pairs of indicators is postively correlated. Hence, replication at the indicator-level is a very strong type of replication, and the proportion of the $a \cdot b$ correlations that are in the expected direction is a relatively useful measure of degree of confirmation.

As can be seen from the formula the correlation r_{xy} between the indices will be zero or negative if all indicator-correlations are zero and negative – in accordance with the requirements in I, 3.2. This should be checked for other correlation measures and other additive indices.

3. *Replication on the value side*

We now assume both units and stimuli to be the same, and shall attack the problem of replication of the variables (i.e., the sets of responses) from another angle: in terms of the values. We assume that we have a variable which in line with current practice has been properly dichotomized or trichotomized in r_1 values. Two types of change are important; subdividing the values so as to get a number $r_2 > r_1$, and changing the position of the cuts while keeping the number of values constant.

Let us call the two sets of cutting points c_1 and c_2 – they are, of course, not the same for different values of r, although there may be an overlap. In other words, we get these possibilities:

Table 5.4.4. *Examples of replication on the value side*

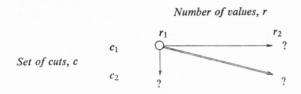

Number of values, r

Set of cuts, c

The most ambitious would be a replication to higher number of values and a completely new set of cutting points, and the general idea is that an hypothesis invariant of changes in number of values and the location of the cutting points receives a higher degree of confirmation. For if it were not it would in most cases be difficult to defend its limitation to a special set of values and a special set of cutting points unless they are both deducible from the same theoretical framework.

We have earlier argued how the transition from $r = 2$ to $r = 3$ may change the conclusion completely, because the gross results obtained by a dichotomy obscure theoretically important variations. If the proposition is 'X increases with Y' it is much easier to falsify this proposition for $r = 3$ than for $r = 2$, for there is a higher proportion of distributions *a priori* that do not confirm the proposition for $r = 3$ than for $r = 2$ (II, 4.2, § 5). This holds *a fortiori* for increasing r. As an example look at these percentages from a Norwegian gallup-sample taken in August 1959 (the hypothesis was 'positive attitudes to governmental initiatives increases with increasing social position'):

		Positive attitude to		
		visit by Khruschev	free trade area	daylight saving time
Social	1 (periphery)	14	9	45
position	2	21	18	56
	3	28	25	57
	4	32	30	66
	5	33	37	77
	6	36	28	80
	7	29	47	86
	8 (center)	40	58	94

The strong confirmation of the hypothesis derives from two sources: horizontal replication on the variable side, and replication in terms of number of values. The latter means, concretely, that the finding holds not only from value 1 to value 2, but also from value 1 to value 3, from value 2 to value 3, etc. The hypothesis is perfectly confirmed for the question of daylight saving time, but for the other two columns there is one percentage in each which is 'wrong'.

A measure of the gain in confirmation can easily be developed. For the sake of simplicity, let us assume that there are no ties in the columns of percentages (a condition that will almost always obtain, at least if one is willing to calculate percentages with decimal places). We then start with the lowest value of the variable and the percentage that corresponds to it. The next (this reasoning presupposes ordinal level of the variable) percentage can be higher or lower; in other words, there are two possibilities. The third percentage has to be placed relative to the pattern already given by the preceding two percentages – which leaves it with three possibilities. The fourth percentage is presented with a pattern of three, and consequently has four possibilities, and so on till the r'th percentage with r possibilities. If we assume all these positions to be equally probable *a priori* we get the simple result that the probability of any one distribution of percentages is $1/r!$, and since there is only one of these distribution that confirms the hypothesis of monotonous correlation the *a priori* probability of *not* confirming fully the hypothesis is $\dfrac{r!-1}{r!}$. Let us look at this as a function of r:

Table 5.4.6. *Gains in falsifiability with increasing r*

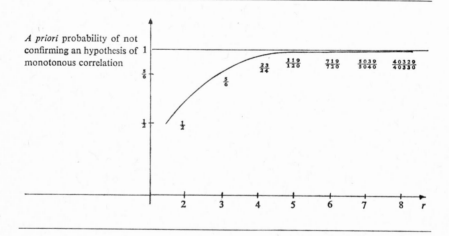

As can be seen, the gains in falsifiability are very quickly made, in fact so quickly that *no important gains are made for $r > 5$*. It may, however, be

446

objected to this reasoning that we do not, in fact, count all the $r! - 1$ distributions that are not exactly according to the pattern of monotonous correlation as disconfirmations, not even as non-confirmations. In practice we would be more tolerant, so the probabilities given above represent upper limits of degrees of falsifiability. The researcher should clarify for himself where the limits of his tolerance or true-set actually are located.

As a measure of relative falsifiability the ratio between probabilities of non-confirmation may be used. And as a measure of *monotonicity,* the degree to which the measures form a never-decreasing or never-increasing function of the independent variable can be used any measure of rank correlation, for instance Kendall's tau. Thus, one would find out how many pairs of measures are in the right order and how many in the wrong order. In data analysis this is a significant measure.

Although the form of data representation discussed above is very important, it is by no means the only form possible. It involves only two variables, where the dependent variable is a dichotomy. Let us now change the attention to percentage differences, for the case of two variables, where X is independent and Y is dependent. We shall discuss three cases: both dichotomies, X a dichotomy and Y a trichotomy, and both trichotomies:

Table 5.4.7. *The falsifiability of hypotheses about percentage differences for the hypothesis 'Y increases with X'*

Case 1: X and Y dichotomies			Case 2: X dichotomy, Y trichotomy			Case 3: X and Y trichotomies			
x_1 x_2	difference		x_1 x_2	difference		x_1 x_2 x_3	difference		
y_1 p_{11} p_{12}	$d_1 = p_{12}-p_{11}$		y_1 p_{11} p_{12}	$d_1 = p_{12}-p_{11}$		y_1 p_{11} p_{12} p_{13}	$d_1 = p_{13}-p_{11}$		
y_2 p_{21} p_{22}	$d_2 = p_{22}-p_{21}$		y_2 p_{21} p_{22}	$d_2 = p_{22}-p_{21}$		y_2 p_{21} p_{22} p_{23}	$d_2 = p_{23}-p_{21}$		
SUM 100 100	0		y_3 p_{31} p_{32}	$d_3 = p_{32}-p_{31}$		y_3 p_{31} p_{32} p_{33}	$d_3 = p_{33}-p_{31}$		
			SUM 100 100	0		SUM 100 100 100	0		

Working with percentage differences as measures of correlation, we are interested in how the column of differences 'behaves'. According to the hypothesis, we should get a tendency towards higher percentage differences with increasing value of y. But if the hypothesis is as stated, this should be necessary, but not sufficient: we should actually request a monotonous series of percentage differences, from negative via (close to) zero to positive. For if not, the hypothesis is only confirmed in a general sense, 'in the large', not 'in the small'; and it will be difficult to find *ad hoc* hypotheses that can explain away the irregularities. This condition implies that there should be one and only one *transition point* (the point where the differences change sign). For if there were more than one, then the differences could not form a monotone series. And since the differences have to add up to zero, we can get the case of no transition from negative to positive or vice versa if and only if all differences are 0, i.e. when there is independence, which would be contrary to the hypothesis of (positive) dependence.

We shall now prove that in case (1), and case (1) only, is monotony in the differences equivalent to monotony in the percentages. For if $d_2 > d_1$, then d_2 is positive, and we have $p_{22} > p_{21}$ (and vice versa), which implies $p_{12} < p_{11}$, and we are essentially back to the preceding case for $r = 2$. But in the other two cases this does not hold. Thus, $d_3 > d_2 > d_1$ implies $p_{32} > p_{31}$ and $p_{12} < p_{11}$, but p_{21} may be less than, equal to, or greater than p_{22} [and similarly for case (3)]. Hence, there is more variety compatible with the hypothesis in the percentages than in the differences. With r differences, i.e. r values of the dependent variable, the variety is $r!$ and the *a priori* probability of falsification is $\frac{r!-1}{r!}$, but for a given series of differences there may be several patterns of relative magnitude of the percentage. It should be noted that this also applies to differences between differences and so on when there is more than one independent variable.

Finally: the variation in cutting points. This is clearly important, since most analysts will have experienced the temptation to maximize correlations *a posteriori* by choosing suitable cutting points. This does no harm if the correlation maintains its sign (and roughly its magnitude) with changes of the cuts, *and* the cuts chosen can be justified as theoretically particularly meaningful. But if there is no independent theoretical basis for the location of the cutting points, degree of confirmation should obviously decrease if one cannot demonstrate that the finding is invariant of the location of the cuts within reasonable limits.

That this is not only a taxonomically deduced point but of analytical importance can easily be demonstrated. Below is a table 3×3 with two cuts for both variables:

8	9	4		8	13		30	6
10	3	2		17	13		8	7
7	1	7		$ad-bc = -120$			$ad-bc = +162$	

This, is, in a sense, rather distressing, since the correlation may vary from high negative via zero to high positive, only depending on the cutting points. Of course, the distribution has to be somewhat strange to permit this variation; but such distributions are often found in practice, particularly if one is working with 'contaminated' variables that are tapping several dimensions.

The conditions the two-dimensional distribution will have to fulfill in order for the measure of correlation to stay within certain limits (e.g. maintain the sign) will obviously depend on the measure, and on the limits and the changes in cutting points. There is no reason to go into the details of this, since the general logic is clear. By requiring invariance under change of cutting points the number of distributions compatible with the hypothesis will be severely reduced, and the *a priori* probability of falsification correspondingly increased – hence, there will be an increase in the degree of confirmation.

In general, the measures of association will depend on the cutting points, but one must at least require their signs to be the same. A distribution that satisfies this weaker requirement is referred to as *isotropic*.

4. *Replication on the data-collection side*

At this point it is considerably more difficult to formalize the procedure. In I, 5.1 a typology of data-collection procedures has been given. But it seems rather obvious that we can at most ask for replicability relative to methods located in the same row or in the same column of Table 5.1.2. Thus, if an hypothesis (e.g., about polarization in a conflict) is confirmed for structured, written data but not for informal, non-verbal data, it is hard to conceive of this as sufficient evidence to reject the hypothesis, or at least not to accept it. Rather, one would say that the two types of data-collection tap different dimensions – which they do, even different universes, – and one is back to the problem of locating the limits for horizontal replication on the variable side.

Thus, as a point of departure we have to presume that we are trying to get at, for the same units, the same variables only by different means. For the survey, all differences in interviewing techniques will be of importance here, including socially relevant characteristics of the interview, of the interview setting, not to mention the form of the instrument. Parallel versions of what is basically the same instrument is a well-known technique, and the parallelism can be used for such important dimensions as wording, whether the question is structured or unstructured, the order of the questions, and the extent to which the question is 'leading'.

As as example, imagine one is studying anti-semitism. Three different kinds of questions lend themselves to this kind of replication: open-ended ('Are there any groups in this country you dislike?'), closed but not leading

('Which of the following groups do you dislike?') and closed, leading ('Do you like Jews, or do you dislike Jews?'). It is well known that these three methods will yield very different estimates of the level of anti-semitism in a country, but that is not the crucial point. The replication consists in examining whether the indicators of anti-semitism obtained by three different methods nevertheless yield correlations in the same direction with other variables. They very often do, but that is no tautology, it will have to be demonstrated.[13]

Since we do not have a good theory of the relations between these methods, we do not see many efforts to measure the degree of confirmation either, except, perhaps, as a kind of horizontal variable replication.

Clearly, what is missing in sociological research more often than not are behavioral data. Replications of findings from verbal data on behavioral data would immensely increase the belief in our propositions. This does not, as many seem to believe, imply a switch from survey methods to observational methods, since much valid information about behavior can be obtained simply by asking people what they do or did instead of always asking them what they mean or meant. Such questions may telescope series of behavior into meaningful statements that can be checked and validated, and hypotheses can be tested independently using behavioral and attitudinal variables. In addition, pure observation data should be used.

In other words, our plea is not for a change from one type of data to another, but to a norm of social research that gives low degrees of confirmation to propositions confirmed for one type of data collection only, and a much higher degree of confirmation when multi-dimensional approaches to the data problem are made use of.

6. Theories

6.1. *Definition of 'theory'*

The methodology of theories and theory-formation is underdeveloped, relative to the methodology of hypotheses and hypothesis-formation. The move away from the level of very concrete empirical work, particularly with statistical tools, makes itself felt in a certain vagueness and a frequent recourse to formulas of the 'to test an hypothesis is a kind of handicraft, to make a theory is to make a work of art' kind. Also, unfortunately, it seems that qualitatively different kinds of scientists and philosophers have been working at these two levels. Nevertheless, it should be feasible to discuss theories within the framework presented without having to use too vague or even undefinable terms.

We shall define a theory as a set of hypotheses structured by the relation of implication or deducibility, or more formally:

> A *theory*, T, is a structure $(\underline{H}, I)$ where
> $\underline{H}$ is a set of hypotheses and
> I is a relation in $\underline{H}$ called 'implication' or 'deducibility',
> so that $\underline{H}$ is weakly connected by I.[1]

One may say that this is only begging the question, for what, after all, is 'implication' or 'deducibility'? First of all, as a relation it is binary, relating antecedent and consequent. We shall symbolize it with an arrow, $\rightarrow$, and a number of structures are possible, such as (the two first are particularly important):

$$H_1 \rightarrow H_2 \quad (H_1 \;\&\; H_2) \rightarrow H_3 \quad H_1 \rightarrow (H_2 \;\&\; H_3) \quad (H_1 \;\&\; H_2) \rightarrow (H_3 \;\&\; H_4)$$

The binary character of the relation may be emphasized, if one so wants, by combining the hypotheses in parentheses to form one single hypothesis, but that changes $\underline{H}$ and is hardly necessary for a discussion. We shall use the standard definition of implication, inference, deduction:

> *P implies Q* or *Q is deducible* from *P*, where *P* and *Q* are hypotheses or conjunctions of hypotheses and $P \neq Q$,[2] if we cannot accept *P* without also accepting *Q* ('Gedankennotwendigkeit').

451

The important thing in this definition is its pragmatic nature: it relates implication to the empirical question of what one can make people accept. P implies Q if and only if 'we' feel we have to accept Q if we also accept P. This is also begging the question, for who are 'we'? How much training, conformism, socialization, etc. goes into this kind of acceptance? But here we may refer to the more general discussion in II, 4.2 of the composition of the competence group; the same reasoning applies to this problem.

The definition of implication makes for an important bridge between physical and sociological theory. Physical theory is certainly more formalized (see II, 6.2), but contemporary sociological theory also has a certain amount of deducibility, even if we call it by its right name, which often is 'acceptability' or 'plausibility'. The difference is one of degree, not of kind, and will be spelt out in the discussion of formalization.

We shall use the symbol T for a theory and the symbol $T \rightarrow H$ for 'T implies H' or 'H can be deduced from T'. This makes for a certain ambiguity in the symbol T; it stands for what has already been deduced as well as for what can be deduced. Since the implication relation is a simple binary relation in the set H it can be classified as *irreflexive* (since we have included the condition $P \neq Q$), *non-symmetric* (if it is symmetric the relation of double implication is called 'equivalence'), *transitive* (a surprising number of people connect logic with the recital of the formula 'if A implies B and B implies C, then A implies C'); but *not strongly connected* (we do not assume that there is an implication relation one way or the other for all possible pairs of hypothesis-sets).

This combination is known as a *weak order relation* if there is no case of equivalence, and we can use it to discuss what is known as the *level of the hypothesis*. Unfortunately, even with these assumptions, the level of an hypothesis is not unambiguous. The graph of the $(\underline{H}, I)$ structure can be used to find the hypotheses that 'only imply but never are implied' (the beginners) and the hypotheses that 'only are implied but never imply' (at least at that stage of the development of the theory). The first kind are the highest level hypotheses, the second kind the lowest level hypotheses. In between are the intermediate levels. If the implication relation were strongly connected and, hence, induced a strong order in H, all hypotheses would be ordered linearly and the level would be the distance from the bottom; as to the left in the figure:

We adopt the convention of counting from the bottom and start with the lowest level as the 'first level' – which would be H_d to the left and H_i, H_j, H_k to the right. To the left there will be no problem in assigning levels, to the right there are problems. Thus, H_a may be a fourth level or fifth level

Diagram 6.1.1. *Strong and weak theory structures*

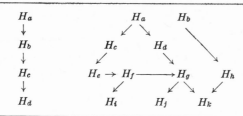

hypothesis depending on which implication-path we follow. However, this difficulty is hardly essential, since we only need a crude concept of order of the hypotheses in terms of level. 'Higher level' and 'lower level' may do, and for any pair of hypotheses there will in general be no doubt as to relative level. For if they are on the same implication-path it is clear. If they are not, they will nevertheless have to be connected somehow, which means that implication-chains on which they are located intersect. If they intersect 'above', the higher hypothesis is the one that is closest to the intersection; and if they intersect 'below', the higher hypothesis is the one farthest away from the intersection. The condition of weak connection ensures comparability, although the picture is complicated by the possibility of intersection of the implication chains both above and below. However, it will hardly pay off to develop more precise concepts here: it should only be noted that the implication structure can take on any form known in graph theory as long as the graph is connected.

Some common concepts can now be defined:

(1) An hypothesis is said to be *tenable* if it is *confirmed*, and is then called a *proposition*.
(2) An hypothesis is said to be *valid* if it is *deducible*, and is then called a *theorem*.
(3) A system of tenable hypotheses is called an *inductive* system.
(4) A system of valid hypotheses is called a *deductive* system.
(5) An *inductive-deductive* (hypothetico-deductive) system or *scientific theory* is a system where some valid hypotheses are tenable, and (almost) none are untenable.
(6) An hypothesis *describes* a phenomenon if the phenomenon confirms the hypothesis (a low level hypothesis 'describes').
(7) A theory *explains* a phenomenon if it implies an hypothesis that describes the phenomenon (a high level hypothesis 'explains').

There are certainly other ways of using these terms, but the list above seems to be in line with current practice. Most important about the list is the breakdown of the use of the word 'true': it does not appear. Instead the words

453

'tenable' (for confirmed hypotheses) and 'valid' (for deduced hypotheses) are used. The first refers to the *correspondence concept of truth,* truth as correspondence (consonance) between an hypothesis and data. The second refers to the *consistency concept of truth,* truth as something transferred by deduction.

For the past centuries the concept of 'science' has been linked to an eclectic combination of inductive and deductive methods. The scientific method is called the hypothetico-deductive or inductive-deductive method, and the goal is to arrive at a set of hypotheses that are 'true' both in the correspondence and consistency senses, both tenable and valid. This is an extremely strong requirement, as will be spelt out later; and for this reason the requirement is weakened in the definition above to 'a system where *some* valid hypotheses are tenable, and (almost) none are untenable'. Thus, except for a certain flexibility where one would not give up a very fruitful theory because of some dissonances, the point is that the valid hypotheses should at least not be untenable, and in part also tenable. But we do not require *all* of them to be tenable: they may, for instance, be not (yet) testable or not (yet) confirmed which is very different from disconfirmed.

We now turn to a more detailed exposition of the relation between a theory and the hypotheses we deduce from it. The relation is one of implication or deducibility, so the question is what can be said about this relation. We have defined it by means of 'Gedankennotwendigkeit' and what we shall loosely call 'transfer of acceptability'. More formally, the properties of the implication relation are stated as follows:[3]

MODUS PONENS: If we accept 1. T and 2. $T \rightarrow H$, then we have to accept H.

MODUS TOLLENS: If we accept 1. $\bar{H}$ and 2. $T \rightarrow H$, then we have to reject T.

Since it is customary to say that a relation is between an *antecedent* and a *consequent, modus ponens* means that if the implication is 'true', then there is a transfer of truth from antecedent to consequent. And *modus tollens* makes use of the equivalence between $T \rightarrow H$ and $\bar{H} \rightarrow \bar{T}$ and is actually an application of *modus ponens* to this second form (the 'contrapositive' form).

Of more importance than this is what we can *not* say. Since an implication $P \rightarrow Q$ does not imply its converse $Q \rightarrow P$, there is no transfer of truth from consequent to antecedent, however true one holds the implication to be. In other words: if a theory implies an hypothesis and this hypothesis is 'true', this does *not* imply the truth of the theory.

So far a basic asymmetry between 'arguing with the arrow' and 'arguing against the arrow' has been pointed out, well known from any elementary book in logistics.[4] Less trivial is the exact meaning given to the expression 'transfer of truth'. What kind of truth? As pointed out, 'truth' is ambiguous. For instance, is it possible to say, using *modus ponens* that (1) given $H_1 \rightarrow H_2$ and (2) H_1 is confirmed, that H_2 is confirmed? Obviously not: confirmation is an empirical operation resting on an infinity of assumptions that all enter the test. The only kind of truth that is transferred via the *modus ponens* mechanism is validity, not tenability. This will be elaborated below, here we shall only state the general point: the relation between the levels of hypotheses in an inductive-deductive system is for reasons of principle a relatively loose one. This has three far-reaching epistemological consequences which we shall now spell out.

(1) *The only way to obtain complete confirmation of T is to confirm independently all hypotheses in $\underline{H}$.* In other words, one can never hope to avoid the task of independent confirmation by entering the theory at a 'strategic' point, confirming some hypotheses at that point, and then affirming that confirmation of the rest 'follows'. There are two reasons for this *principle of independent confirmation:*

(a) *From higher level to lower level hypotheses one may infer validity but not tenability.* The implication relation is a formal relation, and it transfers validity, not tenability. We can not confirm an hypothesis *a priori* by confirming the antecedent, however correctly it is deduced, for we can never be sure *a priori* that the empirical counterparts of the formal elements relate to each other in the same way. This may depend on the validity of our indicators and their combination into indices, or some other validity.

(b) *From lower level to higher level hypotheses one may infer neither validity, nor tenability.* This is only a restatement of the principle that one cannot infer from the truth of the consequent to the truth of the antecedent. Since there is no transfer of validity against the arrow, there will *a fortiori* not be an automatic transfer of confirmation. The antecedent *may* well be confirmed, and valid in terms of its relation to higher level hypotheses, but this does not follow from its relation to the consequent.

(2) *There is in general no limit to the number of theories from which a given set of confirmed hypotheses can be deduced.* Since only a finite number, h, of hypotheses can be confirmed during our finite existence what is said is that this is not sufficient to determine the theory. A heuristically useful illustration of this *principle of variety of theories* is the relation between the finite number of observations and the curve that can be fitted through them. By socialization, Gestalt mechanisms etc. one is conditioned to fit certain curves at the expense of other possibilities through a set of points representing empirical observations:[5]

455

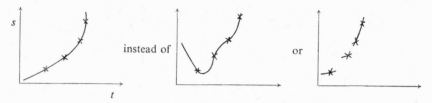

Another illustration of the same point lies in the relationship between rejection and acceptance of statistical hypotheses. The hypothesis that a sample comes from a specified universe can be rejected (with a probability of Type I error equal to the significance level of the test). But if it is not rejected this does not mean that the universe is accepted as an 'explanation' of the sample, for the reason that an unlimited number of neighbor universes might just as well or better have been the origins of the sample.

These examples are of the low level kind, and relate hypotheses to observation-sentences. The same relation of ambiguity holds between higher level and lower level hypotheses, however.[6] Given a set of hypotheses, there is no limit to the number of theories from which they can be deduced. For imagine there were such a limit, that there were only t theories. Then any conjunction of them would also be a theory, which extends the number to $2^t - 1$. But the basic point is that there is no limit to the variety one can obtain specifying the higher level hypotheses, and then combining them in all combinatorically possible ways. However, even though one may not be able to prove it, the variety of theories to be obtained simply by introducing completely new concepts and perspectives seems also to be unlimited – where by 'unlimited' we mean that there is nowhere in the activity of producing theories from which the hypotheses can be deduced, any logical stop-sign, only the limitation imposed by lack of human imagination.

(3) *One does not have to choose between two or more non-contradictory theories from which the same set of hypotheses can be deduced.* In other words, if two or more theories 'explain' the same phenomena, one does not have to choose between them. This *principle of co-existence between theories* is basically a principle of pluralism, contrary to the idea that there is only one explanation, the valid one. Thus, for a phenomenon like the existence of incest taboos and the (consequent or not) relatively low level of observed incest, a variety of theories have been offered.[7] As long as they are not contradictory (i.e., as long as one cannot deduce a proposition as well as its negation from them), and since confirmation of the deduced hypotheses offers no basis for inferences about the rest of the theory (besides, the theories are equal in this regard since the assumption is that the same body of hypotheses can be deduced), at least some theories should coexist in the mind of the investi-

456

gator – and in his publications as well. One particular reason for this is that the theories often point out different aspects of the phenomenon, or different factors that are working so that the principle of coexistence in reality is a principle in favor of multi-factor approaches to the exclusion of one-factor approaches.

This does not mean that *any* particular state of simultaneous coexistence of diverse theories for the same phenomena is desirable, however. There are two different ways to proceed from that point on. One may try to obtain a synthesis between the coexisting theories by integrating the aspects or factors into one theoretical superstructure, where the relative weight as well as the interplay between the factors can be clearly seen. Or, one may try to deduce from the theories new consequences and test them to establish a basis for a choice between the theories. This activity has often the unfortunate consequence that when a theory has been shown to lead to a disconfirmed hypothesis, the whole theory is rejected or given up as a perspective: 'it was wrong'. This is an easy way out for the scientist who wants to simplify the picture he presents of reality. What is needed instead would be some way of assigning, at least on an ordinal scale, measures of relative importance to the factors operating. Besides, it is a very naïve conception of theory-formation that would reject a theory completely because of a single instance of disconfirmation. No doubt, there is something wrong with T as a scientific theory if a disconfirmed hypothesis is deduced, but one cannot think in the absolute terms provided by two-valued logic: true *or* false. Rather, the theory will have to be specified, made more complex, etc., i.e. modified instead of rejected.

What we have called the principles of independent confirmation, of variety of theories, and of coexistence between theories are all unsatisfactory to 'the closed mind'. Authoritarian attitudes in scientific research typically show up in assertions of the opposite: the automatic transfer of confirmation along implication lines, the denial of a variety of theories because 'there must be one right theory', the inability to let two or more non-contradictory but different theories coexist in one's mind. These attitudes are reinforced in most academic settings by the division of research into departments and institutes and by the institutionalization of scientific provincialism: the same phenomenon looks very different to researchers located at different points on the scale from the micro- to the macro-sciences in behavioral science and they reject with ease other perspectives than their own. But, as mentioned, eclecticism is not a goal, it is a means. Criteria for choosing between theories exist and should be used, but like the criteria for choosing between hypotheses, they are continuous rather than dichotomous, which

457

implies much open room for judgment, and especially for temporary suspension of judgment. Of course, just as for hypotheses, the fundamental criterion is confirmation and particularly falsification as a negative criterion. But, as Quine points out,[8] it is difficult to falsify a theory; even if it looks easy according to *modus tollens:*

If this view is right, it is misleading to speak of the empirical content of an individual statement – especially if it is a statement at all remote from the experiential periphery of the field. Furthermore, it becomes folly to seek a boundary between synthetic statements, which hold contingently on experience, and anlytic statements, which hold come what may. Any statement can be held true come what may, if we make drastic enough adjustments elsewhere in the system. Even a statement very close to the periphery can be held true in the face of recalcitrant experience by pleading hallucination or by amending certain statements of the kind called logical laws. Conversely, by the same token, no statement is immune to revision. Revision even of the logical law of the excluded middle has been proposed as a means of simplifying quantum mechanics; and what difference is there in principle between such a shift and the shift whereby Kepler superseded Ptolemy, or Einstein, Newton, or Darwin Aristotle?

Thus, not only is it impossible to confirm completely a theory without confirming independently all the hypotheses that constitute the theory – it is also impossible to falsify completely a theory without independent falsifcation or disconfirmation at all points in the theory. There are always revisions that can be made in this 'field of force whose boundary conditions are experience'. And that is as it should be: modus tollens tells us that the theory *as a whole* has to be rejected if we do not accept one of its consequences, but it does not say that every element in the theory is to be rejected. It remains for the scientist to locate the error, and here he is often in the situation that many small errors or deviations at one point in the structure add up to one flagrantly wrong hypothesis – so that he has to revise at the most strategic point.

6.2. *Dimensions of theories*

By means of the general definition, a theory can be recognized on formal criteria alone, since it can be put on the form $(\underline{H}, I)$. The variety of theories is enormous, however. In this section, theories will be discussed in terms of ten dimensions, as we did for hypotheses in 4.2. All of them imply important methodological and epistemological problems, and all of them are rank-dimensions in the sense that they can be used to evaluate theories. For easy reference, the ten dimensions are these:

(1) Generality
(2) Range
(3) Evaluation of the hypotheses

(4) Formalization
(5) Axiomatization
(6) Relation to other theories

(7) Predictability
(8) Communicability
(9) Reproducibility

(10) Fruitfulness

The basis for the grouping above is as follows: the first three concern the set $\underline{H}$. The following three concern the structure of I. The next three have to do with the relation between theory and investigators. And the last dimension gives, like tenability for hypotheses, a composite evaluation of the theory.

We shall not go so much in detail with these dimensions as we did for hypotheses, partly because these dimensions are less clear, partly because much of this field has already been implicitly covered in II, 4.2. Thus, we shall not attempt to develop more precise ideas by means of operationalization, and shall treat them in groups as they appear in the list above.

(1) *Generality, range and evaluation of the hypotheses*
To compare theories in terms of the number, h, of hypotheses that can be deduced from them makes no sense, even less sense than the comparison of hypotheses in terms of the number, m, of units they describe. The difference lies in the fallacy of concreteness: it makes no sense to count hypotheses, since two hypotheses can be joined into one by conjunction, and one hypothesis can be split into many by specification. For that reason, comparison would have to be done in terms of inclusion of sets: one would clearly prefer T_2 to T_1 if $H_2 \supset H_1$. This is trivial, and gives no guide for the comparison of theories when they have an overlap in deducible hypotheses, but also a specialty of their own.

More basic than generality, perhaps, is *range* of hypotheses. The theory from which one can deduce confirmed hypotheses that cover a wide range of phenomena that *prior to the theory* were considered unrelated receives a high score – provided the hypotheses are confirmed. It should be noticed that the condition obtains only before and when the theory is proposed and the hypotheses are confirmed, for afterwards the phenomena are no longer unrelated – they are related precisely by that theory. It is enough to think of Newton's way of relating terrestrial and celestial mechanics to each other or a theory of incest taboos that could link certain interaction phenomena in small groups, big groups, and international systems to these important intra-family norms. However, even though it is easy to say that 'range' is important and perhaps even more important than 'generality' it seems difficult to progress from this qualitative stage into a stage where theories can be more explicitly evaluated and the two dimensions weighed against each other.

We then turn to a composite dimension called 'evaluation of the hypotheses', in H. 'By their fruits ye shall know them' according to the Bible (Matth. 7:20), and the fruits of the theory are H. Since we have fairly good criteria for judging hypotheses, we already possess an important basis for judging theories – without going as far as this Bible quotation in *only* using the fruits as a basis for the judgment. The obvious rule is to prefer the theory whose hypotheses rank highest, what is less easy would be to evaluate the relative merits of two theories when one dimension leads one to favor T_1 and the other dimension to favor T_2.

This way of thinking, judging theories in terms of their hypotheses, leads to one non-trivial conclusion. If it is applied to dimension (10) in II, 4.2, degree of confirmation, the conclusion is that the theory is preferred for which most hypotheses are confirmed. This is trivial as long as we restrict ourselves to what Quine calls the 'experiential periphery' of the theory (which is only a way of expressing 'lowest level hypotheses' in the language of graphs). But if we apply the criterion of confirmation, *which implies testability*, to hypotheses located high up in the implication hierarchy (close to the center or nucleus of the theory in Quine's language) we have to give scientifically inferior status to *als ob*, *as if* thinking, where higher level hypotheses are used that are not testable or even are disconfirmed (such as assumptions about 'homo economicus', 'homo sociologicus' or ideal type thinking in general). Very often the nucleus of a theory consists of such assumptions that are not testable or have extremely low degree of falsifiability (e.g., the idea that 'Man behaves as if he is seeking self-realization') or, if they are testable, are disconfirmed. Sociologists are usually prone to criticize economists for the rationality of *homo economicus*, citing all kinds of evidence to the effect that economic behavior depends on social position, social pressure, etc. Or they turn their criticism against *homo politicus*, who weighs advantages and disadvantages of all elements in a set of political actions, e.g., when he is about to vote. The sociologist can point out that 80% vote as do their parents, that most vote as do their primary groups, and if parents and primary groups do not agree, this cross-pressure leads to a certain withdrawal.

460

But what about *homo sociologicus?* Here are some properties often attributed to him, forming a set of assumptions:

(a) He tries to maximize the evaluation he receives from others, especially rank (*mobility axiom*).
(b) He tries to minimize the differences between the ranks he receives in different systems (*rank equilibration axiom*).
(c) He tries to avoid conflict by seeking redefinitions of his roles, statuses and status-set (*conflict avoidance axiom*).
(d) He tries to act so as to maximize the sum of the intrinsic value of the act, the personal sanctions deriving from it and the social sanctions (*utility axiom*).
(e) He tries to align his interaction patterns with friends and enemies so as to contribute to polarization (*balance axiom*).

Many others could be cited. The point is merely that although the sociologist deals with more intangible variables than the economist and the political scientist, his *homo sociologicus* nevertheless sounds like a cross-breed between a nineteenth century British merchant, out to maximize profit, and a retired twentieth century executive who wants peace and quiet around himself. Delight in conflict, change and ambivalence is easily disregarded.

As will be taken up in the subsequent paragraph, such perspectives and assumptions are useful, even indispensable, but that does not mean that we would not *ceteris paribus* prefer the theory that can afford high level testing, and not only testing along its periphery. Thus, even if in Quine's words a theory is 'a man-made fabric which impinges on experience only along the edges'[9] one should try to get far away from the 'edges' and towards higher level hypotheses in the effort to test and confirm. For some period one may be satisfied saying that a social phenomenon takes place as if axioms (a)–(e) above were satisfied – but in the long run one should try to get as close to them with a confirmation process as possible.

(2) *Formalization, axiomatization and relation to other theories*

We now turn to the properties of I, the implication relation. So far it has been treated as unproblematic in the sense that is has been taken for granted that we always know where in $\underline{H}$ the implication relations are located. To see how unrealistic this assumption is, all one has to do is to examine almost any piece of social science theory presented in ordinary prose. One finds half-stated hypotheses linked by half-assertions of deducibility, in an unorderly mess. It may be interesting to disentangle it, trying to make the graph structure clear – but the pay-off may be low. One may have to face the fact that there are stages of development of any science, and that at certain stages it would be a disservice to the science to force on it more clarity in theoretical structure than corresponds to the level of insight and knowledge actually found.

By *formalization,* then, we mean any effort that contributes to the explicitation of the structure of a theory, i.e. to bring it on the ($\underline{H}$, I) form. Essentially, this means the explicitation of the rules of deduction, but we prefer a wider concept of 'formalization' that also includes the explicitation of the hypotheses. All this is often confused with symbolization and mathematization.

Symbolization, in turn, implies only the introduction of abbreviations, often in the form of a letter (Greek or Latin) instead of terms or expressions. The argument in favor of symbolization is in terms of economy: it may save time, energy, and printing expenses by suitably abbreviating a lengthy text. More important than this, however, is the reduction of ambiguity: a symbol is less subject to interpretations in terms of surplus values, extra connotations, and is thus more likely to keep its interpretation constant over time and throughout a text. This means that both intra- and inter-subjective communicability are increased.

Mathematization is the introduction of relations and operations, i.e. a calculus, in a set of symbols, so as to arrive at a deductive system. While it may be argued that this does not actually presuppose symbolization, in practice it is always done by means of symbols not found in daily language. This has the great advantage that the mathematical system appears as a purely formal system that may or may not be interpreted. Mathematization stands out as the archetype of formalization because of the explicitness of the rules of inference. To obtain this, symbols may be necessary or useful, but indeed not sufficient, as may be seen by reading Kurt Lewin's works or S. F. Nadel's *Theory of Social Structure* (Glencoe, Ill.: Free Press, 1957).

But the softer techniques should not be forgotten or overshadowed by the use of mathematics. The use of technical terms is one, where the terms are explicitly introduced so that the reader at any point can check whether the author sticks to his criteria for the application of the terms. Another technique is a systematic presentation, where hypotheses are presented in a typographically clear way, numbered or not, instead of being woven into a web of assertions. But the price is well-known: lack of elegance, dullness, and lack of conversion power outside the limited circle of colleagues.

Axiomatization does not presuppose symbolization and mathematization, although the three are often found together. It presupposes, however, at least some level of formalization, and may be said to be implicit as a by-product of formalization as we conceive of it. In the ($\underline{H}$, I) structure there will

usually be hypotheses, at least one, that are not implied but only imply –
we have called them the highest level hypotheses. This set of hypotheses, A,
is called the axiom-set, and a highest level hypothesis an axiom (or a postulate). The implication chains are cut at these points. One may always ask
why exactly at these points, and the possible answers are many. The axioms
may be held to be 'selfevident', apodictic. Or they may represent well-con-
firmed propositions that are used as a basis for new explorations. Or, they
may simply be relatively arbitrary cuts, where the investigator has decided
'let us assume this and see what we get out of it'. 'This', A, may then be a
set of assumptions that simplify a part of reality to make it manageable for
research purposes, often *not* with the idea that the hypotheses derived from
it will be confirmed, but only to serve as a base-line. Thus, a Markov-chain
model of preelection decision-making or social mobility may be extremely
unrealistic, yet quite useful.

But there is more to axiomatization than the explicitation of the highest
level hypotheses, and the formalization of the implication structure. Traditionally, three requirements are made of the set A: the axioms shall be *non-
contradictory, independent* and *complete*. Of these requirements the first two
are trivial and the third largely unobtainable, however – but they are heuristically very useful in directing efforts to axiomatize sociological theories.
More precisely stated:

(a) If it is possible to derive both H and $\bar{H}$ from A, then A is said to be
contradictory. The absence of this condition is the *first requirement*.

(b) If it is possible to derive a subset of A from another subset of A,
the axioms in A are said to be *dependent*. The absence of this is the *second
requirement*; and follows from the definition above of A as the set of the
highest level hypotheses, i.e. hypotheses that are not derived.

(c) If it is possible to decide for any hypothesis H formulated in the
terms used in T (i.e. used in A) whether it can be deduced from A or not,
A is said to be *complete*. This is the *third requirement*.

Of course, the ideal is an axiomatic system that uses a certain set of concepts, C, so that all hypotheses that can be formulated using C can be divided
into two groups, the valid and the invalid – *and* so that all the valid hypotheses are tenable and all the invalid hypotheses are untenable. But even though
this is much easier to say than to achieve, it seems to have been a very useful
goal for all empirical sciences.

By means of the independence criterion, superfluous axioms can be excluded on the grounds that they are implicit as deductions. This does not
mean, however, that it makes sense to add a requirement to the effect that
the number of axioms should be as low as possible. The axioms are hypoth-

eses, and as such not countable; they can be split and joined. An axiomatic system with five independent axioms is reduced to a system with one axiom $A = A_1$ & A_2 & A_3 & A_4 & A_5 by means of conjunction. This, however, does not mean that it is not meritorious to develop a rich theory with an extremely limited axiomatic basis (a pyramid with a broad base and a pointed top). The best recent example is the extremely stimulating work by Duncan Luce, where one axion about choice behavior serves as a basis for the deduction of an impressive variety of hypotheses.[10] His theory is of the base-line type, however.[11]

So far we have been concerned with a theory as an isolated system, with the obvious conclusion that *ceteris paribus,* we prefer the theory with the highest level of formalization and axiomatization. But there seems also to be a rule in methodology to the effect that we prefer the theory that can be deduced from another theory or set of theories to the isolated theory. In practice this means that *ceteris paribus* we prefer theories where the axioms appear as deductions in other theories, for the simple reason that this reduces the total set of axioms in the discipline. The theory is then actually integrated in the other theories, but it may be advantageous for reasons of exposition, division of labor etc., to discuss it as a separate system. The theory, then, receives validity from above and, possibly, confirmation from below.

There is a special case of this that now merits a more detailed discussion: the case where $\underline{H} = H$, where the theory consists of only one hypothesis. In this case, the rule says that *ceteris paribus* we prefer the hypothesis that can be deduced, to the isolated hypothesis. In other terms, although they are unhappy terms unless they are given some relatively precise sense like what we have suggested in II, 4.1: we prefer description with explanation to description alone. That there can be many explanations of the same phenomenon does not enter here as an argument, the choice is between zero or one. It should be noticed that H receives only validity, not confirmation 'from above' – and that however much other consequences of the theory explaining H are confirmed this does not confirm H. But it certainly adds to the fruitfulness of the theory.

(3) *Predictability, communicability and reproducibility*
To require these three virtues of the theory is to require them of the hypotheses in the theory. Hence, we could simply refer to the corresponding passages in II, 4.2 – had it not been for the distinction made between high-level and low-level hypotheses. The question is, do we require all this also of the high-level hypotheses, or does it only apply to the periphery? This can only

be answered in terms of confirmation of high level hypotheses, which is a *desideratum,* but not a requirement. Thus, if confirmation is obtainable, predictability is a virtue, as is reproducibility. But communicability we would require in any case. And in addition the implication relation has to be inter-subjectively communicable and reproducible, as mentioned in 6.1.

(4) *Fruitfulness*

The question is now how this discussion of dimensions for evaluating theories can be summarized in an over-all evaluation of a theory. As mentioned many times this cannot be done in terms of the confirmation values given to the hypotheses in $\underline{H}$, since we do not even require all hypotheses in $\underline{H}$ to be testable, and much less confirmed – we have only said that it is desir-able. In general, a theory cannot be confirmed. The theory is a source for generating hypotheses, and the biblical argument turns into the principle of fruitfulness:

> A theory is *fruitful* to the extent many, different and tenable hy-potheses can be derived from it.

This includes all the criteria discussed under (1) above, but implicitly also the criteria discussed under (2): fruitfulness is linked to derivation, which presupposes formalization and is greatly facilitated by axiomatization. But the formula as such says very little, and should only be taken as a loose slogan to express that a theory is judged in terms of its generating power, not in terms of confirmation, and much less in terms of 'truth'.

Since, in sociology, quasi-theories called 'perspectives' play an important role, methodological research should probably be directed towards what happens when a sociologist 'buys a perspective' and tries to use it to give sense to his data. A perspective is essentially a set of concepts used in a theory with very low degree of formalization, as when the anthropologist decides to analyze a community under the 'how do they keep conflict under control' perspective. At this stage in theory-formation the best strategy, as indicated, is probably to keep formalization low, allow surplus meanings to enter, and use them to enrich the theory – in other words, to allow for looseness as a tool in the free, imaginative search for insights (an 'insight', we presume, is a high level, but relatively untestable, hypothesis). But this pragmatic virtue of the perspective should not be allowed to be interpreted as a methodological virtue: the next phase is the tightening of the system, the explicitation, and all that goes with it to arrive at the goal: the scientific system with a maximum coincidence between validity and tenability.

6.3. *Correlational, causal, and functional analysis*

The difficulty with theory-formation is that nobody really knows how it takes place. There is no difficulty in explaining how a matrix of correlations is established, or how a single correlation is found. But the implication relation between propositions is essentially different from the correlation relation between variables, although they can be presented in a formally similar way. Thus, compare the following:

A *correlation* is an empirical relation between variables. It is established by deciding for each pair of *values* of the variables whether they are empirically realized (i.e. found within the same *unit*). Pairs of values are divided into 'found' not-'found', and if the pairs that are found empirically form a certain pattern, then correlation is said to exist.

An *implication* is a logical relation between propositions. It is established by deciding for each pair of *truth-values* of the propositions whether they are compatible (i.e. found within the same *mind*). If the compatible pairs of truth-values form a certain pattern, then implication is said to exist.

Diagrammatically, we get something like this:

Diagram 6.3.1. *Formal similarity between correlation and implication*

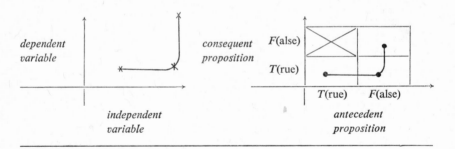

For implication there is one combination that is ruled out: it is not possible to accept the antecedent as true and at the same time reject the consequent as false. This is precisely the meaning of the *Gedankennotwendigkeit* in 6.1: that one cannot at the same time accept the antecedent as true and the consequent as false (but all the remaining three combinations are possible). What is new here is only the idea of filling the right hand side of the diagram with the opinions of many people, i.e. having some kind of vote taken for each combination of truth-values.

This is usually not done explicitly, but is done all the time implicitly, in debates. If one person says that mother-child separation in early childhood

466

leads to crime in adolescence, thus asserting an implication, the argument against would consist in giving a case of childhood-separation, but no crime. But explicit voting among scientists does not seem to belong to contemporary methodology,[12] only informal approval/disapproval in conferences.

Thus, implication is a logical relation for the single individual investigator, but an empirical relation for the investigator of investigators, i.e. he who could imagine studying the distribution of beliefs in the implication in a sample of scientists and/or other people. This may perhaps one day be utilized in an attempt to operationalize the idea of 'degree of implication'. Methodology was greatly aided when the old dichotomy 'true-false' applied to empirical propositions was abandoned in favor of 'degree of confirmation', for instance conceived of as a continuum running from $+1$ to -1. Similarly, instead of talking about implication in dichotomous terms one might conceive of degree of implication as a continuum running from 1 to 0, and one approach might be simply in terms of the proportion who agree that the relation is 'gedankennotwendig'. This proportion will probably be a decreasing function of the distance from the originator of the theory containing the implication, and the acceptance value of the theory can be expressed in terms of how steeply the acceptance decreases as a function of the distance. If the acceptance is limited to the originator alone it is usually not accepted as a scientific theory, since some degree of intersubjectivity is required. But let us leave this aspect aside, and concentrate on the relation between given empirical data and the step into theory-formation.

Three 'methods' will be briefly commented upon. They can be seen as more or less explicit ways of organizing empirical data, starting from the correlation matrix, so that theory-construction may be facilitated. A more correct way of talking would be to refer to three *languages:* (1) the correlation language, (2) the causal language, and (3) the structural-functional language. We shall deal with them in that order.

(1) *The correlation language*

A major weakness of this language is its richness and consequent ambiguity. The number of measures of correlation that order given distributions differently is quite high (II, 2.3 for an indication), so one has always to specify 'correlation as measured by ...'. We shall assume in this discussion that all bivariate intercorrelations of some kind for n variables have been computed and that the variables are at least ordinal, so that it makes sense to distinguish between negative and positive correlation.

The correlation matrix can then be represented by a graph as in II, 3.8, p. 304; with a solid line for positive correlation, no line for independence and a broken line for negative correlation. For detailed information, the numerical size of the correlation may be added – and independence may be defined as an interval around zero, for instance the interval given by some level of significance. Graphs can then be drawn, and the patterns be analyzed for possible ways of grouping the variables together, as dealt with in II, 3.8.

The main relation between correlation and implication is negative and can now be spelt out: *correlation is not in general a transitive relation*, whereas implication is. If it were, one could infer from $C^+(x, y)$ and $C^+(y, z)$ to $C^+(x, z)$. But no such purely logical connection is warranted; correlation is only transitive under certain conditions. If we use product-moment correlation, then a well-known formula relating the magnitude of the three correlations mentioned can be deduced from the formula for the partial correlation (see end of 5.3):

6.3:1.
$$r_{xy.z} = \frac{r_{xy} - r_{xz} r_{yz}}{(1 - r_{xz}^2)^{1/2} (1 - r_{yz}^2)^{1/2}}$$

Since this has to be equal to or less than 1, we get:

6.3:2.
$$r_{xy}^2 + r_{xz}^2 + r_{yz}^2 - 2r_{xy} r_{xz} r_{yz} \leqslant 1$$

This can be seen as a second degree equation in r_{xz}. We get as extreme limits for r_{xz} the two solutions of the equation we obtain by using the equality sign:

6.3:3i
$$r_{xz} = r_{xy} r_{yz} \pm \sqrt{r_{xy}^2 r_{yz}^2 - r_{xy}^2 - r_{yz}^2 + 1}$$

Since this gives us only the limits of the variation of r_{xz}, the lower limit has to be positive for the inference above to be valid. This leads to:

6.3:4.
$$r_{xy}^2 + r_{yz}^2 \geqslant 1$$

which means that the first two coefficients have to be located outside a circle with radius 1 if we shall be certain that r_{xz} is positive. Thus, if we have $r_{xy} \geqslant 0.6$ and $r_{yz} \geqslant 0.8$ then we are guaranteed non-negative r_{xz}. Or we can have both equal to 0.707. This means that relatively strong requirements have to be fulfilled for the relation 'positively correlated as measured by the product moment correlation' to be transitive.

It should be noticed that the relation of independence is not transitive either. If we insert $r_{xy} = r_{yz} = 0$ in 6.3.2, we get the range of variation of r_{xz} from -1 to $+1$, i.e. the maximum possible. If X is independent of Y, and Y is independent of Z, then nothing can be said about the relation between X and Z.

468

The consequence of this for theory-formation is somewhat disheartening. It means, that even if we choose to define our terms so that we feel we can infer from:

H_1: the more X, the more Y

and H_2: the more Y, the more Z

to H_3: the more X, the more Z

this inference will not necessarily be corroborated by empirical evidence if we use product-moment correlation coefficients to measure dependence, even if the data we have are perfectly valid indicators of the variables. If in addition the empirical indicators are not valid, the inference is even less valid (the point made in the preceding section), and the conditions of inference will vary from one correlation measure to the other.

Similar points can be made for percentage differences, and for other co-efficients.[13] One may now argue whether this is a shortcoming of our logic or a shortcoming of the coefficients – the two premises above and the conclusion look so convincing. But this is because we project more into it than is actually warranted. If all we mean is expressed by statistical dependence, then transitivity simply does not obtain. But if we add to this what is approximately expressed by the term 'process', then transitivity may obtain by definition. We now turn to that subject.

(2) *The causal language*

We shall approach the problem of the nature of the causal language through what we shall call *processes* and *mechanisms*.

Any unit of interest to the social scientist can be described by means of an unlimited number of variables, X, Y, Z, ... It is well known from all social experience that variables are related in the sense that if one variable is increased over time (by deliberate intervention or not), then the other variable may (1) increase, (2) decrease, (3) remain constant, or (4) exhibit no definite pattern of these kinds. The latter will in most cases obtain if the range of variation for the first variable is sufficiently large – if the range is limited one of the first three patterns will generally be approximated. If we assume that we are within such a range, then the relation between X and Y can be characterized as $+$, 0 or $-$, depending on whether we get increase, no effect or decrease of Y with increasing X.

We can now reverse the reasoning and let Y vary, with the same division where the behavior of X is concerned. All together we get nine patterns, where the arrows are used instead of $+$, 0 and $-$ (solid arrow for positive covariation, broken arrow for negative covariation):

	Y independent		
X independent	$\rightarrow$ (1) $X \rightleftarrows Y$	(2) $X \rightarrow Y$	$\leftarrow\cdots$ (3) $X \rightleftarrows Y$
	(4) $X \leftarrow Y$	(5) $X \quad Y$	(6) $X \leftarrow\cdots Y$
	$\cdots\rightarrow$ (7) $X \rightleftarrows Y$	(8) $X \dashrightarrow Y$	(9) $X \rightleftarrows Y$

Actually, there are only six patterns different enough to warrant special discussion:

(1) *Two-way positive process* (No. (1) above, positive feed-back). The so-called Richardson process in the theory of arms races is a good example: *X* and *Y* are the armament levels of two antagonists, either of them increases when the other increases. Another example would be the Homans theory of the relation between liking and interaction: more of one leads to more of the other. And there is the well known example of the relation between prejudice and discrimination: more prejudice is translated into more discrimination (trivial), and more discrimination is translated into more prejudice (less trivial, partly to make attitudes consistent with actions, partly because more discrimination makes the prejudice more 'correct').

(2) *Two-way negative process* (No. (9) above, positive feed-back). This is actually the same, since it is highly conventional how we decide the *sign* of a relation. As an example may serve the relation between tax-pressure and investment-rates in certain economies: if the government wants constant income it will have to increase taxes when investments go down because the income yield will be less, but if it increases taxes, the investment will also decrease, and so on. A more sociological example could be as follows: lack of identification in an organization leads to less participation, and less participation leads to less interest – because there is less to be interested in.

Depending on the nature of the end result positive and negative feed-back patterns may be called 'vicious circles' (if we dislike the result) or 'virtuous circles' (if we like it);[14] these are value-loaded terms.

(3) *One-way positive and one-way negative process* (Nos. (3) and (7), negative feed-back). This is the paradigm of the *social control process*. There is deviance that provokes a sanction, and the more deviance, the more sanction, the more sanction the less deviance – until an equilibrium point is found. Of course, it may also be that the sanction has no effect on the deviance, which would give us patterns (2) or (4); or it may even provoke more deviance and we get the positive feed-back of pattern (1). Hence, this is the paradigm of *effective* social control.

(4) *One-way positive processes* (Nos. (2) and (4), no feed-back). An increased investment-rate will probably produce an increase in the share the middle classes have of the population, at least under certain conditions, but the import of people with middle class status and life-style will not necessarily have any effect on the investment-rate. Increased rank-disequi-

libration may lead to radicalism, but increased radicalism may have no effect on the rank-disequilibration.

(5) *One-way negative processes* (Nos. (6) and (8), no feed-back). This is just the same as the preceding case: an increase in rank equilibrium will lead to decrease in radicalism – but not necessarily vice versa.

(6) *No process.* An example might be the relation between social position and conflict ideology in a period of crisis: the ideology cuts through social stratification and makes the population attitudinally homogeneous, so that mobility will not affect ideology.

Actually, there are only four patterns: positive feed-back, negative feed-back, one-way processes and no process at all. Nevertheless, it is useful to spell them out somewhat more, as is done above.

A typical gap now exists in social science between theory, which is often phrased in terms of the patterns above, and methodology, which leads to statements about correlation coefficients. We shall try to do something to bridge this gap by spelling out what the processes mean in terms of correlations.

There is no simple relation.

Imagine a high correlation is found between X and Y. We shall show that we can have correlation without a process and a process without a correlation. If X and Y are two attitudinal dimensions so that we have $C^+(X, Y)$ all we know is that in a sample the two attitudes will tend to be high together and low together. This does not mean that we can get an increase in Y by increasing X, or vice versa.

For imagine the correlation is between readiness to use military pressure and readiness to use corporal punishment of children, pupils, or convicts. This correlation may be a result of particular group formations or a projection of personality types. But the correlation as such gives no basis for inferring that a change in one attitude for an individual leads to a change in the other. The correlation may express a certain situation, a social system at a given point in time, but say nothing about what happens over time. Even if the individuals at one point in time are divided perfectly into 'high-high' and 'low-low', with no dissonant combinations, this does not mean that these combinations ('high-low' and 'low-high') cannot emerge later.

The system *may be* so strongly coupled that either there is no change or change in both at the same time (this may be accompanied by some kind of discontinuity in the personality development, or a change in group affiliation, or both – for instance by a change in reference group orientation). But the system may also be so weakly coupled that individuals can change one of these attitudes with no implication whatsoever for the other. After all, the attitudes refer to different fields of experience that may lead to differ-

471

ent orientations; social and personality control for 'consistency' may be weak or weakened, etc.

Thus, correlations for *many* individuals at *one* point in time is an insufficient basis for inference about what will happen to *one* individual over a *period* of time – although it is certainly a good basis for hypothesis-formation.

To summarize: we shall only infer from a *correlation* to a *process* if two additional conditions are fulfilled:

the correlation holds *if the same unit is measured at several points in time*, not only if many units are measured once, (diachronic correlation), and
the *variables are also correlated with time*, so that the finding actually refers to a covariation between time and two other variables.

In a Richardson process, the unit may be the USA–USSR dyad, and the two variables their armament levels. Yearly measures are given by the military budgets, and they may, at least for certain time intervals, satisfy the conditions. With increasing time, both armament levels increase, so that the observation points are nicely ordered on the regression curve (first comes 1948-1949, then 1949-1950, and so on).[15] But it is easy to imagine a correlation pattern where the first but not the second condition above has been satisfied. Systems may be oscillating so that the time-points appear in all kinds of disorder – the only pattern is a certain tendency for the variables to covary. If not even this tendency is present, there is no structure in the data relevant for our purpose.

The second condition above may be satisfied for small time intervals, and as is well known, the process may have negative feed-back, with a period of positive covariation followed by a period of negative covariation, so that the system or unit is oscillating between two extremes. Data for an extended period of time would show a lack of correlation with time because of the superimposition of all the sub-series of observation. The system may also be so well equilibrated that both variables are constant over time. In this case, data from a number of units may show no correlation at all, because two processes balance each other.

Thus, positive feed-back processes will show up as correlations over time; negative feed-back processes may result in a range of variation so limited that no clear pattern, or a pattern of independence emerges; and the one-way processes show up as correlations.

In short, we may say that there are two reasons why we cannot in general infer from synchronic to diachronic correlation.

First of all, since a synchronic correlation is tied, by definition, to one point in time it does not take into account the possible changes of relevant conditions in the context. These changes may also change the relationship, and this will be seen if we observe the same unit through a period of time. However, it may be objected that we cannot infer from one diachronic correlation to another based on another time interval either – for the context may be different. This is true, but less so than for inferences from synchronic correlation, since diachronic studies will at least sensitize us to the problem.

It may also be objected that we can introduce a *ceteris paribus* assumption and try to infer from the synchronic correlation assuming that the context (i.e., all possible third variables) will remain constant. But this is likely to be a highly untenable assumption, and even if it does not produce bad science, it may produce useless science.

Secondly, there is the difficulty of the time order: synchronic correlation may point to the prevalence of some combinations (such as low, low; medium, medium and high, high) and the exclusion of all the others, but cannot guarantee against discontinuous jumps. Of course, if we are able to manipulate one of the variables from low via medium to high then the other may follow suit, but in social reality the transition may also be from low, low via high, high to medium, medium.

Moreover, neither is it possible, in general, to infer from diachronic correlation to synchronic correlation. Diachronic correlation is for *one* unit, but if the same correlation also holds for the *other* units then synchronic correlation will obtain for any point in time. For diachronic correlation guarantees that only certain combinations of values will be realized. At a given point in time, some units may have realized one combination and other units another combination – but the net result is synchronic correlation.

Imagine now that we add one more condition to the two conditions above:

one of the variables can be manipulated, i.e. we can determine the value (at least within a range of variation).

When this condition is satisfied, we shall say that a *mechanism* has been found. By manipulating the independent variable, desired changes can be brought about in the system, depending on how strong the correlation is and how well-known the processes are. *And this is applied social science,* it must be based on knowledge of mechanisms, not on knowledge of correlations. A correlation alone, however high, is no basis for social engineering: it may not work over time within the same unit, and there may be no variable that is manipulable. In a sense this is trivial, but it is often forgotten; and it has some implications both for data-collection and for theory-formation, if applied science is the goal.

Thus, there should be much more emphasis on longitudinal data in social science, and much less on the synchronic type of study. Further, one should include among the variables an independent variable that is manipulable, as we have argued in I, 1.4 and build the theory around that variable. Otherwise the data and the analysis may have little or no value from the point of view of application – although they may be of considerable value in the understanding of the structure of a system at a given point in time.

Moreover, social theory should be presented in the process language as a set of variables related by one-way or two-way, negative or positive processes (or no process at all), where the theory gets support from correlation statements and social process data. Thus, take the following paradigm of the present East-West arms race situation:

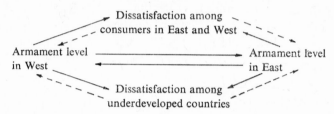

The arms races are positive feed-backs between two armament levels, as is amply demonstrated in the post Second World War situation. But if these were the only processes working one would end up either with war or with the conversion of all resources to military capability. However, we have indicated two simple negative feed-backs that are called into action when the armament levels absorb an increasing fraction of the GNP: demands from the consumers, the inhabitants of the bloc countries, and demands from the developing nations. There is also, of course, a certain negative feed-back due to fear, to what Richardson and Smoker have analyzed as submissiveness, etc. In general this seems to be a valid rule: whenever a positive feed-back is found in a system, look for a negative feed-back coupled to it somewhere – since otherwise the system would have to disintegrate. The example also indicates that negative feed-backs form a much broader category in social science than 'social control'.

One may now speculate about the relation between this and the idea of causation. We have touched the definition of a causal relation in II, 5.3 and here only want to add some comments.

First of all, the causal language is impractical, since the testing of a causal relation not only is a tremendous investment, but also an infinite process. Secondly, the causal language has, since there is no limit to the number of multivariate analyses to be carried out, a degree of absolutism not found in the process language: it presupposes perfect correlation with time (cause shall never occur after the effect), where the complexities of social reality should make us more modest and fully content if a process in our sense is found. And finally, it is often required that the causal mechanism is explained, i. e. is deducible from some other proposition. This seems irrelevant, since a mechanism works as long as it works regardless of whether we 'understand' or not. Hence, we suggest the more pragmatic concept of process to the dogmatic concept of cause and effect. The causal language is too strong and the correlation language too weak to fit the needs of social theory – so something like the process language should be developed.

The problem this raises is of crucial importance to the future development of the social sciences: how is it possible to get more data and more theories about *processes,* if one cannot infer from synchronic to diachronic correlation? The general answer is, of course, to include time as a variable in a maximum number of studies, but some care should be exercised here.

First of all, the *trend study* does not by itself represent a solution, since it does not involve the same unit(s) measured several times. Rather, it is a set of synchronic studies ordered in time, and although much will probably be gained by exploring what kind of inferences one can legitimately make from such data, the trend study should not be confused with diachronic data. On the other hand, as aggregate data about collectivities, for instance as a public opinion trend, this method yields diachronic data at the level of the collectivities that are very valuable.

Secondly, the *panel study* as it is known today does not by itself represent a solution. It is diachronic, but the time interval has to be short in order to avoid excessive panel mortality. This reduces the applicability considerably since one is limited to studies of short-term processes (between two elections, for instance). It may be, however, that the method can be extended considerably by follow-up studies of cohort samples – but then the problem becomes that of duration discussed above.

Thirdly, the *retrospective technique* has severe limitations because of the differential memory effect and the drive towards consistency: people interviewed about their childhood experiences may try to make reports about earlier actions consistent with their present beliefs. Nevertheless, this is probably a very promising method if carried out somewhat like a police interrogation: 'You did like to play that game when you were ten years old. With whom did you do it – did anybody see it' – and then check to validate the data.

These three methods combined should yield much of value. But in addition there are other methods.

First of all, one may concentrate on *quick social processes*. Some nations or parts of nations develop extremely quickly, and a study of their growth processes can be conceived of as a study of the history of more slowly developing societies in a telescoped form. There is of course the problem of whether 'quick history' really corresponds to 'slow history', but this is a problem that can be attacked, probably with the consequence that much of the history of mankind will have to be rewritten in the light of what we today know about socio-economic development processes.

Secondly, even though a process takes long time to unfold itself if we are to follow it as it unfolds itself, we may work backward in time, studying processes that have already taken place, so that we know better which variables to be included. This can be done by using the retrospective technique for quickly developing societies: asking older people what life was like ten, twenty, thirty, fourty, fifty years back and checking what they say. But one is, of course, not limited to interviews or questionnaire methods. The historian's meticulous work with sources, combined with modern sampling methods and the analytic machinery of content analysis so that multi-variate analysis can be carried out should yield much, provided an institutional framework can be found.

Thirdly, and this may be the most promising procedure of them all: processes may be simulated, by computer experiments or experiments with human beings (or both). Through simulation of past history or of contemporary events, processes may be telescoped into amenable sequences, be subjected to analysis, and may lead to the formulation of hypotheses that in turn may be tested. This will solve the time problem, but it remains to be seen how valid the conclusions will be.

And this leads to the final point: for diachronic social science to develop, social scientists must somehow be given the chance to follow social processes as closely as possible, which may mean keeping in contact with the people who are closest to shaping such processes, the politicians. But in order to evaluate this possibility, extra-scientific values will have to be considered. And one such value is the reduction of publication-pressure on young social scientists so that they may engage in lasting diachronic research without losing in the competition with synchronic work.

(3) *The structural-functional language*
We shall not go into any detail with this third language since we have tried to do so elsewhere.[16] Suffice it only to say that it is based on the correlation language, supplemented with one idea: that the variables can be meaningfully divided into *ends* called *functions,* and *means* called *structures.* We may perhaps put it this way: structural-functional analysis is a way of dividing the variables into independent and dependent that uses evaluative criteria,

criteria of importance. Thus, analyses in these terms give us information about to what extent important values, often called social prerequisites, are realized in the structure.

In this language, consequences ('effects', 'results', 'dependent variables') are evaluated, using as yardsticks value-standards. Thus, exogamy is not only said to produce decrease in violence potential (because of ties of multiple loyalties established) but to be 'functional' for this reason, because decrease in violence potential is considered a value. We may say that structural-functional analysis is an effort to establish a language where pure descriptions of how variables relate to each other can be combined with a value-analysis in terms of how different states of society contribute to social survival or to social realization. The approach raises a great number of difficult problems, and is hardly indispensable for social analysis.

In general, it is safe to say that this entire field is far from explored. Lately, some impressive advances have been made,[17] but they are usually based on too strong measures of correlation and are also, perhaps, overly complicated. For that reason we prefer not to review them, but to wait and see till the entire situation is more clarified.

*   *   *

Let us now, as a conclusion to these comments on different approaches to problems of theoretization, try to make some kind of synthesis of the scattered definitions and techniques mentioned here and in the literature.

In I, 2.3 and in II, 4.1, hypotheses and propositions have been defined as having the form $P_S(X_1, X_2, \ldots X_n)$.

In II, 5.3, techniques are given to confront a large variety of hypotheses for different values of n with data; so-called multivariate analysis.

In II, 6.1, theories are defined as sets of hypotheses weakly connected by implication relations. Lower level hypotheses are said to describe the phenomena, higher level hypotheses to explain them. It is pointed out that we can infer validity but not tenability.

In II, 6.3, difficulties with the correlational as well as with the causal language are pointed out, and a process language is suggested. Schemes are indicated to analyze chains of negative and positive feed-back in sets of variables.

A suitable point of departure is now to do what was done in II, 5.3: to focus on n as a major variable. Let us start with $n = 1$. In this case the proposition is one-dimensional; a set of objects or units are distributed on a variable. The lower the dispersion of this distribution, the closer we are to a simple classification of S, where the m objects are given a value: 'All taxis in Santiago are old' or 'Socrates is mortal'.

One standard basis for the deduction of conclusions of this kind is the *syllogism*. Why are taxis in Santiago old? Because (1) the few new cars that exist are used for prestige purposes by rich people, and (2) the taxi-function excludes the prestige-function. The structure of the theory is $(H_1 \& H_2) \rightarrow H_3$, which is the standard format of the syllogisms. A frequently found form is the syllogism *barbara:* H_1: All nations in rank disequilibrium will show aggressiveness, H_2: Developing nations are in rank disequilibrium, hence H_3: Developing nations will show aggressiveness. Both examples show the weakness of the syllogism formats: the favorite expressions of social scientists, 'mainly', 'usually', 'tend to' and other expressions of probabilistic rather than deterministic distributions are excluded. Syllogisms are simple applications of simple set-theoretical relations (the set of new cars is a subset of the set of prestige-cars, and since the set of taxi-cars has no intersection with the set of prestige-cars, no taxi-cars can be new cars, and hence all of them will have to be old cars).

How, then, does one proceed to explain a *distribution* on one variable, when the dispersion is not zero? One method would be to pretend that the distribution is deterministic, and proceed as indicated above. But this requires justification in terms of both central tendencies and dispersions, and this leads us to the second major type of theoretization. Statements of the type 'Danes are over-protective' are short-hand for 'on a scale of protectiveness the distribution of Danes has a higher central tendency than the distribution of non-Danes, and both distributions have relatively low dispersion so that the overlap is not too big'. It makes little sense to explore the vagueness of certain expressions in this statement (and many would not include the second clause), as long as it is clear that the statement has the form $C(X, Y)$. A correlation is asserted between two variables, in this case Dane-non-Dane and protectiveness. It should be noticed in passing that the conclusions in syllogisms also can be put on the form of correlation in a fourfold-table, as a correlation between 'Socrates non-Socrates' and 'mortal non-mortal', in the set of all human beings. What the conclusion specifies is only that the combination 'Socrates non-mortal' is empty.

Imagine now that we start with a correlation statement of the usual $C(X, Y)$ type and we want to explain or interpret the finding. One standard way of doing this, probably the most frequent form of explanation found, is as follows: A variable Z is introduced between the variables X and Y, in a logical sense. We then assert:

$$H_1: \quad C(X, Z)$$
$$H_2: \quad C(Z, Y)$$
$$\overline{H_3: \quad C(X. Y)}$$

The correlation between X and Y is explained by means of their variation with a third variable, Z. Example: 'Later-born siblings are, on the average, more intelligent than first-born siblings', relating birth-order (X) to intelligence (Y). What is needed is a third variable that can serve as a *basis of explanation,* and is related to both of them. One such basis is 'ease of birth', which increases with birth-order and diminishes brain-damage, consequently favoring the physiological basis for intelligence. Another basis is 'number of role-models to imitate', which increases with increasing birth-order, and can be seen as a stimulus (within a certain range) to the development of intelligence. These two bases serve to develop two different theories and are good illustrations of the principle of co-existence; one need not choose between them, unless there are different, and very different, degrees of the falsification when deductions are made in other directions. What seems ideal and scientifically tempting is to try to study the interaction of the factors and construct a theory where they both play a role weighted according to their explanatory power, for instance, using analysis of type 3.2.

We now have five comments to make.

First of all, there is not necessarily 'Gedankennotwendigkeit' in the format given above. If the symbol C is given a process-language interpretation ('if X increases, then Z will increase' and similarly for H_2 and H_3, we think almost all will conceive of the relation between (H_1 & H_2) and H_3 as an implication. But if C is given a wider interpretation, including synchronic correlation, then we have shown earlier in this section that the inference is only valid under certain conditions; and these conditions will depend on the particular correlation measure used. We may, however, assume that C is interpreted so as to be within the range where valid inferences can be made, in which case the statement that '(H_1 & H_2) $\rightarrow H_3$ is an implication' becomes a tautology.

Secondly, much has been said in the literature of the Lazarsfeld school about the role of the time-order of Z relative to X and Y. The two possible three-variable models are[18]

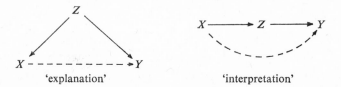

'explanation'   'interpretation'

where either arrow stands for H_1 or H_2 and the broken arrow for H_3. It may be objected that three variables can have 3! or 6 temporal orders relative to each other, but we do not differentiate between X and Y, and the forms

$X \to Y \to Z$ and $Z \to X \to Y$ and other forms are excluded because $C(X, Y)$ enters in the premises and not only in the conclusion. We attach less importance to this type of reasoning since the time-order is only rarely so clear[19] and since concepts of 'cause' and 'effect' seem to play a decreasingly important role.

Thirdly, the simple scheme given is a good illustration of both the need and the possibility of testing at all levels. The 'birth-order intelligence' proposition can be tested directly and the two sets of premises can all be tested.

Fourthly, we can now construct much more complex theories simply building upwards and downwards from the theoretical nucleus. One typical form is as follows:

$$
\begin{array}{c}
\underbrace{H_{11} \ \& \ H_{12}} \\
\downarrow \\
\underbrace{H_{21} \ \& \ H_{22}} \\
\downarrow \\
H_{31} \ \& \ H_{32}
\end{array}
$$

where the conclusion of step n is one of the premises in step $n+1$. The scheme has neither beginning nor end, but one style of theory-construction would be to start in the middle with a verified hypothesis and then build both upwards and downwards, i.e. 'anchor it in both ends'.

Another form is this one:

$$
\ldots \ H_{11} \ \& \ \underbrace{H_1 \ \& \ H_2} \ \& \ H_{21} \ \ldots \\
\underbrace{} \quad \downarrow \quad \underbrace{} \\
H_{111} \quad P \quad H_{221}
$$

Here a start has been made with the proposition P which then has been deduced from $H_1 \ \& \ H_2$ according to the usual scheme (whether it is of the syllogistic or correlational form). We might now test H_1 and H_2 directly and/or deduce consequences from them adding new hypotheses H_{11} and H_{21}, which then in turn may have to be tested the same way.

The two forms can be called *vertical* and *horizontal* extensions respectively, and their combination is a full-fledged theory, verified or not at any point. Such schemes can rapidly grow quite complicated and should be handled with graph-theoretical concepts – but that is beyond our scope here. Also,

480

this format for presenting theories is not necessarily the most efficient one: and that brings us to our final point.

When many variables are involved, a variable-diagram may be a heuristically better device, where tendencies to increase and decrease together can be traced and implications hypothesized. (We say 'hypothesized' because of the difficulty of valid inference with correlations.) The best thing to do in the present stage of theory-formation in the social sciences is probably to use both approaches, sketching both how hypotheses are related by implications, and how variables are related by correlations and particularly by processes.

6.4. *Limitations in contemporary social research*

We are at our journey's end. We have presented what to us appear essential parts of the theory and method of social research, with no claim to have exhausted that vast field, and certainly with no claim to have said the last word on any point. A model of science that presupposes a constant methodology producing a flow of hypotheses and theories is a model of a dead science. Methodology, like a factory, will have to change when there is no longer satisfaction with the kind of products it turns out (but as with a factory, there are certain principles that will have to be respected in re-construction, at least for the time being). In I, 6.4 we have indicated some examples of sources of dissatisfaction.

More is indicated in one of the most important books that has appeared recently in social science literature, Berelson and Steiner: *Human Behavior: An Inventory of Scientific Findings* (New York: Harcourt, Brace World, 1964). The importance of this book lies in presenting, for the first time, an up-to-date answer to the question *où en sommes-nous* in the social sciences (in this case meaning psychology, social psychology, sociology, with some dashes of anthropology and political science). The authors present social science as an inventory of 1045 'findings' or propositions. The number does not matter, as the authors say there 'could have been one fifth as many or five times as many, depending on the criteria' (p. 659). What matters is that anybody can get, quickly, an orderly impression of what today represents relatively well substantiated knowledge of human behavior, with good indications of the empirical evidence. No specialist will be fully content with the treatment of 'his' field: but such inventories are not for specialists but for 'generalists', for people who want a general survey, and for specialists outside their own field.

Berelson and Steiner make some observations on the state of social science knowledge today:

First, we believe that there are some important things wrong with the behavioral sciences at this stage in their development: e. g., too much precision misplaced on trivial matters, too little respect for crucial facts as against grand theories, too much respects for insights that are commonplace, too much indication and too little proof, too little genuine cumulation of generalizations, too little regard for the learning of the past, far too much jargon.

But second, we also believe that, despite all the faults of youth and immaturity, the behavioral sciences have already made important contributions to our understanding of man and will make many more; that they are an indispensable approach to that understanding; that they have already affected man's image of himself, and permanently so; in short, that they are a major intellectual invention of the twentieth century, and largely an American one. (p. 12).

We, and we think many other social scientists, agree with both statements although there may be disagreements about emphasis. However, we want to make use of the dimensions for evaluating hypotheses and theories, developed in II, 4.2 and II, 6.2 to point more concretely at some of the limitations of the sociology of today.

A major shortcoming has to do with the pair 'generality-complexity'. The road forward is relatively clear: generality can be increased by adding to the complexity, thus linking together phenomena that are otherwise not seen as different realizations of basically the same principle. This should not be confused with the problem of collecting data so as to permit generalization: this is solved by suitable sampling and particularly by replication procedures. But the problem of increasing generality by adding to the complexity, by introducing new variables, is not only a theoretical problem: empirical validation will still have to be done. Thus, imagine we observe that recent immigrants to big cities in the USA become members of secondary associations with a relatively anonymous type of relationship to the leaders, whereas similar immigrants in Latin America tend to be absorbed in associations with a more primary type of relationship between leaders and members, if they become members of any association at all. The two findings can perhaps be tied together by using degree of urbanization as a variable. If we assume (1) that secondary associations are more easily developed in a country with a high degree of urbanization because of the social compatibility between the two in terms of, for instance, Parsonian pattern variables, and (2) that a person needs training before he can switch from the primary type organization of the family to the modern and anonymous secondary organization; then the findings are linked together. An implication of this is the nature of a political party in the two Americas. Mobilization of the periphery

482

by means of internal migration and organization membership would lead to parties organized around ideas or issues in countries with a high level of urbanization and parties organized around central persons in countries with a low level of urbanization, and so on. The point is never to give up and say 'the finding for country X is invalid for country Y' – that is a pres-scientific although important kind of statement – but rather ask: 'which are the premises from which we can deduce the findings in both X and Y'. Obviously, when such deductions are made, we should try to increase degree of confirmation by testing the theory on new levels of urbanization, inter-polating or extrapolating from the findings in X and Y. And here the empirical problem of generalization will enter.

To bring isolated findings together is a problem both of hypothesis- and theory-formation. This also applies to the next weak point in contemporary social science: the low levels of specificity and falsifiability. They are closely related to each other, since falsifiability by definition can be increased by only two methods: (1) by increasing the specificity, or (2) by decreasing the number of distributions for which the hypothesis will be accepted. This, again, is a question of (1) sufficiently valid methods of data-collection to permit meaningful classification of units so that fine discriminations can be made, between values and between distributions; and (2) a sufficiently well-developed theory to discriminate better between distributions and delimit better the distributions that confirm the hypotheses. Thus, the days of 'more X, more Y' hypotheses should be running out now, yielding to hypotheses specifying degree and shape of the correlation, more like 'Y will increase rapidly with X up to X_1, then less rapidly to X_2, and keep constant for X higher than X_2, and the average correlation will be at least 0.7 as measured by coefficient so and so'. The next step will obviously be to relate X and Y functionally in relatively precise mathematical terms. But so far the mathematics that corresponds to the level of measurement in the social sciences has not been sufficiently developed.

From a utilitarian, point of view it would also be desirable to bring social theory up to a level where predictions are more successful. But as mentioned, we do not consider this one of the criteria of scientific success; social science should be judged according to its ability to explain and to account for, more than according to its ability to predict. This will be further elaborated below.

The short-comings of theory-formation are equally conspicuous. There is an enormous and relatively empty middle-range, as pointed out by many leading sociologists,[20] between 'grand theory' and 'abstract empiricism', between the remote horizons and 'the small grains of sand on the beach'. To a large extent this is a question of tying together singular propositions in the way described above, by increasing the complexity. But it is also a question of finding new and fruitful nuclei from which a diversified spectrum of hypotheses can be deduced. This, of course, is done all the time in contemporary sociology. An example is the diversity of good hypotheses that have emerged from the simple idea of describing individuals not in terms of one single rank-dimension, but in terms of whether they have consistent ranks or not.[21] Many such nuclei will be found in the future, and the progress of social science will probably mainly depend on whether institutional circumstances permit cooperation between empiricists who confirm singular hypotheses and theoreticians who can tie them together.

However, we have a feeling that all of this and the points mentioned by Berelson and Steiner as well as many other points, will be taken care of; that social science will progress and become more able to account for, explain, and even predict a range of phenomena that will increase both in breadth and depth. But there is another limitation that in a sense is much more important and difficult to tackle, because it is so deeply entangled with basic principles. We are thinking of the relation social science in general and sociology in particular has to human values, ideologies, utopias.

There is a general dogma of *value-neutrality* in science that is difficult to pin down in exact terms. It is usually seen as some kind of constraint on the activities of social scientists, as ruling out something they might otherwise have done. This may inmediately make one somewhat suspicious: constraints in human affairs are rarely random and usually serve some other functions in addition to the functions they are said to serve. Without any implication that somewhere there is or has been a particularly machiavellian person who wanted to keep the social scientists in their place and, hence, pronounced the dictum of value-neutrality that has been repeated with varying degrees of awe by generations of social scientists ever since, it is important to think along these lines. Potentially, the sociologist is encroaching on the traditional fields of other people; the politician, the priest, the ideologist, the humanist, the 'generalist' (each society has its 'generalist', the person who can serve in many contexts, like jurists and journalists) and many others all have a potential competitor in the social scientist.

In the literature and in discussions there is a great variety of interpretations of the doctrine of value-neutrality. The only one that seems acceptable is also either unnecessary or (almost) devoid of meaning. It is the idea that scientific findings should be invariant of the ideology of the scientist. This invariance of the characteristics of the scientists (not only his ideology, but any characteristic) is already expressed in the idea of science as 'intersubjectively communicable and reproducible', so at this level of preciseness, this

484

interpretation of the idea of value-neutrality is not needed. In practice it does not bring us very far. Imagine three persons trained at Columbia, Louvain, and University of Moscow checking each other's writings on the structure and functions of the class system in, say, Italy. What meaning does it have to say that they shall serve as each other's checks? To begin with, they would often not even dream of reading each other's writings. And if they did, they would often disagree with the very premises, the choice of problem, the conceptualization, the methodology, the data or lack of data, the analysis, the theories – everything. At the same time there may very well be a high level of intra-school intersubjectivity, corresponding to a conflict rather than cooperation model of the scientific community. Consistency is brought into this picture by one simple trick: the three schools, explicitly or implicitly, might refuse to refer to each other as scientists.

One could now relax the requirement somewhat by saying: the idea is not that all other scientists in the field should accept everything in the publication, but that they shall come to the same conclusion as the author if they do accept his premises. But which premises? Should the Thomist accept the Hegelian basis in Marxist analysis and then control that the rest follows? Or should the empiricist accept the scholastic basis in Catholic scholarship, with reference to forms and categories and not to what the empiricist would call Data, and then control the rest? Since they would hardly be capable of doing so, the control would be insufficient and much better carried out by somebody inside the same school. Besides, if the disagreement is about precisely these premises, often of a fundamental epistemological nature, then what sense does it make to say that 'findings should be reproducible'?

Rather, we might relax the criterion even further, accepting the idea of three or more ways of explaining the human condition and requesting as a minimum intersubjectivity within, if not between, the camps. This has the advantage of making for a more pluralistic world, if we accept that as a value. For the final consequence of intersubjectivity is a unitary world where science is concerned, which is a considerable value-choice as a consequence of a doctrine of value-neutrality. Today there is little doubt that there is a basic correspondence between the social matrix and the kind of social science it produces, and it is probably also true that styles of scientific pursuit will converge as the social matrices converge.[22] It may well be that a doctrine of value-neutrality, i.e. invariance of value-orientation, will speed up this process. In the meantime, maximum openness between camps to learn other perspectives, and maximum intersubjectivity within camps seem to be the best one can make of the situation. It may also be that the situation never has and never will be as conducive to progress in social science as today: there is both a high level of achievement protected by a sufficient level of consensus, and a challenge from the outside made effective by conferences, travel, informal contact, etc. The three major camps are each other's major source of renewal. It is obvious within which camp the present book has emerged. But to be raised in one tradition should not make one blind to the possible virtues of other lines of thought.

Let us then examine some other interpretations of 'value-neutrality'. By and large they can be ordered on a dimension that corresponds to the scientific process itself: choice of problem, concepts and methodology, data-processing and -analysis, interpretation and theory-formation, conclusions, publication, and finally the activities of the social scientist himself.

First of all, it is obvious that value-neutrality does not mean that the social scientist should not do research *on* values. Nor should it mean that he should not let himself be *guided* by his own values in his *choice of topic* of research. Chances are that the social scientist has more insight, knows more, is more motivated, if his field of research is close to the location of the values he believes in or rejects strongly. No doubt, there is the danger of value-contamination when it comes to how the research is carried out, but unless there is too much homogeneity in the milieu or too little ambivalence in the researcher himself, this can be corrected for. An enormous amount of motivational energy and insight goes unutilized every year because many social scientists feel it is not dignified to combine, say, political interest in X with a study of X. But even if some mistakes are made, we should perhaps be as much on guard against unengaged, unimportant research however well it is done as against value-contamination at every point. Contamination can just as well come from the unengaged conformist as from the engaged deviant – it is only more difficult to discover.

And this brings us to another possible interpretation: the idea that research should not be done on controversial issues (regardless of where the researcher stands), *only on the non-controversial.* It is not difficult to see the protection mechanisms of other social groups in this 'stay in your ivory tower' idea. There are some practical arguments. It is easier to gather data about the non-controversial because people are less cautious; and since the controversial is probably still in process, in development, one can easily go astray. A process that has come to an end, a conflict that has gone through its life-cycle, is more easily and often more profitably studied because conclusions can be drawn with more finality. But these two arguments are arguments for developing new methodology and new theory, not for giving up a certain style of research. On the contrary, the role of the intellectual in general and the sociologist in particular should be to present a deeper, more penetrating image of the social condition, not to run away from it.

The next set of interpretations would start with the basis of social research and ask to what extent there is built into fundamental concepts and methodology certain conclusions that are not value-neutral. An example might be the type of criticism we have mentioned against the survey method in I, 6.4; and the frequent and justifiable criticism against equilibrium models (see II, 6.3). Science progresses by means of this criticism, but we are not convinced that the criticism has to be subsumed under the heading of value-neutrality. There are enough other bases for the evaluation of hypotheses and theories. If important phenomena go unexplained, one does not have to invoke a doctrine of value-neutrality to explain this omission. From the point of view of the sociology of sociology one might be more interested in using value-biases to explain why important phenomena have not become topics of scientific study (for instance, the scientific study of the conditions conducive to peace). But in the scientific process itself the built-in checks stemming from the idea of intersubjectivity are sufficient, provided there is enough inter-school contact – so that the professor is not 'checked' only by students he has trained himself.

This also applies to biases in data-processing and -analysis, interpretation and theory-formation, and the conclusions drawn from the study. The mistakes that can be made are, of course, numerous. Some of them are correlated with lack of training, some of them with lack of intelligence, and some of them with ideological bias that makes the researcher blind to certain interpretations while too eager to jump on others.[23] But to single out the latter kind of errors more than others seems unwarranted. Let science be judged on its merits, i.e. the finished product, not on some *a priori* characteristic of the investigator, such as amount and quality of training, intelligence, and ideology. A social science monopolized by the uncommitted, bright young men trained at some universities rather than others is an impoverished social science.

But there is another aspect of social theory that is less trivial in its value-implications, and less frequently noticed. The moment the social scientist turns from explanation to prediction, he passes judgments on what the future is going to look like. This, by itself, is not a value-judgment, but in their consequences they may function like one. A prediction and a value-standard have this in common: given the set of *a priori* possible states of the world at some point in the future, a value-standard rules out some of them as undesirable and focuses on others, and a prediction rules out some of them as impossible or improbable and also focuses on others (i.e., the states that are predicted). *Both limit the potential richness of human existence by applying some principle of exclusion.* But this is not a neutral action in its consequences even if it is guided by no (explicit) value-standard at all in the case of the social scientist.

Thus, we can imagine two different ways in which the social scientist can relate himself to the future:

he may ask: given a certain set of conditions, C, what is the most likely state, S, of the world that will follow from C; or

he may ask: given a state S^* of the world, which are the conditions, C^*, that are most likely to produce S^*?

In the first case he works from C to S, in the second from S^* to C^*. In both cases the implications will have to be based on data from past and present and on general theory. Thus, in both cases serious errors may be made by reading the doctrine of 'uniformity of nature' (implicit in much physical research, it is the invariance-of-space-and-time doctrine) as a 'uniformity of society' doctrine. If C has led to S in the past we do not know for certain that it will continue to do so in the future, not because of indeterminacy in human affairs, but because the *ceteris paribus* condition. In the past other circumstances may have been equal, in the future they may change and combine into a world where C does not lead to S but to some other state. This state may have been approximated before, so we may be approximately right in our theory – but the margin of errors may be serious in human affairs.

The difference between the two perspectives is important. The former limits the range of variation in human affairs, the second leaves it open. In principle, it should even enlarge the range: the social scientist should have at his disposal concepts and insights that enable him to construct worlds that have never existed, societies nobody dreamt of, and even indicate the conditions that may lead to them. But in practice the social scientist may be as limited in his vision as anybody else, or even more: he may become so tied to his analysis of contemporary society that he falls prey to the cheap cynicism of 'plus ça change, plus c'est la même chose'. It should be pointed out to that type of social scientist that the second style above is no less scientific than the first, since it also permits empirical confirmation and disconfirmation. It has, moreover, the virtue of not necessarily leaving the definition of S to the politicians (making of the social scientist a kind of Weberian servant) but giving the social scientist a voice in the chorus defining the future states – not only predict them. And he can give policy advice, i.e. how to change C into C^* so as to obtain S^* rather than S.

We next turn to the problem of publication. Publication is a social act, because science is supposed to be public and accessible to all – at least, according to some traditions. As such the publication may create a new situation, it may please some more than others, it may favor some more than others: all consequences that, however unintended, are not value-neutral. And then, what if the consequences are even intended?

Theoretically, there are a number of positions one may take on this knotty issue. The two extremes are

The restrictive position: the scholar should do nothing of relevance to other than scientific values.

The permissive position: the scholar can do anything he wants as a citizen, but his scholarly work should be evaluated on its scientific merits only.

The first position is, of course, only value-neutral on paper. In practice it is value-loaded, because it leads to a number of important acts by omission, failure to take a stand, an apolitical attitude which is usually in the interest of the establishment and the *status quo,* etc. The second position is one of complete liberty, i.e. the scientist has the same liberty as anybody else to do what is value-relevant whenever he wants – but *qua* scholar he shall, of course, be evaluated on his scientific merits. This includes the right (1) to *intend* to promote values, and (2) to *combine this with scientific work,* for instance in the same book or article.

Intermediate positions would cut out either or both of these two points, maintaining, for instance, that the scholar has his liberty only in other contexts (outside working hours, outside the institute, writing in newspapers, not in scientific journals); and if his scientific activity is directly value-relevant, it should at least not be intended. This latter position is relatively frequently held, but we know only one good argument in its favor: under the present circumstances, it may well be that better social science is done under the banner of value-neutrality than under some ideological heading.

But this can change. Society may become more permissive, the social scientist may be more able to combine the two roles, and he may be more able to translate into social theory his experiences from social practice, and test his theories in clinical practice, like engineers and physicians. The latter is highly important: there is, in the long run, something anomalous about a political sociology by people who have never made politics the basis of their existence, industrial sociology by people who only know a factory as a place where interviewees can be found, medical sociology by people who have never been in hospitals in any of the roles found there, a sociology of prisons by people who have never been prisoners (only administrators if anything), a sociology of development by people who have barely visited poor countries, etc. We do not intend by this to say that the sociologist should only write about what he knows from his own experience, limiting sociology to the sociology of university institutes, for it is obvious that the outsider as analyst can be as good as or better than the insider. But both sources of insight are better than one alone, and the insider's knowledge is not yet fully utilized.

Thus, to conclude where we started: we feel the basic limitations of contemporary social research are not so much in methodology or theory, although there are important things to do. The basic limitation lies in the relation the social scientist has to his society. Many of the constraints he is working under, and has even internalized, pass under the heading of 'value-neutrality'. We suggest that society relinquish this value-loaded norm and opens its gates even more to the social scientist, to collect data, to analyze them, to publish his findings. We make a plea for his right to be engaged, to participate. In return, the social scientist should oblige himself to be exposed to the criticism of his colleagues, learned or lay, at any point. And he should oblige himself to hand back to society what it will always need most: a true and rich picture of society, past, present, and future – where nothing is taken for granted.

APPENDIX C

Sheets for data-processing

To facilitate data-processing it is recommendable to use some standard formats of *code-books* and sheets for *coding,* for ordering *cross-runs,* for *ordering indices* and for *tables.* Social scientists often differ as to how these sheets should be constructed. We have found the formats given in this appendix valuable, and shall give some brief comments on them.

(1) *Code-book* (p. 494)

The code-book is a dictionary where questions or variables are translated into columns and answers or values are translated into punches. Here as elsewhere it is important to remember the number of the deck of cards, in case there are so many variables that one card becomes insufficient. After the data have been processed, it is often useful to make some code-books where not only the code but also the marginal distributions with percentages are given.

If the interview-guide/questionnaire is well done, the code-book is actually superfluous, as indicated in I, 6.1. The number of the question/variable will also be the number of the column, and the punch will be written under or next to the answer/value or be found by counting from the left and above.

(2) *Code-sheets* (p. 495)

The sheets are self-explanatory. They come in two versions, one for one card per sheet and the other one for two cards per sheet. The choice will depend on two considerations: how much paper one is willing to have around and how much one wants to economize, and whether one would like to use the extra space in the first version to indicate what goes into the columns. For this purpose all one has to do is to make a new stencil for every project and type over the appropriate boxes the name of the field. For instance if age with two digits is to be coded in columns 13 and 14, all one has to do is to type age over the two boxes 13 and 14. In principle this should be unnecessary with a good code-book, in practice it may be useful as a reminder, to check coding quickly – and may also make the code-book superfluous if the coding itself is obvious.

These forms should not make one oblivious of the possibilities of punching directly from the interview-guide/questionnaire or using perforated margins or other techniques mentioned in II, 1.1, so as to make separate code-sheets superfluous.

(3) *Order-sheets for cross-runs* (p. 496)

The function of this sheet is to obtain the data needed for (multi-variate) analysis. The first column serves for the researcher as a place where he can put down some words to remind himself of why he was interested in that particular table – for that reason he should always make a copy and keep one for himself. The next column is for deck-identification. And then follow four (sets of) columns.

The idea here is to use the four for increasingly dependent variables, so that the *most* dependent variable(s) is (are) put in the very last column. If pure straight runs are wanted nothing more has to be done than writing the number of the column in the extreme right column: the 'to-column'. But this should be avoided, pure straight runs are rarely an economic way of using machines and data.

For simple bi-variate cross-runs the column for the independent variable is indicated in the 'from-column'. The number of the column may be sufficient, but if one is not interested in all values, or would like to have the values regrouped, this can be indicated under 'punch'. For control purposes it may be advisable to add the N. Thus, age may be coded in ten-year intervals from 0 (0-9 years) to 9, but the hypothesis may be about how adolescents compare with adults, or between 1-2 and 3-9. If this reformulation of the variable will be used often it will, of course, be better to punch it in a new column – but not if it is for a few runs only.

For tri-variate tables the most independent variable, for instance profession, should be indicated under 'column' for 'keep constant'. And if four variables are used the variable should be indicated under 'columns' for 'subgroups'. Apart from this the comments for the 'from-column' all apply. It should be noticed that under 'subgroups', 'keep constant' and 'from' only one column should be written at the time; under 'to' many columns can be indicated. One can, of course, 'run from' more columns, but a new line on the order-sheet should be used.

The sheet serves only up to four-variate analysis which is usually enough, and the fourth variable is usually a 'subgroup', for instance different parts of the sample (schools, villages, factories). By combining two variables into the definition of subgroups (old males, old females, young males, young females) the sheet can be used for five-variate analysis, and so on.

(4) *Order-sheet for indices* (p. 497)

Since additive indices play a fundamental role in the methodology presented here, a separate order-sheet is included. It provides space for as many as ten items, but in general around five should be sufficient. Further, the sheet can handle items that are trichotomized by giving them the values, 0, 1, and 2 – but in general dichotomous items may be preferable (the '2-column' will then be left blank).

For each item its column number is written, its content is also mentioned verbally to facilitate understanding, and under 0, 1, and 2 are written the punches that shall be given these weights respectively. With this scheme the maximum range for the index will be from 0 to 20, and the operator should write down the frequencies for each index value for later inspection of the distribution. The analyst and the operator may then decide how to simplify the index by combining adjacent values into 'low', 'medium', 'high' or something similar, for instance according to the principle of uniform distribution. The values of the simplified index are then indicated, and the column number for the new index given. The original index with its 0-20 range will rarely be punched into the card.

(5) *Cross-run sheets* (p. 498)

This sheet can be used advantageously by the person using a sorter-counter – he can write the figures into the sheet as they appear, and also write in the interpretation of the punch values. Lines are provided for comments.

(6) *Table-sheets* (p. 499)

For multivariate analysis this sheet may be useful. The table element is a bivariate table where the variables have four values each (a trichotomy and a DK, NA category). For bivariate analyses one such table will do. For trivariate analysis where the third variable also has four values the whole sheet must be used. But the sheet can also be used for four-variate analyses provided variables numbers 3 and 4 both are dichotomies. Thus the two top tables may be used for 'men', the left hand table for 'young' and the right hand table for 'old'; and the two bottom tables for 'women', in the same way.

Usually these tables will be filled with frequencies that come from the table-sheets of a data-processing machine, but are suitably collapsed for analysis. Percentages will then be calculated with the appropriate bases, and we have made no special provision for columns of percentages since that would complicate the sheet too much. It is recommendable to use different pencils, for instance always use red pencil for percentages.

INSTITUTION

Project:

Code book

Schedule no.   Card no.

No. 1 question	Column no.		N	%
answer *a*	punch 1			
answer *b*	punch 2			
DK	punch 9			
		SUM		100 %

No. 2 variable	Column no.		N	%
value *m*	punch 1			
value *n*	punch 2			
no information	punch 9			
		SUM		100 %

INSTITUTION

Project: Deck: Project: Deck:

1	21	41	61
2	22	42	62
3	23	43	63
4	24	44	64
5	25	45	65
6	26	46	66
7	27	47	67
8	28	48	68
9	29	49	69
10	30	50	70
11	31	51	71
12	32	52	72
13	33	53	73
14	34	54	74
15	35	55	75
16	36	56	76
17	37	57	77
18	38	58	78
19	39	59	79
20	40	60	80

1	21	41	61
2	22	42	62
3	23	43	63
4	24	44	64
5	25	45	65
6	26	46	66
7	27	47	67
8	28	48	68
9	29	49	69
10	30	50	70
11	31	51	71
12	32	52	72
13	33	53	73
14	34	54	74
15	35	55	75
16	36	56	76
17	37	57	77
18	38	58	78
19	39	59	79
20	40	60	80

Coder: Date: Verifier: Date: Coder: Date: Verifier: Date:

Puncher: Date: Verifier: Date: Puncher: Date: Verifier: Date:

INSTITUTION

Project: _____

Table order

Com- ments	Deck	Sub-groups			Keep constant			from			to
		col.	punch	N	col.	punch	N	col.	punch	N	Columns

Ordered by: _____   Performed by: _____

Date: _____   Date: _____

INSTITUTION

Project: _____   Card: _____

Index order

Column	Content	0	1	2

Index-value	0	1	2	3	4	5	6	7	8	9	10	11	12	13	14	15	16	17	18	19	20
Frequencies																					
Simplified index punch																					

Index to be punched in column: _____

Ordered by: _____   Executed by: _____

Date: _____   Date: _____

32 *

INSTITUTION

Project: _____   Deck: _____

Question _____ Question _____

Col. no. _____ Col. no. _____

	C o d e	1	2	3	4	5	6	7	8	9	0	x	y	R	SUM
Code															
	1														
	2														
	3														
	4														
	5														
	6														
	7														
	8														
	9														
	0														
	x														
	y														
	R														
	SUM														

_____

_____

_____

Operator: _____ Date: _____

Verifier: _____ Date: _____

498

Project_____

Table sheet

_____   _____

					Sum
Sum					

					Sum
Sum					

_____   _____

					Sum
Sum					

					Sum
Sum					

_____

_____

_____

APPENDIX D

Styles of social science in United States, Europe and Latin America

Much is said, and often, about different styles of intellectual endeavour in the social sciences in various parts of the world. Since the present text represents one among several approaches to studies of social reality, we felt it might be interesting to study more empirically the distribution of different styles of social science research. The present report gives one approach to this problem; while limited in scope and method, it is nevertheless indicative of something.

A total of 97 volumes of social science periodicals in the library of one regional social science institution were examined for their content.[1] 50% of them were from the United States, 8% from Latin America and 42% from Europe. Although one institution's library certainly is not the ideal sampling criterion, this particular institution had the advantage of having an international faculty from the three regions mentioned, so that at least three regions were well represented in the library. The center of gravity was in sociology: 71% of the volumes were in that branch of social science, with 9% in psychology, 9% in general social science, 6% of a more general nature, 3% in political science and 2% in anthropology. What we were interested in knowing was how such independent variables as *region, subject,* and *year of publication* were related to such dependent variables as *percentage of articles with statistical data* (in each volume), *average number of units* (per article with statistical units), *average level of multivariate analysis,* and *type of units* used in the analysis. The results are more or less as one would expect, but this does not make them less valid as sources of insights into the process of diffusion in social science.

The statistical orientation of social sciences in the United States is clearly evidenced in the first part of Table D.1, with Europe in-between as expected, and Latin America close to Europe and quite far from the United States.

More or less the same pattern is seen in the second part of the Table, about the level of analysis used. Since the averages are between 2 and 3 in most cases, most tables presented in the journals are in terms of 2 or 3 variables. Typically, the evolutionary pattern here is as follows: first the presentation of some marginal distributions, secondly bivariate distributions but with very traditional background variables as one of the variables (everything is 'run against' sex, although sex may be completely irrelevant relative to the theoretical framework). Then follows a phase where background variables are correlated or attitudinal variables are correlated and some indices are constructed, but from there on the step to three-variate

Table D.1. *The difference between the regions*

% articles with statistical data,	United States	Europe	Latin America
low (0 %–30 %)	35 %	63 %	75 %
medium (31 %–60 %)	35 %	27 %	25 %
high (61 %–100 %)	30 %	10 %	0 %
SUM	100 %	100 %	100 %
Maximum number of variables used in one table, average			
low (less than 2.10)	23 %	59 %	50 %
medium (2.11–2.50)	54 %	22 %	37 %
high (more than 2.50)	23 %	19 %	13 %
SUM	100 %	100 %	100 %
Number of units			
less than 500 units	60 %	34 %	75 %
501–900 units	11 %	9 %	25 %
above 900 units	27 %	54 %	0 %
census data	2 %	3 %	0 %
SUM	100 %	100 %	100 %
Type of units			
individuals	39 %	47 %	29 %
groups	29 %	19 %	35 %
nations	13 %	11 %	7 %
content analysis	8 %	3 %	0 %
others	11 %	20 %	29 %
SUM	100 %	100 %	100 %

analysis is still difficult. The distributions for Europe or Latin America actually both have their medians below 2.0, which corresponds to an average of bivariate analysis. This means that the amount of insight supplied by empirical social science is relatively limited. In practical terms it also means that the articles produced in social science have relatively little to offer that is new and provocative, since a high percentage of bivariate findings are of a kind that the more intuitive analyst and observer of social affairs will feel, or at least say, that he knew in advance. And this, in turn, is often used to reject empirical social science.

As to number of units, the situation is somewhat more complicated. Most samples in the Latin American articles are very small. But why is Europe above the United States? One reason is simply that when statistical methods are used at all, then the samples are big, of the types used in professional surveys. There is less of a tendency towards refined use of small and highly controlled samples of the types found very frequently in US journals. As can be seen from the distributions for US and Europe, samples either tend to be small or to be big – there is less of a tendency to use samples in the middle range. This reflects the division between the big, national sample of the gallup poll variety on the one hand and the small sample of the experimental variety – and the Table seems to indicate that the latter represents a later stage if we accept the general tendency for the US to be the *avant garde*.

Types of units also vary to some extent, with much more dispersion for the United States. This is borne out even more clearly if one counts for each volume how many types of statistical units are used:

Table D.2. *Number of types of units used per volume*

	United States	Europe	Latin America
1 type	15 %	34 %	50 %
2–3 types	70 %	54 %	50 %
4 types	15 %	12 %	0 %
SUM	100 %	100 %	100 %

Here the pattern is more clear: the trend, all the time using US as a guide, is above all towards dispersion, towards pluralism in the choice of type of data. That this represents a tremendous strength because it permits multi-level analysis of what is, structurally, the same phenomenon, is obvious.

Comparisons of different fields of social science brought out what one would expect: sociology is still less empirical than psychology, but when it is empirical it works with bigger samples – but this is to some extent compensated for by the circumstance that psychology works with analyses at higher levels of complexity.

We then made a special analysis of the *American Sociological Review* and the *Social Forces,* since we had data about them for a sufficient time-span to permit a longitudinal analysis. We were interested in seeing to what extent the synchronic analysis given above is reflected in the diachronic patterns: in other words, to what extent one may say that Europe and Latin

America represent past stages of a development that has taken place relatively recently in the United States.

For the *ASR,* 1939/1941, 1949-1952, and 1961-1962 were compared; and for the *SF* 1949 was compared with 1959/1961-1962, just to arrive at the general trends. The numbers are too small to merit a write-up in tabular form, but it makes sense to calculate the averages. For the *ASR* they were as follows:

Table D.3. *The trends in the American Sociological Review*

Averages	around 1940	around 1950	around 1960
% articles with statistical data	30	23	45
average no. of units	950	750	600
average level of analysis	2.10	2.28	2.70
average no. of types of units	3.5	2.8	4.0

Using *Social Forces* as a control we get the same trends, but less pronouncedly. This is probably due to the fact that there is a lag between the leading journal and a more peripheral journal in any field. The trend is typically towards smaller samples and more refined analysis. As to the latter, the trend is monotone, from low level to high level, and this is reflected synchronically. But where size of sample is concerned, the trend seems to be A-shaped: Sociology gets money and national elections are imitated in big samples, polls. This is probably the point where Europe is now, according to Table D.1. Then theory becomes more refined: research becomes less focused on the discovery of one's own society and its opinion structure, and more on theoretically well-defined problems that can be studied by means of smaller samples and replications. At the same time, multivariate analysis is introduced, and complexity of analysis is used to compensate for smaller samples. Thus, if one should make a prediction for Latin American social science, it is that it will work towards ever bigger samples, keeping complexity more or less constant in some years to come; and then gradually build up the complexity and reduce the sample sizes. A condition for this prediction to come true is increasing interest in cooperation between academic institutes of social science on the one hand and commercial or political pollsters on the other.

Apart from the strange dip in the trends around 1950, for which we would only have very *ad hoc* explanations to offer, the all over ASR trend is towards more articles with statistical data and more pluralism in the choice of units. Hence, with the general parallelism between the synchronic and the diachronic analysis it is rather safe to predict that this will be the trend in European and Latin American social science as well.

We should, ideally, have had some data that could give some information about the cultural diffusion in the opposite direction, if there is any. Is there any trend, for instance towards refined structural analysis, where Europe or Latin America are on an upward curve with the US lagging behind? Perhaps, but this is not reflected in our data which focus only on the growth of empirical social science of a particular variety.

It is interesting to compare this with the investigation made by Gold in 1959.[2] He found that of 743 articles published in the *American Sociological Review* 1944-1953, 272 or 37% of the articles could be said to be 'statistical' articles; if in addition one included the 11% dealing with demography, population, and census analysis the total is 48%. Of the 272 articles, however, only 73 or 27% present 'some statement or direct question concerning the nature of the relationship among three or more qualitative variables but no accompanying statistical analysis involving more than two variables. That is, not even the joint frequencies for more than two variables simultaneously were presented'. Gold concludes his report by saying that 'what the sociologist most needs are appropriate measures of association, measures of differences between contingency tables, descriptive measures that will perform a task somewhat analogous to multiple and partial correlation. In other words, he needs statistical techniques for describing the nature of the relationship among qualitative variables'. We very much agree, and it is in that spirit that the techniques in II, 5.3 have been presented.

1 This does not mean that the solution is trivial or easily arrived at. The chemist has an ideal case in mind, 'pure' sulphur or any compound which is defined as having only one kind of molecules. Whether a given substance is 'pure' can only be ascertained indirectly, by sampling from the material and testing a number of indicators (melting characteristics, refraction, scatter, etc.). But the indicators may not discriminate sufficiently, or the sampling be too permissive. The methodology is not too different from social science methodology, but the social scientist often does not even have a pure case concept in mind, not to mention any method to approximate it operationally.

2 Often a big number is necessary to 'get the differences out' at all.

3 Sorokin *(Social and Cultural Dynamics* (Boston: Porter Sargent, 1957), pp. 57 ff.) makes this observation against the position that human events are unique: 'No unique historical process can be narrated without the admission, explicit or implicit, that many essential traits are repeated. – Let us take, for example, Roman religion. If any moment of any historical event or socio-cultural process is unique, a difficulty arises at once: what moment of Roman religion is to be described? Is it to be Roman religion of 8 P.M., July 1, 321 B.C., or 7 A.M., May 10, 322 B.C.? –'. There are invariances in the 'uniqueness', otherwise no description would be possible. But, there are also variations, and our approach would be to cut the process in suitable pieces, units, and collect as much information about each single one as possible, including *time*. Different cuts will yield different results, and these results would have to be compared. Similarly with synchronic social science: one would make cuts in *space* (see 2.2.) and exploit the variations analytically. Thus, to test hypotheses one would get a sample from the units concerned and test the hypothesis systematically. McClelland, in *The Achieving Society* (Princeton, 1961), contrasts this effectively with the traditional quotation/illustration methodology, where cases are picked that are in accordance with the hypothesis – and hypotheses are rejected if one deviant case is found. This is a very naive conception of social science propositions; if only perfect correlations should be permitted social science would not have come very far.

4 For an introductory discussion, see Goode, Hatt: *Methods in Social Research* (New York: McGraw-Hill, 1952) ch. 5, particularly p. 42.

5 This is discussed in Galtung, Johan: 'An Inquiry Into the Concepts of "Reliability", "Intersubjectivity" and "Constancy"', *Inquiry,* 1959, pp. 107-125.

6 Behind the sociological model is an important tradition phrased in normative terms by Durkheim: 'The determining cause of a social fact should be sought among the social facts preceding it and not among the states of the individual consciousness' *(The Rules of Sociological Method* (Glencoe: Free Press, 1950), p. 110). Today this would be referred to as a 'structural' proposition or theory as against propositions/ theories in terms of values with varying degrees of internalization. And today one would, hopefully, be less concerned with the definition of the realm of one particular social science, and more concerned with the development of research models that combine the virtues of approaches from several disciplines.

7 In Christie and Jahoda: *Studies in the Scope and Method of 'The Authoritarian Personality'* (Glencoe: Free Press, 1954), pp. 50-122.

8 When this scheme can be so easily extended to nations, which means from thinking in psychology and sociology to thinking in political science and international relations, it is because of a basic similarity between these pairs of sciences. Thus, the four sciences can be classified as follows (see 2.1 for further explanation):

		Type of variable used	
		absolute, comparative	*relational*
Type of units used	*individuals*	psychology	sociology
	nations	political science	international relations

The "background variables", thus, place the units in the structure in which they are embedded, whether this is an individual or international interaction structure. The "personality" variables describe the unit *per se,* and the "behavioral" variables get at their interaction patterns. In model I, at both levels, this behavior is related to position in the structure; in model II, to internal structure. Thus, acts of nations may be explained by their position on the international rank scale, or by the structure of their political system. Models III and IV combine these two perspectives into more complex types of analysis, and model V is concerned with how internal structure relates to external position. All this can then be generalized further to a general methodology of system analysis, but that would lead outside the present scope of analysis.

9 This is closely linked to the ideology of our age, in industrial countries. We have no hesitation when it comes to changing a person's behavioral pattern by setting him in a different social context, as when he changes his style of life after (or prior to) a promotion. But behavioral change caused by change of personality seems to be acceptable only if the change is slow and not too efficient, as during a process of education or socialization, or when psychotherapy is used. Bio-chemical approaches to personality change meet with resistance, unless they can be defined as 'cures'. Findings that use personality variables as independent variables are either useless or too useful: there is a very narrow range between the two.

10 One can easily imagine a culture, dominated by Koestler's yogis (as opposed to his commissars) or Sorokin's ideationals (as opposed to his sensates) where personality variables would always be used as independent variables. Another question is whether that culture would produce social science at all.

2. *Units (pp. 37–71)*

1 'On the Relation Between Individual and Collective Properties', in Etzioni, A., ed.: *Complex Organizations, A Sociological Reader* (New York: Holt, 1961), pp. 422-440. Also see: Lazarsfeld and Kendall: 'The Relation Between Individual and Group Characteristics in "The American Soldier"', in *The Language of Social Research,* (Glencoe: The Free Press, 1955) pp. 290-296.

2 ibid., p. 440.

3 ibid., p. 433.

4 Or vice versa: even if 'democratic personality' disposes for peaceful behavior, one cannot infer that democracies are less bellicose than dictatorships. The discussion of ecological fallacies usually concentrate on fallacies 'downward', and neglects the equally important fallacies 'upwards'.

5 The literature on the ecological fallacy started with the very important article by Robinson, W.S.: 'Ecological Correlations and the Behavior of Individuals', *ASR,* vol. 15 (1950), pp. 351-357; and the comment by Herbert Menzel: 'Comment', *ASR,* 15 (1950), p. 674.
   Also see: Goodman, Leo: 'Ecological Regressions and Behavior of Individuals',

ASR, 18 (1953), pp. 663-664; and Duncan, O.D. and Davis, B.: 'An Alternative to Ecological Correlation', *ASR,* 18 (1953), pp. 665-666.

6 Cochran, W.: *Sampling Techniques* (New York: Wiley, 1953), p. 5. New edition 1963. For a good introduction to sampling in social science, see Kish, L.: 'Selection of the Sample', in Festinger, Katz: *Research Methods in the Behavioral Sciences* (New York: Dryden, 1953), pp. 175-239.

7 See Wald, A.: *Statistical Decision Functions* (New York: Wiley, 1950), pp. 28-31.

8 For an example of such expense, see Kish, op. cit., p. 202.

9 Hyman and Sheatsley, op. cit. p. 67.

10 In Galtung, Johan: *Members of two Worlds* (Oslo: International Peace Research Institute, mimeo 1962), Section 3.5.

11 Galtung, Johan: 'Foreign Policy Opinion as a Function of Social Position', *Journal of Peace Research,* vol. 1, nr. 3-4, 1964.

12 Berelson, Bernard: 'Content Analysis', Ch. 13 in Lindzey (ed.): *Handbook of Social Psychology,* vol. I (Cambridge: Addison-Wesley, 1954), p. 489. Also by same author: *Content Analysis in Communication Research* (Glencoe, Free Press, 1952). For a recent text, see North, Holsti, Zaninovich, Zinnes: *Content Analysis* (Evanston: Northwestern University Press, 1963).

13 Berelson refers to this as a separate distinction, op. cit., p. 508, and says (p. 509) that 'More than one unit of analysis can profitably be employed in a single study'.

14 See Stempel, G.H.: 'Increasing Reliability in Content Analysis', *Journalism Quarterly,* 1955, pp. 449-455 for a good study of reliability of content analysis.

15 Galtung, Johan: *Kontakt, konflikt og toppmøte* (Oslo: forthcoming), Ch. II gives an example of a content analysis of this kind.

16 See e.g. Brody, Richard A., Holsti, Ole R., and North, Robert C.: 'Measuring Affect and Action in International Reaction Models: Empirical Materials from the 1962 Cuban Crisis', *Journal of Peace Research,* vol. 1, no. 3-4, 1964.

3. *Variables (pp. 72–89)*

1 For a good treatment of the theory of classification, see Cohen, Nagel: *An Introduction to Logic and Scientific Method* (New York: Harcourt, Brace, 1934), ch. XII.

2 Figures from *Situação Social da America Latina* (Rio de Janeiro: Centro, 1961), p. 104.

3 In Rostow, W.W.: *The Stages of Economic Growth* (Cambridge: University Press, 1961), p. 7.

4 For one good presentation see Coombs: 'Theory and Methods of Social Measurement', in Festinger & Katz (eds.): *Research Methods in the Behavioral Sciences* (New York: Holt, 1953), pp. 411-488.

5 For one way of using this term that corresponds to what we shall call 'dimension' or 'cluster', see Guttman: 'A Basis for Scaling Qualitative Data; *ASR* 1944, pp. 139-150.

6 Zeisel, Hans: *Say It With Figures* (New York: Harpers, 1957), ch. X. An excellent study in the field is Kendall, P.: *Conflict and Mood: Factors Affecting Stability of Responses* (Glencoe: Free Press, 1954). Specifically dedicated to the problem of the effect of repeated interviewing is Bandage, C.H.: 'Are research panels wearing out?', *Journal of Marketing,* 1956, pp. 397-401. The conclusion was that people did not wear out after the three waves, and this is also the experience of the present author but the study has to interest the respondents (such as a study about integration).

7 The classical text is Moreno: *Who shall survive?* (Washington: Beacon House, 1953, rev. ed.).

8 The classical text is Bales, R.F.: *Interaction Process Analysis* (Reading, Mass.: Addison-Wesley, 1950).

[9] The classical text is Leontieff, W.: *The Structure of American Economy 1919-29* (New York: Oxford Univ. Press, 2nd ed., 1951).

[10] For a discussion of these types of social analysis, see Galtung, Johan: *An Introduction to Mathematical Sociology* (Santiago: FLACSO, mimeographed, 1963), chs. 2 and 5.

[11] For details, see the excellent introduction given by Zeisel, op.cit., in chapter V, where he uses sociometric examples among others in his discussion of indices.

4. *Values (pp. 90–108)*

[1] Used in Gross, Mason, McEachern: *Explorations in Role Analysis* (New York: Wiley, 1958), for instance p. 102.

[2] Described in Murphy, Gardner and Likert, Rensis: *Public Opinion and the Individual* (New York: Harper, 1938).

[3] Described in Osgood, Suci, and Tannenbaum: *The Measurement of Meaning* (Urbana: University of Illinois Press, 1957).

[4] Described in L. L. Thurstone and E. J. Chave: *The Measurement of Attitude* (Chicago: University of Chicago Press, 1929).

[5] Described in Cantril, Hadley: *The Pattern of Human Concerns* (New Brunswick: Rutgers University Press, 1965) pp. 22-24.

[6] For an elaboration of this, see Coombs, Clyde: 'Theory and Methods of Social Measurements', in Festinger, Katz, eds.: *Research Methods in the Behavioral Sciences* (New York: Holt, 1953), pp. 492 ff.

[7] See Luce, D.: *Individual Choice Behavior* (New York: Wiley, 1959), pp. 5 ff.

5. *Collection (pp. 109–128)*

[1] Of particular importance here has been the discussion of the technique used by Festinger and his colleagues in *When Prophecy Fails* (University of Minnesota Press, 1956), where social scientists disguised themselves as sect members waiting for doomsday to come, to record the reaction when doomsday did not materialize.

[2] For an example, see the articles by Borgatta, E. F. and Bales, R. F.: 'The Consistency of Subject Behavior and the Reliability of Scoring in Interaction Process Analysis', *ASR,* 1958, pp. 566-568. Also see Davis, F. J. and Hagedorn, R.: 'Testing the Reliability of Systematic Field Observations', *ASR,* 1954, pp. 345-348, where an almost experimental technique shows that a reasonable degree of reliability can be obtained.

[3] One way of examining the problem of validity, according to some authors, is to compare the results obtained by recording non-verbal and verbal data (one may object: 'what if they make the same mistake?'). This was done in Campbell, D. T.: 'The Informant in Quantitative Research', *AJS,* 1955, pp. 299-342, where the morale of ten submarine crews was assessed in three different ways: by informants, by officers, and by means of a 30-item morale questionnaire. The rank correlation between the first and the third method was 0.9. In a study reported in Vidich, A. J. and Shapiro, G.: 'A Comparison of Participant Observation and Survey Data', *ASR,* 1955, pp. 28-33, a prestige hierarchy in a community of 1500 was established by an anthropological field worker and sociometric techniques, and the correspondence was 'remarkably strong'. Also see Vidich, A. J. and Bensman, J.: 'The Validity of Field Data', *Human Organization,* 1954, pp. 20-27, for interesting evaluation of the same project from a methodological point of view.

[4] For problems in conducting a public opinion survey in Ghana, see Birmingham, W. B. and Jahoda, G.: 'A Pre-election Survey in a Semi-Literate Society', *Public Opinion Quarterly,* 1955, pp. 140-152. Such problems as '– there is no map of Accra

which shows all street names, – neither names nor surnames are firmly and unambiguously attached to individuals' are mentioned, where particularly the latter problem would be rather vexing. However, the authors conclude that survey techniques can be applied despite the radical differences.

Of course, the problem of universality also applies to interviews, as will be developed further in I, 6.4. For an excellent collection of articles discussing problems in interviewing particular groups, such as Frenchmen, pentecostalists, medical students, and homosexuals, see the special issue of the *American Journal of Sociology*, September 1956.

5 Some examples of this literature: In one of the major works on interviewing, Hyman, H. et al., *Interviewing in Social Research* (Chicago: University of Chicago Press, 1954), there is an extensive discussion of the problem. Data on the impact of the ideology of the interviewers are contradictory: in some cases there is no effect, in other cases there is (pp. 129-134). A study by Rice, S. S.: 'Contagious Bias in the Interview', *AJS*, 1929, where 2000 'destitute' men were interviewed, shows a tendency for prohibitionists to report alcohol as the cause of the misery, whereas socialists would blame the economic conditions. Of course, interviewers are themselves influenced by the ideology expressed, as shown by the famous experiment where interviewers were asked to code some unclear answers in the middle of tape-recorded interviews, one with an isolationistic and the other with an interventionist tendency – the answers were coded accordingly (Hyman, pp. 99-105). But their own ideology did not seem to count here, or at least not so much as the expectation structure created by the context.

Hyman discusses (pp. 208-221) the influence of having majority or minority views, and it looks as if interviewers with the majority point of view project this view into the respondents, both because of an ideology effect and an expectation effect. Interviewers with a minority ideology will project their ideology but also their expectation that the respondent will have the majority ideology, and will tend to use 'don't know' categories. Both effects are only appreciable when the answers are ambiguous.

The book contains a wealth of data and theory. One conclusion is 'Although there is undoubtedly a great deal of random or situational error in interviews, it still seems very possible that different interviewers may exert differential net biases on given respondents or subgroups of respondents. These individual biases may cancel out to a large extent when the total assignment per interviewer contains a number of respondents or a number of groups of respondents'. We agree with Hyman that this may apply to the marginal frequency distributions, but if the errors are systematic it will not apply to data obtained from more refined analysis. – In addition to ideology, background factors (sex, age, race) are known to influence heavily; personality factors likewise – in general, one cannot rule out salient interviewer variable as irrelevant for the result of the interview. Thus, Boyd, H. W. and Westfall, R., 'Interviewers as a Source of Error in Surveys', *Journal of Marketing*, 1955, pp. 311-324, discusses a number of sources of error in interviews and calls interviewers 'a major source of error'.

As a curiosity may be mentioned the study by Hildum, D. C. and Brown, R. W.: 'Verbal Reinforcement and Interviewer Bias', *Journal of Abnormal and Social Psychology*, 1956, pp. 108-111, where telephone interviews were used to control for such interfering variables as facial expressions, clothing, social manners, etc. Respondents were interviewed about a certain educational philosophy, and divided into four groups, two ways. Two groups got 'good' as interviewer reaction, two groups got the more neutral 'Mm-hmm'; two groups got the reaction when what they said was in favor of the educational philosophy, two groups when their responses were contra. The difference between good-pro and good-anti was significant ($p < .01$

but even mm-hmm-pro vs. mm-hmm-anti produced an effect (p < .20). Thus, it is almost impossible not to influence the respondents.

6 Nevertheless, there is much research to indicate that repeated surveys based on interviews give very similar results. Hadley Cantril, in his article 'Do Different Polls Get the Same Results?', *Public Opinion Quarterly*, 1945, pp.61-69, compares different polls where the same question has been asked, altogether 99 comparisons, and finds an average percentage difference of 3.25%. The difference depends on *time* (3.05 when the questions were asked with an interval of less than 10 days, 3.41 when the interval was from 11 to 70 days), and on *content* (3.15 for political questions, 3.43 for unpolitical questions – probably because the former are more crystallized and anchored in ideological and other systems). Cantril concludes that the differences are not 'unduly high', and Stephan and McCarthy agree *(Sampling Opinions,* New York: Wiley, 1958).

7 Allen H.Barton, in 'Asking the Embarrassing Question', *Public Opinion Quarterly,* 1958, pp.67-68, mentions 8 techniques that can be used for the really difficult question: (1) the casual approach, (2) the numbered card, (3) the 'everybody' approach, (4) the 'other people' approach, (5) the sealed ballot technique, (6) the projective technique, (7) the Kinsey technique and (8) putting the question at the end of the interview. Some of these require interviews, some are better with questionnaires. Nevertheless, Hyman *(Interviewing in Social Research,* pp.139-149) gives a number of examples where questionnaires prove to be superior. In a study of 'love relationships', interviews were compared with questionnaires; and less acceptable emotions (jealousy, sadism, masochism, aggression, very strong sexuality) appeared in the latter. On p.144 is shown that this also applies to ordinary census questions. Also compare *The American Soldier* (Princeton: Princeton University Press, 1950), vol.IV, pp.718-719; Stephan, McCarthy, p.365.

8 No doubt, social scientists could use more imagination in creating artificially 'natural' settings. Thus, Stanton, Back and Litwak, in 'Role-Playing in Social Research', *AJS,* 1956-57, pp.172-176, report on three studies where role-playing has been used to get survey-type data reliably, quickly, and perhaps also with more validity.

9 A good example of an investigation of the problem of constancy (unfortunately called 'reliability' in the title of the article and 'consistency' in the article) is Morton, J.S., Blake, R.R., and Fruchter, B.: 'The Reliability of Sociometric Measures', *Sociometry,* 1955, pp.7-48. The article surveys 8 test-retest sociometric studies and finds constancy of choices to vary between 27% and 77%. Constancy is seen to depend on time interval (negatively), age (positively), relevance of sociometric criterion (positively), number of values in the variable (our r) (positively, the more discriminations that can be made, the more constant the choice or rather, the higher the test-retest correlation).

10 Hyman (in *Interviewing in Social Research,* Chicago: Chicago University Press, 1954, pp.190-201) gives data that show higher percentages of errors, both 'bias' and 'non-bias', and more technical errors for unstructured than for structured interview-guides. For another point of view, see Achal, A.P.: 'Relative Value of Poll-End and Open-End Questions in Search for Reasons of a Problem', *Educ. and Psychol.,* 1958, pp.55-60. It was concluded that the choice of the respondents was biased by the alternatives presented, and that this effect is off-set by age and education. Also see the report in Stephan, McCarthy, op.cit., p.365 of a paper by R.L. Kahn, 'A Comparison of Two Methods of Collecting Data: The Fixed-Alternative Questionnaire and the Open-Ended Interview'.

11 This reasoning is basic to an anthropological/sociological research project on the effect of technical assistance on two villages in southern India, carried out by Arne Martin Klausen and Johan Galtung at the International Peace Research Institute, Oslo.

510

12 For general literature on problems of reliability and validity, see Lindquist, E.F.: *Educational Measurement* (Washington: American Council on Education, 1951), chs.15, 16; Jahoda, Deutsch, Cook, Selltiz, ch.5; Guilford, J.P.: *Psychometric Methods* (New York: McGraw-Hill, 1954), ch.14; Green, B.F.: 'Attitude Measurement' in Lindzey, G.: *Handbook of Social Psychology* (Cambridge: Addison-Wesley, 1954) pp.338-341; Festinger, Katz, pp.41-51; Stevens, S.S.: *Handbook of Experimental Psychology* (New York: Wiley, 1951); Stouffer, S.A., Guttman, L., Suchman, E.A., Lazarsfeld, P.F., Star, Shirley and Clausen, J.A.: *Measurement and Prediction* (vol.IV in *The American Soldier*).

13 *The Pre-election Polls of 1948* (New York: Social Science Research Council, Bulletin 60, 1949).

14 'Validity of Responses to Survey Questions', *Public Opinion Quarterly,* 1950, pp.61-80.

15 New York: McGraw-Hill, 1951.

16 'Validity of Readership Studies', *Journal of Marketing,* 1953, pp.26-32.

17 'Response Errors in the Collection of Wage Statistics By Mail Questionnaire', *Journal of American Statistical Association,* 1954, pp.240-253.

18 There is an interesting literature on how to improve the technique of mail questionnaires, which undeniably is a very attractive method since it leaves so much of the work to an outside bureaucracy, the mail system, at a moderate cost. In Bradt, K., 'The Usefulness of a Post Card Technique in a Mail Questionnaire Study', *Public Opinion Quarterly,* 1955, pp.218-222 the idea is presented of asking mail questionnaire respondents to return a pre-paid card when they have returned the questionnaire – but separately so that anonymity is preserved. This gives a rapid check of the representativeness of the return, and also information about where to insist. After 2 mailings and 14 weeks a return of 80 % of a sample of 5,356 persons was obtained; without such techniques a 20 % return is not uncommon (but, of course, unacceptable). Goldstein, H. and Kroll, B.H., 'Methods of Increasing Mail Response', *Journal of Marketing,* 1957, pp.55-57, recommend the inclusion of new copies of the questionnaire for each follow-up, inclusion of return-addressed and postage-paid envelopes for each follow-up, and the use of extra-rate mail to stimulate return (rather expensive in the long run). Similar recommendations are made by Longworth, D.S., 'Use of a Mail Questionnaire', *ASR,* 1953, pp.310-313. A word of caution about bias in representativity is voiced by Wallace, D., 'A Case For and Against Mail Questionnaires', *Public Opinion Quarterly,* 1954, pp.40-52.

19 'Validity and Reliability in Measurements of Message Diffusion', *Proceedings of Pacific Sociological Society,* 1955, pp.110-120.

20 In II, 3.7 we shall return to the problem of validity.

6. *Surveys (pp. 129–160)*

1 For an excellent discussion of this see the section 'The disposition concept' in Lazarsfeld, P.F.: 'Latent Structure Analysis'; in Koch, S., ed.: *Psychology: A Study of a Science* (New York: McGraw-Hill, 1959), vol.III, pp.476-543.

2 One discussion of this is found in Parsons and Bales: *Family, Socialization and Interaction Processes* (Glencoe: Free Press, 1955), ch.II.

3 The classical article in the field is Cronbach, L.J.: 'Response-set and Test Validity', *Educational and Psychological Measurement,* 1946, pp.475-494. For a more recent article see Hare, P.A.: 'Interview Responses: Personality or Conformity', *POQ,* 1960, pp.679-685, with interesting findings and extensive references.

4 A most distressing article for the less critical believer in interview methods is Ehrlich, J.S. and Riesman, D.: 'Age and Authority in the interview', *POQ,* 1961, pp.39-56. The authors did a secondary analysis of a study of adolescent girls where

women had been used as interviewers, and introduced as their main variable in the secondary analysis not a property of the interviewees, but the age of the interviewer. By means of this variable they were able to explain a sizable proportion of the variance between the answers given by the interviewees. For other studies in the same tradition see Hyman, H. et.al.: *Interviewing in Social Research* (Chicago: Chicago Univ. Press, 1954) and Benney, M., Riesman, D. and Star, S.: 'Age and Sex in the Interview', *AJS,* 1956, pp.143-152.

[5] An example of the general section of an interview guide is given in Appendix A.

[6] For one discussion of the refusal problem, see Stephan and McCarthy: *Sampling Opinions* (New York: Wiley, 1958), pp.261 ff.

[7] Etzioni, A.: *A Comparative Analysis of Complex Organizations* (Glencoe: Free Press, 1961), p.5.

[8] Lazarsfeld, P.F. and Kendall, P.L.: 'We are warned that there are many pitfalls in the investigation of 'intangibles', and it is suggested that these are impossible to remedy. What the critic does not realize is that sophisticated research technicians are well aware of these dangers. But they do not accept them as inevitable –'. For a masterly review of some of these problems, see 'Problems of Survey Analysis', Part II, in Merton, Lazarsfeld, eds.: *Continuities in Social Research* (Glencoe: Free Press, 1950), pp.168-196. Quotation from p.168.

[9] For different kinds of criticism, see, for instance, Veron, Eliseo: 'Sociologia, ideologia y subdesarrollo', *Cuestiones de Filosofia,* 1962, pp.13-40; Rozitohner, Leon: 'Persona, Cultura y Subdesarrollo', *Rev. de la Univ. de Buenos Aires,* 1961, pp.75-98; Touraine, A.: 'Le traitement de la société globale dans la sociologie américaine contemporaine', *Cahiers Internationaux de Sociologie,* pp.126-145; Aron, R.: 'La Société Américaine et sa sociologie', *Cahiers Internationaux de Sociologie,* pp.55-80; and of course Mills, C.W.: *The Sociological Imagination* (New York: Oxford Univ. Press, 1959), and Sorokin, P.: *Fads and Foibles* (Chicago: Henry Regnery Co., 1956).

[10] For a discussion of this technique, see Merton, R.K. and Kendall, P.L.: *The Focused Interview* (Glencoe: Free Press, 1956).

[11] A suggestion often given is to interview heads of households in developing areas (see, for instance, the special issue of *POQ* (no. 3, 1958) called 'Attitude Research in Modernizing Areas', esp. pp.224-274, and about this topic pp.237-238, or article by Neurath, P.: 'Social Research in Newly Independent Countries: An Indian Example'. *POQ,* 1960, pp.670-674. We have done so in studies in Sicily and in Kerala, India, and can confirm the general impression that it is difficult to get below the level of the head of household if one wants to reach down in society. But however 'low class' one may be operating on, one should not fool oneself into believing that this is the true periphery of society. The heads of household in traditional societies are likely to be the link between the household and the rest of the society, and for that reason much more centrally located than class position may lead one to believe. For the same reason a study of male, urban industrial workers will not qualify as a study of the periphery. With this technique, thus, one gets at the middle range, and not at the lower range of the dimension of total social position.

[12] A valuable discussion is found in 'Opinion Surveys in Developing Countries', *Int. Social Science Journal,* 1963, pp.7-110, especially Jones, E.L.: 'The Courtesy Bias in South-East Asian Surveys', pp.70-76.

[13] For an excellent account of some of the problems encountered as well as ways of handling them, see Robinson, J.A.: 'Survey Interviewing Among Members of Congress', *POQ,* 1960, pp.127-138. Robinson also has references to other articles dealing with the types of elites. It is worth noting that in the most famous elite study, Mills, C.W.: *The Power Elite* (New York: Oxford Univ. Press, 1957) many data are given, but never based on surveys taken for the purpose of the study.

For another article on this topic see 'Interviewing Political Elites in Cross-cultural Comparative Research', *AJS*, 1964, pp. 59-68, by W. H. Hunt (a sample of 76 members of the French National Assembly), W. W. Crane (a sample from the legislature of lower Australia), and J. C. Wahlke (474 of the 504 members of the legislatures of California, New Jersey, Ohio, and Tennessee). The conclusion of the authors is optimistic both in the sense that they 'feel that their most valuable asset was the highly structured and uniform interview schedule' – which, of course, is the most reliable instrument (and sometimes also the most valid instrument). They have an interesting comment: 'The fact that possibly indiscreet or inapplicable questions could be read from a standard form was also a valuable asset, since it tended to lead respondents to blame someone other than the interviewer for possible embarrassment and thus to increase their tolerance for the process of being interviewed.' (p. 68).

[14] On the other hand, questionnaires may also serve as scape-goats: "It says that I shall ask this question"; whereupon interviewer and interviewee may join in an alliance against "they" who constructed the quenstionnaire.

[15] The reader is referred to Appendix B for presentation and discussion of the data.

[16] For a discussion of some of the problems in refugee samples, see 'Some Considerations of Method and Methodology', in Inkeles, A. and Bauer, R. A.: *The Soviet Citizen* (Cambridge: Harvard Univ. Press, 1961).

Appendix B (pp. 164–165)

[1] I am indebted to Juan Planas Crespell for his assistance with the data collection.

[2] *POQ* has more data, but it does not appear in article form.

Part II: Data Analysis
1. *Processing (pp. 169–180)*

[1] The best recent text seems to be Borko, H.: *Computer Applications in the Behavioral Sciences* (Englewood: Prentice-Hall, 1962).

[2] But before using these punches, machine operators should always be consulted. A "classical" sorter-counter works very well with double punches, 11 and 12, and if it is advantageous to have all data about one unit on one card then such punches should be used – since only variables on the same card can be cross-tabulated. With modern machines, comparability of variables from different cards is obtained at the expense of a rigid "one-and-only-one-punch-in-each-column"-principle. x and y punches must be avoided, but then there is less reason to force data into one card only – and that generally increases the possibilities.

[3] See Ashby, W. R.: *An Introduction to Cybernetics* (New York: Wiley, 1957), p. 189, for a better measure of distortion, called 'equivocation'.

[4] A closer inspection of Table 1.2.2 shows clearly that the gains in eliminating one step are small as long as there are many steps, but that the returns or rewards are in fact increasing for each step one eliminates. Thus, elimination of one step, for a noise per step level of 0.10, yields only a gain of 0.03 as long as the elimination is from seven down to six steps, but as much as 0.08 when the transition is from two steps to one only. And this is even more clear when it is expressed in relative terms: in the first case the relative gain is 0.03 relative to 0.40 or 7.5 %, in the second case it is 0.08 relative to a noise level of 0.18 or 44.5 %. This has to do with the convergence of the product matrix towards the matrix of maximum noise (with all cells 0.50).

[5] Special code-sheets exist where the coding is done by means of horizontal bars with a special pencil, to be put in precisely indicated places. The code-sheets are

then put in a machine and the punching of the cards is automatic. Thus, punching can be said to be eliminated as a source of error, since the cards will be punched exactly as the code-sheets are coded. But there has to be a transfer of the code to this special sheet, which is both time-consuming and error-producing. With a questionnaire one will have to evaluate carefully what is better, to code and punch directly from the questionnaires (elimination of transfer) or to code, transfer to special code-sheets and then have automated punching (elimination of punching). One may obtain both by recording answers directly on the code-sheet, where answer categories will have to be printed – and this is probably the method for the future.

2. *Distribution (pp. 181–239)*

1 The best treatment of the topic of percentaging in the methodological literature is found in Zeisel, Hans: *Say It With Figures* (New York: Harpers, 1957), Chs. I and II.

2 Of course, percentages calculated on the basis of the total *N* will always be useful as bivariate relative frequencies. They yield information about the proportion in the sample that have any value-combination, but they are useless as means to trace the impact one variable has on another variable.

3 For classification of variables, see I, 1.4. For further discussion of this point, see Zeisel, op.cit., ch. II.

4 See Goodman, L.A. and Kruskal, W.H.: 'Measures of Association for Cross Classifications', *Journal of the American Statistical Association,* December 1954, pp.732-764, esp. section 6.2.

5 See the analysis of Weber's work given in Samuelsson, Kurt: *Religion and Economic Action* (New York: Basic Books, 1961), where Weber's thesis is attacked heavily. Samuelsson presents raw data (p.139), and a recalculation of his percentages yields percentage differences of 3 and 5 instead of 6 and 8.

6 The mathematical difficulty is the following: if r^2 gives the percentage of variation that depends, then $1-r^2$ should give the percentage that does not depend – and it does. But if r gives the percentage that depends, then $1-r$ says nothing. According to the equation:

$$\frac{s_{res}}{s_y} = \sqrt{1-r^2} , \text{ not } 1-r - \text{whereas } \frac{s^2_{res}}{s^2_y} = 1-r^2.$$

Thus, there is additivity if we use s^2 and r^2, not if we use s and r. See also Stouffer, S.A.: *Social Research To Test Ideas* (Glencoe: Free Press, 1962), p.269.

7 A good discussion of the whole interval scale family of correlation measures is found in Edwards, A.: *Statistical Methods for the Behavioral Sciences* (New York: Rinehart, 1954), chs. 8 and 10.

8 Kendall, M.G., *Rank Correlation Methods* (New York: Haffner, 1955), ch. 1.

9 Goodman, Kruskal, op.cit., 1954. Also see Kruskal, W.: 'Ordinal Measures of Associaonti', *Journal of the American Statistical Association,* 1958.

10 Somers, R.: 'A New Asymmetric Measure of Association for Ordinal Variables', *ASR,* 1962, pp.799-811.

11 Kendall, op.cit. p.36; and Somers, op.cit. p.803.

12 Kendall, op.cit. p.47; and Somers, op.cit. p.804.

13 Goodman, Kruskal, 1954. For an excellent introduction see Zelditch, M.: *A Basic Course in Sociological Statistics* (New York: Holt, 1959), ch. 7.

14 Goodman, Kruskal, 1954. Also see Zelditch, op.cit. pp.178ff.

15 For an analysis of the whole problem of agreement measurement see Galtung, Johan, *The Measurement of Agreement* (forthcoming). Scott's measure is described in 'Reliability of Content Analysis: The Case of Nominal Scale Coding', *Public*

Opinion Quarterly, vol. 19, pp. 321-325. Robinson's articles are found in *American Sociological Review,* 'The Statistical Measurement of Agreement' (vol. 22, pp. 17-25) and 'The Geometric Interpretation of Agreement' (vol. 24, pp. 338-345).

16 More details are found in Galtung, Johan, 'Rank and Social Integration: A Multidimensional Approach', in Berger, Zelditch, Anderson, *Sociological Theories in Progress*: (Boston Houghton, Mifflin Co., 1966), pp. 145-198.

17 The basic article is Cantril, Hadley: 'The Intensity of an Attitude', *Journal of Abnormal and Social Psychology,* 1946, pp. 129-135. For political science interpretations of various curve shapes, see Dahl, R.A., *A Preface to Democratic Theory* (Chicago: University of Chicago Press, 1956), pp. 90-119.

3. *Patterns (pp. 240–308)*

1 For an excellent introduction to index theory, see Zeisel, H.: op.cit., ch. V; and Section I in *Language of Social Research,* eds. Lazarsfeld, P. and Rosenberg, M. (Glencoe: The Free Press, 1955). In survey research there is a special meaning given to index formation. Anyone who has constructed a questionnaire will know that one often throws in a question as a 'control', with the idea that only if the response to the control question is positive will some other positive response(s) be taken seriously. In other words, it is the *pattern* of consistent responses that matters, not the single response. An index can easily be constructed to measure the degree of consistency, for instance simply by counting the number of positive responses (this would be a dichotomous, additive index; see II, 3.2.)

2 Let us call the number of different mappings when R patterns are mapped on $R(r)$. The number we look for is $R(2) + R(3) + \ldots + R(R-1)$.

Here we have:

$$R(2) = 2^R - \binom{2}{1}R(1)$$
$$R(3) = 3^R - \binom{3}{1}R(2) - \binom{3}{2}R(1)$$
$$R(4) = 4^R - \binom{4}{1}R(3) - \binom{4}{2}R(2) - \binom{4}{3}R(1)$$

and in general: $R(r) = r^R - \binom{r}{1}R(r-1) - \binom{r}{2}R(r-2) \ldots - \binom{r}{r-2}R(2) - \binom{r}{r-1}R(1)$

where we always subtract the number of illegitimate indices. Thus, with two dichotomies we get $4(3) = 36$ trichotomous indices.

3 If, however, the variables have a very high correlation – so high that a good proportion of the units in fact have the patterns 'low-low- ... -low' and 'high-high- ... -high', then the index might still be very useful. But this is a strong requirement as with be shown in 3.2.

4 In the Likert scale it is customary to give some of the items a negative form to avoid response-set. This means that a 'disagree' to a negative item is counted as an agree to a positive item. A negative item has a -1 instead of a $+1$ in the weight vector. But it may be that this mathematics is too simple to reflect semantics; it may be that disagreeing with something negative is not quite the same as agreeing with something positive. The researcher may find it advisable to test the respondents to find out whether they feel this way about the use of the words 'not' and 'disagree' or whether they feel that disagreement with something negative may be 'less than' full agreement.

5 For a penetrating criticism, see Merton, R.K.: 'Fact and Factitiousness in Ethnic Opinionnaires', *ASR,* 1940, pp. 13-28. Also see his rejoinder to Jessie Bernard, ibid., pp. 647-648.

6 For increasing n, the distribution will approximate the normal distribution, according to the central limit theorem in statistics. As we can see from the number pyramids, the approximation is already good for moderate n, if the variables are independent. For high n this holds also when the variables are dependent, which means

that it is very difficult to avoid A-shaped distributions. In practice U-shaped distributions will only occur for low *n* and a very high degree of dependence between the variables.

7 The method of paired comparisons can also be seen as a special case of a much more general methodology. The respondent is presented not with one stimulus but with a set of stimuli and asked to evaluate some *relation* between them. One such relation is the relation of preference, as applied to pairs in the method of paired comparisons and to other sets in the comparative approach called ranking in general (what is typical of paired comparison is only that *all* pairs are used, similarly one might have triple comparisons, etc.). But there are other relations, as when the respondent is presented with two names and asked to say whether the relation between them is one of friendship, indifference or animosity. The stimulus is still an 'object' in our sense (I, 1.1.) but at the relation level instead of element level.

8 See Guttman, L.: 'A Basis for Scaling Qualitative Data', *ASR,* 1944, pp. 139-150, and 'The Basis for Scalogram Analysis', vol. 4 *The American Soldier,* pp. 60-90. Also see Torgerson, W.: *Theory and Methods of Scaling* (New York: Wiley, 1958), ch. 12.

9 Goodenough, W. H.: 'A Technique for Scale Analysis', *Educational Psychology Measurement,* 1944, pp. 174-190. See also the excellent introduction in Edwards, A. L.: *Techniques of Attitude Scale Construction* (New York: Appleton, 1957), ch. 7.

10 An interesting study of the effect of order of presentation of the items in a cumulative scale is found in Haynes, D. P., 'Item order and Guttman Scales', *AJS,* 1964, pp. 51-58. His thesis is that the tendency towards reduction of cognitive dissonance will cause respondents to try to integrate their answers so as to obtain consistency. While this in itself, of course, represents no methodological problem, since it is one of the mechanisms by which a cumulative scale is produced, the effect will vary with the order of presentation: 'Applied to attitudes, where an attitude structure is already well formed, the first of a set of related attitude questionnaire statements serves as a figure against the ground of the previously established attitude structure. Where no attitude previously existed, the first statement of the questionnaire becomes the ground for the second'. Thus, the paper treats empirically the effect of a particular kind of response-set relevant for cumulative or nearly cumulative items.

11 To take one study among the many using cumulative scales: Alan Richardson studied 'The Assimilation of British Immigrants in a Western Australian Community' (*R.E.M.P. Bulletin,* vol. 9, January/June 1961, Hague) and found six items measuring satisfaction that formed a scale (ibid., pp. 12 ff). Since satisfaction of immigrants is typically a question of *process* (not necessarily monotone, and certainly not linear) this is only what should be expected. On the one hand, one should design items that reflect different stages in the assimilation process; on the other hand, items that do form a scale should be inspected to see whether they might shed some light on the assimilation *process* and whether in fact there is a correlation with time in the life of the single individual. But items that are 'simultaneous' may also form a scale, only that no interesting interpretation of this kind is available. To feel, however, that this index is more 'valid' than an ordinary aditive index is, in our opinion, a misunderstanding of the idea of validity.

12 The weights should preferably not be given only by the investigator, but by a panel of judges according to some modification of the Thurstone method, or by the respondents themselves.

13 Coombs, C. H.: 'Theory and Methods of Social Measurement', in Festinger and Katz eds., *Research Methods in the Behavorial Sciences* (New York: Holt, 1953), ch. 11, pp. 471-535, and, above all, *A Theory of Data* (New York, 1964).

14 Torgerson, W. S.: 'Models for Comparative Response Data', in *Theory and Methods of Scaling* (New York: John Wiley & Sons, 1958), ch. 14, pp. 403-417.

516

15 Torgerson, ibid, p.413.

16 loc.cit.

17 But if people are asked about their income, M, and we have reasons to believe that on the average they are conditioned for tax reasons to reduce it by 25 %, the transformation (linear, deterministic) $L = \frac{4}{3} M$ is nevertheless useful.

81 The central limit theorem in statistics, in our view, is no justification for the assumption of a normal distribution, since it is difficult to see that it excludes anything. It is difficult to conceive of phenomena that cannot be analyzed in terms of n components that jointly produce the phenomenon (they do not have to be independent or to combine according to an additive formula for the theorem to be valid – but then the appronximatio is not so good for low n).

19 Lazarsfeld, P.F.: 'Latent Structure Analysis', in Koch, S. ed: *Psychology: A Study of a Science* (New York: McGraw-Hill, 1959), vol. III, pp.476-543. – Torgerson, W.S.: 'Probability Models for Categorical Data', in *Theory and Methods of Scaling* (New York: Wiley, 1958), ch. 13, pp.361-402. Guttman's facet analysis should also be consulted in this connection.

20 For an important exploration of this theme, see Flament, Claude: 'Modèle à caracteristiques non-monotones dans l'étude d'un questionnaire', *Revue Française de Sociologie,* 1963, no. 2.

21 See Lazarsfeld, op.cit. pp.495-506.

22 ibid., p.495.

23 ibid., p.524.

24 Torgerson, op.cit. p.371.

25 For the Gram-Charlier and Edgeworth series, see Cramér, H.: Mathematical Methods of Statistics (Princeton, 1946), chs. 17.6 and 17.7.

26 Lazarsfeld, op.cit. p.526.

27 Torgerson, op.cit. p.373.

28 For an example, see Lazarsfeld, op.cit. pp.529ff.

29 Galtung, J.: *Verdiorientering og sosial posisjon* (Oslo: International Peace Research Institute, 1961, mimeo), pp.85-87.

30 Galtung, J.: *The Measurement of Agreement,* section 3.2.

31 ibid., section 3.3.

32 ibid., section 3.4.

33 A study that made systematic use of this technique was *The Authoritarian Personality* (pp.77-83). The interval level condition was not satisfied, however, which makes the authors' reasoning somewhat fictitious.

34 A good presentation of the whole problem of item selection is found in Edwards, A.: *Techniques of Attitude Scale Construction* (New York: Appleton-Century-Crofts, 1957), pp.152-156. For Likert's own presentation of the discriminatory power technique, see Murphy, G. and Likert, R.: *Public Opinion and the Individual* (New York: Harper, 1937). For more technical but in our opinion also too restrictive discussions, see Guilford, J.P.: *Psychometric Methods* (New York: McGraw-Hill, 1954), pp.417-443; Gulliksen, H.: *Theory of Mental Tests* (New York: Wiley, 1950), ch. 21, pp.263-395 ('Item Analysis'); Dubois, P.H.: *Multivariate Correlational Analysis* (New York: Harper, 1957), pp.36-44; Solomon, H.: 'Measures of Worth in Item Analysis and Test Design', in Arrow, K. et al., *Mathematical Methods in the Social Sciences* (Stanford: Stanford Univ. Press, 1960), pp.36-44.

35 See Galtung, J.: *An Introduction to Mathematical Sociology,* section 3.4 (forthcoming).

36 For this condition guarantees transitivity of correlation; if V_1 is highly correlated with V_2 and V_2 with V_3, then there is also a high correlation between V_1 and V_3. As will be shown in II, 6.3. this does not occur always.

37 See Tryon, R.C.: *Cluster Analysis: Correlation Profile and Orthometric (Factor)*

517

Analysis for the Isolation of Unities in Mind and Personality. (Ann Arbor: Edwards Bros., 1939); and Holzinger, K.J. and Harman, H.H.: *Factor Analysis: A Synthesis of Factorial Methods* (Chicago: Univ. of Chicago Press, 1941). However, a six-page, completely sufficient account of the method is given in Fruchter, B.: *Introduction to Factor Analysis* (New York: van Nostrand, 1954), pp.12-17.

38 Fruchter, op.cit. p.14.

39 For instance, this is the case with the example given by Fruchter, op.cit. p.15.

40 For an easy introductory presentation, see Fruchter, Benjamin: op.cit. The fundamental classic in the field is Thurstone, L.L.: *Multiple Factor Analysis* (Chicago: Chicago University Press, 1947). Two highly important manuals are Cattell, R.B.: *Factor Analysis* (New York: Harper, 1952) and Harmon, Harry H.: *Modern Factor Analysis* (Chicago: Chicago University Press, 1960).

41 An especially attractive example is found in Alker, Hayward R. Jr., 'Dimensions of Conflict in the General Assembly', *American Political Science Review,* 1964, pp. 642-657; he also gives references to other articles of the same nature. Voting patterns lend themselves particularly well to factor analysis since one can talk meaningfully about interval scales. It goes without saying that factor analysis can be used for any type of units, for instance to classify nations, as is frequently done by the Political Data Program at Yale University.

4. Hypotheses (pp. 309–389)

1 Galtung, J.: *Norm, Role and Status* (Santiago: FLACSO, 1963), section 1.3.

2 The most important reference here is to Popper, Karl R.: *The Logic of Scientific Discovery* (London: Hutchinson, 1959), Ch. 4. Also consider this quotation from Rudolf Carnap: *Symbolische Logik* (Wien: Springer, 1954), p.20:
  "Ein Satz besagt dadurch etwas über die Welt, dass er bestimmte Fälle, die an sich möglich wären, ausschliesst, d.h., dass er uns mitteilt, dass die Wirklichkeit nicht zu den ausgeschlossenen Fällen gehört. Je mehr Fälle ein Satz ausschliesst, um so mehr besagt er. Daher erscheint es als plausibel, den *Gehalt* eines Satzes zu definieren, als die Klasse der möglichen Fälle, in denen er nicht gilt ..."

3 See Popper, op.cit.

4 This is easily achieved through a combination of the formulae for T and T^*, for instance:

$$T^{**} = \frac{n_T(n_T+n_F)n_F}{E^3}$$

which is zero when and only when we are on the coordinate axes. But the formula is far from simple.

5 See Coleman, J.: *Community Conflict* (Glencoe: Free Press, 1957).

6 See Asch, Solomon: *Social Psychology* (New York: Prentice-Hall, 1952), ch. 16.

7 In the words of Rudolf Carnap in 'Testability and Meaning', Feigl and Brodbeck, Eds.: *Readings in the Philosophy of Science* (New York: Appleton-Century-Crofts, 1953), pp.48ff.
  "Now a little reflection will lead us to the result that there is no fundamental difference between a universal sentence and a particular sentence with regard to verifiability, but only a difference in degree. Take for instance the following sentence: 'There is a white sheet of paper on this table'. In order to ascertain whether this thing is paper, we may make a set of simple observations and then, if there still remains some doubt, we may make some physical and chemical experiments. Here as well as in the case of the law, we try to examine sentences which we infer from the sentence in question. These inferred sentences are predictions about future observations. The number of such predictions which we can derive from the sentence

518

given is infinite, and therefore the sentence can never be completely verified. To be sure, in many cases we reach a practically sufficient certainty after a small number of positive instances, and then we stop experimenting. But there is always the theoretical possibility of continuing the series of test-observations. Therefore here also *no complete verification is possible,* but only a process of gradually increasing *confirmation.* We may, if we wish, call a sentence disconfirmed to a certain degree if its negation is confirmed to that degree."

8 See Galtung, J.: *The Measurement of Agreement* (Oslo, forthcoming), section 3.2 for a discussion of similar problems.

9 New York: McGraw-Hill, 1956.

10 But it should be noticed that classical tests involving parameters often can be derived from more general principles.

11 See Siegel, op.cit., pp.35-47, pp.95-111, pp.175-179, pp.196-202.

12 See Robert S. Lee: *The Function of Fins in the Flattening of Images* (New York: Bureau of Applied Social Research, Columbia University, ditto, 1957).

13 'Modifications of the Dorn-Stouffer-Tibbitts Method for Testing the Significance of Comparisons in Sociological Data', *AJS,* 1961, pp.355-363.

14 'The Multivariate Analysis of Dichotomized Variables', *AJS,* 1965, pp.455-466. This article also has an excellent bibliography.

15 'On Methods for Comparing Contingency Tables', *Journal of the Royal Statistical Society,* 1963, pp.94-108.

16 op.cit. p.461.

17 See Blalock, H.M.: 'A Double Standard in Measuring Degree of Association', *ASJ,* 1963, pp.988-989.

18 Leo A. Goodman and W.H. Kruskal, 'Measures of Association for Cross Classifications: III. Approximate Sampling Theory', *Journal of the American Statistical Association,* 1963, pp.310-364. Most importantly, the article gives estimates for the variance of gamma. For the tau family the most important reference is still Kendall's original work, *Rank Correlation Methods* (London: Griffin, 1955), especially chapter 4.

19 op.cit., p.3.

20 Also quoted by Selvin, 14, p.8.

21 I am indebted to mag.art. Else Øyen for the collection of these data, and to the Institute of Sociology, University of Oslo, for support.

22 In a similar investigation by David Gold ('A Note on Statistical Analysis in the *American Sociological Review*', *ASR,* 1957, pp.332-333) all articles published in the *ASR* 1944-1953 were examined. 48 % of them 'reported data that conceivably could be subjected to some kind of statistical analysis', whereas for 1959 the corresponding figure is 68 % – an increase indicative of the growth in empirical/statistical research in the 'fifties.

24 One good example is Oscar Lewis, *Life in a Mexican Village, Tepoztlán Restudied* (Urbana: University of Illinois Press, 1963).

25 Galtung, Johan: 'Summit Meetings and International Relations', *Journal of Peace Research,* 1964, p.44.

26 A survey undertaken by the author, with the assistance of mag.art. Else Øyen, of most standard texts in statistics in the behavioral sciences showed that use of statistics was considered as unproblematic apart from what will be referred to here as 'technical difficulties'. Two widely dispersed texts that do discuss 'hypothetical' universe are Hagood, Price: *Statistics for Sociologists* (New York: Holt, 1952, rev.ed.), pp.293-294 and pp.419-423, where arguments are presented in the form of a dialogue, with the authors in a wait-and-see position; and Yule and Kendall, who also have a discussion of the issue, in *An Introduction to the Theory of Statistics,* 14th edition (London: Chas. Griffin, 1958), chapter 16.

27 In an article 'Common Errors in Sampling', *Social Forces,* 1933, pp. 521-525, T. J. Woofter makes most of these points. Thirty years later the situation is not very much different: see for instance the chapter by Leo Festinger on 'Use of Statistics in Jahoda, Deutsch, Cook: *Research Methods in Social Relations,* vol. II (New York: Holt, 1952).

28 *Sample Survey Methods and Theory* (New York: Wiley, 1956), vol. I & II.

29 See Cochran, op. cit., chapter 8.

30 See Selvin (10, p. 523) and (2) and (6).

31 A warning here about chi square. If the deviations $f_i - t_i$ are kept constant and the sample size is increased, chi square will decrease, because chi square is based on absolute, not relative frequencies. See Edwards, *Statistical Methods for the Behavioral Sciences,* pp. 364-370.

32 See, for instance, 2, p. 430, 'What should be tested is the significance of the total set of interlocking tables'.

33 Edwards has a good discussion of this, op. cit, pp. 391-393.

34 For excellent discussions see Selvin, (13, 14); Kendall (6, p. 303) and Coleman (2, p. 430).

35 For a discussion of these problems also see Camilleri, Santo F.: 'Theory, Probability, and Induction in Social Research', *ASR,* 1962, pp. 170-178, especially pp. 174 ff. The article does not make any clear distinction between substantive hypothesis and generalization hypothesis, however.

36 See for instance, (10, p. 527) and (2, p. 432).

37 See, for instance, (6, p. 303) and (10, p. 524).

38 See the articles by Kish (7.8).

39 The classical work is *Sequential Analysis,* by Abraham Wald (New York: Wiley, 1949). Also see the chapter in Mood, A. M., *Introduction to the Theory of Statistics* (New York: McGraw-Hill, 1950).

40 See Wald, *Statistical Decision Functions* (New York: Wiley, 1950).

41 See (2, p. 429) and (10, p. 526).

42 R. A. Fisher in *The Design of Experiments* (London: Oliver and Boyd, 1953), p. 43.

43 Edwards, op. cit. develops an approximate chi square technique for this situation (pp. 392-393). The sign test and the Wilcoxon matched-pairs test are also useful, see Siegel, pp. 68-83.

5. Data analysis (pp. 390–450)

1 Investigations using collectivities, especially provinces, nations or other units for which census data etc. exist, are rapidly increasing in number. Particularly important are the research traditions coming out of the Human Relations Area File and the Political Data Program at Yale University, as well as the Dimensions of Nations Project at the University of Hawaii.

2 See Appendix D for an analysis of styles of social science in United States, Europe and Latin America in terms of types of analysis that are used.

3 See Kendall, P. L. and Lazarsfeld, P. F.: 'Problems of survey analysis' in Merton, Lazarsfeld, eds.: *Continuities in Social Research* (Free Press, 1950), Lazarsfeld, P. F.: 'Interpretations of Statistical Relations as a Research Operation', in Lazarsfeld, Rosenberg, eds.: *The Language of Social Research* (Free Press, 1955); Chs. VI and VII in Hyman, H.: *Survey Design and Analysis* (Free Press, 1955), and Ch. 2 in Simon, H.: *Models of Man,* (Wiley 1957.) For important elaboration and criticism, se Nowak, Stefan, 'Some Problems of Causal Interpretation of Statistical Relationships', *Philosophy of Science,* vol. 27, pp. 23-38.

4 Nowak, op. cit., p. 33.

5 For an example of an analysis of that kind, see Galtung, Johan: 'Foreign Policy Opinion as a Function of Social Position', *Journal of Peace Research,* 1964, p.220.
6 For a good exposition the reader is referred to Edwards, A. L.: *Experimental Design in Psychological Research* (New York: Rinehart, 1959).
7 It should be noted that two irrelevant criticisms against the correlation coefficient would be in terms of normality of the conditional distributions of D and homoscedasticity for these distributions. These objections are irrelevant since they refer to conditions to be satisfied for certain statistical tests to be applicable, not to the development of a measure of association or, in this case 'degree of accounting for'. Here we are concerned with substantive measures and not with such generalization measures as significance levels.
8 One might suggest using Somers' generalization of the percentage differences for this purpose (II, 2.3). But it is much more complicated to calculate and in addition attains its maximum and minimum values under conditions that are less intuitive than the conditions we have obtained here.

Besides, it will not be sensitive to the conditions of semi-monotonicity that are crucial in this connection.
9 On the other hand, multiple regression analysis has also been adjusted to meet the exigencies of social science research. "Dummy" variables have been introduced to recast the variables into interval form, product terms have been employed to take care of the problem of interaction. However, the total machinery tends to be over-complicated and difficult to interpret.
10 See his discussion in 'Evidence and Inference in Social Research', *Daedalus,* 1958, pp.105-109.
11 See Stouffer, S. *Communism, Conformity and Civil Liberties* (New York: Doubleday, 1955), Appendix D: 'even when no individual pair of percentages is significantly different, a pattern of such differences, most of them in the same direction, may be highly significant' (p.273). Statistically yes, but in the theoretical sense only if the differences refer to items that are not too similar – if they are very similar a pattern does not help us much.
12 For an excellent discussion, see Curtis, Richard F. and Jackson, Elton F. 'Multiple Indicators in Survey Research', *AJS,* September 1962.
13 See Germani, Gino: *Antisemitismo ideologico y antisemitismo tradicional* (Buenos Aires: Cuadernos de Comentario, 1963).

6. Theory formation (pp. 451–490)

1 By the condition 'weakly connected' we mean that there are no isolated hypotheses or sets of hypotheses that are not linked somehow to the rest. If there were, they would form a theory of their own.
2 Since each hypothesis or proposition implies itself, the minimum theory will consist of one hypothesis, but this is clearly an improper case which we prefer to exclude.
3 Tarski, A.: *Introduction to Logic* (New York: Oxford Univ. Press, 1946), pp.47-48.
4 For an excellent discussion, see Tarski, op.cit. pp.23-32.
5 It is an elementary mathematical fact that through any finite collection of points an infinite number of curves may be drawn.
6 See, for instance, Naess, Arne: *Hypothetico-deductive Methodology in its Relation to Probabilism and Possibilism,* unpubl. MS (University of Oslo: Institute of Philosophy and History of Ideas): 'The crucial points in these methodological views are (1) the reduction of explanations, or rather the logic of explanation, to deductions of certain kinds, and (2) the application of the logical theorem that one cannot in a true implication infer the truth of the antecedent from the truth of the con-

521

sequent, or in an inference, infer the truth of the premises from the truth of the conclusion. There may be infinitely many sets of equivalent premises which permit us to infer the same conclusions. Thus, if the conjunction of accepted observation-sentences represents the conclusion, there are an infinity of different hypotheses, theorems, principles, Laws of Nature, explanations, Randbedingungen, etc. from sets of which the observation-sentences can be deduced'.

Historically, one of the most important formulations of the principle comes from Poincaré, Henri *(Électricité et Optique,* Paris; Georges Carré, 1890, p. XIV): 'Si ... un phénoméne comporte une explication mécanique compléte, il en comportera une infinité d'autres qui rendront également bien compte de toutes les particularités révélées par l'expérience'.

[7] Aberle, D. F. et al.: 'The Incest Taboo and the Mating Patterns of Animals', *American Anthropologist,* 1963, pp. 253-265.

[8] Quine, W. O.: *From a Logical Point of View* (Cambridge: Harvard University Press, 1953), p. 43.

[9] Quine, op. cit., p. 42.

[10] Luce, R. Duncan: *Individual Choice Behavior* (New York: Wiley, 1959).

[11] Hans Zetterberg has done sociology a great service by arguing the case of axiomatization with a number of good examples. See *On Theory and Verification in Sociology* (Stockholm: Almquist & Wiksell, 1954), ch. 2; 'Theorie, Forschung und Praxis in der Soziologie' in König, R. ed.: *Handbuch der empirischen Sozialforschung* (Stuttgart: Ferdinand Enke Verlag, 1962), pp. 65-104 and 'Notes on Theory Construction and Verification in Sociology', paper presented at the Work Group on Theory and Model Construction, Fifth World Congress of Sociology. Zetterberg is, however, in our mind too optimistic as to the possibility of obtaining transfer of confirmation, not only validity, by testing a theory at some strategic points in the $(\underline{H}, I)$ structure only.

[12] On the borderline of science such votes may be interesting. Psychologists have been polled as to their opinion about 'extra-sensory perception', showing an almost four times higher belief in it among younger psychologists (but only 4 % believing it is an established fact). See Berelson and Steiner, *Human Behavior* (New York: Harcourt, Brace, 1964), p. 127.

[13] For an excellent article on this general problem with corresponding results for inferences based on Yule's Q, see Costner, H. L. and Leik, R. K.: 'Deductions from "Axiomatic Theory"', *ASR,* 1964, pp. 819-835.

[14] The positive feed-back patterns are what Myrdal refers to as patterns of 'circular and cumulative causation' in his extremely stimulating 'The principle of circular and cumulative causation' in Myrdal, G.: *Economic Theory and Underdeveloped Regions* (London: Duckworth, 1957), pp. 11-22. Myrdal attacks, rightly we believe, the belief in the stable equilibrium assumption (here called negative feed-back), the idea that 'a change will regularly call forth a reaction in the system in the form of changes which on the whole go in the opposite direction of the first change' (p. 13). But Myrdal overstates his case: his cure for the illness of using negative feed-back models is to prescribe positive feed-back models. 'in the normal case there is no such tendency towards automatic self-stabilisation in the social system' (p. 13). Myrdal has no empirical basis for so saying; and if it were true, human society would certainly not have survived. We prefer an eclectic view, viewing the patterns we have described as an arsenal for the formation of theory in terms of both kinds of cycles.

[15] See Smoker, Paul: 'Fear in the Arms Race', *Journal of Peace Research,* 1964, pp. 55-64.

[16] Galtung, Johan: *Structural-functional Analysis* (forthcoming).

[17] The most important contributions seem to be Wold, Herman, 'Causal Inference from Observational Data: A Review of Ends and Means', *Journal of the Royal*

Statistical Society, Series A, 1956, pp.28-61; Simon, Herbert, 'Causation and In-fluence Relations', Part I in *Models of Man* (New York: Wiley, 1957); a number of articles by Hubert M. Blalock, see his *Causal Inferences in Nonexperimental Research* (Chapel Hill: University of North Carolina Press, 1964), also see the discussion in *ASR,* 1962, pp.539-548; Pelz, D.C. and Andrews, F.M., 'Detecting Causal Priorities in Panel Study Data', *ASR,* 1965, pp.836-848; and the article by Costner and Leik quoted above.

18 See Lazarsfeld, Kendall: 'Problems of Survey Analysis' in Merton, Lazarsfeld, eds., *Studies in the Scope and Method of 'The American Soldier'* (Glencoe: The Free Press, 1951), p.157.

19 The two cases called 'explanation' and 'interpretation' put Z in the two logically possible orders relative to *X* and *Y,* preceding both or intervening between them. The terms are unfortunate, both terms can be used for either and are used for either.

20 For instance Thomas Marshall, Robert Merton, C.Wright Mills.

21 For an excellent example, see Jackson, E.F.: 'Status Consistency and Symptoms of Stress', *ASR,* 1962, 469-480.

22 For an analysis of some patterns of Latin American social sciences in these terms, see Galtung, J. 'Los factores socioculturales y el desarrollo de la sociologia en America Latina' in *Revista Latinoamericana de Sociologia,* 1965, pp.72-102; English version in *Social Sciences Information,* 1966, pp.7–33.

23 Particularly important here is the asymmetry between the expected and the un-expected. An expected finding, whether it is expected on the basis of ideology, traditions, or predictions, will easily be accepted, whereas the unexpected or even falsifying finding may be 'explained away' by questioning and criticising at any or all points in the process of data-collection, processing, and analysis.

Appendix D (pp. 500–504)

1 I am indebted to the outstanding students of the third promotion at FLACSO, Santiago, for their helpfulness in carrying out this project.

2 Gold, David: 'A Note on Statistical Analysis in the *American Sociological Review*', *ASR,* 1957, pp.332-333.

INDEX

n *means reference to a note;* II. n *refers to a note in Part II.*

Hagedom, R., n. 5.2
Hagood, P., II. n. 4.26
Handbook of Experimental Psychology, n. 5.12
Handbook of Social Psychology, n. 2.12, n. 5.12
Handbuch der empirischen Sozialforschung, II. n. 6.11
Hansen, 370
Hare, P. A., n. 6.3
Harman, H. H., 305; II. n. 3.37, n. 3.40
Haynes, D. P., II. n. 3.10
Heteroscedasticity, 416
Hierarchy analysis, 88
  matrices, 89
Hildum, D. C., n. 5.5
Holsti, O. R., n. 2.12, n. 2.16
Holzinger, K. J., 305; II. n. 3.37
Homan's theory, 470
Homo economicus, 460
  politicus, 460
  sociologicus, 461
Homoscedasticity, 416; II. n. 5.7
Horizontal analysis. *See* Indices, Patterns of values, Response set
Horizontal replication, 439-444
Hudson, C., 417
Human Behavior, 481; II. n. 6.12
Human Relations Area File, II. n. 5.1
Hunt, W. H., n. 6.13
Hurwitz, 370
Hyman, H. H., 34, 53, 127, 410; n. 2.9, n. 5.5, n. 5.7, n. 5.10, n. 6.4; II. n. 5.3
Hypergeometric distribution, 347, 350
Hypotheses, 309-389
  communicability, 334-335
  complexity, 317-318
  definition, 309-315
  determinacy, 321-323
  dimensions, 315-340
  falsifiability, 322-324, 333-334, 338
  generality, 316-317
  predictability, 328-334
  reproducibility, 335-336
  specificity, 318-320
  tenability, 336-339
Hypothetical universes, 366-369; II. n. 4.26
Hypothetico-deductive Methodology in its Relation to Probabilism and Possibilism, II. n. 6.6
Hypothetico-deductive system, 453

Identification of IBM cards, 144-146
Ideographic sciences, 22-27
Immigration, 482-483
Implication, 451-452, 454, 466-467, 468
Independent variables, 193, 318, 392-393, 394. *See also* Multivariate analysis
Indicator, 78, 80, 81, 122, 292-301
Indices, 80, 132, 179-180, 235-236, 240-308 *pass.*, 395, 442. *See also* Patterns of values
Individual Choice Behavior, n. 4.7; II. n. 6.10
Induction, finite, 330
Inductive system, 453
Information theory in evaluation, 104, 105-106, 107
  in data processing, 174-178
  in measurement, 214, 322
  noise, 105, 176
Inkeles, A., n. 6.16
Inner-directedness, 151
Instrument of sampling, 130-137
Integration, 133
Intension in selecting variables, 77-78, 246
  of evaluation, 90
Interaction Process Analysis, n. 3.8
Interaction, social, 30, 37, 88, 89, 112-113
  statistical, 356, 414-437 *pass.*
Interchangeability of indices, 442
Intersubjectivity, 29, 85, 121, 169
Interval scale, 73-76, 98, 186, 282, 425
  family of parameters, 214-218
  for parameters, 209, 210, 305, 308
  in analysis of variance, 414
  in latent structure analysis, 284, 290
  in multiple regression analysis, 436
  in test-theory, 344
Interview, 161-163
Interview method. *See* Survey method
Interviewers, 145-146, 147, 155-156; n. 5.5
Interviewing in Social Research, n. 5.5, n. 5.7, n. 5.10, n. 6.4
Intrasubjectivity, 29, 85, 121, 170
Introduction to Cybernetics, An, II. n. 1.3
Introduction to Factor Analysis, II. n. 3.37, 3.38, 3.39, 3.40
Introduction to Logic, II. n. 6.3, n. 6.4
Introduction to Logic and Scientific Method, An, n. 3.1
Introduction to Mathematical Sociology, An, n. 3.10; II. n. 3.35
Introduction to the Theory of Statistics, II. n. 4.39

34 *

Riesman, D., n. 6.4
Robinson, J. A., n. 6.13
Robinson, W. S., n. 2.5; II. n. 2.15
Robinson's measure, 228; II. n. 2.15
Roper, E., 127
Rosenberg, M., II. n. 3.1
Rostow, W. W., 73 (take-off stage); n. 3.3
Rozitohner, L., n. 6.9
Rules of Sociological Method, The, n. 1.6

Sample Survey Methods and Theory, II. n. 4.28
Sampling, 48-67, 130, 138, 164-165, 364
  fraction, 57
  instrument, 130-137
  parameter distributions, 208
  replications, 66-67
  size of sample, 59-64
  typology, 56
Sampling, biased, 52-54, 56, 82-84
  cluster, 56, 58
  deviant case, 56
  disproportionate, 56
  extreme case, 56
  factorial design, 56
  heterogenous, 51-52, 56, 138
  homogenous, 56
  multi-stage, 56, 57, 81
  one-stage, 56, 57
  probability, 54-55, 82
  proportionate, 56, 83
  purposive, 56
  quota –, 52, 55, 56
  random, 55, 56, 57, 344
  representative, 51-52, 56
  stratified, 56
  structural, 56
  systematic, 56, 143
  time-oriented, 65-66
  unbiased, 52, 56
  See also Statistical hypotheses, Surveys
Sampling Opinions, n. 5.6, n. 5.7, n. 5.10, n. 6.6
Samuelsson, K., II. n. 2.5
Say it With Figures, II. n. 2.1, n. 2.3, n. 3.1
Scale level. *See* Levels of measurement
Scales, 95-98, 254. *See also* Levels of measurement, Measurement, Variables
Scatter-diagram, 182, 275
Scientific theory, 453, 454
Scott's measure, 227; II. n. 2.5
Selection of variables, 80-84
Selltiz, C., n. 5.12

Selvin, H., 390; II. n. 4.20, n. 4.30, n. 4.34
Sequential Analysis, II. n. 4.39
Sexual Behavior in the Human Male and Female, 149, 359, 386
Shapiro, G., n. 5.3
Sheatsley, P. B., 34, 53; n. 2.9
Shirley, n. 5.12
Siegel, S., 340, 345, 352; II. n. 4.9, n. 4.11, n. 4.43
Significance level, 199-200, 342, 349, 351, 366-369 *pass.*, 372-375 *pass.*, 375-376, 378, 379-381, 382-383, 387-388. *See also* Statistical hypotheses
Significant others, 151
Simon, H., II. n. 5.3, n. 6.17
Simulation, 476
Situação Social da America Latina, n. 3.2
Sixfold-tables, 192, 194-195, 427-429
Skewness, 205. *See also* Curve chape analysis
Smoker, P., II. n. 6.15
Social and Cultural Dynamics, n. 1.3
Social change, 154
Social conflict, 158, 160
Social control process, 470
Social network analysis, 88
Social Research to Test Ideas, II. n. 2.6
Social structure, 398
Social Structure, Theory of, 462
Socialization, 123
Society structure, 398
Socio-economic status, 247
Sociological Imagination, The, n. 6.9
Sociological Theories in Progress, II. n. 2.15
Sociometric analysis, 88, 89
Solomon, H., II. n. 3.34
Somers, R., 218; II. n. 2.10, n. 2.11, n. 2.12, n. 5.8
Somers' measure, 208, 224, 295, 357; II. n. 5.8
Sorokin, P., n. 1.3, n. 1.10, n. 6.9
Soviet Citizen, The, n. 6.16
Spaeth, J. L., 417
Spearman's rho, 208, 218-220
Specificity, 113, 319-321
Split-half technique, 440
Spurious correlation. *See* Correlation
Stages of Economic Growth, The, 73; n. 3.3
Stanton, n. 5.8
Star, n. 5.12
Star, S., n. 6.4
Statistical Decision Functions, II. n. 4.40

532

533

534